INTERPERSONAL COMMUNICATION

RELATING TO OTHERS

INTERPERSONAL COMMUNICATION

RELATING TO OTHERS

Steven A. Beebe

SOUTHWEST TEXAS STATE UNIVERSITY

Susan J. Beebe

SOUTHWEST TEXAS STATE UNIVERSITY

Mark V. Redmond

IOWA STATE UNIVERSITY

Carol Milstone

UNIVERSITY OF OTTAWA

Allyn and Bacon Canada

SCARBOROUGH, ONTARIO

Canadian Cataloguing in Publication Data

Interpersonal communication: relating to others.

Canadian ed.

ISBN 0-205-26896-X

1. Interpersonal communication.
2. Interpersonal relations.
3. Nonverbal communication (Psychology).
I. Beebe, Steven A..

BF637.C45I68 1997   153.6   C96-932029-9

 © 1997 Prentice-Hall Canada Inc., Scarborough, Ontario
A Division of Simon & Schuster/A Viacom Company

Allyn and Bacon, Inc., Needham Heights, Massachusetts
Prentice-Hall, Inc., Upper Saddle River, New Jersey
Prentice-Hall International (UK) Limited, London
Prentice-Hall of Australia, Pty. Limited, Sydney
Prentice-Hall Hispanoamericana, S.A., Mexico City
Prentice-Hall of India Private Limited, New Delhi
Prentice-Hall of Japan, Inc., Tokyo
Simon & Schuster Southeast Asia Private Limited, Singapore
Editora Prentice-Hall do Brasil, Ltda., Rio de Janeiro

ISBN 0-205-26896-X

Vice-President, Editorial Director: Laura Pearson
Acquisitions Editor: Cliff Newman
Developmental Editor: Imogen Brian
Production Editor: Susan James
Copy Editor: Jem Bates
Editorial Assistant: Carol Whynot
Production Coordinator: Deborah Starks
Permissions/Photo Research: Marijke Leupen
Cover Design: Mary Opper
Cover Image: The Stock Illustration Source/Tana Powell
Page Layout: Debbie Fleming

Original edition published by Allyn & Bacon Inc.
A Simon & Schuster Company
Needham Heights, MA 02194-2315
Copyright © 1996 by Allyn & Bacon.

1 2 3 4 5   CC   01 00 99 98 97

Printed and bound in the U.S.A.

Visit the Prentice Hall Canada Web site! Send us your comments, browse our catalogues, and more. **www.phcanada.com** Or reach us through e-mail at **phabinfo_pubcanada@prenhall.com**

Brief Contents

Contents

Part IV
Bridging Differences in
Interpersonal Relationships   287

Part V
Developing Relationships with Family,
Friends, Lovers, and Colleagues   363

Preface

*I*nterpersonal Communication: Relating to Others, Canadian Edition, is designed to help students understand, and improve their effectiveness in, the special variety of human communication that takes place within interpersonal relationships. We agree with H. D. Duncan, who said, "We do not relate and then talk, but relate in talk." Conversation is the tool we use to initiate and sustain relationships, and all interpersonal communication takes place within the context of a relationship. We emphasize this link throughout the text, addressing students' innate desire for knowledge about how to improve their relationships as they study the self, language, nonverbal communication, conflict management, and communication with family, friends, lovers, and colleagues.

Throughout the book we emphasize that there are no sure-fire prescriptions for achieving satisfying relationships or peak communication experiences. But we do believe that, armed with a solid grasp of principles, students can adapt research-based strategies to their own purposes and become more skilled at initiating and managing interactions with others.

This book is designed to feature unique Canadian contexts throughout its contents, in order to provide "at home" relevance to all the topics covered in the book, and to facilitate personal identification with these lessons by Canadian students. These objectives are achieved through the following features:

- excerpts from reports of noted Canadian research institutions

- quotations and anecdotes from prominent Canadians

- presentation of relevant Canadian statistics

- photographic images which are identifiably Canadian, e.g., Canadian entertainers, R.C.M.P., sports teams, tourism images, etc.

Our Approach to Teaching Interpersonal Communication

An Other-Oriented Approach. We also believe that considering the thoughts and feelings of others is a prerequisite for improving interpersonal communication. Becoming other-oriented involves not a single skill, but rather a composite of skills and principles. Foremost among them are self-awareness and self-knowledge; throughout the book we stress that true empathy and sensitivity are possible only when we feel secure about our own identity.

To help students develop an other orientation, we include in each chapter a feature called "Considering Others" (see description below), along with research conclusions that emphasize the importance of being other-oriented. We also highlight other-oriented skill instruction and principles with a special icon in the margin.

Throughout the text, our other-oriented approach encompasses all of the classic principles and skills in a typical interpersonal communication course curriculum. But we stress throughout that real understanding and meaningful communication occur when we link our own perceptions, thoughts, and feelings to those of our communication partners.

An Emphasis on Diversity. In recent years, the body of research on gender- and culture-based differences in communication behaviour has grown by leaps and bounds. We now recognize that many interpersonal difficulties stem from these differences, and a whole industry has grown up around efforts to compensate for them. For this reason, we have integrated an examination of diversity issues into every chapter, in special "Understanding Diversity" boxes (see description below) as well as in text discussions.

A Focus on Relationships. Students are consistently curious about how to improve their relationships with others. We link communication skills with principles that help explain and predict how relationships begin, develop, and sometimes decline. As suggested by our subtitle, *Relating to Others*, we stress the importance of cultivating relationships by developing increased awareness of and sensitivity to others.

Plan of the Book

This book is organized into five units. Unit one, Foundations of Interpersonal Communication, focuses upon the prerequisites for an understanding of interpersonal communication. Chapter 1 traces the evolution of interpersonal communication theory, defines key concepts, and begins exploring the link between interpersonal communication and relationships. Chapter 2 encourages students to examine their own self-concept and self-esteem as they study theoretical frameworks and constructs. Chapter 3 examines the perception process, emphasizing tendencies that interfere with relational development and suggesting ways to combat them.

The second unit, Interpersonal Communication Skills, homes in on the basic skills and competencies required for effective interpersonal relationships: listening and responding with accuracy and empathy (Chapter 4); perceiving and interpreting nonverbal cues (Chapter 5); and understanding the power of language and verbal messages (Chapter 6).

Unit Three, Interpersonal Relationships, focuses on the ways that communication leads to and affects relationships. Chapter 7 defines and classifies different types of relationships, then examines their dynamics. Chapters 8 and 9 focus upon the ways relationships are initiated and maintained, and on how they sometimes deteriorate.

Unit Four, Bridging Differences in Interpersonal Relationships, presents principles and strategies that help bridge the inevitable differences that arise when we communicate with others. Chapter 10 defines the elements of conflict and offers strategies for effectively managing interpersonal differences. As we explained above, we have integrated an examination of issues relating to gender and diversity in every chapter of the book. But Chapter 11 takes a broader look at the spectrum of challenges involved in intercultural communication. We examine the ways that culture, race, gender, disability, and ethnicity influence our thoughts, emotions, speech, and behaviours, suggesting ways to bridge the differences they engender.

Finally, our last unit, Developing Relationships with Family, Friends, Lovers, and Colleagues, takes a look at special types of interpersonal relationships. We present research conclusions and emphasize skills that help students understand the dynamics of communication within the family (Chapter 12), with friends and lovers (Chapter 13), and with colleagues (Chapter 14).

Our Partnership with Instructors

With this book we form a partnership with the instructor to help students learn principles and skills of interpersonal communication. We recognize that a textbook alone cannot do the job. Learning how to understand and improve interpersonal communication is an active process that involves *comprehending, applying, experiencing,* and ultimately *evaluating* the appropriateness of interpersonal communication principles and skills. But this book, along with our *Instructor's Annotated Edition,* and our *Instructor's Manual,* provide guidance for every stage of the process.

Students will begin to comprehend the discipline as they read our digest of communication research conclusions, along with the examples, illustrations, stories, and sample dialogues that help them apply those conclusions to their own lives. They will have an opportunity to practice applying their understanding through our "Communication Experiences"—self-tests, learning activities and skill-building exercises integrated into the text. We also provide additional activities and suggestions for journal assignments at the end of each chapter. Most of the latter are based on the students' own experiences. They heighten self-awareness and encourage students to observe and analyze their own interactions within relationships. All of these exercises and activities encourage students to evaluate their mastery of the material in conjunction with feedback from their instructors.

Text Features

We designed this text to give instructors a high degree of flexibility in tailoring the approach and style of classroom instruction to their students' needs, building an array of pedagogical features to help stimulate and facilitate learning. These teaching-learning components, which are described in greater detail in the "How to Use This Book" section, include the following:

- Chapter outlines—immediately preceding each chapter, these provide a quick preview of the contents for both instructor and students.
- Chapter-opening objectives—designed to help students predict and review essential elements of the chapter.
- Recaps—distillations of essential principles and skills, these are excellent tools for class review, group discussion, and exam preparation.
- Communication Experiences—in-text group and individual learning activities linked to key principles and skills.
- Considering Others—special features that appear in each chapter to help students develop an other-orientation in their interpersonal communication behaviour.
- Understanding Diversity—features that highlight the ways factors in our backgrounds affect interpersonal communication and relationships.
- Electronic Connections—special material that explores interpersonal communication's new frontier—technology—and its impact on relationships.
- Essays, articles, cartoons, and art—support materials keyed to text topics that can be used to generate class discussion.
- Glossaries—terms highlighted in boldface that appear in chronological order at the end of each chapter. A comprehensive glossary arranged in alphabetical order appears at the end of the book.
- End-of-chapter exercises—these discussion and review questions focus on three areas:
  - *Comprehension*—to help students assess whether they understand key ideas.
  - *Critical Thinking*—to give students an opportunity to extend their understanding to new situations.
  - *Ethical Issues*—to help students apply their interpersonal insights and skills responsibly.
- For Your Journal—questions and assignments that encourage self-observation, reflection, and analysis.
- Learning with Others—collaborative learning activities that promote cooperative

interaction and skills practice.

In addition to this cornucopia of in-text pedagogical features, we provide an additional resource to help instructors:

- Instructor's Manual. This resource includes teaching suggestions, suggested course syllabi, guidelines for using the complete teaching-learning package, and a set of test questions.

- You can send your comments on this book to **phabinfo_pubcanada@prenhall.com**.

The authors are grateful to those colleagues who acted as reviewers for this edition, including Jenepher Lennox Terrion of the University of Ottawa, Christina Gauthier of Centennial College, Geoffrey Gurd of the University of Ottawa, and Brigitte Wiebe of the University of Manitoba.

Steven A. Beebe
Susan J. Beebe
Mark V. Redmond
Carol Milstone

How to Use This Book:
A Guide to Special Features

The main purpose of this text is to help you improve the quality of your daily interactions with others. In addition to discussions about skills and principles, we've incorporated a variety of special features to make your learning easier and more enjoyable. We've also built in several that you can combine to use as a study guide for exams. Below, we'll suggest ways you can use each feature to the best advantage.

Other-Oriented Icon

As our subtitle implies, this book emphasizes the importance of considering and responding to others in all of your interpersonal communications. To encourage your development of a strong "other orientation," we highlight text passages that provide specific tips for becoming other-oriented or that emphasize the value of considering others in your interactions. Watch for the special icon in the margins. You can read an explanation about this icon on page 25 in Chapter One.

Provide Information about Yourself

Disclosing information about yourself allows the other person to make an informed decision about whether or not to continue the relationship. Remember, both of you need to be in a position to make such a decision. You might have found out what you want and decided that you have a lot in common with the other person, but he or she might not have reached that same point. However, you need to be careful not to violate the script or cultural expectations about what is appropriate to disclose in an initial conversation. You have probably had the experience of someone you have just met telling you his or her problems. As we mentioned earlier, such disclosures usually alienate the other, rather than advancing the relationship.

Chapter Outline

Use this list of the chapter's main headings to preview the contents. As you scan the headings, try turning them into questions to investigate as you read. For example, you can change "Words and Meaning" into "What can affect the meaning of words?"

Chapter Objectives

Each chapter opens with a list of objectives that you can use as learning goals. Keep them in mind as you read the chapter. When you finish your reading, use them as a self test to ensure that you've fulfilled your goals.

Initiating and Establishing Relationships

After studying this chapter, you should be able to:

1. Explain what interpersonal attraction is.

2. Describe the elements that contribute to interpersonal attraction.

3. Explain the relationship between attraction and interpersonal communication.

4. Describe the principles of self-disclosure.

5. Construct the two models of self-disclosure.

6. Summarize the eight suggestions for starting relationships.

■ INTERPERSONAL ATTRACTION: THE SPARK FOR A RELATIONSHIP

■ SELF-DISCLOSURE: THE FUEL FOR A RELATIONSHIP

How to Use This Book:
A Guide to Special Features

Recap

Interspersed throughout the text, these capsule summaries of essential skills and principles will help you process and remember what you've read. In combination with the Chapter Summaries and Glossaries (described below), they also provide an excellent way to review key points before an exam. And use them to refresh your knowledge of specific topics as you face new interpersonal communication challenges in your daily life. For a complete list of Recaps, consult the inside front cover of this book.

RECAP	Critical Management Styles
NONCONFRONTATIONAL STYLE	Avoids conflict by placating (agreeing), distracting, computing (becoming emotionally detached), or withdrawing from the conflict.
CONTROLLING STYLE	Wants to manipulate others by blaming and making threats; sets up win-lose framework.
COOPERATIVE STYLE	Seeks mutually agreeable resolutions to manage differences. Works within an other-oriented, win–win framework: ■ Separates people from the problem. ■ Focuses on shared interests. ■ Generates many options to solve problems. ■ Bases decisions upon objective criteria.

Chapter Summary

Use this brief review of key principles in combination with the Recaps and Glossaries (described on the next page) to reinforce your understanding of chapter material and review for exams.

Summary

The words we use have great power to affect our self-image and to influence the relationships we establish with others. English words are symbols that refer to objects, events, people, and ideas. They are arbitrary. We interpret their meaning through the context and culture to which they belong. Communication is complex because most words have both denotative (literal) meanings and connotative (subjective) meanings, and because words range from concrete to abstract.

The power of words stems from their ability to create images and to influence our thoughts, feelings, and actions. There is also an important link between the words we use and our culture. Language shapes culture and culture shapes language. Our view of the world is influenced by our vocabulary and the categories we have created with words.

Several word barriers can contribute to misunderstanding in interpersonal communications. Bypassing occurs when a word means one thing to one person and another to someone else. Our verbal expressions may lack clarity, either because we make language errors or because the meaning we want to convey is not clear to us. Allness statements can mislead and alienate listeners because the speaker falsely implies that he or she knows all there is to know about something. Another barrier, static evaluation, fails to take changes into account and uses outdated labels and

Glossary

Throughout the text, we've highlighted in **boldface** those terms that are critical to an understanding of interpersonal communication. A Glossary at the end of each chapter defines these terms in the order in which they appear in the chapter. Refer to it as you read; when you finish each chapter, use it to check your understanding of key terms. Together with the Recaps and Chapter Summaries, these Glossaries are excellent tools for exam preparation.

▪ GLOSSARY

SYMBOL: A word, sound, or visual device that represents a thought, concept, or object.

REFERENT: The thing that a symbol represents.

THOUGHT: The mental process of creating a category, idea, or image triggered by a referent or symbol.

HIGH-CONTEXT CULTURE: A culture in which the meaning of messages is highly dependent upon context and nonverbal cues.

LOW-CONTEXT CULTURE: A culture that relies primarily on language to communicate messages.

SYMBOLIC INTERACTION: A theory that suggests societies are bound together through common use of symbols.

DENOTATIVE MEANING: The restrictive or literal meaning of a word.

CONNOTATIVE MEANING: The personal and subjective meaning of a word.

LINGUISTIC DETERMINISM: A theory that describes how use of language determines or influences thoughts and perceptions.

WORLD VIEW: A culturally acquired perspective for interpreting experiences.

Considering Others

In each chapter we present special thought-provoking selections and activities to strengthen your development of other-oriented interpersonal communication. Try the self-checks and role-plays in these boxes to deepen your understanding of the book's most important theme.

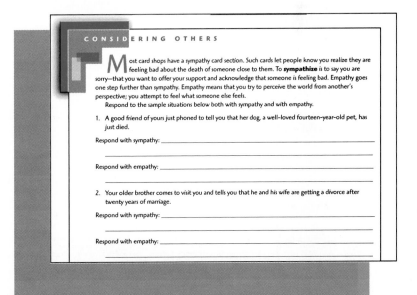

CONSIDERING OTHERS

Most card shops have a sympathy card section. Such cards let people know you realize they are feeling bad about the death of someone close to them. To **sympathize** is to say you are sorry—that you want to offer your support and acknowledge that someone is feeling bad. Empathy goes one step further than sympathy. Empathy means that you try to perceive the world from another's perspective; you attempt to feel what someone else feels.

Respond to the sample situations below both with sympathy and with empathy.

1. A good friend of yours just phoned to tell you that her dog, a well-loved fourteen-year-old pet, has just died.

Respond with sympathy: _____

_____

Respond with empathy: _____

_____

2. Your older brother comes to visit you and tells you that he and his wife are getting a divorce after twenty years of marriage.

Respond with sympathy: _____

_____

Respond with empathy: _____

_____

How to Use This Book:
A Guide to Special Features

Electronic Connections

The new frontier in interpersonal communication is electronically mediated interaction. Around the globe, people are striking up relationships over the Internet and other networking systems. This special feature explores some of the changes and conventions that this new form of communication has spawned.

ELECTRONIC CONNECTIONS

The Power of Confirming Responses

A Disabled Writer Finds a Friend Along the Information Superhighway

To Chris Young, e-mail is the great equalizer. Nearly 10 years ago, my wife, Pamela, "met" Chris through the engaging messages he'd posted in CompuServe's Issues Forum. Chris's thoughts and writing style caught Pamela's eye; she happened to mention how much she enjoyed the postings to forum administrator Georgia Griffith, who, in turn, relayed her compliments to Chris.

"When Georgia wrote [via e-mail] to tell me, I laughed out loud," Chris recalls today. That was partly because he'd never

of his right hand and types by poking the computer keys, one laborious letter at a time, with a wooden pointer.

"Years ago," he says, "when I first started using e-mail, I was shocked when I realized that some of my on-line acquaintances didn't know about my disability. For the first time in my life, people had the opportunity to meet the real me before seeing my disability, which doesn't happen when I meet someone face to face." Often, however, Chris chooses to tell people on-line about his disability. "I'm not fully myself without my disability," says Chris. "It gives me a unique perspective on life that I can share with others."

Chris and Pamela began a regular e-mail correspondence.

my personal journals have been in the form of e-mail that begins 'Dear Pamela,'" Chris says. "It's somehow more significant to me knowing a real live human being is on the other end of the line than it would be pouring my soul onto pages that might never see the light of day. Also the distance between us provides some safety. Pamela will likely never meet most of the characters in my life, so I am totally free to speak my mind about them."

Chris credits Pamela's support for inspiring him to pursue his writing professionally. Over the past few years, several of his articles have appeared in technical computer magazines. His first book, *Ray Tracing Creations*, about computer graphics, was recently published

Understanding Diversity

Differences in culture, gender, and ethnicity affect our interpersonal communications. Supplementing discussions woven throughout the text, these special boxes provide additional insight into diversity issues as well as practical suggestions for bridging gaps.

UNDERSTANDING DIVERSITY

When Gay Parents Come Out

Three years ago, Julie was convinced that Larry, her husband of 20 years was seriously ill. For four months he couldn't eat or sleep. He was losing weight. He was pale and clammy.

When he announced that he was going to the doctor, she knew he would come home with news that he was dying.

Instead, Larry told Julie and soon afterward their two sons and daughter that he is gay. Reactions ran the gamut, from relief, then rage, then compassion on the part of Julie to confusion but acceptance on the part of their youngest son, then 9.

Initially, their daughter, then 15, wanted nothing to do with her dad and stormed out of the room. Months of therapy have changed some of her feelings.

Their middle son, 16, continues struggling to accept Larry's sexual orientation. He attended

names not be used for this story. If they knew it would not upset him, they said, they would be completely open. They've declined invitations to tell their story on national talk shows.

Now divorced, Julie and Larry remain close friends, often spending holidays together or socializing over dinner.

Larry, who lives with a male partner, tries to spend as much time as possible with his kids, taking them to the movies, attending their athletic events, and spending time at his former home with them.

Their youngest son occasionally spends the night at Larry's house, and has accompanied him and his companion on business trips.

Larry and Julie won't go so far as to say they are living happily ever after, but they will say that things are working out better than they could have imagined.

"Not many stories are this good," said Larry, who with Julie credits therapy as well as a series

Gay and lesbian activism is prompting more homosexuals to come out of the closet. When they do, their straight spouses and children are often shocked and traumatized. The straight partner often feels rejected sexually and deceived, as if their marriage has been a lie. Typically, they believe that they are alone in feeling such pain.

When Julie looks back on the day that Larry told her the news, she said she felt a sense of relief knowing that he wasn't ill: Soon after, though, the anger set in.

"There's a sense of betrayal, a sense of mistrust. I was very angry at Larry. I was like a volcano. I remember at one point saying, 'We were living a lie,' and he said, 'We didn't live a lie. We loved each other and we still do.'

"We've had the benefit of some really good therapy. He's allowed me to yell at him and let out all my venom and that's what has gotten me through. As for the kids, I thought they should be privy to the same

Sidebars, Illustrations, Cartoons

Throughout the book we offer a wealth of stories, articles, poetry, fine art, and cartoons to broaden and strengthen your understanding of material discussed in the text. Read these supplementary offerings carefully to add new dimensions to your knowledge of interpersonal communication.

This afternoon there will be meetings in the North and South ends of the church—Children will be baptized on both ends.

These are funny examples, but in fact unclear language can launch a war or sink a ship. It is vital to remember that *meanings are in people, not in words.* We give symbols meaning; we do not receive inherent meaning *from* symbols. If you are other-oriented, you will assess how someone else will respond to your message and try to select those symbols that he or she is most likely to interpret as you intend.

For most communication, the object is to be as specific and concrete as possible. Vague language creates confusion and frustration. Consider this example:

Derrick: Where's the aluminum foil?

Ha ha ha, Biff. Guess what? After we go to the drugstore and the post office, I'm going to the vet's to get tutored.

...stricted code that has a mean-...nvolves the use of words that ...r example, most children ...metimes we develop abbrevi-...ial terms that relate to read-...now that "a screamer" is ...CAPITAL LETTERS. Ham ...rwaves. Yet, in each instance ...n outsider. In fact, groups that ...ness because of this shared ...ons" box on page 181 ...ge of a restricted group of ...guard against lapsing into

...time, they may also use ...on overleaf is an example of ...hat no outsider could ever

---

Figure 7.2
Model of Relational Stages

Up	Down
Intimacy	Turmoil or stagnation
Intensification	De-intensification
Exploration	Individualization
Initiation	Separation
Pre-Interaction Awareness	Post-Interaction Effects
Escalation	**De-escalation**

him or her without having any direct interaction. Gaining information about others without directly interacting with them is a *passive strategy* for acquiring knowledge.[12] Through your passive observations, you form an initial impression. You might not move beyond the pre-interaction awareness stage if that impression is not favourable or the circumstances aren't right.

If you are attracted to the other person and the circumstances are right, you might proceed to the *initiation stage,* one of the first turning points in a relationship. In this stage, the interaction typically is routine; you might each respond to a large number of standard questions during the first four minutes of conversation,[13] sticking to safe and superficial topics, and presenting a "public self" to the other person. Your partner is now riding on the elevator with you, and any decision about whether the elevator should go up, down, or nowhere is a mutual one for the rest of the ride. You can never return to the initiation stage. Once you make an initial contact, you have created a relational history on which you will continue to build.

If you decide to go to the next floor, *exploration,* you will begin to share more in-depth information about yourselves. But you will have little physical contact, maintain your social distance, and limit the amount of time you spend together. This stage can occur in conjunction with the initiation stage.

If you proceed to the *intensification stage,* you will start to depend upon each other for self-confirmation and engage in more risky self-disclosure. You will spend more time

As couples proceed from exploration to intensification, they have more physical contact and begin sharing more activities and confidences. Does it seem as if this couple is heading into the intensification stage? (Sandra Rice)

How to Use This Book:
A Guide to Special Features

Communication Experience

These lively, interactive, in-chapter exercises encourage you to apply principles and skills while they're fresh in your mind. Some are self-tests to help you assess the skills you already have and pinpoint areas for improvement. Others are designed for collaborative learning with your classmates.

For Discussion and Review

These issues and questions that appear at the end of each chapter are divided into three sections:

Focus on Comprehension tests your understanding of the chapter material and provides yet another tool for exam preparation;

Focus on Critical Thinking invites you to use your newly acquired knowledge to make connections and draw conclusions in the context of your own life and experience;

Focus on Ethics encourages you to think through the ethical implications of important interpersonal communication activities.

COMMUNICATION EXPERIENCE

Supportive-Defensive Communication Charades

Divide into groups of two to four people. Each team or group should prepare a short play depicting one of the supportive or defensive communication responses described in this chapter. Perform your play for the class or another team to see if they can identify the type of supportive or defensive communication behaviour your team is portraying. Consider one of the following situations or develop one of your own:

Speaking with a professor about a grade.

Returning a broken item to a store.

Talking with your child about his or her grades.

Responding to a telemarketing salesperson who calls you during dinner.

Talking with one of your employees who made a work-related mistake.

Re-booking a flight because your flight was cancelled by the airline.

Taking an order from a customer at a fast-food restaurant.

Receiving a complaint from a customer about poor service.

Talking with someone who has knocked on your door inviting you to his or her church.

Asking someone to turn down the stereo or TV while you are trying to study.

Variation: Instead of illustrating supportive and defensive communication, roleplay an example of one of the confirming or disconfirming communication behaviours discussed in this chapter.

For Discussion and Review

■ FOCUS ON COMPREHENSION

1. How do words create meaning for others?

2. What are some barriers to effective understanding, and what are strategies for overcoming these barriers?

3. What are the characteristics of a supportive communicator?

4. What are confirming communication responses? Describe a few.

5. What are disconfirming communication responses? Describe a few.

■ FOCUS ON CRITICAL THINKING

6. Marge and Paul are having an argument. Paul shouts, "You're constantly criticizing me! You don't let me make any important decisions!" How could Paul communicate how he feels in a more supportive way?

7. Alan asked Jessie to pick him up after work at the circle drive at 5:30 P.M. Jessie waited patiently at the circle drive on the other side of campus and finally went home at 6:30 P.M., having seen no sign of Alan. Alan was waiting at the circle drive behind his office rather than at the one on the other side of the campus. What word barriers do you think led to this misunderstanding?

8. Rephrase the following statements to use less biased language:

A. I'd like to introduce Mr. Russell Browne and his wife Muriel.

B. In an office memo: "Several gals have been leaving their purses at their desks."

9. Rephrase the following statements, using the skill of indexing.

A. All politicians want power and control over others.

B. All teachers are underpaid.

C. All Vancouverites like to brag about how great their city is.

■ FOCUS ON ETHICS

10. If you really don't want to listen to your co-worker go into detail about her latest vacation trip or provide details about the recent escapades of her children or grandchildren, is it appropriate to tell her that you'd rather not hear her "news"? Support your response.

For Your Journal

Journal suggestions at the end of each chapter encourage you to record interpersonal events and translate your understanding of skills and principles into writing.

Even if your instructor does not require that you keep a journal, you can use these suggestions for discussion and review.

Learning with Others

These group learning exercises at the end of each chapter provide opportunities to translate your new knowledge into action, using your classmates as communication partners.

Above all, keep in mind that we designed this text to help you understand and reap the rewards of well-managed interactions and relationships. Study hard, but also work hard to apply what you read to your daily life.

For Your Journal

1. Keep a log of examples of word barriers you experience or encounter. Note examples of bypassing, lack of precision in language, bafflegab, and other uses of words that inhibit communication. The examples could come from your own verbal exchanges or those that you observe in the conversations of others.

2. Make a list of words that are in your vocabulary today but were not in your vocabulary five years ago. Include new vocabulary words that you may have learned in school as well as words that were not generally used or that have been coined in the last half-decade (e.g., CD-ROM).

3. Record a sample dialogue between you and a good friend that illustrates some of the confirming responses described on pages 190–191.

■ FOCUS ON ETHICS

8. How ethical is it for a person who is very skilled at compliance gaining to convince another person to escalate the relationship if that person has a strong initial resistance to escalation?

9. Under what circumstances might it be ethical for a person in an intimate relationship to use sudden death withdrawal as a strategy for ending a relationship? Under what circumstances would it be unethical?

Learning with Others

1. Working in groups of four or five students, use your own experiences to develop an answer to the following question: Do the reasons for breaking up a relationship change as the relationship becomes more intimate? To answer this question, start with casual relationships and identify reasons that people end those relationships. Next, talk about friendships, and discuss reasons for ending them. And finally, talk about intimate relationships and the reasons they break up. What are the similarities and differences among these different types of relationships and why they break up?

2. In groups of four or five, develop a survey of questions about what skills are critical for maintaining close relationships. Have each student conduct this survey with four or five of their friends. Then come back together as a group and total your survey results. How many of the communication skills that we identified in this chapter were named by the respondents? What new skills were identified? Report your results to the rest of the class.

3. In groups of four or five, videotape a five-minute conversation between two of your team members who know each other the best. They should try to carry on as natural a conversation as they can over anything they want. Watch the replay of the videotape, stopping it as necessary, as you evaluate which forms of adaptation from the list in Table 9.2 were present. Which types were easiest to identify? Why? Which were hardest? Why? How much of the time did the two team members actually adapt what they were saying to one another? What effect did adapting have upon the interaction?

Building Foundations of Interpersonal Communication

The first three chapters present fundamental concepts that frame our study of interpersonal communication. In Chapter 1 you will learn answers to these questions: What is interpersonal communication? What is the connection between interpersonal communication and interpersonal relationships? Why is it important to study relationships? What can I do to improve my relationships with others? Chapter 2 offers concepts and skills to help you understand more about who you are and how your self-concept and sense of self-worth influence your relationships. In Chapter 3 you will learn that perception plays a key role in effective interpersonal communication. By recognizing the factors that influence your perceptions and actively analyzing the meaning of perceptual information, you can become more adept at sharing your sense of the world with others.

■ CHAPTER 1:
Introduction to Interpersonal Communication

■ CHAPTER 2:
Communication and Self

■ CHAPTER 3:
Interpersonal Communication and Perception

1

Introduction to
Interpersonal Communication

After studying this chapter, you should be able to:

1. Compare and contrast definitions of communication, human communication, and interpersonal communication.

2. Compare and contrast communication as action, interaction, and transaction.

3. Describe the key components of the communication process.

4. Identify four communication principles.

5. Describe three goals of communication.

6. Explain why it is useful to study interpersonal communication.

7. Discuss seven characteristics of interpersonal relationships.

8. List strategies that can improve your communication effectiveness.

■ WHAT IS INTERPERSONAL COMMUNICATION?

■ AN EVOLVING MODEL FOR HUMAN AND INTERPERSONAL COMMUNICATION

■ INTERPERSONAL COMMUNICATION'S NEW FRONTIER

■ FOUR PRINCIPLES OF INTERPERSONAL COMMUNICATION

■ THREE GOALS FOR INTERPERSONAL COMMUNICATION

■ WHY STUDY INTERPERSONAL COMMUNICATION?

■ HOW DO WE CHARACTERIZE INTERPERSONAL RELATIONSHIPS?

■ HOW CAN YOU IMPROVE YOUR OWN INTERPERSONAL COMMUNICATION?

he stout woman in the oddly shaped hat kept beckoning to her; a faint smile played on her lips. She was trying to tell her something, but a rush of wind swept the sound away. Slowly, Cathy began moving towards the figure, pleading with it, "Who are you? Where are we going?"

But with her first step, a whining roar, followed by the clatter of metal against concrete, jolted her into consciousness. The shadowy figure dissolved in the warm yellow light of morning. "What was she trying to tell me?" pondered Cathy, glancing enviously at the blanket-swaddled figure next to her who slept on, unperturbed. Throwing on a robe, she pushed up the window and saw two young men standing before the yawning maw of a garbage truck, poised to hurl another empty can down onto the sidewalk.

Suppressing an urge to unleash a barrage of curses and insults, Cathy smiled and called out cheerfully, "Good morning, friends!" The two men looked up and waved. "Could you be a little gentler with the cans? Some of us are resting up to face other kinds of garbage later today," she said, thinking of her bulging briefcase. She kept the smile glued on tightly.

"Sorry if we disturbed you," the men called back. Cathy crept back to bed and wrested some covers from the snoring mound at her side. "What was she saying?" she asked herself again, squeezing her eyes shut for a moment, struggling to recapture the image in her mind's eye.

"Mommy! Wake up! I had a bad dream!" Suddenly, her arms were full of warm, clinging four-year-old. Once more Cathy opened her eyes. Sighing inaudibly, she began her day's work. "Tell me all about it," she said softly, planting a light kiss on Matthew's soft black hair.

Interpersonal communication is at the core of our existence. Even when we close our eyes for sleep, we dream of interacting with others. Each day we have fleeting conversations with others, such as Cathy's brief exchange with the men who noisily emptied her garbage cans. And also like Cathy, we may sometimes think of what we'd really like to say, but then censor ourselves, perhaps to soften our message. Cathy's clinging child and her sleeping partner sent unspoken messages to her, the meaning of which she understood. Most of us have a similar understanding with the people closest to us. Like Cathy, each day we formulate, interpret, and share messages with others through interpersonal communication.

Think of the number of times you communicated with someone today, as you worked, ate, studied, shopped, or went about your other daily activities. Most people spend between 80 and 90 percent of their waking hours engaging in some form of interpersonal communication.[1] It is through these exchanges that we develop interpersonal relationships with others.

Because these relationships are so important in our lives, later chapters will focus on the communication skills and principles that explain and predict how we develop, sustain, and sometimes end them. We'll explore such questions as: Why do we like some people and not others? How can we interpret other people's unspoken messages with greater accuracy? Why do some relationships blossom and others deteriorate? How can we better manage disagreements with others? How can we better understand our relationships with our family, friends, and co-workers?

This chapter charts the course ahead, addressing key questions about what interpersonal communication is and why it is important. We will begin by seeing how our understanding of the interpersonal communication process has evolved. And we will conclude by examining how we initiate and sustain relationships through interpersonal communication.

What Is Interpersonal Communication?

In order to understand interpersonal communication, we must begin by understanding how it relates to two broader categories: communication in general and human communication. Scholars have attempted to arrive at a general definition of communication for decades. One research team counted more than 126 published definitions,[2] and experts cannot agree upon a single one. But, in the broadest sense, **communication** is the process of acting upon information.[3] Someone does or says something, and others think or do something in response to the action or the words as they understand them.

Communication is not unique to humans. It is possible, for example, for you to act upon information from your dog. He barks; you feed him. This definition also suggests that your dog can act upon information from you. You head for the cupboard to feed him; he wags his tail and jumps up in the air anticipating his

The relationship between horse and rider for members of the Royal Canadian Mounted Police's Musical Ride is close, and the communication between them is precise and reliable. What distinguishes this form of communication from *interpersonal communication*, which is the focus of this textbook?

dinner. Researchers do study communication between species as well as communication systems within single animal species, but these fields of study are beyond the scope of this book. The focus of our study is upon a form of **human communication**: people communicating with other people. To refine this definition, we can say that human communication is the process of making sense out of the world and sharing that sense with others.[4] We learn about the world by listening, observing, tasting, touching, and smelling; then we share our conclusions with others. Human communication encompasses many media: speeches, songs, radio and television broadcasts, E-mail, letters, books, articles, poems, advertisements.

Interpersonal communication is a special form of human communication that occurs when we interact simultaneously with another person and mutually influence each other. *Simultaneous interaction* means that the communication partners are both acting upon the same information at the same time. *Mutual influence* means that both partners are affected by the interaction: it affects their thoughts, their feelings, and the way they interpret the information they exchange.

Our definition of interpersonal communication covers a broad range of human contexts. The simultaneous interaction and mutual influence may or may not involve words. It may be fleeting or enduring. Suppose you catch someone's eye in a crowded bus; the person smiles, you smile back. No words are exchanged, but you have communicated simultaneously and with mutual influence—one smile led to another; the second smile sustained the first. At the other end of the spectrum is the conversation-filled simultaneous interaction and mutual influence you've enjoyed a thousand times over with your closest friend, as you've gone through life sharing joys and sorrows.

Whether the interpersonal communication lasts for seconds or decades, it is a meaningful experience that we share with another human being. It is also the tool we use to forge and maintain relationships with others.

The shared experience of interpersonal communication is vital to our well-being. In fact, social isolation is so uncomfortable that solitary confinement has been used for centuries as a severe form of punishment. Without interpersonal communication, people suffer and even die. Recluses, hermits, and those isolated in solitary confinement dream and hallucinate about talking with others face-to-face.[5]

For this reason, Russian linguist Mikhail Bakhtin even suggests that interpersonal communication and being are synonymous:

> To be *means to communicate. Absolute death is the state of being unheard, unrecognized, unremembered. To* be *means to be for another, and through the other, for oneself. Monologue is finalized and deaf to the other's response, does not expect it and does not acknowledge in it any decisive force. The single adequate form for verbally expressing authentic human life is the open-ended dialogue.*[6]

RECAP	**Comparing Key Definitions**
Term	**Definition**
Communication	The process of acting upon information.
Human Communication	The process of making sense out of the world and sharing that sense with others.
Interpersonal Communication	The process of interacting simultaneously and sharing mutual influence with another person.

When we cease to communicate, we cease to exist. To study interpersonal communication is to study an essential aspect of what makes us human.

An Evolving Model for Human and Interpersonal Communication

Today, we know that interpersonal communication involves more than simply transferring or exchanging messages with others; it is a complex process of creating meaning. To understand this process, it is useful to see how our perspective on the human communication process has evolved over the past half century. We will begin with the simplest and oldest model of the human communication process.

Human Communication as Action: Message Transfer

"Did you get my message?" This simple sentence summarizes the communication-as-action approach to human communication. Communication takes place when a message is sent and received. Period. It is a way of transferring meaning from sender to receiver. In 1942, Harold Lasswell summarized the process as follows:

Who (sender)

Says what (message)

In what channel

To whom (receiver)

With what effect.[7]

Figure 1.1 shows a basic model formulated in 1949, seven years after Lasswell's summary, that depicts communication as a linear input/output process. Today, although they view the process differently, researchers still define most of the key components in this model in basically the same way.

■ INFORMATION SOURCE AND TRANSMITTER
The **information source** for a communication can be a thought or an emotion. The transmitter (now called the **source**), the originator of that thought or emotion, puts it into a code that can be understood by a receiver. Translating ideas, feelings, and thoughts into a code is called **encoding**. Vocalizing a word, gesturing, or establishing eye contact are signals that we use to encode our thoughts into a message that can be **decoded** by someone. Decoding is the opposite process of encoding. The words or unspoken signals are interpreted by the receiver.

In face-to-face encounters, we simultaneously exchange both verbal and nonverbal messages that result in shared meanings. Through this kind of interaction, we build relationships with others. (John Eastcott/The Image Works)

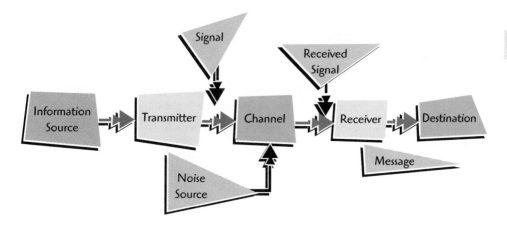

Figure 1.1

A Model for Communication as Action.
From: *The Mathematical Theory of Communication* by Claude E. Shannon and Warren Weaver. Copyright 1949 by the Board of Trustees of the University of Illinois. Used by permission of the University of Illinois Press.

RECEIVER

The **receiver** is the person who decodes and attempts to make sense out of what the source encoded. Think of a radio station with a source broadcasting to a receiver that picks up the station's signal. In human communication, however, there is something in between the source and the receiver: we filter messages through past experiences, attitudes, beliefs, values, prejudices, and biases.

SIGNAL, RECEIVED SIGNAL, AND MESSAGE

Today, all of these components are simply called the message. **Messages** are the written, spoken, and unspoken elements of communication to which we assign meaning. You can send a message intentionally (talking to a professor before class) or unintentionally (falling asleep during class); verbally ("Hi. How are you?"), nonverbally (with a smile and a handshake), or in written form (this book).

CHANNEL

A message is communicated from sender to receiver via some pathway called a **channel**. Channels correspond to your senses. When you call your mother on the telephone, the channel is an auditory one. When you talk with your mother face-to-face, the channels are many. You see her: the visual channel. You hear her: the auditory channel. You may smell her perfume: the olfactory channel. You may hug her: the tactile channel.

NOISE

Noise is interference. Without noise, all of our messages would be communicated with sublime accuracy. But noise is always present. It can be literal—the obnoxious roar of a gas-powered lawn mower—or it can be psychological. Instead of concentrating on your teacher's lecture, you may start thinking about the chores you need to finish before the end of the day. Whichever kind it is, noise gets in the way of the message and may even distort it. Communicating accurate messages involves minimizing both external and psychological noise.

While the action approach is simple and straightforward, it has a key flaw: human communication rarely, if ever, is as simple and efficient as "what we put in is what we get out." Others cannot automatically know what you mean just because you think you know what you mean. Although by Lasswell's time, communication scholars had already begun identifying an array of key elements in the communication process, the action approach overlooked their complexity.

Human Communication as Interaction: Message Exchange

The next big leap in our understanding of human communication came in the late 1940s and early 1950s. The communication-as-interaction perspective used the same elements as the action models but added two new ones: feedback and context.

Think of a Ping-Pong game. Messages, like a Ping-Pong ball, bounce back and forth. We talk; someone listens and responds. We respond to their response, and so forth. This perspective can be summarized using a physical principle: For every action there is a reaction.

Feedback is the response to the message. Without feedback, communication is rarely effective. When you order your black olive pizza and the server says in response, "That's a black olive pizza, right?" he has provided feedback to ensure that he encoded the message correctly.

Feedback is really a response message. Like other messages, it can be intentional (applause at the conclusion of a symphony) or unintentional (a yawn as you listen to your uncle tell his story about bears again); verbal ("That's a black olive pizza, right?") or nonverbal (blushing after being asked to dance).

A second component recognized by the interaction perspective is **context**, the physical and psychological communication environment. All communication takes place in some context. As the cliché goes, "Everyone has to be somewhere." A conversation with your good friend on the beach would likely differ from one the two of you may have in a funeral home. Context encompasses not only the physical environment but also the number of people present and their relationship with the communicators, the communication goal, and the culture in which the communicators are steeped.

This approach, as shown in Figure 1.2, is more realistic, but it still has limitations if we think about interpersonal communication in specific. It still views communication as a linear, step-by-step sequence of events. Although it emphasizes feedback and context, it does not quite capture the complexity of the process if the communication takes place simultaneously. In interpersonal situations, both the source and the receiver send and receive messages at the same time.

Figure 1.2

A Model of Communication as Interaction
Interaction models of communication include feedback as a response to a message sent by the communication source. From: *Invitation to Effective Speech Communication*, by John T. Masterson, Steven A. Beebe and Norman H. Watson, Scott, Foresman and Company, 1989.

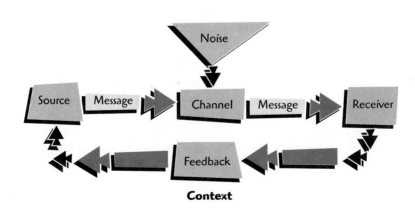

Human Communication as Transaction: Message Creation

The communication-as-transaction perspective, developed in the 1960s, acknowledges that when we talk to another, we are constantly reacting to what our partner is saying. Most scholars today view it as the most realistic model for interpersonal communication. It uses the same components to describe communication such as action and interaction. But in this model, all of the interaction is simultaneous. As Figure 1.3 indicates, we send and receive messages concurrently. Even as we talk, we are also interpreting our partner's nonverbal and verbal responses.

As we send messages, we monitor the degree to which the other person understands each message. We mutually define the symbols we use. If one partner misunderstands a message, both can work to clarify the meaning. For example, if I ask you to hand me the book off my desk and you hand me a pad of paper, we have failed to create a shared meaning. I might then say, "No, not the pad of paper, the red book next to the phone"; you then would hand me the book. Your action would require me to explain and be more specific. We would not simply transfer or exchange meaning; we would create it during a communication transaction.

One researcher says that interpersonal communication is "the coordinated management of meaning" through **episodes**, during which the message of one person influences the message of another.[8] Technically, only the sender and receiver of those messages can determine where one episode ends and another begins.

Figure 1.3

Communication as Simultaneous Transaction

Interpersonal Communication's New Frontier

The transactional model confirms the definition we presented earlier: in interpersonal communication, the partners engage in simultaneous interaction and have mutual influence upon each other. Whether the simultaneous interaction is fleeting or enduring, verbal or nonverbal, it represents a significant link between two human beings. It is the means we use to form and sustain relationships with others.

Although most of the time this form of human communication is "up close and personal," today's technological advances are creating new contexts for interpersonal exchanges. In the future, our model may continue to evolve. We can now communicate with other humans via a bewildering assortment of devices: fax, telephone, computer terminals, and video exchanges. These mediated message exchanges sometimes do permit mutual influence and often constitute a relationship. We can certainly initiate, maintain, or terminate relationships when we are not in one another's presence, as we have done for years using the telephone. Of course, without visual nonverbal cues, we can misunderstand one another more easily, and our messages tend to lose their emotional richness. At present, the most effective interpersonal communication still occurs when there are no media filters to interfere with the clarity of the message or to delay feedback from the receiver of the message. For this reason, our key focus in this book will be upon unmediated interaction between people.

But we will also begin to explore the new frontier in interpersonal communication. In special Electronic Connections features throughout the text, we will highlight the ways that today's technology is affecting our relationships. As the following example illustrates, E-mail allows intimate relationships to develop between people who are separated by thousands of miles.

RECAP   **Components of the Human Communication Process**

Term	Definition
Source	Human being who has an idea or emotion.
Receiver	The person or group toward whom the source directs messages, intentionally or unintentionally.
Message	The written, spoken, and unspoken elements of communication to which we assign meaning.
Channel	The pathway through which messages pass between source and receiver.
Noise	Anything that interferes with the clear reception and interpretation of a message.
Encode	The translation of ideas, feelings, and thoughts into a code.
Decode	The interpretion of ideas, feelings, and thoughts that have been translated into a code.
Context	The physical and psychological communication environment.
Feedback	Verbal and nonverbal responses to messages.

ELECTRONIC CONNECTIONS

Today's technology makes it possible for people to develop relationships with others without meeting face-to-face. Glen is an elementary school teacher in the coastal fishing village of Port Simpson, in northern British Columbia. His wife Cathy is a full-time homemaker and mother to their five young children. They were drawn to this remote community from Vancouver eight years ago "to get away from it all."

For Cathy, however, their alternative lifestyle quickly became one of isolation and loneliness. Three years ago, Cathy's sister visited with gifts of a computer, a modem, and a lesson on the Internet. Since that visit, Cathy has been able to "converse" daily with family and friends throughout the country. She has also made connections and formed close bonds with new acquaintances as far away as Norway. "Since I've been 'online,'" explains Cathy, "life in Port Simpson has gone from boring and lonely to worldly."

For people like Cathy, E-mail provides a form of correspondence that is comparable to, yet also worlds apart from, old-fashioned letter-writing. The difference, of course, is that partners can measure the intervals between these "letters" in nanoseconds instead of days or weeks. Although such exchanges are not simultaneous, they certainly can have the kind of spontaneity that we usually associate with interpersonal communication.

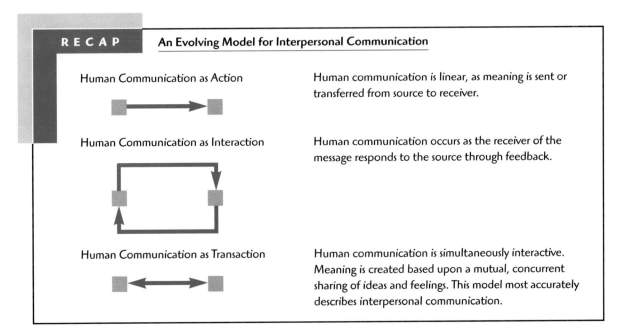
Four Principles of Interpersonal Communication

We have seen how interpersonal communication relates to other communication categories, and we have examined how our understanding of it has evolved over the last half century. Now we can begin looking at the practical side of interpersonal communication. How does it work in real life? What can we expect from it? Underlying our current understanding of interpersonal communication are four principles: interpersonal communication is inescapable, interpersonal communication is irreversible, interpersonal communication is complicated, and interpersonal communication is contextual.[9]

Interpersonal Communication Is Inescapable

We can't not communicate. Even before we are born, we respond to movement and sound. With our first cry, we begin the process of announcing to others that we are here. And once we make contact with other humans, we communicate and continue to do so until we die. Even though many of our messages are not verbalized, we nonetheless intentionally, and sometimes unintentionally, send them to others. Try to think of a time when you are not communicating. Even as you silently stand in a crowded elevator, your lack of eye contact with others communicates your unwillingness to interact with fellow passengers. If, after a long night of studying, you nod off to sleep as your daughter is excitedly trying to tell you about her upcoming field trip, she will think you are ignoring her. Your unspoken messages, even when you are asleep, provide cues to which others react. Remember: people judge you by your behavior, not your intent.

Interpersonal Communication Is Irreversible

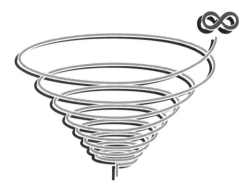

"Disregard that last statement made by the witness," instructs the judge. Yet the clever lawyer knows that once her client has told the jury that her husband gave her a black eye during an argument, the client cannot really "take it back." This principle applies to all forms of oral communication. We may try to modify the meaning of a spoken message by saying something like, "Oh, I really didn't mean it." But in most cases, the damage has been done. Once created, communication has the physical property of matter; it can't be uncreated. As the helical model in Figure 1.4 suggests, once interpersonal communication begins, it never loops back on itself. Instead, it continues to be shaped by the events, experiences, and thoughts of the communication partners. A Russian proverb nicely summarizes the point: "Once a word goes out of your mouth, you can never swallow it again."

Figure 1.4

Interpersonal Communication Is Irreversible
This helical model shows that interpersonal communication never loops back on itself. It expands as the communication partners contribute their thoughts and experiences to the exchange.
Copyright © F.E.X. Dance in *Human Communication Theory*. Holt, Rinehart and Winston, 1967, p. 294. Reprinted with permission.

Interpersonal Communication Is Complicated

No form of communication is simple. If any were, we would know how to reduce the number of misunderstandings and conflicts in our world. Because of the number of variables involved in interpersonal exchanges, even simple requests are extremely complex. Communication theorists have noted that whenever we communicate with another person, there are really at least six "people" involved: (1) who you think you are; (2) who you think the other person is; (3) who you think the other person thinks you are; (4) who the other person thinks he or she is; (5) who the other person thinks you are; and (6) who the other person thinks you think he or she is.[10] Whew! And when you add more people to the interaction, it becomes even more involved.

Moreover, when we humans communicate, we interpret information from others as symbols. A **symbol** is merely a representation of something else, and it can have various meanings and interpretations. Language is a system of symbols. In English, our symbols do not resemble the words they represent. The word (symbol) for *cow* does not look at all like a cow; someone, somewhere decided that *cow* should mean a beast that chews a cud and gives milk. Our reliance upon symbols to communicate poses a communication challenge; we are often misinterpreted. Sometimes we don't know the code. Only if you are conversant with *Canadian* English will you know that "riding" refers to an electoral district; "allophone" refers to a Quebecker who speaks neither French nor English; and "poutine" is french fries with cheese curds and gravy.

Messages are not always interpreted as we intend them. Osmo Wiio, a Scandinavian communication scholar, points out the messiness of communicating with others when he suggests the following maxims:

"I'm afraid you misunderstood . . .
I said I'd like a mango."

If communication can fail, it will.

If a message can be understood in different ways, it will be understood in just that way which does the most harm.

There is always somebody who knows better than you what you meant by your message.

The more communication there is, the more difficult it is for communication to succeed.[11]

While we are not as pessimistic as Professor Wiio, we do suggest that the task of understanding each other is challenging.

Surrealist René Magritte symbolized the complexity of communication in this painting, *The Art of Conversation*. The word *rêve* is French for *dream*. (Courtesy: New Orleans Museum of Art)

Interpersonal Communication Is Contextual

We've already noted that every communication encounter occurs in a context. For discussion, we can identify five: psychological, relational, situational, environmental, and cultural.

The **psychological context** is you. Who you are and what you bring to the interaction affect how you will interpret the messages of others. Your needs, desires, values, personality, self-concept, self-esteem—all the factors that make you uniquely you—form the psychological context. The other person also has a psychological context that he or she brings to the interaction. Interpersonal communication is the bridge between these two psychological contexts.

The **relational context** concerns your reactions to the other person—the level of trust, the degree of self-disclosure, levels of power and control, and the history you share.

The **situational context** is the event or reason that you are communicating. This context may be a classroom where you meet someone because you are taking the same course. When you meet that person after class for a cup of coffee, the situational context changes, and it affects what you say and how you communicate messages.

The physical surroundings in which people communicate constitute the **environmental context**. The furniture, other people, the location, the temperature, time of day, and day of the week are all part of the environmental context.

Finally, the **cultural context** includes all the elements of the culture (learned behaviours and rules) that affect the interaction. Do you come from a culture that takes a tea break each afternoon at 4:00 P.M.? Does your culture value hard work and achievement or relaxation and enjoyment? Obviously, your cultural background influences how you interact with others. Throughout this text, and especially in Chapter 11, we will examine how cultural differences affect communication. Special Understanding Diversity boxes, like the one on page 40, will provide additional insights as well as suggestions for bridging gaps in communication.

Every interaction you have with another person takes place in these five contexts simultaneously. Although they affect the individuals in a relationship in different ways, understanding their impact can reduce misunderstanding and improve your interpersonal effectiveness.

1. Working in small groups, compare the names you use for popular foods—for example, carbonated drinks, sandwiches made on long rolls, drinks made with ice cream—with the names that other people in your group use for them. Discuss possible origins for these names and the cultural or regional differences that they reflect.

2. Choose a few simple common nouns such as dog, house, road, table, and so on. Ask each person in turn to describe the image that pops into his or her head. Question the person about where the image came from and how it is connected with his or her life. When each person has had a turn, discuss how the differences in these images may complicate a conversation based on that word.

3. Choose a partner and try to verbalize your impressions about the "six people" involved in your exchanges with that person.

RECAP   **Principles of Interpersonal Communication**

	Implication
Interpersonal Communication Is Inescapable	You cannot not communicate.
Interpersonal Communication Is Irreversible	Once a message is sent, you cannot take it back.
Interpersonal Communication Is Complicated	You cannot completely understand others.
Interpersonal Communication Is Contextual	Communication occurs in psychological, relational, situational, environmental, and cultural contexts.

Three Goals for Interpersonal Communication

Although it is difficult to communicate effectively, it is not impossible. As with other challenges in life, setting goals for our communication with others can help us to overcome the obstacles. Researchers have identified three goals that we can apply to all our interpersonal interactions:[12]

- Make sure your message is understood.
- Make sure your message has the effect you intended.
- Make sure your message is ethical.

Make Sure Your Message Is Understood

The following true story of an international communication misunderstanding demonstrates the importance of making sure that the message being conveyed is the message intended: Not long ago a delegation of Canadian business people visited Japan to promote international trade. As a spontaneous gesture of goodwill toward their Japanese hosts, one of the Canadian delegates decided to sport a decorative shirt that bore some Japanese characters on an ornate background. Only toward the end of a dinner reception was the Canadian delegate informed by a Japanese journalist that the characters were an advertisement message equivalent to "Eat at Joe's Diner." Surely some of the Japanese business hosts must have interpreted the Canadian's "goodwill" gesture as an inappropriate form of cheap advertising.

Environmental context has a strong influence upon the quality of our interpersonal communication. What factors make this a positive setting for effective conversation? (G. Mancuso/Stock Boston)

The same kinds of misunderstandings can happen in interpersonal exchanges. Meanings are fragile. Consider the following exchanges between two good friends, Paula (an anglophone) and Marie-Joseph (a francophone):

Paula:	It was just the way my boss *looked* at me during my presentation; he says it went well, but I'm not so sure.
Marie-Joseph:	Paula, maybe you are being a bit too *sensible*.
Paula:	I sure wish I could find a copy of Peter C. Newman's latest book, to buy for my father's birthday.
Marie-Joseph:	Have you tried the *library* on Broadview Street?

Only if Paula knows French would she realize that *sensible* is the French word for *sensitive*, which is the message Marie-Joseph wished to convey in the first dialogue. *Librairie* is the French word for *bookstore*, which is what Marie-Joseph was actually referring to in the second dialogue. It's always wise to question your communication partners to make sure they share your understanding of a word or symbol.

Make Sure Your Message Has the Effect You Intended

When you communicate intentionally with others, it is for a specific purpose: to share information, to persuade, to solve a problem, to establish trust, to entertain your listener, or sometimes just to converse for fun. Establishing, maintaining, or ending a relationship with another person is often what we seek to achieve. Because different purposes require different strategies for success, being aware of your purpose can enhance the probability of your achieving it.

Suppose, for example, that you had purchased an expensive sleeping bag for a two-week backpacking trek on Vancouver Island's rugged west coast. During the trek, the bag met all your expectations for warmth and softness. But when you returned home and followed the washing instructions, you found yourself extracting from the washer an unidentifiable, frayed, sodden lump. Before calling the outfitter who sold you the bag, you would want to determine your purpose. Do you want simply to vent your frustration? Do you want to suggest that the store discontinue selling that particular item? Or do you want a store credit or refund?

Whether you are attempting to close a sale, get a date, give directions to the mall, or tell a joke, to communicate effectively, you should consider your goal. The purpose of interpersonal communication is not always to get or receive something tangible. Sometimes it is simply to make human contact, to establish a relationship, or just to be with someone.

Make Sure Your Message Is Ethical

Ethical communication is other-oriented. An ethical message considers the needs and rights of your communication partner. Interpersonal communication can be used to manipulate, bully, and coerce others, or it can permit the listener to make his or her own choice. Ethical communication gives listeners freedom of choice, does not decrease their feelings of self-worth, and promotes trust. Unethical communication does just the opposite: it forces views on others and demeans their integrity.

Another attribute of ethical communication is honesty. If you knowingly withhold key information, lie, or distort the truth, then you may not be communicating ethically or effectively. Only by considering the *motive* for the deception, as well as its *effects* and the *alternatives* can a determination be made as to the deception's ethical justification.[13] For example, when Art did not show up for his history class to take the test, he later told his professor that his grandmother had died and he had to attend the funeral. Art's professor obliged and allowed him to make up the test. Art's message was understood by his professor and also achieved the effect he wanted. Art's grandmother, however, is alive and well. According to our criteria for effective communication, Art's dishonesty would qualify his interaction as inappropriate and unethical.

Communicating ethically also means keeping confidences. Although we love to read about scandals in the tabloid press, we do not want our friends to reveal personal information that we told them in private. Because these issues are so important, we will return to them throughout the book as we discuss each new aspect of interpersonal communication. At the end of each chapter we will also explore ethical issues for discussion and review.

R E C A P   **Three Goals for Interpersonal Communication**

Make sure your message is understood

Make sure your message has the effect you intended

Make sure your message is ethical

Why Study Interpersonal Communication?

Until now, we have touched only briefly on the link between interpersonal communication and interpersonal relationships. In fact, one of the main purposes of this book is to explore that link in depth. We agree with H. D. Duncan, who said, "We do not relate and then talk, but relate in talk." Close relationships are one of the most important reasons for being. They serve as our compass as we navigate our way through the world; they are critical to maintaining good health and happiness.

As we have seen, the process of meeting, talking, listening, responding, and reacting to others results in more than information exchange or sharing; it enables you to form relationships with others. In some relationships the emotional connection is minimal; if you are waiting for a bus with a stranger, you may simply be aware of another's presence. Your relationship with the person who delivers your mail or waits on you each morning when you order breakfast at your local fast-food restaurant may hold no deep emotional attachment or commitment. But your relationships with your mother, father, spouse, child, colleagues, and best friends are emotionally rich. To understand and improve these relationships is to make your life more worthwhile. That is why we will examine interpersonal communication within the context of these important ties. The following sections briefly describe the benefits you can reap from your study.

Improve Relationships with Family

Our earliest communication relationships take place within our families. Psychologist Sven Wahlroos observed, "The greatest happiness and the deepest satisfaction in life, the most intense enthusiasm and the most profound inner peace all come from being a member of a loving family."[14] And even if family life is not always harmonious or peaceful, it is still where we learn how to relate to others. It is there that we learn how to cooperate and compete. In her classic work about family relationships, *Peoplemaking*, Virginia Satir calls family communication "the largest single factor determining the kinds of relationship [we make] with others."[15] And we maintain our family relationships despite physical distance; for many of us, almost half of our most important relationships are with family members who live away from us (mother, father, siblings).[16] Learning about communication can help us better understand and enhance the quality of our relationships with family members.

If you have had to ride in the back seat of the car on a long trip with brothers or sisters, perhaps you have learned the art of negotiating. Determining who got to sit by a window or what music was played on the car stereo may have tested your communication and persuasion skill. Your interaction with your parents deeply affected your self-concept. Did they praise or ignore achievements and accomplishments? As we will learn in the next chapter, your self-concept plays a major role in determining how you interact with others.

Improve Relationships with Friends

We cannot choose our biological families, but we do choose our friends. Friends are people we choose to be with because we like them and usually they like us. We expect friends to be honest, open, and affectionate; to confide in us, respect us, and constructively work through disagreements.[17] We depend on them to fill many roles. According to one researcher, friends provide useful information (about job vacancies, where to shop, the best places to eat, etc.); needed services (help us when we need it); companionship; emotional support; and even financial assistance.[18] We also develop unique meanings, private jokes, and other coded messages that only our friends can understand.[19] Why do we choose some people as friends and develop a reciprocal mistrust with others? The quality of our relationships with others hinges on the quality of our communication. Therefore, learning communication patterns, principles, and prescriptions can help answer this question and improve our relationships with the friends we have.

For unmarried people, developing friendships and falling in love are the top-rated sources of satisfaction and happiness in life.[20] Conversely, losing a relationship is among life's most stressful events.[21] Most individuals between the ages of nineteen and twenty-four report that they have had from five to six romantic relationships and have been "in love" once or twice.[22] Of course, the most intense human relationships involve both psychological and sexual intimacy, and they follow predictable patterns of courtship, escalation, and de-escalation. What we reveal about ourselves, the activities we pursue, and what we talk about in these relationships determine how successful they will be. Studying interpersonal communication may not unravel *all* of the mysteries of romantic love, but it can offer insight into our behaviours.

Improve Relationships with Colleagues

In many ways, our colleagues at work are like family members. Although we choose our friends and lovers, we don't always have the same flexibility in choosing whom we work with or for. Understanding how relationships develop on the job can help us avoid conflict and stress and increase our sense of satisfaction. In addition, our success or failure in a job often hinges upon how well we get along with our supervisor and our peers. Most job performance reviews give the boss a chance to make comments about how well we work with others. Moreover, recent studies have shown that training workers to relate and communicate as a team improves quality and productivity in many occupations, so more and more workplaces are adopting teamwork as a management strategy.

Improve Your Physical and Emotional Health

Intimate interpersonal relationships are vital to your health. Research has shown that the lack or loss of a relationship can lead to ill health and even death. Physicians have long observed that patients who are widowed or divorced experience more medical problems such as heart disease, cancer, pneumonia, and diabetes than do married people.[23] Grief-stricken spouses are more likely than others to die prematurely,[24] especially around the time of the departed spouse's birthday or near their wedding anniversary.[25] Being childless can also shorten your life. One research team found that middle-aged, childless wives were almost two and one-half times more likely to die in a given year than those who had at least one child.[26] Terminally ill patients with a limited number of friends or no social support die sooner than those with stronger ties.[27] Loneliness can kill.

Research findings are similar for mental illness: widowed and divorced individuals are more likely to experience mental illness, especially depression, than those in ongoing relationships. Being widowed or divorced often means being unhappy.[28]

On the positive side, however, establishing a quality social support system can be a major factor in improving and maintaining your health. One study suggests that the more attached we are to at least one other person, the longer we live.[29]

All of these findings show that the stress of loneliness can make us sick, but if we have support from people who care about us, we can adjust to life's tumbles and challenges. By learning more about effective communication, you are paving the way for closer, more satisfying relationships, and a longer life.

How Do We Characterize Interpersonal Relationships?

Now that we've seen that interpersonal communication is the key to forming and improving relationships that are vital to our well-being, we can look at some of the characteristics we use to describe a relationship. This set of descriptions is just a beginning. In Chapter 7 we will look at other ways that researchers define and classify relationships, and Chapters 8 and 9 will explore the ways we develop, maintain, and terminate them.

We have already seen that an **interpersonal relationship** is the ongoing connection we make with another person through interpersonal communication. We carry that connection in our minds (and metaphorically, in our hearts), whether the other person is present or not.

Interpersonal communication and interpersonal relationships are connected in a number of ways. Each interpersonal interaction adds to an interpersonal relationship. We start at ground zero with no relationship and begin communicating. Over time, if we continue to engage in interpersonal communication, the relationship evolves. Each time we communicate, we add richness to the relationship, sometimes by great amounts (such as in the initial stages) and sometimes by infinitesimal amounts (as in highly developed intimate relationships).

Relationships range from impersonal to intimate and emphasize both message content and human emotions. They are complementary or symmetrical. They are anchored in culturally based rules, and evolve in stages. And individuals in a relationship can focus either upon themselves or upon others. We will examine each of these characteristics next.

Interpersonal Relationships Range from Impersonal to Intimate

When you buy a pair of socks at a clothing store, you have a two-person, face-to-face, relatively brief interaction with someone who influences you and whom you influence. You communicate. Yet that interchange could hardly be described as intimate. Researchers Gerald Miller and Michael Sunnafrank suggest that the kind of information the participants use to relate to one another determines where any given interaction lies along a continuum from impersonal to intimate. **Cultural information** is general information about language and dominant values that we assume someone shares even if we know little about him or her. Relating to someone simply on the basis of cultural information represents impersonal communication.

Sociological information is based upon what we know about another person's membership in certain groups. These can be large demographic groups, such as people who live in the inner city, or smaller special interest groups, such as the local bowling league. These groups provide information that allows us to make additional predictions about the other person's reactions. But sociological information is fairly general, and communication based on it is still fairly impersonal.

Psychological information is specific information about the unique person with whom we are interacting. It distinguishes individuals from their cultural and social groups. When we base our predictions of another's responses on psychological information, then we are communicating in a more intimate way.[30]

Other researchers place more emphasis on the unique relational rules that two people establish as they communicate and on the degree to which they treat each other as unique people. In their view, the more we recognize an individual as unique, the more intimate is our communication. According to this approach, even interaction with close friends might be impersonal at times if we are operating on the basis of certain cultural or sociological assumptions. For example, you might automatically suggest sharing a chicken instead of a pork dish when you go to a restaurant with your Jewish friend.

Conversely, the interaction between a salesclerk and customer buying socks can become more intimate if both decide to alter the rules. If the customer were to inquire about where to have a good meal and eventually invite the sock seller to lunch, the relationship would shift into another gear.

Interpersonal Relationships Emphasize Both Content and Emotions

What you say and how you say it—your tone of voice, amount of eye contact, facial expression, and posture—can reveal a great deal about the emotional makeup of a relationship.[31] Interpersonal exchanges provide clues about how intimate a relationship is, and also about the power structure within the relationship. If your mother yells, "CLEAN YOUR ROOM NOW!" and your father says gently, "Would you please clean your room?" both are delivering a message with the same goal. But the two messages have different relationship cues. The first one suggests that your mother sometimes resorts to exerting power and control. The second message suggests that your father tries to treat you more like an equal.

Interpersonal Relationships May Be Complementary, Symmetrical, or Parallel

Interpersonal interaction involves give-and-take, speaking and responding, influencing and being influenced. These patterns of interaction may be **complementary**. The partners' styles may fit together in a compatible way because one partner usually dominates and the other usually submits: one likes to listen and the other likes to talk; one likes someone to dictate a schedule and the other likes to control the agenda. Although these patterns of interaction complement each other, their inherent imbalance of power or influence may be unacceptable to some couples. We will discuss the implications of interpersonal power further in Chapter 7.

In a **symmetrical** relationship, both partners behave in similar ways.[32] In a **competitive symmetrical** relationship, each partner seeks to dominate the other. For example, each may try to control which TV programs the partners watch together or insist on participating in every spending decision. When both partners are consistently competing for equal power, they are bound to clash.

In contrast, some partners have **submissive symmetrical** relationships, in which each tries to relinquish control. The following snatch of conversation illustrates submissive symmetry:

Bea: What movie do you want to rent?

Vic: Oh, I don't care. You decide.

Bea: No, you decide. I don't care either.

Most relationships, however, are neither purely complementary nor purely symmetrical; they are **parallel**. In a parallel relationship, the partners' styles allow them to shift power back and forth in accordance with the situation or interaction. For example, if one partner knows a great deal about cars, then the other may be willing to bow out of the decision about which car to purchase. But that same partner may take the upper hand when it comes to discussing restaurants, and the other partner may defer to his or her judgment.

Interpersonal Relationships Are Governed by Rules

According to Susan Shimanoff, a rule is "a followable prescription that indicates what behaviour is obligated, preferred, or prohibited in certain contexts."[33] These rules, which help define appropriate and inappropriate communication in any given situation, may be explicit or implicit. For this class, explicit rules are probably spelled out in your syllabus. But your instructor has other rules that are more implicit. They are not written or verbalized because you learned them long ago: only one person speaks at a time; you raise your hand to be called; you do not pass notes.

Interpersonal relationships are also shaped by both explicit and implicit rules. You may explicitly ask your friend not to phone you after 9:00 P.M. There are also implied rules that most people follow as a relationship develops. In an early stage of a relationship, for example, we usually don't reveal private family secrets or our incomes. At a later stage, an intimate friend might be offended if we do *not* reveal these things. Understanding rules helps you understand what is expected in a relationship.

Rules are developed by those involved in the interaction and by the culture in which the individuals are interacting. It is interesting to note how the social rules in French society of the 1700s, listed below, remain appropriate today. We develop and modify the rules so that we can achieve the goals of the relationship.[34] One research team asked individuals to identify general rules for relationship development and maintenance and then rate their importance. Here are the most important rules:[35]

- Partners should respect each other's privacy.
- Partners should not reveal each other's secrets.
- Partners should look each other in the eye during conversation.
- Partners should not criticize each other publicly.

Most of us learn these relationship rules from experience, by observing and interacting with family members and then friends. Individuals who grow up in environments where these rules are not observed may not know how to behave in close relationships.

Interpersonal Relationships Evolve in Stages

Your best friend probably did not become your best friend the first time you met. It takes time for intimacy and honesty to develop in a relationship. Researchers have identified predictable patterns in relationship development. The early stage includes a period of testing, experimenting, and exploring. As the relationship intensifies, greater intimacy and sharing occur. Some researchers use the term bonding to describe more intense interpersonal relationships. There are also patterns in the way relationships end. Individuals may become dissatisfied, avoid each other, and then decide to end the relationship either by explicit agreement (such as a legal divorce) or by drifting away from each other. Rarely do people cut off contact abruptly. We will present more detailed models of relationship development and deterioration in Chapter 7.

Rules of Civility and Decent Behaviour

The following rules of "Civility and Decent Behavior in Company and Conversation" were taken by George Washington from an English translation of a French book of manners, moral virtues, and social relations. Most of the over two-hundred-year-old rules for appropriate interpersonal communication are still appropriate today.

Every action done in company ought to be with some sign of respect to those that are present.

When in company, put not your hands to any part of the body not usually discovered.

Show nothing to your friend that may affright him.

In the presence of others sing not to yourself with a humming noise, nor drum with your fingers or feet.

If you cough, sneeze, sigh, or yawn, do it not loud but privately; and speak not in your yawning, but put your handkerchief or hand before your face and turn aside.

Spit not in the fire, nor stoop low before it. Neither put your hands into the flames to warm them, nor set your feet upon the fire, especially if there be meat before it.

Turn not your back to others especially in speaking.

The gestures of the body must be suited to the discourse you are upon.

Let your countenance be pleasant, but in serious matters somewhat grave.

Use no reproachful language against any one; neither curse nor revile.

Be not apt to relate news if you know not the truth thereof.

From: *George Washington's Rules of Civility and Decent Behavior in Company and Conversation* (Applewood Books, Bedford, MA).

Interpersonal Relationships Range from Self-Oriented to Other-Oriented

In a self-oriented relationship, at least one of the partners is primarily focused on him or herself. The goal of the relationship is to maximize his or her rewards and to fulfill personal needs, rather than to meet the needs of the other person. In an other-oriented relationship, one or both partners focus on understanding the needs, desires, and goals of the other person. To do that, an individual needs skills in observing, interpreting, and empathizing with others. In 1951 Carl Rogers wrote a pioneering book called *Client-Centered Therapy*, which transformed the field of psychotherapy. In it Rogers explains how genuine positive regard for another person and an open and supportive communication climate lay the foundation for trusting in relationships. Rogers emphasized the importance of listening in connecting to another human being. He suggests we are often egocentric—we focus on our own thoughts, fears, and feelings—instead of being other-oriented.

How Can You Improve Your Own Interpersonal Communication?

Now that we have previewed the study of interpersonal communication and interpersonal relationships, you may be asking yourself, "Well, that's all well and good, but what do I have to do to improve my own interpersonal communication?" We suggest a five-part strategy.

Be Knowledgeable

By reading this chapter, you have already begun improving your communication skills. Competent communicators are knowledgeable. They know how communication works. They understand the components, principles, and rules of the communication process. As you read on in this book, you will learn theories, principles, concepts, and rules that will permit you to explain and predict how humans communicate.

Understanding these things is a necessary prerequisite for enhancing your interpersonal effectiveness, but this kind of knowledge alone does not make you competent. You would not let someone fix your car's carburetor if he or she had only read a book. Knowledge must be coupled with skill. And we acquire skill through practice.

Be Skilled

Competent communicators know how to translate knowledge into action. You can memorize the characteristics of a good listener but still not listen well. To develop skill requires practice and helpful feedback from others who can confirm the appropriateness of your actions.

Learning a social skill is not that different from learning how to drive a car or operate a computer.[36] To learn any skill, you must break it down into subskills that you can learn and practice. "Hear it, see it, do it, correct it" is the formula that seems to work best for learning any new behaviours.[37] In this book we will examine the elements of complex skills such as listening, offer activities that will let you practice the skill, and provide opportunities for you to receive feedback and correct your application of the skill.

Be Motivated

Practicing skills requires work. You need to be motivated to use your information and skill. You must want to improve, and you must have a genuine desire to connect with others if you wish to become a competent communicator. You may know people who understand how to drive a car and have the skill to drive, yet are reluctant to get behind the wheel. Or maybe you know someone who took a course in public speaking but is still too frightened to stand in front of a crowd. Similarly, someone may pass a test about interpersonal communication principles with flying colours, but unless they are motivated to use their newfound skills, their interactions with others may not improve.

Be Flexible

In this book, we do not identify tidy lists of strategies that you can use to "win friends and influence people," as Dale Carnegie has. The same set of skills is not effective in every situation, so competent communicators do not assume that "one size fits all." Rather, they assess each unique situation and adapt their behaviour to achieve the desired outcome. They examine the context, the situation, and the needs, goals, and messages of others to establish and maintain relationships.

Be Other-Oriented

Most of us are egocentric—self-focused; our first inclination is to protect ourselves. Scholars of evolution might argue that it is our tendency to look out for number one that ensures the continuation of the human race.

Yet when we focus *exclusively* on ourselves, it is difficult to communicate effectively. If we fail to adapt our message to our listener, we may not be successful in achieving our intended communication goal. Adapting messages to others does not mean that we tell them only what they want to hear; that would be unethical. Nor does being considerate of others mean we abandon all concern for our own interests. Other-oriented communication suggests that we consider the needs, motives, desires, and goals of our communication partners while still maintaining our own integrity. The choices we make in forming the message and selecting the time and place to deliver it should consider the other person's thoughts and feelings.

How do you become other-oriented? We will devote considerable discussion throughout the book to developing this essential communication skill. Becoming other-oriented involves a two-step process: **decentring**—consciously thinking about another's thoughts and feelings—and **empathizing**—responding emotionally to another's feelings. What does your boss think and feel when you arrive late for work? What would your spouse think and feel if you brought a dog home as a surprise gift? To decentre is to try to understand your partner's thought processes and emotional reactions.[38]

Sometimes the information we use to think about someone else's thoughts and feelings is based upon our immediate observations or past memories. If we have no direct experiences to rely upon, we then may have to use our imagination to make educated guesses. For example, if you know how your best friend felt when her favourite uncle died, you could apply that knowledge to predict her behaviour in a new, unknown situation. You could make an educated guess about how she would feel if a classmate were to die. If you can predict your friend's behaviour, you are likely to be more tolerant of it. The decentring process, which involves conscious thinking, will open the door to an emotional response, or empathy. If you can understand a person's emotions, you may be able to "feel for" that person. Perhaps

BUILDING FOUNDATIONS OF INTERPERSONAL COMMUNICATION

Figure 1.5

Two relationships:
One which is other-
oriented and one which
is not.

Shared understanding and
feelings—other orientation

No shared understanding or
feelings—no other orientation

you would provide comfort and reassurance for your friend because you would actually have a sense of her grief. The less experience-based information we have, the more dependent we are upon our imaginations to fill the information void. Men, for instance, can never personally know what it is like to be pregnant and give birth. However, they can imagine what those things might be like, and those who have coached a woman through a birth have more experiences upon which to draw.

Empathy—the ability to put yourself in someone else's shoes in order to feel what that person is feeling—is an important quality for listening, responding, and observing nonverbal messages. We will discuss the way it affects these fundamental communication skills in Chapters 4, 5, and 6. And throughout the book we will emphasize the importance of developing an other orientation in your communication activities. As we explained in the "How to Use this Book" section at the beginning of this text, when we come to sections that will help you with this development, we will place a symbol in the margin to alert you. You may already have noted a few marked passages in this chapter (see page 16). As you can see in Figure 1.5, this symbol represents the sharing of thoughts and feelings in an interpersonal exchange. We have also incorporated special Considering Others features in all of the chapters to help you understand the meaning of this important quality.

CONSIDERING OTHERS

With a communication partner, role-play the following interpersonal situations in two ways. First, role-play an interaction in which the communicators are other-oriented; they decentre by thinking about what the other person may be thinking or feeling, and they display empathy toward one another. Then role-play the same scene as self-centred communicators. Present your scenes to the class and discuss the interactions.

Suggested situations:

- Try to return a broken VCR to a department store salesperson.

- Correct a grocery store cashier who has scanned an item at the wrong price.

- Meet with a teacher who gave your son or daughter a failing grade.

- Ask your professor for a one-day extension on a paper that is due tomorrow.

- Ask someone for a donation to a worthy cause.

- Ask a professor for permission to get into a class that has reached its maximum enrollment.

- Accept an unappealing compact disc as a gift from a friend.

- Remind your son or daughter that he or she needs to practice the piano.

Summary

Communication is the process of acting upon information. Human communication is the process of making sense out of the world and sharing that sense with others. Interpersonal communication is the process of interacting simultaneously and sharing mutual influence with another person. Early models viewed human communication as a simple message transfer process. Later models evolved to view communication as interaction and finally as transaction. Contemporary approaches to interpersonal communication emphasize the simultaneous nature of influencing others. They identify seven key components in the interpersonal communication process: source, receiver, message, channel, noise, context, and feedback. Electronic media may encourage further evolution of our models for interpersonal communication.

Interpersonal communication is inescapable, irreversible, complicated, and contextual. Rarely, if ever, are our thoughts and feelings interpreted by others *exactly* as we intended. We should try to ensure that the messages we communicate are understood by others, that they achieve their intended effect, and that they are ethical.

If we understand interpersonal communication and the relationships it promotes, then we can improve our relationships with family, friends, and colleagues. Interpersonal relationships affect our overall health and well-being. Interpersonal relationships range from impersonal to intimate, are complementary or symmetrical, and are governed by rules and evolve in stages. The goal of this book is to help you improve your interpersonal skills and relationships. The most effective interpersonal communicators are knowledgeable, skilled, motivated, flexible, and other-oriented. Learning to connect with others—by decentring and developing empathy—is the key to establishing satisfying relationships.

For Discussion and Review

█ FOCUS ON COMPREHENSION

1. Discuss key differences among the communication as action, interaction, and transaction models.

2. Define communication, human communication, and interpersonal communication. Discuss the differences among them.

3. What are the four principles of communication discussed in this chapter?

4. Identify the characteristics of interpersonal relationships.

█ FOCUS ON CRITICAL THINKING

5. Analyze a recent interpersonal exchange with someone that did not go well. Write down some of the dialogue. Did the other person understand you? Did your communication have the intended effect? Was your message ethical?

6. Make a relationship scale on a piece of paper and label it "impersonal" at one end and "intimate" at the other. Place your family members and closest friends on the scale; then compare and discuss your entries with your classmates.

7. What rules govern your relationship with your mother? Your father? Your communication teacher? Your roommate or spouse?

█ FOCUS ON ETHICS

8. Think about your primary goal for this course. Is it to develop strategies to achieve your own personal goals? Is it to develop sensitivity to the needs of others? What is behind your desire to achieve your goal? Is your purpose ethical?

9. Your parents want you to visit them for the holidays. You would rather spend the time with a friend. You don't want to hurt your parents' feelings so you tell them that you have an important project that you are working on; you won't be able to come home for the holidays. Your message is understood. It achieves the intended effect; you don't go home. Explain why you think your message is ethical or unethical.

For Your Journal

1. Try to identify at least three personal goals for improving your interpersonal relationships. Write several specific objectives that you hope to accomplish by the end of this course.

2. Briefly describe a recent communication exchange that was not effective. Perhaps you or your communication partner did not understand the message, or the message may not have achieved its intended goal, or it may have been unethical. Analyze the communication exchange, applying the components of communication discussed in this chapter. For example, what was the communication context? What were sources of internal and external noise? Did you have problems encoding and decoding? Were there problems with the communication channel?

3. Keep a one-day log of your electronically mediated interactions (e.g., phone calls, E-mail messages, fax messages). Describe each one, noting whether there was a greater emphasis on the content or emotional elements of the messages you exchanged during the interaction.

■ LEARNING WITH OTHERS

1. Working with a group of your classmates, develop a five-minute lesson to teach one of the following concepts to your class:

   A. Human communication as action

   B. Human communication as interaction

   C. Human communication as transaction

   D. Differences between complementary and symmetrical relationships

   E. How interpersonal relationships are governed by rules

   F. How interpersonal relationships range from impersonal to intimate

   G. How to improve communication effectiveness

2. Working with a group of your classmates, develop your own model of interpersonal communication. Include all of the components that are necessary to describe how communication between people works. Your model could be a drawing or an actual object (like a Slinky toy) that symbolizes the communication process. Share your model with the class, describing the decisions your group made in developing it. Illustrate your model with a conversation between two people, pointing out how elements of the conversation relate to the model.

COMMUNICATION: The process of acting upon information.

HUMAN COMMUNICATION: The process of making sense out of the world and attempting to share that sense with others.

INTERPERSONAL COMMUNICATION: The process of interacting simultaneously and sharing mutual influence with another person.

INFORMATION SOURCE: The thought or emotion that triggers communication.

SOURCE: The originator of a thought or emotion who puts it into a code that can be understood by a receiver.

ENCODE: To translate ideas, feelings, and thoughts into a code.

DECODE: To interpret ideas, feelings, and thoughts that have been translated into a code.

RECEIVER: The person who decodes a message and attempts to make sense out of what the source has encoded.

MESSAGE: The written, spoken, and unspoken elements of communication to which people assign meaning.

CHANNEL: The pathway through which messages are sent.

NOISE: Information, either literal or psychological, that interferes with the accurate reception of the communication of the message.

CONTEXT: The physical and psychological communication environment.

FEEDBACK: The response to a message.

EPISODE: A sequence of interaction between individuals during which the message of one person influences the message of another.

SYMBOL: A representation of something else.

PSYCHOLOGICAL CONTEXT: Elements that an individual brings to a relationship, including needs, desires, values, personality, and self-concept.

RELATIONAL CONTEXT: All those factors that evolve when two people meet and continue a relationship: level of trust, degree of self-disclosure, level of power and control, and the history of the relationship.

SITUATIONAL CONTEXT: The event or reason two people are communicating with one another.

ENVIRONMENTAL CONTEXT: The physical surroundings in which people communicate.

CULTURAL CONTEXT: All elements within a culture, such as learned rules, behaviours, and values, that affect the interaction.

INTERPERSONAL RELATIONSHIP: The connection we forge with another human being through interpersonal communication.

CULTURAL INFORMATION: Information about language and dominant values learned in a given culture that we assume someone shares even if we know little about him or her.

SOCIOLOGICAL INFORMATION: Information based upon what we know about another person's membership in certain groups.

PSYCHOLOGICAL INFORMATION: Information about the unique person with whom we are interacting.

COMPLEMENTARY RELATIONSHIP: A relationship in which the partners' communication styles fit together in a compatible way; one willingly turns over power to the other (e.g., one person likes to talk, the other person likes to listen).

SYMMETRICAL RELATIONSHIP: A relationship in which both partners behave in similar ways while striving for equal power when they communicate.

COMPETITIVE SYMMETRICAL RELATIONSHIP: A relationship in which each partner seeks to dominate and control the other (e.g., both individuals like to talk and monopolize the conversation).

SUBMISSIVE SYMMETRICAL RELATIONSHIP: A relationship in which each partner strives to relinquish control (e.g., each may try to convince the other person to make a decision about something that affects both—such as which TV program to watch).

PARALLEL RELATIONSHIP: A relationship in which the partners are willing to shift power back and forth in accordance with the communication situation or interaction.

BONDING: The process of emotionally and psychologically becoming attached or enmeshed with another person.

DECENTRING: The process of thinking about another person's thoughts and feelings.

EMPATHY: The ability to "feel for" another person, or to "stand inside another's shoes."

Communication and Self

After studying this chapter, you should be able to:

1. Define, compare, and contrast the meanings of self-concept and self-esteem.

2. Identify factors that shape the development of your self-concept.

3. Describe how your self-concept affects your relationships with others.

4. Identify the effects of your communication style upon your relationships with others.

5. List and describe strategies for improving your self-esteem.

■ SELF-CONCEPT: WHO ARE YOU?

■ SELF-ESTEEM: YOUR SELF-WORTH

■ HOW SELF-CONCEPT AND SELF-ESTEEM AFFECT INTER-PERSONAL COMMUNICATION AND RELATIONSHIPS

■ IMPROVING YOUR SELF-ESTEEM

hilosophers suggest that there are three basic questions to which we all seek answers: (1) Who am I? (2) Why am I here? and (3) Who are all these others? In this chapter we will focus on these essential questions. We view them as progressive. Grappling with the question of who you are and seeking to define a purpose for your life are fundamental to understanding others and becoming other-oriented in your interpersonal communication and your relationships.

Fundamentally, all of your communication starts or ends with you. When you are the communicator, you intentionally or unintentionally code your thoughts and emotions to be interpreted by another. When you receive a message, you interpret the information through your own frame of reference. Your self-image and self-worth, as well as your needs, values, beliefs, and attitudes, serve as filters for your communication with others. As you develop and establish relationships, you may become more aware of these filters, and perhaps you will have the desire to alter them. A close relationship often provides the impetus for change.

To better understand the role that self-concept plays in interpersonal communication, we will explore the first two basic questions, Who am I? and Why am I here?, by trying to discover the meaning of self. We will examine the multifaceted dimensions of our self-concept, learn how it develops, and compare self-concept to self-esteem. Then we will move to the third basic question, Who are all these others? We will discuss the effect of our self-concept on our communication with others, focusing on how our individual communication styles affect our interpersonal relationships.

Self-Concept: Who Are You?

ou can begin your journey of self-discovery by trying the following Communication Experience.

How did you answer the question, Who are you? Perhaps your self-descriptions identify activities in which you participate. Others may describe groups and organizations to which you belong or some of the roles you assume, such as student, child, or parent. All of these things are indeed a part of yourself, the sum total of who you are. Karen Horney defines self as "that central inner force, common to all human beings and yet unique in each, which is the deep source of growth."[1]

Your answers are also part of your **self-concept**. Your self-concept is your subjective description of who you *think* you are—it is filtered through your own perceptions.

Consider this question: Who are you? More specifically, ask yourself this question ten times. Write your responses in the spaces provided here or on a separate piece of paper. It may be challenging to identify ten aspects of yourself; the Spanish writer Cervantes said, ". . . to know thyself . . . is the most difficult lesson in the world." But your answers will help you begin to explore your self-concept and self-esteem in this chapter.

I am _____   I am _____

I am _____   I am _____

I am _____   I am _____

I am _____   I am _____

I am _____   I am _____

For example, you may have great musical talent, but you may not believe in it enough to think of yourself as a musician. We can view self-concept as the labels we consistently use to describe ourselves to others.

Who you are is also reflected in the attitudes, beliefs, and values that you hold. These are learned constructs that shape your behaviour and self-image. An **attitude** is a learned predisposition to respond to a person, object, or idea in a favourable or unfavourable way. Attitudes reflect what you like and what you don't like. If you like school, butter pecan ice cream, and your mother, you hold positive attitudes toward these things. You were not born with a fondness for butter pecan ice cream; you learned to like it just as some people learn to enjoy the taste of snails, raw fish, or puréed turnips.

Beliefs are the way in which you structure your understanding of reality—what is true and what is false. Most of your beliefs are based on previous experience. You trust that the sun will rise in the morning and that you will get burned if you put your hand on a hot stove.

How are attitudes and beliefs related? They often function quite independently of one another. You may have a favourable attitude toward something and still believe negative things about it. You may believe, for example, that your school football team will not win the national championship this year, although you may be a big fan. Or you may believe that God exists, yet not always like what God does. Beliefs have to do with what is true or not true, while attitudes reflect likes and dislikes.

Values are enduring concepts of good and bad, right and wrong. Your values are more resistant to change than either your attitudes or your beliefs. They are also more difficult for most people to identify. Values are so central to who you are that it is difficult to isolate them. For example, when you go to the supermarket, you may spend a few minutes deciding on whether to buy regular or cream-style corn, but you probably do not spend much time deciding whether you will steal the corn or pay for it. Our values are instilled in us by our earliest interpersonal relationships; for almost all of us, our parents shape our values. The chart in Figure 2.1 shows that values are central to our behaviour and concept of self, and that what we believe to be true or false stems from our values. Attitudes are at the outer edge of the circle because they are the most likely to change. You may like your co-worker today but not tomorrow, even though you *believe* the person will come to work every day and you still *value* the concept of friendship.

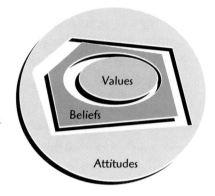

Figure 2.1

Values, Beliefs, and Attitudes in Relation to Self

Values

Beliefs

Attitudes

RECAP	Who You Are Is Reflected in Your Attitudes, Beliefs, and Values		
	Definition	**Dimensions**	**Example**
ATTITUDES	Learned predispositions to respond favourably or unfavourably toward something.	Likes–Dislikes	You like ice cream, incense, and cats.
BELIEFS	The way in which we structure reality.	True–False	You believe your parents love you.
VALUES	Enduring concepts of what is right and wrong.	Good–Bad	You value honesty and truth.

One or Many Selves?

Shakespeare's famous line, "To thine own self be true," suggests that you have a single self to which you can be true. But do you have just one self? Or is there a more "real you" buried somewhere within? "I'm just not myself this morning," sighs Sandy, as she drags herself out the front door to head for her office. If she is not herself, then *who is she?* Most scholars conclude that we have a core set of behaviours, attitudes, beliefs, and values that constitute our self—the sum total of who we are. But our *concept* of self can and does change, depending upon circumstances and influences.

In addition, our self-concepts are often different from the way others see us. We almost always behave differently in public than we do in private. Sociologist Erving Goffman suggests that, like actors and actresses, we have "on stage" behaviours when others are watching and "backstage" behaviours when they are not.

Perhaps the most enduring and widely accepted framework for describing who you are was developed by the philosopher William James. He identified three components of the self: the material self, the social self, and the spiritual self. We will continue our exploration by examining these components.

As this sculpture implies, each of us dons a series of masks for our "on stage" interactions with others throughout the day. (Sandra Rice)

Perhaps you've heard the statement "You are what you eat." The **material self** goes a step further by suggesting, "You are what you have." The material self is a total of all of the tangible things you own: your possessions, your home, your body. As you examine your list of responses to the question "Who are you?" note whether any of your statements refers to one of your physical attributes or something you own.

One element of the material self gets considerable attention in our culture: the body. Do you like the way you look? Most of us, if we're honest, would like to change something about our appearance. When there is a discrepancy between our desired material self and our self-concept, we may respond to eliminate the discrepancy. We may try to lose weight, change the shape of our nose, or acquire more hair. The multibillion-dollar diet industry is just one of many that profit from our collective desire to change our appearance. Anna Quindlen's essay "The Barbie Doll, Now 35 Years Old," points out how a pop culture image of the "ideal" can affect self-image.

We also attempt to keep up with the proverbial Joneses by wanting more expensive clothes, cars, and homes. By extension, what we own becomes who we are. The bigger, better, and more luxurious our possessions, we may subconsciously conclude, the better *we* are.

The Barbie Doll, Now 35 Years Old

My theory is that to get rid of Barbie you'd have to drive a silver stake through her plastic heart. Or a silver lamé stake, the sort of thing that might accompany Barbie's Dream Tent.

This is not simply because the original Barbie, launched 35 years ago, was more than a little vampiric in appearance, more Natasha of "Rocky and Bullwinkle" than the "ultimate girl next door" Mattel describes in her press kit.

It's not only that Barbie, like Dracula, can appear in guises that mask her essential nature: surgeon, astronaut, UNICEF ambassador. Or that she is untouched by time, still the same parody of the female form she's been since 1959.

She's said by her manufacturers to be "eleven and one-half stylish inches" tall. If she were a real live woman she would not have enough body fat to menstruate regularly. Which may be why there's no PMS Barbie.

The silver stake is necessary because Barbie—the issue, not the doll—simply will not be put to rest.

"Mama, why can't I have Barbie?"

"Because I hate Barbie. She gives little girls the message that the only thing that's important is being tall and thin and having a big chest and lots of clothes. She's a terrible role model."

"Oh, Mama, don't be silly. She's just a toy."

It's an excellent comeback, if only it were accurate. But consider the recent study at the University of Arizona investigating the attitudes of white and black teenage girls toward body image.

The attitudes of the white girls were a nightmare. Ninety percent expressed dissatisfaction with their own bodies and many said they saw dieting as a kind of all-purpose panacea. "I think the reason I would diet would be to gain self-confidence," said one. "I'd feel like it was a way of getting control," said another.

And they were curiously united in their description of the perfect girl. She's 5 feet 7 inches, weighs just over 100 pounds, has long legs and flowing hair. The researchers concluded, "The ideal girl was a living manifestation of the Barbie doll."

While the white girls described an impossible ideal, black teenagers talked about appearance in terms of style, attitude, pride and personality. White respondents talked "thin," black ones "shapely."

Seventy percent of the black teenagers said they were satisfied with their weight, and there was little emphasis on dieting. "We're all brought up and taught to be realistic about life," said one, "and we don't look at things the way you want them to be. You look at them the way they are."

There's a quiet irony in that. While black women correctly complain that they are not sufficiently represented in advertisements, commercials, movies, even dolls, perhaps the scarcity of those idealized and unrealistic models may help in some fashion to liberate black teenagers from ridiculous standards of appearance.

When the black teenagers were asked about the ideal woman, many asked: Whose ideal? The perfect girl projected by the white world simply didn't apply to them or their community, which set beauty standards from within. "White girls," one black participant in the Arizona study wrote, "have to look like Barbie dolls."

There are lots of reasons teenage girls have such a distorted fun-house mirror image of their own bodies, so distorted that one study found that 83 percent wanted to lose weight, although 62 percent were in the normal range.

Fashion designers still showcase anorexia chic; last year the supermodel Kate Moss was reduced to insisting that, yes, she did eat.

But long before Kate and Ultra Slimfast came along, hanging over the lives of every little girl born in the second half of the 20th century was the impossibly curvy shadow (40-18-32 in lifesize terms) of Barbie. That preposterous physique, we learn as kids, is what a woman looks like with her clothes off.

"Two Barbie dolls are sold every second," says Barbie's résumé, which is more extensive than that of Hillary Rodham Clinton. "Barbie doll has had more than a billion pairs of shoes . . . has had over 500 professional makeovers . . . has become the most popular toy ever created."

Has been single-handedly responsible for the popularity of the silicone implant?

Maybe, as my daughter suggests while she whines in her Barbie-free zone, that's too much weight to put on something that's just a toy. Maybe not. Happy birthday, Babs. Have a piece of cake. Have two.

—ANNA QUINDLEN

Look at your "Who are you?" list once more. How many of your responses relate to your **social self**, the part of you that interacts with others? William James believed that you have many social selves—that depending on the friend, family member, colleague, or acquaintance with whom you are interacting, you change the

way you are. A person has, said James, as many social selves as there are people who recognize him or her. For example, when you talk to your best friend, you are willing to "let down your hair" and reveal more thoughts and feelings than you would in a conversation with your communication professor, or even your parents. Each relationship that you have with another person is unique because you bring to it a unique social self.

Artists Frida Kahlo and Egon Schiele sought to explore their self dimensions by painting their own portraits. What qualitites do each of these self-portraits reveal? (The Granger Collection)

■ THE SPIRITUAL SELF

Your **spiritual self** consists of all your internal thoughts and introspections about your values and moral standards. It is not dependent upon what you own or with whom you talk; it is the essence of who you *think* you are, and of your *feelings* about yourself, apart from external evaluations. It is an amalgam of your religious beliefs and your sense of who you are in relationship to other forces in the universe. Your spiritual self is the part of you that answers the question "Why am I here?"

RECAP	William James's Dimensions of Self	
	Definition	**Examples**
MATERIAL SELF	All of the physical elements that reflect who you are.	Possessions, car, home, body, clothes.
SOCIAL SELF	The self as reflected through your interactions with others; actually a variety of selves that respond to changes in situations and roles.	Your informal self interacting with your best friend; your formal self interacting with your professors.
SPIRITUAL SELF	Introspections about values, morals, beliefs.	Belief or disbelief in God; regard for life in all its forms.

Take another look at your responses to the question "Who are you?" Divide your list according to James's description of self-concept as material, social, or spiritual self. If, for example, nothing on your original list relates to your spiritual self, make an entry here so that you have a response for each of the three "selves."

Material Self
References to the physical elements that reflect who you are.

Social Self
References to interactions with others that reflect who you are.

Spiritual Self
References to your reflections about values, morals, and beliefs.

Example:
I collect antiques.

I am a member of the Chess Club.

I believe the *Book of Mormon* is an inspired book.

_____   _____   _____

_____   _____   _____

_____   _____   _____

_____   _____   _____

_____   _____   _____

How Your Self-Concept Develops

James's three elements define the dimensions of the self, but they do not tell us where our "Who am I?" responses come from. In truth, we can only speculate about their origins. But some psychologists and sociologists have advanced theories that suggest we learn who we are through four basic means: (1) our interactions with other individuals, (2) our association with groups, (3) roles we assume, and (4) our own labels. Like James's framework, this one does not cover every base in our study of self, but its constructs can provide some clues about how our own self-concepts develop.

INTERACTION WITH INDIVIDUALS

In 1902, Charles Horton Cooley first advanced the notion that we form our self-concepts by seeing ourselves in a kind of figurative **looking glass**: we learn who we are by interacting with others, much as we look into a mirror and see our reflection. Like Cooley, George Herbert Mead also believed that our behaviour and our sense of who we are are a consequence of our relationship with others. And Harry Stack Sullivan theorized that from birth to death our self changes primarily because of how people respond to us. One sage noted, "We are not only our brother's keeper; we are our brother's maker."

The process begins at birth. Our names, one of the primary ways we identify ourselves, are given to us by someone else. During the early years of our lives, our parents are the key individuals who reflect who we are. If our parents encouraged us to play the piano, we probably play now. As we become less dependent on our parents, our friends become highly influential in shaping our attitudes, beliefs, and values. And friends continue to provide feedback on how well we perform certain tasks. This, in turn, helps us shape our sense of identity as adults—we must acknowledge our talents in math, language, or art in our own minds before we say that we are mathematicians, linguists, or artists.

Fortunately, not *every* comment affects our sense of who we think we are or our own self-worth. We are likely to incorporate the comments of others into our self-concept under three conditions:

First, we are more likely to believe another's statement if he or she repeats something we have heard several times. If one person casually tells us we have a good ear for singing, we are not likely to launch a search for an agent and a recording contract. But if several individuals tell us on many different occasions that we have a talent for singing, we may decide to do something about it.

Second, we are more likely to value another's statements if he or she has already earned our confidence. If we believe the individual is competent, trustworthy, and qualified to make a judgment about us, then we are more likely to believe it. You would be more likely to think you were a talented singer if you heard it from opera star Luciano Pavarotti rather than your Aunt Sally. Again, while we are very young, our parents are the dominant voices of credibility and authority. If they tell us repeatedly that we are spoiled and sloppy, then we will probably come to view ourselves that way. If they tell us we are loving, gifted, and charming, we are likely to believe it.

Third, we are likely to incorporate another's comments into our own concept of self if the comments are consistent with other comments and our own experience. If your boss tells you that you work too slowly, but for years people have been urging you to slow down, then your previous experience will probably encourage you to challenge your boss's evaluation.

■ ASSOCIATION WITH GROUPS

I'm a Liberal. I'm a Girl Guide. I'm a rabbi. I'm a coach. I'm a member of the Sweet Adelines. Each of these self-descriptive statements has something in common. They answer the "Who are you?" question by providing identification with a group or organization. Reflect once more on your responses to the "Who are you?" question. How many associate you with a group? Religious groups, political groups, ethnic groups, social groups, study groups, and occupational and professional groups play important roles in determining our self-concept. Some of these groups we are born into; others we choose on our own. Either way, these group associations are significant parts of our identities.

As we have already noted, peer pressure is a powerful force in shaping attitudes and behaviour, and adolescents are particularly susceptible to it. But adolescents are not alone in allowing the attitudes, beliefs, and values of others to shape their expectations and behaviour. Most adults, to varying degrees, ask themselves, "What will the neighbours think? What will my family think?" when they are making choices.

■ ROLES WE ASSUME

Look again at your answers to the "Who are you?" question. Perhaps you see words or phrases that signify a role you often assume. Father, aunt, sister, uncle, manager, salesperson, teacher, and student are labels that imply certain expectations for behaviour, and they are important in shaping self-concept. Couples who live together before they marry often report that marriage alters their relationship. Before, they may have shared domestic duties such as doing dishes and laundry. But when they assume the labels of "husband" and "wife," they slip into traditional roles. Husbands don't do laundry. Wives don't mow the grass. These stereotypical role expectations that they learned long ago may require extensive discussion and negotiation. Couples who report the highest satisfaction with marriage have similar role expectations for themselves and their spouses.

One reason we assume traditional roles automatically is that our gender group asserts a powerful influence from birth on. As soon as parents know the sex of their child, many begin placing their children in the group by following cultural rules. They paint the nursery pink for a girl, blue for a boy. Boys get a catcher's mitt, a train set, or a football for their birthdays; girls get dolls, frilly dresses, and tea sets. These cultural conventions and expectations play a major role in shaping our self-concept and our behaviour. We describe male babies as strong, solid, and independent; little girls are cute, cuddly, and sweet.[2] Recent research suggests that up until the age of three, children themselves are not acutely aware of sex roles. Between the ages of three and

Very young children are not highly aware of sex differences. By age seven, however, boys and girls may think it's embarrassing to play with one another in public. (John Lee/Stock Boston)

five, however, masculine and feminine roles begin to emerge,[3] and they are usually solidified between the ages of five and seven.

Although it is changing, North American culture is still male-dominated. What we consider appropriate and inappropriate behaviour is often different for males than it is for females. For example, in group and team meetings, task-oriented, male-dominated roles are valued more than feminine, relationship-building roles.[4] We applaud fathers who work sixty hours a week as "diligent and hard working," but criticize mothers who do the same as "neglectful and selfish." The list on page 43 illustrates more of these contrasts.

The groups we choose are our microenvironments, but our gender groups represent the expectations of an even larger group: the culture into which we are born. We do, however, make choices about our gender roles. One researcher developed an inventory designed to assess whether you play traditional masculine, feminine, or androgynous roles.[5] Because an **androgynous** role is both masculine and feminine, this role encompasses a greater repertoire of actions and behaviours. Take the inventory in the Communication Experience below, to see what role you have assumed.

COMMUNICATION EXPERIENCE

Bem Sex-Role Inventory[6]

Indicate the degree to which each statement is true of you.

Write 1 if the statement is never or almost never true of you.

Write 2 if it is usually not true of you.

Write 3 if it is sometimes but infrequently true of you.

Write 4 if it is occasionally true of you.

Write 5 if it is usually true of you.

Write 6 if it is always or almost always true of you.

_____ 1. I am self-reliant.

_____ 2. I am cheerful.

_____ 3. I am independent.

_____ 4. I am affectionate.

_____ 5. I have a strong personality.

_____ 6 I am sympathetic.

_____ 7. I act as a leader.

_____ 8. I am eager to soothe hurt feelings.

_____ 9. I am analytical.

_____ 10. I am warm.

Odd-numbered items are stereotypes for masculine traits; even-numbered items are stereotypical feminine traits. Total your score for masculine and feminine items. A score of 22 for either masculine or feminine is high; below 22 is low. If you scored high on both traits, you have a high androgynous score, suggesting you have a wide range of behaviours. No single test can definitively categorize you as either masculine or feminine, but your scores may give you some sense of the role you have assumed. This test is designed to help you describe yourself, rather than to prescribe a certain way for you to behave.

From: *Connecting: A Culture-Sensitive Approach to Interpersonal Communication Competency,* by Roy M. Berko, Lawrence B. Rosenfield, and Larry A. Samovar. Copyright © 1994 by Harcourt Brace & Company. Reproduced by permission of the publisher.

SELF LABELS

Although our self-concept is deeply affected by others, we are not blank slates for them to write on. The labels we use to describe our own attitudes, beliefs, values, and actions also play a role in shaping our self-concept.

Where do we acquire our labels? We interpret what we experience; we are self-reflexive. **Self-reflexiveness** is the human ability to think about what we are doing

Stereotypical Labels for Males and Females

Terms for Males	Terms for Females
Aggressive	Appreciative
Arrogant	Considerate
Assertive	Cooperative
Conceited	Dependent
Dominant	Feminine
Forceful	Fickle
Frank	Friendly
Handsome	Frivolous
Hard-headed	Helpful
Outspoken	Submissive
Strong	Timid

From: Judy C. Pearson, Lynn H. Turner, and William Todd-Mancillas, *Gender & Communication* (Dubuque, IA: William C. Brown, 1991).

while we are doing it. We talk to ourselves about ourselves. We are both participants and observers in all that we do. This dual role encourages us to use labels to describe who we are.

When you were younger, perhaps you dreamed of becoming an all-star hockey player or a movie star. Your coach may have told you that you were a great player or a terrific actress, but as you matured, you probably began observing yourself more critically. You scored no goals; you did not get the starring role in the local production of *Annie*. So you self-reflexively decided that you were not, deep down, a hockey player or an actress, even though others may have labelled you as "talented." But sometimes, through this self-observation, we discover strengths, which encourages us to assume new labels. One woman we know never thought of herself as "heroic" until she went through seventy-two hours of labour before giving birth and then nursed her baby right after delivery.

We all have the ability to view ourselves almost as if we were another person. We may be harsher on ourselves than we are on others in judging skills, talents, and virtues, or we may have an inflated self-concept. Either way, the point is that we make judgments about ourselves and simplify them into labels we use to describe ourselves to others. As the study described in the reading below shows, our labels have a powerful effect on our feelings and behaviour.

One researcher suggests that we develop our self-concept by comparing our "real" self with an idealized view of who we think we should be and how we think we should act. The result of this comparison determines our level of self-esteem.

Passionate Women Feel More Romance

LOS ANGELES—Women who see themselves as passionate and sexually liberated have a much "greater capacity for love and romance" than those who are embarrassed or self-conscious about sex, according to a new study.

The research, by scientists Barbara Andersen and Jill Cyranowski, suggests a direct correlation between openness to sexual experiences and the ability to fall deeply in love.

The study, to be published in the *Journal of Personality and Social Psychology*, showed: Ninety-seven percent of the women studied who had "positive sexual self-concepts" had been in love sometime in their lives, compared to only 78 percent of women with a negative concept—those who described themselves as inhibited, embarrassed, or self-conscious about sex.

Women in the study who had a positive image of sex reported having had more romantic partners—an average of 2.1— than women who felt inhibited about sex—who reported 1.4 partners.

Women with a positive image of sex described themselves as friendly and likable, and other people as trustworthy. "Negative-rated women tended to describe themselves as aloof and skeptical of others or overly eager to commit themselves to the relationships," the researchers said.

Andersen said it also was significant that women with a positive view of their sexuality rated their own sexuality as above average, regardless of whether they had a current partner. On the other hand, negative-rated women described themselves as more sexual only if they currently had a partner.

"Women with a positive self-concept have a much more stable view of themselves as sexual women," Andersen said at the American Psychological Association's annual convention. "Their self-concept isn't dependent on having a romantic partner around."

The researchers interviewed and followed 174 college students. A secondary study, with 31 women, ages 25 to 46, found similar results, Andersen said.

To do the study, the researchers had to develop a measure of sexual self-concept. College women were asked to evaluate 300 words as to whether they described "a sexual woman." That list was pared to 26 adjectives, which had the most relevance to women's sexuality. Words that subjects said described a sexual woman included "passionate, stimulating, arousable, romantic, revealing, and loving."

The 174 women were later asked to rate, on a scale of 0 to 6, how much those adjectives described themselves. Women with a positive sexual self-concept were those who described themselves as passionate and stimulating. Women with a negative sexual self-concept described themselves using words like timid, inexperienced, and self-conscious.

Andersen said women develop the sexual attitudes long before beginning sexual relations, through "messages from parents and other adults about what sex is all about."

Andersen said she is now studying sexual self-concepts in men, but it is premature to tell how men differ from women in this regard.

Cox News Service. Reprinted by permission.

Self-Esteem: Your Self-Worth

Your **self-esteem** is closely related to your self-concept. Through your self-concept you *describe* who you are. Through your self-esteem, you *evaluate* who you are. The term **self-worth** is often used interchangeably with *self-esteem*. We derive our sense of self-worth from comparing ourselves to others: I'm good at playing soccer (because I beat others); I can't cook (because others cook better than I do); I'm not good at meeting people (most people I know seem to be more comfortable interacting with others); I can't fix a broken toilet (but my brothers and my mom and dad can). Each of these statements implies a judgment about how well or badly you can perform certain tasks, with implied references to how well others perform the same tasks. A belief that you cannot fix a broken toilet or cook like a chef may not in itself lower your self-esteem. But if there are *several* things you can't do well, or *many* important tasks that you cannot seem to master, these shortcomings may begin to colour your overall sense of worth.

Psychologist Eric Berne developed the concept of a **life position** to describe our overall sense of our own worth and that of others.[7] He identified four life positions: (1) "I'm OK, you're OK," or positive regard for self and others; (2) "I'm OK, you're not OK," or positive regard for self and low regard for others; (3) "I'm not OK, you're OK," or low self-regard and positive regard for others; and (4) "I'm not OK, you're not OK," or low regard for both self and others. Your life position is a driving force in your relationships with others. People in the "I'm OK, you're OK" position have the best chance for healthy relationships because they have discovered their own talents and also recognize that others have been given talents different from their own. Virginia Satir's "Declaration of Self-Esteem" below illustrates an "I'm OK" point of view.

Declaration of Self-Esteem

I am me.

In all the world, there is no one else exactly like me. There are persons who have some parts like me, but no one adds up exactly like me. Therefore, everything that comes out of me is authentically mine because I alone chose it.

I own everything about me—my body, including everything it does; my mind, including all its thoughts and ideas; my eyes, including the images of all they behold; my feelings, whatever they may be—anger, joy, frustration, love, disappointment, excitement; my mouth, and all the words that come out of it, polite, sweet or rough, correct or incorrect; my voice, loud or soft; and all my actions, whether they be to others or to myself.

I own my fantasies, my dreams, my hopes, my fears.

I own all my triumphs and successes, all my failures and mistakes.

Because I own all of me, I can become intimately acquainted with me. By so doing I can love me and be friendly with me in all my parts. I can then make it possible for all of me to work in my best interests.

I know there are aspects about myself that puzzle me, and other aspects that I do not know. But as long as I am friendly and loving to myself, I can courageously and hopefully look for the solutions to the puzzles and for ways to find out more about me.

However I look and sound, whatever I say and do, and whatever I think and feel at a given moment in time is me. This is authentic and represents where I am at that moment in time.

When I review later how I looked and sounded, what I said and did, and how I thought and felt, some parts may turn out to be unfitting. I can discard that which is unfitting, and keep that which proved fitting, and invent something new for that which I discarded.

I can see, hear, feel, think, say, and do. I have the tools to survive, to be close to others, to be productive, and to make sense and order out of the world of people and things outside of me.

I own me, and therefore I can engineer me.

I am me and I am okay.

—VIRGINIA SATIR

RECAP   **Comparison of Self-Concept and Self-Esteem**

SELF-CONCEPT   Your subjective *description* of who you are—your beliefs, attitudes, values, and behaviours.

SELF-ESTEEM   Your subjective *evaluation* of your worth based on skill, talent, appearance, and other factors.

How Self-Concept and Self-Esteem Affect Interpersonal Communication and Relationships

Your self-concept and self-esteem act as filters in every interaction with others. They determine how you approach, respond to, and interpret messages. Specifically, your self-concept and self-esteem affect your ability to be sensitive to others, your overall expectations through self-fulfilling prophecy, your interpretation of messages, and your typical communication style.

Self and Others

We have suggested the importance of becoming other-oriented—being sensitive to the thoughts and feelings of others—as a requisite for developing quality interpersonal relationships with others. As we saw in Chapter 1, the process of becoming other-oriented begins with decentring—consciously thinking about another person's thoughts and feelings. But before you begin to *decentre*, to try to understand another person from another perspective, it is important for you to feel *centred*—to know yourself and to understand how others see you.

To become other-oriented involves recognizing that your "self" is different from others. As the Peanuts cartoon reminds us, the world does not revolve around our solitary selves. Others influence our actions and our self-image. George Herbert Mead suggests that we develop an "I," which is based upon our own perspective of ourselves, and a "Me," which is an image of ourselves based upon the collective responses we receive and interpret from others. Being aware of how your concept of self ("I") differs from the perceptions others have of you ("Me") is an important first step in developing an other-orientation.

When we begin the decentring process, we often interpret our assumptions about others using our own selves as a frame of reference, especially if we do not know the other person well.[8] For example, if you are nervous and frightened when you have to take a test, you might assume that your friend will react the same way. You may need to remind yourself that the other person is separate from yourself and has a different set of responses.

When you use a **specific-other** perspective, you rely on information that you have observed or that you can imagine about a particular person to predict his or her reactions. For example, if you know firsthand that your sister hates it when someone eats off her plate during dinner, you may use that experience to conclude that she would dislike sharing a bag of popcorn at the movies.

Sometimes a **generalized-other** perspective will be more useful. When you decentre, you can apply knowledge and personal theories that you have about people in general or about specific subgroups to the person with whom you are interacting. For example, you might think that your economics professor, who holds a Ph.D., would prefer to be addressed as *Professor* rather than as *Mister* because almost all of your other professors with doctorates prefer to be called *Professor*.

PEANUTS

PEANUTS reprinted by permission of UFS Inc.

Your ability to predict how others will respond to you is based upon your ability to understand how your sense of the world is similar to, and different from, their own. First you must know yourself well. Then you can know and understand others. The best way to improve your ability to decentre is to notice how others respond when you act on the predictions and assumptions you have made about them. You may discover that you have not moved out of your own frame of reference enough to make an accurate prediction about another person.

Self-Fulfilling Prophecy

While you are considering whether a person's behaviour matches the predictions that you make about him or her, it is also important to remember that people interpret messages in a way that confirms what they already think of themselves. For example, suppose you think of yourself as an overly controlling person. If your sister surprises you by offering to share her popcorn at the movies, you may feel guilty

---

CONSIDERING OTHERS

As discussed in Chapter 1, empathy is an emotional capability that often grows out of a conscious decentring process. It is the ability to move away from yourself enough to "feel for" another person. But it does not mean abandoning your own self. On the contrary, empathetic people often have a strong self-concept and high self-esteem, which enable them to be generous with others. Take this short test to assess your empathy. Respond to each statement by indicating the degree to which the statement is true regarding the way you typically communicate with others. When you think of how you communicate, is the statement always false (answer 1), usually false (answer 2), sometimes false and sometimes true (answer 3), usually true (answer 4), or always true (answer 5)?

_____ 1. I try to understand others' experiences from their perspectives.

_____ 2. I follow the Golden Rule ("Do unto others as you would have them do unto you") when communicating with others.

_____ 3. I can "tune in" to emotions others are experiencing when we communicate.

_____ 4. When trying to understand how others feel, I imagine how I would feel in their situation.

_____ 5. I am able to tell what others are feeling without being told.

_____ 6. Others experience the same feelings I do in any given situation.

_____ 7. When others are having problems, I can imagine how they feel.

_____ 8. I find it hard to understand the emotions others experience.

_____ 9. I try to see others as they want me to.

_____ 10. I never seem to know what others are thinking when we communicate.

To find your score, first reverse the responses for the even-numbered items (if you wrote 1, make it 5; if you wrote 2, make it 4; if you wrote 3, leave it as 3; if you wrote 4, make it 2; if you wrote 5, make it 1). Next, add the numbers next to each statement. Scores range from 10 to 50. The higher your score, the more you are able to empathize.

From: William Gudykunst, *Bridging Differences*, 2d ed. (Thousand Oaks, CA: Sage Publications, 1994).

---

and wonder if she is just giving in to your bullying, instead of assuming that she is expressing affection for you. This extends into the realm of action as well. What we believe about ourselves often comes true because we expect it to come true. We refer to this as **self-fulfilling prophecy**. If you think you will fail the math quiz because you have labelled yourself inept at math, then you must overcome not only your math deficiency, but also your low expectations of yourself. As Professor Henry Higgins argues in George Bernard Shaw's play *Pygmalion*, "If you treat a girl like a flower girl, that's all she will ever be. If you treat her like a princess she may be one." Your attitudes, beliefs, and general expectations about your performance have a powerful and profound effect upon your behaviour.

The medical profession is learning the power that our attitudes and expectations have over healing. Dr. Bernard Siegel, in his book *Love, Medicine, and Miracles*,[9] provides convincing evidence that patient attitudes about the healing process have a direct effect upon becoming well. Patients who have a positive, cooperative spirit are likely to recover from illness more quickly than those who assume the worst. As the article below about positive attitudes and heart disease illustrates, your state of mind may influence your state of health.

Don't Worry, Be Happy: Study Shows Optimism Helps Fight Heart Disease

A healthy outlook helps heal the heart, scientists say in a study that found pessimism can be a killer.

The study identified optimism as a powerful predictor of who will live and who will die after the diagnosis of heart disease. It is the most recent in a series of recent reports showing that people's emotions and friendships play a critical role in recovery.

"Optimism is a good thing," Dr. Daniel Mark said. "When people give up and feel they are not going to make it, it's usually a self-fulfilling prophecy."

Mark, a heart specialist at Duke University, based his findings on a follow-up on 1,719 men and women who had undergone heart catheterization, a common procedure used to check the arteries for clogging. He outlined the results at a meeting of the Society of Behavioural Medicine in Rockville, Md.

The patients typically underwent the test because of chest pain, and all had heart disease. When interviewed, 14 percent said they doubted they would recover enough to resume their daily routines. After one year, 12 percent of these pessimists had died, compared with 5 percent of those who were optimistic about getting better.

Even when the severity of people's conditions was taken into account, outlook was a crucial factor in survival. In fact, optimism often seemed to have little bearing on how sick people were. In his study, pessimism appeared to be even more damaging to recovery than depression, which is also shown to be bad for heart patients.

Dr. Nancy Frasure-Smith of the Montreal Heart Institute presented follow-up data on the effect of negative emotions on 222 patients, most of them in their 60s, who were recovering from heart attacks.

They were given a psychological test that measures feelings of sadness and depression. Those who scored high on this were eight times more likely than more upbeat folks to die during the following 18 months. Feeling anxious tripled the risk, as did holding in anger.

Less clear, however, is what to do about these black moods in heart patients.

"We don't know how to change negative emotions," Frasure-Smith said. "And if we try to intervene, we don't know if we will change the prognosis."

How emotions harm the heart is unclear. Heart attacks usually occur when a bit of fatty buildup, called plaque, breaks in a heart artery. A blood clot sticks to this wound, plugging the artery and choking off the heart's oxygen supply. Researchers speculate that emotions may increase levels of hormones that put strain on the artery walls or make the blood more likely to clot.

—DANIE Q. HANEY

Cox News Service. Reprinted by permission.

Self and Interpretation of Messages

Do you remember Eeyore, the donkey from the stories about Winnie-the-Pooh and his friends? Eeyore lived in the gloomiest part of the Hundred Acre Wood and had a self-image to match. In one story, which used to be a favourite of one of your author's sons, all of the animals congregated on a stormy night to check on Eeyore:

> . . . they all came to the part of the forest known as Eeyore's gloomy place. On this stormy night it was terribly gloomy indeed—or it would have been were it not for Christopher Robin. He was there with a big umbrella.
>
> "I've invited Eeyore to come and stay with me until the storm is over," said Christopher Robin.
>
> "If it ever is," said Eeyore, "which doesn't seem likely. Not that anybody asked me, you understand. But then, they hardly ever do."[10]

Perhaps you know or have known an Eeyore—someone whose low self-esteem colours how he or she interprets messages and interacts with others. According to research, such people are more likely to have the following traits:[11]

■ Be more sensitive to criticism and negative feedback from others.

■ Be more critical of others.

■ Believe they are not popular or respected by others.

■ Expect to be rejected by others.

■ Not like to be observed when performing.

■ Feel threatened by people who they feel are superior.

■ Expect to lose when competing with others.

■ Be overly responsive to praise and compliments.

■ Evaluate their overall behaviour as inferior to that of others.

The Pooh stories offer an antidote to Eeyore's gloom in the character of the optimistic Tigger, who assumes that everyone shares his exuberance for life:

> *... when Owl reached Piglet's house, Tigger was there. He was bouncing on his tail, as Tiggers do, and shouting to Piglet. "Come on," he cried. "You can do it! It's fun!"*[12]

If, like Tigger, your sense of self-worth is high, research suggests you will:

- Have higher expectations for solving problems.

- Think more highly of others.

- Be more likely to accept praise and accolades from others without feeling embarrassed.

- Be more comfortable having others observe you when you perform.

- Be more likely to admit you have both strengths and weaknesses.

- Be more comfortable when you interact with others who view themselves as highly competent.

- Expect other people to accept you for who you are.

- Be more likely to seek opportunities to improve skills that need improving.

- Evaluate your overall behaviour more positively than would people with lower self-esteem.[13]

Reflecting the assumption that our self-concept influences our behaviour is the principle of **selective exposure**, which suggests that we tend to place ourselves in situations consistent with who we think we are. Whom do you usually find at a Baptist church on Sunday morning? Baptists. Who are the attendees at a Liberal convention? Liberals. If you view yourself as a good student who wants an A in the class, where are you likely to be during class time? We behave in ways that reinforce our perception of self, both in our interpretation of messages and our behaviour.

Self and Communication Style

Our self-concept and self-esteem affect not only the way we feel about ourselves, the way we interpret messages, and our personal performance; they also influence the way we *deliver* messages and treat other people. Each of us has a **communication style** or **social style** that is identifiable by the habitual ways in which we behave toward others. The style we adopt helps others interpret our messages. As they get to know you, other people begin to expect you to behave in a certain way, based upon previous associations with you. The table on the following page lists nine styles that researcher Robert Norton has identified, along with the behaviour that illustrates each style.[14]

In reality, most of us use several of these communication styles, depending upon the situation; we do, however, develop a "style profile" that includes two or more related styles.

The Wilson Learning Corporation classifies our communication styles by the degree to which we display assertive and responsive behaviours.[15] **Assertiveness**, according to the Wilson Learning model, refers to our efforts to control others: for

Style	Description of Behaviour
Dominant	Talks a lot. Takes charge. Comes on strong. Controls conversations.
Dramatic	Tells stories and jokes. Often exaggerates. Acts out illustrations for dramatic effect.
Contentious	Argues with others. Likes to debate. Demands evidence from others to support their arguments. Tenacious when arguing a point; difficult to turn off.
Animated	Uses a variety of facial expressions when talking. Uses many gestures. Emotionally expressive, particularly around the face and eyes.
Impression-leaving	Says things in a memorable way. Uses words effectively.
Relaxed	Seems cool, calm, centred, collected when talking with others even when under stress. Not easily affected by anxiety-producing situations.
Attentive	Listens well. Maintains eye contact and body posture that communicates interest in what others are saying. Good at paraphrasing what others have said.
Open	Easily expresses emotions and shares personal information with others.
Friendly	Often provides compliments, encouragement, and support to others. Helps others feel valued and affirmed.

Adapted from: Robert Norton, "Foundations of a Communicator Style Construct," *Human Communication Research* 4 (1978): 99–112.

example, trying to change their behaviour; asking them to take actions; trying to lead rather than follow. **Responsiveness** refers to our efforts to place the feelings of others above our own: for example, focusing attention on them; expressing interest in what they say; reaching out emotionally.

As Figure 2.2 shows, these two dimensions, assertiveness and responsiveness, contribute to one of four basic social styles. Each of the four styles—driver, expressive, amiable, and analytical—is based on a different combination of two anchoring response styles.

Drivers, at one extreme, are the highly assertive. They are aloof, cool, abrupt, and highly task-oriented; they control their emotions and even design their living space to focus on work and accomplishment, displaying awards and plaques that symbolize achievement. They strive for efficiency. When you visit a driver's office, you will probably sit across from the driver, with a desk or table between you, rather than face-to-face without a barrier.

Analyticals are also high on assertiveness and low on responsiveness. They, too, are task-oriented and focus on the job to be done rather than on relationships. Analyticals like structures and systems, so their offices and homes may have lots of cubbyholes and be highly organized. Analyticals are more comfortable accomplishing tasks than working with others.

Expressives are high in both assertiveness and responsiveness. While they often feel a need to control relationships, they may also be emotive and respond on impulse. Expressives tell and/or show others how they feel. Their offices and homes may be more dishevelled and disorganized than a driver's. Expressives may express

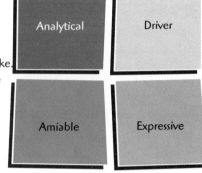

Task–Responsive
- Reserved, unresponsive.
- Wants facts and details.
- Eyes serious.
- Limited gestures.
- Limited exposure of personal feelings, story-telling, or small talk.
- Preoccupied or vigilant.

Ask–Assertive
- Little use of voice to express ideas.
- Deliberate, studied, or slow in speech.
- Indifferent handshake.
- Asks questions more often than makes statements.
- Vague about what is wanted.
- Tends to lean backwards.

Tell–Assertive
- Emphasizes ideas by tone change.
- Quick, clear, or fast paced.
- Firm handshake.
- Makes statements more often than asks questions.
- Lets others know what is wanted.

People–Responsive
- Animated, uses facial expressions.
- Actions open or eager.
- Little effort to push for facts.
- Friendly gaze.
- Varied gestures.
- Shares personal feelings.
- Attentive, responsive, enjoys the relationship.

Figure 2.2

Four Primary Communication Styles (Copyright 1990 by Wilson Learning Corporation)

their feelings with signs, slogans, and bumper stickers. Expressives, like drivers, want to get the job done, but they go about it in a more emotional way.

Amiables are the most responsive and least assertive types. They are more concerned with relationships than work; they want to meet people's social needs. Their goal is to make others feel welcome and comfortable. An amiable is likely to converse with others while seated at a round table or in chairs without a table.

You can see that the first three styles in Norton's classification system—dominant, dramatic, and contentious—encompass a number of assertive behaviours. Other styles in Norton's system reflect a more amiable approach to interactions—relaxed, open, friendly—similar to the amiable style identified by Wilson Learning Corporation. Both systems are ways of describing similar types of behaviour.

According to the Wilson Learning model, each of us has a predominant communication style, and we tend to interact most effectively with others who have a similar style. But we also have a **backup communication style** that we may use under stress if our primary style does not achieve the desired results. Under pressure, an amiable may become more assertive and move toward an expressive style. If a driver is unsuccessful in pushing others without regard to their feelings, he or she may become less assertive and move closer to an amiable style. Cultivating this kind of flexibility in responding to others can enhance the effectiveness of communication.

What's Your Communication Style?

1. Rate how often you use each style listed below. Ask friends or classmates to give you feedback on your self-descriptions or to rate you using the same scales. Ask them for specific examples that led to their observations.

Norton's Communication Styles

	Often Used	Sometimes Used	Uncertain if Used	Little Used	Rarely Used
Dominant	5	4	3	2	1
Dramatic	5	4	3	2	1
Contentious	5	4	3	2	1
Animated	5	4	3	2	1
Impression-leaving	5	4	3	2	1
Relaxed	5	4	3	2	1
Attentive	5	4	3	2	1
Open	5	4	3	2	1
Friendly	5	4	3	2	1

2. Now determine your communication style using the Wilson Learning Corporation model. For each of the scales below, place an X on the scale nearest the description that best fits you.

Task-Responsive
I restrict my actions around others. I keep my emotions to myself. I don't express my feelings to others.

Scale A

Expressive and People-Responsive
I am animated and expressive. I talk about my feelings and emotions when given the opportunity.

Ask-Assertive
I tend to make slow and deliberate actions. I tend to ask questions rather than make statements.
I am not assertive.

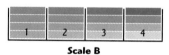
Scale B

Tell-Assertive
I am quick and decisive. I tend to make statements rather than ask questions. I am assertive.

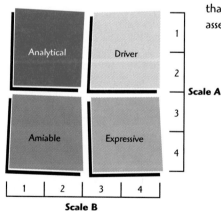
Scale B

3. Transfer your responses on scales A and B to the grid and then plot your social style.

Both Norton's system and the Wilson model help us see how our interaction with others is based upon learned assumptions regarding how we should behave that are closely tied to our self-concept and self-esteem. Recognizing the styles that you and others use will help you adapt your messages to others. We are not suggesting that you should, or even that you *can,* completely forsake the style that comes naturally to you. You can, however, develop flexibility and sensitivity to feedback, using it to enhance your self-concept and learn more about your own behaviour.[16]

RECAP	**How Self-Concept and Self-Esteem Affect Interpersonal Communication and Relationships**	
	Definition	**Examples**
MESSAGE INTERPRETATION AND INTERACTION	Feelings of high or low self-esteem affect how you understand and react to messages.	If you have high self-esteem, you are more likely to accept praise without embarrassment.
SELF-FULFILLING PROPHECY	What you believe about yourself will come true because you expect it to come true.	You expect to have a rotten time at a party and you behave in ways so that you don't enjoy the party.
COMMUNICATION STYLE	Your self-concept and self-esteem contribute to habitual ways of responding to others.	Your image of yourself influences your expressive or assertive behaviour toward others.

Improving Your Self-Esteem

We have already seen how low self-esteem can affect our own communication and interactions. In recent years teachers, psychologists, ministers, rabbis, social workers, and even politicians suggest that many of our societal problems as well stem from our collective feelings of low self-esteem. Our feelings of low self-worth may contribute to our choosing the wrong partners, to becoming dependent on drugs, alcohol, or other substances, and to experiencing problems with eating and other vital activities. So we owe it to society, as well as ourselves, to maintain or develop a healthy sense of self-esteem.

While no simple list of tricks can easily transform low self-esteem into feelings of being valued and appreciated, you can make improvements in the ways you think about yourself and interact with others. We'll explore seven proven techniques that have helped others.

Self-Talk

Intrapersonal communication is communication within yourself. Your level of self-esteem influences the way you talk to yourself about your abilities and skills. Perhaps you remember the children's story *The Little Engine That Could*, in which the pint-sized hero repeated, "I think I can. I think I can," to overcome a seemingly

"I'm on a diet today. How 'bout a shred of dignity and an ounce of respect?"

impossible challenge. Although becoming your own cheerleader may not enable you to climb your own metaphorical mountains quite so easily, there is evidence that self-talk, both positive and negative, does in fact influence behaviour. Realistic, positive self-talk can have a reassuring effect upon your level of self-worth and therefore your interactions with others. Conversely, repeating negative messages about your lack of skill and ability can keep you from trying and achieving.

For example, imagine that you have an algebra test coming up. If you are not optimistic about your performance on the test, you may be tempted to let your self-fulfilling prophecy come true by not studying. But by reminding yourself (talking to yourself) about the importance of study and effort, you may be able to change your defeatist outlook. If you tell yourself, "I don't have to fail if I study," or "If I seek help from the teacher and spend more time on algebra, I can master these formulas," you may motivate yourself to improve your performance. Improved performance can enhance your confidence and self-worth. Of course, blind faith without hard work won't succeed. Self-talk is not a substitute for effort; it can, however, keep you on track and help you ultimately to achieve your goal.

Visualization

Visualization takes the notion of self-talk one step further. Besides just telling yourself that you can achieve your goal, you can actually try to "see" yourself conversing effectively with others, performing well on a project, or emphasizing some other desirable behaviour. Recent research suggests that an apprehensive public speaker can manage his or her fears not only by developing skill in public speaking, but also by visualizing positive results when speaking to an audience. If you are one of the many people who fears speaking in public, try visualizing yourself walking to the lectern, taking out your well-prepared notes, and delivering an interesting, well-received speech. This visualization of positive results enhances confidence and speaking skill. The same technique can be used to boost your sense of self-worth about other tasks or skills. Of course, your visualization should be realistic and coupled with a plan to achieve your goal. Visualizing yourself performing well can yield positive results in changing long-standing feelings of inadequacy.

Avoiding Comparisons

Even before we are born, we are compared with others. The latest medical technology lets us see sonograms of fetuses still in the womb, so parents may begin comparing children with their siblings or other babies before birth. For the rest of our lives we are compared with others, and rather than celebrating our uniqueness, comparisons usually point up who is bigger, brighter, and more beautiful. Most of us have had the experience of being chosen last to play on a sports team, passed over for promotion, or standing unchosen against the wall at a dance.

In North American culture we may be tempted to judge our self-worth by our material possessions and personal appearance. If we know someone who has a newer car (or simply a car, if we rely on public transportation), a smaller waistline, or a higher grade point average, we may feel diminished. Comparisons such as "He has more money than I have," or "She looks better than I look," are likely to deflate our self-worth. One-hundred-and-one-year-old Sadie and one-hundred-and-three-year-old Besie Delaney, sisters who have endured racial prejudice, have inspired many by their refusal to let what they didn't have deter their sense of personal accomplishment. In their best-seller, *Having Our Say*, these two family matriarchs write of the value of emphasizing what we have, rather than comparing our lack of resources with the abundance of others who have more.

Rather than finding others who seemingly are better off, focus on the unique attributes that make you who you are. Avoid judging your own value in comparison to that of others. A healthy, positive self-concept is fueled not by judgments of others, but by a genuine sense of worth that we recognize in ourselves.

Reframing

Reframing is the process of redefining events and experiences from a different point of view. Just as reframing a work of art can give the picture a whole new look, reframing events that cause us to devalue our self-worth can change our perspective. Research suggests that in times of family stress, individuals who are able to engage in self-talk and describe the event from someone else's perspective manage stress more successfully. For example, if you get a report from your supervisor that says you should improve one area of your performance, instead of listening to the self-talk that says you're bad at your job, reframe the event within a larger context: tell yourself that one negative comment does not mean you are hopeless as a worker.

Of course, all negative experiences should not be lightly tossed off and left unexamined, because you can learn and profit from your mistakes. But it is important to remember that our worth as human beings is not contingent on a single letter grade, a single response from a prospective employer, or a single play in a football game. Looking at the big picture—what effect this small event will have on your whole life, on society, on history—places negative experiences that we all have in a realistic context. The reading that follows is a good reminder to maintain this longer perspective.

People Who Were Told, "You'll Never Amount to Much"

Einstein was four years old before he could speak and seven before he could read. Isaac Newton did poorly in grade school, and Beethoven's music teacher once said of him, "As a composer he is hopeless." When Thomas Edison was a boy, his teachers told him he was too stupid to learn anything. F. W. Woolworth got a job in a dry goods store when he was 21, but his employers would not let him wait on a customer because he "didn't have enough sense." A newspaper editor fired Walt Disney because he had "no good ideas." Caruso's music teacher told him, "You can't sing. You have no voice at all." The director of the Imperial Opera in Vienna told Madame Schuman-Heink that she would never be a singer and advised her to buy a sewing machine. Leo Tolstoy flunked out of college; Wernher von Braun flunked ninth-grade algebra. Admiral Richard E. Byrd had been retired from the Navy as "unfit for service" until he flew over both Poles. Louis Pasteur was rated as "mediocre" in chemistry when he attended the Royal College. Abraham Lincoln entered the Black Hawk War as a captain and came out as a private. Louisa May Alcott was told by an editor that she could never write anything that had popular appeal. Fred Waring was once rejected for high school chorus. Winston Churchill failed the sixth grade.

From Milton E. Larson, "Humbling Cases for Career Counselors," *Phi Delta Kappan,* 54, no. 6 (February 1973), 374.

Developing Honest Relationships

Having at least one other person who can help you objectively and honestly reflect on your virtues and vices can be extremely beneficial in fostering a healthy, positive self-image. As we noted earlier, other people play a major role in shaping our self-concept and self-esteem. The more credible the source of information, the more likely we are to believe it. Having a trusted friend, colleague, clergy member, or counsellor who can listen without judging you and give you the straight scoop about yourself can help you avoid "pity parties." Prolonged periods of self-pity left unchecked and unconfirmed can lead to feelings of inferiority. Later in the book we will discuss how honest relationships are developed through the process of self-disclosure.

Letting Go of the Past

Your self-concept is not a fixed construct. Nor was it implanted at birth to remain constant for the rest of your life. Things change. You change. Others change. Individuals with low self-esteem may be locking on to events and experiences that happened years ago and tenaciously refusing to let go of them. Someone wrote, "The lightning bug is brilliant, but it hasn't much of a mind; it blunders through existence with its headlight on behind." Looking back at what we can't change only reinforces a sense of helplessness. Constantly replaying negative experiences in our mental VCR only serves to make our sense of worth more difficult to change. Becoming aware of the changes that have occurred and can occur in your life can assist you in developing a more realistic assessment of your value. If you were overweight as a child, you may have a difficult time accepting that your worth does not hinge upon pounds you carried years ago. Being open and receptive to change in self-worth is important to developing a healthy self-concept. Longfellow's advice to let go of the past remains wise advice today: "Look not mournfully into the past. It comes not back again. Wisely improve the Present. It is thine. Go forth to meet the shadowy future, without fear . . ."

Seeking Support

Some of your self-image problems may be so ingrained that you need professional help. A trained counsellor, clergy member, or therapist can help you sort through them. Therapists usually take a psychoanalytic approach, inviting you to search for experiences in your past that may help you first to understand your feelings and then to change them. Other counsellors use different techniques. If you are not sure to whom to turn for a referral, you can start with your school counselling services. Or, if you are near a medical school teaching hospital, you can contact the counselling or psychotherapy office there for a referral.

Because you have spent your whole lifetime developing your self-esteem, it is not easy to make big changes. But as we have seen, talking through our problems can make a difference. As communication researchers Frank E. Dance and Carl Larson see it, "Speech communication empowers each of us to share in the development of our own self-concept and the fulfillment of that self-concept."[17]

Summary

We all seek answers to three questions: Who am I? Why am I here? Who are all these others? William James answered the first question by dividing the self into three parts. The material self includes our bodies and those tangible possessions we own that give us identity. The social self is the part that engages in interaction with others. The spiritual self consists of thoughts and assumptions about values, moral standards, and beliefs about forces that influence our lives. Other theorists conclude that our self-concept develops through interaction with other people. The groups we belong to also give us identity. Our roles as sister, brother, student, and parent are important in how we view who we are; the roles we assume provide labels for who we are. We also self-reflexively make our own observations about ourselves apart from others, and about groups or roles we assume. Our gender plays a key part in affecting our view of who we are in relationship to others.

Your self-concept and self-esteem affect how you interact with others. Self-concept is who you think you are; self-esteem is your evaluation of your self-worth. Your life position—whether you view yourself as OK or not OK in relationship to others—is a reflection of your self-worth. Our self labels are powerful influences upon our actions, and our self-understanding also affects how we send and receive interpersonal messages. Our personality and style of relating to others is also influenced by our concept of self. One researcher has identified nine different communication styles: dominant, dramatic, contentious, animated, impression-leaving, relaxed, attentive, open, and friendly. Another framework for categorizing our style of interacting identifies our communication styles based on varying degrees of assertiveness and responsiveness: driver, expressive, amiable, and analytical. Few of us adopt one style in all situations.

Assessing Your Skills for Enhancing Your Self-Esteem

Evaluate your skill for improving your self-esteem using the scales below. Scores of 35–25 suggest that you have skills which can help you improve your self-esteem. Scoring 25–15 means you may have some skill or you may be uncertain as to whether you possess these skills. A score below 15 suggests that you are not confident of your skills for enhancing your self-esteem.

	Highly Skilled	Somewhat Skilled	Uncertain of Skill	Little Skill	No Skill
Self-Talk	5	4	3	2	1
Visualization	5	4	3	2	1
Avoiding Comparisons	5	4	3	2	1
Reframing	5	4	3	2	1
Developing Honest Relationships	5	4	3	2	1
Letting Go of the Past	5	4	3	2	1
Seeking Support	5	4	3	2	1

RECAP   Strategies for Improving Your Self-Esteem

SELF-TALK	If you're having a bad hair day, tell yourself that you have beautiful eyes and lots of friends who like you anyway.
VISUALIZATION	If you feel nervous before a meeting, visualize everyone in the room congratulating you on your great ideas.
AVOID COMPARISON	Focus on what you can do to enhance your own talents and abilities.
REFRAME	If you experience one failure, keep the larger picture in mind rather than focusing on that isolated incident.
DEVELOP HONEST RELATIONSHIPS	Cultivate friends in whom you can confide and who will give you honest feedback for improving your skills and abilities.
LET GO OF THE PAST	Talk yourself out of your "old tapes"; focus on ways to enhance your abilities in the future.
SEEK SUPPORT	Talk with professional counsellors who can help you identify your gifts and talents.

It is difficult to alter your self-esteem, but seven techniques have been helpful to others: positive self-talk, visualizing success, avoiding comparisons with others, reframing events and relationships from a different perspective, developing honest relationships with others, letting go of the past, and seeking professional help.

For Discussion and Review

■ FOCUS ON COMPREHENSION

1. List and describe the three selves identified by William James.

2. Define, compare, and contrast the terms self-concept and self-esteem.

3. Identify and describe four factors that explain how our self-concept develops.

■ FOCUS ON CRITICAL THINKING

4. Joel, who is 30 years old, married, and has two children, suffers from feelings of low self-esteem. Although he has many friends and a wife who loves him, he feels that others perform much better than he does at work. What strategies would help Joel enhance his self-esteem?

5. Make a list of all of the groups, clubs, and organizations to which you belong. Rank order them from most important to least important. What does your rank ordering tell you about these groups in reference to your self-concept?

6. Provide an original example of how visualization might help you enhance your self-esteem. Describe the positive scene.

■ FOCUS ON ETHICS

7. Discuss the ethical implications of using untrue flattery to enhance a friend's self-esteem.

8. There are many self-help books on the market that claim to enrich your social life by providing sure-fire techniques for enhancing self-esteem. Do you think these claims are ethical? Why or why not?

9. Aelish has long planned to attend a top-notch graduate program in Psychology. Her grades, however, are only in the C and B range. Her SAT scores are average. Should she try to reframe this factual information or deal with her problem in another way?

For Your Journal

1. Record goals for your self-talk and note your self-talk messages day by day. You might want to organize your journal around specific topics such as academic achievement, personal appearance, or social skills. Under academic achievement

you could write: "I will monitor my self-talk messages to keep myself on track while I study for two hours each day." Your personal appearance self-talk goal may be to tell yourself something positive about your appearance instead of only thinking about what you don't like.

2. Write the ten responses you wrote for the Communication Experience on page 34 in your journal. At the end of the course, again write ten responses to the "Who are you?" question without looking at your earlier responses. What are the differences in your responses? How do you explain them?

3. If someone were to walk into one of your favourite rooms in your home, dorm, or apartment, what conclusions might he or she draw about your social style? Are you neat and well-organized? Or does your room have the characteristics of an expressive personality? Write a brief description of who you are from a social style perspective based upon the clues in your room.

Learning with Others

1. Place the following list of values in rank order from one to twelve. In a group with other students, compare your answers. Discuss how your personal ranking of these values influences your interaction with others.

_____	Honesty	_____	Justice
_____	Salvation	_____	Wealth
_____	A comfortable life	_____	Beauty
_____	Good health	_____	Equality
_____	Human rights	_____	Freedom
_____	Peace	_____	Mercy

2. You are going to make a shield of your life. Draw a large outline of a shield that fills up an entire sheet of paper. Divide your shield into four equal sections. In the upper right-hand section of your shield, draw or symbolize something at which you have skill or talent. In the upper left-hand section draw or symbolize something you are trying to improve or a new skill you are learning. In the lower right-hand section, draw or symbolize your most prized material possession. Finally, in the lower left-hand section, write three words that you hope someone would use to describe you.

   Share your shield with other students. Tell your classmates why you drew what you did. Discuss how your shield reflects your attitudes, beliefs, and values.

3. Go through your personal music library of tapes or CDs and identify a selection that best symbolizes you. Your selection may be based upon either the lyrics or the music. Bring your selection to class and play it for your classmates. (Your instructor will bring a tape or CD player.) Tell why this music symbolizes you. Discuss with classmates how today's music provides a glimpse of our culture and a vehicle for self-expression.

SELF: The sum total of who a person is; a person's central inner force.

SELF-CONCEPT: A person's subjective description of who he or she is.

ATTITUDES: Learned predispositions to respond to a person, object, or idea in a favourable or unfavourable way.

BELIEFS: The ways in which you structure your understanding of reality—what is true and what is false.

VALUES: Enduring concepts of good and bad, right and wrong.

MATERIAL SELF: Your concept of self as reflected in a total of all the tangible things you own.

SOCIAL SELF: Your concept of self as developed through your personal, social interactions with others.

SPIRITUAL SELF: Your concept of self based upon your thoughts and introspections about your values and moral standards.

LOOKING-GLASS SELF: A concept that suggests we learn who we are based upon our interactions with others that are reflected back to us.

ANDROGYNOUS ROLE: A gender role that includes both masculine and feminine qualities.

SELF-REFLEXIVENESS: The human ability to think about what we are doing while we are doing it.

SELF-ESTEEM (SELF-WORTH): Your evaluation of your worth or value as reflected in your perception of such things as your skills, abilities, talents, and appearance.

LIFE POSITIONS: Your feeling of being either "OK" or "Not OK" as reflected in your sense of worth and self-esteem.

SPECIFIC-OTHER PERSPECTIVE: The process of relying upon information that a person observes or imagines about another person that is used to predict a person's behaviour.

GENERALIZED-OTHER PERSPECTIVE: The process of relying upon observed or imagined information about many people or people in general that is used to predict a person's behaviour.

SELF-FULFILLING PROPHECY: The notion that predictions about your future actions are likely to come true because you believe that they will come true.

SELECTIVE EXPOSURE: A principle that suggests we tend to place ourselves in situations that are consistent with our self-concept and self-esteem.

COMMUNICATION STYLE (SOCIAL STYLE): Your consistent way of relating to others based upon your personality, self-concept and self-esteem.

ASSERTIVENESS: A dimension of the Wilson Learning social style model that describes a personal quality that refers to an individual's effort to control others.

RESPONSIVENESS: A dimension of the Wilson Learning social style model that describes a personal quality of placing the feelings of others above our own and expressing those feelings.

DRIVER STYLE: A communication style characterized by high achievement, assertiveness, and controlled emotions.

ANALYTICAL STYLE: A communication style characterized by high assertiveness and low expressiveness, considerable attention to detail and task achievement.

EXPRESSIVE STYLE: A communication style characterized by a high degree of expressiveness and assertiveness; there is a tendency both to control others and to respond emotionally or impulsively.

AMIABLE STYLE: A communication style characterized by a high degree of expressiveness and sensitivity toward others and a minimum of assertiveness.

BACKUP COMMUNICATION STYLE: The communication style we often use when we are under stress or when our primary style does not achieve the desired results.

INTRAPERSONAL COMMUNICATION: Communication within yourself that includes your self-talk.

VISUALIZATION: A technique of imagining that you are performing a particular task in a certain way. Positive visualization can enhance your self-esteem.

REFRAMING: The process of redefining events and experiences from a different point of view.

Interpersonal Communication and Perception

After studying this chapter, you should be able to:

1. Define perception and interpersonal perception.

2. Identify and explain the three stages of interpersonal perception.

3. Describe the relationship between interpersonal communication and interpersonal perception.

4. Explain the interpersonal perception processes of impression formation, implicit personality theory, attribution theory, and constructs.

5. Identify the ten factors that distort the accuracy of our interpersonal perceptions.

6. Identify seven suggestions for improving your interpersonal perceptions.

■ UNDERSTANDING THE INTER-PERSONAL PERCEPTION PROCESS

■ PERCEPTION AND INTERPER-SONAL COMMUNICATION

■ HOW WE ORGANIZE AND INTERPRET INTERPERSONAL PERCEPTIONS

■ BARRIERS TO ACCURATE PERCEPTIONS

■ IMPROVING YOUR PERCEPTUAL SKILLS

Look at the picture in Figure 3.1. What is happening and what has happened? What is the relationship among the individuals in the painting? You probably have deduced that the boy was running away from home, the policeman found him, and then he took the boy into the local coffee shop for ice cream or some other treat. Perhaps you think that the counterman is wistfully recalling his own days of running away as a child. What are your feelings about the policeman? Do you see him as a friendly and caring person who has a good understanding of kids?

As human beings we interpret and attribute meaning to what we observe or experience, particularly if what we are observing is other people. We tend to make inferences about their motives, personalities, and other traits based on their physical qualities and behaviours. The types of conclusions you draw from observing the picture in Figure 3.1 exemplify the process we call interpersonal perception. Through interpersonal perception we piece together various bits of information about other people and draw conclusions that may or may not be accurate. Because our feelings and responses to other people are based on our perceptions, those who are skilled at making observations and interpretations have a head start in developing effective interpersonal relationships.

Most of the time, we are unaware of our own perception process. For example, you may not have realized that you were drawing conclusions about the painting until you read the questions above. But we may become aware of the process when differences in perception cause a conflict or disagreement. For example, at the end of the movie *Thelma and Louise,* the two main characters drive off the edge of the Grand Canyon. The scene sparked a lot of arguments between friends because some people perceived it as a tragic ending, whereas others perceived it as an uplifting one because the two characters maintained the freedom they had finally come to realize. In truth, no two individuals ever perceive the same thing in exactly the same way. Fortunately, communication tools such as conversation allow us to create shared meanings despite the differences in our perceptions.

Our perceptions are influenced by who we are, including the accumulation of our experiences. If you have had several bad experiences with the

Figure 3.1

The Runaway. Original oil painting for a *Saturday Evening Post* cover, September 20, 1958. Old Corner House Collection, Stockbridge, Massachusetts.

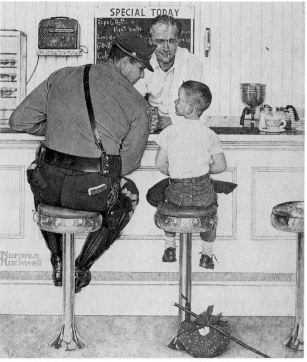

police, for example, you may not view the policeman in Figure 3.1 as a friendly person. Or if you know something about the life and work of Norman Rockwell, the illustrator who painted the picture, you may view all his works as representations of an idyllic American culture and society that existed only in his mind. As we saw in Chapter 2, everything we perceive is filtered through our self-concept.[1] It is important to recognize and examine factors that might distort the accuracy of our interpretations. We can also reduce inaccuracies by applying an other-oriented approach as we interact with people. By focusing on how others perceive the world, we can reduce the amount of distortion that our own self-concepts impose on our perceptions.

Before we turn to the role that perception plays in interpersonal communication, let's first take a closer look at the interpersonal perception process itself.

Understanding the Interpersonal Perception Process

What is perception? On the most general level, **perception** is simply the arousal of any of our senses. A sound vibrates the air, vibrates in our eardrum, activates the nerves, and sends a signal to the brain. A similar sequence of events takes place when we see, smell, feel, or taste something. Perception also includes organizing and interpreting information provided by the senses. You come out of a building and see wet pavement and puddles of water, hear thunder, smell a distinct odour caused by ions, and observe drops of water falling in front of you. You integrate all those bits of information and conclude that it is raining, and has been for a while.

Our perceptions of people, however, include analysis and interpretation that goes beyond simple interpretation of sensory information. **Interpersonal perception** is the process by which we decide what people are like and give meaning to their actions. It includes making judgments about personality and drawing inferences from what we observed.[2] When you meet someone new, you *select* certain information to attend to: you note whether the person is male or female, has an accent, smiles, uses a friendly tone of voice, as well as particular personal information (she is from St. John's, Newfoundland). You then *organize* the information under some category that is recognizable to you, such as "a friendly Maritimer." Then you *interpret* the organized perceptions: this person is trustworthy, honest, hardworking, and likable.

In our discussion, we will focus on this kind of interpersonal perception, which relates to understanding our observations of other people. We will begin by examining the three stages of the interpersonal perception process that we described above: selecting, organizing, and interpreting what we observe.

Stage One: Selecting or Simplifying the Stimuli

Sit for a minute after you read this passage and try to tune in all the sensory input you are receiving: consider the feel of your socks against your feet, the pressure of the floor on your heels, the pressure of the piece of furniture against your body as you sit, the buzzing sounds from various sources around you—this "white noise" might come from a refrigerator, personal computer, fluorescent lights, water in pipes, voices, passing traffic, or your own heartbeat or churning stomach. What do you smell? What do you see? Without moving your eyes, turn your awareness to the images you see in the corner of your vision. What colours do you see? What shapes? What taste is in your mouth? How do the pages of this book feel against your fingertips? Now stop reading and consider all these sensations. Try to focus on all of them at the same time. You can't.

The number of sensations we can attend to at any given time is limited. Therefore, we are selective about which sensations make it through to the level of awareness. Perhaps you close your eyes or sit in the dark as you listen to music. This allows you to select more auditory sensations because you are eliminating visual ones. Individuals who have an impaired sense often become more tuned in to input from other senses because they have fewer sensations vying for their attention.

This selectivity can also cause us to fail to perceive information that is important. Imagine that you are standing with your back to an open hallway door talking to a friend and complaining about your roommate or spouse just as that roommate or spouse walks in the door. Your friend tries to signal with her hand that the other person has just entered, but you miss this cue and go on to say things that you later wish your roommate or spouse had not heard. You missed the signal because you failed to perceive the gesture. Because you were simplifying the stimuli to which you attended, you did not process the hand gesture.

During the selection stage, we attempt to simplify the stimuli that flood in through our senses using various techniques. We use perceptual filters to screen out constant sensations that we have learned are unimportant, such as the sensations of our clothes against our skin and the surrounding white noise and smells. However, we do attend to the sensation of the elastic bands of our underclothes if they pull too tight, because a threshold of arousal is crossed, forcing the brain to attend to that stimulus. Each of our senses has such a threshold.

Directing our attention to specific stimuli and consequently ignoring others is called **selective perception**. In our interactions with others we may choose to focus on specific cues such as gestures or foot movement. What specific qualities or features do you tend to focus on when you first meet others? Do you pay particular attention to handshakes, smiles, eye contact, body posture, gestures, or tone of voice? Sometimes we exercise selective perception when we are listening for a specific piece of information. As in the example above of missing your friend's hand signal, our selective focus might prevent us from perceiving other important cues.

We also simplify stimuli by categorizing information and inventing stereotypes. We create categories to reduce the amount of information to which we have to attend or remember. If you learn that your communication partner is a parent, you may put him or her into a "mother" or "father" category that contains stored information, which you then could apply to this person. You may automatically attribute qualities to this person that you typically associate with parenthood: being loving, responsible, committed, and tired. This saves you the trouble of selecting and perceiving the individual pieces of information that you would otherwise need to draw these conclusions. Try to think about some of the categories into which you place people: jocks, teachers, partyers, high school students, women, and men. The more we interact with a variety of individuals, the greater the number of categories we can potentially create and use in this simplification process.

Human beings are as diverse as they are numerous. Placing people into rigid categories can keep us from understanding and appreciating their individual qualities. (Mark Burnett/Photo Researchers, Inc.)

Despite its efficiency, however, this simplification process can create significant problems. We easily may attribute inaccurate qualities to an individual because of these stereotypes. The word *stereotype* is a printing term; it refers to a metal plate that was cast from type set by a printer. The plate would print the same page of type over and over again. When we stereotype people, we place them into inflexible, all-compassing categories. We "print" the same judgments on anyone placed into a given category. We may even choose to ignore contradictory information that we receive directly from the other person. Instead of adjusting our conception of that person, we adjust our perception. That is, we see what we want to see, rather than seeing what is really there.

Categorizing individuals is not an inherently bad thing to do, but it is harmful to hang on to a stereotypical image of another person in the face of contradictory information. For example, not all mothers are responsible or loving. Because North American culture reveres motherhood, we may not process easily our perceptions of a mother who is abusive or negligent.

One of the most general ways to categorize people is according to those we like and those we don't like. When we observe people we like, there is often a **halo effect**; we attribute a variety of positive qualities to them because we like them. If you like me, then you will assume I have nothing except angelic qualities: I am nice to other people, warm and caring, fun to be with, and have a great sense of humour. On the other hand, if you don't like me, you may think of me as the Devil, attributing to me a variety of negative qualities. This is called the **horn effect**.

Stage Two: Organizing and Imposing Structure on What We Observe

Look at the four items in Figure 3.2. What does each of them mean to you? If you are like most people, you will perceive item A as the word *interpersonal*, item B as a circle, C as a rabbit, and D as a telephone number. Strictly speaking, none of those perceptions is correct. We'll discuss why after we explore the second stage of perception: organization.

After we select what stimuli we are going to attend to and process, we start to organize them into convenient, understandable, and efficient patterns that allow us to make sense of what we have observed. Organizing makes it easier for us to process complex information, because it allows us to impose the familiar onto the unfamiliar, and because we can easily store and recall simple patterns. For example, when you looked at item C in Figure 3.2, you see the pattern of dots that you label a rabbit because *rabbit* is a concept you know and to which you attach various meanings. The set of dots would not have meaning for you in and of themselves, nor would it be meaningful for you to attend to each particular dot or to the dots' relationship to one another. It would be possible to create a mathematical model of the dots indicating their placement on an X-Y grid, but such a model would be extremely complex and difficult to observe and remember. It's much easier to organize the dots in a way that refers to something stored in your memory: a rabbit. For similar reasons, we organize patterns of stars in the sky into various animals and familiar shapes like the bear, the crab, and the Big and Little Dippers. As we do for the pattern of dots making up the rabbit, we search for and apply patterns to our perceptions of people.

The way we organize information depends partly upon the way we punctuate it. Item D in Figure 3.2 looks like a telephone number because it has three numbers followed by four numbers. You might also remember that 555 is the prefix you use for calling long-distance information. However, the digits could just as easily represent two totally independent numbers: five hundred and fifty-five followed by the number four thousand, four hundred and thirty-three. How we interpret the numbers depends upon how we punctuate[3] or separate them. When we record information, we use commas, periods, dashes, and colons to signal meanings and interpretations. In our minds, sometimes we impose punctuation marks where we believe they should be. For example, we put a dash between 555 and 4433 even though no dash appeared there.

When it comes to punctuating relational events and behaviours, we each develop our own separate set of standards. You will sometimes experience difficulties and disagreements because of differences in how you and your partner choose to punctuate a conversational exchange or shared sequence of events.[4] For example, suppose you and a friend have been talking about her recent school problems. After a few moments of silence, you assume that your conversation on that topic has ended, so you start talking about your recent job interview. Later on, you find out that you offended your friend because she had not punctuated the conversation the same way. She believed that her problems should still have been the focus of the conversation.

Looking again at Figure 3.2, you can see that our inclination to impose structure and consistency on what we observe also leads us to create a familiar word from the meaningless assemblage of letters in item A, and to label the figure in item B a circle, even though circles are continuous lines without gaps on the right side. We apply the same principles in our interactions with people. When we have an incomplete picture of another human being, we impose a pattern or structure, classify the person on the basis of the information we do have, and fill in gaps.

A. N T R P R S N L

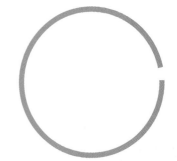

B.

C.

D. **5 5 5   4 4 3 3**

Figure 3.2

What Do You See?

Stage Three: Interpreting or Attributing Meaning to What We Observe

Once we have organized stimuli into familiar patterns, we are ready to interpret what they mean. We attach meaning to all that we observe. We learn through socialization and our own recurring experiences to attribute particular meaning to particular stimuli. In some cases the meanings are fairly standardized, as they are for language, for example. But others are much more personalized. As the excerpt from "The Greek Interpreter" shows, the fictional detective Sherlock Holmes was noted for his ability to apply exacting interpretations to what he observed. In general, the heroes in mysteries usually excel in their ability to observe, organize, and interpret the stimuli around them. Sherlock and Mycroft Holmes possess an ability to attend to specific cues that you and I may miss. They also are able to organize the cues to create a unique meaning and interpretation. Seeing that the man in dark mourning clothes is carrying a baby's toy and picture-book takes on special meaning when the various clues are combined.

Sherlock Holmes and His Brother Mycroft Make Some Observations

In this excerpt, Sherlock Holmes is visiting his brother Mycroft. Both are looking out a window when Mycroft asks Sherlock what he makes of a very small, dark fellow with his hat pushed back and several packages under his arm standing on the street corner. Dr. Watson records their conversation:

"An old soldier, I perceive," said Sherlock.

"And very recently discharged," remarked his brother.

"Served in India, I see."

"And a non-commissioned officer."

"Royal Artillery, I fancy," said Sherlock.

"And a widower."

"But with a child."

"Children, my dear boy, children."

"Come," said I, laughing, "this is a little too much."

"Surely," answered Holmes, "it is not hard to say that a man with that bearing, expression of authority, and sun-baked skin, is a soldier, is more than a private, and is not long from India."

"That he has not left the service long is shown by his still wearing his ammunition boots, as they are called," observed Mycroft.

"He had not the cavalry stride, yet he wore his hat on one side, as is shown by the lighter skin on that side of his brow. His weight is against his being a sapper [army engineer]. He is in the artillery."

"Then, of course, his complete mourning shows that he has lost someone very dear. The fact that he is doing his own shopping looks as though it were his wife. He has been buying things for children, you perceive. There is a rattle, which shows that one of them is very young. The wife probably died in childbed. The fact that he has a picture-book under his arm shows that there is another child to be thought of."

From: Sir Arthur Conan Doyle, *The Greek Interpreter.*

Although all of us may not possess Sherlock Holmes's perceptual talents, we do all attribute meaning to what we observe. If you shake someone's hand and it feels like a wet, dead fish, what is your reaction and interpretation? If you notice someone you don't know winking at you from across a room, what do you think? If a toddler is crying in a room full of people and a woman comes over and picks the child up, what do you assume about the woman? If you see a student glance over at another student's exam paper and then record an answer, what do you think the student has done? All of these are examples that show we impose meaning on what we observe to complete the perceptual process.

COMMUNICATION EXPERIENCE

Find a place where you can sit and watch people for a while. Write down as many points as you can that you are able to observe about the people that pass by or that are seated nearby. Try to make some interpretations based upon your observations, just as Sherlock Holmes might have. What do you notice about their clothing, their shoes, the manner in which they walk? What are they carrying with them? Do they seem to be in a hurry? Can you tell which are students, teachers, or members of other professions? If you are watching other students, can you tell what their majors are?

If you get the chance, you might approach some of these people and see how accurate your observations are. People are generally open to hearing positive perceptions about themselves. You may want to hold back on sharing negative perceptions.

RECAP   The Interpersonal Perception Process

Term	Explanation	Examples
Perception	The arousal of any of our senses.	Hearing a dog bark, smelling roses, or tasting saltwater.
Interpersonal Perception	The process of piecing together information about people and drawing conclusions about them.	A stranger passing in a car waves a hand at you, and you decide the person is friendly.
Selection	The first stage in the perceptual process in which we select sensations for our awareness.	Responding to someone calling your name. Ignoring background noise to hear someone talking.
Organizing	The second stage in the perceptual process in which we assemble stimuli into convenient and efficient patterns.	Labelling someone as "funny" because we observe him or her telling jokes and clowning around.
Interpreting	The final stage in perception in which we assign meaning to what we have observed.	Deciding that when someone stood you up for a date, it meant that he or she did not really like you.

Perception and Interpersonal Communication

Interpersonal perception is a two-way street when it comes to interpersonal communication. Our perceptions of others affect the ways in which we communicate with them, and their perceptions of us affect the way they communicate with us.

We continually modify the topics, the language, and the manner in which we communicate according to the perceptions we have of others. For example, if you observe a woman in a tracksuit running in a park, you may conclude that she is a physical fitness fanatic. Then, if you strike up a conversation with her, you may bring up topics such as physical fitness, sports, and diet. But if she informs you that she knows nothing about those things and has just started jogging to offset the time she spends watching videos and eating potato chips, then you would probably shift your focus according to a revised perception. You might start talking about movies and the relative merits of rippled versus plain potato chips. Similarly, if you were talking to a child, you would probably use simple language rather than complex technical terminology. If you were talking to an elderly person, you might slow down your speech and raise your speaking volume if you perceived that he or she had hearing problems (a perception that is often inaccurate).

The way that others talk and behave also tells us a great deal about how they perceive us. Maybe you can remember the first time someone younger than you called you Mister, Ms., Mrs., or Miss (if it hasn't happened yet, it will). It probably surprised you to realize that someone perceived you as "old," or as someone with authority. We also analyze others' reactions to us for clues about their conception of who we are. For example, suppose your new college friends go out to play basketball, your favourite sport, but do not invite you. When you later ask them why, they say they always thought of you as the unathletic, studious type. Sometimes others' perceptions of us are surprising. If we never ask, we may never discover that they are inaccurate. The degree to which others have a conception of us that is different from our own is often a measure of the quality of the relationship. The stronger the interpersonal relationship, the closer our self-perceptions are to the perceptions others have of us.[5]

How much we notice about another person's communication behaviour relates to our level of interest and need. Perception can be either a passive or an active process. **Passive perception** occurs simply because our senses are in operation. We see, hear, smell, taste, and feel things around us without any conscious attempt to do so. We've all heard noises that startle us and make us wonder, "What was that?" We then try to recall the sound and identify it, or we might investigate—seek out additional information. We are constantly bombarded by stimuli to our senses. Think of all the things you potentially could select for your awareness while interacting with a friend: words you hear with variations in the tone, rate, and so forth; behaviours you see with variations in eye contact, gestures, body movement, and facial expressions. As we have seen, because of the overwhelming amount of potential information that is available to our senses, we usually don't catch it all.

If we feel uncertain about a given situation or interaction, we become motivated to select particular information through **active perception**. If you need to know whether someone is lying to you about why he was late for a meeting, you might watch his eyes, look for nervous body movements, and listen for hesitation in his voice. We try to reduce uncertainty because we want to control and predict the world around us in order to accomplish our personal goals, and we need accurate and complete information to make plans and develop strategies toward that end.[6] If you can gain information about others, then you can predict their reactions and behaviours, adapt your behaviours and strategies, and therefore maximize the likelihood of fulfilling your social needs. Although this might sound calculating, it really isn't. If you enjoy outdoor activities such as camping and hiking, one of your goals in establishing social relationships is probably to find others who share your interest. So observing, questioning, and processing information to determine a potential friend's interests can help you assess whether the relationship will meet your goals.

How We Organize and Interpret Interpersonal Perceptions

As we collect information about others, we organize and interpret that information in various ways. Interpersonal perception involves three processes: forming impressions of others; applying implicit personality theories and the use of mental constructs, which we use to organize information about people; and finally, developing attribution theories, which help us explain why people behave the way they do.

Impression Formation

Impressions are collections of perceptions about others that we maintain and use to interpret their behaviours. Impressions tend to be very general: she seemed nice, he was very friendly, or what a nerd. We form these impressions through perceptions of physical qualities and behaviour, information people disclose about themselves, and information that third parties tell us. We select, organize, and interpret all of these perceptions to create a general impression. We tend to form these impressions readily and part with them reluctantly. When we first meet someone we form a first impression without having much information, and we often hold on to this impression throughout the relationship.

In one study conducted by Solomon Asch, individuals were asked to provide an evaluation of two people based on two lists of adjectives.[7] The list for the first person had the following adjectives: intelligent, industrious, impulsive, critical, stubborn, and envious. The list for the other person had the same adjectives, but in reverse order. Although the content was identical, respondents gave the first person a more positive evaluation than the second. One explanation for this is that the first words in each list created a first impression that respondents used to interpret the remaining adjectives. In a similar manner, the first impressions we form about someone often affect our interpretation of subsequent perceptions of them.

This effect of attending to the first pieces of information that we observe is called the **primacy effect**. We also tend to put a lot of stock in the last thing we observed, which is called the **recency effect**.[8] For example, if you think for years that your friend is honest, but today you discover that she lied to you about something important, that lie will have a greater impact on your impression of her than the honest behaviour she has displayed for years. The primacy and recency effects explain why you are more likely to remember information at the beginning or end of a paragraph than you are to remember information in the middle.

Implicit Personality Theory

In addition to developing impressions about specific people we come to know, we also organize our perceptions by developing our own implicit theories to explain how people in general behave. Suppose you are walking along in front of some stores with a number of other shoppers. You notice that a man walking ahead of you has dropped a five dollar bill without realizing it. A teenage boy following behind the man picks up the money. What do you think the boy will do next? Will he put the money in his own pocket or will he catch up with the man and return the money? While a number of factors, such as the boy's nonverbal cues and clothing, would affect your response, your answer might also reflect your general belief system about the way people behave. If you believe that people are generally selfish and out to make a fast buck, you will probably predict that the boy will keep the money. If you believe that people are generally honest and kind, then you will predict that the boy will return it.

Your **implicit personality theory** is your own set of beliefs and hypotheses about what people are like.[9] We each develop an implicit personality theory over time that changes as we make more and more observations about people. These theories allow us to make sense of people whom we do not know very well. They affect our perceptions and actions. As we discussed in Chapter 2, we see the world in a way that is generally consistent with what we believe, and we act in accordance with our beliefs about other people.

COMMUNICATION EXPERIENCE

Elements of Your Implicit Personality Theory

Generate a series of statements that you believe are true about people in general.

- People are basically _____.
- I believe people are _____.
- In general, people will _____.
- One thing people seem to have in common is _____
_____.

- One nice thing about people is that they generally _____
_____.

- One thing I don't like about people in general is their tendency to
_____.

Constructs

Another way that we organize our perceptions of others is to create a set of specific qualities called constructs. **Personal constructs** represent qualities that allow us to categorize people into one of two groups of polar opposites: friendly or unfriendly, intelligent or unintelligent, athletic or klutzy, extrovert or introvert, funny or serious, conservative or liberal, overachiever or underachiever, playful or studious. The better you know someone and the more cognitively complex you are, the more constructs you use to interpret her or his messages and behaviours. Your set of constructs about each person you know will contain constructs that are common to several people, and some that are distinctive.

COMMUNICATION EXPERIENCE

Constructs

Think of two people you know, one a very close friend, and the other a more casual friend or acquaintance. For two minutes write down all the attributes (constructs) that you associate with your friend. Then for two minutes write down all the attributes you associate with your acquaintance. Now compare the two lists. You should have been able to write a longer list for your friend. How many qualities does the acquaintance have that are not on your friend's list, and how many qualities does your friend have that are not on the acquaintance's list? How do these constructs affect your interactions with your friend and acquaintance?

If you get a chance, compare your list with those of some of your classmates. What is different or the same? What do those similarities and differences tell you about your ability to generate constructs?

Attribution Theory

This theory relates to the third stage of the perception process: interpreting. We attribute specific motives and causes to the behaviours we observe. For example, suppose you see a student sitting next to you in class who gets up in the middle of the lecture and walks out. Why did the student leave? Did the student become angry at something the instructor said? No, the lecturer was simply describing types of cloud formations. Was the student sick? You remember noticing that the student looked a little flushed and occasionally winced. Maybe the student has an upset stomach. Or maybe the student is just a bit of a rebel, and often does strange things like leaving in the middle of a class.

Fritz Heider said that we are "naive psychologists,"[10] because we all seek to explain the motives people have for their actions. We are naive because we do not create these explanations in a systematic or scientific manner, but rather by applying common sense to our observations. Developing the most credible explanation for the behaviour of others is the goal of the **attribution process**. According to one attribution theory, **Correspondent Inference Theory**, we try to determine the intentionality of the person in causing the effect.[11] In determining how intentional the act was, we may take into account what other choices the person had available to him or her, how desirable the action was, and whether we believe the person changed his or her behaviour in an attempt to impress us. What did the student intend to accomplish in leaving the class?

Causal Attribution Theory identifies three potential causes for any person's action: circumstance, a stimulus, or the person herself or himself.[12] Attributing to *circumstance* means that you believe a person acts in a certain way because the situation leaves no choice. This way of thinking places responsibility for the action outside of the person. You would be attributing to circumstance if you believed the student quickly left the classroom because of an upset stomach. Concluding that the student left because the instructor said something inappropriate would be attributing the student's action to the *stimulus* (the instructor). But if you knew the instructor hadn't said anything out of line, and that the student was perfectly healthy, you would place the responsibility for the action on the student. Attributing to the *person* means that you believe there is some quality about the person that caused the observed behaviour. Attributions to the person are the ones we are most concerned with in this text because they are factors in our impressions of others.

A number of factors affect the accuracy of our attributions: our ability to make effective and complete observations; the degree to which we are able to directly observe the cause and the effect; the completeness of our information; and our ability to rule out other causes. It is also helpful to know how unique the person's response is to the particular stimulus, to compare the person's response to how other people typically respond, and to know whether the person usually responds each time in the same way to the stimulus. Even with the most complete information, however, we can never completely understand another person's action because we cannot become the other person. Fortunately, we can improve our level of understanding by using decentring and by becoming more sensitive to the assumptions or theories we use to make attributions.

RECAP	How We Organize and Interpret Interpersonal Perceptions	
Term	**Definition**	**Examples**
Impression Formation	We form global perspectives we have of others based upon general physical qualities, behaviours, and disclosed information.	Categorizing people as nice, friendly, shy, or handsome.
Implicit Personality Theory	We form our own personal general theory about the way people think and behave.	"I've never met a person I didn't like."
Personal Constructs	We associate specific qualities or attributes with each person we know.	"My friend Fred is caring, smart, strong, and devoted."
Attributions	We develop reasons to explain the behaviours of others. We attribute others' actions to the circumstance, a stimulus, or to the person.	"I guess she didn't return my call because she doesn't like me." "He's just letting off steam because he had a bad week of exams."

Barriers to Accurate Perceptions

Think about the most recent interaction you have had with a stranger. Do you remember the person's age, sex, race, or body size? Did the person have any distinguishing features such as a beard, wild clothing, or a loud voice? The qualities you recall will most likely serve as the basis for attributions you make about that person's behaviour. But these attributions, based upon your first impressions, might be highly inaccurate. We each see the world from our own unique perspective. That perspective is clouded by a number of distortions and barriers that contribute to inaccurate interpersonal perception. We'll examine these barriers next.

Focusing on appearances may distract us from attending to details about people's messages and behaviour. What assumptions do you make based on the appearance of the people in this photo? (Robert Harbison)

Ignoring Details

We give too much weight to information that is obvious and superficial.[13] We tend to explain the motives for a person's actions on the basis of the most obvious information rather than on in-depth information we might have. This means we tend to lump people into general categories and make biased statements about them: "He acts that way because he's a man"; "I guess you can expect that behaviour from someone his age"; and "Of course, it was a woman driver." When meeting someone new, we perceive his or her physical qualities first: colour of skin, body size and shape, age, sex, and other obvious physical characteristics. We over-attribute to these qualities because they are so vivid and available. We have all been victims of these kinds of attributions; some of us more than others. Often we are unaware that others are making biased attributions because they do not express them openly. But sometimes we can tell by the way others react to us and treat us.

One female student described a job interview in which the male interviewer talked at her for fifteen minutes and then abruptly dismissed her without asking a single question. A male friend of hers with less distinguished academic qualifications and work experience spent forty minutes fielding questions from this same interviewer. Did the interviewer have a sex bias? Probably. Looking only at the female student's gender, he attributed qualities to her that he decided would make her unsuitable for the job. Instead of looking at the more specific information her résumé provided, he simply disregarded it. As discussed earlier, this tendency reflects our desire to simplify stimuli, but it can be dangerous and unfair.

Overgeneralizing

We treat small amounts of information as if they were highly representative.[14] This tendency also leads us to draw inaccurate, prejudicial conclusions. For example, your authors may talk to two students from your school, and then generalize the impression we have of those two students to the entire student population. In a similar way, we tend to assume that the small sampling we have of another person's behaviour is a valid representation of who that person is. As we saw in Figure 3.2, we create a rabbit even when we have only a few dots on which to base our perception.

Holding on to Preconceptions

We distort or ignore information that violates our expectations or preconceptions.[15] We see what we want to see, hear what we want to hear. Earlier in this chapter we talked about how we develop impressions and constructs. Once we develop them, we have preconceptions about what we expect from another person. These preconceptions can be so strong that we will distort the way we process our perceptions in order to remain constant to them. The halo and horn effects discussed earlier are reflections of this tendency. For example, if an instructor gets an excellent paper from a student that she has concluded is not particularly bright or motivated, she may tend to find errors and shortcomings that are not really there, or she may even accuse the student of plagiarism.

Imposing Consistency

We overestimate the consistency and constancy of others' behaviours. When we organize our perceptions, we also tend to ignore fluctuation in people's behaviours, and see them as consistent. We believe that if someone acted a certain way one day, he or she will continue to act that way in the future. In an episode of the TV series *Ellen*, the main character had been fixed up on a blind date, and because of a series of unexpected events, Ellen's date perceived her as weird. Despite her efforts to correct this impression, the man kept perceiving every behaviour as weird, and finally chose to terminate the relationship.

In fact, everyone's behaviour varies from day to day. Some days we are in a bad mood, and our behaviour on those days does not represent what we are generally like. As intimacy develops in relationships, we interact with our partners in a variety of activities that provide a more complete picture of their true nature.

Preconnecting Causes and Effects

We rely on pre-existing ideas about underlying causes and what we observe. We've already seen how preconceptions about a person can shape our attributions. We also develop a particular type of preconception that reflects both our implicit personality theory and our personal constructs. We create beliefs about what particular causes are linked to what particular effects. This keeps us from investigating and collecting additional information to explain an individual's action. For example, suppose you take a two-hour lunch one day because your child falls off the monkey bars at school and you have to rush her to the doctor. You return to work and your boss screams that people who take long lunches (effect) are lazy, irresponsible, or alcoholic (cause), and refuses to listen to your explanation. To avoid imposing your own preconceptions on others, you must be ready to listen to alternative explanations.

Think about your own preconceptions about cause-effect relationships. For each of the following, think about what your first explanation of the cause would be:

■ A person not calling back after a first date.

■ A waitress giving you lousy service.

■ Your car not being repaired after paying a high service fee.

■ A teacher being late for class.

■ A child who beats up on other kids.

■ A student who copies test answers from the student next to him.

■ A mother who refuses to let her teenage son drive the car on Friday nights.

Now go back and generate as many alternative explanations for each behaviour as you can. How can you be sure which explanation is correct?

Simplifying

We prefer simple explanations to complex ones. When Terry picks you up late to go to a movie, she says, "Sorry, I lost track of the time." The next day, Christine also picks you up late to go to a movie. She says, "Sorry. You wouldn't believe how busy I've been. I ran out of hot water when I was showering and my hair dryer must be busted. It kept shutting off. Then I stopped to get something to eat and it took forever to get my order. And then it turned out they had it all messed up and had to redo it." Whose explanation can you accept more easily, Terry's or Christine's?

Usually we prefer simple explanations; they tend to be more believable and easier to use in making sense of another's actions. But in reality our behaviours are affected by a multitude of factors, as Christine's explanation indicates. Unfortunately, it takes a lot of effort to understand what makes another person do what he or she does—more effort than we are typically willing to give.

Ignoring Circumstances

We diminish the effect of external circumstances on another's behaviour.[16] Although we tend to explain our own negative actions in terms of circumstances, we tend to attribute others' actions to their personality. If we are late for an appointment, it is because of traffic or the need to wrap up a project, and so on. But if others are late, it is because they are unpunctual and have intentionally chosen to treat us rudely. Again, this tendency represents our desire for simplification. We are often unaware of the circumstances that affect others, and we do not want to take the trouble to investigate them.

We also fail to compare one person's behaviour with that of others under the same circumstances. Suppose you have a close friend who has flunked out of school because of personal problems, financial difficulties, and insufficient college preparation. You gain many insights into his motives and emotions as you spend time providing support. However, if you meet someone else who flunked out of school, you may not compare this other person's situation with your friend's. Usually, we come to appreciate the effect of circumstances on the behaviours of those we know intimately,

but we discard that knowledge when we encounter it in someone else, preferring to attribute the behaviour to the person.

Crediting Irrelevant Information

We treat irrelevant information as if it were relevant. Have you ever sat and analyzed a conversation after it was finished, considering what each word, gesture, and intonation really meant? In truth, most exchanges are filled with irrelevant information, and it requires skill and experience to separate the irrelevant information from information that really does help explain another's actions. Imagine eating at a restaurant where the waitress seems rude and impatient. Later you may ask yourself, "Why was that waitress so rude to me? Did I take too long in placing my order? Was she upset when I asked for a second order of fries? Maybe she thinks I'm not going to leave a tip? Didn't she realize I was joking around when I placed my order for 'ground cow on a wheat bun'?" Such questions relate to information that may have nothing to do with her behaviour. The waitress may have worked a double shift, had problems with the kitchen staff, or had personal problems at home.

If a waitress fails to laugh at your corny jokes, the reason may have little to do with you and a great deal to do with her own mood and problems. Too often we attribute others' behaviour to factors that are, in truth, irrelevant. (Al Harvey)

Focusing on the Negative

We give more weight to negative information than to positive information.[17] Job interviewers often ask interviewees to describe their strengths and weaknesses. If you describe five great strengths and one weakness, it is likely that the interviewer will attend more to the one weakness you mention than to the strengths. We seem to recognize this bias and compensate for it when we first meet someone by sharing only positive information about ourselves.

In another of the Solomon Asch experiments on impression formation, participants heard one of the following two lists of terms describing a person: (1) intelligent, skillful, industrious, warm, determined, practical, cautious; or (2) intelligent, skillful, industrious, cold, determined, practical, cautious.[18] The only difference in these two lists is the use of "warm" in the first list, and "cold" in the second. Despite the presence of six other terms, those with the "cold" list had a much more negative impression of the person than those with the "warm" list. One piece of negative information can have a disproportionate effect on our impressions and negate the effect of several positive pieces of information.

Seeing Good or Bad

We distort our attributions to match our like or dislike for someone. A small dog comes running up to a person. The person kicks at the dog, sending it yelping away. The person is someone you don't like. Why do you think he or she behaved this way? You would probably say something like, "That person is mean." You would attribute the behaviour to an internal cause. But what if that person was a close friend who you liked a lot? Then you would probably say, "My friend is afraid of dogs," or "That dog was about to bite her—what else could she do?" You relieve your friend of responsibility by attributing her action to external causes. By the same token, if someone we like does something positive, we attribute it to his or her personality, but when those we dislike do something positive, we attribute it to external reasons or to some darker motivation.

We explain our own behaviour in a similar way: the things we do that people like about us are because of who we are; the things we do that are undesirable, we attribute to circumstance. For example, if you fail an exam, you are likely to blame some external cause—the exam was unfair, you had to work, or your roommates were noisy when you were studying. But if you ace the exam, it is because you are smart and studious.

RECAP	Barriers to Accurate Perceptions
IGNORING DETAILS	We give too much weight to information that is obvious and superficial.
OVERGENERALIZING	We treat small amounts of information as if they were highly representative.
HOLDING ON TO PRECONCEPTIONS	We distort or ignore information that violates our expectations or preconceptions.
IMPOSING CONSISTENCY	We overestimate the consistency and constancy of others' behaviours.
PRECONNECTING CAUSES AND EFFECTS	We rely on pre-existing ideas about the underlying causes for what we observe.
SIMPLIFYING	We prefer simple explanations to complex ones.
IGNORING CIRCUMSTANCES	We diminish the effect of external circumstances on another's behaviour. We fail to compare one person's behaviour to that of others under the same circumstances.
CREDITING IRRELEVANT INFORMATION	We treat irrelevant information as if it were relevant.
FOCUSING ON THE NEGATIVE	We give more weight to negative information than to positive information.
SEEING GOOD OR BAD	We distort our attributions to match our like or dislike for someone.

Improving Your Perceptual Skills

With so many barriers to perceiving and interpreting other people's behaviour accurately, what can you do to improve your perceptual skills? Increasing your awareness of the factors that lead to inaccuracy will help initially, and you will find further suggestions in this section. Ultimately, your improvement will depend upon your willingness to do three things: (1) to grow as you expand your experiences, (2) to communicate about your perceptions with others, and (3) to seek out and consider others' perceptions of you.

Increase Your Understanding of the Perceptual Process

Study this chapter well because it will help you to understand many of the elements that affect your perception. You need to understand the process through which you make sense of the world and other people. Don't take your conclusions about others for granted. Question your perceptions and analyze the process through which you arrive at perceptual conclusions. Emulate Sherlock Holmes: use your knowledge of the perceptual process to sharpen your own perceptions and conclusions.

Increase Your Observational Acuity

Your senses are constantly bombarding you with information, much of which you ignore. You can increase the amount of information that you process from your senses by consciously attending to the input. When you interact with others, try to identify one new thing each time to focus on and observe. Watch their gestures, their eyes, the wrinkles around their eyes, their foot movements; listen to their tone of voice. Each observation will provide information that potentially can improve the quality of your interactions. You may create additional problems, however, if you focus so narrowly on one element that you miss others or overestimate the meaning of irrelevant information. Try to notice as much detail as possible, but keep the entire picture in view.

Recognize the Elements to Which You Attribute Meaning

As we have seen, the third stage in the perception process involves attributing meaning to what we perceive. We do this so automatically that we often fail to realize that we have attributed meaning to something. Therefore, we also fail to recognize the effect it might have on what we do and say. Try to become aware of the stimuli to which you attribute meaning. For instance, if you shake a man's hand that is weak and clammy, you might quickly withdraw your hand and form an impression of the man as wimpy and aloof without realizing that you have attributed meaning to the handshake. Take an inventory of your own perceptual tendencies. Do you pay particular attention to eye contact, gestures, facial expressions, clothing, accents, or vocal intonations? When you become more aware of what you attend to and when you are attributing meaning, you can then decide whether you are giving proper weight to the elements you are perceiving.

Check Your Perceptions

You can check out the accuracy of your perceptions and attributions indirectly and directly. **Indirect perception checking** involves seeking additional information through passive perception to either confirm or refute your interpretations. If you suspect someone is angry at you but is not admitting it, for example, you could look for more cues in his or her tone of voice, eye contact, and body movements to find more cues to confirm your suspicion. You could also ask questions or listen more intently to the person's words and language.

Direct perception checking involves asking straight out if your interpretations of a perception are correct. This often is not easy to do for several reasons: we don't like to admit uncertainty or suspicions to others; we might not trust that they will respond honestly; if our interpretations are wrong, we might suffer embarrassment or anger. But asking someone to confirm a perception shows that you are committed to understanding his or her behaviour. If your friend's voice sounds weary and her posture is sagging, you may assume that she is depressed or upset. If you ask, "I get the feeling from your tone of voice and the way you're acting that you are kind of down and depressed; what's wrong?" Your friend can then either provide another interpretation, "I'm just tired; I had a busy week"; or expand on your interpretation, "Yeah, things haven't been going very well. . . ." Your observation might also be a revelation: "Really? I didn't realize I was acting that way. I guess I am a little down."

Increase Your Awareness of Perceptual Inaccuracies and Compensate for Them

As you read through the list of distorting factors earlier in this chapter, some of them should have struck a familiar chord. Keep in mind which distortions tend to colour your perceptions of others and be aware of their effect. For example, if you know that you are likely to interpret the behaviour of people you don't like in a negative way, regardless of their intent, then you can question your interpretations and correct them if necessary.

Increase Your Awareness of Others' Perceptions of You and Seek Honest and Constructive Feedback

The best athletes don't avoid hearing criticisms and observations from their coaches. Instead, they seek out as much feedback as they can about what they are doing right and wrong. Olympic training often involves the use of videotaped replays and computer analysis so that athletes can see themselves as others see them and use that perspective to improve their performance. It is difficult to be objective about our own behaviour, so feedback from others can help us with our self-perceptions. The strongest relationships are those in which the partners are both willing to share and be receptive to the perceptions of the other.

Write down a list of some recent interpretations you've made about others' behaviours. Identify the specific behaviour or quality that you have observed and the resulting interpretation. For example, Joe is a really big man (quality), therefore he must be a football player (interpretation).

Identify which interpretations might have been affected by any of the biases we've talked about (e.g., giving weight to information that is obvious and superficial).

See if you can find out the validity of those interpretations by collecting additional information. Ask Joe if he plays football or look on the football roster for his name.

Develop Decentring, Empathy, and Other Orientation

Effective interpersonal perception depends upon our ability to understand where others are coming from, to get inside their head, to see things from their perspective. These abilities allowed Ernie to empathize with the caller in the story below. We have already talked about the importance of decentring and empathy in interpersonal communication. They enable us to increase our understanding of others, and they improve our ability to predict and adapt, to increase our communication effectiveness, and to achieve our interpersonal goals.[19] To improve your ability to decentre, strive for two key goals: (1) gather as much knowledge about the circumstances that are affecting the other person as possible; and (2) gather as much knowledge about the other person as possible. Try asking and answering the following ten questions the next time you interpret someone's actions:

Those who educate and deal with children acknowledge the importance of empathy. The following reading is from a child's storybook created in cooperation with the producers of *Sesame Street*. Ernie demonstrates a strong aptitude for being empathic as he listens to an emotion-filled story. As you read through it, try to think of times when you have been emotionally involved and empathic with what another person told you.

Ernie's Telephone Call

RING!

"I'll answer the telephone, Bert," called Ernie.

"Hello?" he said, after picking up the receiver. "No I didn't hear what happened to you today. Tell me. What was it?

"This morning you were unhappy because you went on a picnic? . . . And the weather was great? . . . And you had baloney sandwiches and soda and cake?

"And you played softball and hit a home run? No wonder you were HAPPY! It makes me happy just to hear about it!

"And then it rained and they called off the softball game? How SAD!

"So you grabbed your baloney sandwich and ran under a tree . . . And then you were really sad because the picnic was ruined. Gee! It makes me sad, too.

"And while you were standing there, you were SURPRISED to see climbing down toward you . . . A GIANT GORILLA!

"And the gorilla had huge eyes? . . . And big sharp teeth? . . . And you were AFRAID!! I'm scared already!

1. What factors or circumstances are affecting the person?

2. How can I determine whether there are factors I don't know about or don't fully understand?

3. What do I know about this person that explains his or her behaviours and feelings?

4. What is going through the other person's mind at this time?

5. What are the other person's feelings at this time?

6. What other explanations could there be for the person's actions?

7. What would I think if I were in the same situation?

8. How would I feel if I were in the same situation?

9. What would other people think if they were in that situation?

10. What would other people feel if they were in that situation?

"And the gorilla reached down and grabbed your baloney sandwich! . . . And then you got angry!

"And ANGRIER! . . . and ANGRIER!!

"Then the gorilla said he was sorry? And to show you he was friendly, he picked you up and carried you on his shoulders? . . . And when everybody saw how you had made friends with a giant gorilla, they cheered? . . . And you felt very PROUD? Boy, I'd feel proud, too!

"What's that? . . . Really? . . .

Oh, that's all right. It was nice talking to you anyway. Good-bye."

"Wait a minute, Ernie," said Bert. "Let me get this straight. You were just talking to somebody who was HAPPY at a picnic . . . then who was SAD because it started to rain and the picnic was ruined . . . then was SURPRISED when a giant gorilla appeared . . . then who was AFRAID because the gorilla had big eyes and sharp teeth . . . then who was ANGRY because the gorilla grabbed the baloney

sandwich . . . and who was PROUD when they made friends and everybody cheered!

"Ernie, that's the most amazing story I've ever heard! Tell me, who was that who just called you?"

"Gee, Bert, I don't know. It was a wrong number."

Ernie's Telephone Call, by Ray Sipherd, © Children's Television Workshop, 1978. Ernie & Bert © Jim Henson Productions, Inc.

Summary

Interpersonal perception is a fundamental element of interpersonal communication. Our communication and interpersonal relationships are affected by the way we perceive those with whom we interact. Interpersonal perception is more than just the arousal of the senses; it also involves selecting, organizing, and interpreting what we observe in order to decide what people are like and give meaning to their actions.

Our perceptions of others affect how we communicate, and how others perceive us affects how they communicate with us. Interpersonal perception can be a passive or active process. It is passive when only our senses are in operation; it is active when we feel a need for information and intentionally seek it. We are motivated to seek information in situations that have high amounts of uncertainty. Perception of information helps reduce uncertainty and provides us with more control of the situation.

Interpersonal perception affects and is affected by the development of impressions, our own implicit personality theories, constructs, and attributions. Our general impressions of individuals are often affected by primacy and recency effects; we pay particular attention to the first things we notice and the most recent things we notice about others. In our interactions with others we all seem to operate as "naive psychologists," developing and applying our own implicit personality theories. These implicit personality theories represent the general way we believe people behave. We develop specific personal constructs that represent the qualities we associate with specific people we know. Finally, we try to explain the actions and behaviours of others through the process of attribution. According to attribution theorists, we seek to find out the intent and cause of a person's action; we see a person's action as a response to a given circumstance, a particular stimulus, or the person's own personality. To make rational and accurate attributions, we must overcome perceptual barriers. We can identify ten specific tendencies that distort the accuracy of our attributions, such as focusing on obvious or negative information.

The following suggestions will help you to improve your interpersonal perception: (1) increase your understanding of the perceptual process; (2) increase your observational acuity; (3) recognize the elements to which you are attributing meaning; (4) check out your perceptions directly and indirectly; (5) increase your awareness of perceptual biases and compensate for them; (6) increase your awareness of others' perceptions of you and seek honest and constructive feedback; and (7) develop your ability to decentre and empathize.

Questions for Discussion and Review

FOCUS ON COMPREHENSION

1. In what ways does interpersonal perception affect our interpersonal communication and relationships?

2. Identify and describe the three stages of the interpersonal perception process.

3. Explain the relationships among impressions, implicit personality theory, constructs, and attributions.

4. Identify and explain three barriers to accurate perception.

5. How can you improve your perceptual skills?

FOCUS ON CRITICAL THINKING

6. Think about some of your recent interpersonal conflicts. How would you describe your perception of the problem? How do you think the others would describe their perceptions of it? What role did perception play in contributing to or resolving the conflict?

7. What do you think contributes to the development of the tendencies that cause us to perceive people inaccurately? How might the effects of those factors be minimized or eliminated?

FOCUS ON ETHICS

8. Do you have a right in an intimate relationship to expect your partner to share his or her perceptions of you, whether those perceptions are positive or negative? Explain your reasoning.

9. If you are aware of how you are distorting your own perceptions and attributions, should you try to change them? Is it a moral obligation? Explain your reasoning.

For Your Journal

1. As you interact with a friend, try to assess your awareness level of the cues that are being communicated. Ask your friend to confirm your interpretation of the cues that you have observed. How effective and accurate were you at picking up information?

2. Use the list of barriers to accurate perception to do a self-analysis. Which barriers influence your perceptions the most? What problems do those distortions create in your interactions with others?

3. Choose two of the suggestions for improving your perceptions. Develop a plan for what you will do in your next interaction to apply that suggestion. Try the suggestion; then write an evaluation of how well you applied the suggestion, how well the suggestion worked, and how you might modify your plan to apply the suggestion in the future.

Learning with Others

1. Choose an advertisement, magazine illustration, photograph, or painting that shows a group of people and bring it to class. In groups of four or five, pass around the pictures. For each picture, write down a few words to describe your perceptions about what you see in the picture. What are the people doing? What is their relationship to one another? What is each one like? How is each one feeling? Why are they doing what they are doing? After you have finished, share with one another what you wrote down. Try to determine why there were differences. What factors influenced your perceptions?

2. Pair up with someone in class whom you do not know and have not interacted with before. Without saying anything to each other, write down the words from the following list that you think apply to the other person. Now converse for five minutes. In a separate section of your paper, write down any additional words that you believe apply to the person. You can go back and put a line through any of the words in the first list that you now think are inaccurate. Share with your partner what words you put down before and during the conversation, and what words you changed. Have your partner share his or her perceptions of you. Discuss, as best you can, the reasons you chose each word.

Intelligent	Athletic	Artistic	Studious
Nice	Funny	Conceited	Friendly
Introvert	Extrovert	Hard worker	Shy
Talented	Popular	Inquisitive	Moody
Emotional	Happy	Brave	Responsible
Leader	Follower	Uncertain	Confused

GLOSSARY

PERCEPTION: The arousal of any of our senses.

INTERPERSONAL PERCEPTION: The process of selecting, organizing, and interpreting our observations of other people.

SELECTIVE PERCEPTION: Directing our attention to specific stimuli and consequently ignoring other stimuli.

HALO EFFECT: Attributing a variety of positive qualities to those we like.

HORN EFFECT: Attributing a variety of negative qualities to those we dislike.

PASSIVE PERCEPTION: Perception that occurs because our senses are in operation.

ACTIVE PERCEPTION: Seeking out specific information through intentional observation and questioning.

IMPRESSION FORMATION: The process of forming a general collection of perceptions about another person.

FIRST IMPRESSIONS: The product of a set of perceptions we gather upon meeting another person.

PRIMACY EFFECT: Placing heavy emphasis upon the first pieces of information that we observe about another to form an impression.

RECENCY EFFECT: Placing heavy emphasis on the most recent information we have observed about another to form or modify our impression.

IMPLICIT PERSONALITY THEORY: Our own set of beliefs and hypotheses about what people are like.

PERSONAL CONSTRUCTS: Specific qualities or attributes we associate with each person we know.

COGNITIVE COMPLEXITY: The level of ability to develop a sophisticated set of personal constructs.

ATTRIBUTIONS: The reasons we develop to explain the behaviours of others.

CORRESPONDENT INFERENCE THEORY: One theory of attribution that is based on determining how intentional a person's actions are.

CAUSAL ATTRIBUTION THEORY: One theory of attribution that is based upon determining whether a person's actions are caused by circumstance, a stimulus, or the person.

INDIRECT PERCEPTION CHECKING: Seeking additional information to confirm or refute interpretations you are making through passive perception.

DIRECT PERCEPTION CHECKING: Asking for confirmation or refutation from the observed person of an interpretation of a perception about him or her.

Learning Interpersonal Communication Skills

People judge you by your behaviour, not by your intentions. The following three chapters focus on research-based communication skills that will help you monitor and shape your behaviour to improve the quality of your relationships. Chapter 4 offers tips and strategies for listening to others and confirming your understanding of what you hear. Chapter 5 focuses on the scope and importance of unspoken messages. We will explore the implications of the adage, Actions speak louder than words. Then in Chapter 6 we will explore how the words we use and misuse affect our relationships with others. Meanings, as we'll learn, are in people, not in words themselves. Becoming other-oriented involves both listening to the words and reading the behaviour cues of others.

Listening and Responding

A fter studying this chapter, you
should be able to:

1. Describe four elements of the listening process.

2. Understand why we listen and list
   several important barriers to effective listening.

3. Identify ways to improve your other-
   orientation and listening skills.

4. Identify responding skills and understand strategies for improving them.

Conversation overheard at Jimmie's Bar and Grill last Thursday:

Terry: So, let's get down to the details. Where are we gonna hold this party?

Bonnie: I can't think about it now, Terry. I'm too upset over a fight I had with Alex this morning.

Terry: Why don't you get rid of that husband, kiddo? You're always fighting. Find someone who treats ya with more respect. Now come on, just think about the best place—here at Jimmie's or over at Nate and Carmen's house?

Roseanne: What did you fight about, Bonnie?

Bonnie: He wants me to quit my job—which I don't like so much anyway—and have a baby. But I'm not sure I feel ready for such a big move, although I'd love to stop working there.

Roseanne: So you're feeling torn because you'd like to quit your job, but not to have a baby.

Bonnie: Well, I don't know. But if I did decide to have a baby, I wouldn't want to do it just to please him.

Terry: Don't give in to him, Bonn. He'll never stop pushing you around. I think maybe Nate and Carmen's. They've got that big barbecue pit.

Roseanne: Let's go over to my house where there's no jukebox and talk this over, Bonnie. It sounds like you're not really dismissing the idea, are you?

Bonnie: No. I would like to talk.

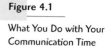

Figure 4.1

What You Do with Your Communication Time

Can you identify the skilled listener in this snatch of conversation? Probably. Can you describe the skills that she is using? Probably not. But you will be able to by the time you finish this chapter.

You spend more time listening to others than almost anything else you do. As the pie chart in Figure 4.1 shows, people typically spend more than 80 percent of an average day communicating with other people, and they spend 45 percent of that communication time listening to others.[1] Ironically, most people's formal communication training focuses on writing, the activity to which we devote the least amount of communication time. Chances are that up until now, you have had no training in listening. In this chapter, we will focus on this often neglected, yet quintessential skill for developing quality interpersonal relationships. As we have seen, becoming other-oriented means learning about the needs,

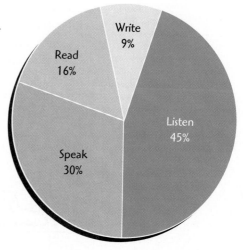

hopes, concerns, and joys of another in order to enhance the quality of your relationship. And listening is the process by which you can learn the most about another person. In addition, we will explore ways to respond to others and check your perceptions of their comments.

Listening Defined

"**D**id you hear what I said?" demanded a father who had been lecturing his teenage son on the importance of hanging up his clothes. In fact, the boy did *hear* him, but he may not have been *listening*. **Listening** is a complex process we use to make sense out of what we hear. **Hearing** is the physiological process of decoding sounds. You hear when the sound vibrations reach your eardrum and buzz the middle ear bones: the hammer, anvil, and stirrup. Eventually, the sound vibrations are translated into electrical impulses that reach the brain. In order to listen to something, you must first select that sound from competing sounds. To truly listen involves four activities—selecting, attending, understanding, and remembering. We confirm that listening occurs by responding.

Selecting

To **select** a sound is to focus on one sound as you sort through the various sounds competing for your attention. As you listen to another in an interpersonal context, you focus on the words and nonverbal messages of your partner. Even now, as you are reading this book, there are undoubtedly countless noises within earshot. Stop reading for a moment and sort through the various sounds around you. Do you hear music? Is there noise from outside? How about the murmur of voices, the tick of a clock, the hum of a computer, the whoosh of an air conditioner or furnace? To listen, you must select which of these sounds will receive your attention.

Attending

After selecting a sound, you then focus on it. Attention can be fleeting. You may **attend** to the sound for a moment and then move on or return to other thoughts or other sounds. Typically, you attend to those sounds and messages that meet your needs or are consistent with what you think you should be focusing on. If you are

hungry, you may select and then attend to a commercial for a sizzling burger or a crispy-crust pizza. Information that is novel, humorous, intense, or that somehow relates to you, also may capture your attention. Almost 25 years later, many Canadians still recall Prime Minister Trudeau's "fuddle-duddle": The prime minister had been accused of violating parliamentary rules by mouthing a particular four-letter word beginning with "f", while making a matching hand gesture, in the House of Commons. Trudeau's quick response to his accusers ("I may have just mouthed 'fuddle-duddle'") became a shared joke among the Canadian media and public alike, even sparking a boom in "fuddle-duddle" T-shirts. The collective attention of the nation had been temporarily drawn away from more pressing issues of the time, which by now are forgotten by most.

In general, conflict, humour, new ideas, and real or concrete things command your attention more easily than abstract theories that do not relate to your interests or needs. In addition, when someone invites you to participate or respond, you listen much more attentively than you do when someone just talks at you. One of your authors recently attended a day-long series of lectures at Oxford University on life in England during the Middle Ages. As a paleoanthropologist droned on about femur measurements and Harris lines, I struggled to stay awake. But when the lecturer produced several recently unearthed skeletons and invited the audience to participate in drawing conclusions about their lives and environment, I was all ears.

Understanding

Whereas hearing is a physiological phenomenon, **understanding** is the process of assigning meaning to the sounds you select and to which you attend. There are several theories about how you assign meaning to words you hear, but there is no universally accepted notion of how this process works. We know that people understand best if they can relate what they are hearing to something they already know. For this reason the use of analogy and comparison is effective when explaining complex material or abstract ideas.

A second basic principle about how people understand others is that the greater the similarity between individuals, the greater the likelihood for more accurate understanding. Individuals from different cultures who have substantially different religions, family lifestyles, values, and attitudes often have difficulty understanding each other, particularly in the early phases of a relationship. In a scene from her novel *The Joy Luck Club*, Amy Tan describes a culturally based misunderstanding between Jing-mei's Chinese mother and American boyfriend:

> As is the Chinese cook's custom, my mother always made disparaging remarks about her own cooking. That night she chose to direct it toward her famous steamed pork and preserved vegetable dish, which she always served with special pride.
>
> "Ai! This dish not salty enough, no flavour," she complained, after tasting a small bite. "It is too bad to eat."
>
> This was our family's cue to eat some and proclaim it the best she had ever made. But before we could do so, Rich said, "You know, all it needs is a little soy sauce." And he proceeded to pour a riverful of the salty black stuff on the platter, right before my mother's horrified eyes.[2]

You understand best that which you also experience. Perhaps you have heard the Montessori school philosophy: I hear, I forget; I see, I remember; I experience, I understand. Hearing alone does not provide us with understanding. We hear over one billion words each year, but we understand a fraction of that number. In Chapter 3 we discussed the processes involved in perception and observed that different people can reach dramatically different conclusions about the same events and messages, based on their previous experiences. A key to establishing relationships with others is trying to understand those differences in experience in order to arrive at a common meaning for the messages we exchange.

Remembering

To **remember** is to recall information. Some researchers theorize that you store every detail you have ever heard or witnessed; your mind operates like a video camera. But you cannot retrieve or remember all of the tapes. Sometimes you are present, yet you have no recollection of what occurred.

Our brains have both short-term and long-term memory storage systems. Short-term memory is where you store almost all the information you hear. You look up a phone number in the telephone book, mumble the number to yourself, then dial the number only to discover that the line is busy. Three minutes later you have to look up the number again because it did not get stored in your long-term memory. Our short-term storage area is very limited. Just as airports have just a few short-term parking spaces, but lots of spaces for long-term parking, our brains can accommodate a few things of fleeting significance, but acres of important information. Most of us forget hundreds of snips and bits of insignificant information that pass through our brains each day.

The information we store in long-term memory include events, conversations, and other data that are significant for us. We tend to remember dramatic and vital information, as well as seemingly inconsequential details connected with such information. Most Canadians over the age of thirty-five know exactly where they were

Donovan Bailey's 1996 run for Olympic gold is unforgettable. (Canadian Olympic Association)

in 1972 when the winning goal was scored and Canada won the hockey series against the former U.S.S.R. Many can recall in poignant detail how Wayne Gretzky tearfully announced his trade from the Edmonton Oilers to the Los Angeles Kings. Do you remember the day that runner Ben Johnson was detected with steroids after winning the gold medal for Canada at the 1988 Olympic Games? Donovan Bailey's recent world-record sprint to bring Canada an Olympic gold medal will likely be another indelible image in the collective memory of Canadians. Information makes it to long-term memory because of its significance to us.

Responding

Interpersonal communication is interactive; it involves both talking and responding. You **respond** to people to let them know you understand their messages. Responses can be nonverbal; direct eye contact and head nods let your partner know you're tuned in. Or you can respond verbally by asking questions to confirm the content of the message: "Are you saying you don't want us to spend as much time together as we once did?" or by making statements that reflect the feelings of the speaker: "So you are frustrated that you have to wait for someone to drive you where you want to go." We will discuss responding skills in more detail later in the chapter.

RECAP	What Is Listening?
SELECTING	Sorting through various sounds that compete for your attention.
ATTENDING	Focusing on a particular sound or message.
UNDERSTANDING	Assigning meaning to messages.
REMEMBERING	Recalling information that has been communicated.
RESPONDING	Confirming your understanding of a message.

Why You Listen

Why do we listen to others? As the great explorer Sir Edmund Hillary replied when asked why he climbed Mount Everest—because it's there. You listen because words are there. But you also listen because you have a need to connect with other humans; it is through listening that you develop and maintain relationships. You listen to enjoy, to learn, to evaluate, and to empathize with others.

Listening to Enjoy.
Many people tune in to popular entertainers such as Alanis Morissette just for the fun of it.

Listening to Enjoy

Often, you listen to others just for the fun of it. Perhaps one of the reasons your friends are your friends is that they are entertaining storytellers or clever wisecrackers. You select TV programs, movies, music, and other forms of entertainment for the same reason. Listening is part of the pleasure of being with others. You enjoy going to parties, dining with friends, and getting together just to hang out because you can share the joys and humorous events of life by listening and being listened to.

Listening to Learn.
You probably listen to the national news regularly to keep abreast of important current affairs.

Listening to Learn

Not all listening is for pleasure. Nothing snaps a class to attention more quickly than a professor's proclamation that, "This next point will be covered on the test." Another key reason we listen is to learn. Since the days you began watching *Sesame Street* (if you grew up in North America during the 1970s) until now, as you pursue a degree, you have been challenged to understand and remember what you hear. The more motivated you are to learn, the more likely it is that you listen.

You do most of your listening and learning outside the classroom, though. You probably listen to the news regularly to keep abreast of important current affairs. In interpersonal situations, you listen for everyday information, such as who will pick up the kids after school and where and when to pick up the laundry. You also listen to find out about the daily activities of others. Your phone calls to family members when you are separated by distances are often motivated by wanting to find out what's happening. It is through listening that we learn.

Listening to Evaluate

Besides listening to accumulate information, you also listen to acquire information that you can then use to solve problems and to make critical decisions and judgments. The job interview is a classic situation in which both people listen to gather information to make a critical decision. The interviewer listens to the applicant's responses to determine whether the person can do the job well and get along with others. The applicant also seeks information and listens to evaluate whether the work will be suitable and the boss a reasonable manager for him or her. As we saw in Chapter 3, often, because of the barrage of information coming at you each day, you make snap judgments. These first impressions are based upon information we hear, and upon our own biases and backgrounds. As the saying goes, you never get a second chance to make—or to form—a first impression.

We use critical thinking skills to evaluate the messages of others. If we are adept at separating facts from inferences, identifying fallacies in reasoning, and analyzing evidence, then our evaluations of others' messages can be reasonably accurate.

Listening to Empathize

The word *empathy* comes from a Greek word for "passion" and a translation of the German word *einfühlen*, which means "to feel with." Empathy involves emotions. As we discussed in Chapter 1, to **empathize** with someone is to try to feel what he or she is feeling, rather than just to think about or acknowledge the feelings.

When your friends have "one of those days," perhaps they seek you out to talk about it. They may not have any real problems to solve—perhaps it was just a day filled with miscommunication and squabbles with their partners or co-workers. But

LEARNING INTERPERSONAL COMMUNICATION SKILLS

they want to tell you the details. Do you listen empathically, without giving advice? That is what they are seeking—a listener who focuses attention on them and understands what they are saying. We are willing to listen empathically for the same reasons that we like to give our friends gifts. It makes us feel good to show others that we value them. Carl Rogers summarized the value of empathy when he said, "A high degree of empathy in a relationship is possibly the most potent factor in bringing about change and learning."

One of our best motivations for listening is a desire to provide support and understanding for others by actually experiencing what they feel. What clues in this photo signal that the listening is empathic? (Superstock)

CONSIDERING OTHERS

Most card shops have a sympathy card section. Such cards let people know you realize they are feeling bad about the death of someone close to them. To **sympathize** is to say you are sorry—that you want to offer your support and acknowledge that someone is feeling bad. Empathy goes one step further than sympathy. Empathy means that you try to perceive the world from another's perspective; you attempt to feel what someone else feels.

Respond to the sample situations below both with sympathy and with empathy.

1. A good friend of yours just phoned to tell you that her dog, a well-loved fourteen-year-old pet, has just died.

Respond with sympathy: _____

_____

Respond with empathy: _____

_____

2. Your older brother comes to visit you and tells you that he and his wife are getting a divorce after twenty years of marriage.

Respond with sympathy: _____

_____

Respond with empathy: _____

_____

3. A friend tells you that she just got fired from her job.

Respond with sympathy: _____

_____

Respond with empathy: _____

_____

From William Gudykunst, *Bridging Differences,* 2d ed. (Thousand Oaks, CA: Sage Publications, 1994). Reprinted by permission of Sage Publications, Inc.

Reasons for Listening

Why We Listen	Example
Listening for Enjoyment	Listening to friends and relatives tell stories.
Listening to Learn	Getting directions to a friend's house.
Listening to Evaluate	Sorting through a persuasive sales pitch to buy a new car.
Listening to Empathize	Listening to a good friend talk about the death of a cherished pet.

COMMUNICATION EXPERIENCE

Assessing Your Listening Behaviour

The purpose of this questionnaire is to assess your listening behaviour. Respond to each statement with a number as follows: 1 for always false, 2 for usually false, 3 for sometimes false, 4 for usually true and 5 for always true.

_____ 1. I have a difficult time separating important and unimportant ideas when I listen to others.

_____ 2. I check new information against what I already know when I listen to others.

_____ 3. I have an idea what others will say when I listen to them.

_____ 4. I am sensitive to others' feelings when I listen to them.

_____ 5. I think about what I am going to say next when I listen to others.

_____ 6. I focus on the process of communication that is occurring between me and others when I listen to them.

_____ 7. I cannot wait for others to finish talking so I can take my turn.

_____ 8. I try to understand the meanings that are being created when I communicate with others.

_____ 9. I focus on determining whether others understand what I said when they are talking.

_____10. I ask others to elaborate when I am not sure what they mean.

To find your score, first reverse your responses for the *odd-numbered* items (if you wrote 1, make it 5; if you wrote 2, make it 4; if you wrote 3, leave it as 3; if you wrote 4, make it 2; if you wrote 5, make it 1). Next, add the numbers next to each statement. Scores range from 10 to 50. The higher your score, the better your listening behaviour.

From: William Gudykunst, *Bridging Differences*, 2d ed. (Thousand Oaks, CA: Sage Publications, 1994). Reprinted by permission of Sage Publications, Inc.

Listening Barriers

Even though we spend so much of our communication time listening, most of us don't listen as well as we should. Twenty-four hours after we hear a speech, a class lecture, or a sermon, we forget more than half of what was said. And it gets worse. In another twenty-four hours we forget half of what we remembered, so we really remember only a quarter of the lecture.

Our interpersonal listening skills are not much better. If anything, they may be worse. When you listen to a speech or lecture, you have a clearly defined listening role; one person talks and you are expected to listen. But in interpersonal situations, you may have to alternate quickly between speaking and listening. This takes considerable skill and concentration. Often you are thinking of what you want to say next rather than listening.

One study found that even in the most intimate relationships, our listening skills are not highly developed. Couples who had been married for at least five years were placed in separate rooms and researchers asked the wives, "During the last six months have you and your spouse talked about who would be responsible for some of the household chores such as taking out the garbage and other domestic responsibilities?" "Yes," recalled at least 71 percent of the wives. Interestingly, when the same question was put to their husbands, only 19 percent recalled a discussion of domestic duties. Intrigued, the researchers next asked a more personal question of the wives: "In the last six months have you and your spouse discussed the possibilities of increasing the size of your family? Have you talked about having children?" An overwhelming majority, 91 percent, of the wives responded affirmatively. Curiously, only 15 percent of the husbands recalled having a conversation about having more children. While one anecdotal study does not prove conclusively that all intimate relationships suffer from listening lapses, it does illustrate the problem. And as the Understanding Diversity box on p. 104 reiterates, often the problem is gender related.

Another surprising study found that we sometimes pay more attention to strangers than to intimate friends or partners.[3] Married couples in the study tended to interrupt each other more often and were generally less polite to one another than were strangers involved in a decision-making task. Apparently, we take listening shortcuts when communicating with others in close relationships.

Who Listens Better: Men or Women?

Research provides no definitive answer to this question. There is evidence that men and women listen differently and have different expectations about the role of listening and talking. Deborah Tannen suggests that one of the most common complaints wives have about their husbands is "He doesn't listen to me anymore" along with, "He doesn't talk to me anymore." Another scholar noted that complaints about lack of communication were usually at the top of women's lists of reasons for divorce but mentioned much less often by men. Since both men and women are participating in the same conversation, why are women often more dissatisfied with the listening and talking process than men? Tannen's explanation: women expect different things from conversations than men do.

One researcher suggests that men and women may have different attention styles. When men listen, they may be looking for a new structure or organizational pattern, or to separate bits of information they hear. They continually shape, form, observe, inquire, and direct energy toward a chosen goal. Men's attention style is reported to be more emotionally controlled than women's attention style. Women are described as more subjective, empathic, and emotionally involved as they listen. They are more likely to search for relationships among parts of a pattern and to rely upon more intuitive perceptions of feelings. They are also more easily distracted by competing details. Females may hear more of the message because they reject less of it. These differences in attention styles and the way men and women process information, suggests the researcher, can potentially affect listening, even though we have no direct evidence linking attention style to listening skill.

Another researcher suggests that when men listen, they listen to solve a problem; men are more instrumental and task oriented. Women listen to seek new information to enhance understanding. There is additional evidence that men may be more goal oriented when they listen. What are the implications of these research studies? It may mean that men and women focus on different parts of messages and have different listening objectives. These differences can affect relationship development. Males may need to recognize that while they are attending to a message and looking for new structure to solve a problem or achieve a goal, they may hear less of the message and therefore listen less effectively. And even though many females may hear more of the message, they may need to make connections between the parts of the information they hear to look for major ideas, rather than just focus on the details. In any case, gender-based differences in attention style and information processing may account for some of the relational problems that husbands and wives, lovers, siblings and male–female pairs experience.[4]

Most interpersonal listening problems can be traced to a single source—ourselves. While listening to others, we also "talk" to ourselves. Our internal thoughts are like a play-by-play sportscast. We mentally comment on the words and sights that we select and to which we attend. If we keep those comments focused on the message, they may be useful. But we often attend to our own internal dialogues instead of others' messages. Then our listening effectiveness plummets.

Inattentive listening is a bit like channel surfing when we watch TV—pushing the remote control button to switch from channel to channel, avoiding commercials and focusing for brief periods on attention-grabbing program "bites." When we listen to others, we may fleetingly tune in to the conversation for a moment, decide that the content is uninteresting, and then focus on a personal thought. These thoughts are barriers to communication, and they come in a variety of forms.

Barrier: Focusing on a Personal Agenda

Most of us have had the experience of waiting our turn in a conversation, formulating what we were going to say next. This focus on an internal message can keep us from selecting and attending to the other person's message. If you are supposed to be listening to Aunt Mae tell about her recent trip to the Navan Country Fair, but you are eager to hit her up for a loan, your personal agenda will serve as a barrier to your listening ability. Or you may simply decide that Aunt Mae's monologue is boring and unimportant and give yourself permission to tune out as she drones on. Like humorist James Thurber's famous daydreamer, Walter Mitty, you may eventually find yourself unable to respond cogently, lost in your own world:

> "Not so fast! You're driving too fast!" said Mrs. Mitty. "What are you driving so fast for?"
>
> "Hmmm?" said Walter Mitty. He looked at his wife, in the seat beside him, with shocked astonishment. She seemed grossly unfamiliar, like a strange woman who had yelled at him in a crowd.[5]

How do you short-circuit this listening problem? First, diagnose it. Note consciously when you find yourself drifting off, thinking about your agenda rather than concentrating on the speaker. Second, throttle up your powers of concentration when you find your internal messages are distracting you from listening well. If you notice that you are "telling" yourself that Aunt Mae's anecdote is boring, you can also mentally remind yourself to listen with greater energy and focus.

Barrier: Emotional Noise

Words are powerful symbols that affect our attitudes, our behaviour, and even our blood pressure. Words arouse us emotionally. **Emotional noise** occurs when our emotional arousal interferes with communication effectiveness. If you grew up in a home in which R-rated language was never used, then four-letter words may be distracting to you. In the essay "Mind Your Tongue, Young Man," the author describes a scene in which obscene language created a barrier to maintaining a civil customer relationship. Words that insult your religious or ethnic heritage can also be fighting words. Most of us respond to certain trigger words like a bull to a waving cape; we want to charge in to correct the speaker or perhaps even do battle with him or her.

Mind Your Tongue, Young Man

We have become indifferent to cussing in everyday language.

It was one of those days filled with the little vexations of life. In the morning, insult was added to injury when I got a speeding ticket after having a root canal. At work, the computer fouled me up by going down. By noon, the banana I'd brought for lunch had turned black and squishy, and finally, as I sped for home at the end of the day, the needle on the car's fuel indicator shook convulsively in its demand for a thirst-quenching gulp of gas.

Although I don't remember that I uttered any profanities upon encountering the day's irritations, in all likelihood I did. Like most people, I've never been known to have a lily-white mouth.

On that particular evening, I was eager to get home because I was giving a dinner party. However, my main concern was that I couldn't make it without first obliging the car's needs. I whipped off the freeway and headed for the nearest convenience store, only to find all eight pumps taken.

"Damn," I remember exclaiming as I impatiently waited my turn. But I soon found myself using another expletive when a cheeky woman in a Volvo tried to nudge ahead of me and cheat me of my already established territorial rights.

Eventually I was able to sidle up to a pump and fill the tank. Then I darted inside to pay—only to have to wait in line for the privilege of forking over money. As I stood, swearing under my breath about another delay in my life, I was only vaguely aware of a young man in front of me. He had plunked a Pepsi on the counter and was reaching into his pocket for money.

"Ninety-four cents, please," declared the middle-aged clerk. "Oh, and I'll take this pack of cigarettes, too," the young man stated matter-of-factly, as he pitched his selection on the counter.

"ID," countered the clerk, in a tone that suggested he had made this request many times before. The casual command caused me to focus on the person ahead of me. He was extremely slight with delicate features and a face as smooth as a baby's heel. I silently agreed with the clerk's decision to question his age. He could have been 18—or he could have been 15. It was impossible to tell.

"ID," said the clerk a second time, after the customer failed to respond with anything but a surly look.

Apparently the question about his age was more than he could stand, and upon being asked twice, the young man burst forth with a string of verbal garbage. "Goddamn it! I don't have any f—-ing identification with me. I don't haul the f—-ing thing everywhere I go!" To which the clerk calmly remarked, "Then, it will be 94 cents for the Pepsi. No ID, no cigarettes."

With that rejection, the angry young man spewed a stream of obscenities that have become part of today's vocabulary. "I just ain't got my f—-ing ID with me today. I told you."

I'd been observing the exchange more out of a sense of indifference than anything. All I wanted was to pay for my gas and get on my way. But my indifference vanished when the clerk, reacting to the profanity, suddenly reached across the counter with both arms, grabbed the fellow by the collar and literally plucked him off the floor. With fire in his eyes and passion in his voice, he growled, "That is enough! You watch what you say in here, do you understand? There's a lady present!" Then he shoved the guy away with obvious contempt.

The foul-mouthed offender was stunned. So was I! Instinctively, I looked around to see where the "lady" was. I glanced up and down the nearby aisles and peered high into the corners where mirrors reveal all activity in the store. I had an image of some little old woman in a housedress, shuffling along in sturdy orthopedic shoes, her white hair done up in a bun, her purse dangling from her arm. I didn't see her anywhere.

All I saw in the mirror was the reflection of the two combatants—and my own. The obvious hit me hard. *I* was the "lady." I was flabbergasted by the clerk's stern admonition on my behalf. No one had tried to protect me from offensive language before.

With considerable speed the astonished young man paid for his drink and scurried from the store. I did likewise, still so startled by the clerk's actions that I didn't respond to his gallantry.

It was only after I began driving from the convenience store that I realized the significance of the episode. Profanity seems to be one of those problems about which almost everyone agrees something should be done. Yet few of us ever do anything about it. On the contrary, most of us contribute, if not to its proliferation, at least to its continuation, by swearing ourselves or making no attempt to curb it in others.

I recalled with guilt all the less-than-delicate language that had rolled off my tongue through the years—when I was mad, when I was glad, when I was trying to be dramatic and, yes, even when I had to wait in line for a few seconds. But nothing as crass as what I'd just heard.

And now, in an act of omission myself, I had failed to respond. Why hadn't *I* told the culprit to knock it off when the first raunchy words foamed out of his mouth? Why hadn't I given so much as a second thought to rebuking him about his language? It's so familiar that it passes unnoticed, just runs off our backs. At the very least, why hadn't I thanked the clerk for taking a stand against offensive language in his store?

Recently I read a newspaper article that stated although most people do have a concern about all the unbridled profanity around us every day, the reality is that we are swearing more, hearing it less.

Unfortunately, there must be some truth to the story—as shown by my experience in the convenience store. Granted it seems only natural that someone might be in shock after being subjected to a string of raw expressions while waiting to pay for gas. What surprises me is how much more astonished I was by the store clerk's gallant intervention and stand against vulgarity in his establishment than by the cussing of an angry young punk denied a pack of cigarettes.

—SANDRA FLAHIVE MAURER

Sometimes it is not specific words, but rather concepts or ideas that cause an emotional eruption. Some talk-radio hosts try to boost their ratings by purposely using demagogic language that elicits passionate responses. Although listening to such conflict can be interesting and entertaining, when your own emotions become aroused, you may lose your ability to converse effectively. Strong emotions can interfere with focusing on the message of another.

The emotional state of the speaker may also affect your ability to understand and evaluate what you hear. One researcher found that if you are listening to someone who is emotionally distraught, you will be more likely to focus on his or her emotions, than on the content of the message.[6] Another researcher advises that when you are communicating with someone who is emotionally excited, you should remain calm and focused, and try simply to communicate your interest in the other person.[7]

Your listening challenge is to avoid emotional sidetracks and keep your attention focused upon the message. When your internal dialogue is kicked into high gear by objectionable words or concepts, or by an emotional speaker, make an effort to quiet it down and steer back to the subject at hand.

COMMUNICATION EXPERIENCE

Identifying Emotional "Hot Buttons"

Following are some listening situations and phrases that may cause you to be emotional. Check those that are "hot buttons" for you as a listener, and add others that strongly affect you, positively or negatively.

_____ "You never/always . . ."

_____ Know-it-all attitudes

_____ Individuals who smoke cigarettes or cigars while talking to you

_____ "Shut up!"

_____ Being ignored

_____ Bad grammar

_____ "You never listen."

_____ Obscene language

_____ Whining

_____ "What you should do is . . ."

_____ Being interrupted

Others:

_____

_____

_____

Knowing what your emotional hot buttons are can help prevent your overreacting when they are pushed.

Adapted from Diane Bone, *The Business of Listening*, p. 52.

Barrier: Criticizing the Speaker

Mother Teresa once said, "If you judge people, you have no time to love them." Being critical of the speaker may distract us from focusing on the message. As we learned in Chapter 3, most people are especially distracted by appearances, forming impressions of others based solely on nonverbal information. Superficial factors such as clothing, body size and shape, age, and ethnicity all affect our interpretation of a message.

It is important to monitor your internal dialogue to make sure you are focusing on the message rather than criticizing the messenger. Good listeners say to themselves, "While it may be distracting, I am simply not going to let the appearance of this speaker keep my attention from the message."

Barrier: Speech Rate vs. Thought Rate

Your ability to think faster than people speak is another listening pitfall. The average person speaks at a rate of 125 words a minute. Some folks talk a bit faster, others more slowly. You, on the other hand, have the ability to process up to 600 or

800 words a minute. The difference between your mental ability to handle words and the speed at which they arrive at your cortical centres can cause trouble, giving you time to daydream, tune the speaker in and out, and give you the illusion that you are concentrating more attentively than you actually are.[8]

You can turn your listening speed into an advantage if you use the extra time instead to summarize what a speaker is saying. By periodically sprinkling in mental summaries during a conversation, you can dramatically increase your listening ability and make the speech-rate/thought-rate difference work to your advantage.

Barrier: Information Overload

We live in an information-rich age. We are all constantly bombarded with sight and sound images, and experts suggest that the volume of information competing for our attention is likely to become even greater in the future. Incoming messages and information on computers, Fax machines, car phones, and other technological devices can interrupt conversations and distract us from listening to others.

Be on the alert for these information interruptions when you are talking with others. Don't assume that because you are ready to talk, the other person is ready to listen. If your message is particularly sensitive or important, you may want to ask your listening partner, "Is this a good time to talk?" Even if he or she says yes, look for eye contact and a responsive facial expression to make sure the positive response is genuine.

Barrier: External Noise

As you will recall, all of the communication models we saw in Chapter 1 include the element of noise—distractions that take your focus away from the message. Many households seem to be addicted to noise. Often there is a TV on (sometimes more than one), a computer game beeping, and music emanating from another room. These and other sounds compete with your attention when you are listening to others.

Besides literal noise, there are other potential distractors. A headline in your evening paper about the latest details in a lurid sex scandal may "shout" for your attention just when your son wants to talk with you about his latest science fiction story. A desire to listen to your new compact disk of "Pacific Overtures" may drown out your spouse's overtures to a heart-to-heart about your family's budget problems. The lure of music, TV, books, or Nintendo can all distract you from your listening task.

Distractions make it difficult to sustain attention to a message. You have a choice to make. You can attempt to listen through the labyrinth of competing distractions, or you can modify the environment to reduce them. Turning off the stereo, setting down the paper, and establishing eye contact with the speaker can help to minimize the noise barrier.

Although a noisy party may be a great place to have fun, it isn't the best setting for effective listening. When it's important to focus on the content of your partner's messages, choose a quiet place with few distractions. (Roswell Angier/Stock Boston)

The following listening activities can help you sharpen your listening skills.

1. Make a list of "red flag" words that have derailed your listening ability in the past. Ask another student to make up a paragraph about an important issue, using these words, and read it aloud to you. Monitor your reactions to the words and see whether you can steer your internal conversation back to the issue. Also notice how you begin to feel about the speaker and what you do about those feelings.

2. In a group, assign one student to speak very slowly on a difficult subject. Write down short summaries during pauses in the speech, then compare the summaries with those of others in the group.

3. List the things in your home—TVs, stereos, computers, newspapers, and so on—that might distract from conversation. Bring a radio into class and try conversing with a partner with music and news broadcasts in the background. Then have a conversation without the extra noise. Compare the results.

RECAP   Overcoming Barriers to Listening

Listening Barriers	To Overcome the Barrier
Focusing On Our Personal Agenda	Consciously become aware of the self-focus and shift attention.
Emotional Noise	Use self-talk to manage emotions.
Criticizing the Speaker	Focus on the message, not the messenger.
Information Rate	Use the difference between speech rate and thought rate to mentally summarize the message
Information Overload	Realize when you or your partner is tired or distracted and not ready to listen.
External Noise	Take charge of the listening environment by eliminating the distraction.

Improving Your Listening Skills

Many of the listening problems we have identified stem from focusing on ourselves rather than on the messages of others. You can begin improving your listening skills by following three steps you probably first encountered on an elementary school chart: (1) stop, (2) look, and (3) listen. Simple as they may seem, these steps can provide the necessary structure to help you refocus your mental energies and improve your listening power. Let's consider each step separately.

Stop

In order to select and attend to the messages of others, we must tap into our internal dialogue and stop our own running commentary about issues and ideas that are self-focused rather than other-focused. As we learned in Chapter 1, decentring is the term that describes the process of stepping away from our own concerns to think about the thoughts and feelings of our partner. If we treat decentring as a skill, we can learn to shift our internal dialogue to focus on others, although at first it will require conscious effort.

A model of how we learn any skill, attributed by many to Abraham Maslow, suggests that we operate at one of four skill levels:

- Unconscious incompetence

- Conscious incompetence

- Conscious competence

- Unconscious competence

The first level—*unconscious incompetence*—means we are unaware of our own incompetence. We don't know what we don't know. For example, before you read this chapter, you may simply not have been aware that you are distracted by your internal dialogue when you interact with others.

The second level is *conscious incompetence*. Here we become aware or conscious that we are not competent; we know what we don't know. You may now be aware that you are an easily distracted listener, but you do not know how to solve the problem.

Level three is *conscious competence*; we are aware that we know something, but it has not yet become an integrated habit. You might have to work at decentring when you first begin using it as you listen.

The final level of skill attainment is *unconscious competence*. At this level your skills have become second nature to you. After the age of six, most people who were raised in Canada are unconsciously competent at tying their shoes; it is automatic. In the same way, you may become so skilled in the decentring process that you do it as the rule rather than as an exception. At this level, you will also probably have the capacity to empathize, or "feel with," others as you listen. The article on page 112 points out that doctors, despite their high level of professional training, do not always have highly developed listening skills. If they took time to *stop* and listen, says the writer, they would be far more effective at treating their patients. As a wise person once said, "Take a tip from nature—your ears aren't made to shut, but your mouth is."

Look

Nonverbal messages are powerful. As the primary ways we communicate feelings, emotions, and attitudes, they play a major role in the total communication process, particularly in the development of relationships. Facial expressions and vocal cues, as well as eye contact, posture, and use of gestures and movement, can dramatically colour the meaning of a message. When the nonverbal message

Doctors Must Address More Than Physical Complaints

What's wrong with this picture: An 80-year-old woman visits her doctor, the same one she has been seeing for a long time. He asks about her health, and she starts talking about not being happy in her new apartment after 41 years living in the same house.

The apartment is in a different part of town and she misses her former neighbors, who used to pick up items for her at the grocery store. Buying furniture has posed a problem, especially because her failing eyesight makes it difficult to drive places. She also worries about making her retirement money stretch as far as she needs. She says she is so lonely.

The doctor says "Mmm-hmm" and "That's too bad" at the appropriate times during her story. Then he steers the conversation toward the woman's heart condition and whether she has been experiencing any pain or other symptoms.

Stop right there, says Dr. Howard Waitzkin, an internal-medicine physician and sociologist at the University of California at Irvine. He says the doctor is focused on the physical symptom (a weak heart) and not listening to what is really disrupting this woman's life (the loss of community).

"Social problems almost always come up when doctors and patients are talking," Waitzkin says, "but they tend to be marginalized in the conversation."

This added work [of taking more time to listen] may seem a burden for busy doctors, but Waitzkin insists such careful listening has long-term benefits: it helps address patients' underlying concerns in one visit rather than let a stressful situation linger at the potential expense of the patient's health.

Bob Condor, *Chicago Tribune*, Thursday, January 5, 1995. Copyright © Chicago Tribune Company. All rights reserved. Used with permission.

RECAP   The Skill Learning Process

Levels of Learning a Skill	Definition	Explanation
Unconscious Incompetence	We don't know that we don't know.	We are not aware that we have self-centred listening habits.
Conscious Incompetence	We know that we don't know.	We know we have self-centred listening habits, yet we don't know how to improve them.
Conscious Competence	We know a skill yet must think and work deliberately to perform it.	We understand the decentring process. When we are consciously aware, we can put it into action.
Unconscious Competence	The performance of the skill has become second nature to us.	We have practiced the decentring process so often that it has become second nature to us. We can now listen with understanding and even empathy.

contradicts the verbal message, we almost always believe the nonverbal message. In listening to others, it is vital that you focus not only on the words, but also on the nonverbal messages. Listen with your eyes as well as your ears.

Another reason to look at another person is to establish eye contact, which signals that you are focusing your interest and attention on him or her. If your eyes are darting over your partner's head, looking for someone else, or if you are constantly peeking at your watch, your partner will rightfully get the message that you're not really listening. One researcher found that we telegraph our desire to change roles from listener to speaker by increasing our eye contact, using gestures such as a raised finger, and shifting our posture.[9] So it is important to maintain eye contact and monitor your partner's nonverbal signals when you are speaking as well as listening.

It is important, however, not to be distracted by nonverbal cues that may prevent us from interpreting the message correctly. A research team asked one group of college students to listen to a counsellor, and another group to both view and listen.[10] The students then rated the counsellor's effectiveness. Students who both saw and heard the counsellor perceived him as *less* effective because his distracting nonverbal behaviours affected their evaluations. We will provide more information about how to enhance your skill in interpreting the nonverbal messages of others in Chapter 5.

Listen

After making a concerted effort to stop distracting internal dialogue and to look for nonverbal cues, you will then be in a better position to understand the verbal messages of others. To listen is to do more than focus on facts; it is to search for the essence of the speaker's thoughts. We recommend a two-pronged approach to good listening.

1. *Mentally summarize the details of the message.* This suggestion may seem to contradict the suggestion to avoid focusing only on facts, but it is important to have a grasp of the details your partner provides. As we noted earlier, you can process words much more quickly than a person speaks. So periodically summarize the names, dates, and locations in the message. Organize the speaker's factual information into appropriate categories or try to place events in chronological order. Without a full understanding of the details, you will likely miss the speaker's major point.

2. *Mentally weave these summaries into a focused major point or series of major ideas.* Facts usually make the most sense when we can use them to help support an idea or major point. So as you summarize, try to link the facts you have organized in your mind with key ideas and principles. Use facts to enhance your critical thinking as you analyze, synthesize, evaluate, and finally summarize the key points or ideas your listening partner is making.[11]

In addition to these three steps—stop, look, listen—there are other strategies you can use to improve your listening ability. These suggestions build upon the assumption that listening is a challenging activity that requires sustained concentration, especially if you must overcome bad listening habits you have developed over the years.

Read the following situation. If you are alone, read it only once and then write the details in the message as well as the key idea. Or, as a real test of listening, have a roommate, friend, or family member read the situation out loud. Check your answers by rereading the situation.

Imagine that you are working in a fast-food restaurant. Your boss approaches you with a concerned look on his face and says: "We have a problem. I have had three customers in the past hour call and complain that they have been given the wrong order when they left the drive-thru window. We have to correct this problem immediately. The first incident happened at ten this morning. We had another problem at ten-thirty. I just had another call a few minutes ago. I think Jan is working the drive-thru now. I'd like you to investigate and let me know what you find out."

What are the details in the message? _____

_____

_____

_____

_____

_____

What is the main point? _____

_____

Components of the Human Communication Process

Listening Skills	Definition	Action
Stop	Tune out distracting, competing messages.	Become conscious of being distracted; use self-talk to remain focused.
Look	Become aware of the speaker's nonverbal cues; monitor your own nonverbal cues to communicate your interest in the speaker.	Establish eye contact; avoid fidgeting or performing other tasks when someone is speaking to you. Listen with your eyes.
Listen	Comprehend the meaning of facts and details in your partner's message.	Mentally summarize details; link these details with main ideas.

Have you ever spoken to someone who communicates in sign language, or in a language other than yours? The communication between two people who speak different languages is typically facilitated through the use of an interpreter. What are the specific norms for communication through an interpreter?

The Canadian Hearing Society recommends the following points of protocol for communicating with a deaf person who is signing, where an interpreter is used. These points also apply to communicating with interpreters of other languages.

Do I need to speak slowly?

Speak at your natural pace but be aware that the interpreter must hear and understand a complete thought before signing it. Taking turns in a conversation may be different from what you are used to, owing to the lag time necessary for the interpreting process.

Should I look at the interpreter?

Look and speak directly to the deaf person. Do not say "tell him" or "tell her." The deaf person will be watching the interpreter and glancing back and forth at you.

Where should I sit?

Usually it is best to position the interpreter next to you (the hearing person), opposite the deaf person. This makes it easy for the deaf person to see you and the interpreter in one line of vision.

What about group situations?

Semicircular seating arrangements are best for discussion formats. For large group situations, such as conferences or performances, be sure to reserve a "deaf participants and their friends" seating area near the front for clear visibility of the interpreter.

Do I need any special visual aids?

Visual aids such as xeroxed handouts or writing on a chalkboard can be a tremendous help to both the interpreter and the deaf person, ensuring correct spelling of vocabulary or names.

Can I ask the interpreter about the deaf person or sign language?

The interpreter is present to facilitate communication. If you have questions about the deaf person or sign language, ask the deaf person directly and the interpreter will interpret (but not answer) your questions.

Excerpt from *How to Use Sign Language Interpreters Effectively*, The Canadian Hearing Society, Toronto, Ont.

Transform Listening Barriers into Listening Goals

If you can transform the listening barriers you read about earlier into listening goals, you will be well on your way to improving your listening skill. Make it a goal not to focus on your personal agenda. Make it a goal to use self-talk to manage emotional noise. Set a goal not to criticize the speaker. Remind yourself before each conversation to do mental summaries that capitalize on the differences between your information processing rate and the speaker's verbal delivery rate. And make it your business to choose a communication environment that is free of distraction from other incoming information or noise.

Practice Listening to Challenging Material

To improve or even maintain any skill, you need to practice it. Listening experts suggest that our listening skills deteriorate if we do not practice what we know. Listening to difficult, challenging material can sharpen our listening skills, so good listeners practice by listening to documentaries, debates, and other challenging material rather than mindless sitcoms and other material that entertains but does not engage them mentally.

Determine Your Listening Goal

As we saw earlier in this chapter, you listen to other people for several reasons—to learn, to enjoy yourself, to evaluate, or to provide support. With so many potential listening goals and options, it is useful to decide consciously what your listening objective is.

If you are listening to someone give you directions to the city park, then your mental summaries should focus on the details of when to turn left and how many streets past the courthouse you go before you turn right. The details are critical to achieving your objective. If, on the other hand, your neighbour is telling you about her father's triple bypass operation, then your goal is to empathize. It is probably not important that you be able to recall when her father checked into the hospital or other details. Your job is to listen patiently and to provide emotional support. Clarifying your listening objective in your own mind can help you use appropriate skills to maximize your listening effectiveness.

Responding with Empathy

Above all, good listening is an other-oriented ability. Good listening is active, not passive. To listen passively is to avoid displaying any behaviour that lets the speaker know we are listening.[12] Passive listeners sit with a blank stare or a frozen facial expression. Their thoughts and feelings could be anywhere, for all the speaker knows. **Active listeners**, in contrast, respond mentally, verbally, and nonverbally to a speaker's message. This serves several specific functions. First, it can be a measure of how accurately you understood the message. If you burst out laughing as your friend tells you about losing his house in a flood, he'll know you misunderstood what he was saying. Second, your responses indicate whether you agree or disagree with the comments others make. If you tell your friend that you do not approve of her comments on abortion, she'll know your position on the information she shared. Finally, your responses tell speakers how they are affecting others. Like radar that guides high-tech weapons, your feedback provides information to help others decide whether or not to correct the course of their messages.

As you can see, responding is something we do for others that holds out great benefits for us. It is the key to exchanging mutually understood, emotionally satisfying messages. Responding is especially critical if you are listening to provide support. Of course, listening to empathize is only one of the possible listening goals you may have. We are not suggesting that ferreting out someone's emotions is the goal of every listening encounter. That would be tedious for both you and your listening partners. But when you do want to listen empathically and respond, you must shift the focus to your partner and try to understand the message from his or her perspective.[13] We will discuss four strategies you can use to accomplish this.

Understand Your Partner's Feelings

If your goal is to empathize or "feel with" your partner, you might begin by imagining how you would feel under the same circumstances. If your spouse comes home dejected from being hassled at work, try to recall how you felt when that happened to you. If a friend calls to tell you his mother died, try to imagine how you would feel if the situation were reversed. Of course, your reaction to these events might be different from your spouse's or your friend's. You may need to decentre and remember how your partner felt in other similar situations, to understand how he or she is feeling now.

Ask Questions

Sometimes when others share a momentous occurrence, the story may tumble out in a rambling, disorganized way. You can help sort through the story if you ask questions to identify the sequence of events. "What happened first?" and "Then what happened?" can help both you and your partner clarify what happened.

If your partner is using words or phrases that you don't understand, ask for definitions. "He's just so lackadaisical!" moans Mariko. "What do you mean by lackadaisical? Could you give me an example?" asks Reggie. Sometimes asking for an example helps the speaker sort through the events as well.

Of course, if you are trying to understand another's feelings, you can ask how he or she is feeling, or how the event or situation made him or her feel. Often, however, nonverbal cues are more revealing than a verbal disclosure about feelings and emotions.

Reflect Content by Paraphrasing

After you try to imagine how you would feel under similar circumstances and to make sure you have an accurate understanding of the events that occurred, you need to check your understanding of the facts. Respond with a statement such as:

"Are you saying . . ."

"You seem to be describing . . ."

"So the point you are making seems to be . . ."

"Here is what I understand you to mean . . ."

"So here is what seemed to happen . . ."

Then summarize the events, details, or key points you think the speaker is trying to convey. This is not a word-for-word repetition of what the speaker has said, nor do you need to summarize the content of *each* phrase or minor detail. Rather, it is a **paraphrase** to check the accuracy of your understanding. Here is an example:

Steven: This week I have so much extra work to do. I'm sorry if I haven't been able to help keep this place clean. I know it's my turn to do the dishes tonight, but I have to get back to work. Could you do the dishes tonight?

Brigid: So you want me to do the dishes tonight and for the rest of the week. Right?

Steven: Well, I'd like you to help with the dishes tonight. But I think I can handle it for the rest of the week.

Brigid: OK. So I'll do them tonight and you take over tomorrow.

Steven: Yes.

Research conducted in clinical counselling settings found that when a listener paraphrases the content and feelings of a speaker, the speaker is more likely to trust and value the listener.[14] Remember the conversation at the beginning of this chapter? Roseanne cultivates trust by paraphrasing, whereas Terry focuses on her own issues and dispenses unsolicited advice. Paraphrasing to check understanding is also a vital skill to use when you are trying to reconcile a difference of opinion. Chapter 10 will show you how to use it in that context.

Reflect Feelings by Paraphrasing

The bottom line in empathic responding is to make certain that you accurately understand how the other person is feeling. Again, you can paraphrase, beginning with such phrases as:

"So you are feeling . . ."

"You must feel . . ."

"So now you feel . . ."

"Emotionally, you must be feeling . . ."

In the following example of empathic responding, the listener asks questions, summarizes content, and summarizes feelings.

David: I think I'm in over my head. My boss gave me a job to do and I just don't know how to do it. I'm afraid I've bitten off more than I can chew.

Mike: (Thinks how he would feel if he were given an important task at work but did not know how to complete the task, then asks for more information.) What job did she ask you to do?

David: I'm supposed to do an inventory of all of the items in the warehouse on the VAX computer system and have it finished by the end of the week. I don't have the foggiest notion of how to start. I've never even used that system.

Mike: (Summarizing feelings.) So you feel panicked because you may not have enough time to learn the system and do the inventory.

David: Well, I'm not only panicked, I'm afraid I may be fired.

Mike: (Summarizing feelings.) So your fear that you might lose your job is getting in the way of just focusing on the task and seeing what you can get done. It's making you feel like you made a mistake in taking this job.

David: That's exactly how I feel.

Note that toward the end of the dialogue Mike has to make a couple of tries to summarize David's feelings accurately. Also note that Mike does a good job of just listening and responding without giving advice. Just by being an active listener, you can help your partner clarify a problem.

We have discussed responding and the active listening process from a tidy step-by-step textbook approach. In practice, you may have to back up and clarify content, ask more questions, and rethink how you would feel before you attempt to summarize how someone else feels. Conversely, you may be able to summarize feelings *without* asking questions or summarizing content if the message is clear and it relates to a situation with which you are very familiar. Overusing this skill can slow down a conversation and make the other person uncomfortable or irritated. But if you use it judiciously, paraphrasing can help both you and your partner keep focused on the issues and ideas at hand.

Reflecting content or feeling through paraphrasing can be especially useful in the following situations:

■ Before you take an important action.

■ Before you argue or criticize.

■ When your partner has strong feelings or wants to talk over a problem.

■ When your partner is speaking "in code" or using unclear abbreviations.

■ When your partner wants to understand *your* feelings and thoughts.

■ When you are talking to yourself.

■ When you encounter new ideas.[15]

If you do decide to use reflecting skills, researchers suggest you keep the following guidelines in mind:

■ Use your own words.

■ Don't go beyond the information communicated by the speaker.

■ Be concise.

■ Be specific.

■ Be accurate.

Do *not* use reflecting skills if you aren't able to be open and accepting; if you do not trust the other person to find his or her own solution; if you are using these skills as a way of hiding yourself from another; or if you feel pressured, hassled, or tired.[16] And as we have already discussed, overuse of paraphrasing can be distracting and unnatural.

Don't be discouraged if your initial attempts to use these skills seem awkward and uncomfortable. Any new skill takes time to learn and use well. The instructions and samples you have seen here should serve as a guide, rather than as hard-and-fast prescriptions to follow during each conversation.

Listening and Reflecting Content and Emotion

Working in groups of three, ask person A to briefly identify a problem or conflict that he or she is having (or has had) with another person (co-worker, supervisor, spouse, or family member). Person B should use questioning, content paraphrasing, and emotion paraphrasing skills to explore the problem. Person C should observe the discussion and evaluate person B's listening and reflecting skills, using the Observer Checklist. Make a check mark next to all of the skills that person B uses effectively.

Observer Checklist

Nonverbal Skills

Direct Eye Contact	_____
Open, Relaxed Body Posture	_____
Uncrossed Arms	_____
Uncrossed Legs	_____
Appropriate Hand Gestures	_____
Reinforcing Nods	_____
Responsive Facial Expression	_____
Appropriate Tone of Voice	_____
Appropriate Volume	_____

Verbal Skills

Effective and Appropriate Questions	_____
Accurate Paraphrase of Content	_____
Accurate Paraphrase of Emotion	_____
Timely Paraphrase	_____
Appropriate Lead-In ("So," or "You seem to be saying")	_____
Didn't interrupt the speaker	_____

RECAP   How to Respond with Empathy

Responding with Empathy	Action
Understand Your Partner's Feelings	Ask yourself how you would feel if you had experienced a similar situation or recall how you *did* feel under similar circumstances. Or recall how your *partner* felt under similar circumstances.
Ask Questions	Seek additional information to better understand your partner's message.
Reflect Content by Paraphrasing	Summarize the essence of the information for your partner as you understand it.
Reflect Feelings by Paraphrasing	When appropriate, try to summarize what you think your partner may be feeling.

Listen

When I ask you to listen to me and you start giving advice,
you have not done what I asked.
When I ask you to listen to me and you begin to tell me why I shouldn't feel that way
you are trampling on my feelings.
When I ask you to listen to me and you feel you have to do something

to solve my problems, you have failed me, strange as that may seem.

Listen! All I asked, was that you listen. Not talk or do—just hear me.

Advice is cheap: 50 cents will get you both Dear Abby and Billy Graham

in the same newspaper.

And I can do for myself; I'm not helpless. Maybe discouraged and faltering,

but not helpless.

When you do something for me that I can and need to do for myself, you contribute

to my fear and weakness.

But when you accept as a simple fact that I do feel what I feel,

no matter how irrational, then I quit trying to convince you

and can get about the business of understanding what's behind this irrational feeling.

And when that's clear, the answers are obvious and I don't need advice.

Irrational feelings make sense when we understand what's behind them.

Perhaps that's why prayer works, sometimes, for some people

because God is mute, and doesn't give advice or try to fix things,

God just listens and lets you work it out for yourself.

So, please listen and just hear me, and, if you want to talk,

wait a minute for your turn: and I'll listen to you.

—ANONYMOUS

Improving Your Responding Skills

E ven if providing support is not your main goal, responding skills are crucial to the success of most interactions. Here are some additional suggestions for becoming an active listener.

Provide Well-Timed Responses

Feedback is usually most effective when you offer it at the earliest opportunity, particularly if your objective is to teach someone a skill. For example, if you are teaching your friend how to make your famous egg rolls, you provide a step-by-step commentary as you watch your pupil. If he makes a mistake, you don't wait until the egg rolls are finished to tell him that he left out the cabbage. He needs immediate feedback to finish the rest of the sequence successfully.

Sometimes, however, if a person is already sensitive and upset about something, delaying feedback can be wise. Use your critical thinking

When you are teaching someone a new skill, the timing of your feedback is just as important as what you say. When should this grown-up tell the child he is helping how to improve his handstand? (Robert Harbison)

skills to analyze when feedback will do the most good. Rather than automatically offering immediate correction, use the just-in-time (JIT) approach, and provide feedback just before the person might make another mistake. If, for example, your daughter typically rushes through math tests and fails to check her work, remind her right before her next test to double-check her answers, not immediately after the one she just failed. To provide feedback about a relationship, select a mutually agreeable place and time when both of you are rested and relaxed; avoid hurling feedback at someone "for his own good" immediately after he offends you.

Provide Usable Information

Perhaps you've heard this advice: Never try to teach a pig to sing. It wastes your time. It doesn't sound pretty. And it annoys the pig. When you provide information to someone, be certain that it is useful and relevant. How can you make sure your partner can use the information you share? Be other-oriented; put yourself in your partner's mind-set. Ask yourself, "If I were this person, how would I respond to this information? Is it information I can act on? Or is it information that may make matters worse?" Under the guise of effective feedback, we may be tempted to tell others our complete range of feelings and emotions. But research suggests that selective feedback is best. In one study, married couples who practiced selective self-disclosure were more satisfied than couples who told everything they knew or were feeling.[17] Immersing your partner in information that is irrelevant or that may be damaging to the relationship may be cathartic, but it may not enhance the quality of your relationship or improve understanding.

Avoid Unnecessary Details

When you are selecting meaningful information, also try to cut down on the volume of information. Don't overwhelm your listener with details that obscure the key point of your feedback. Hit only the high points that will benefit the listener. Be brief.

Be Descriptive Rather Than Evaluative

"You're an awful driver!" shouts Doris to her husband Frank. While Doris may feel she has provided simple feedback to her spouse about his skills, Frank will probably not respond warmly or even listen closely to her feedback. If Doris tries to be more descriptive and less evaluative, then he might be inclined to listen: "Frank, you are travelling seventy miles an hour in a fifty miles an hour zone" or "Frank, I get very nervous when you zigzag so fast through the freeway traffic" are less offensive comments. They describe Frank's behaviour rather than render judgments about him that are likely to trigger a defensive, passive listening reaction.

RECAP	**Suggestions for Improving Responding Skills**
Provide Well-Timed Responses	Sometimes immediate feedback is best; at other times provide a just-in-time (JIT) response when it will do the most good.
Provide Meaningful Information	Select information that your partner can act on rather than making vague comments or suggestions that are beyond his or her capabilities.
Avoid Unnecessary Details	Avoid information overload; don't bombard the listener with too much information; keep your comments focused on major points.
Be Descriptive	Don't evaluate your listening partner; focus on behaviour rather than personality.

Summary

Listening effectively to others is the quintessential skill required for establishing other-oriented relationships. Listening, the process of making sense out of what we hear, includes selecting, attending, understanding, remembering, and responding to others. Most of us listen for a variety of reasons: to enjoy, to learn, to evaluate, and to empathize with and support others.

Most of us don't listen effectively because we are self-oriented instead of other-oriented. Barriers to effective listening include focusing on our personal agendas, being distracted by emotional noise, criticizing the speaker, daydreaming, and being distracted by information overload and external noise.

To become more other-oriented, we can pursue three seemingly simple steps: stop, look, and listen. To stop means to avoid tuning in to our own distracting messages and to become mindful of what others are saying. To look is to observe and interpret unspoken messages. Nonverbal communication skills and principles will be discussed in greater detail in the next chapter. After stopping and looking, we can then listen more effectively to others by focusing on details and the speaker's key ideas. Being other-oriented does not mean you should abandon your own convictions or values, but that you should make a conscious effort to pay attention to the needs and concerns of others.

We can check the accuracy of our listening skill by reflecting our understanding of what our partner has said. Responding skills are especially important if our goal is to empathize with and support others. These skills include understanding the feelings of others, asking questions, and reflecting the message's content and the speaker's feelings through paraphrasing. Responding effectively does not mean consistently parroting or repeating what the speaker has said. Instead, judicious use of responding skills can enhance our understanding of the message, and tell the speaker whether he or she is communicating the intended message. The most effective responses to others are carefully timed, provide usable information, avoid unnecessary details, and are descriptive rather than evaluative.

For Discussion and Review

■ **FOCUS ON COMPREHENSION**

1. What are some differences between hearing and listening?

2. What strategies can we follow to respond with empathy?

3. What are key listening barriers that keep people from listening well?

4. What are suggestions for effectively reflecting the content of interpersonal messages?

■ **FOCUS ON CRITICAL THINKING**

5. Identify two situations during the past twenty-four hours in which you were an effective or ineffective listener. What factors contributed to your listening skill (or lack of skill)?

6. Miranda and Salvador often disagree about who should handle some of the child-rearing tasks in their home. When they have discussions on these issues, what are some effective listening skills and strategies that they could use to make sure they understand one another?

7. Jason and Chris are roommates. They both work hard each day and come home exhausted. What suggestions would you offer to help them listen effectively even when they are tired?

■ **FOCUS ON ETHICS**

8. Is it possible for paraphrasing and active listening to become a way to manipulate others? Support your answer.

9. Your friend asks you how you like her new dress. You really feel it is a bit too revealing and may embarrass your friend. But it is time to leave for your evening activity. Should you respond honestly even though it may mean that you and your friend will be late for important engagements?

10. Your roommate wants to tell you about his day. You are tired and really don't want to hear all of the details. Should you fake attention so that you won't hurt his feelings or should you simply tell your roommate that you are tired and would rather not hear about the details of his life?

For Your Journal

1. Keep this checklist, first published in the *International Listening Association Newsletter,* with you one full day to monitor your listening problems.

Today I . . .

Interrupted other people _____ times.

Misunderstood other people _____ times.

Lost track of a conversation _____ times.

Stopped making eye contact with a speaker _____ times.

Asked someone to repeat himself/herself _____ times.

Let my mind wander while listening to someone _____ times.

Changed the subject in the middle of a conversation _____ times.

Jumped to a conclusion about what someone was going to say _____ times.

Reacted emotionally to what someone was saying before they finished _____ times.

After keeping track of your personal listening statistics, what changes would you like to make in your listening behaviour?

2. Monitor and then jot down notes about your own self-talk during a conversation with another person. What competing thoughts and ideas occurred to you while you were conversing with your partner? What did you do to refocus on the message?

Learning with Others

1. Place a check mark beside all of the communication barriers that affect you. Identify the action you will take to manage the barrier. Discuss your results with your classmates.

HOW WILL YOU OVERCOME LISTENING BARRIERS?

Barrier	Action
Focusing on a Personal Agenda	_____
	_____
Emotional Noise	_____
	_____
Criticizing the Speaker	_____
	_____
Speech Rate vs. Thought Rate	_____
	_____

Information Overload   _____

                                        _____

Outside Distractions   _____

                                        _____

2. Charting Your Listening Cycle

Are you a morning person or an evening person? Use the chart shown here to plot your listening energy cycle. Draw a line starting at 6:00 A.M. showing the highs and lows of your potential listening effectiveness. For example, if you are usually still asleep at 6:00 A.M., your line will be at 0 and start upward when you awake. If you are a morning person, your line will peak in the morning. Or perhaps your line will indicate that you listen best in the evening.

After you have charted your typical daily listening cycle, gather in small groups with your classmates to compare listening cycles. Identify listening strategies that can help you capitalize on your listening "up" periods. Also, based upon the chapter and your own experiences, identify ways to enhance your listening when you traditionally have low listening energy.

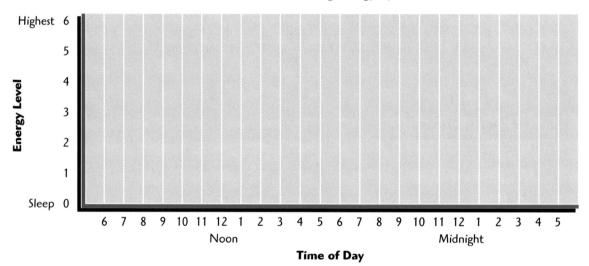

Your Listening Energy Cycle

LISTENING: The process of selecting, attending, understanding, remembering, and responding to sounds and messages.

HEARING: The physiological process of decoding sounds.

SELECTING: The process of sorting through various sounds competing for your attention.

ATTENDING: The process of focusing on a particular sound or message.

UNDERSTANDING: Assigning meaning to messages.

REMEMBERING: Recalling information that has been communicated.

RESPONDING: Confirming your understanding of a message.

EMPATHIZE: To feel what others are feeling, rather than just to acknowledge that they are feeling a certain way.

SYMPATHIZE: To acknowledge that someone may be feeling bad.

EMOTIONAL NOISE: A form of communication caused by emotional arousal.

ACTIVE LISTENING: The interactive process of responding mentally, verbally, and nonverbally to a speaker's message.

PARAPHRASING: Checking the accuracy of your understanding by offering a verbal summary of your partner's message.

Communicating Nonverbally

A fter studying this chapter, you should be able to:

1. Explain why nonverbal communication is an important and challenging area of study.

2. Describe the functions of nonverbal communication in interpersonal relationships.

3. Summarize research findings that describe codes of nonverbal communication behavior.

4. Describe three bases for interpreting nonverbal behaviour.

5. Formulate a strategy for improving your ability to interpret nonverbal messages accurately.

Eddie: Lisa, will you get the telephone?

Lisa: Get it yourself!

*Eddie: Hey! Why so testy? All I asked you
to do was answer the phone!*

f we could view a videotape of Eddie and Lisa's interaction, we could more clearly see the source of the conflict. Eddie's tone of voice and his scowling facial expression made his simple request seem more like an order.

As we noted in Chapter 1, communication has both content and emotional dimensions. Our tone of voice, eye contact, facial expressions, posture, movement, vocal cues, appearance, use of personal space, manipulation of the communication environment, and other nonverbal clues reveal how we feel toward others. We can define **nonverbal communication** as behaviour other than written or spoken language that creates meaning for someone. In this chapter we will focus on how nonverbal communication affects the quality of our interpersonal relationships. As we identify the functions and codes of nonverbal cues, we will also explore ways to improve our skill in interpreting the nonverbal messages of others.

Why Learn about Nonverbal Communication?

When you are sitting in a public place such as a shopping mall, airport, or bus stop, do you make assumptions about what other people might be like as you observe their nonverbal behaviour? Most of us are people watchers, and we rely on nonverbal communication clues to predict how others may feel about and react to us. Nonverbal communication plays a major role in relationship development because it is also the main channel we use to communicate our feelings and attitudes toward others. But because much of our nonverbal communication behaviour is unconscious, most of us have limited awareness or understanding of it. We can begin examining nonverbal communication by looking at the ways we use it.

Nonverbal Messages Communicate Our Feelings and Attitudes

Daryl knew that he was in trouble the moment he walked into the room. His wife Sandra gave him a steely stare. Her brow was furrowed and her arms were crossed. On the table was a dish of cold lobster Newburg, extinguished candles burnt to nubs, and dirty dishes in all but one spot: his. Daryl was in the doghouse for forgetting the special meal his wife had prepared, and he needed no words to sense the depth of her displeasure.

Albert Mehrabian concluded that as little as 7 percent of the emotional meaning of a message is communicated through explicit verbal channels.[1] The most significant source of emotional communication is our face—according to Mehrabian's study, it channels as much as 55 percent of our meaning. Vocal cues such as volume, pitch, and intensity, communicate another 38 percent of our emotional meaning. In all, we communicate approximately 93 percent of the emotional meaning of our messages nonverbally. Although these percentages do not apply to every communication situation, the results of Mehrabian's investigation do illustrate the potential power of nonverbal cues in communicating emotion.

When we interact with others, we base our feelings and emotional responses not upon what our partner says, but rather upon what he or she does. We also alter our nonverbal communication to suit different relationships. With good friends you let down your guard; you may slouch, scratch, and take off your shoes to show you trust them. But if you were interviewing for a job or meeting your fiancé's parents for the first time, your posture would probably be stiffer and your smiles more carefully controlled as you tried to convey the impression that you are mature, competent, and respectable.

Nonverbal Messages Are More Believable

"Honey, do you love me?" asks Brenda.

"OF COURSE I LOVE YOU! HAVEN'T I ALWAYS TOLD YOU THAT I LOVE YOU? I LOVE YOU!" shouts Jim, keeping his eyes glued to his morning newspaper.

Brenda will probably feel less than reassured by Jim's pledge of affection. The contradiction between his spoken message of love and his nonverbal message of irritation and disinterest will leave her wondering about his true feelings.

Actions speak louder than words. This cliché became a cliché because nonverbal communication is more believable than verbal communication. Nonverbal messages are more difficult to fake. One research team concluded that we use the following cues, listed in order of most to least important, to help us discern when a person is lying.[2]

Greater time lag in response to a question

Reduced eye contact

Increased shifts in posture

Unfilled pauses

Less smiling

Slower speech

Higher pitch in voice

More deliberate pronunciation and articulation of words

It is difficult to manipulate an array of nonverbal cues, so a skilled other-oriented observer can see when our true feelings leak out. One research team has identified the face, hands, and feet as key sources of nonverbal leakage cues.[3] Are you aware of what your fingers and toes are doing as you are reading this book? Even if we become experts at masking and manipulating our faces, we may first signal disinterest or boredom with another person by finger wiggling or toe wagging. Or we may twiddle a pen or pencil. When we become emotionally aroused, the pupils of our eyes dilate, and we may blush, sweat, or change our breathing patterns.[4] Lie

LEARNING INTERPERSONAL COMMUNICATION SKILLS

detectors rely on these unconscious clues. A polygraph measures a person's heart and breathing rate, as well as the electrical resistance of the skin (called galvanic skin response), to determine whether he or she is giving truthful verbal responses.

Nonverbal Communication Plays a Major Role in Interpersonal Relationships

As we learned in Chapter 1, you cannot not communicate; one researcher suggests that as much as 65 percent of the social meaning in our messages is based upon nonverbal communication.[5] Of course, the meaning that others interpret from your behaviour may not be the one you intended, and the inferences they draw based upon nonverbal information may be right or wrong.

We learned in Chapter 3 that we begin making judgments about strangers just a fraction of a second after meeting them, based upon nonverbal information. Within the first four minutes of interaction we scope the other out and draw conclusions about him or her.[6] Another research team found that you may decide whether a date is going to be pleasant or dull during the first thirty seconds of meeting your partner; before your partner has had time to utter more than "Hello."[7] Nonverbal cues are the ones that form first impressions, accurate or not.

Noverbal cues are important not only when we initiate relationships, but also as we maintain and develop mature relationships with others. In fact, the more intimate the relationship, the more we use and understand the nonverbal cues of our partners. Long-married couples spend less time verbalizing their feelings and emotions to each other than they did when they were first dating; each learns how to interpret the other's subtle nonverbal cues. If your spouse is silent during dinner, you may know that the day was a tough one, and you should give her a wide berth. And if, when you put on your new kelly green pants, your husband grimaces as he asks, "New pants?" you may understand that he does not love them. In fact, all of us are more likely to use nonverbal cues to convey negative messages than to explicitly announce our dislike of something or someone. We also use nonverbal cues to signal changes in the level of satisfaction with a relationship. When we want to cool things off, we may start using a less vibrant tone of voice and cut back on eye contact and physical contact with our partner.

Although we do rely heavily on nonverbal messages, they do not operate independently of spoken messages in our relationships. Instead, verbal and nonverbal cues work together in two primary ways to help us make sense of others' messages.

First, nonverbal cues substitute for, repeat, contradict, or regulate verbal messages. An extended thumb signals that a hitchhiker would like a ride. A circle formed by the thumb and index finger can either signal that everything is A-OK or convey an obscene message. When someone asks, "Which way did he go?" we can silently point to the back door. In these instances, we are substituting nonverbal cues for a verbal message.

Portrait artists play close attention to nonverbal cues such as posture, facial expression, and gesture to capture their subjects' personalities. What do the nonverbal cues reveal about this Spanish dancer? (John Singer Sargeant, *Belle Epoque.* Erich Lessing/Art Resource)

We can also use nonverbal cues to repeat or reinforce our words. "Where is the personnel department?" asks a job applicant. "Three flights up. Take the elevator," says the security guard, pointing to the elevator. The guard's pointing gesture repeats her verbal instruction and clarifies the message.

"Sure, this is a good time to talk about the Henrikson merger," says the business executive, nervously looking at her watch, stuffing papers into her attaché case, and avoiding eye contact with her co-worker. In this instance, the nonverbal cues contradict the verbal ones. And as we learned earlier, the nonverbal message is almost always the one we believe.

We also use nonverbal cues to regulate our participation in verbal exchanges. In most informal meetings it is not appropriate or necessary to signal your desire to speak by raising your hand. Yet somehow you are able to signal to others when you'd like to speak and when you'd rather not talk. How does this happen? You use eye contact, raised eyebrows, an open mouth, or perhaps a single raised index finger to signal that you would like to make a point. If your colleagues do not see these signals, especially the eye contact, they know you are not interested in talking.[8]

The second way in which nonverbal cues work together with verbal ones is in accenting and complementing emotional messages. "Unless we vote to increase our tax base," bellows Mr. Coddlington, "we will not have enough classroom space to educate our children." While delivering his impassioned plea to the school board, Mr. Coddlington also loudly slaps the lectern to accent his message, and reinforce its intensity. A scolding mother's wagging finger and an angry supervisor's raised voice are other nonverbal cues that accent verbal messages.

Complementary nonverbal messages that we deliver simultaneously with a verbal message can also help to colour the emotion we are expressing or the attitude we are conveying. The length of a hug while you tell your son you are proud of him provides complementary information about the intensity of your pride. The firmness of your handshake when you greet a job interviewer can complement your verbal claim that you are eager for employment.

RECAP   **Reasons to Study Nonverbal Communication**

1. Nonverbal communication is the primary way in which we communicate feelings and attitudes toward others.

2. Nonverbal messages are usually more believable than verbal messages.

3. Nonverbal communication plays a major role in relationship development.

   - Nonverbal cues substitute for, repeat, contradict, or regulate verbal messages.

   - Nonverbal cues accent and complement emotional messages.

The Challenge of Studying Nonverbal Communication

Even though we have made great claims for the value of studying nonverbal behaviours, it is not always easy to decipher unspoken messages. We have dictionaries to help us interpret words, but we have no handy reference book to help us decode nonverbal cues. To help you with the decoding process, we are going to attempt to classify some common types of nonverbal behaviours. But first, you should be aware of some of the difficulties inherent in attempting a classification.

Nonverbal Messages Are Often Ambiguous

Most words carry a meaning that everyone who speaks the same language can recognize. But the meaning of nonverbal messages may be known only to the person displaying them. Perhaps even more importantly, that person may not intend for the behaviour to have any meaning at all. And some people have difficulty expressing their emotions nonverbally. They may have a frozen facial expression or a monotone voice. Or they may be teasing you, but their deadpan expressions lead you to believe that their negative comments are heartfelt. Often it is tough to draw meaningful conclusions about another person's behaviour, even if we know him or her quite well.

Nonverbal Messages Are Continuous

Words are discrete entities; they have a beginning and an end. You can point to the first word in this sentence and underline the last one. Our nonverbal behaviours are not as easily dissected. Like the sweep of a second hand on a watch, nonverbal behaviours are continuous. Some, such as a slap or a hand clap, have definite beginnings and endings. But more often than not, your nonverbal behaviour unfolds without clearly defined starting and stopping points. Gestures, facial expressions, and even eye contact can flow from one situation to the next with seamless ease. Researchers have difficulty studying nonverbal cues because of this continuous stream, so trying to categorize and interpret them will be challenging for us as well.

Nonverbal Cues Are Multichannelled

Have you ever tried to watch two or more TV programs at once? Some televisions let you see as many as eight programs simultaneously so that you can keep up with three ball games and two soap operas and view commercials on the three other channels. Like the multichannel TV, nonverbal cues come to our perception centre from a variety of sources simultaneously. And just as you can really watch only one channel at a time on your multichannel television—although you can move among them very rapidly—so too can you actually attend to only one nonverbal cue at a time. One researcher suspects that negative nonverbal messages (frowns, grimaces,

Research investigating nonverbal communication in a variety of cultures confirms that individuals interpret nonverbal messages from their unique cultural perspective. Note the following conclusions:[9]

FACIAL EXPRESSIONS One research team found that facial expressions conveying happiness, sadness, anger, disgust, and surprise were the same in 68 to 92 percent of the cultures examined. All humans probably share the same neurophysiological basis for expressing emotions, but we learn different rules for sending and interpreting the expressions. For example, the Japanese culture does not reinforce the show of negative emotions; it is important for Japanese to "save face" and to help others save face as well.

EYE CONTACT There seems to be more eye contact in interpersonal interactions between Arabs, South Americans, and Greeks than between people from other cultures. There is evidence that some African Americans look at others less than do whites when sending and receiving messages. One of the most universal expressions among cultures appears to be the eyebrow flash (the sudden raising of the eyebrows when meeting someone or interacting with others).

GESTURES Hand and body gestures with the most shared meaning among Africans, North Americans, and South Americans include pointing, shrugging, head nodding, clapping, thumbs down, waving hello, and beckoning. There are, however, regional variations within cultures; it is not wise to assume that all people in a given culture share the same meaning for certain gestures. The OK gesture made by forming a circle with the thumb and finger has sexual connotations for some South American and Caribbean countries. In France the OK sign means worthless.

SPACE Arabs, Latin Americans, and Southern Europeans seem to stand closer to others than people from Asia, India, Pakistan, and Northern Europe. If you have been to Britain you know that people queue or wait for buses in orderly straight lines. In France, however, queuing is less orderly and individuals are more likely to push forward to be the next customer or get the next seat on the bus. As with gestures, however, there are regional variations in spatial preferences.

lack of eye contact) command attention before positive messages when the two compete.[10] Moreover, if the nonverbal message contradicts the verbal message, then we may have trouble interpreting either one correctly.[11]

Nonverbal Interpretation Is Culture Based

There is some evidence that humans from every culture smile when they are happy and frown when they are unhappy.[12] We also all raise or flash our eyebrows when meeting or greeting others, and young children in many cultures wave to signal they want their mothers, raise their arms to be picked up, and suck their thumbs for comfort.[13] All this suggests that there is some underlying basis for expressing emotion. Yet each culture may develop unique rules for displaying and interpreting these gestures and expressions.

There is no common cross-cultural dictionary of nonverbal meaning. However, there are well-established norms for nonverbal behaviour for each culture, and conscientious travellers will make an effort to learn these norms for the culture they are visiting. How accurate is the advice given in the "Communication Experience" box on p. 135, for visitors to Canada? Given Canada's rapidly changing immigrant population (discussed in Chapter 11), how long can these norms be expected to remain valid?

Taming Your Feelings: Digesting Gut Reactions

You've experienced it at least once in your life: You've met someone and, without knowing a thing about the person, taken an immediate dislike to him or her.

Or you've felt an instant rapport with someone right after exchanging "hellos."

These are gut reactions, and they tell us more about ourselves than about the people who inspire them.

If you've had a negative gut reaction to someone you'll be in regular contact with, here are some tips to help you accept him or her.

- Figure out what you don't like about the person. Pushiness? Egotism? Wussiness? Putting a name on what you're reacting to will help you bring it to a conscious level.

- If you're having trouble naming the source of your irritation, try saying to yourself, "What I see in this person that I see in me and don't like is _____."

- Take a look at the times you exhibit this behaviour. How does it help you? You may come to understand that, however unpleasant certain behaviours are, we do them because they work for us at times. Let's face it, pushy people often get what they want. We are not recommending that you become obstinate, only that you seek to understand why others may push and shove to get their way.

From: Loraine O'Connell, *The Orlando Sentinel.*

What are the rules for nonverbal communication in Canada? In a recent "bible" of protocol for doing business in sixty different countries, readers are provided the following advice on nonverbal rules of behaviour with Canadians.

- In Canada, the standard greeting is a smile, often accompanied by a nod, wave, and/or verbal greeting.
- In business situations, a handshake is used upon greetings or introductions.
- Canadian business people expect a firm handshake (web-to-web contact), direct eye contact, and an open, friendly manner. A weak handshake may be taken as a sign of weakness.
- Older men usually wait for women to offer their hand before shaking.
- French Canadians also have a fairly firm handshake. And they shake hands more often: upon greetings, introductions, and departures, even if the person has been greeted earlier that day.
- Good friends and family members sometimes embrace, especially among the French. A kissing of both cheeks may also occur, especially among the French.
- Note that the French do not finish an embrace with a pat or two on the back, as many U.S. citizens do.
- The standard distance between you and your conversation partner should be two feet. British Canadians are uncomfortable standing any closer to another person. French Canadians may stand slightly closer.
- Canadians, especially those of British descent, do not tend toward frequent or expansive gesturing.
- In general, friends of the same sex do not hold hands. Only French Canadians commonly touch during conversation.
- The backslap is a sign of close friendship among British Canadians. It is rarely used among the French.
- Direct eye contact shows that you are sincere, although it should not be too intense. Some minorities look away to show respect.
- When sitting, Canadians often look very relaxed. Men may sit with the ankle of one leg on the knee of the other or prop their feet up on chairs or desks.
- In business situations, maintain good posture and a less casual pose.
- In most of Canada, to call the waiter or waitress over, briefly wave to get his or her attention. To call for the check, make a writing gesture. In Quebec, it is only necessary to nod the head backwards or to make a discreet wave of the hand.

From T. Morrison, W.A. Conaway, and G.A. Borden, *Kiss, Bow, or Shake Hands: How to Do Business in Sixty Different Countries* (Holbrook, Mass.: Bob Adams, Inc., 1994).

Nonverbal Communication Codes

Keeping all of these challenges to our understanding in mind, we can begin looking at the categories of nonverbal information that researchers have studied: movement and gestures, eye contact, facial expressions, use of space and territory, touch, and personal appearance.[14] Although we will concentrate on the codes that fall within these categories in mainstream Western culture, we will also try to look at codes for other cultures and subcultures.

Body Movement, Posture, and Gestures

In 1771, when English explorer Captain Cook arrived in the New Hebrides, he didn't speak the language of the natives. His only way of communicating was sign language. Through gestures, pointing, and hand waving, he established contact with the natives. There is evidence that people have used gestures to communicate since ancient times—especially to bridge cultural and language differences. The first record of using sign language to communicate is found in Xenophon's *The March Up Country,* in which unspoken gestures were used to help the Greeks cross Asia Minor in about 400 B.C. Even when we do speak the same language as others, we use gestures to help us make our point.[15]

Kinesics is the study of human movement and gesture. It was Francis Bacon who noted, "As the tongue speaketh to the ear, so the hand speaketh to the eye." We have long recognized that the movement and gestures we exhibit provide valuable information to others. Various scholars and researchers have proposed paradigms for analyzing and coding these movements and gestures as we do for spoken or written language.[16]

One paradigm identifies four stages of "quasi-courtship behaviour."[17] The first stage is *courtship readiness.* When we are attracted to someone, we may suck in our stomach, tense our muscles, and stand up straight. The second stage includes *preening behaviours*: we manipulate our appearance by combing our hair, applying makeup, straightening our tie, pulling up our socks, and double-checking our appearance in the mirror. In stage three we demonstrate *positional cues*, using our posture and body orientation to be seen and noticed by others. The classic Norman Rockwell painting below shows teenagers illustrating typical preening and positional cues.

One researcher recently found fifty-two gestures and nonverbal behaviours that women use to signal an interest in men. Among the top unspoken flirting

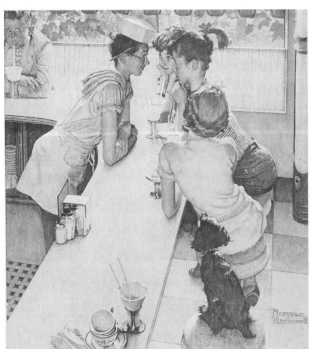

Can you identify the quasi-courtship behaviour in this painting?

Nonverbally play the roles of both a good listener and a bad listener. First, imagine that you are listening to someone talk. As a good listener, how would you communicate your interest in what the person is saying without uttering a word? Note your posture, eye contact, presence or lack of hand movement. Are your arms and legs crossed?

Now roleplay a poor listener—someone who appears to be bored or even irritated by what a speaker is saying. What are the differences in the cues you use? Use the space below or write your responses on a sheet of paper to describe the differences.

Nonverbal Behaviours of a Good Listener

Posture: _____

_____

Body Orientation: _____

_____

Eye Contact: _____

_____

Gestures: _____

_____

Movement: _____

_____

Nonverbal Behaviours of a Poor Listener

Posture: _____

_____

Body Orientation: _____

_____

Eye Contact: _____

_____

Gestures: _____

_____

Movement: _____

_____

cues were: smiling and surveying a crowded room with the eyes, and moving closer to the object of our affection.[18] We intensify these cues in the fourth stage, *appeals to invitation*, using close proximity, exposed skin, open body positions, and eye contact to signal our availability and interest. Subjects in one study reported that they were aware of using all these techniques to promote an intimate relationship. In fact we use these quasi-courtship behaviours to some extent in almost any situation in which we are trying to gain favourable attention from another.

Another team of researchers focused on nonverbal behaviours that make us label a person warm and friendly or cold and distant.[19] They found that "warm" people face their communication partners directly, smile more, make more direct eye contact, fidget less, and generally make fewer unnecessary hand movements. "Cold" people make less eye contact, smile less, fidget more, and turn away from their partners.

Posture and body orientation reveal important information. Open body posture (uncrossed arms and legs) communicates that we are receptive and responsive listeners. When we are trying to decrease our contact with someone, say at a party or family gathering, we are likely to turn away from the individual we want to avoid. As you will find when you participate in the following Communication Experience, your body orientation and posture provide important cues as to your interest and willingness to continue or end communication with someone.

Albert Mehrabian has identified the nonverbal cues that contribute to perceptions of liking.[20] He found that an open body and arm position, a forward lean, and a more relaxed posture communicate liking. When we are attempting to persuade someone, we typically have more eye contact and a more direct body orientation; we are more likely to lean forward and closer to others.

Another team of researchers tried to classify movement and gestures according to their function. They identified five categories: emblems, illustrators, affect displays, regulators, and adaptors.[21]

EMBLEMS

Nonverbal cues that have specific, generally understood meanings in a given culture and may actually substitute for a word or phrase are called **emblems**. When you are busy typing a report that is due tomorrow and your young son bounces in to ask for permission to buy a new computer game, you turn from your computer and hold up an open palm to indicate your desire for uninterrupted quiet. To communicate your enthusiastic enjoyment of a violin soloist at a concert, you applaud wildly. You want your children to stop talking in the library, so you put an index finger up to your pursed lips.

ILLUSTRATORS

We frequently accompany a verbal message with **illustrators** that either contradict, accent, or complement the message. Slamming a book closed while announcing, "I don't want to read this anymore" or pounding a lectern while proclaiming, "This point is important!" are two examples of nonverbal behaviours that accent the verbal message. Typically, we use nonverbal illustrators at the beginning of clauses or phrases.[22] TV newscasters, for example, turn a page to signal that they are moving to a new story or topic. Most of us use illustrators to help us communicate information about the size, shape, and spatial relationships of objects. You probably even use them when you talk on the phone, although probably not as many as you use in face-to-face conversation.[23]

AFFECT DISPLAYS

Nonverbal movements and postures used to communicate emotion are called **affect displays**. As early as 1872, when Charles Darwin systematically studied the expression of emotion in both humans and animals,[24] we have recognized that nonverbal cues are the primary ways we communicate emotion. Our facial expressions, vocal cues, posture, and gestures convey the intensity of our emotions.[25] If you are happy, for example, your face will telegraph your joy to others. But the movement of your hands, the openness of your posture, and the speed with which you move will tell others *how* happy you are. Similarly, if you are feeling depressed, your face will probably reveal your sadness or dejection, while your slumped shoulders and lowered head will indicate the intensity of your despair. When we are feeling friendly, we use a soft tone of voice, an open smile, and a relaxed posture.[26] When we feel neutral about an issue, we signal it by putting little expression on our face or in our voice. When we feel hostile, we use a harsh voice, frown with our teeth showing, and keep our posture tense and rigid.

REGULATORS

We use **regulators** to control the interaction or flow of communication between ourselves and another person. When we are eager to respond to a message, we make eye contact, raise our eyebrows, open our mouth, raise an index finger, and

While facial expressions of basic emotions are thought to be universal, most nonverbal communication codes are culture-specific. How fluent are you in the nonverbal communication codes of the four most popular points of origin for Canada's newest citizens?

In *Hong Kong*, for example, members of the same sex may hold hands to signify friendship, but members of the opposite sex may not. Patting people on the shoulder is not appreciated, and men should sit with both feet on the floor. "Come here" is signified by turning the palm face down and waving the fingers.

In *China*, any form of touching by strangers or by younger or less important people is offensive. The Chinese avoid exaggerated facial expressions, and they do not use their hands when speaking. Putting your hands in your mouth is considered disgusting.

In the *Philippines*, staring has various nuances, most of them negative. Looking down, even in a crowd, is useful to avoid giving offence. Filipinos rarely indicate objects or directions by pointing with their fingers; instead, they indicate with a glance or by pursing their lips.

In *India*, it is not uncommon to see two men holding hands while talking. The head is considered the seat of the soul, hence someone else's head should never be touched—not even to pat a child's hair. And a sideways nod of the head indicates "yes." Indians point with their chins, and never their fingers. The ears are considered sacred appendages, and the grasping of one's ears designates sincerity or repentance. Never point your feet at someone, as they are considered unclean; if your shoes or feet touch another person, apologize.

From T. Morrison, W.A. Conaway, and G.A. Borden, *Kiss, Bow, or Shake Hands: How to Do Business in Sixty Different Countries* (Holbrook, Mass.: Bob Adams, Inc., 1994).

lean forward slightly. When we do not want to be part of the conversation, we do the opposite: we avert our eyes, close our mouth, cross our arms, and lean back in our seats or away from the verbal action.

ADAPTORS

When we are cold, we reach for a sweater or wrap our arms around our chests to keep warm. When it's 102 degrees Fahrenheit in the shade without a breeze, we reach for a fan to make our own breeze. These behaviours are examples of **adaptors**—nonverbal behaviours that help us to satisfy a personal need and adapt to the immediate situation. When you adjust your glasses, scratch a mosquito bite, or comb your hair, you are using movement to help you manage your personal needs.

THE FIVE CATEGORIES AND INTERPERSONAL COMMUNICATION

How will understanding these five categories of nonverbal behaviour help you understand others and your own interpersonal communication? They give you a new and more precise way to think about your own behaviour. By noting how often you use emblems instead of words to communicate a message, you can recognize how important emblems are in your relationships with others. The more you rely upon emblems that have unique meanings for you and your partner, the more intimate the interpersonal relationship. Also start to notice whether your nonverbal behaviour contradicts what you say. Monitoring your use of illustrators can help you determine whether you are sending mixed signals to others. Be aware of how you display affect. Knowing that your face and voice communicate emotion, and that posture and gesture indicate the intensity of your feelings, can help you understand how others make inferences about your feelings and attitudes. If other people have difficulty interpreting your emotional state, you may not be projecting your feelings nonverbally. And finally, notice how you use adaptors. Individuals who do not learn the cultural norms of displaying adaptors can have a difficult time socially. For example, if you were never taught not to comb your hair or belch at the table, you may find you receive few dinner invitations.

Since nonverbal cues are ambiguous, it's not a good idea to use them to achieve a specific objective. But as you have seen, people are more likely to respond in predictable ways if you use behaviours they can recognize and interpret easily.

RECAP — Categories of Movement and Gestures

Category	Definition	Examples
Emblems	Behaviours that have specific, generally understood meaning.	A hitchhiker's raised thumb.
Illustrators	Cues that accompany verbal messages and provide meaning for the message.	A public speaker's pounding the podium to emphasize a point.
Affect Displays	Expressions of emotion.	Hugging someone to express love.
Regulators	Cues that control and manage the flow of communication between others.	Looking at someone when you wish to speak.
Adaptors	Behaviours that help you adapt to your environment.	Scratching, combing your hair.

Eye Contact

Subtle power. Whether you choose to look at someone or avert your gaze has an enormous impact on your relationship with that person. Researchers have identified four functions for eye contact in interpersonal interactions.[27]

First, it serves a *cognitive* function because it gives you information about another person's thought processes. For example, if your partner breaks eye contact after you ask him or her a question, you will know that he or she is probably thinking of something to say.

Second, we use eye contact to *monitor* the behaviour of others. We receive a major portion of the information we obtain through our eyes. We look at others to determine whether they are receptive to our messages. In fact, this search for feedback is implicit in the word for the centre part of the eye, pupil, which comes from the Latin word *pupilla* or "little doll." When you look into someone's eyes, you can see a miniature reflection of yourself.[28]

Third, eye contact is one of the most powerful *regulatory* cues we use to signal when we want to talk and when we don't want to communicate. Your authors have noticed that when they ask questions such as, "Who can tell me the four functions of eye contact?" students quickly yet unobtrusively avert their eyes to signal, "Don't call on me." When we do want to communicate with others, say when we're standing in line at the bakery, we fix our eyes on the clerk to signal, "My turn next. Please wait on me."

Finally, the area around our eyes serves an *expressive* function. The eyes have been called the "mirror of the soul" because they reveal our emotions to others. We may cry, blink, and widen or narrow our gaze to express our feelings.

What are the reasons we look or don't look at others? The following list from one researcher provides some insight.[29]

You are most likely to look at your partner when you:

- are physically distant from him or her
- are discussing easy, impersonal topics
- have nothing else to look at
- are interested in your partner's reactions—that is, you are interpersonally involved
- are interested in your partner—that is, like or love your partner
- are trying to dominate or influence your partner
- are from a culture that emphasizes visual contact in interaction
- are an extrovert
- have high affiliative or inclusion needs
- are dependent on your partner (and the partner has been unresponsive)
- are listening rather than talking
- are female

You are less likely to look at your partner when you:

- are physically close
- are discussing difficult, intimate topics
- have other relevant objects, people, or backgrounds to look at
- are not interested in your partner's reactions
- are talking rather than listening
- are not interested in your partner—that is, you dislike him or her
- are from a culture that imposes sanctions on visual contact during interaction
- are an introvert
- are low on affiliative or inclusion needs
- have had a mental disorder like autism, schizophrenia, or the like
- are embarrassed, ashamed, sorrowful, sad, submissive, or trying to hide something

When we do establish eye contact with others, it may seem that our gaze is constant. Yet research suggests that we actually spend the majority of our time looking at something other than the person's eyes. One research team found that we focus on something else, including our partner's mouth, 57 percent of the time.[30] Not surprisingly then, facial expressions are another rich source of information in our communication with others.

RECAP   **Functions of Eye Contact**

COGNITIVE FUNCTION   Provides cues about our thinking and thought processes.

MONITORING FUNCTION   Provides information about how others are responding to us; we monitor to seek feedback.

REGULATORY FUNCTION   Manages the flow of communication; we use eye contact to signal when we do and do not want to interact with another person.

EXPRESSIVE FUNCTION   Provides information about feelings, emotions, and attitudes.

Facial Expressions

You tell your parents that you will not be able to spend the holidays with them because you have decided to take your children skiing. You present your fiancée with a new abstract art painting that you would like to hang in your bedroom after you are married. As the personnel director reviews your résumé, you sit in silence across from her desk. In each of these situations you would be eagerly awaiting some reaction from your partner. And what you would be scanning is his or her face. The face is the exhibit gallery for our emotional displays. And although we often try to manipulate our facial cues to project a premeditated feeling, our faces may still betray our true emotions to others.[31]

To interpret our partner's facial expressions accurately, we need to put our other orientation skills to work, focusing on what the other person may be thinking or feeling. It helps if we know the person well, can see his or her whole face, have plenty of time to watch it, and understand the situation that prompted the emotion.[32] But it is also helpful to know the cues for "reading" facial expressions.

Your face is versatile. According to one research team, it is capable of producing over 250,000 different expressions.[33] Research suggests that women have greater variety in their emotional expressions and spend more time smiling than men.[34] But all of our expressions can be grouped under six primary emotional categories; the following list describes the changes that occur on our faces for each one.[35]

Surprise: Wide-open eyes; raised and wrinkled brow; open mouth.

Fear: Open mouth; tense skin under the eyes; wrinkles in the centre of the forehead.

Disgust: Raised or curled upper lip; wrinkled nose; raised cheeks; lowered brow; lowered upper eyelid.

Anger: Tensed lower eyelid; either pursed lips or open mouth; lowered and wrinkled brow; staring eyes.

Happiness: Smiling; mouth may be open or closed; raised cheeks; wrinkles around lower eyelids.

Sadness: Lip may tremble; corners of the lips turn downward; corners of the upper eyelid may be raised.

As the Electronic Connections box below shows, it is possible to provide expressions of emotions via your computer by cleverly using punctuation marks to represent facial expressions.

How accurately do we interpret emotions expressed on the face? Several studies have attempted to measure subjects' skill in identifying emotional expressions of others. They have found that reading facial expression is a tricky business. According to one research team, even though our faces provide a great deal of information about emotions, we have learned how to control our facial expressions.[36] In addition, our facial expressions also seem to be contagious.

ELECTRONIC CONNECTIONS

A kiss is just a : *, a sigh is just a : - (

Electronic-mail writers have adopted a lighthearted system of shorthand known as "emoticons." These clever combinations of keyboard characters punctuate a message with just the right spirit. To read them, simply look at the line with your head tilted slightly to the left.

For example, in the most basic emoticon, the smiley face, a colon, hyphen, and a right parenthesis become the eye, nose, and mouth of glee : -).

Here's a sample of some frequently used emoticons that will help you get across the nuances of your message:

: - |)	smiley with a mustache	| -)	hee hee
: D	big smile	| - D	ho ho
; -	wink	: /	not funny
: - @	scream	: - }	smirk
: X	keeping mouth shut	: - o	shocked (or singing the national anthem)
: - &	tongue-tied	: |	bored
: - J	tongue in cheek or joking	> : - <	angry
: P	sticking out tongue or giving a raspberry	< : -)	dumb question or dumb person
: *	kiss	(: - $	sick person or person is sick
: * * :	returning kiss	: - (	sad
( )	hug	: -	really sad
(((((())))))	lots of hugs	:' (	crying
: -)8	sharply dressed person	; - ?	licking your lips
: - >	hey hey		

From: Charles Bowen, *HomePC*, January 1995, p. 109.

COMMUNICATION EXPERIENCE

Facial Expression Quiz

Divide into teams of two people. Person A should select one of the six primary emotions communicated by the face and attempt to display the emotion to person B. The six primary emotions are happiness, sadness, surprise, disgust, anger, and fear. Communicate all six emotions *in random order*.

Person B should attempt to identify the emotions expressed by person A and list them in order below.

When person A has communicated all six emotions, he or she can reverse roles with person B.

1. _____
2. _____
3. _____
4. _____
5. _____
6. _____

Vocal Cues

Try this. Say "John" to communicate the following emotions: anger, sadness, disgust, happiness, fear, surprise. If you are reading this in a public place, stop reading for a moment and give it a try even if you have to whisper. What happened to your voice? Like your face, your voice is a major vehicle for communicating your emotions. The pitch, rate, and volume at which we speak, and our use of silence, all provide important clues to our feelings.

Your voice is a primary tool for communicating information about the nature of relationships between you and others.[37] We use our voices to present one message on the surface (with words) and usually a more accurate expression of our feelings with our vocal quality. Say the following sentence out loud: "This looks great." Now say it sarcastically; you really don't think it looks great: "This looks great." Clearly, your vocal cues provide the real meaning. Some vocal expressions of emotion are easier to identify than others. Expressions of joy and anger are obvious ones, whereas shame and love are the most difficult emotions to identify based on vocal cues alone.[38] We are also likely to confuse fear with nervousness, love with sadness, and pride with satisfaction. As an example of how the intonation of a single word can convey rich meaning, read the excerpt below from *A Lesson Before Dying*. In this story, a black schoolteacher is collecting money to buy a radio for a black man unfairly condemned to death by a white jury in Louisiana in the late 1940s.

> I ate the food hungrily because I had not had dinner, and I sopped up the gravy with the light bread. Thelma watched me all the time. When I was finished, she put a wrinkled ten-dollar bill on the counter by my plate.
> "Here."
> It was the kind of "here" your mother or your big sister or your great-aunt or your grandmother would have said. It was the kind of "here" that let you know this was hard-earned money but, also, that you needed it more than she did, and the kind of "here" that said she wished you had it and didn't have to borrow it from her, but since you did not have it, and she did, then "here" it was, with a kind of love. It was the kind of "here" that asked the question, "When will all this end? When will a man not have to struggle to have money to get what he needs 'here'? When will a man be able to live without having to kill another man 'here'?"
> I took the money without looking at her. I didn't say thanks. I knew she didn't want to hear it.
>
> —ERNEST J. GAINES,
> A Lesson Before Dying

Our voices also provide information about our self-confidence and our knowledge of the subject matter in our messages. Most of us would conclude that a speaker who mumbles, speaks slowly, consistently mispronounces words, and uses "uhs" and "ums" is less credible and persuasive than one who speaks clearly, rapidly, and fluently.[39] Even though mispronunciations and vocalized pauses ("ums" and "ahs") seem to have a negative effect on credibility, they do not seem to be a major impediment to attitude change. People may, for example, think that you are less knowledgeable if you stammer, but you may still be able to get your persuasive message across.

In addition to providing information about emotions, self-confidence, and knowledge, vocal cues also serve a regulatory function in interpersonal situations, signalling when we want to talk and when we don't. When we are finished talking, we may lower the pitch of our final word. When we want to talk, we may start by interjecting sounds such as "I . . . I . . . I . . ." or "Ah . . . Ah . . . Ah . . ." to interrupt the speaker and grab the verbal ball. We also may use more cues such as, "Sure," "I understand," "Uh-huh," or "OK" to signal that we understand the message of the other person and now we want to talk or end the conversation. These *back channel* cues are particularly useful in telephone conversations when we have no other nonverbal cues to help us signal that we would like to get off the phone.

Sometimes it is not what we say, or even how we say it, that communicates our feelings. Being silent may communicate volumes. One researcher, in commenting about the importance of silence in speech, said: "Silence is to speech as white paper is to this print. . . . The entire system of spoken language would fail without [people's] ability to both tolerate and create sign sequences of silence-sound-silence units."[40]

Why are we sometimes at a loss for words? There are many possible reasons. We may simply not know what to say. Or, there is evidence that when someone tells a lie, he or she may need a few moments to think of a credible ruse. We may be silent because we want to distance ourselves from those who are around us; we want to communicate that we really don't want to be involved in the conversation. Or perhaps we just need some time to think about what we want to contribute to the conversation. Silence, too, may be a sign of respect. Some children were raised with the message, Be seen and not heard. They were taught that those in authority should maintain control of the talking process. At other times you are silent with someone because words would diminish the experience you are sharing. Walking hand-in-hand on the beach, watching the sun set, or sitting on a balcony overlooking a spectacular mountain vista may call for silence; trying to translate the experience into words would diminish it.

Would you be comfortable just sitting silently with a good friend? Sidney Baker's theory of silence suggests that the more at ease we are when we share a silence with a close friend, the more comfortable we are with just being together and enjoying each other's companionship. People need to talk until there is nothing left to say; the uncertainty has been managed. In most long-term relationships, partners may not feel a need to fill the air with sound. Just being together to enjoy each other's company may be most fulfilling. Baker calls such moments "positive silence."[41]

Personal Space

Imagine that you are sitting alone in a booth at your local pizza parlour. As you sit munching your thin-and-crispy pepperoni pizza, you are startled when a

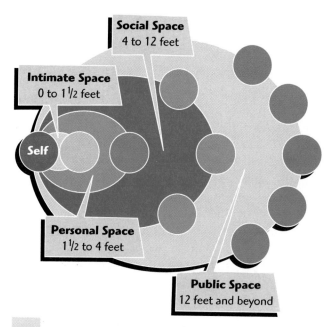

Social Space
4 to 12 feet

Intimate Space
0 to 1½ feet

Self

Personal Space
1½ to 4 feet

Public Space
12 feet and beyond

Figure 5.1

Edwin T. Hall's Four Zones of Space

complete stranger sits down in your booth directly across from you. With several empty tables and booths in the restaurant, you feel very uncomfortable that this unknown individual has invaded "your" area.

Normally, we do not think much about the rules we observe regarding personal space, but in fact every culture has fairly rigid ways of regulating space in social interactions. Violations of these rules can be alarming and, as in the preceding scenario, even threatening. How close we are willing to get to others relates to how well we know them and to considerations of power and status.

One of the pioneers in helping us understand the silent language of personal space was Edward T. Hall. His study of **proxemics** investigated how close or how far away we arrange ourselves around people and things.[42] Hall identified four spatial zones that we unconsciously define for ourselves, as shown in Figure 5.1. When we are between zero and and one and one-half feet from someone, we are occupying **intimate** space. This is the zone in which the most intimate interpersonal communication occurs. It is open only to those with whom we are well acquainted, unless we are forced to stand in an elevator, a fast-food line, or some other crowded space.

The second zone, which ranges from one and one-half to four feet, is called **personal space**. Most of our conversations with family and friends occur in this zone. If someone we don't know well invades this space on purpose, we may feel uncomfortable.

Zone three, called **social space**, ranges from four to twelve feet. Most group interaction, as well as many of our professional relationships, take place in this zone. The interaction tends to be more formal than that in the first two zones.

Public space, the fourth zone, begins at twelve feet. Interpersonal communication does not usually occur in this zone, and many public speakers and teachers position themselves even more than twelve feet from their audience.

The specific space that you and others choose depends upon several variables.[43] The more you like someone, the closer you will stand. We allow individuals with high status to surround themselves with more space than we allow for people with lower status. Large people also usually have more space around them than smaller ones, and women stand closer to others than men do.[44] All of us tend to stand closer to others in a large room than we do in a small room.

In a group, who's in charge, who's important, and who talks to whom are reflected by the spatial arrangement we self-select. The more dominant group members tend to select seats at the head of a table, while shyer individuals often select a corner seat at a rectangular table.[45]

Interaction: Spatial Communication

Here are diagrams of tables and chairs. Imagine that you are in the cafeteria and that this is the only unoccupied table. In the space marked X is the seated person described next to the diagram. Place an X in the circle where you would sit.

1. Your boss is at the table. You need to talk about why you were not able to finish the project he or she assigned you.

2. Your boss is at the table. You are planning a weekend camping trip together.

3. A person you once dated is at the table. You had a miserable time that night and you would never date him or her again.

4. Your co-worker is at the table. You are working on a project together, and you like him or her.

5. Your co-worker is at the table. You are competing with your co-worker for a promotion, and you do not like him or her.

6. The chief executive officer of your company is seated at the table. You've met her once, but don't know her well at all.

7. The janitor who cleans your office is seated at the table. You know him well enough to ask how his kids are doing.

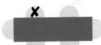

8. A member of your immediate family (e.g., spouse, son, daughter, or parent) is at the table.

9. A stranger is at the table. You do not know this person. You do not want to get to know this person.

10. A stranger is at the table. You do not know this person, but you would like to get better acquainted with him or her.

Adapted from: *The Interpersonal Comunication Book*, 7th edition by Joseph A. De Vito. Copyright © 1995 by Joseph A. De Vito. Reprinted by permission of HarperCollins Publishers, Inc.

	RECAP	Edward T. Hall's Classification of Spatial Zones	
		Definition	Examples
	ZONE ONE	Intimate space	Zero to one and one-half feet
	ZONE TWO	Personal space	One and one-half to four feet
	ZONE THREE	Social space	Four to twelve feet
	ZONE FOUR	Public space	Twelve feet and beyond

Territory

Territoriality is the study of how animals use space and objects to communicate occupancy or ownership of space. You assumed "ownership" of the booth in the pizza parlour and the accompanying "right" to determine who sat with you, because you and your pizza were occupying the booth. In addition to invading your personal space, the intrusive stranger broke the rules that govern territoriality.

We announce our ownership of space with territorial markers—things which signify that the area has been claimed—much as explorers once planted a flag claiming uncharted land for the king. When you are studying at the library, for example, and need to hop up and check a reference at the computerized card catalogue, you might leave behind a notebook or a pencil. In rural areas, landowners post signs at the borders of their property to keep hunters off their territory. Signs, locks, electronic security systems, and other devices secure our home and office territories.

We also use markers to indicate where our space stops and someone else's starts. "Good fences make good neighbors," wrote the poet Robert Frost. When someone sits too close, we may try to erect a physical barrier, such as a stack of books or a napkin holder, or we might use our body as a shield by turning away. If the intruder does not get the hint that "this land is our land," we ultimately resort to words to announce that the space is occupied.

Touch

Standing elbow to elbow in a crowded elevator, you may find yourself in physical contact with total strangers. As you stiffen your body and avert your eyes, a baffling sense of shame floods over you. If you are sitting at a conference table and you accidentally brush the toes of your shoes against your colleague's ankle, you may jerk away and even blush or apologize. Why do we react this way to unpremeditated touching? Normally, we touch to express intimacy. When intimacy is not our intended message, we instinctively react to modify the impression.

Countless studies have shown that intimate touching is vital to our personal development and well-being.[46] Infants and children need it to confirm that they are valued and loved. Many hospitals invite volunteers in to hold and rock newborns whose mothers cannot do it themselves. Advocates of breastfeeding argue that the intimate touching it entails strengthens the bond between mother and child.[47]

The amount of touch we need, tolerate, receive, and initiate depends upon many factors. The amount and kind of touching you receive in your family is one big influence. If your mom or dad greets you with hugs, caresses, and kisses, then you probably do this to others. If your family is less demonstrative, you may be restrained yourself. Studies show that most of us are more likely to touch people when we are feeling friendly, happy, or under other specific circumstances:[48]

- when we ask someone to do something for us

- when we share rather than ask for information

- when we try to persuade someone to do something

- when we are talking about intimate topics

- when we are in social settings that we choose rather than in professional settings that are part of our job

- when we are thrilled and excited to share good news

- when we listen to a troubled or worried friend

Appearance

In all of our interactions with others, appearance counts. Our culture places a high value upon how much we weigh, the style of our hair, and the clothes we wear; these things are particularly important in the early stages of relationship development. Attractive females have an easier time persuading others than do those who are perceived as less attractive. In general, we think attractive people are more credible, happier, more popular, more sociable and even more prosperous than less attractive people.[49]

It was in Chapter 2 that we discussed the link between our self-concept and personal appearance. The shape and size of your body also affects how others perceive you. Heavier and rounder individuals are often perceived to be older, more old-fashioned, less good-looking, more talkative, and more good-natured than thin people, who are perceived to be more ambitious, more suspicious of others, more uptight and tense, more negative, and less talkative. Muscular and athletically fit folks are seen as better looking, taller, and more adventurous. These perceptions are, in fact, so common that they have become easily recognizable stereotypes, on which casting directors for movies, TV shows, and plays rely in selecting actors and actresses. And, as the article below, "Exercise Has Its Limits," points out, it is a challenge to change our basic body type.

Appearances Count.
What role do you think appearance plays in the selection of television hosts?

Exercise Has Its Limits

Let's face it. Not everyone can look like Mr. World or Twiggy.

When it comes to body types, all men (and women) are not created equal. They come in different sizes and shapes unique to their genetics, gender, and lifestyle.

If you are exercising with the goal of reshaping your body, it's important to be realistic about the changes that are possible. An exercise program should fit your needs, desires, and body type.

Everyone is born with a particular body type. Here are characteristics of the three basic types:

Endomorph. Soft roundness predominates on the endomorph body. A higher-than-desired percentage of body fat is distributed at and below the waist. Thick legs, narrow shoulders, and a large chest also are common. Extreme example: Roseanne.

Mesomorph. A well-proportioned physique with heavy bones and solid muscular development is dominant in the mesomorph. Muscular chest and broad shoulders typify this stocky shape. Body fat is usually in the desirable range or lower. Extreme example: Arnold Schwarzenegger.

Ectomorph. The ectomorph is lean and fragile with a delicate bone structure. He or she is tall with long arms and legs and a thin musculature. Body fat is usually low. Extreme example: Kate Moss.

Many people can be classified as a combination of two of the standard body types. For instance, an individual who is naturally muscular and well-proportioned but has excess overall body fat would be a meso-endo. This body type is typical of heavy power lifters and sumo wrestlers.

Assessing and accepting your own body type will help you personalize your workouts. If you are tall and have a lean musculature, striving for a bodybuilder's physique is probably not realistic. Similarly, if you are short and stocky, a dancer or runner's lean build may be out of your reach.

A pear-shaped endomorph has a hard time losing body fat, especially in the hips and thighs. Fat in the hips and thighs is more stable in women because of hormones. Frequent low-impact aerobic activities will help control body fat, and strength training can help with reshaping the body. Patience is important because you may not see the muscle you are developing due to body fat you still need to shed.

Ectomorphs have an easy time reducing body fat but find it difficult to develop muscular definitions without heavy weight training. Strength training can help ectomorphs add muscle tone and curves.

Instead of trying to measure up to some artificial ideal, try to learn more about your own body. By accepting and developing your body's potential, you'll be on the road to being the best you can be.

—LEE ANN BROUSSARD

Reprinted by permission of Knight-Ridder Tribune News Service.

Aside from keeping us warm and within the legal bounds of decency, our clothes also affect how others perceive us. In institutional settings, an individual's rank is typically denoted by his or her uniform, as with the orders of dress for the Royal Canadian Mounted Police. On a less formal level, "social" rank is also inferred by the clothes we wear. For example, one study found that a man who jaywalked while dressed in nice clothes attracted more fellow violators than he could when he was shabbily attired.[50] Studies have attempted to identify a "power" look and magazines are constantly giving us prescriptions for ways to be attractive and stylish; however, outside of uniformed institutions, there really is no formula for dressing for success. Styles and expectations about appearances change. We have only to look at the clothing norms of the 1950s, 1960s, or 1970s to note how they are different from those of today.

Clothes Affect Perceptions.
How is the superior status of senior-ranking R.C.M.P. officers conveyed through their orders of full dress?

COMMUNICATION EXPERIENCE

Visit a public place where social interaction takes place, such as a restaurant, bar, or sports event. Make notes about the quasi-courtship behaviours you observe (see page 136). Compare your observations with those of your classmates.

RECAP Codes of Nonverbal Communication

MOVEMENTS AND GESTURES	Communicate information, status, warmth, credibility, interest in others, attitudes, liking.
EYE CONTACT	Serves cognitive, monitoring, regulatory, and expressive functions.
FACIAL EXPRESSIONS	Express emotions.
VOCAL CUES	Communicate emotion through pitch, rate, volume, and quality, and modify the meaning of messages.
PERSONAL SPACE	Provides information about status, power, and intimacy.
TERRITORY	Provides cues to our use, ownership, or occupancy of space.
TOUCH	Communicates intimacy, affection, or rejection.
APPEARANCE	Influences perceptions of credibility and attraction.

There is evidence that men and women display and interpret nonverbal cues differently.[51]

EYE CONTACT:

Women usually have a more prolonged gaze with others than do men. Women, however, are less likely to just stare at someone; they break eye contact more frequently than men. In general, women receive more eye contact from others than do men.

SPACE:

Men tend to have more space around them than do women. Women both approach and are approached more closely than men. And when conversing with others, women seem to prefer side-by-side interactions.

FACIAL EXPRESSION:

Research suggests that women smile more than men. It is also reported that women tend to be more emotionally expressive with their faces than men; this is perhaps related to the conclusion that women are more skilled at both sending and interpreting facial expressions.

GESTURE AND POSTURE:

Overall, women appear to use fewer and less expansive gestures than men. Women are more likely, for example, to rest their hands on the arms of a chair while seated; men are more likely to use gestures. Men and women cross their legs differently: women cross their legs at the knees or ankles while men are more likely to sit with their legs apart.

TOUCH:

Men are more likely to initiate touch with others than are women. Women are touched more than men. Men and women also attribute different meaning to touch; women are more likely to associate touch with warmth and expressiveness than are men.

VOCAL CUES:

Vocal patterns may be more related to biological differences in the vocal register than other nonverbal behaviours. Women speak in both higher and softer tones than do men. Women also use their voice to communicate a greater range of emotions than do men. Women are also more likely to raise their pitch when making statements; some people interpret the rising pattern (as in asking a question) as an indication of greater uncertainty.

Interpreting Nonverbal Communication

So what does it all mean? How do we make sense out of the postures, movements, gestures, eye contact, facial expressions, uses of space and territory, touch, and appearance of others? Albert Mehrabian has found that we synthesize and interpret nonverbal cues along three primary dimensions: *immediacy, arousal,* and *dominance.*[52]

Immediacy

Sometimes we are not able to put our finger on the precise reason we find a person likable or unlikable. Mehrabian believes that immediacy cues are a likely explanation. **Immediacy** cues are behaviours that communicate liking and engender feelings of pleasure. The principle underlying immediacy is simple: we move toward persons and things we like and avoid or move away from those we dislike. Immediacy cues physically increase our sensory awareness of others.

Our use of space and territory is not the only cue that contributes to positive or negative feelings. Mehrabian has noted several other nonverbal cues that increase immediacy. One of the most powerful is touch; others include a forward lean, increased eye contact, and an open body orientation. The meaning of these behaviours is usually implied rather than explicitly spelled out in words.

In brief, to communicate that we like someone, we use these cues:[53]

Proximity:	Close, forward lean
Body Orientation:	Direct, but could be side-by-side
Eye Contact:	Eye contact and mutual eye contact
Facial Expression:	Smiling
Gestures:	Head nods, movement
Posture:	Open, arms oriented toward others
Touch:	Cultural- and context-appropriate touch
Voice:	Higher pitch, upward pitch

Arousal

The face, voice, and movement are primary indicators of **arousal**. If we see arousal cues, we conclude that another person is responsive to and interested in us. If the person acts passive or dull, we conclude that he or she is uninterested.

When you approach someone and ask whether he or she has a minute or two to talk, that person may signal interest with a change in facial expression and more animated vocal cues. People who are aroused and interested in you show animation in their face, voice, and gestures. Forward lean, a flash of the eyebrows, and a nod of the head are other cues that implicitly communicate arousal. Someone who says, "Sure, I have time to talk with you," in a monotone and with a flat, expressionless face is communicating the opposite. Think of arousal as an on-off switch. Sleeping is the ultimate switched-off state.

Dominance

The third dimension of Mehrabian's framework for implicit cues communicates the balance of power in a relationship. **Dominance** cues communicate status, position, and importance. A person of high status tends to have a relaxed body posture when interacting with a person of lower status.[54] When you talk to a professor, she may lean back in her chair, put her feet on the desk, and fold her hands behind her head during the conversation. But unless your professor is a colleague or a friend, you will maintain a relatively formal posture during your interaction in her office.

Another dominance cue is the use of space. High-status individuals usually have more space around them; they have bigger offices and more "barriers" protecting them. A receptionist in an office is usually easily accessible, but to reach the president of the company you may have to navigate through several corridors, past several secretaries and administrative assistants who are "guarding" the door.

Other power cues that communicate feelings of dominance include our use of furniture, clothing, and locations. You study at a table in the library; the college president has a large private desk. You may wear jeans and a T-shirt to class; the head of the university wears a business suit. Your dorm may be surrounded by other dorms; the president's residence may be a large house surrounded by a lush, landscaped garden in a prestigious neighbourhood. We use space, territory, posture, and artifacts such as clothing and furniture to signal feelings of dominance or submissiveness in the presence of others.

Michael Argyle summarizes the nonverbal cues that communicate dominance:[55]

Use of Space:	Height (on a platform or standing)
	Facing a group
	More space
Eye Contact:	Less with lower status
	More when talking
	More when initially establishing dominance
	More when staring to establish power
Face:	No smile, frown, mature adult features
Touch:	Initiating touch
Voice:	Loud, low pitch, greater pitch range
	Slow, more interruptions, more talk
	Slight hesitation before speaking
Gesture:	Pointing at the other or at his or her property
Posture:	Standing, hands on hips, expanded chest, more relaxed

RECAP — Dimensions for Interpreting Nonverbal Behaviour

Dimension	Definition	Nonverbal Cues
Immediacy	Cues that communicate liking and pleasure.	Eye contact, touch, forward lean, close distances.
Arousal	Cues that communicate active interest and emotional involvement.	Eye contact, varied vocal cues, animated facial expressions, forward lean, movement.
Dominance	Cues that communicate status and power.	Protected space, relaxed posture, status symbols.

Improving Your Ability to Interpret Nonverbal Messages

As we have already cautioned, there are no universal dictionaries to which we can turn for help in interpreting specific nonverbal behaviours. There are some principles and key skills, however, that we can use to enhance our interpretive ability.

Consider Nonverbal Cues in Context

Just as quoting an expert out of context can change the meaning of a statement, trying to draw conclusions from an isolated snatch of behaviour or a single cue can lead to misinterpretations. Beware of looking at someone's folded arms and concluding that he or she does not like you or is not interested in what you are saying. It could be that the air conditioner is set too low and the person is just trying to keep warm.

Look for Clusters of Nonverbal Cues

Instead of focusing on a specific cue, look for corroborating cues that can lead us to a more accurate conclusion about the meaning of a behaviour. Is the person making eye contact? Is he or she facing you? How far away is he or she standing from you?

Always consider nonverbal behaviours in conjunction with other nonverbal cues, the environment, and the person's verbal message.

Consider Past Experiences When Interpreting Nonverbal Cues

Familiarity may breed contempt, but it also increases our ability to interpret another's nonverbal behaviour. You may have learned, for example, that when your mother started crying when you played the piano, it meant she was proud of you, not melancholy. Family members can probably interpret one another's nonverbal cues more accurately than can those from outside the family. But after knowing someone over a period of time, you begin to increase your sensitivity to certain glances, silences, movements, and vocal cues that might be overlooked or misunderstood by others.

Check Your Perceptions with Others

You judge others by their behaviour, not by their intent. The only way to know what people intend is to ask them whether you have interpreted their behaviour correctly. But before you blurt out a hunch, first consider the context and confirming cues; think about this person's previous behaviour. Then, if you are still confused or uncertain about the meaning of a behaviour, ask for clarification.

For example, if you receive a tremendous job offer that requires you to move to a new province, and your spouse greets your enthusiastic announcement with silence,

Nonverbal Skill Assessment

R ate your current level of skill attainment
(10 = High; 1 = Low) on the following factors:

	Rating Today	Desired Rating
1. I know the functions of nonverbal messages when I communicate with others.	_____	_____
2. I know how to interpret other people's postures and movements to determine whether people like me or feel more powerful than I am.	_____	_____
3. I know how to interpret the use of space around me and others to assess whether people like me or feel more powerful than I am.	_____	_____
4. I know the role voice plays in communicating my emotions and others' emotions.	_____	_____
5. I know the role facial expressions play in communicating and interpreting emotions.	_____	_____
6. I know how to interpret the eye contact of other people to assess dynamics of power, control, leadership, and credibility.	_____	_____
7. I know the nonverbal cues that communicate that people like me and that I like them.	_____	_____
8. I know the nonverbal cues that communicate power and status relationships.	_____	_____
9. I know the nonverbal cues that communicate that people are interested and responsive to me and my message.	_____	_____

Overall Nonverbal Assessment

	Rating Today	Desired Rating
10. I do an excellent job of interpreting nonverbal messages.	_____	_____

you could ask, "Does your silence mean that you're opposed to the move, or are you speechless with excitement?" Then wait for a response.

Or suppose you work in the kitchen all day to make fish stew for your friend from Iowa. After her first bite you see her eyes open wide and her lips purse up. So you ask, "Does that mean you don't like it, or did you taste something new and different?"

This key skill is called **perception checking**. As we saw in Chapter 3, you can follow three steps to check someone's perception. First, observe the nonverbal cues, making a point to note such variables as amount of eye contact, posture, use of gestures, facial expression, and tone of voice. Second, try to interpret what the individual is expressing through his or her nonverbal behaviour. Finally, check your perception by asking him or her if it is accurate. Of course, we are not suggesting that you need to go through life constantly checking everyone's nonverbal cues. Overusing this skill would be irritating to most people. We are suggesting, however, that when you are uncertain of how someone feels, and it is important to know, a perception check may be in order. Consider this example:

Deonna: Hi Mom. I'm sorry Erik and I missed the family reunion last week. It's been a hectic week. The kids had something goin' on every night and we just needed to rest.

Muriel: (Frowns, has little eye contact, folds her arms, and uses a flat voice.) Oh, don't worry about it.

Deonna: I know you said don't worry about it, Mom, but it looks like you are still upset. I know that look of yours. I also hear in your voice that you are not really pleased. Is it really OK, or are you still a little miffed?

Muriel: Well, yes, to be honest, Dad and I were really looking forward to getting all of the kids together.

Deonna: I'm sorry, Mom. We will make an effort to be at the next one. Thanks for sharing with me how you really felt.

Addressing your question to a specific nonverbal cue will help you interpret your partner's behaviour in future interactions as well. As we noted earlier, evidence suggests that the longer couples are married, the more they rely upon nonverbal behaviour to communicate. One study claims that most couples spend less than eleven minutes a week in sustained conversation.[56] Even in marriages of fifty years, however, conversation is still required occasionally to clarify nonverbal responses.

RECAP   **How to Check Your Perceptions of Others' Nonverbal Cues**

Steps	Consider
1. Observe their nonverbal behaviour.	Are they frowning? Do they have eye contact? Are their arms crossed? What is their tone of voice? What is their posture?
2. Mentally, form an impression of what you think they mean.	Are they happy, sad, angry? Is the nonverbal message contradicting the verbal message?
3. Ask to check whether your perception is accurate.	"Are you upset? You look angry." "Your expression and your voice suggest you don't believe me. Do you think I'm lying?" "The look on your face tells me you really like it. Do you?"

Summary

Unspoken messages have a major effect upon interpersonal relationships. The primary way in which you communicate feelings, emotions, and attitudes is through nonverbal cues. When there is a contradiction between your verbal and nonverbal messages, others almost always believe the nonverbal one. But nonverbal messages are usually more ambiguous than verbal messages. While some nonverbal messages have a definite beginning and ending, most are part of a seamless flow of

Practice checking your perceptions of nonverbal information by asking questions. Look at the photographs below. Then formulate the perception-checking question requested next to each photograph.

Photo one:

Perception-checking question the teacher could ask her student:

_____

_____

_____

Photo two:
Perception-checking question the father could ask his son:

_____

_____

_____

Photo three:

Perception-checking question the salesperson could ask his customer:

_____

_____

_____

movement, gestures, glances, and inflections. Also, there are culture-based differences in the way we learn and interpret unspoken messages.

Nonverbal cues can be categorized and studied to reveal the codes to our unspoken communication. Movement, posture, and gestures communicate both content and expressive information when we use them as emblems, illustrators, affect displays, regulators, and adaptors. Eye contact is an important code for regulating interaction in interpersonal exchanges. Facial expressions and vocal cues provide a wealth of information about our emotions. Our use of personal space and territory communicates a variety of messages relating to power, status, and other relational concerns. Touch is one of the most powerful cues to communicate liking; and our appearance telegraphs to others how we wish to be treated and how we perceive our role in relation to them.

One of the prime fascinations with nonverbal messages is the potential to understand hidden meaning communicated through unspoken codes. It is difficult to read nonverbal cues as easily as reading the words on this page, but there is a general framework that can help you assess the nonverbal messages of others, as well as your own nonverbal expressions. Researchers have identified three primary dimensions for interpreting nonverbal messages: Immediacy cues provide information about liking and disliking. Arousal cues tip others off as to our interest and level of engagement with them; and position, power, and status are often communicated through dominance cues.

To enhance your skill in interpreting nonverbal messages, always consider the context in which you observed the cues and look for clusters of nonverbal behaviours. The longer you have known someone, the easier it is to interpret his or her unspoken messages. But in order to verify whether you understand someone's nonverbal behaviour, you should ask whether your interpretation is accurate.

For Discussion and Review

■ FOCUS ON COMPREHENSION

1. What is nonverbal communication?

2. Why is it important to study nonverbal communication?

3. Describe nonverbal emblems, illustrators, affect displays, regulators, and adaptors.

4. What are the nonverbal communication codes presented in this chapter?

5. What are the nonverbal cues that communicate immediacy, arousal, and power?

■ FOCUS ON CRITICAL THINKING

6. Sasha has had difficulty getting hired as a manager. One of her best friends suggested that she pay more attention to her nonverbal behaviour when she is interviewed for a job. What advice would you give Sasha to ensure that she monitors her nonverbal interview behaviour?

7. Greg has been told that he sometimes comes across as cold, aloof, and standoffish. What could Greg do to communicate his sincere desire to be interpersonally warm and approachable?

■ FOCUS ON ETHICS

8. Donald really wants to be hired as a salesperson. He hires a fashion consultant to recommend what he should wear and determine how he should look when he interviews for a job. In general, is it ethical to manipulate your appearance so that you can impress others?

9. Is it appropriate to draw definitive conclusions about another's personality and attitudes based only upon a "reading" of his or her other nonverbal cues? Support your answer.

10. Is it ethical for salespersons, politicians, and others who wish to make favourable impressions to alter their nonverbal messages to get you to like them, vote for them, or buy their products? Explain your answer.

For Your Journal

1. Videotape fifteen minutes of a TV drama or situation comedy. View the program with the sound turned off. Using the four principles of interpreting nonverbal messages, describe the meaning of the nonverbal messages you watch. After you have made written observations in your journal, view the program with full sound and determine how accurate your interpretations were.

2. Mehrabian has suggested that we convey 55 percent of our emotional meaning through facial expressions, 38 percent through vocal cues, and only 7 percent through verbal statements. Spend thirty minutes observing four or five people in a public place, such as a mall, airport, or student centre, and attempt to prove or disprove Mehrabian's conclusions. Before you begin your people watching, design a method for recording your observations in your journal.

Learning with Others

1. Go on a nonverbal communication scavenger hunt. Your instructor will ask you to observe your family members and friends to find one or more of the following sets of nonverbal communicators:

   A. Examples of emblems, illustrators, affect displays, regulators, and adaptors.

   B. Examples of how people use the four zones of personal space.

   C. Examples of pleasure, arousal, and dominance.

   D. Examples of the cognitive, monitoring, regulatory, and expressive functions of eye contact.

   E. Examples of clothing that reveals intentions or personality traits.

2. Divide into groups of three or four people. Use the following evaluation form to evaluate a room or public space. Each person in your group should evaluate the same room. It could be your own room, a cafeteria, classroom, fast-food restaurant, or even a hotel lobby. Compare your answers with other group members. You could also give a report to the class on your results.

Environment Analysis

1. Briefly describe the environment you analyzed:

   A. How big is the space?

   B. Describe the movable objects in the space provided. (A brief diagram may clarify your description.)

   C. Describe the predominant colours.

   D. Describe the sounds in the environment; what did you hear?

   E. Describe the lighting.

   F. Make a note of any unique structural or aesthetic design features (e.g., artwork, plants, windows, etc.).

2. Rate the room you observed using the following scales:

   formal   __ __ __ __ __ __ __   informal

   warm   __ __ __ __ __ __ __   cold

   pleasant   __ __ __ __ __ __ __   unpleasant

   useful   __ __ __ __ __ __ __   not useful

   beautiful   __ __ __ __ __ __ __   ugly

3. Describe the probable effects the room design has upon communication interaction patterns (e.g., does it encourage or discourage communication?).

   _____

   _____

   _____

   _____

4. Based upon your observations, is the room appropriately designed for its intended use? Explain.

   _____

   _____

   _____

   _____

NONVERBAL COMMUNICATION: Behaviour other than written or spoken language that creates meaning for someone.

KINESICS: The study of human movement and gestures.

EMBLEMS: Nonverbal cues that have specific, generally understood meanings in a given culture and may substitute for a word or phrase.

ILLUSTRATORS: Nonverbal behaviour that accompanies a verbal message and either contradicts, accents, or complements it.

AFFECT DISPLAY: Nonverbal behaviour that communicates emotions.

REGULATORS: Nonverbal messages that help to control the interaction or level of communication between people.

ADAPTORS: Nonverbal behaviours that help satisfy a personal need and help a person adapt or respond to the immediate situation.

PROXEMICS: The study of how close to or far away from people and objects we position ourselves.

INTIMATE SPACE: Zone of personal space most often used for very personal or intimate conversation, ranging from zero to eighteen inches.

PERSONAL SPACE: Zone of personal space most often used for conversation, ranging from one and one-half to four feet.

SOCIAL SPACE: Zone of personal space most often used for group discussion, ranging from four to twelve feet.

PUBLIC SPACE: Zone of personal space most often used by public speakers or one speaking to many people, ranging beyond 12 feet.

TERRITORIALITY: The study of how animals and humans use space and objects to communicate occupancy or ownership of space.

IMMEDIACY: The feelings of liking, pleasure, and closeness communicated by such nonverbal cues as eye contact, forward lean, touch, and open body orientation.

AROUSAL: The feelings of interest and excitement communicated by such nonverbal cues as vocal expression, facial expressions, and gestures.

DOMINANCE: The feelings of power, status, and control communicated by such nonverbal cues as a relaxed posture, greater personal space, and protected personal space.

PERCEPTION CHECK: The skill of asking someone whether your interpretation of his or her nonverbal behaviour is accurate.

Communicating Verbally

After studying this chapter, you should be able to:

1. Describe the relationship between words and meaning.

2. Understand how words influence us and our culture.

3. Identify word barriers and know how to manage them.

4. Discuss how the words we use affect our relationships with others.

5. Understand supportive approaches to relating to others.

6. Understand how to confirm other people's sense of themselves.

■ WORDS AND MEANINGS

■ WORDS HAVE POWER

■ WORD BARRIERS

■ USING WORDS TO ESTABLISH SUPPORTIVE RELATIONSHIPS

■ USING WORDS TO VALUE OTHERS

ords are powerful. Those who use them skillfully can exert great influence with just a few of them. Consider these notable achievements:

> Shakespeare expressed the quintessence of the human condition in Hamlet's famous "To be or not to be" soliloquy—363 words long.

> Several of our great religions adhere to a comprehensive moral code expressed in a mere 297 words: the Ten Commandments.

Words have great power in our private lives as well. In this chapter we will examine ways to use them more effectively in interpersonal relationships. We'll investigate how to harness the power that words have to affect your feelings, thoughts, and actions, and we'll describe links between language and culture. We will also identify communication barriers that may keep you from using words effectively and note strategies and skills for managing those barriers. Finally, we will examine the role of speech in establishing supportive relationships with others. In one of his pessimistic moments, the poet Robert Frost said, "Half the world is composed of people who have something to say and can't, and the other half who have nothing to say and keep on saying it." This chapter is designed to help you prove him wrong, to help you become a person who has something to say and can say it well.

Words and Meaning

As you read the printed words on this page, how are you able to make sense out of these black marks? When you hear words spoken by others, how are you able to interpret those sounds? Although there are several theories that attempt to explain how we learn language and ascribe meaning to both printed and uttered words, there is no single universally held view that neatly clarifies the mystery. We can, however, better understand the nature of words by taking a closer look at what words are and how they function.

Figure 6.1

Triangle of Meaning

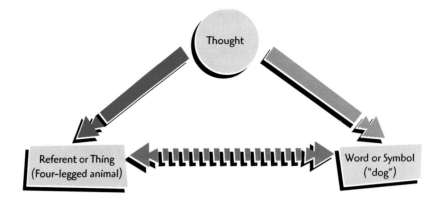

Words Are Symbols

As we noted in Chapter 1, words are symbols that represent something else. A printed word triggers an image, sound, concept, or experience. Take the word *cat*, for instance. The word may conjure up in your mind's eye a hissing creature with bared claws and fangs. Or perhaps you envision a cherished pet curled up by a fireplace.

The classic model in Figure 6.1 was developed by one pair of researchers to explain how we use words as symbols, noting relationships between **symbols** (words), *referents*, and *thoughts*.[1] **Referents** are the things the symbols (words) represent. **Thought** is the mental process of creating a category, idea, or image triggered by the referent or the symbol. So these three elements, words, referents, and thoughts, become inextricably linked. Although some scholars find this model too simplistic to explain how we link all words to a meaning, it does illustrate the process for most concepts, people, and tangible things.

Words Are Arbitrary

In English, as in all languages, words arbitrarily represent something else. The word *dog*, for example, does not *sound* like a dog or *look* at all like a dog. There is no longer a logical connection between the beast and the symbol. Figure 6.2 shows the language tree that charts the evolution of, and links among, one group of human languages. As you can see, the English language evolved from a mixture of Indo-European tongues. The humorous inventions of Rich Hall, in the following selection of "Sniglets," demonstrate that English is a living language. It will continue to evolve as we develop the need to name and describe new phenomena.

False generalizations based on gender and race are still rampant in North American culture. Statements such as, "Women don't know anything about fixing cars" are inaccurate as well as insulting to women. (R. Sidney/The Image Works)

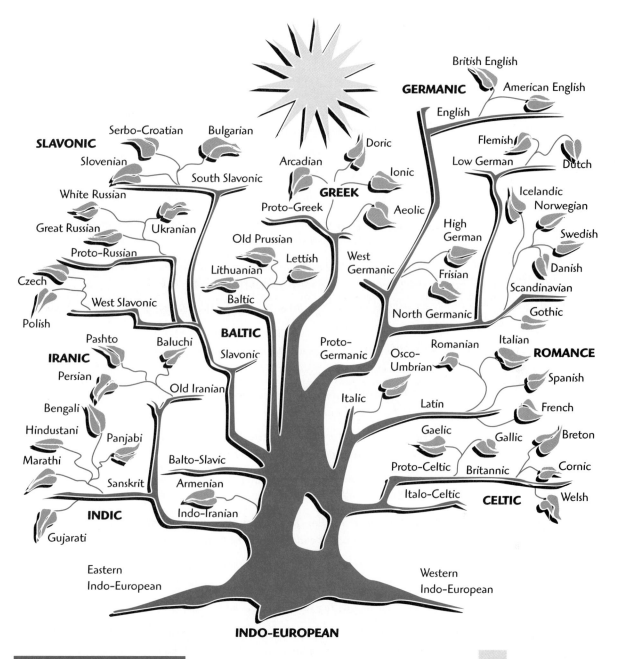

The "Language Tree"

British English
American English
GERMANIC
English
SLAVONIC
Serbo-Croatian
Bulgarian
Flemish
Slovenian
Doric
Low German
Dutch
South Slavonic
Arcadian
Ionic
Icelandic
White Russian
GREEK
Norwegian
Great Russian
Ukranian
Proto-Greek
West
High
Swedish
Ukranian
Aeolic
German
Proto-Russian
Old Prussian
West
German
Frisian
Danish
Czech
Lithuanian
Lettish
Germanic
Scandinavian
West Slavonic
Baltic
North Germanic
Gothic
Polish
BALTIC
Pashto
Baluchi
Proto-
Romanian
Italian
ROMANCE
IRANIC
Slavonic
Germanic
Osco-
Umbrian
Persian
Old Iranian
Spanish
Italic
Latin
Bengali
Hindustani
Panjabi
French
Gaelic
Gallic
Breton
Marathi
Balto-Slavic
Proto-Celtic
Britannic
Cornic
Sanskrit
Armenian
Italo-Celtic
CELTIC
Welsh
INDIC
Indo-Iranian
Gujarati
Eastern
Indo-European
Western
Indo-European
INDO-EUROPEAN

Words Are Context Bound

Your English or speech communication teacher has undoubtedly cautioned you that taking something out of context changes its meaning. Symbols derive their meaning from the situation in which they are used. As Mark Twain once said, "The difference between the right word and almost the right word is the difference between lightning and the lightning bug." Adding the word *bug* after the word *lightning* completes the context and dramatically changes your mental image. The words *old man* could refer to a male over the age of seventy, your father, your teacher, your principal, or your boss. We would need to know the context of the two symbols *old* and *man* in order to decipher their specific meaning.

Figure 6.2

The "Language Tree"
Copyright © 1994 by Allyn and Bacon. Adapted by permission.

Sniglets

What do you call a pencil covered with teeth marks? Or the act of pushing eyeglasses back up on the nose? "Sniglets" are words that, figuratively speaking, don't exist but should. The following examples, created by Rich Hall and friends, illustrate how anyone, with a little imagination, can invent the right word.

ALPOPUCK (al' po puk) n: Any empty dish pushed around the kitchen floor by a dog trying to get the last morsel.

BEAVO (bee' vo) n: A pencil with teeth marks all over it.

BURGACIDE (burg' uh side) n: When a hamburger can't take any more torture and hurls itself through the grill into the coals.

CHUBBLE (chub bul) n: The aerobic movement combining deep-knee bends and sideward hops used when trying to fit into panty hose.

CRAYOLLIA (kray oh' lee uh) n: The area on the refrigerator where kindergarten drawings are displayed.

DIMP (dimp) n: A person who insults you in a cheap department store by asking, "Do you work here?"

DOWN PAUSE (down' pawz) n: The split second of dry weather experienced when driving under an overpass during a storm.

FICTATE (fik' tayt) v: To inform a television or screen character of impending danger under the assumption he can hear you.

GREEDLING (gree' dling) v: Pretending to read the inscription on the birthday card when you really just want to know how much the check is for.

MALTIAN (mat' shun) n: The alien beside you with concave cheeks, bulging forehead veins, and clearly outlined skull who is sucking on a too thick milk shake.

MOTODRIFT (mow toh drift) n: The mistaken belief at a stoplight that your car is moving backward when, actually, the car beside you is moving forward.

OPUP (op' uhp) v: To push one's glasses back on the nose.

PREMADERCI (pree muh dayr' chi) n: The act of saying good-bye to someone, then running into him again moments later (usually accompanied by a lame quip such as, "You following me?").

SOMNAMBAPOLOGIST (som nam ba pol uh jist) n: Person too polite to admit he was sleeping even when awakened at three in the morning.

TOOLCENTRIC (tewl sen' trik) adj: Describes any tool that, when dropped, rolls to the exact center of the car's underside.

—RICH HALL AND FRIENDS

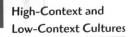

High-Context and Low-Context Cultures

Some cultures place great emphasis on the verbal context—the explicit importance of words—in a message. Others place more emphasis on the nonverbal context. Renowned anthropologist Edward T. Hall categorized these distinctions as **high context** (emphasis on the nonverbal) and **low context** (emphasis on the verbal).[2] The chart in Figure 6.3 depicts cultures arranged along a continuum from high to low context.[3]

Individuals from high-context cultures find nonverbal cues extremely important in helping them interpret the messages of others. Consequently, individuals from high-context cultures are usually more skilled at decoding nonverbal messages than individuals from low-context cultures. In addition, because context plays a major role in communicating meaning, they may use fewer words and spend less time speaking than do individuals from low-context cultures.

Larry Samovar and Richard Porter found that individuals from high-context cultures often perceive those from low-context cultures as less attractive, knowledgeable, and trustworthy. They find typical low-context requests such as "Say what you mean," "Don't beat around the bush," and "Tell it to me straight" particularly annoying because they expect others to be as skilled as they are in interpreting unspoken, contextual cues.

Novelist Amy Tan notes:

I try to explain to my English-speaking friends that Chinese language is more strategic in manner, whereas English tends to be more direct; an American business executive may say, "Let's make a deal," and the Chinese manager may reply, "Is your son interested in learning about your widget business?" Each to his or her own purpose, each with his or her own linguistic path.[4]

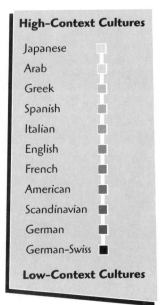

High-Context Cultures

Japanese
Arab
Greek
Spanish
Italian
English
French
American
Scandinavian
German
German-Swiss

Low-Context Cultures

Figure 6.3

Cultures arranged along the high-context/low-context dimension. Figure from Larry Samovar and Richard Porter, *Communication Between Cultures* (Belmont, CA: Wadsworth, 1991) 235.

Words Are Culturally Bound

Culture consists of the rules, norms, values, and mores of a group of people, which have been learned and shaped from one generation to the next. The meaning of a symbol such as a word can change from culture to culture. A few years ago General Motors sold a car called a Nova. In English, *nova* means bright star—an appropriate name for a car. In Spanish, however, the spoken word *nova* sounds like the words "no va," which translates, "It does not go." As you can imagine, this name was not a great sales tool for the Spanish-speaking market.

Because words reflect the values, beliefs, and norms of a given culture, business transactions that cross linguistic boundaries frequently engender confusion on both sides. (Susan Van Etten/Stock Boston)

The study of words and meaning is called semantics. One important body of semantic theory known as **symbolic interaction** suggests that as a society we are bound together because of our common use of symbols. Originally developed by sociologists as a way of making sense out of how societies and groups are linked together,[5] the theory of symbolic interaction also illuminates how we use our common understanding of symbols to form interpersonal relationships. Common symbols foster links in understanding and therefore lead to satisfying relationships. Of course, even within a given culture we misunderstand each other's messages. But the more similar the cultures of the communication partners, the greater the chance for a meeting of meanings.

Words Have Denotative and Connotative Meaning

Language is the vehicle through which we share our sense of the world with others. Through language we transfer our experience into symbols and then use the symbols to share our experience. But as we learned in Chapter 1, the process of symbol sharing through language is not just a simple process of uttering a word and having its meaning clearly understood by another. Messages convey both content and feelings. So our language conveys meaning on two levels: the denotative and the connotative.

The **denotative** level conveys content. The denotation of a word is its restrictive or literal meaning. For example, here is one dictionary definition for the word *school*:

An institution for the instruction of children; an institution for instruction in a skill or business; a college or a university.[6]

This definition is the literal or denotative definition of the word *school*; it describes what the word means in North American culture.

The **connotative** level of language conveys feelings. Words also have personal and subjective meanings for us. The word *school* to you might mean a wonderful, exciting place where you meet your friends, have a good time, and occasionally take tests and perform other tasks that keep you from enjoying fellowship with your chums. To others, *school* could be a restrictive, burdensome obligation that stands in the way of making money and getting on with life. The connotative meaning of a word is more specialized. The denotative or objective meaning of the word *school* can be found in your *Webster's, Oxford, or Gage* dictionary; your subjective response to the word is probably not contained there.

Denotative and Connotative Meaning

Level	Definition	Examples
DENOTATIVE	The literal, restrictive definition of a word.	Mother: the female person who gave birth to you.
CONNOTATIVE	The personal, subjective reaction to a word.	Mother: the warm, caring woman who nurtured and loved you; or the cold, distant woman who always implied that you were not measuring up to her standards.

Words Communicate Concrete or Abstract Meaning

Words can be placed along a continuum from abstract to concrete. We call a word concrete if we can experience its referent with one of our senses; if we can see it, touch it, smell it, taste it, or hear it, then it's concrete. If we cannot do these things with the referent, then the word is abstract. We can visualize the progression from abstract to concrete as a ladder:

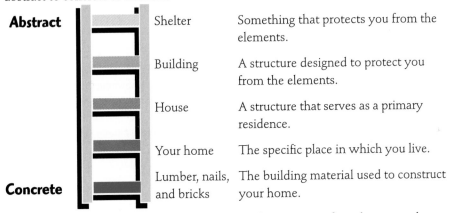

Abstract

	Shelter	Something that protects you from the elements.
	Building	A structure designed to protect you from the elements.
	House	A structure that serves as a primary residence.
	Your home	The specific place in which you live.
Concrete	Lumber, nails, and bricks	The building material used to construct your home.

In general, the more concrete the language, the easier it is for others to understand. As the following passage explains, professional writers apply this principle to written words.

> Look at the work of any professional writer and notice how constantly he is moving from the generality, the abstract statement, to the concrete example, the facts and figures, the illustrations. If he is writing on juvenile delinquency, he does not just tell you that juveniles are (it seems to him) delinquent and that (in his opinion) something should be done about it. He shows you juveniles being delinquent, tearing up movie theatres or smoking marijuana. And more than likely he is moving toward some specific remedy, not just a general wringing of the hands.
>
> It is no doubt possible to be *too* concrete, too illustrative or anecdotal, but few inexperienced writers err this way. For most the soundest advice is to be

seeking always for the picture, to be always turning general remarks into seeable examples. Don't say, "Sororities teach girls the social graces." Say, "Sorority life teaches a girl how to carry on a conversation while pouring tea, without sloshing the tea into the saucer." Don't say, "I like certain kinds of popular music very much." Say, "Whenever I hear Gerber Sprinklittle play 'Mississippi Man' on the trombone, my socks creep up my ankles."

—PAUL ROBERTS
UNDERSTANDING ENGLISH

COMMUNICATION EXPERIENCE

1. Provide both denotative (literal) and connotative (personal) definitions for the following terms. Compare your answers with those of your classmates.

	Denotative Definition	Connotative Defintion
WINTER		
PROM		
PIANO		
CAR		
SPRING BREAK		

2. Practice describing something, starting with an abstract description, and then becoming more concrete. Make this a game you play with one or more of your classmates. Think of something concrete, such as the name of your communication teacher or your provincial premier. Make your first clue an abstract hint such as "person" or "human," and then provide increasingly more concrete clues.

Words Have Power

Sticks and stones may break my bones,
But words can never hurt me.

This old schoolyard chant may provide a ready retort for the desperate victim of name-calling, but it is hardly convincing. With more insight, the poet Robert Browning wrote, "Words break no bones; hearts though sometimes." And in his book *Science and Sanity*, mathematician and engineer Alfred Korzybski argued that the words we use (and misuse) have tremendous effects upon our thoughts and actions.[7] Browning and Korzybski were right. As we said at the beginning of this chapter, words have power.

Words Have Power to Create

"To name is to call into existence—to call out of nothingness,"[8] wrote French philosopher Georges Gusdorff. Words give us a tool to create our world by naming and labelling what we experience. You undoubtedly learned in your elementary science class that Sir Isaac Newton discovered gravity. Perhaps it would be more accurate to say that he labelled rather than discovered it. His use of the word *gravity* gave us a cognitive category; we now converse about the pull of the earth's forces that keeps us from flying into space. Words give us the symbolic vehicles to communicate our creations and discoveries to others.

When you label something as "good" or "bad," you are using language to create your own vision of how you experience the world. If you tell a friend that the movie you saw last night was vulgar and obscene, you are not only providing your friend with a critique of the movie; you are also communicating your sense of what is appropriate and inappropriate.

As we noted in Chapter 2, you create your self-worth largely with self-talk and with the labels you apply to yourself. One theorist believes that you also create your moods and emotional state with the words you use to label your feelings.[9] If you get fired from a job, you might say that you feel angry and helpless, or you might declare that you feel liberated and excited. The first response might lead to depression, and the second to happiness. One fascinating study conducted over a thirty-five-year period found that people who described the world in pessimistic terms when they were younger were in poorer health during middle age than those who had been optimistic.[10] Your words and corresponding outlook have the power to affect your health.

Words Have Power to Affect Thoughts and Actions

How about some horse meat for supper tonight? Most of us find such a question disgusting. Why? Horse meat is not something we typically eat. One theorist argues that horse meat is not a featured delicacy at the local supermarket simply because we have no other word for it. Your butcher does not advertise pig meat or cow meat; labelling the meat as pork chops, ham, and sausage, or as steak and ribs, makes it sound more appetizing. Advertisers have long known that the way a product is labelled affects our propensity to purchase it.

Words also have the power to affect policies and procedures. Consider the words of Supreme Court of Canada judge Claire L'Heureux-Dubé, who participated in a human rights conference on the topic of government budget cuts. How are Justice L'Heureux-Dubé's personal values about human rights reflected in the words of her speech? What power do these words have in shaping Canadian policy on human rights protection? What is the ultimate power of a judge's words or court rulings on the making and interpretation of laws in Canada?

Human Rights Outweigh Debt Cutting, Top Judge Says

VICTORIA—A Supreme Court of Canada judge says the push to cut government debt and deficits is one of the greatest threats to human rights in Canada.

In an interview Tuesday, Justice Claire L'Heureux-Dubé said the protection of equality should supersede short-term economic considerations.

"In the short term you may think that you are saving money, but in the long term the damage that it does to society without human rights creates more problems and it costs more.

"You have no justification to ask the cost of justice when you haven't figured out the cost of injustice.

"When you don't see the results [of human rights commissions] immediately ... then there's a great temptation to cut resources. Justice should be at the forefront of politicians' agendas....

"In an era of diminishing public resources and increasing global competition, the real question is not whether we can afford to eliminate discrimination but whether we can afford not to.... [T]he equal dignity of every member of the community is a value of the highest order, and I would hope that money is not a measure of that dignity."

Excerpts from article by Jim Beatty, Southam Newspapers (*The Vancouver Sun*), as it appeared in *The Ottawa Citizen*, June 5, 1996, A1.

In the late 1960s a California sociology professor conducted an experiment to demonstrate that words have power to affect behaviour.[11] He divided his class into two groups. To one group he distributed a bumper sticker that boldly displayed the words, "I support the Black Panthers." At that time, many members of the students' local community thought the Panthers were using unnecessary force to promote their agenda. Students in this first group had to drive around for a week with the stickers on their cars. The other group drove around as usual, without stickers.

It took only a few hours to prove the professor's point: words do affect attitudes and behaviour. Students who had the stickers were harassed by other motorists and issued traffic tickets at an alarming rate. The other group had no increase in hassles. By the end of the study, seventeen days later, the "Panther" group had received thirty-three traffic citations.

Words Have Power to Affect and Reflect Culture

About a decade before the sociology professor's bumper sticker experiment, two anthropologists simultaneously began to refine a theory called **linguistic determinism**, which had originated in the nineteenth century.[12] Their version is based on a hypothesis of reciprocity: language shapes your culture and culture shapes your language. To understand your culture, theorize these anthropologists, you should study the words you use. If an impartial investigator from another culture were to study a transcript of all of your spoken utterances last week, what would he or she learn about you and the culture in which you live? If you frequently used words like *CD* and *rollerblades*, the investigator would know that these things are important to you. But he or she might not know what they mean if they are not also part of his or her culture.

Words not only reflect your culture; there is evidence that they mold it. Perhaps you've heard there are twenty-three different words for snow in Inuktitut. As the

What's in a Name?

For most people, the most attention-catching word is their name. Given the power that words have to create and affect thoughts and actions, consider the implications of names.

1. Rank the following names according to status (1 = most status), then share and discuss the results with your classmates.

Mr. Smith _____

Miss Smith _____

Ms. Smith _____

Mrs. Smith _____

Fr. Smith _____

Dr. Smith _____

Prof. Smith _____

Officer Smith _____

Smith _____

2. If you marry, should you change your name? Imagine that John Smith marries Mary Jones. Discuss the communication implications of the following names with your classmates. Which name would you prefer? Explain your choice.

John Smith-Jones/Mary Smith-Jones

John Jones-Smith/Mary Jones-Smith

John Smith and Mary Smith

Mr. John Smith/ Mrs. Mary Jones

Mr. and Mrs. Smith-Jones

Mr. John Smith/ Ms. Mary Jones

John Jones/ Mary Jones

Mr. and Mrs. John Smith

article "The Melting of a Mighty Myth" points out, there really aren't quite that many, even though there is evidence that Inuktitut has more words for snow than most other languages.

These examples also show that the words we use and listen to affect our **world view**—how we interpret what we experience. If you were to don someone else's prescription glasses, the world would literally look different to you, and the glasses would either enhance or inhibit your ability to see the world around you. In a sense, your world view is your own set of prescription glasses, which you formulate over time, based upon your experiences, attitudes, beliefs, values, and needs. The words you use to describe your view of the world reflect and further shape your perspective. And you, in turn, help to shape your culture's collective world view through your use of language.

The Melting of a Mighty Myth

Guess what: Eskimos don't have 23 words for snow

Once in a while science makes a breakthrough so revolutionary that it changes forever the way we think about reality, like the discovery that hay fever usually isn't caused by hay. To the great iconoclasts of science, one can add anthropologist Laura Martin of Cleveland State University, who has had the audacity to assert that *Eskimos don't actually have any more words for "snow" than anyone else.*

This will be shattering news to millions of people who attended college after about 1958, when the theories of the great amateur linguist Benjamin Lee Whorf began to appear in college psychology texts. Whorf held that Eskimos—living in daily contact with snow in its variously slushy, dry, powdery or crusty forms—use different words for substances that English speakers call just "snow." (Whorf didn't specify how many words, but he implied there were around seven.) It is not hard to see why this mundane observation should have emerged as one of the handful of facts most liberal-arts majors retained from their educations. Simple to grasp, it had implications so profound that anyone who stayed awake through his introductory psychology course could feel like another Descartes. For if the Eskimos use many different words for things that English speakers lump into one category, does it not follow that they actually perceive the world differently? That Eskimos do not grasp the unity among all forms of frozen precipitation, while non-Eskimos do not see the differences, at least until they try to lift a shovelful of slush? Like, is that heavy—the idea, not the shovel—or what?

It would be, if only it were true. Martin, along with the linguist Geoffrey K. Pullum, author of *The Great Eskimo Vocabulary Hoax,* has traced the story's progress from learned exotica to the world of Sunday-supplement Astounding Facts, showing how it became more incredible along the way. Most of the references Martin found put the number of Eskimo snow words at 17 to 23, but the *New York Times* once casually referred to 100. The misunderstanding seems to have arisen because Eskimos do indeed have more than one word for snow and snow-related phenomena. Anthony Woodbury of the University of Texas at Austin puts the number at around a dozen. But, he adds, the proper comparison to English is not with the single noun "snow," but a list of at least 10 words, including "blizzard," "dusting," and "avalanche." Martin admits that her efforts are unlikely to get the public to drop such a charming myth. But she was disappointed in the reaction of her colleagues when she pointed out the fallacy; most, she says, took the position that true or not, "it's still a great example."

Well, so it is. To play Descartes for a minute, does it perhaps provide an example of how language can be used to change how we perceive reality? If a lack of vocabulary can cause us to overlook the differences between kinds of snow, then maybe we could learn to ignore the differences between human races by unlearning the names for them. Just a thought: we are all, after all, much more alike than, say . . . powder, hardpack, and slush.

Word Barriers

According to theologian and educator Ruel Howe, a communication barrier is "something that keeps meaning from meeting."[13] Words have the power to create monumental misunderstandings as well as deep connections. Let's identify some of the specific barriers to understanding that we can create through language.

Bypassing: One Word, Two Thoughts

A student pilot was on his first solo flight. When he called the tower for flight instructions, the control tower said, "Would you please give us your altitude and position?"

The pilot said: "I'm five feet ten inches, and I'm sitting up front."

Bypassing occurs when the same words mean different things to different people.

In another amusing example of this phenomenon, an Englishwoman who was looking for permanent accommodations in a Swiss town asked the schoolmaster if he could recommend any rooms. He took her to see several. When everything was arranged, the woman returned to her home to make final preparations for the move. On arriving home, she suddenly realized that she had not seen a water closet (a toilet). She immediately wrote a note to the schoolmaster, asking him if there was a W.C. around the place. Knowing only limited English, the schoolmaster asked the parish priest if he could help out in this matter. Together they tried to discover the meaning of the letters W.C. The only solution they could come up with was "Wayside Chapel." The schoolmaster wrote the following letter to the woman:

> Dear Madam:
>
> I take great pleasure in informing you that a W.C. is situated nine miles from your house, in the centre of a beautiful grove of pine trees, surrounded by lovely grounds.
>
> It is capable of holding two hundred and twenty-two persons and is opened on Sundays and Thursdays only. As there are a great number of people expected during the summer months, I would advise you to come early. Although there is usually plenty of standing room, this is an unfortunate situation, particularly if you are in the habit of going regularly.
>
> You will no doubt be glad to hear that a great number of people bring their lunch and make a day of it, while others who can afford to, go late and arrive just in time. I would especially advise your ladyship to go on Thursday when there is an organ accompaniment. The acoustics are excellent, and often the most delicate sounds can be heard everywhere.
>
> It may interest you to know that my daughter was married in the W.C. It was there she met her husband. I can remember the rush there was for seats. There were ten people to seats usually occupied by one. It was wonderful to see the expressions on their faces.
>
> The newest attraction is the bell donated by a wealthy resident of the district. It rings every time a person enters. A bazaar is to be held to provide the plush seats for all, since the people believe it is a long-felt need.
>
> My wife is rather delicate so she cannot attend regularly. It is almost a year since she last went. Naturally, it pains her very much not to be able to go more often. I shall be delighted to reserve the best seat for you if you wish, where you will be seen by all. For the children there is a special time and place so they will not disturb the elders.
>
> Hoping to have been of service to you.
>
> Sincerely yours,
> Father Franz

Meaning is fragile. And the English language is imprecise in many areas. One researcher estimated that the 500 words we use most often in our daily conversations with others have over 14,000 different dictionary definitions. And this number does not take into account personal connotations. So it is no wonder that bypassing is a common communication problem.

We all know that Pavlov's dog salivated when he heard the bell that he learned to associate with food. Sometimes we respond to symbols the way Pavlov's dog did to the bell, forgetting that symbols (words) can have more than one meaning.

Bafflegab: High-Falutin Use of Words

Do you suffer from bafflegab? Here is an example of it: Bafflegab is multiloquence characterized by consummate interfusion of circumlocution or periphrasis, inscrutability, incognizability, and other familiar manifestations of abstruse expatiation commonly used for promulations implementing procrustean determinations by governmental bodies. Whew! What a mouthful. Why do some people use such highly abstract language? Perhaps they are just trying to dazzle their listener with evidence of their education, or they may simply not be other-oriented. Bafflegabbers may be focused on impressing the receiver rather than on conveying meaning. Other-oriented speakers use clear words that the listener can understand. Another reason people use big words, overly formal language, or evasive phrases is to hide their ignorance.

Lack of Precision: Uncertain Meaning

Alice Roosevelt Longworth writes about the investigation of a merchant seaman. "Do you," asked the interrogator, "have any pornographic literature?"

"Pornographic literature!" the sailor burst out indignantly. "I don't even have a pornograph!"

At a ceremony in a university chapel, an old lady buttonholed an usher and commanded, "Be sure you get me a seat up front, young man. I understand they've always had trouble with the agnostics in the chapel!"

Each of these examples, along with the Far Side cartoon opposite, illustrates a **malapropism**—a confusion of one word or phrase for another that sounds similar to it. You have probably heard people confuse such word pairs as *construction* and *instruction*, and *subscription* and *prescription*. Although this confusion may at times be humorous, it may also result in failure to communicate clearly. So, too, can using words out of context, using inappropriate grammar, or putting words in the wrong order. Confusion is the inevitable result, as these sentences taken from letters to a welfare department illustrate:

I want my money as quickly as I can get it. I've been in bed with the doctor for two weeks, and it didn't do me any good. If things don't improve, I will have to send for another doctor.

And the following statements appeared in church bulletins:

The eighth-graders will be presenting Shakespeare's Hamlet in the church basement on Friday at 7:00 P.M. The congregation is invited to attend this tragedy.

This afternoon there will be meetings in the North and South ends of the church—Children will be baptized on both ends.

These are funny examples, but in fact unclear language can launch a war or sink a ship. It is vital to remember that *meanings are in people, not in words.* We give symbols meaning; we do not receive inherent meaning *from* symbols. If you are other-oriented, you will assess how someone else will respond to your message and try to select those symbols that he or she is most likely to interpret as you intend.

For most communication, the object is to be as specific and concrete as possible. Vague language creates confusion and frustration. Consider this example:

Derrick: Where's the aluminum foil?

Pam: In the drawer.

Derrick: What drawer?

Pam: In the kitchen.

Derrick: But where in the kitchen?

Pam: By the fridge.

Derrick: But which one? There are five drawers.

Pam: Oh, the second one from the top.

Derrick: Why didn't you say so in the first place?

Is it possible to be too precise? It is if you use a restricted code that has a meaning your listener does not know. A **restricted code** involves the use of words that have a particular meaning to a subgroup or culture. For example, most children grow up learning their own family's secret words. Sometimes we develop abbreviations or specialized terms that make sense and save time when we speak to others in our group. Musicians, for example, use special terms that relate to reading and performing music. Most computer hackers know that "a screamer" is someone who sends messages in cyberspace in ALL CAPITAL LETTERS. Ham radio operators use codes to communicate over the airwaves. Yet, in each instance this shorthand language would make little sense to an outsider. In fact, groups that rely upon restricted codes may have greater cohesiveness because of this shared "secret" language or **jargon**. The "Electronic Connections" box on page 181 describes how computer jargon is the rarefied language of a restricted group of knowledgeable insiders. Whatever your line of work, guard against lapsing into phrases that can only be interpreted by a few.

When people have known one another for a long time, they may also use restricted codes for their exchanges. The Blondie cartoon overleaf is an example of how married couples can communicate using a code that no outsider could ever interpret.

Ha ha ha, Biff. Guess what? After we go to the drugstore and the post office, I'm going to the vet's to get tutored.

Allness: The Language of Generalization

The tendency to use language to make unqualified, often untrue generalizations is called **allness**. Allness statements deny individual differences or variations. Statements such as "All women are poor drivers" and "People from the South love iced tea" are generalizations that imply that the person making the pronouncement has examined all the information and has reached a definitive conclusion. Although our world would be much simpler if we *could* make such statements, reality rarely, if ever, provides evidence to support sweeping generalizations.

For example, although research conclusions document differences between the way men and women communicate, it is inaccurate to say that all women are more emotional and that all men are task oriented. Empathic, other-oriented speakers avoid making judgments of others based only upon conventional wisdom or traditionally held attitudes and beliefs. If you respond to others (of a different gender, sexual orientation, or ethnicity) based on stereotypical concepts, you will diminish your understanding and the quality of the relationship.

One way to avoid untrue generalizations is to remind yourself that your use and interpretation of a word is unique. Saying the words "to me" either to yourself or out loud before you offer an opinion or make a pronouncement can help communicate to others (and remind yourself) that your view is uniquely yours. Rather than announcing, "Curfews for teenagers are ridiculous," you could say, "To me, curfews for teenagers are ridiculous."

Indexing your comments and remarks is another way to help you avoid generalizing. To index is to acknowledge that each individual is unique. Rather than announcing that all doctors are abrupt, you could say, "My child's pediatrician spends a lot of time with me, but my internist never answers my questions." This helps you remember that doctor number one is not the same as doctor number two.

Greek or Geek? To Apply Here, You Must Speak Geek

Unlike most other job sectors, jobs in Canada's high-tech sector are easy to obtain. Or are they? Before even beginning to consider a job in Canada's state-of-the-art silicon sector, an individual must be fluently bilingual—in English as well as in "geek," the esoteric language of constructing the superhighway.

How fluent are you in the **restricted code** or **jargon** of "geek"? Although the following job descriptions may seem "Greek" to you, they are actually from a typical page in the High-Tech Career Ads of *The Globe and Mail*.

Static Evaluation: The Language of Rigidity

You change. Your world changes. An ancient Greek philosopher said it best: "You can never step in the same river twice." A **static evaluation** is a statement that fails to recognize change; labels in particular have a tendency to freeze-frame our awareness. Ruby, known as the class nerd in high school, is today a successful and polished business person; the old label does not fit.

In addition, some of us suffer from hardening of the categories. Our world view is so rigid that we can never change or expand our perspective. But the world is a technicolour moving target. Just about the time we think we have things neatly figured out and categorized, something moves. Our labels may not reflect the buzzing, booming, zipping process of change. It is important to acknowledge that perception is a process, and to avoid trying to nail things down permanently into all-inclusive categories.

General semanticists use the metaphorical expression "the map is not the territory" to illustrate the concept of static evaluation. Like a word, a map symbolizes or represents reality. Yet our road system is constantly changing. New roads are built, old ones are closed. If you were to use a 1949 map to guide you from St. Andrew's, New Brunswick, to Winnipeg, Manitoba, the current highway system would not even be on it, and you would probably lose your way. Similarly, if we use old labels and do not adjust our thinking to accommodate change, we will be semantically lost.

Perhaps you have a parent who still uses "old maps" when you come home to visit, expecting that you will be there for dinner each night and will still eat four helpings at every meal. Your parent may not understand that you have changed, and his or her old map does not function well in your new territory. You may have to help construct a new one.

To avoid static evaluation yourself, try dating your observations and indicate to others the time period from which you are drawing your conclusion. If your second cousin comes to town for a visit, say, "When I last saw you, you loved to listen to Patti Smith." This allows for the possibility that your cousin's tastes may have changed during the last few years. But most importantly, try to observe and acknowledge changes in others. If you are practicing what you know about becoming other-oriented, you are unlikely to erect this barrier.

Polarization: The Language of Extremes

Describing and evaluating what we observe in terms of extremes, such as good or bad, old or new, beautiful or ugly, brilliant or stupid is known as **polarization**. General semanticists remind us that the world in which we live comes not in black and white but in a variety of colours, hues, and shades. If you describe things in extremes, leaving out the middle ground, then your language does not accurately reflect reality. And because of the power of words to create, you may believe your own pronouncements.

"You either love me or you don't love me," says Jerome.

"You're *always* trying to control me," replies Lisa.

Both people are overstating the case, using language to polarize their perceptions of the experience.

Family counsellors who listen to family feuds find that the tendency to see things from an either-or point of view is a classic symptom of a troubled relationship. Placing the entire blame on your partner for a problem in your relationship is an example of polarizing. Few relational difficulties are exclusively one-sided.

Fact-Inference Confusion: Jumping to Conclusions

Imagine this scene. You are a detective investigating a death. You are given the following information: (1) Leo and Moshia are lying together on the floor; (2) Leo and Moshia are dead; (3) they are surrounded by water and broken glass; (4) on the sofa near Leo and Moshia is a cat with its back arched, apparently ready to defend itself. Given these sketchy details, do you, the detective assigned to the case, have any theories about the cause of Leo and Moshia's demise? Perhaps they slipped on the water, crashed into a table, broke a vase, and died (that would explain the water and broken glass). Or maybe their attacker recently left the scene, and the cat is still distressed by the commotion. Clearly, you could make several inferences (conclusions based upon partial information) as to the probable cause of death. Oh yes, there is one detail we forgot to mention: Leo and Moshia are fish. Does that help?

We often spin grand explanations and hypotheses based upon sketchy details. Acting upon inferences, we may act as though the "facts" clearly point to a specific conclusion. Clearly determining the difference between a fact and an inference can help us more accurately use language to reach valid conclusions about what we see and experience.

What makes a fact a fact? Most students, when asked this question, respond by saying, "A fact is something that has been proven to be true." If that is the case, *how* has something been proven to be true? In a court of law, a fact is something that has been observed or witnessed. Anything else is speculation or inference.

"Did you see my client in your house, taking your jewellery?" asks the wise attorney.

"No," says the plaintiff.

"Then you do not know for a fact that my client is a thief."

"I guess not," the plaintiff admits.

The semantic problem occurs when we respond to something as if it were a fact (something observed), when in reality it is an inference (a conclusion based upon speculation):

"It's a fact that your mother doesn't like me."

"It's a fact that you will be poor all of your life."

"It's a fact that you will fail this course."

Each of these statements, although it might very well be true, misuses the term *fact*. If you cannot recognize when you are making an inference instead of stating a fact, you may give your judgments more credibility than they deserve.

Biased Language: Insensitivity Toward Others

Using words that reflect your biases toward other cultures or ethnic groups, or someone's gender, can create a word barrier for your listeners. Although TV, radio, and magazine articles may debate the merits of political correctness, it is clear that sexist or racially stereotypical language can offend others. In addition, such language ignores the fact that the world is constantly changing. Sexist language can reflect stereotypical attitudes or describe roles in exclusively male or female terms. Words such as alder*man*, mail*man*, and *man*kind ignore the fact that women are part of the workforce and the human race. Contrast these with city councillor, letter carrier, and humankind, which are gender neutral and allow for the inclusion of both men and women. Or, rather than eliminating the word *man* from your vocabulary, try to use appropriate labels when you know the gender of the subject. A male police officer is a policeman; a female police officer is a policewoman. Rather than salesperson, you could say salesman or saleswoman, depending upon the gender of the seller.

O'Donnell found that even dictionaries fall into patterns of describing men and women with discriminatory language.[14] Included in the *Oxford English Dictionary* definition for *woman* were (1) an adult female being, (2) female servant, (3) a lady-love or mistress and (4) a wife. Men were described in more positive and distinguished terms: (1) a human being, (2) the human creation regarded abstractly, (3) an adult male endowed with many qualities, and (4) a person of importance of position.

Many of our social conventions also diminish or ignore the importance of women:

Sexist	Unbiased
I'd like you to meet Dr. and Mrs. John Chao.	I'd like you to meet Dr. Sue Ho and Dr. John Chao. They are husband and wife.
	or
	I'd like you to meet John Chao and Sue Ho. They're both doctors at Mercy Hospital.
Let me introduce Mr. Tom Bertolone and his wife Beverly.	Let me introduce Beverly and Tom Bertolone.

We have, however, made more substantial progress in reflecting changes and changed attitudes toward women in the professional arena. Compare the terms we use to describe workers now with those used in the 1950s:

Terms Used Today	Terms Used in 1950s
Flight attendant	Stewardess
Fire fighter	Fireman
Police officer	Policeman
Physician	Female doctor
Women at the office	Girls at work
Ms.	Miss/Mrs.
People/humans	Mankind

Consciously remembering to use nonsexist language will result in several benefits.[15] First, nonsexist language reflects nonsexist attitudes. Your attitudes are reflected in your speech and your speech affects your attitudes. Monitoring your speech for sexist remarks can help you monitor your attitudes about sexist assumptions you may hold. Second, using nonsexist language will help you become more other-oriented. Monitoring your language for sexist remarks will reflect your sensitivity to others. Third, nonsexist language will make your speech more contemporary and unambiguous. By substituting the word *humankind* for *mankind*,

LEARNING INTERPERSONAL COMMUNICATION SKILLS

for example, you can communicate that you are including all people, not just men, in your observation or statement. And finally, your nonsexist language will empower others. By eliminating sexist bias from your speech, you will help confirm the value of all the individuals with whom you interact.

In addition to monitoring your language for sexual stereotypes, avoid racial and ethnic stereotypes. Monitor your speech so that you are not, even unconsciously, using phrases that depict a racial group or ethnic group in a negative, stereotypical fashion. The underlying principle in avoiding biased language is to be other-oriented and to imagine how the listener might react to your words. As we shall see in the next section, this is also the underlying principle in strategies for establishing supportive relationships with others.

RECAP   **Word Barriers**

Barrier	Definition	Examples
Bypassing	Misinterpreting a word that evokes different meanings for different people.	W. C. might mean wayside chapel to a Swiss and water closet to someone from England.
Bafflegab	Unnecessary use of many abstract words.	"Please extinguish all smoking materials" instead of "No Smoking."
Lack of Clarity	Words used inappropriately or in imprecise ways.	Sign in Acapulco hotel: The manager has personally passed all the water served here.
Allness	Lumping things or people into all-encompassing categories.	All Texans drive pickup trucks and hang a rifle in their back windows.
Static Evaluation	Labelling people, objects, and events without considering change.	You call your twenty-eight-year-old nephew a juvenile delinquent because he spray-painted your fence when he was eleven.
Polarization	Description in either-or terms— good or bad, right or wrong.	You're either for me or against me.
Fact-Inference Confusion	Pronouncing something as a fact without directly observing it or verifying it through the authority of an expert's research or observation.	It is a fact that cats are smarter than dogs.
Biased Language	Language that reflects gender, racial, or ethnic biases.	My mom is a mailman.

Using Words to Establish Supportive Relationships

Imagine that you are a corporate manager attending a professional meeting. A counterpart from another company approaches you and says, "I'm Harvey

Michaels. I read your letter to the editor of the *Ottawa Citizen* yesterday, and I don't think you understand the first thing about the future of our industry." This stranger's critique more than likely makes you feel defensive: you want to protect yourself or strike back. Or you want to run away. The climate is not conducive to developing a quality relationship.

For more than three decades Jack Gibb's observational research has been used as a framework for both describing and prescribing verbal behaviours that contribute to feelings of either supportiveness or defensiveness.[16] Gibb spent several years listening to and observing groups of individuals in meetings and conversations, noting that some exchanges seemed to create a supportive climate, whereas others created a defensive one.

Words and actions, he concluded, are tools we use to let someone know whether we support them or not. In Chapter 5, we saw how nonverbal cues can affect the quality of relationships. Now let's consider how you can use words to create a supportive climate rather than an antagonistic one.

Describe Your Own Feelings Rather Than Evaluate Others

Most of us don't like to be judged or evaluated. Criticizing and name-calling obviously can create relational problems, but so can our attempts to diagnose others' problems or win their affection with insincere praise. In fact, any form of evaluation creates a climate of defensiveness. As Winston Churchill declared, "I am always ready to learn, although I do not always like being taught." Correcting others, even when we are doing it "for their own good" can raise their hackles.

One way to avoid evaluating others is to eliminate the accusatory *you* from your language. Statements such as, "You always come in late for supper," or "You need to

---

COMMUNICATION EXPERIENCE

Practice Using *I* Language

An essential skill in being supportive rather than defensive is describing what you want with *I* language rather than *you* language. Rephrase the following *you* statements into *I* statements.

You Language	*I* Language
1. You are messy when you cook.	_____
2. Your driving is terrible.	_____
3. You never listen to me.	_____
4. You just lie on the couch and never offer to help me.	_____
5. You always decide what movie we see.	_____

pick up the dirty clothes in your room," attack a person's sense of self-worth and usually result in a defensive reaction.

Instead, use the word *I* to describe your own feelings and thoughts about a situation or event: "I find it hard to keep your supper warm when you're late," or "I don't enjoy the extra work of picking up your dirty clothes." When you describe your own feelings instead of berating the receiver of the message, you are in essence taking ownership of the problem. This approach leads to greater openness and trust because your listener does not feel rejected or as if you are trying to control him or her.

Solve Problems Rather Than Control Others

When you were younger, your parents gave you rules to keep you safe. Even though you may have resented their control, you needed to know what was hot, when not to cross the street, and not to stick your finger in a light socket. Now that you are an adult, when people treat you like a child, it often means they are trying to control your behaviour, to take away your options. In truth, we have little or no control over someone else's behaviour.

Most of us don't like to be controlled. Someone who presumes to tell us what's good for us, instead of helping us puzzle through issues and problems, is likely to engender defensiveness. Open-ended questions such as, "What seems to be the problem?" or "How can we deal with the issue?" create a more supportive climate than critical comments such as, "Here's where you are wrong" or commands such as, "Don't do that!"

Be Genuine Rather Than Manipulative

To be genuine means that you honestly seek to be yourself rather than someone you are not. It also means taking an honest interest in others and considering the uniqueness of each individual and situation, avoiding generalizations or strategies that focus only on your own needs and desires. A manipulative person has hidden agendas; a genuine person uses words to discuss issues and problems openly and honestly.

Empathize Rather Than Remain Detached from Others

Empathy is one of the hallmarks of supportive relationships. As we learned earlier, empathy is the ability to understand the feelings of others and to predict the emotional responses they will have to different situations. The opposite of empathy is neutrality. To be neutral is to be indifferent or apathetic toward another. Even when you express anger or irritation toward another, you are investing some energy in the relationship.

After an unsuccessful attempt to persuade his family to take a trip to Banff National Park, Preston declared, "I don't care what you think, that's where we're going." His proclamation reflects a disregard for the feelings of others in his family. This insensitivity is self-defeating. The defensive climate Preston creates with his words will probably prevent the whole family from enjoying the vacation.

Be Flexible Rather Than Rigid Toward Others

Most people don't like someone who always seems certain that he or she is right. A "you're wrong, I'm right" attitude creates a defensive climate. This does not mean that you should have no opinions and go through life blithely agreeing to everything. And it doesn't mean that there is *never* one answer that is right and others that are wrong. But instead of making rigid pronouncements, you can use phrases such as, "I may be wrong, but it seems to me . . .," or "Here's one way to look at this problem." This manner of speaking gives your opinions a softer edge that allows room for others to express a point of view.

Present Yourself as Equal Rather Than Superior

You can antagonize others by letting them know that you view yourself as better or brighter than they are. You may be gifted and intelligent, but it's not necessary to announce it. And although some people have the responsibility and authority to manage others, "pulling rank" does not usually produce a cooperative climate. With phrases such as, "Let's work on this together," or "We each have a valid perspective," you can avoid erecting walls of resentment and suspicion.

Also, avoid using bafflegab to impress others. Keep your messages short and clear, and use informal language. When you communicate with someone from another culture, you may need to use an **elaborated code** to get your message across. This means that your messages will have to be more explicit, but they should not be condescending. Two of your authors remember vividly trying to explain to a French exchange student what a fire ant was. First, we had to translate *ant* into French, and then we had to provide scientific, descriptive, and narrative evidence to help the student understand how these tiny biting insects terrorize people in the southern part of the United States.

RECAP   **Using Words to Value Others**

Describe your feelings instead of evaluating the behaviour of others.

Keep the focus on problem solving, not control.

Be genuine rather than manipulative in your approach.

Show that you understand another person's point of view.

Make it clear that you do not have all the answers.

Present yourself as equal rather than as a superior.

Using Words to Value Others

just don't feel appreciated any more," confides Charlene during her counselling session. "My husband Gailyn just doesn't let me know he cares for me." One of the key skills in maintaining a long-term relationship is to know how to demonstrate that you value the other person. It's not just *nice* to know that someone cares about us; it is vital that we know others have genuine feelings of concern for us. In addition to acts of kindness, it is our words that let others know we appreciate them.

Researchers have identified ways we use language to confirm or disconfirm others.[17] A **confirming response** is a statement that causes others to value themselves more. Conversely, a **disconfirming response** is one that causes others to value themselves less.

The words we select to communicate our feelings *do* affect our relationships with others. The Electronic Connections box below illustrates how confirming responses can bolster another person's self-esteem and lead to a meaningful relationship.

ELECTRONIC CONNECTIONS

The Power of Confirming Responses

A Disabled Writer Finds a Friend Along the Information Superhighway

To Chris Young, e-mail is the great equalizer. Nearly 10 years ago, my wife, Pamela, "met" Chris through the engaging messages he'd posted in CompuServe's Issues Forum. Chris's thoughts and writing style caught Pamela's eye; she happened to mention how much she enjoyed the postings to forum administrator Georgia Griffith, who, in turn, relayed her compliments to Chris.

"When Georgia wrote [via e-mail] to tell me, I laughed out loud," Chris recalls today. That was partly because he'd never thought of himself as a writer, but it was also because he knew Pamela had no idea what a physical challenge each of his messages posed. Chris was born with a congenital neuromuscular disease similar to muscular dystrophy and he spends his days in a motorized wheelchair. He has never walked, has limited use

of his right hand and types by poking the computer keys, one laborious letter at a time, with a wooden pointer.

"Years ago," he says, "when I first started using e-mail, I was shocked when I realized that some of my on-line acquaintances didn't know about my disability. For the first time in my life, people had the opportunity to meet the real me before seeing my disability, which doesn't happen when I meet someone face to face." Often, however, Chris chooses to tell people on-line about his disability. "I'm not fully myself without my disability," says Chris. "It gives me a unique perspective on life that I can share with others."

Chris and Pamela began a regular e-mail correspondence. In Chris's messages—each are thousands of words long and represent hours of painstaking labor—the young computer programmer shared his life stories with the grace, insight and humor of a seasoned writer.

"Where some people spill their guts onto blank pages starting with the words 'Dear Diary,'

my personal journals have been in the form of e-mail that begins 'Dear Pamela,'" Chris says. "It's somehow more significant to me knowing a real live human being is on the other end of the line than it would be pouring my soul onto pages that might never see the light of day. Also the distance between us provides some safety. Pamela will likely never meet most of the characters in my life, so I am totally free to speak my mind about them."

Chris credits Pamela's support for inspiring him to pursue his writing professionally. Over the past few years, several of his articles have appeared in technical computer magazines. His first book, *Ray Tracing Creations*, about computer graphics, was recently published by The Waite Group; the dedication reads, "To my friend, Pamela, who convinced me I could write."

Confirming Responses

The adage, People judge us by our words and behaviour rather than by our intent, summarizes the underlying principle of confirming responses. Those who receive your messages determine whether they have the effect you intended. Formulating confirming responses requires careful listening and attention to the other person. We will describe several kinds of confirming responses here:

■ DIRECT ACKNOWLEDGMENT

When you respond directly to something another person says to you, you are acknowledging not only the statement, but also that the person is important.

Joan: It certainly is a nice day for a canoe trip.

Mariko: Yes, Joan, it's a great day to be outside.

■ AGREEMENT ABOUT JUDGMENTS

When you confirm someone's evaluation of something, you are also affirming that person's sense of taste and judgment.

Nancy: I think the steel guitar player's riff was fantastic.

Victor: Yes, I thought it was the best part of the performance.

■ SUPPORTIVE RESPONSE

When you express reassurance and understanding, you are confirming a person's right to his or her feelings.

Lionel: I'm disappointed that I only scored a 60 on my interpersonal communication test.

Sarah: I'm sorry to see you so sad, Lionel. I know that test was important to you.

Complimenting someone for a job well done is a powerful way to confirm that person's self worth. (Jeff Person)

■ CLARIFYING RESPONSE

When you seek greater understanding of another person's message, you are confirming that he or she is worth your time and trouble. Clarifying responses also encourage the other person to talk in order to explore his or her feelings.

Larry: I'm not feeling very good about my family situation these days.

Tyrone: Is it tough with you and Margo working different shifts?

■ EXPRESSION OF POSITIVE FEELING

We feel confirmed or valued when someone else agrees with our expression of joy or excitement.

Lorraine: I'm so excited! I was just promoted to associate professor.

Dorette: Congratulations! I'm so proud of you! Heaven knows you deserve it.

▪ COMPLIMENT

When you tell people you like what they have done or said, what they are wearing, or how they look, you are confirming their sense of worth.

Jean Christophe: Did you get the invitation to my party?"

Manny: Yes! It looked so professional. I didn't know you could do calligraphy. You're a talented guy.

In each of these examples, note how the responder provides comments that confirm the worth or value of the other person. But we want to caution that confirming responses should be sincere. Offering false praise is manipulative, and your communication partner will probably sniff out your phoniness.

RECAP   **Responses That Confirm Another Person's Self-Worth**

Directly acknowledge something someone has said.

Agree with the person's judgments.

Be supportive; let the other person know you are trying to understand how he or she feels.

Ask questions to help clarify another person's statements if you are not sure you understand.

Express positive feelings to echo those of the other person.

Compliment the person if you can be sincere.

Disconfirming Responses

Some statements and responses can undermine another person's self-worth. We offer these categories so that you can avoid using them and also recognize when someone is trying to chip away at your self-image and self-esteem.

▪ IMPERVIOUS RESPONSE

When a person fails to acknowledge your statement or attempt to communicate, even though you know he or she heard you, you may feel a sense of awkwardness or embarrassment.

Rosa: I loved your speech, Harvey.

Harvey: (No response, verbal or nonverbal.)

▪ INTERRUPTING RESPONSE

When people interrupt you, they may be implying that what they have to say is more important than what you have to say. In effect, they could also be implying that they are more important than you are.

Anna: I just heard on the news that . . .

Sharon: Oh yes. The stock market just went down 100 points.

■ IRRELEVANT RESPONSE

An irrelevant response is one that has nothing at all to do with what you were saying. Chances are your partner is not listening to you at all.

Arnold: First we're flying down to Rio, and then to Quito. I can hardly wait to . . .

Peter: They're predicting a hard freeze tonight.

The real message Peter is sending is, "I have more important things on my mind."

■ TANGENTIAL RESPONSE

A tangential response is one that acknowledges you, but that is only minimally related to what you are talking about. Again, it indicates that the other person isn't really attending to your message.

Richard: This new program will help us stay within our budget.

Samantha: Yeah. I think I'll save some bucks and send this letter by regular mail.

■ IMPERSONAL RESPONSE

A response that intellectualizes and uses the third person distances the other person from you and has the effect of trivializing what you say.

Diana: Hey, Bill. I'd like to talk with you for a minute about getting your permission to take my vacation in July.

Bill: One tends to become interested in recreational pursuits about this time of year, doesn't one?

■ INCOHERENT RESPONSE

When a speaker mumbles, rambles, or makes some unintelligible effort to respond, it may leave you wondering if what you said was of any value or use to the listener.

Paolo: George, here's my suggestion for the merger deal with Canatech. Let's make them an offer of forty-eight dollars a share and see how they respond.

George: Huh? Well . . . So . . . Well . . . hmmm . . . I'm not sure.

■ INCONGRUOUS RESPONSE

As we saw in Chapter 5, when a verbal message is inconsistent with nonverbal behaviour, we usually believe the nonverbal message, but we usually feel confused as well. An incongruous response is like a malfunctioning traffic light with flashing red and green lights—you're just not sure whether the speaker wants you to go or stay.

Sue: Honey, do you want me to go grocery shopping with you?

Steve: (Shouting) OF COURSE I DO! WHY ARE YOU ASKING?

Supportive-Defensive Communication Charades

Divide into groups of two to four people. Each team or group should prepare a short play depicting one of the supportive or defensive communication responses described in this chapter. Perform your play for the class or another team to see if they can identify the type of supportive or defensive communication behaviour your team is portraying. Consider one of the following situations or develop one of your own:

Speaking with a professor about a grade.

Returning a broken item to a store.

Talking with your child about his or her grades.

Responding to a telemarketing salesperson who calls you during dinner.

Talking with one of your employees who made a work-related mistake.

Re-booking a flight because your flight was cancelled by the airline.

Taking an order from a customer at a fast-food restaurant.

Receiving a complaint from a customer about poor service.

Talking with someone who has knocked on your door inviting you to his or her church.

Asking someone to turn down the stereo or TV while you are trying to study.

Variation: Instead of illustrating supportive and defensive communication, roleplay an example of one of the confirming or disconfirming communication behaviours discussed in this chapter.

The key to shared understanding is to focus on the needs, goals, and mind-set of your communication partner. Throughout this chapter we have emphasized how to develop an other-oriented approach to communicating verbally. You can use a few slogans to remind yourself of what you have read:

Slogan # 1: *Meanings are in people not in words.*

Words are arbitrary, contextually and culturally bound symbols that can have denotative and connotative, concrete or abstract meaning. Focus on what the words may mean to your partner.

Slogan # 2: *Think before you speak.*

Words have power to create and affect feelings and actions, as well as to affect and reflect culture. Before you speak, consider the impact your words will have on others. Remember that words can hurt—and once spoken, words cannot be taken back.

Slogan # 3: *Say what you mean and mean what you say.*

Given the complexity of the meaning creation process, it is a wonder that we communicate as accurately as we do. When speaking with others, be mindful of the potential for miscommu-nication and misunderstanding. Use precise language and be accurate in conveying your true feelings. Remember that you are responsible for what you communicate. The spoken word belongs half to the person who speaks and half to the person who understands.

Slogan # 4: *Speak to others as you wish to be spoken to.*

Our words can engender a supportive communication climate or create defensiveness, which can lead to misunder-standing. Always try to put yourself in your partner's place.

Although it may be impossible to eliminate all disconfirming responses from your repertoire, becoming aware of the power of your words and monitoring your conversation for offensive phrases may help you avoid unexpected and perhaps devastating consequences.

Summary

The words we use have great power to affect our self-image and to influence the relationships we establish with others. English words are symbols that refer to objects, events, people, and ideas. They are arbitrary. We interpret their meaning through the context and culture to which they belong. Communication is complex because most words have both denotative (literal) meanings and connotative (subjective) meanings, and because words range from concrete to abstract.

The power of words stems from their ability to create images and to influence our thoughts, feelings, and actions. There is also an important link between the words we use and our culture. Language shapes culture and culture shapes language. Our view of the world is influenced by our vocabulary and the categories we have created with words.

Several word barriers can contribute to misunderstanding in interpersonal communications. Bypassing occurs when a word means one thing to one person and another to someone else. Our verbal expressions may lack clarity, either because we make language errors or because the meaning we want to convey is not clear to us. Allness statements can mislead and alienate listeners because the speaker falsely implies that he or she knows all there is to know about something. Another barrier, static evaluation, fails to take changes into account and uses outdated labels and categories. Polarization is the language of extremes; when someone thinks in black and white, many shades of meaning disappear. Confusing facts with inferences results in jumping to conclusions that are not based upon direct observations. Finally, biased language that is insensitive to others creates noise that interferes with the meaning of a message.

The words you use can enhance or detract from the quality of relationships you establish with others. Supportive communication is descriptive rather than evaluative, problem oriented rather than control oriented, genuine rather than contrived or manipulative, empathic rather than neutral, flexible rather than rigid, and equal rather than superior. The words we use can either confirm or undermine another's sense of self-worth. If you directly acknowledge people, agree with their judgments, voice support when they feel bad, ask them to clarify their messages, affirm their positive feelings, and compliment them sincerely, then you may help them boost their self-image. Conversely, our responses can be disconfirming if we are impervious, interrupt someone, or use irrelevant, tangential, impersonal, incoherent, or incongruous messages.

For Discussion and Review

■ FOCUS ON COMPREHENSION

1. How do words create meaning for others?

2. What are some barriers to effective understanding, and what are strategies for overcoming these barriers?

3. What are the characteristics of a supportive communicator?

4. What are confirming communication responses? Describe a few.

5. What are disconfirming communication responses? Describe a few.

■ FOCUS ON CRITICAL THINKING

6. Marge and Paul are having an argument. Paul shouts, "You're constantly criticizing me! You don't let me make any important decisions!" How could Paul communicate how he feels in a more supportive way?

7. Alan asked Jessie to pick him up after work at the circle drive at 5:30 P.M. Jessie waited patiently at the circle drive on the other side of campus and finally went home at 6:30 P.M., having seen no sign of Alan. Alan was waiting at the circle drive behind his office rather than at the one on the other side of the campus. What word barriers do you think led to this misunderstanding?

8. Rephrase the following statements to use less biased language:

   A. I'd like to introduce Mr. Russell Browne and his wife Muriel.

   B. In an office memo: "Several gals have been leaving their purses at their desks."

9. Rephrase the following statements, using the skill of indexing.

   A. All politicians want power and control over others.

   B. All teachers are underpaid.

   C. All Vancouverites like to brag about how great their city is.

■ FOCUS ON ETHICS

10. If you really don't want to listen to your co-worker go into detail about her latest vacation trip or provide details about the recent escapades of her children or grandchildren, is it appropriate to tell her that you'd rather not hear her "news"? Support your response.

11. Is it ethical to correct someone when he or she uses sexist language or makes a stereotypical remark about someone's race, gender, or sexual orientation? What if that person is your boss or your teacher? Explain your answer.

12. Is it ethical to mask your true feelings of anger and irritation with someone by using supportive statements or confirming statements when what you really want to do is tell him or her "the truth" in no uncertain terms?

For Your Journal

1. Keep a log of examples of word barriers you experience or encounter. Note examples of bypassing, lack of precision in language, bafflegab, and other uses of words that inhibit communication. The examples could come from your own verbal exchanges or those that you observe in the conversations of others.

2. Make a list of words that are in your vocabulary today but were not in your vocabulary five years ago. Include new vocabulary words that you may have learned in school as well as words that were not generally used or that have been coined in the last half-decade (e.g., CD-ROM).

3. Record a sample dialogue between you and a good friend that illustrates some of the confirming responses described on pages 190–191.

Learning with Others

1. Think of a bypass miscommunication that you've experienced. Share your recollection with a small group and compare your feelings and responses with those of others.

2. In your group, choose one person to play a recently divorced person whose spouse is not abiding by a child custody agreement and insists on seeing the children at odd hours. Another person should play the role of a trusted friend who only listens and responds. Ask the trusted friend to use the skills he or she learned in this chapter along with effective listening skills presented in Chapter 4. Then do a group evaluation of his or her response.

3. To practice separating facts from inferences, read each of the following stories. Assume that all the information presented is accurate, and refer to the story whenever you wish.

   Next read the statements and mark whether the statement is definitely true on the basis of the information in the story (T) or definitely false (F). The ? means that you cannot be certain on the basis of the information in the story; mark this if any part of a statement is doubtful.

Story A

As you step onto your front porch from your living room, you observe a delivery truck approaching along the street. You see that your next-door neighbour is backing her car from her garage into the street in the path of the approaching truck. You see the truck swerve, climb over the curb, and come to a stop against a tree, which crumples one of the truck's front fenders.

■ STATEMENTS ABOUT STORY A

1. Your next-door neighbour was backing her car into the street in the path of an approaching truck.   **T   F   ?**

2. The delivery truck was travelling at a reasonable speed.   **T   F   ?**

3. The only damage resulting from the incident was to the truck's fender.   **T   F   ?**

4. You saw the truck swerve and climb over the curb.   **T   F   ?**

5. Your neighbour across the street was backing her car out of the garage.   **T   F   ?**

6. The truck suffered no damage.   **T   F   ?**

7. You saw the truck approaching as you stepped onto your front porch from your living room.   **T   F   ?**

8. The man who drove the delivery truck swerved and ran his truck up over a curb.   **T   F   ?**

9. The delivery truck driver swerved in order to miss a child playing in the street.   **T   F   ?**

Story B

A husband, wife, and their sons aged eleven and fourteen drove cross-country on a vacation trip in their three-year-old automobile. They started the trip on a Friday, the thirteenth of the month. The wife said she did not like the idea of leaving on that day and the man laughed at her statement. In the course of the trip the following mishaps occurred:

The automobile radiator sprang a leak.
The eleven-year-old boy became carsick for the first time in his life.
The wife was badly sunburned.
The husband lost his fishing rod.

■ STATEMENTS ABOUT STORY B

1. There were fewer than two children in the family.   **T   F   ?**

2. The sedan's radiator sprang a leak.   **T   F   ?**

3. The wife really didn't mind leaving on Friday the thirteenth.	**T**	**F**	**?**
4. A fishing reel was lost.	**T**	**F**	**?**
5. The family's trip began on Friday the thirteenth.	**T**	**F**	**?**
6. The eleven-year-old boy lost his fishing rod.	**T**	**F**	**?**
7. The story mentions the name of the family taking the trip.	**T**	**F**	**?**
8. The make of the automobile in which the family made the trip was not mentioned in the story.	**T**	**F**	**?**
9. The husband laughed at his wife's fears of Friday the thirteenth.	**T**	**F**	**?**

Story C

John and Betty Smith are awakened in the middle of the night by a noise coming from the direction of their living room. Smith investigates and finds that the door opening into the garden, which he thought he had locked before going to bed, is standing wide open. Books and papers are scattered all over the floor around the desk in one corner of the room.

■ STATEMENTS ABOUT STORY C

1. Mrs. Smith was awakened in the middle of the night.	**T**	**F**	**?**
2. Smith locked the door from his living room to his garden before going to bed.	**T**	**F**	**?**
3. The books and papers were scattered between the time Mr. Smith went to bed and the time he was awakened.	**T**	**F**	**?**
4. Smith found that the door opening into the garden was shut.	**T**	**F**	**?**
5. Mr. Smith did not lock the garden door.	**T**	**F**	**?**
6. John Smith was not awakened by a noise.	**T**	**F**	**?**
7. Nothing was missing from the room.	**T**	**F**	**?**
8. Mrs. Smith was sleeping when she and Mr. Smith were awakened.	**T**	**F**	**?**
9. The noise did not come from their garden.	**T**	**F**	**?**
10. Smith saw no burglar in the living room.	**T**	**F**	**?**
11. Mr. and Mrs. Smith were awakened in the middle of the night by a noise.	**T**	**F**	**?**

Developed by T. Richard Chetham and Robert Sherman for *Oral Communication Handbook* (Warrensbury, MO: Central Missouri State University, 1972).

SYMBOL: A word, sound, or visual device that represents a thought, concept, or object.

REFERENT: The thing that a symbol represents.

THOUGHT: The mental process of creating a category, idea, or image triggered by a referent or symbol.

HIGH-CONTEXT CULTURE: A culture in which the meaning of messages is highly dependent upon context and nonverbal cues.

LOW-CONTEXT CULTURE: A culture that relies primarily on language to communicate messages.

SYMBOLIC INTERACTION: A theory that suggests societies are bound together through common use of symbols.

DENOTATIVE MEANING: The restrictive or literal meaning of a word.

CONNOTATIVE MEANING: The personal and subjective meaning of a word.

LINGUISTIC DETERMINISM: A theory that describes how use of language determines or influences thoughts and perceptions.

WORLD VIEW: A culturally acquired perspective for interpreting experiences.

BYPASSING: The same words mean different things to different people.

MALAPROPISM: The confusion of one word or phrase for another that sounds similar to it.

RESTRICTED CODE: Using words that have a meaning to a person, group, or culture.

JARGON: Another name for restricted code; specialized terms or abbreviations whose meaning is known only to members of a specific group.

ALLNESS: The tendency to use language to make unqualified, often untrue generalizations.

INDEXING: A way of avoiding allness statements by separating one situation, person, or example from another.

STATIC EVALUATION: Pronouncing judgment on something without taking changes into consideration.

POLARIZATION: Describing and evaluating what we observe in terms of extremes such as good or bad, old or new, beautiful or ugly.

ELABORATED CODE: Using many words and various ways of describing an idea or concept to communicate its meaning.

CONFIRMING RESPONSE: A statement that causes another person to value himself or herself more.

DISCONFIRMING RESPONSE: A statement that causes another person to value himself or herself less.

Understanding Interpersonal Relationships

hy are we attracted to some people and not to others? How do we begin relationships, and what are the best strategies for keeping them alive? What makes some relationships last for years and some fall apart? These are just some of the questions we will explore in this unit as we build upon our understanding of interpersonal communication skills and principles. Chapter 7 reviews classic principles that can help explain and predict why we develop relationships with others. Chapter 8 discusses how we initiate and nurture relationships. Chapter 9 explains the sometimes mysterious process of how relationships mature and die.

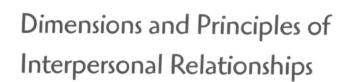

Dimensions and Principles of Interpersonal Relationships

After studying this chapter, you should be able to:

1. Explain relationships of circumstance and relationships of choice.

2. Describe three dimensions of interpersonal relationships.

3. Identify the qualities associated with communication in interpersonal relationships.

4. Explain the model of the stages of relational development.

5. Discuss eight principles of interpersonal relationships.

■ RELATIONSHIPS OF CIRCUMSTANCE AND RELATIONSHIPS OF CHOICE

■ TRUST, INTIMACY, AND POWER IN RELATIONSHIPS

■ COMMUNICATION QUALITIES OF INTERPERSONAL RELATIONSHIPS

■ STAGES OF INTERPERSONAL RELATIONSHIPS

■ PRINCIPLES OF INTERPERSONAL RELATIONSHIPS

Pat: Hi, aren't you in my communication course?

Chris: Oh, yeah, I've seen you across the room.

Pat: What do you think about the course so far?

Chris: It's okay but I feel a little intimidated by some of the class activities.

Pat: I know what you mean. It gets kind of scary to talk about yourself in front of everyone else.

Chris: Yeah. Plus some of the stuff you hear. I was paired up with this one student the other day who started talking about being arrested last year on a drug charge.

Pat: Really? I bet I know who that is. I don't think you have to worry about it.

Chris: Don't mention that I said anything.

Pat: It's okay. I know that guy, and he just likes to act big.

This interaction between Pat and Chris illustrates the reciprocal nature of interpersonal communication and interpersonal relationships. As you learned in Chapter 1, **interpersonal relationships** are connections that we develop with other people as a direct result of our interpersonal communication with them. The character and quality of interpersonal communication is affected, in turn, by the nature of the relationship.

The conversation between Pat and Chris begins with a casual acknowledgment but quickly proceeds to a higher level of intimacy. Chris confides in Pat. Pat, an other-oriented listener, offers confirmation and support; this response encourages Chris to confide even more. In this brief encounter, Pat and Chris have laid the groundwork for transforming their casual acquaintanceship into an intimate relationship.

In the next three chapters, we will explore the dynamic link between interpersonal communication and interpersonal relationships. Drawing from the understanding of communication you have acquired from the first six chapters, you will learn about the nature of relationships, their development from initiation to termination, and the specific communication skills you can apply to maintaining them.

In this chapter we will examine the nature of interpersonal relationships, building on the descriptions presented in Chapter 1. Then we will explore the stages of a relationship as it moves from ground zero to intimacy, and perhaps to termination. And finally, we will examine the principles that describe how relationships work.

Relationships of Circumstance and Relationships of Choice

In Chapter 1 an interpersonal relationship is defined as an ongoing connection we make with another person that we carry in our minds (and metaphorically, in our hearts), whether the other person is present or not. These ongoing connections can be formed either because of unintentional circumstances or because of intentional choice. **Relationships of circumstance** form not because we choose them, but simply because our lives overlap with others' in some way. Relationships with family members, teachers, classmates, and co-workers fall into this category. In contrast, when we seek out and intentionally develop a relationship with someone, that is a **relationship of choice**. These relationships might include acquaintances, friends, lovers, spouses, or counsellors.

It is chance that makes brothers but hearts that make friends.

—VON GEIBEL

We act and communicate differently in these two types of relationships because the stakes are different. The effect of the same interpersonal communication behaviour on different relationships can be dramatic. If we act in foolish or inappropriate ways, our friends might end the relationships. If we act the same way within the confines of our family, our relatives may not like us much, but we will still remain family.

Of course, these categories are not mutually exclusive. Relationships of circumstance can also be relationships of choice: your brother or sister can also be your best friend. You can break off interacting with family members or quit your job to sever your relationships with fellow employees. In addition, the other individual can define and redefine the relationship. Your boss might fire you, a relative might cut you off, or a lover might desert you.

RECAP	**Categories of Interpersonal Relationships**	
Term	Definition	Examples
Relationships of Circumstance	Those that exist because of the situation in which we find ourselves.	Mother, father, sister, subordinate, teacher, boss, waiter.
Relationships of Choice	Those we choose to initiate, maintain, and terminate.	Husbands and wives, best friends, and lovers.

Trust, Intimacy, and Power in Relationships

We can further examine interpersonal relationships along three dimensions that are always present in varying degrees: trust, intimacy, and power. Although we have touched upon these elements in other discussions, we will now examine more closely the role that they play in forming and maintaining relationships. You should recognize the importance interpersonal communication has in the development of these dimensions.

Trust

Think about the kind of trust you have in people who are important to you. What does it mean when you trust your doctor? Your lover or spouse? Your accountant? More than likely, each of these relationships involves a different kind of trust, as shown in Table 7.1.

In most interpersonal relationships, especially intimate ones, the last two categories of trust listed in Table 7.1 are the most important. Basically, **interpersonal trust** is the degree to which we feel safe in disclosing personal information to another person. We exhibit a variety of trusting behaviours: revealing intimate information about ourselves; displaying our vulnerability to another; displaying confidence in him or her.[1] As a relationship develops, we look for proof that our partner is **trustworthy**. We look for behaviours to assure us that he or she accepts our feelings and won't exploit them, and that he or she will protect our vulnerability and remain in the relationship. These behaviours include such things as not cheating, protecting information we have disclosed about ourselves, and continuing to show affection and closeness even when we reveal negative or threatening information. Our partner, in turn, expects the same from us. To sustain a close interpersonal relationship, both participants need to exhibit and expect trusting and trustworthy behaviour.[2]

Table 7.1

Types of Trust

Types of Trust	Explanation
Trust in someone's ability (accountant):	You believe that the person has the skill, knowledge, will, and ethical standards to do a good job or fulfill some role expectation.
Trust in someone's regard for your welfare (doctor):	You believe that this person will not cause you harm as you place your health, welfare, resources, and security in his or her hands.
Trust in someone's regard for privileged information (counsellor or friend):	You believe that the person to whom you have disclosed personal information will not use this information against you.
Trust in someone's relational commitment (lover or partner)	You believe that when you disclose personal information, the other will acknowledge your feelings and vulnerability, will not exploit you, and will remain in the relationship.

There is a direct correlation between how much we trust someone and how much we can potentially gain from a relationship. The more we trust, the more information we are willing to share about ourselves, and the closer the relationship becomes. Sometimes this sharing is selective. Students may tell their professors about very personal family problems, yet they would never tell them if they cheated on an exam. You may tell your parents about your finances and your academic progress, but you may be reluctant to tell them about the development of each of your new intimate relationships.

Intimacy

You have already seen that relationships range from nonintimate to intimate. But what does *intimate* mean, exactly? Sometimes the term refers to the sexual activity in a relationship, but that is not the way we are using the term intimacy here. Instead, **intimacy** means the degree to which we can be ourselves in front of another person and still be accepted by him or her. We can measure intimacy by the extent to which other people let us know that they see us the same way we see ourselves and express positive feelings about who we are. We depend upon intimate relationships to bolster our self-confidence. The more intimate the relationship, the more the individuals depend upon each other for acceptance and confirmation of their self-image.[3] During periods when we might not have very intimate relationships, it is sometimes hard to maintain a strong self-image.

We communicate our sense of intimacy directly and indirectly, verbally and nonverbally. We might tell another person how we feel about him or her and how much we value the relationship. We might also use a variety of nonverbal cues such as close physical proximity, eye contact, word selection, tone of voice, physical contact, and spending time together.

The more intimate a relationship, the stronger the emotional bond and the greater the mutual trust in relational commitment. Because we are placing confirmation of our self into another person's hands, there is a great deal of emotionality associated with developing and ending intimacy. The feeling of "being in love" can create a variety of emotional responses, depending upon the way we have been raised to deal with emotions, our emotional experiences, and our emotional self-image. We might welcome a growing sense of intimacy with excitement and enthusiasm, or turn away from it in fear.

Emotions sometimes fly in the face of reason. That is why we say that people are "blinded by love" or "infatuated." The roles that different emotions play in the development of intimacy are so many and varied that researchers and scholars have achieved little understanding of them. There is evidence that sharing and discussing emotions leads to a healthier life; generally, it is a good idea to talk about emotions with your partners as you attempt to understand and respect one another's needs and preferences.

As the following Arabian proverb so aptly puts it, intimacy is not simply a quality between lovers but also between good friends.

> *A friend is one*
> *to whom one may pour*
> *out all the contents*
> *of one's heart,*
> *chaff and grain together*
> *knowing that the*
> *gentlest of hands*
> *will take and sift it,*
> *keep what is worth keeping*
> *and with a breath of kindness*
> *blow the rest away.*

Partners in intimate relationships communicate their acceptance and affection for one another through both verbal and nonverbal cues. What signs of intimacy can you identify in this photo? (John Coletti)

Power

The third dimension in interpersonal relationships, power, might be the most significant of all. We might not realize it, but distributing power between partners requires a lot of subtle negotiation. Furthermore, our ability to do it successfully is a major factor in relational development. Power and control have been defined in a variety of ways,[4] but for our purposes **interpersonal power** means the ability to influence another in the direction you desire—to get another person to do what you want.

All interactions involve power. If you ask some friends to go to the movies with you, you are attempting to influence them. If they say no, they are mustering resistance and, in essence, demonstrating their power over you. If you get upset by their rejection, you might offer to buy your friends' tickets, or to drive. We will discuss the issue of interpersonal persuasion in Chapter 9. We will also discuss power when we examine the nature of conflict in Chapter 10, because power negotiations often create or intensify conflict.

Every relationship you have with another person falls on the continuum shown in Figure 7.1. At one extreme you have more power than your partner; at the other your partner has more power than you.

In some relationships, such as teacher to student or doctor to patient, there is a predefined imbalance of power. In Chapter 1, we referred to some relationships as complementary; in such relationships, one partner willingly hands over power to the other. For example, if one partner has trouble making decisions, he or she may feel comfortable letting the other partner make most of the purchases and plan most of the activities for the household. In a parallel relationship, power continually shifts from one partner to the other, depending upon the nature of the interaction or situation. For instance, if one partner is in charge of keeping the finances straight, he or she will have more power in budgetary decisions. If the other partner is a better cook, he or she probably will exert more power over decisions about diet and menus. When we try to equalize power in our relationships, we attempt to make them symmetrical. Although this might seem like an ideal to strive for, in fact, such attempts often backfire. When partners feel as if they have equal power over every decision, sometimes they compete with one another; neither one is willing to give in to the other person. The negotiation process can be time-consuming and ineffective when quick decisions are needed.

In all of these types of relationships, the balance of power affects how we talk and what we talk about; it is reflected in every message we convey. Read the sample interactions below to see if you can tell who has more power in each exchange.

■ INTERACTION ONE

Fong: Do you want me to sweep up the floor now?

Pearl: No, not yet. Go into the freezer and get me another container of fudge caramel.

Fong: Okay.

■ INTERACTION TWO

Mickey: So, do you want to go to a movie tonight, or just sit home and watch TV?

Sarah: I don't know. What movies are showing?

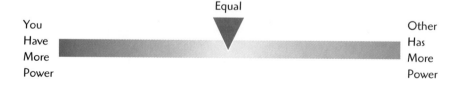

Figure 7.1

Interpersonal Power

III   UNDERSTANDING INTERPERSONAL RELATIONSHIPS

Mickey: Not much. Nothing new has come out for a few weeks.

Sarah: Why don't we just stay home?

▆ INTERACTION THREE

Al: I can't believe I failed that test. I don't think it was very fair. Should I go in and complain to the instructor?

Tika: Hey, you're the one who went out partying instead of studying.

Al: Don't remind me. Whose side are you on anyway? I don't need that kind of scolding.

Tika: You're always criticizing me for what I say to you. If you don't want my opinion, don't ask for it.

Al: Okay, I won't. Forget I said anything.

Interaction One is between an employee and a boss. Clearly, Pearl has more power than Fong in this situation. In Interaction Two, the power tends to shift back and forth, but Sarah makes the final decision. In the third interaction the power balance is less obvious, but the last two statements seem to indicate that Tika has the upper hand. In all of these interactions, the messages have both an obvious meaning and a more subtle one that reflects the power negotiation process. In the first interaction, Pearl easily could have surrendered power by telling Fong, "You can decide if it needs it now." We can always empower others by turning decision-making requests back to them.

When we communicate, we also affect the balance of power by exchanging information. Information is a source of power. Possessing special information or knowledge serves as the basis for expert power, which we will discuss in Chapter 10. In addition, when we trust another person enough to disclose information about ourselves, we give up control of that information, and empower the other person. If you reveal to a co-worker at a bank that you were arrested at your last job for embezzlement, sharing that information gives your co-worker a certain degree of power over you. He or she might threaten to tell your boss about your record in an attempt to force you to comply with a request. Typically, however, as relationships move toward intimacy, both partners share information with the other in a fairly equal manner, which gives both power over one another. We will discuss the process of disclosing personal information in more detail in Chapter 8.

Nonverbal behaviours and speech patterns also reflect an individual's perception of his or her power relative to the person with whom he or she interacts. Traditionally, our cultural norms classify men's speech patterns as more powerful than women's. To be masculine is to be loud and forceful; to speak in deeper tones; to swear often; and to be authoritarian and blunt. Feminine speech, in contrast, is gentle, smooth, friendly, warm, quick, gossipy, high pitched, nonverbally expressive, and frequent. In truth, however, individuals of both sexes are apt to adopt either style. Table 7.2 lists behaviours that our culture classifies as "powerful" and "powerless."

Table 7.2

Cues That Indicate Powerful and Powerless Speech

"Powerful" Speaker	"Powerless" Speaker
Talks first	Talks second if at all
Dominates speaking time	Doesn't talk much
Initiates conversations	Lets others initiate
Makes longer statements	Makes short statements/replies
Talks over others	Makes frequent hedging statements (Ah..., Um...)
Interrupts	Adds qualifiers (...if that's okay. Maybe)
Asks questions	Uses disclaimers (I'm not very good at...)
Uses expletives	Makes nervous gestures
	Makes frequent gestures
	Uses overly formal grammar
	Uses polite language (Please, Thanks)

COMMUNICATION EXPERIENCE

Form groups of three students. Student A and student B will engage in a debate. Student A will argue that all eighteen- to twenty-year-olds should do compulsory government service for a year. Student B will argue against that proposal. Student C should carefully listen and watch the other two, recording powerful and powerless speech cues. After three to five minutes, stop, and trade roles. Student A will record the power cues while student B argues that all incoming college students should be required to own a personal computer and student C argues against it. Again, stop after three to five minutes, and switch again. Student B will record while students A and C take opposite sides to debate whether we should extend the length of the elementary and high school year by an additional month.

After you have completed all three debates, share your observations about power cues. Which powerful and powerless cues did people use most often? What effect did the topic have upon the use of these cues? What effect did switching roles have? To what degree was each of you affected by your partner's use of powerful or powerless speech?

RECAP — Dimensions of Interpersonal Relationships

TRUST	The degree to which we are comfortable disclosing personal information about ourselves to another.
INTIMACY	The degree to which individuals depend upon each other for acceptance and confirmation of their self-image.
POWER	The ability to influence another person in a desired direction.

The following chart lists the qualities associated with friendship (and their importance) for three cultures. These qualities reflect inherent values of each culture, and, as you can see, vary widely.

North America	Korea	Nigeria
Trust (high)	Generosity (high)	Tolerance (high)
Respect (high)	Intelligence (high)	Honesty (high)
Authenticity (high)	Congeniality (moderate)	Caring (high)
Psychological support (low)	Sympathy (moderate)	Trust (high)
	Unselfishness (moderate)	Responsibility (moderate)
Responsibility (moderate)	Humor (low)	
Honesty (moderate)	Intelligence (low)	

From A. M. Nicotera[5]

Communication Qualities of Interpersonal Relationships

One of the most important ways to examine relationships is according to the communication qualities that are associated with them. As we saw in the dialogue between Pat and Chris at the beginning of this chapter, the way we interact with others reflects the nature of the relationship, and the relationship, in turn, affects the way we interact. The research team of Irwin Altman and Dalmas Taylor identified eight communication qualities that vary according to the level of intimacy or the stage of development for an interpersonal relationship.[6] Table 7.3 shows that as a relationship becomes more intimate, the communication moves from the eight restricted and impersonal qualities (left column) to their open and personal counterparts (right column). As a relationship decays, the reverse happens; communication becomes less open and less personal. Most interactions lie somewhere between the two poles, and all individual interactions can be categorized differently, even if they take place within the same relationship.

Think of the last time you visited a relative, for example, an uncle or aunt who you hadn't seen for a while. The conversation was probably narrow and public in style. You probably talked about school, past family activities, and other relatives, but really didn't get into personal matters. However, given your familiarity with each other, the communication might have been smooth, efficient, flexible, and unique. The pattern of conversation with this relative is probably much the same each time you visit with him or her. In general, the more stable a relationship, the more the qualities remain constant across interactions.

Table 7.3

Qualitites of Communication in Interpersonal Relationships[7]

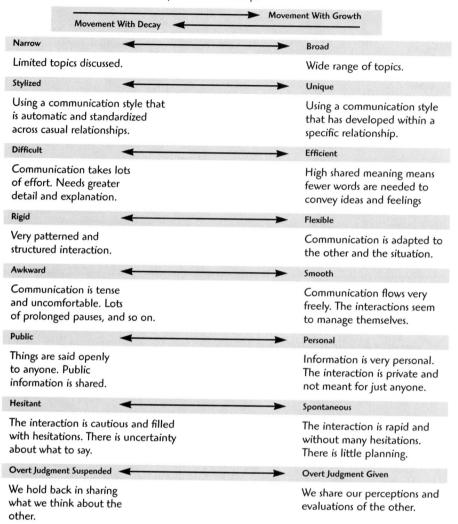

	Movement With Growth
Movement With Decay ←	→

Narrow ← →	**Broad**
Limited topics discussed.	Wide range of topics.

Stylized ← →	**Unique**
Using a communication style that is automatic and standardized across casual relationships.	Using a communication style that has developed within a specific relationship.

Difficult ← →	**Efficient**
Communication takes lots of effort. Needs greater detail and explanation.	High shared meaning means fewer words are needed to convey ideas and feelings

Rigid ← →	**Flexible**
Very patterned and structured interaction.	Communication is adapted to the other and the situation.

Awkward ← →	**Smooth**
Communication is tense and uncomfortable. Lots of prolonged pauses, and so on.	Communication flows very freely. The interactions seem to manage themselves.

Public ← →	**Personal**
Things are said openly to anyone. Public information is shared.	Information is very personal. The interaction is private and not meant for just anyone.

Hesitant ← →	**Spontaneous**
The interaction is cautious and filled with hesitations. There is uncertainty about what to say.	The interaction is rapid and without many hesitations. There is little planning.

Overt Judgment Suspended ← →	**Overt Judgment Given**
We hold back in sharing what we think about the other.	We share our perceptions and evaluations of the other.

Another research team synthesized these eight qualities into three more general characteristics: personalization, synchronization, and difficulty.[8] **Personalization** is the degree to which the communication incorporates things known only to the individuals, the use of terms that have special meanings for the individuals, and general adaptation to each other.

Just as synchronized swimmers coordinate their motions and gestures, so do **synchronized** communicators interact in a smooth, flowing, and effortless way. When you are in sync with someone, the communication seems to roll along without pauses or awkwardness.

Finally, **difficulty** in the form of tension or problems is inherent in human communication, even in the most intimate relationships. When you have a conflict with a close friend, interaction becomes difficult, no matter how personalized or synchronized your communication is normally.

Think of three different interactions you have had with a family member (FM), a close friend (CF), and a new friend (NF). Using the qualities in Table 7.3, draw eight continua, then place each interaction on each of the continua to indicate how much of each quality was present in each of the interactions. For example, your first continuum might look like this:

Narrow———NF———————————FM————CF——Broad

What differences do you see among the relationships? How do you explain these?

RECAP   **Communication Qualities of Interpersonal Relationships**

Term	Definition	Examples
Personalization	Degree to which the communication incorporates things known only to the individuals and their relationship.	Use of personal names and examples. Sharing private information.
Synchronization	Degree to which two individuals are coordinated in the flow and management of their interaction.	Nonstop talking. Quick and easy movement from topic to topic.
Difficulty	The level of tension and problems that are manifested in an interaction. Decreased eye contact.	Increased volume. Name-calling. Personal attacks.

Stages of Interpersonal Relationships

In Chapter 1 you learned that relationships go through discernible stages as they move toward and away from greater intimacy. This process is referred to as **relational development**. Table 7.4 lists some of the terms and stages researchers have used to describe relational development. Note that, although they use different terms and different numbers of stages, all agree that relational development does proceed in discernible stages. Understanding these stages is important to your studies because interpersonal communication is affected by the stage of the relationship. As you might have concluded after doing the Communication Experience above, individuals in an intimate stage discuss topics and display nonverbal behaviours that do not appear in the early stages of a relationship. We use interpersonal communication to move a relationship forward as we proceed from acquaintances, to friends, to lovers. Outsiders usually can tell what stage a relationship is in by observing the interpersonal communication.

As a relationship moves from stage to stage, we use markers to indicate a change in the definition of the relationship. We might exchange tokens or rings to let friends know that we are "going steady" or engaged. Often these markers signify **turning**

Table 7.4

Comparison of Models of Relational Stages[9]

Our Model	Knapp	DeVito	Ruben	Wood
Pre-Interaction Awareness				Individuals Alone and receptive.
Initiation	Initiating	Contact	Initiation	Invitational communication
Exploration	Experimenting		Exploration	Explorational communication
Intensification	Intensifying	Involvement	Intensification	Intensifying Revising
Intimacy	Integrating Bonding	Intimacy	Formalization Redefinition	Bonding Navigating
Turmoil/ Stagnation	Differentiating			Differentiating
De-intensification	Circumscribing Stagnating	Deterioration	Deterioration	Disintegrating
Individualizing	Avoiding			Stagnating
Separation	Terminating	Dissolution		Terminating
Post Interaction Effects				Individuals

points—specific events or interactions that are associated with positive or negative changes in a relationship.[10] A first meeting, first date, first kiss, first sex, saying "I love you" for the first time, meeting a partner's family, going away together somewhere, making up after a conflict, moving in together, providing help in a crisis, or providing a favour or gift might all be turning points that indicate a relationship is moving forward. A pair of researchers found that 55 percent of the time, these turning points inspired a discussion about the nature of the relationship.[11] Such discussion helps the partners reach mutual agreement about the definition of the relationship.

We can think of the stages, from first meeting to intimacy, as the floors in a high-rise. Relational development is an elevator that stops at every floor. As you get to each floor, you might get off and wander around for a while before taking the elevator to the next floor (see Figure 7.2). Each time you get on, you don't know how many floors up the elevator will take you, or how long you will stay at any given floor. In fact, sometimes you will never get back on the elevator, electing instead to stay at a particular stage of relational development. But, if you fall head over heels in love, you might want to move quickly from floor to floor toward intimacy. Part of the time you share this elevator with your partner, and the two of you make decisions about how high you will ride the elevator, how long to stay at each floor, and when and whether to ride the down elevator.

Relational Escalation

As you can see in the model in Figure 7.2, the first floor is the *pre-interaction awareness stage*. Here, you might observe someone or even talk with others about

Figure 7.2

Model of Relational Stages

Up ▲	**Down** ▼
Intimacy	Turmoil or stagnation
Intensification	De-intensification
Exploration	Individualization
Initiation	Separation
Pre-Interaction Awareness	Post-Interaction Effects
Escalation	**De-escalation**

him or her without having any direct interaction. Gaining information about others without directly interacting with them is a *passive strategy* for acquiring knowledge.[12] Through your passive observations, you form an initial impression. You might not move beyond the pre-interaction awareness stage if that impression is not favourable or the circumstances aren't right.

If you are attracted to the other person and the circumstances are right, you might proceed to the *initiation stage*, one of the first turning points in a relationship. In this stage, the interaction typically is routine; you might each respond to a large number of standard questions during the first four minutes of conversation,[13] sticking to safe and superficial topics, and presenting a "public self" to the other person. Your partner is now riding on the elevator with you, and any decision about whether the elevator should go up, down, or nowhere is a mutual one for the rest of the ride. You can never return to the initiation stage. Once you make an initial contact, you have created a relational history on which you will continue to build.

If you decide to go to the next floor, *exploration*, you will begin to share more in-depth information about yourselves. But you will have little physical contact, maintain your social distance, and limit the amount of time you spend together. This stage can occur in conjunction with the initiation stage.

If you proceed to the *intensification stage*, you will start to depend upon each other for self-confirmation and engage in more risky self-disclosure. You will spend more time

As couples proceed from exploration to intensification, they have more physical contact and begin sharing more activities and confidences. Does it seem as if this couple is heading into the intensification stage? (Sandra Rice)

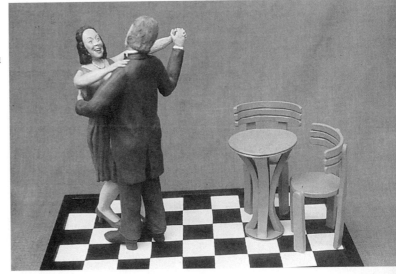

together, increase the variety of activities you share, adopt a more personal physical distance, engage in more physical contact, and personalize your language. Also, you may discuss and redefine the relationship often in this stage, perhaps putting a turning-point label on yourselves such as "going steady," "good buddies," or "best friends." Other turning points associated with this stage include decisions to date each other exclusively, to become roommates, or to spend time with each other's families.

The top floor in the building is the *intimacy stage*. In this stage the two partners turn to each other for confirmation and acceptance of their self-concept. Their communication is highly personalized and synchronized. They talk about anything and everything. There is a free flow of information and self-disclosure. There is a commitment to maintaining the relationship that might even be formalized through marriage or some other agreement. The partners share an understanding of one another's language and nonverbal cues, and have a great deal of physical contact. They use fewer words to communicate effectively, and they have a clearer definition of their roles and of the relationship. Reaching this stage takes time—time to build trust, time to share personal information, time to observe each other in various situations, and time to build a commitment and emotional bond.

COMMUNICATION EXPERIENCE

Think of an interpersonal relationship that you have had for at least a year. On the graph at right, plot the development of that relationship from stage to stage reflecting the relative amount of time you spent in each stage. You can also indicate whether you backed up to a previous stage at any point.

If possible, have your relational partner fill out a similar graph and compare your perceptions of how the relationship has developed. What differences are there and why?

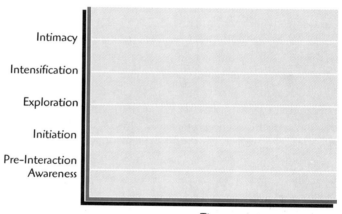

You also might want to share your graph with those of classmates to compare how different relationships develop. What can you tell from the graphs about the nature of their relationships?

Relational De-Escalation

Sometimes, for a variety of reasons, you might decide that you want to leave an intimate relationship. But as you may already know, the process of ending it is not as simple as going down the same elevator you came up on; it is not a reversal of the formation stage.[14]

You can hardly make a friend in a year, but you can lose one in an hour.

—CHINESE PROVERB

When an intimate relationship is not going well, it usually enters the **turmoil** or **stagnation** stage. Turmoil involves an increase in conflict, as one or both partners tend to find more faults in the other. The definition of the relationship seems to lose its clarity, and mutual acceptance declines. The communication climate is tense and exchanges are difficult.

Stagnation occurs when the relationship loses its vitality and the partners become complacent. Communication and physical contact between the partners decrease; they spend less time together, but do not necessarily fight. Partners in a stagnating relationship tend to go through the motions of an intimate relationship without the commitment; they simply follow their established relational routines.

As with the up elevator, individuals can stop at this point on the down elevator and decide to quit descending. The relationship can remain in turmoil or stagnate for a long time, or the individuals can repair, redefine, or revitalize the relationship and return to intimacy.

If the turmoil or stagnation continues, however, the individuals might move down to the **de-intensification stage**, decreasing their interactions; increasing their physical, emotional, and psychological distance; and decreasing their dependence upon the other for self-confirmation. They might discuss the definition of their relationship, question its future, and assess each partner's level of satisfaction or dissatisfaction. The relationship can be repaired and the individuals can move back up to intensification and intimacy, but that is more difficult to accomplish now.

On the next floor down, the *individualization stage*, the partners tend to define their lives more as individuals and less as a couple. Neither views the other as a partner or significant other anymore. Interactions are limited. The perspective changes from "we" and "us" to "you" and "me," and property is defined in terms of "mine" or "yours" rather than "ours." Both partners turn to others for confirming their self-concepts.

In the *separation stage*, individuals make an intentional decision to eliminate further interpersonal interaction. If they share custody of children, attend mutual family gatherings, or work in the same office, the nature of their interactions will change. They will divide property, resources, and friends. Early interactions in this stage are often tense and difficult, especially if the relationship has been intimate. For relationships that never went beyond exploration or intensification, however, the negotiation is often relatively painless.

For former intimates, one of the awkward things about separating is their extensive personal knowledge about one another. Their talk is limited to superficial things, although they still know a lot about each other. This tends to make the interactions fairly uncomfortable. Over time, of course, each partner knows less about who the other person has become. For example, even after spending just a few years away from your high school friends, you might have difficulty interacting with them because the knowledge you both share is out of date.

Although interaction may cease altogether, the effect of the relationship is not over. Our relational stages highrise is like something out of the old TV series, *Twilight Zone*: once you enter it, you can never leave it. The bottom floor on the down elevator, where you remain, is the **post-interaction stage**. This floor represents the lasting effects the relationship has on your self, and therefore on your other interactions and relationships. Steve Duck claims that in this final stage of terminating relationships we engage in "grave-dressing."[15] We create a public statement for people who ask why we broke up and also come to grips with losing the relationship. Sometimes our sense of self gets battered during the final stages of a relationship, and we have to work hard to regain a healthy sense of self.

Of course, we are all aware of people who hop on an express elevator to get out of a relationship, bypassing all the normal stages of decline. One study found that among the various ways to terminate a relationship, abandoned partners most dislike the quick exit without discussion.[16]

Principles of Interpersonal Relationships

Now that we have discussed some definitions, dimensions, and stages associated with interpersonal relationships, we are ready to examine the principles that describe more specifically how relationships work. As you will see, many of them amplify the principles of communication that you learned in Chapter 1. In Chapters 8 and 9, you will learn more about how relationships work, and also about the skills you can develop to initiate and maintain them effectively.

Principle 1: Interpersonal Relationships Are Processes

Interpersonal relationships are not static; besides moving from one stage to another, they also change as the individuals in them grow and change. As children mature, their relationships with their parents shift dramatically; these shifts can be painful as each person struggles to adjust. In relationships of circumstance, we usually negotiate to resolve issues arising from these relational changes, but we may decide to terminate a relationship of choice if it has changed too radically.

In Chapter 1 you learned that communication is an irreversible and complex process. The same is true of interpersonal relationships. Although you can choose to get out of a relationship, you can never reverse what has occurred within it. Nor can you undo the effects of a relationship, although they might diminish over time. Some scholars conceptualize the self as the product of all the relationships we have had in our lives.

In addition, interpersonal relationships are cumulative. Any given moment in a relationship represents the aggregate of experiences that preceded that moment. The helix that we used to represent the communication process in Chapter 1 also depicts the way a relationship progresses, growing larger with each interaction. The history of your relationship with another person affects the way you communicate in the present and future. You use information that you acquire about the other as the basis for your next interaction. For example, the interactions among you, the other students, and the instructor in this course are undoubtedly quite different than they were on the first day of class because of what you know about one another now. The relationships, the communication climate, and the communication have changed.

If you forget that relationships are processes, you can slip into a taking-the-other-for-granted mode, expecting the same thing from the relationship tomorrow that you got from it yesterday. If you hold on to this view too tightly, you soon may find yourself without a friend or a partner. Adapting to changes helps you successfully maintain your interpersonal relationships.

Principle 2: Interpersonal Relationships Are Systems

A *system* is a set of interconnected elements; a change in one element affects all of the other elements. For example, a change in the mood of one of your friends will affect your feelings and your interactions with him or her. In a highly empathic relationship, you may actually feel the same emotional response as a friend does in response to his or her situation.

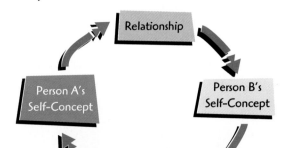

Figure 7.3

Relationship as a System

Interpersonal relationships are open systems; that is, they are subject to change from outside influences. If an external influence affects one partner's self-concept, then those changes will in turn alter the nature of the relationship, and that alteration will in turn affect both people's self-concept. This circular sequence is shown in Figure 7.3.

Principle 3: Interpersonal Relationships Are Mutually Defined and Agreed Upon[17]

As in communication, relationships are transactive—both participants need to acknowledge the existence of some bond between them. If you are attracted to someone, but she or he doesn't even know you exist, then there is no communication and therefore no relationship. You remain at the pre-interaction stage. Once involved in a relationship, both partners participate in defining its nature; one partner cannot unilaterally decide that the relationship is intimate.

We rarely talk directly about the nature of the relationship, but we constantly send cues to our interaction partners about our perceptions and definitions for it. They then respond with cues of acceptance, rejection, or modification.[18]

Suppose you have a friend, Lynn, with whom you would like to have a closer relationship. You see Lynn only occasionally at work or at parties of mutual friends. You call Lynn to suggest that you go to a movie together. This sends a message that you want to escalate the relationship. An agreement to go out with you signals Lynn's acceptance of your new definition for the relationship. After the movie, suppose you ask Lynn back to your house. Lynn declines, unwilling to escalate the definition of the relationship. No matter how much you may want a closer friendship, Lynn will have to share your desire before it can happen. In essence, you both have to push the elevator button to move the relationship to the next floor.

Principle 4: Interpersonal Relationships Are Continually Renegotiated

As your relationship with Lynn continues, you might suggest a weekend camping trip or a visit to your family; you might offer more personal information, attempt more physical contact, or try to spend longer periods of time together as a way of moving the relationship toward intimacy. Each of your moves might be accepted, rejected, or modified by Lynn. We continually redefine the nature of our relationships—even old ones. For example, your relationship with your best friend probably has changed, or will change, when one of you gets married. You and your friend must renegotiate the nature of the relationship in light of the new circumstances.

Even couples who have been married for years find that they must renegotiate their roles periodically. No matter how old we grow, our goals and desires never stop changing. (Superstock)

Principle 5: Interpersonal Relationships Cast Us in a Variety of Roles

A **role** is a set of expected behaviours that we associate with a particular situation. These sets of behaviours reflect the rules that, as you saw in Chapter 1, govern relationships. Often your role in a relationship is defined by the situational context. The relationship between you and your instructor is defined by the situational context of the classroom. If that instructor also happens to be your advisor, then when you go into his or her office to discuss your future, you both adjust your roles to suit the new relationship. In our more intimate relationships, we play several roles, depending upon the demands of the situation. We might play counsellor, companion, advisor, substitute parent, lover, helper, problem solver, or leader.

Principle 6: Interpersonal Relationship Partners Perceive the Relationship Differently

This principle might seem to contradict principle 3, but individuals never have exactly the same perception of a relationship. If the differences in perceptions are abundant or significant, then the partners will probably negotiate or terminate the relationship.

As relationships become more successful and more intimate, the partners spend more time aligning their perspectives. Researchers suggest that a couple's ability to share the same perceptions of their relationship determines how successful the relationship will be.[19] Achieving a shared perception and understanding of the relationship requires effective interpersonal communication. To achieve a shared perception, both partners need to adopt an other-oriented perspective. They need to ask about, and also appreciate, the other person's perception of the relationship. As the relationship becomes more intimate, it becomes more and more important to be

Understanding Others

Find a friend who is willing to do the following activity with you and with whom you feel comfortable talking about your relationship. Each of you should write down your answers to the following:

1. Describe your perception of the relationship.

2. Describe what you think your friend's perception of the relationship is.

3. Describe what you think your friend will say is your perception of the relationship.

After you are both done, compare your responses. How similar are your responses to question 1? What made them different? How closely were you able to predict the other's perception of the relationship (compare your response to question 1 to his or her response to question 2)?

What does it tell you about the relationship if all three responses are similar? Different?

sure that your perceptions are closely aligned and that you define the relationship the same way.

Principle 7: Past Interpersonal Relationships Define Current and Future Ones

We depend upon knowledge we gain from prior relationships to help define expectations and behaviours in our current and future relationships. If your most recent first date was successful, you probably will act that way again. If it was a disaster, you probably will use the knowledge gained in that experience to modify your behaviour the next time. Although every relationship is unique, each provides us with a better understanding of relationships and helps us to improve our ability to manage them. This text and the course you are taking are based on this premise.

Principle 8: Each Interpersonal Relationship Represents a Balance Between Comfort and Intimacy

Social exchange theorists use a cost-benefit model to explain relationships.[20] As we increase intimacy in a relationship, we incur greater costs in terms of risk and commitment of more personal resources (e.g., time, money, or fewer interactions with others). But the potential for rewards—confirmation and acceptance of our self, social satisfaction, or pleasure—is also greater. Because there is no guarantee that moving toward more intimacy will produce these rewards, we don't attempt to make every relationship an intimate one. Instead, we seek to optimize the amount of intimacy while also optimizing our level of comfort.

If our movement toward intimacy in a given relationship results in a loss of comfort, we will no longer pursue that relationship. Sometimes, even in intimate relationships, the costs eventually come to outweigh the rewards. We then choose to de-escalate or terminate the relationship. Our movement from one floor to another in the relationship highrise may involve movement up and down between several floors as we attempt to find the right floor on which to stabilize the relationship.

Summary

We can classify interpersonal relationships as relationships of circumstance—those that occur because the surrounding conditions cause us to interact with someone else; and relationships of choice—those that we seek out to establish and intentionally develop. We can also distinguish among relationships by looking at the degrees of trust, intimacy, and power in each one. Although there are many types of trust, interpersonal trust generally involves a belief that you can disclose information about yourself to another person because he or she accepts who you are and is committed to the relationship. Intimacy is the degree to which your sense of self is accepted and confirmed by another person. Power is the degree to which you can influence another in the direction you desire.

We can classify interpersonal relationships by looking at the nature of the communication that takes place within them. Two researchers identified eight pairs of adjectives to describe variables in communication behaviour. Another researcher grouped these pairs into three major categories: personalization, synchronization, and difficulty. These qualities describe how interpersonal communication varies according to the level of intimacy in a relationship. Communication in intimate relationships is typically personal, smooth, flexible, and efficient; covers a broad range of topics; and uses a personalized relational language.

Relationships progress through stages, and the movement from one stage to another is often signalled by turning points. As relationships escalate, they progress from pre-interaction awareness to initiation, to exploration, to intensification, and finally, to intimacy. Relationships also de-escalate as we move to redefine or terminate them, moving from turmoil or stagnation, to de-intensification, to individualization, to separation, and finally, to post-interaction. Even after we end a relationship, its effects remain with us to shape our feelings and responses in other relationships.

Interpersonal relationships operate according to principles. They are processes and they function as systems. They are mutually defined and agreed upon by the partners, who also renegotiate those definitions. We play a variety of roles in our relationships, and each partner perceives the relationship differently. Our past relationships define our current and future ones. We seek a balance between comfort and intimacy in our relationships.

For Discussion and Review

FOCUS ON COMPREHENSION

1. Distinguish relationships of circumstance from relationships of choice.

2. Define trust, intimacy, and power.

3. What are the five stages of relational escalation and the five stages of relational de-escalation?

4. What are the eight principles of interpersonal relationships?

FOCUS ON CRITICAL THINKING

5. What connections can you draw between the relational dimensions of trust, intimacy, and power and the interpersonal communication dimensions of synchronization, personalization, and difficulty? For example, would the level of trust you have in a person affect the level of synchronization in your interactions?

6. Trace two close relationships that you have had—one with a friend of the same sex, and one with a friend of the opposite sex—through the applicable stages of relational escalation and de-escalation. What differences and similarities do you find at each stage? How can you explain them?

7. Many of the issues covered in the eight principles of interpersonal relationships overlap. See if you can boil those principles down into two or three broad principles.

8. Under what circumstances is it inappropriate for a person to use the power he or she has over another person to satisfy personal goals?

9. Lynn and Chris have had an intimate relationship and have been living together for over a year. The relationship seemed to be comfortable for both of them. One day Lynn comes home from work and finds that all of Chris's belongings are gone. A note from Chris says, "I couldn't bring myself to tell you I'm leaving. Sorry. Good-bye." Is Chris's behaviour ethical?

For Your Journal

1. Monitor a face-to-face conversation between two or three of your friends that is at least four minutes long. You should play the role of a quiet observer. Write down all of the ways in which your friends attempted to gain or concede power during the interaction. Include examples of the language they used and the nonverbal cues they exchanged.

2. Keep track of your interactions with two friends for five or six days. Identify and discuss the way you redefined or negotiated the relationship during that period.

3. Describe and evaluate two of your existing relationships according to the principles and concepts discussed in this chapter. In what ways do the relationships differ? In what ways are they the same?

Learning with Others

1. In class, form at least five pairs of students. Each pair should choose a particular stage of relational development without telling the rest of the class. Then each pair should spend two minutes discussing plans for the upcoming weekend in a way that communicates the stage they have chosen. The rest of the class should write down what stage they think each pair is portraying. After all the pairs have finished their dialogues, score each other's responses. Which stage was easiest to portray and identify? Which stage was most difficult? How easy is it to see differences in communication behaviour at various stages?

2. In small groups, brainstorm some of the turning points that each of you has experienced in important relationships. Identify the relational stages that they led to. Which stages crop up most often? Least often? What does the frequency tell you about those stages?

INTERPERSONAL RELATIONSHIPS: Those connections we make with other people through interpersonal communication.

RELATIONSHIPS OF CIRCUMSTANCE: Interpersonal relationships that exist because of the circumstances in which we are born, circumstances in which we work or study, and so on.

RELATIONSHIPS OF CHOICE: Interpersonal relationships we choose to initiate, maintain, and terminate.

INTERPERSONAL TRUST: A quality of a relationship represented by the degree to which the partners believe it is safe to disclose personal information.

TRUSTWORTHY: A quality we use to describe an individual who can be trusted to accept personal information without exploiting it, support vulnerabilities, and remain in a relationship.

INTIMACY: A quality of a relationship represented by the degree to which a person's sense of self is accepted and confirmed by another person.

INTERPERSONAL POWER: A quality of a relationship represented by the degree to which one person can influence another in the direction he or she desires.

PERSONALIZATION: The degree to which interpersonal communication concerns things known only to the individuals and their relationship.

SYNCHRONIZATION: The degree to which two individuals coordinate the management of their interaction.

COMMUNICATION DIFFICULTY: The level of tension and problems manifested in an interaction.

RELATIONAL DEVELOPMENT: The process of moving from one stage to another as a relationship moves toward or away from greater intimacy.

TURNING POINT: A specific event or interaction associated with positive or negative changes in a relationship.

RELATIONAL ESCALATION: The upward movement of a relationship toward intimacy through five stages pre-interaction awareness, initiation, exploration, intensification, and intimacy.

RELATIONAL DE-ESCALATION: The downward movement of a relationship away from intimacy through five stages: turmoil or stagnation, de-intensification, individualization, separation, and post-interaction.

ROLE: A set of expected behaviours that we associate with a particular situation.

Initiating and Establishing Relationships

A fter studying this chapter, you should be able to:

1. Explain what interpersonal attraction is.

2. Describe the elements that contribute to interpersonal attraction.

3. Explain the relationship between attraction and interpersonal communication.

4. Describe the principles of self-disclosure.

5. Construct the two models of self-disclosure.

6. Summarize the eight suggestions for starting relationships.

■ INTERPERSONAL
ATTRACTION:
THE SPARK FOR
A RELATIONSHIP

■ SELF-DISCLOSURE:
THE FUEL FOR A
RELATIONSHIP

. . . I found myself looking straight at Everard Bone, who was coming in at that moment. He looked back at me but without any sign of recognition. I suppose I was indistinguishable from many another woman in a neutral winter coat and plain hat and I was thankful for my anonymity. But he was unmistakable. His tall figure, his well-cut overcoat, his long nose and his fair hair were outstanding in this gathering of mediocrity.[1]

ildred Lathbury's unrequited admiration of Everard Bone in Barbara Pym's novel, *Excellent Women*, seems an inauspicious start to their friendship and eventual marriage. Yet it illustrates the kind of pre-interaction awareness and attraction that often precedes actual interaction between people. As you learned in Chapter 7, we may be attracted to someone if we have the opportunity to observe or collect information about him or her in some indirect way. The amount of information affects the depth of our impression.

Research indicates that we prefer to observe individuals in informal social interactions, rather than in formal or individual activity.[2] In other words, we learn more by observing someone at a party than we do by observing a person studying at a table in the library. The more information we have, the more substantive the basis for attraction or repulsion.

In this chapter we will explore the nature of the attraction that leads us to initiate relationships, and then discuss the role of self-disclosure in fueling relationships.

Interpersonal Attraction: The Spark for a Relationship

hat does it mean to say that you are attracted to another person? Interpersonal attraction is the degree to which you desire to form or maintain an interpersonal relationship with a person. Interpersonal attraction occurs in the early stage of relational development as short-term initial attraction, and in the later stages of relational development as long-term maintenance attraction.

You can understand the difference between the two by looking at your own relationships. Think of the dozens of people whom you initially found attractive but with whom you never developed an intimate relationship. **Short-term initial attraction** is the degree to which we sense a *potential* for developing an interpersonal relationship. For instance, you might find one of your classmates to be physically attractive, but never move to introduce yourself. The information you gather in your first interaction with someone can also generate a short-term initial attraction for a relationship, which you may or may not pursue, depending upon the circumstances. **Long-term maintenance attraction**, on the other hand, is the type that sustains relationships like your best friendships. It refers to a level of liking or positive feeling that motivates us to maintain or escalate a relationship. Short-term attraction gives way to long-term attraction as a relationship develops through the stages we discussed in Chapter 7.

Think about your best friend. How did that relationship start? Perhaps it was because he or she was physically attractive, or perhaps you observed your friend laughing and joking with others and found that quality attractive. Why are you still friends with this person? Rarely (except in movies or TV shows) do we commit to, and maintain, a long-term intimate relationship such as marriage solely because we find another person physically attractive.[3] Perhaps you have discovered that you and your friend have a lot in common, or that you complement each other's personalities. For instance, your friend's calm, even disposition might balance your fiery temper.

Elements of Interpersonal Attraction

Why do we feel attracted to some people and not to others? The explanations are complex, but researchers have identified seven elements that influence our feelings of attraction. As you read about them, try to analyze your own feelings about people you find attractive.

PHYSICAL ATTRACTION

The degree to which we find another person's physical self appealing represents our **physical attraction** to him or her. That appeal might be based on size, height, clothing, hairstyle, makeup, jewellery, vocal qualities, gestures, and so forth. The old adage, "Beauty is in the eye of the beholder," is particularly true in terms of explaining physical attraction. Each culture has its own definition of the physical ideal, which it teaches and perpetuates. In North America, for instance, advertisements and TV programs promote a slender ideal for both males and females. This certainly contributes to our society's fixation on losing weight and staying fit. However, in some cultures, and at various times throughout history, physical attractiveness was synonymous with bulkiness.

Physical attractiveness acts as a convenient filter to reduce relationship possibilities.[4] In general, we tend to seek out individuals who represent the same level of physical attractiveness as ourselves. Suppose you are really into physical conditioning and have a personal philosophy about good eating habits, exercise, avoiding drugs, and not smoking. You will probably seek out and attract a physically fit person to be your partner. To a certain degree, the physical image a person presents can reflect more substantive qualities. For example, there is a good possibility that a physically fit individual's philosophy about eating and exercise would be similar to yours. That similarity might serve as the basis for a long-term maintenance attraction. As you learned in Chapter 3, we use superficial information to make inferences about personality with varying degrees of accuracy, but whether we decide to escalate a relationship depends upon what happens in the initial interaction and subsequent interactions.

CREDIBILITY, COMPETENCE, AND CHARISMA

Most of us are also attracted to individuals who seem competent and credible. We like those who are sure of themselves, but not full of themselves. We assume they are competent if they seem skilled, knowledgeable, and experienced. We find people credible if they display a blend of enthusiasm, trustworthiness, competence, and power. Competence, credibility, and sometimes physical attractiveness are all important elements in the composite quality we call *charisma*, which inspires strong attraction and allegiance. Political and other types of leaders often depend upon their charisma to attract supporters who are motivated to form relationships with them and willing to devote themselves to a chosen cause.

■ PROXIMITY

We are more likely to be attracted to people who are physically close to us than to those who are farther away. In this class, you are more likely to form a relationship with classmates sitting on either side of you than with someone seated at the opposite end of the room. This is partly because physical **proximity** increases communication opportunities. We tend to talk with someone on a casual, offhand basis because he or she is right next to us. We are more likely to talk, and therefore to feel attracted to, neighbours who live right next door than those who live down the block. Any circumstance that increases the possibilities for interacting is also likely to increase attraction.

Physical proximity plays a pivotal role in interpersonal attraction. We are much more inclined to find our next-door neighbours to our liking than to be attracted to someone who lives a block away. (Catherine Karnow / Woodfin Camp & Associates)

In impromptu surveys of students in our classes over the years, your authors have found that a high percentage form close friendships with dormitory roommates who were randomly assigned. There is a good chance that two individuals will become good friends simply because they share living accommodations. In one study on attraction, a researcher told pairs of people about one another, describing to each the other's dissimilar attitudes on a particular topic.[5] The participants were then asked to rate their attraction to the other person. All of the ratings were low. Then the partners were introduced to one another and allowed to interact. Even when they discussed only the attitude on which they disagreed, they had significantly more attraction for one another. Clearly, the information exchange that communication affords increases our ability to make an informed decision about pursuing a relationship. In addition, in both of these examples, the interaction was between two college students—two individuals who already have a great deal in common. That commonality is the source of the next form of attraction.

■ SIMILARITY

In general, we are attracted to people whose personality, values, upbringing, personal experiences, attitudes, and interests are **similar** to ours. We seek them out through shared activities. For example, you may join a folk dance group because you know the members share a dance interest with you. Within the group, you would be especially attracted to those who have a similar sense of humour, who share the same attitudes on certain issues, or who enjoy some of the same additional activities that you do. As we interact, we discover both similarities and differences between ourselves and others. We assess the relative weight of those similarities and differences and arrive at a level of attraction that may change over time as we continue to discover more information.

In the initial stages of a relationship, we try to emphasize positive information about ourselves to create a positive and attractive image.[6] We reveal those aspects of ourselves that we believe we have in common with the other person, and the other person does the same thing. Think about your initial interactions with strangers; typically you spend the first few minutes trying to find topics of mutual interest. You discover that the person is from a place near your hometown, has the same musical tastes, likes the same sports, frequents the same restaurants, has been to your favourite campground, has the same attitude about school, has had the same instructor for history class, and on and on. But the depth of this information is limited. We save our revelations about important attitudes and issues for a later stage in the relational development process.[7] Attitude similarity is more likely to be a source of long-term maintenance attraction than of short-term initial attraction.

COMPLEMENTARY NEEDS

You have heard the adage, "Opposites attract." Although we like people with whom we have much in common, most of us wouldn't find it very exciting to be stuck for the rest of our lives with someone who had identical attitudes, needs, values, and interests. Most of us look instead for someone with **complementary needs**. Schutz identified three interpersonal needs that motivate us to form and maintain relationships with others: inclusion, control, and affection. *Inclusion* represents the need to include others in your activities, or to be included in theirs. *Control* represents the need to make decisions and take responsibility, or the willingness to accept others' decision making. *Affection* represents the need to be loved and accepted by others, or the willingness to give love and acceptance to others.

If you have a high need to control and make decisions, and little respect for others' decision making, you will be more compatible with someone who does not have similar needs—someone who wants others to make decisions for him or her. In essence, we can view pairs of individuals as a team in which both sides complement the other side's weaknesses. If you're not very good at keeping track of your bills and balancing your chequebook, you might pair up with someone who is good at maintaining a budget to create a strong personal finance team. In reality, there are no "perfect" matches, only degrees of compatibility relative to needs.

RELATIONSHIP POTENTIAL

We need interpersonal relationships to confirm our self-image. **Predicted Outcome Value theory** claims that we assess the potential for any given relationship to meet this relational need and then weigh that assessment against the potential costs.[8] We are attracted to others with whom a relationship may yield a high outcome value (the rewards might exceed the costs). Over time, our assessments may change. In the movie *When Harry Met Sally*, for example, the main characters both thought initially that their relationship had little potential of meeting their needs. Over time, Harry and Sally developed a friendship that did meet certain needs. At that point they both thought the relationship had gone as far as it could. In the end, however, they discovered that they could have a more intimate relationship with a high outcome value.

Evaluate your level of interpersonal needs for each of the following by putting your first initial along the rating scale.

1. How much do you like to include others in the activities you do?

   Very little 1————2————3————4————5————6————7————8————9————10 A great deal

2. How much do you like to be included by others when they are involved in activities?

   Very little 1————2————3————4————5————6————7————8————9————10 A great deal

3. How much do you like to take responsibility for decision making?

   Very little 1————2————3————4————5————6————7————8————9————10 A great deal

4. How much do you like to let others make decisions for you?

   Very little 1————2————3————4————5————6————7————8————9————10 A great deal

5. How much do you feel a need to be accepted and loved by others?

   Very little 1————2————3————4————5————6————7————8————9————10 A great deal

6. How much do you feel a need to accept others and to give love to others?

   Very little 1————2————3————4————5————6————7————8————9————10 A great deal

Now think of two close friends. Go back and place their first initials along each rating scale to indicate how much each item applies to them. Or ask your friends to initial the scale for themselves. Compare your ratings with those of your friends. Are there areas where you are similar? Complementary? Are there differences that cause difficulties in the relationship, e.g., you both want to make decisions rather than accept others' decisions?

Like Harry and Sally, most of us begin predicting outcome values in initial interactions and continually modify our predictions as we learn more and more about the other person. We pursue attractions beyond the initial interaction stage if we think they can yield positive outcomes, and generally avoid or terminate relationships for which we predict negative outcomes.[9]

RECIPROCATION OF LIKING

We like people who like us. One way to get other people to **reciprocate** is to show that we like them. However, in initial interactions we are often reluctant to let other people know that we are attracted to them. We may hold back from showing our interest because we fear rejection or fear that we may give the other person a certain amount of power over us.

A study conducted by one of your authors and a colleague found that we often underestimate how much a new acquaintance is attracted to us.[10] Pairs of male and female college students interacted for the first time and then indicated their level of attraction for their partner, as well as their perception of how attracted their partner was to them. Most of the students significantly underestimated the amount of attraction the other person felt for them. It is unclear whether we underestimate because we don't have much confidence that others will like us as much as we like them, or because we, as North Americans, in general do not communicate effectively our level of attraction for others. Even in long-term relationships, people sometimes hold back in expressing their continued attraction for their friends or mates. As you interact with new acquaintances, keep in mind that they probably are more attracted to you than you realize, so you might want to adapt your decision making accordingly.

RECAP	**Elements of Interpersonal Attraction**	
Term	**Explanation**	**Examples**
Physical Attraction	The degree to which we find another's physical self appealing.	Body type and size, mannerisms, height, hairstyle, jewellery, facial features, clothes.
Credibility, Competence, and Charisma	We are attracted to individuals whom we perceive as being enthusiastic, knowledgeable, skilled, and trustworthy.	We find teachers, athletes, movie and TV stars attractive because we see them as skillful or credible.
Proximity	Physical proximity encourages attraction.	We are more attracted to immediate neighbours than to those who live down the block.
Similarity	We are attracted to those who share similarities with us.	We make friends with people who have personalities, interests, values, beliefs, attitudes, and needs that are similar to ours.
Complementary Needs	We seek out people whose needs complement our own.	Those who want to control pair up with those who want to surrender control.
Relationship Potential	We are attracted to those with whom we see the potential for a rewarding relationship.	As Humphrey Bogart said to Claude Rains in the movie *Casablanca*, "You know, Louie, this could be the beginning of a beautiful friendship."
Reciprocation of Liking	We are attracted to those who are attracted to us.	If someone indicates an interest in us, we tend to find him or her attractive.

Attraction and Communication

In general, the more we are attracted to someone, the more we attempt to communicate with him or her, although sometimes circumstances limit our ability to act upon our attraction. Communication is one of the ways we indicate our attraction. We avoid people we do not like and seek out those we do. Usually, the amount of communication and interaction we have with a person indicates the level of attraction in the relationship. We try to interact most often with people whom we find attractive.

As we saw in Chapter 7, two people define a relationship through a negotiation process. There will be more need for negotiation if the level of attraction is not the same for both partners, and the negotiation might be difficult and unsuccessful. An imbalance in attraction levels between the two participants in the relationship can be awkward and uncomfortable.

■ COMMUNICATING ATTRACTION

When we are attracted to people, we use a number of strategies to communicate our liking. First, we communicate our level of attraction through nonverbal cues, especially immediacy cues (see page 232). We tend to reduce the physical distance between us; increase our eye contact and use of touch; lean forward; keep an open body orientation; and smile. We also use the courtship readiness behaviours, preening behaviours, positional cues, and appeals to invitation described in Chapter 5.

In addition, we communicate our attraction through language. We use informal and personal language, addressing the person by his or her first name and often referring to "you and I," and "we." We ask questions to show interest, probe for details when our partner shares information, listen responsively, and refer to information shared in past interactions. All of these confirming behaviours demonstrate that we regard what the other person is saying as valuable.

Finally, sometimes we simply tell other people we like them. Most of us don't do this very often. But think about how you feel when a friend tells you that he or she likes you. It raises your self-esteem; you feel valued. You can make others feel that way by communicating your liking for them; although in the early stages of relational development, there are social mores against doing so. We communicate liking verbally in other more subtle ways as well. We might tell someone that we like a particular trait or ability, such as the way she tells jokes, or the way he handled an irritating customer. Or we might compliment someone's outfit, hairstyle, or jewellery. Each of these messages communicates attraction for the other person and is likely to elicit a positive response from him or her.

■ AFFINITY SEEKING

We also use other **affinity seeking** strategies to get people to like us. Table 8.1 summarizes the strategies that one research team identified.[11] Often, the methods just described to communicate attraction double as affinity-seeking strategies. In addition to using immediacy cues and self-concept confirmation, we often try to establish mutual trust, be polite, show concern and caring, and involve others in our activities. Apparently, these strategies do work. The researchers found that individuals who seemed to use many affinity-seeking strategies were perceived by others as likable, socially successful, and satisfied with their lives.

■ UNCERTAINTY REDUCTION

For a long time father, whom Joe Kane had never seen before, remained silently gazing at his visitor. He was no doubt suffering from an attack of stage fright. As so often happens in life he had thought so much and so often of the situation that now confronted him that he was somewhat nervous in its presence.

For one thing, he did not know what to do with his hands. He thrust one of them nervously over the counter and shook hands with Joe Kane. "How-de-do," he said. Joe Kane put his newspaper down and stared at him.[12]

Most of us can relate to the embarrassed awkwardness that "father," a restaurant proprietor in Sherwood Anderson's short story, "The Egg," displays upon meeting someone with a reputation. Meeting strangers and starting relationships is rarely

Table 8.1

Affinity Seeking Strategies

1. Control	Present yourself as in control, independent, free-thinking; show that you have the ability to reward the other person.	"I'm planning on going to grad school, and after that I'm going to Japan to teach English." "You can borrow my notes for the class you missed if you'd like."
2. Visibility	Look and dress attractively; present yourself as an interesting, energetic, and enthusiastic person; increase your visibility to the other person.	"Wow, that was a great show about Chinese acrobats. I do gynmastics too. Would you like to come watch me next week in our dual meet?"
3. Mutual Trust	Present yourself as honest and reliable; display trustworthy behaviours; show that you trust the other person by self-disclosing.	"That guy you're having problems with called me and asked about you. I told him I didn't have anything to say." "I've never told anyone this, but I'd really like to be an astronaut."
4. Politeness	Follow appropriate conversational rules; let the other person assume control of the interaction.	"I'm sorry, I interrupted. I thought you were done. Please, go on." "No you're not boring me at all; it's very interesting. Please tell me more about it."
5. Concern and Caring	Show interest in and ask questions about the other person; listen; show support and be sensitive; help the other person accomplish something or feel good about him- or herself.	"How is your mother doing after her operation?" "I'd like to help out at the benefit you're chairing this weekend." "That must have been really hard for you, growing up under those conditions."
6. Other-Involvement	Put a positive spin on activities you share; draw the other person into your activities; display nonverbal immediacy and involvement with the other person.	"This is a great party, I'm glad you came along." "A group of us are going to get a midnight snack; how about coming along?"
7. Self-Involvement	Try to arrange for encounters and interactions; engage in behaviours that encourage the other person to form a closer relationship.	"Oh hi! I knew your class ended at two, so I thought I'd try to catch you." "It would really be fun to go camping together this summer; I have this favourite place."
8. Common-alities	Point out similarities between yourself and the other person; try to establish equality (balanced power); present yourself as comfortable and at ease around the other person.	"I've got that computer game too. Don't you love the robots?" "Let's both work on the project together. We're a great team." "It's so easy to talk to you. I really feel comfortable around you."

Adapted from Bell and Daly, "The Affinity Seeking Function of Communications."

Write down at least ten different social situations you can recall having been in, such as attending weddings, funerals, hockey games, going to your grandmother's for dinner, visiting your best friend's parents for the first time, or meeting your new roommate. Next to each one, indicate how nervous you felt in that situation. Use a scale from 1 to 10, with 1 being calm and cool, and 10 being highly apprehensive. After you have rated each situation, go back and rate each one on how familiar or unfamiliar the situation was. Again use a scale of 1 to 10, with 1 being very familiar and 10 being very unfamiliar.

According to uncertainty reduction theory, there should be a strong correlation between your level of anxiety and the level of familiarity. Which situations caused the most anxiety? To what degree did your unfamiliarity with the situation affect your level of anxiety? What were you most uncertain about in each situation? In which situations were you most comfortable and why? Did you feel uncomfortable under some circumstances even though the situation was familiar? Why?

easy. We all seem to share a fear of the unknown, and this includes interactions with strangers whose behaviour we cannot predict. The research team of Charles Berger, Richard Calabrese, and James Bradac[13] developed a theory to explain relational development. Their theory is based upon one basic cause-effect assumption: we like to have control and predictability in our lives; therefore, when we are faced with uncertainty, we are driven to gain information to reduce that uncertainty.

We are most comfortable in predictable situations because we can call upon familiar strategies to handle the situation. In initial interactions we often follow predictable, scripted behaviour that reduces uncertainty. What if you approached a stranger and said "Hello," and the stranger responded by saying, "Bananas"? You would probably feel a little leery. You would feel even more uneasy if you then asked for the stranger's name, only to get the same reply: "Bananas." At this point you'd probably look for the nearest exit. If a person's response does not follow the normal initiation script, it might create so much anxiety that you will stop interacting.

Usually, however, we reduce uncertainty by gathering either cognitive or behavioural information about others.[14] Cognitive information relates to thoughts, attitudes, and opinions. Behavioural information relates to reactions and remarks in various situations. As we have seen, we gather some of this information during the pre-interaction stage of a relationship through observations and conversations with others who know the person. Later, we can directly observe the other's behaviours in our interactions with him or her, and also ask direct questions. Usually we gather behavioural information through observation and cognitive information through interactions.

We are particularly motivated to gain information early in a relationship when uncertainty is greatest, and when we are trying to evaluate the predicted outcome value.[15] We also are likely to seek out information if others behave in an unexpected way.[16] If your close friend who watches "The National" every night suddenly begins reading during that time slot, you will probably ask why. Whether the friend shares with you what is going on will depend upon how comfortable he or she is in revealing information about him- or herself.

Term	Explanation	Examples
Communicating Liking	We communicate to others our liking for them through nonverbal cues, our language choices, and direct statements.	We move closer to the person, use "I," "you and I," and "we," or directly state "I like you."
Affinity Seeking	We use various strategies to try to get others to like us, encourage openness, and listen carefully.	We follow conversational rules, ask questions.
Uncertainty Reduction	We seek information about others so we can increase our ability to predict their behaviours and thoughts, thus reducing uncertainty.	We observe the person interacting with friends. We ask others about the person. We question the person directly.

Self-Disclosure: The Fuel for a Relationship

> . . . in college I was unjustly accused of being a politician, because I was privy to the secret griefs of wild, unknown men. Most of the confidences were unsought—frequently I have feigned sleep, preoccupation or a hostile levity when I realized by some unmistakable sign that an intimate revelation was quivering on the horizon; . . .[17]

Unlike Nick Carraway, the dispassionate narrator of *The Great Gatsby*, most of us seek to hear and make "intimate revelations" in our relationships with others. Without a sharing of personal information or mutual self-disclosure, a relationship cannot proceed to a very intimate level. When we **self-disclose**, we provide information that others would not learn if we did not tell them. For example, others can learn our *approximate* age, height, and weight by just observing us. But they cannot learn our *exact* age, height, or weight unless we disclose it.

Self-disclosure serves a relational function. We develop relationships through self-disclosure, and we define relationships by their degree of mutual self-disclosure. Your best friends are those with whom you have shared your most personal information.

COMMUNICATION EXPERIENCE

Rules for Self-Disclosing

Each culture has its own special rules about self-disclosure. In some cultures, individuals are open about sharing personal information, whereas in other cultures it is considered rude to even talk about yourself. Imagine that an individual from another country is coming to visit you and wants to know the "self-disclosure rules" in your culture. Write down as many rules as you can think of, including such things as the type of information that is appropriate to disclose in each of the relational escalation stages: initiation, exploration, intensification, and intimacy. What happens when the rules are violated? What are the exceptions to the rules?

Principles of Self-Disclosure

Because self-disclosure plays such an important role in our relationships, we will look at some of the ways it functions in more detail. Most of the principles discussed here have been identified in research on self-disclosure in the United States and are limited in their cross-cultural application. Before reading this section, be sure to do the preceding Communication Experience.

■ SELF-DISCLOSURE IS A BUILDING BLOCK FOR INTIMACY

As relationships move toward intimacy, they typically include periods of high self-disclosure early in the relationship. However, the *amount* of information that is disclosed decreases as the relationship becomes more and more intimate. In other words, there is generally more self-disclosing activity earlier in a relationship than later. As a relationship proceeds, we begin sharing low-risk information fairly rapidly, move on to share higher risk information, and then finally, to share our most intimate disclosures. The more intimate the relationship becomes, the more intimate the information that is disclosed. The sculpture below represents the way we reveal ourselves when we are with close friends. Holding back from sharing intimate information signals a reluctance to escalate the relationship. The amount of information that we have to share about ourselves is finite, so we slow down as we have less left to disclose.

Graph A in Figure 8.1 illustrates a typical disclosure pattern over the course of a long and intimate relationship. The peaks and valleys represent periods of variable disclosure. Note that most of the disclosure takes place in the beginning of the relationship. Not all relationships progress this way, however. The relationship in graph B represents two individuals who started to get to know each other but were interrupted before they became close friends. They might have stopped because of some conflict, indecisiveness about pursuing the relationship, or external circumstances that limited opportunities for interacting. When the disclosure resumed, it became more intense. Graph C represents two individuals who probably knew each other as acquaintances for some time but never really had the opportunity or inclination to self-disclose. Once they did begin to escalate the relationship, however, there was a steep rise in self-disclosure. This graph might represent two co-workers who eventually start dating, or two students who have shared a class or two together before striking up a friendship.

Generally, a dramatic increase or decrease in self-disclosure reflects some significant change in the relationship. Even long-term relationships have significant increases and decreases in disclosure that signify changes. Before the birth of a first child, for example, both parents might disclose their fears and expectations about child rearing, and the information might have a profound effect on the relationship.

Interpersonal relationships cannot achieve intimacy without self-disclosure. Without true self-disclosure, we form only superficial relationships. You can confirm another person's self-concept, and have your self-concept confirmed, only if both you and your partner have revealed your selves to each other.

As we develop a relationship we reveal more of ourselves, removing the masks that we routinely use with strangers. (Sandra Rice)

Figure 8.1

**Self-Disclosure
and Relational
Development**

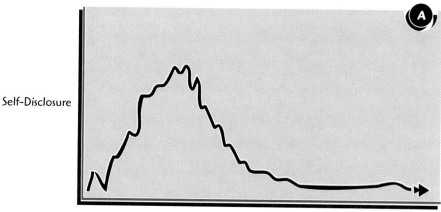

Self-Disclosure

Length of Relationship

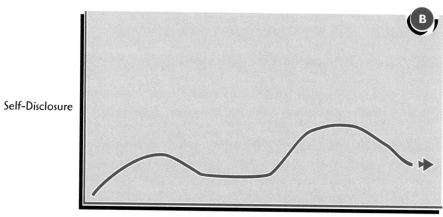

Self-Disclosure

Length of Relationship

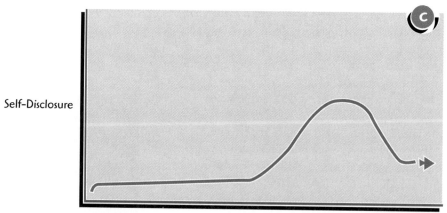

Self-Disclosure

Length of Relationship

Self-Disclosure Patterns

Think about two of your current relationships and draw a graph like those in Figure 8.1 to show how the self-disclosure has progressed in each of them. How do the patterns compare? What do the differences or similarities reflect about the two relationships? What caused the peaks and valleys? Were there times when you or your partner tried to increase the rate of self-disclosure, and the other person rejected that attempt? What happened?

Self-Disclosure

Length of Relationship

WE EXPECT SELF-DISCLOSURE TO BE RECIPROCAL AND APPROPRIATE

One rule that you might have noted in the Communication Experience on page 239, is that in mainstream Canadian culture, when we share information about ourselves, we expect the other person to share similar information about her or himself. If you introduce yourself to someone, by giving your name, you expect that person to respond by telling you his or her name. This cultural rule allows us to use disclosure as a strategy for gaining information and reducing uncertainty.

If the other person does not reciprocate, however, both people might feel resentful. Sharing information about yourself gives others a certain amount of power over you. If the other person reciprocates and discloses similar information, it helps maintain an equal balance of power. But if one person shares information and the other doesn't, the resulting imbalance causes discomfort. To use another example from *The Great Gatsby*, after spending the summer of 1922 with Jay Gatsby and the Buchanans, Nick Carraway declares, "I wanted no more riotous excursions with privileged glimpses into the human heart." Perhaps you can recall how you felt when an acquaintance chose to relate his or her troubles to you, a relative stranger. We do not necessarily want to know the deep dark secrets of those with whom we have a limited relationship.

Sometimes these unwanted disclosures occur because one person misjudges the nature of the relationship. In the Communication Experience on page 236, you probably identified some kinds of information that are inappropriate to disclose at an early stage, but appropriate to disclose later on in a relationship. You must assess the relationship and situation to determine the appropriateness of any given disclosure.

■ WE ASSESS SELF-DISCLOSURE RISKS DIFFERENTLY

What is high self-disclosing for one person might be low self-disclosing for another and vice versa. In judging what and when to disclose, you need to realize that different people have different standards. For instance, some individuals are quite comfortable talking about their sex lives with relative strangers, whereas others find such discussions appropriate only in the most intimate relationships. For some women, sharing a name or phone number with a stranger can seem risky. Obviously, the context in which the disclosure is made affects the risk level. Giving your name and phone number to a stranger at a bar might be riskier than sharing that same information with a new member of your church group or a classmate needing an assignment.

Be sensitive to the other person when you choose what and when to disclose. Consider how the other person will react to the information. Although you may not feel certain information is intimate, the other person may. Conversely, when your partner reveals information, try to determine whether it is highly personal to her or him. You could upset the other person if you fail to treat the information appropriately. If you share that information with others, for example, your partner may feel betrayed.

The research findings about differences between male and female self-disclosure are contradictory. Some research shows that males give more information to strangers than females, but that the information is not very intimate. Females are reportedly more intimate in their disclosures with friends. Other studies found that both males and females prefer to disclose to females.[18] These findings are consistent with cultural stereotypes in our society: both men and women perceive women as more sensitive, empathic, and supportive; whereas they consider men aggressive and control oriented. We perpetuate these stereotypes in our interactions when we expect someone to behave in a certain way because of his or her sex.

There is nothing inherent in men or women that leads them to self-disclose more or less. In truth, some men are highly self-disclosing and some women are quite closed. You will be most effective in your communication with others if you treat each person as an individual, putting aside stereotypical expectations about their self-disclosing behaviour. If you find that someone is reluctant to disclose, don't attribute that behaviour to his or her sex; look for an explanation in the person's background, upbringing, or past relationships.

■ WE BASE SELF-DISCLOSURE ON AN ANALYSIS OF COSTS AND REWARDS

As we have seen, self-disclosure is not without its costs and risks. When we disclose, we make ourselves vulnerable, we forfeit control of information, we might hurt or insult the other by saying things he or she finds offensive, we risk signalling an unintended level of intimacy, and we risk damaging the relationship with ill-timed and inappropriate disclosures. Typically, we seek a balance between the potential risks and rewards. In each stage of relational development, there is an optimum level of self-disclosure with which the individuals are comfortable. As Figure 8.2 indicates, if we go beyond that level, one or both partners might become less satisfied.

III UNDERSTANDING INTERPERSONAL RELATIONSHIPS

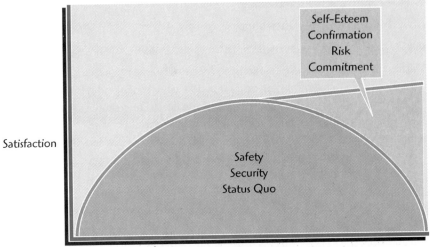

Satisfaction

Self-Disclosure

Safety
Security
Status Quo

Self-Esteem
Confirmation
Risk
Commitment

Figure 8.2

Too Much Disclosure Can Lower Satisfaction From Shirley Gilbert, "Empirical and Theoretical Extension of Self-Disclosure," p. 210. In Explorations in *Interpersonal Communication*, p. 197–215, edited by Gerald R. Miller. Copyright © 1975 by Sage Publications. Reprinted by permission of Sage Publications, Inc.

How do we achieve a balance between rewards and costs? In general, we make disclosures because we believe that the benefits will be greater than the costs. The benefits might not be immediate. We might disclose some negative piece of information about ourselves that initially upsets our partner, but we do it because we believe that in the long run it will be better for the relationship. We trust that our partner will still accept us, even with the negative disclosure, and will eventually appreciate our honesty and openness. Relational development is filled with such judgments. We base our estimates of benefits and costs upon past and present relational experiences. You are likely to share information about yourself with someone if you have found it rewarding to do so in the past. You will be reluctant to self-disclose if you have been harmed, either in your relationship with him or her, or in other relationships.

RECAP	**Principles of Self-Disclosure**
Principle	**Explanation**
Self-disclosure is a building block for intimacy.	We disclose most about ourselves early in the relationship. We disclose more risky information when the relationship is more intimate.
We expect self-disclosure to be reciprocal.	If we share information about ourselves, we expect the other person to share similar information.
We assess self-disclosure risks differently.	What is risky information for one person to disclose might not be risky for someone else.
We base self-disclosure on an analysis of costs and rewards.	We disclose when we believe the benefit will be greater than the costs or risks.

Two Models for Self-Disclosure

We have already seen that we self-disclose in order to move a relationship toward intimacy. One pair of researchers, Irwin Altman and Dalmas Taylor, developed a model of **social penetration** to illustrate how much and what kind of information we reveal in various stages of a relationship.[19] Their model starts with a circle which represents all the potential information about your self that you could disclose to someone (see Figure 8.3, circle A). This circle is divided like a pie into many pieces, with each piece of pie representing a particular aspect, construct, or dimension of your self. For instance, some of the constructs in your personality pie might relate to athletic activities, religion, family, school, recreational activities, political interests, and fears. These pieces of pie represent the breadth of information available about you.

In addition, the concentric circles in the pie represent the depth of information. The smallest circle represents the most personal information. Each of your relationships represents a degree of social penetration, or the extent to which the other person has penetrated your concentric circles (depth) and shared pieces of your pie (breadth). For example, the shading on circle B shows a relationship that involves a high degree of penetration, but on only one aspect of your self. Perhaps you have a good friend with whom you study and go to the library, but do not socialize. You

Figure 8.3

Social Penetration Models

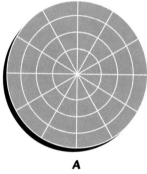

A

Your "self" with all its various dimensions. The pies represent the breadth of your "self," and the rings represent depth.

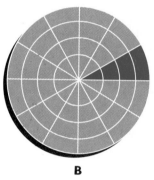

B

A limited relationship in which one dimension of your "self" has been disclosed to another person.

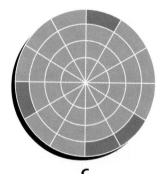

C

A relationship with greater breadth than B but with no intimacy.

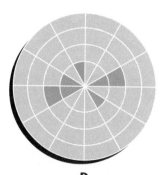

D

A highly intimate, close relationship in which there has been extensive breadth and depth of disclosure.

might have disclosed a depth of information to that friend about your academic skills and weaknesses, but nothing about your family, hobbies, politics, or other aspects of yourself.

Your relationships with your instructors probably look a little like circle B, with its limited breadth. In circle C, more pieces of the pie are shaded, but the information is all fairly safe, surface information about yourself. This would probably be the kind of disclosure associated with a new or limited friendship. Circle D represents almost complete social penetration, the kind we achieve in an intimate, well-developed relationship, in which a large amount of self-disclosure has taken place.

The **Johari Window** in Figure 8.4 is another model of how self-disclosure varies from relationship to relationship. It also reflects various stages of relational development, degrees of self-awareness, and others' perceptions of us. Its name comes from the first names of the two men who developed it (Joe and Harry) and from its windowlike appearance.[20] The window, like the circles in the social penetration model, represents your self. This self encompasses everything about you, including things even you don't see or realize. One axis is divided into what you have come to know about your self and what you don't yet know about your self. The other axis represents what some particular person knows about you and doesn't know about you. The intersection of these categories creates a four-paned window.

Figure 8.4

Johari Window

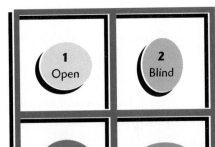

The OPEN quadrant represents that part of your self that you know and which you have revealed to the other person. As a relationship becomes more intimate, the OPEN quadrant grows larger. The HIDDEN quadrant is information you know about yourself but have not shared with the other person. This quadrant is fairly large initially, but as you disclose to another, it shrinks as the OPEN quadrant grows. The information in the UNKNOWN quadrant is that part of your self which you have yet to discover or realize. As we learn and self-disclose more about ourselves, or as others learn more about us, this quadrant becomes smaller and smaller. Individuals who are not very introspective and do not have a very well-developed sense of self will have larger UNKNOWN areas than those who have made a concerted effort to come to know themselves.

Because we can never know ourselves completely, the UNKNOWN quadrant will always exist; we can only guess at its current size because the information it contains is unavailable to us. But sometimes our friends observe things about us that we don't realize or perceive about ourselves. This kind of unintentional self-disclosure is represented by the BLIND quadrant. This quadrant does not include misperceptions about us, but rather real aspects of ourselves that we fail to recognize. The BLIND quadrant is usually small when someone doesn't know us very well, and it grows larger as that person observes more and more information that is in our UNKNOWN quadrant. However, as the relationship becomes more intimate, the other person is more likely to reveal his or her perceptions of us, so the UNKNOWN and the BLIND quadrants shrink as the information becomes known and accessible to us. As you can see, then, intimate relationships play an important role in the growth of self-knowledge.

As we did with the social penetration model, we can draw Johari Windows to represent each of our relationships (see Figure 8.5). Window A depicts a new or very restricted relationship for someone who is probably young or at least not very self-aware. Very little information has been disclosed or observed by the other, so the OPEN and BLIND quadrants are small. Window B also shows a new or restricted relationship for someone who knows him- or herself very well. Again, the OPEN and BLIND quadrants are small, but the UNKNOWN quadrant is also small. Window C represents a relationship that has evolved into a good friendship, and window D shows a very intimate relationship in which both individuals are open and disclosing.

By looking at a collection of your own Johari Windows, you can learn a great deal about your general approach to relationships. If you are reluctant to disclose information to others, and you do not reveal a great deal about yourself through your behaviours, your windows will consistently look like window A or window B in Figure 8.5. If you have a very outgoing and open personality, your windows will resemble window D. We can also examine the status of a particular relationship by drawing a window. Then we can see whether one member has disclosed more of him- or herself than the other (and has a larger OPEN quadrant) or whether one member has more complete self-knowledge (and a smaller UNKNOWN quadrant).

Figure 8.5

Variations on Johari Windows

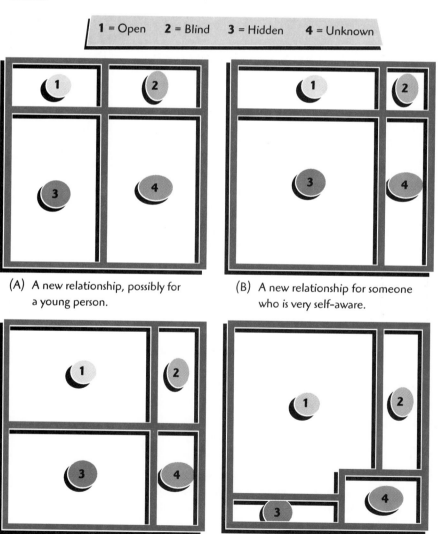

1 = Open   2 = Blind   3 = Hidden   4 = Unknown

(A) A new relationship, possibly for a young person.

(B) A new relationship for someone who is very self-aware.

(C) A good friendship.

(D) An intimate relationship.

Johari Window

1. Make two Johari Windows for yourself, one that depicts one of your relationships two years ago, and one that shows the same relationship today. How much information has moved from your UNKNOWN quadrant to your HIDDEN quadrant? To your OPEN quadrant? What observations can you make about the relationship?

2. Think of another relationship with a friend. Draw a window for your self as it would appear in this relationship. Then draw a window for your partner (or have him or her draw it). Next, draw windows to reflect your relationship with a parent or other relative.

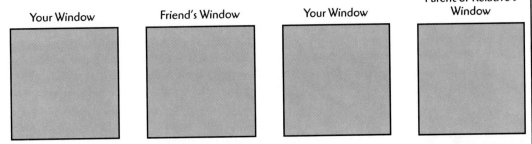

Your Window   Friend's Window   Your Window   Parent or Relative's Window

What are the differences between your friend's window and your window? What effects do these differences have upon the relationship? How have the two windows changed most recently?

What are the differences between your parent or relative's window and your window? How do these windows compare with the windows you drew for the friend relationship? How are the differences reflected in the way you communicate in these two relationships?

Getting Started: Suggestions for Initiating Relationships

In Chapter 7 and so far in this chapter, we have seen how relationships progress in stages and we have seen what makes them grow. The movement from initial attraction to initiation of interaction is not always an easy one. As we have discussed, there is a lot of uncertainty and apprehension involved in approaching a stranger and starting a conversation. In this section, we will look at some suggestions on how to get started.

Adopt an Other-Oriented Perspective

When you were frightened by an encounter with a wild animal or a neighbour's pet as a child, your parents probably told you, "It's just as afraid of you as you are of it." These words reflect an other-orientation and are useful to remember when we encounter new people as well. For all of us, meeting someone for the first time generally produces some degree of anxiety. When this happens to you, try to

ELECTRONIC CONNECTIONS

Carrying on conversations is not an easy task. We must learn to adapt to the other person, to follow the flow of the interaction, to pick up cues from the other person and incorporate them into the exchange, and to achieve a balance between asking for and offering information. There are no hard-and-fast rules. In fact the task is so complex that computer programmers cannot replicate our ability to carry on conversations.

A 1994 annual contest at California State University at San Marcos again proved that making conversation is an art not a science. The objective of the competition was for computer programmers to create a software program in an attempt to fool judges that they're communicating with another person. As they have in the past three years of the competition, the computers fooled no one. All of the judges correctly identified whether they were interacting with a computer or a person. The contest is structured so that 10 judges have conversations with 10 different computer terminals. Half of the judges were interacting with people, the other half were connected to computers programmed to respond to questions and statements from the judge. The computers were programmed to talk about such things as pets, the *Star Trek* television series, environmental issues, and the O.J. Simpson trial. The people who were interacting with the judges conversed about such things as American history, classical music, cryonics, comics, and the Rolling Stones. Artificial intelligence creators still have some work to do before they can emulate the complex and sometimes challenging process of talking with another human being.

Adapted from David L. Wilson, *The Chronicle of Higher Education.*

People use an array of nonverbal cues to let others know whether or not they want to be engaged in conversation. What cues are being sent here to encourage social interaction?

remember what other people did to make you comfortable in past encounters. They probably smiled a lot, actively listened, showed interest in you but didn't put you on the spot, disclosed information about themselves, and kept the conversation light. Try to use these techniques yourself to put your partner at ease.

Also, try to think about how you appear to the other person. For instance, if you are speaking to someone you just hired, he or she may feel nervous and uncomfortable because of the power and status differences between you. Do your best to minimize the differences; for example, sit in chairs that face each other without a desk between them. In general, try to apply all the information you have and that you observe about the other person to make decisions about your own behaviour. Don't just react; take the initiative to make the first interaction pleasant and satisfying to you both.

Observe and Act upon Approachability Cues

Sky Train riders in Vancouver learn to avoid eye contact because it is a signal for approachability. Other ways we can signal approachability include sustaining eye contact, turning toward another person, smiling, being animated (versus sitting very still), taking an open body posture, winking, and waving. In the absence of these cues, we generally conclude that a person wants to be left alone.

Sometimes circumstances prevent us from exchanging approachability cues. The seating arrangements in your class, for example, might discourage nonverbal exchanges. So instead, you may try to develop some sensitivity to the way other people respond to your greetings. Saying "Hello" lets people know that you are approachable, and it tests approachability. If the other person responds with a warm smile and a few words, such as, "Have you finished today's assignment yet?" then the door might be open for further interaction. But if the person gives you a silent half smile and hurries on, you can take this as a signal that the door is closed.

Identify and Use Conversation Starters

We all give off a certain amount of "free" information that others can easily observe. You can use that information as a starting point for a conversation. Noting that someone is wearing a T-shirt from Jasper National Park, for example, you can ask when she or he went there and how she or he liked it. If someone is walking a dog of the same breed as your childhood pet, you can approach him or her to discuss the breed's peculiarities. If someone is carrying a book from a class you took last semester, ask him or her how the course is going. Look at the painting at right to practice identifying conversation starters.

You will probably want to incorporate a greeting into your conversation starter, such as, "Hi, I see from the book you're carrying that you're taking the dreaded Dr. Bellfinger's class." You might also want to include an open question: "How do you like it?" Using an open question (e.g., "What . . . ," or "How . . . ") is an effective strategy because it requests a more complete response than Yes or No. Open questions encourage the disclosure of additional information, which in turn provides opportunities for you to follow up with more questions.

What conversation starters might either of the two people in this picture use to initiate a relationship?

Edward Hopper, *Sunlight in a Cafeteria*
Yale University Art Gallery, Bequest of Stephen Carlton Clark, B.A. 1903

Follow Initiation Norms

Many of the early interactions in a relationship are almost ritualistic, or at least scripted. In our culture, when two strangers meet for the first time they typically follow this pattern of conversation:[21]

Greetings: Say "Hello," "Hi," or "How are you?"

Introductions: Exchange names and pleasantries.

Topic 1: Discuss the present situation or weather.

Topic 2: Discuss current or past residences (where they live, hometown, etc.).

Topic 3: Determine whether they know people in common.

Topic 4: Discuss their educational backgrounds or occupations.

Topic 5: Discuss general topics such as TV, movies, music, family, sports, books, and/or travel.

Discuss Further Meeting (Optional): Say something like, "Let's get together some time."

Exchange Pleasantries: Say, "Nice to meet you," "Hope to see you again," and so on.

Close Conversation: Indicate the intent to end the conversation with such statements as, "See you later," "Got to go to class now," or "Give me a call."

Good-byes: Make final statements, "Bye," and move in different directions.

Following the script provides some comfort and security because both partners are able to reduce the level of uncertainty. If you deviate too much from this script, you might undermine your partner's sense of security and discourage him or her from pursuing a relationship.

As you follow the script, however, you should take advantage of opportunities to expand and develop the conversation in safe ways. Listen for details about the person's background and interests that you can inquire about, and share information about your own interests.

Provide Information about Yourself

Disclosing information about yourself allows the other person to make an informed decision about whether or not to continue the relationship. Remember, both of you need to be in a position to make such a decision. You might have found out what you want and decided that you have a lot in common with the other person, but he or she might not have reached that same point. However, you need to be careful not to violate the script or cultural expectations about what is appropriate to disclose in an initial conversation. You have probably had the experience of someone you have just met telling you his or her problems. As we mentioned earlier, such disclosures usually alienate the other, rather than advancing the relationship.

Present Yourself in a Positive Way

This may seem like a pretty obvious strategy. We tend to find people attractive who have positive self-images. And as we have mentioned, it is also against our cultural norms to disclose negative information early on in a relationship. But this doesn't mean that you should act cocky or that you should try to act ebullient if you are not that way by nature. Do not try to provide false information about yourself, but simply be selective about the information you share. Also keep in mind that we all have weaknesses and foibles, so the person interacting with you is probably also attempting to present a positive image. Practice the social decentring process you learned in Chapter 2 to think about the other person's thoughts and feelings as you listen to what he or she puts forward for your consideration. Being kind and responsive will win you more points than trying to act sarcastic and clever.

Ask Questions

Asking questions will accomplish two goals: first, it will help you learn about the other person, and second, it will let the other person know that you are interested in her or him. Keep your questions open and noninvasive; don't interrogate the other person. Focus on things you know you have in common and that are safe. Use the situation as a resource for questions. For example, if you are standing in line to purchase tickets for an upcoming rock concert, you could ask the person next to you how he or she got interested in the group, which of their songs he or she likes best, how many live concerts he or she has seen, and so on.

Don't Put Too Much into the Initial Interaction

Initial interactions do not necessarily determine the future of a relationship. In movies, such as *Speed*, initial interactions between the hero and the heroine are often brusque and unfriendly, but after sharing a traumatic experience, eventually they find love. Although real life does not usually work this way, keep in mind that the scripted nature of an initial interaction limits the opportunity for you and your partner to achieve an in-depth understanding of one another. Relax and arrange another meeting if you feel the spark of attraction. It will probably take a few interactions before you can make a sound cost-benefit analysis of the relationship.

Initiating conversation is only one step in the process of developing an interpersonal relationship. In the next chapter we will examine ways to escalate a relationship once it gets started, and in the last three chapters of the book, we will learn strategies for strengthening relationships with family members, friends, lovers, and colleagues.

RECAP **Getting Started**

Rule	Examples
1. Adopt an other-oriented perspective.	How does the other person perceive this situation? How would you like to be treated if someone approached you?
2. Observe and act upon approachability cues.	Watch for smiles, eye contact, or someone turning toward you.
3. Identify and use conversation starters.	"I see your T-shirt is from Paris. Have you been there?" "Isn't that the new Danielle Steele novel you've got there?"
4. Follow initiation norms.	Use the script that begins with a greeting, proceeds through a series of socially acceptable topics, and ends in "Good-bye."
5. Provide information about yourself.	Your name, interests, major, hometown, family background.
6. Present yourself in a positive way.	Be positive in tone. Smile. Tell about your successes and accomplishments without bragging.
7. Ask questions.	"Where are you from?" "What's that place like?" "What do you do in your spare time?"
8. Don't put too much into the initial interaction.	"I've enjoyed talking with you. I'd love to hear more about your summer in Paris some time."

Summary

This chapter focuses on the initial stages of relational development, specifically looking at attraction and self-disclosure. Short-term initial attraction leads us to initiate interaction with another, and long-term maintenance attraction sustains our liking for another person. Researchers have identified six elements that contribute to attraction: physical attraction, credibility and competence, proximity, similarity, complementary needs, relationship potential, and reciprocation of liking. Communication plays a significant part in the development of attraction. Through communication we learn about each other's attitudes, values, and beliefs. When we view the information we learn positively, we become attracted. We use communication for affinity seeking, signalling our attraction by initiating interactions. We use nonverbal cues, such as smiling and eye contact, in combination with verbal messages, such as, "I like you," to convey attraction. We also try to get others to like us by attentively listening to them, moving close to them, complimenting them, encouraging them to confide in us, and by other means.

Sometimes we know little about individuals with whom we initiate interactions, and this uncertainty creates anxiety. We are motivated to reduce this uncertainty by finding out more about them. Part of the process of finding out about others involves self-disclosure, or sharing information that others would not learn if you did not tell them. The four principles of self-disclosure show that it is a building block for intimacy, that we expect it to be reciprocal in a relationship, that people have different standards for self-disclosing, and that we assess costs and benefits before we self-disclose. Two models relate self-disclosure to the development of relationships. The social penetration model shows the depth and breadth of what we disclose to different people. The four quadrants in the Johari Window (OPEN, HIDDEN, UNKNOWN, and BLIND), reflect how much information we and others know about our selves. As we develop relationships, the sizes of these windows change relative to one another.

You may find the following suggestions helpful in initiating relationships: adopt an other-oriented perspective; act on approachability cues; follow initiation norms and scripts; provide information about yourself; present yourself in a positive manner; identify and use conversation starters; ask questions; and do not put too much into an initial encounter. Once you initiate a relationship, you embark on an exciting journey, which may or may not lead to a long-lasting, intimate relationship.

For Discussion and Review

■ FOCUS ON COMPREHENSION

1. Define short-term initiation attraction and long-term maintenance attraction.

2. What are the elements that contribute to interpersonal attraction?

3. In what ways is attraction related to communication?

4. What are the principles for self-disclosure?

■ FOCUS ON CRITICAL THINKING

5. What is the relationship between interpersonal attraction and self-disclosure?

6. Under what circumstances in an intimate relationship might a person's OPEN quadrant in a relationship with another person actually become smaller?

7. How do the rules for getting a conversation started relate to uncertainty reduction and affinity seeking?

8. How can you judge whether information that has been disclosed to you is privileged and private information not to be shared with others? When is it okay to tell other people what you know about someone?

9. Under what conditions is it ethical or unethical to approach (a) a co-worker, (b) a subordinate, or (c) a superior for the purposes of developing an interpersonal relationship because you feel attracted to him or her?

For Your Journal

1. For five or six days, keep track of the people you observe or interact with for whom you feel some level of attraction. Divide those interactions into two categories: short-term initial attraction and long-term maintenance attraction. Analyze the various elements that contribute to the attraction: physical attraction, proximity, similarity, complementary needs, relationship potential, and/or reciprocation. What elements contributed the most to each type of attraction?

2. At the end of a day, reflect upon your interactions with others. For each interaction you can recall, write down what you disclosed. What factors affected what you chose to disclose? How did the differences in your relationships with the various people involved affect your decisions about self-disclosure?

Learning with Others

1. In groups, combine your responses to the Communication Experience in which you identified rules of self-disclosure into a "manual" that might be given to an international student. Discard any rules that don't seem valid or that are too specific. Prioritize the rules from the most important to the least important. How does your manual compare to those of other groups in your class?

2. Divide into groups of four or five students. As you go around your group, have each student respond to the following request: Describe the most successful conversation starter that has been used on you, or which you have used. What made it successful? What did you like about it? What was the outcome? Next, go around and describe the worst conversation starter that has been used on each of you, or by each of you. What made it the worst? What was the outcome?

SHORT-TERM INITIAL ATTRACTION: The degree to which we sense a potential for an interpersonal relationship.

LONG-TERM MAINTENANCE ATTRACTION: A liking or positive feeling that motivates us to sustain a relationship.

PHYSICAL ATTRACTION: The degree to which we find another person's physical self appealing.

PROXIMITY: That quality which promotes attraction because of being physically close to another and therefore in a position to communicate easily.

SIMILARITY: We are attracted to people whose personality, values, upbringing, personal experiences, attitudes, and interests are similar to ours.

COMPLEMENTARY NEEDS: We are attracted to those whose needs complement our own; one person's weakness is the other person's strength.

RELATIONSHIP POTENTIAL (PREDICTED OUTCOME VALUE THEORY): We are most attracted to those relationships that potentially have greater rewards or benefits than costs.

RECIPROCATION OF LIKING: We like people who like us.

COMMUNICATING ATTRACTION: We communicate our attraction toward other people by the use of nonverbal cues, language, and direct declarations.

AFFINITY SEEKING: Strategies used to get other people to like us.

UNCERTAINTY REDUCTION: We seek to reduce our uncertainty about what to expect from other people by attempting to gain information about them.

SELF-DISCLOSURE: Providing information about ourselves that another person would not learn if we did not tell them.

SOCIAL PENETRATION: A model of self-disclosure and relational development that reflects sharing information that has both depth and breadth.

JOHARI WINDOW: A model of self-disclosure that reflects the movement of information about our self from BLIND and UNKNOWN quadrants to HIDDEN and OPEN ones.

APPROACHABILITY CUES: Signals from another person that he or she is open to initiating a conversation.

Escalating, Maintaining, and Terminating Relationships

After studying this chapter, you should be able to:

1. Explain the difference between escalating, maintaining, and terminating a relationship.

2. Describe three strategies people use for maintaining relationships.

3. Identify and describe effective interpersonal communication skills for maintaining and escalating relationships.

4. Describe three paths relationships follow when coming to an end.

5. Identify direct and indirect strategies for ending relationships.

6. Explain three major causes for breakups.

7. Identify and explain the four elements in a model for ending a relationship.

8. Discuss some of the signals for identifying trouble in a relationship.

■ ESCALATING RELATIONSHIPS

■ MAINTAINING RELATIONSHIPS

■ INTERPERSONAL COMMUNICATION SKILLS FOR ESCALATING AND MAINTAINING RELATIONSHIPS

■ DE-ESCALATING AND ENDING RELATIONSHIPS

■ IDENTIFYING AND ACTING UPON TROUBLE SIGNS IN RELATIONSHIPS

Justin: Hi. It's Andy, isn't it? We met at Marilyn's party, remember? It's good to see you again.

Andy: Sure, sure. I was hoping we'd run into each other again. I enjoyed our conversation at Marilyn's. Been to any good games lately?

Justin: No, I've been swamped with work. I am going to the Jays game on Saturday, though. Come to think of it, I have an extra ticket because my son cancelled out on me. Would you like to go?

Andy: Sure, that'd be great. Let's figure out where to meet.

This relationship might have gone no further than the initiation stage at Marilyn's, but these two new acquaintances have made a mutual decision to escalate the relationship to the next stage: exploration. In this stage, they will share additional information and observe each other's behaviours more closely. After the game, they might escalate the relationship even further and move toward an intimate and close friendship.

This chapter focuses on specific skills that people like Justin and Andy use to build successful relationships and encourage intimacy. It also looks at strategies for maintaining a relationship at a particular stage. And finally, it examines the way we de-escalate, redefine, and end relationships.

Escalating Relationships

In Chapters 7 and 8, we saw that as partners escalate a relationship, they increase the level of intimacy and self-disclosure. And in Chapter 5 we learned that as relationships become more intimate, the partners learn to read each other's nonverbal expressions more accurately. As they share more common experiences, they also develop shared associations for certain words. As we saw in Chapter 6, many couples develop a language that is specific to the relationship. As the relationship becomes more intimate and remains intimate, that language expands.

Other changes occur as well. As partners learn more and more through self-disclosure and shared experiences, they often are able to predict each other's reactions and behaviours. Remember the "script" that we outlined in Chapter 8 for initial interactions with strangers? As we move from this predictable phase into exploration, the predictability level takes a nosedive. But as we get to know a person, we develop specific relational scripts, and predictability increases. For example, the interaction between a married couple upon returning home from work tends to follow a script of sorts:

She: How was your day?

He: Fine. How was yours?

She: Fine. Got any ideas for dinner?

He: No. What'd you have for lunch?

We also become more trusting as a relationship escalates. We are willing to share increasingly risky and revealing information. As we increase our openness about our weaknesses, faults, past mistakes, and problems, we trust that the other person will remain committed to the relationship. We are more comfortable being ourselves, and we increase our dependence upon the other person for confirming and accepting our self-concept.

As a relationship escalates, partners face and resolve a variety of control issues. They clarify their roles and responsibilities. They establish relational norms for making decisions. For example, one partner may assume responsibility for dealing with the apartment and the landlord, while the other partner tends to take the lead in arranging weekend outings and social engagements.

As we saw in Chapter 7, the partners also assess the relationship as it develops. They weigh benefits against costs and attempt to stabilize the relationship when they feel they have achieved a good balance. Stabilizing a relationship means we attempt to stay with some achieved definition of the relationship; we try to maintain the same levels of intimacy, trust, and power. Stabilized relationships remain at a particular stage of development without escalating or de-escalating. We stabilize most relationships at the exploration or intensification stage. We have hundreds of day-to-day relationships during our lives that we are content to maintain as acquaintanceships and friendships. The Electronic Connections box opposite tells how a pair of cousins used E-mail to escalate their relationship beyond this stage. But whether a relationship is intimate or not, it requires care and attention to remain alive.

Maintaining Relationships

To maintain a relationship, we must sustain the forces that hold a relationship together.[1] The best tool we have for doing this, as researcher Steve Duck claims, is talk.[2] Talk allows partners to verify that they share a common appreciation of the relationship. They generally do this not by talking directly about the relationship, but through day-to-day small talk. The article on page 258 describes the integral role communication plays in one married couple's relationship. Partners note what they have in common, confirm their connectedness, and affirm their shared conception of the relationship. Talk also lets us know when the relationship is in trouble. If we don't confirm what we have in common, we know that we have work to do.

Thanks to my computer, I now have a baby sister.

I've known my cousin Kathy Castner all her life. If I close my eyes, I can still conjure up the sight of her as a leggy, tanned 9-year-old sitting in Grandma Robertson's old house in Ashland, Ky., her round, brown eyes fixed on me as I played the guitar a few days before my wedding. As I recall that moment, my memory quickly flashes years ahead; once again, Kathy's staring at me as I'm playing my guitar, but this time she's all grown up and we're at *her* wedding. These are fond memories of a favorite cousin, but it certainly wasn't my guitar playing that made me her honorary brother. Our closeness grows from the freewheeling heart-to-heart dialogues we carry on over electronic mail.

Kathy and I kept in touch over the years but we live about 200 miles apart, so until we began our computerized correspondence, our direct contacts were too infrequent for us to think of each other as confidantes. Now, e-mail renders the geographical distance meaningless—our messages fly at lightning speed over the Internet, the global network that links millions of computers, including the one in my home office and the one at the junior high school where Kathy teaches. Once we

discovered e-mail our figurative distance vanished. In no time, we fell into an easygoing gabfest about our favorite subject: Us!

Much of our chatter is small talk about how the day is going: How was the movie? What did the plumber say? Who's coming to town for your dad's party? We pepper our notes with "emoticons," keyboard creations like :^) that resemble faces when you tilt your head to the left.

But that familiarity makes it easier to discuss the big stuff, too. The immediacy of e-mail lets us cry on each other's shoulders, applaud our accomplishments, share secrets and pester one another to think as highly of ourselves as we do of each other. In short, it's just the sort of nagging/bragging, bullying/boosting I've always imagined I'd have had with a sibling, but as an only child I never had the chance.

Of course, we like to hear each other's voice, too, so we pick up the phone to talk once a month or so. But thanks to e-mail, we check in with each other most days, and for far less money than that one long-distance phone call (the computer connection is governed by local billing rates).

Although e-mail depends on the written word, it's somehow more intimate than traditional

letters. Kathy thinks it's the immediacy that makes it special.

"I love knowing that I'm reading what you're thinking and feeling right now, rather than two or three days ago, as it is when you're relying on the Post Office," she says.

One day last spring, for instance, I received a distressed e-mail message from Kathy; she'd lost her wedding ring when she'd taken her class outside. After she berated herself for being so emotional, I reminded her that everyone in our family is sentimental. "Don't fight it, darlin'," I reassured her. "We're a clan of softies."

A few hours later, a second electronic message arrived: A student touched by Kathy's predicament had gotten hold of a metal detector and searched the grounds until he found her ring. Kathy and I swapped several e-mail messages that day. I shared Kathy's joy at the recovery of her ring, and in the next breath we were discussing what position her son was going to play in Little League.

Electronic conversations like ours never really end. One story spurs comments and reflections, which send the discussion off in unforeseen directions that can keep our dialogue going all day long.

Plenty of Communication Strengthens the Bond

"I just heard on television that married couples talk to each other an average of 11 minutes per day," my husband told me. "Obviously the people who did the study hadn't heard about us."

When he said this we were 2,000 miles apart and talking long-distance.

We had limited ourselves to half an hour to keep the cost down, and each of us had made a list so we wouldn't forget anything we wanted to say.

I said I couldn't imagine that, but the idea actually conjured up memories of my first marriage, when the daily exchange between my husband and me centered on what was in the mail, who had gone to the bank and what time to pick up the kids from basketball practice.

When that marriage was over, I said I'd never do it again and I meant it, but then I met a man whose only promise was that he'd be my friend. For several months we went to movies and dinner, telling all our friends we were not dating but just enjoyed one another's company. That much was true—we enjoyed it so much we got married.

From the beginning, the centerpiece of our relationship has been conversation. Back in those "just friends" days we talked for hours about a movie we'd seen or a restaurant we'd tried. We hashed over whatever was in the news and discussed the problems of our mutual friends.

When we began to consider marriage, I told him how important it was to me to have a buddy I could talk to.

"What if we ever have problems?" I asked him, "Will you still talk to me then?"

"Especially then," he told me. "We'll talk until we solve them."

After that our talks deepened to include where we wanted to live, feelings about our work, and how we planned to spend our money. My children would tell you we can't sneeze or have a glass of water without talking it over.

On a couple of occasions our penchant for discourse has caused us some distress. Once, my son, by that time grown, was coming into town with some friends. He said to expect them late on a Saturday afternoon.

That morning we made breakfast and carried it on a tray out to the deck. Still in our bathrobes, we read the paper and started to chat. It seemed like only a short time later when we heard car doors slamming in the driveway. It was 5 in the afternoon, and we'd been caught.

Another time I was in London on business and he was at home. We figured out that with an eight-hour time difference, we could conveniently call each other twice a day. I rang in the morning to tell him good night just as he was going to bed. At bedtime, just as he was coming home from work, I called again, to tell him about my day.

It made the most sense for me to phone him since he could never be certain when I'd be in my hotel room. That was our first mistake. Our second was in not watching the time, but the fact is it's impossible to spend an entire day in London and describe it in three minutes. And that didn't even count his telling me what had happened at school.

The morning I checked out, my bill was so astronomical I genuinely thought someone had made a mistake. I'm still too embarrassed to say how much it was, but we had talked an average of two hours per day for five days at prime-time international rates from a hotel. Suffice it to say it would have been cheaper to fly him to London and talk to him face to face.

For a while I thought this fascination with dialogue might be genetic. Bored with most young men her own age, my daughter finally met someone with whom she could carry on a conversation.

"He's so wonderful," she gushed into the telephone after they had dated a few

||| UNDERSTANDING INTERPERSONAL RELATIONSHIPS

times. "We talk for hours on end, I don't even know what we talk about. He's just so fascinating, and no matter what subject comes up, he makes it interesting."

I thought I had been exonerated—that at last she understood how a couple could be found talking in their nightclothes far into the afternoon or running up a phone bill that would go a long way toward squaring the national debt.

But then they broke up and she came home for a weekend. When she got up on Saturday morning, my husband and I were already camped on our patio with the newspaper and the coffee pot. While she silently munched a doughnut and drank some tea, we covered how to landscape our back yard, what birthday gift to buy my mother, and how foreign policy might be affected as a result of the changes in Congress.

Eventually she grew tired of listening and stood up to leave. Apparently the stimulating all-night discussions about which she had so recently enthused had already slipped her mind. "Geez, you two are boring," she grumbled. "Married all this time, and you still talk every subject to death."

From: Glenda Winders, *San Marcos Daily Record*

Every sustained relationship requires maintenance activity by both partners. The amount required depends upon the nature of the relationship. Usually, the more intimate the relationship, the more effort we are willing to put into maintaining it.[3] We will continue to put forth this effort as long as we reap appropriate benefits. If our maintenance efforts become too costly (require a lot of effort and resources), we will probably de-escalate or terminate the relationship.

Sometimes external factors prevent us from maintaining relationships effectively.[4] If you recently moved from another town to attend college, perhaps you are finding it more and more difficult to maintain relationships with friends who are attending other colleges or whom you left behind. The physical distance between you and your friends increases the costs involved in maintaining a relationship with them. Whether you are willing to make the necessary effort to sustain your friendships will depend upon the level of benefits you reap from each one.

One researcher found that people respond to the challenge of maintaining relationships in three ways.[5] Some people are **avoiders**. They are frightened that the relationship might change, so they systematically ignore or avoid opportunities to discuss or redefine it. For example:

Jim: You know, we've been dating for over six months now, and I was thinking that maybe we should decide to see each other exclusively from now on.

Kelley: Maybe. Let's go get dinner at that new restaurant down on Fifth Street. I'll treat.

Other people are more **direct**. They come out and say that they want things to stay the same. And then they pressure their partners to stay on course by reminding them about relationship decisions they've already made together. For example, here's a direct response to Jim's suggestion:

Kelley: When we first went out, I told you that I didn't want to get into any heavy relationship right now in my life. You said that was fine with you. I still feel the same way. I have a lot of fun with you, but I don't want to make any commitment.

A third approach is to strive for **balance** in the relationship. Some people make an effort to understand their partner's moods and maintain a constant level of emotional support. They also do favours for the other person without trying to escalate the relationship. This approach tends to be the most successful because the person derives rewards from his or her own behaviour without depending heavily on what the partner does or does not do. Table 9.1 summarizes these three approaches.

Other researchers note that people who are successful in maintaining relationships share certain behavioural patterns. They set a *positive tone* by being cheerful and noncritical; they provide *assurances* of their continued involvement and caring; they *share tasks*, such as housekeeping, to show their commitment; and they have supportive *social networks* of family and friends who reinforce the value of the relationship.[6]

In general, however, different stages of the relationship require different degrees of maintenance and different strategies.[7] We mix and match elements of the three strategies—avoidance, directness, and balance—to suit each situation. Even if two relationships are at the same stage of development, we might devote different amounts of time and energy to each, depending upon the quality that needs maintenance work.[8] For example, if you have violated an expectation in the relationship by being late or missing a date, then you will need to work hard to restore your friend's trust.

Relational maintenance often requires conflict management skills, which we will discuss in the next chapter. The needs of a given relationship are a product of each

Table 9.1

Strategies for Maintaining a Relationship[9]

Avoidance

1. Ignore things that might change the relationship.
2. Avoid doing things that might change the relationship.
3. Try to prevent your partner from doing things that might change the relationship.

Directness

1. Directly state that your relationship should remain the same.
2. Remind your partner about relationship decisions made in the past.
3. Directly tell your partner how you feel about the relationship.

Balance

1. Try to maintain a constant level of emotional support.
2. Provide favours on a recurring basis for your partner.
3. Try to understand your partner's moods and compensate for them.

partner's unique qualities. The most successful friendships are maintained by choosing strategies that match specific characteristics of the relationship and partners. For instance, you might have one friend who is very open to talking directly about the relationship, and another friend who is very uncomfortable with direct discussions. It would be best to use different strategies for maintaining these two relationships.

Interpersonal Communication Skills for Escalating and Maintaining Relationships

In addition to the three strategies just discussed, you can apply many of the interpersonal skills you learned in Chapters 1 through 6, as well as others that you will study in Chapters 10 through 14, as you develop and maintain relationships. As you read through the descriptions that follow, try to assess your own level of competence and identify areas for improvement. But remember that you can also form satisfying relationships by seeking out partners with skill levels similar to your own.[10] For example, if you are not particularly comfortable with expressing emotions, you can have a successful relationship with a partner who is not overly expressive. In other instances, your partner's strengths might complement your weaknesses. Although these discussions present ideals for communication and relationships, it is important to remember that we all operate at less than the ideal level, and that many of us do it quite successfully.

Monitor Your Perceptions, Listen Actively, and Respond

We devoted two earlier chapters to perception and to listening and responding because of their importance to interpersonal communication. The skills we discussed in these chapters are also keys to success in ongoing relationships. If, for example, you can consciously attend to more of the cues you receive from others, you can learn more about how they react to different situations and then shape your relationship maintenance behaviours accordingly. By becoming more sensitive to your biases and working to counterbalance them, you can avoid overreacting to things your partner says and does. If you make a practice of checking the accuracy of your perceptions of others, you can avoid stewing and fretting over imagined slights and misunderstandings.

Listening skills are also crucial for developing and maintaining relationships. Listening clues you into others' needs, wants, and values and it enables you to respond to them in appropriate ways. In the initial stages of a relationship, partners share a great deal of information. The amount of information tapers off in the later stages and as a relationship continues over time. This tapering off creates the illusion that you don't have to listen as much or as well as you did early on. But listening is a way to demonstrate ongoing interest in another person. Even in long-term relationships, we do not know everything our partners have to say. It is still important to stop, look, and listen—to put down the newspaper or turn off the radio when our close friend begins talking to us.

You also need to listen actively and provide confirming responses. In Chapter 6 we discussed the notions of confirming and disconfirming responses. Using confirming responses increases your partner's sense of self-worth and communicates the value you place upon him or her. In addition, if you can develop an awareness of the biases that prevent you from responding with empathy, you can work deliberately to overcome them as you ask questions and paraphrase your partner's messages.

Be Open and Express Emotions

As we discussed in Chapter 8, for a relationship to develop, both partners have to self-disclose. And both must be sensitive to the timing and appropriateness of the disclosure. Failing to disclose or disclosing the wrong thing at the wrong time can damage a relationship. In a study of forty-six committed, romantic couples (couples who were married, cohabiting, engaged to be married, or who had been "serious" for an extended period of time), researchers found that the number one problem in such relationships is an inability to talk about negative feelings.[11] For example, partners often made the following types of observations, "When she gets upset she stops talking"; "He never lets me know when he's upset with something he doesn't like"; and "He just silently pouts."

In committed relationships, partners generally want to know how the other person is feeling, especially if those feelings are negative. However, many of us have difficulty expressing emotions. Some people equate expressing emotions with being weak; or they feel that it makes them too vulnerable. Even if we are willing to share positive feelings with others, we might feel it is risky to share negative ones. And as you saw in Chapter 8, that concern is not unfounded. Too much negative disclosure can reduce satisfaction in a relationship. There is value in sharing negative emotions, but the sharing must be at appropriate times and with appropriate language in order to be constructive.

Empathize and Adapt

The processes you learned in Chapters 1 and 3 for decentring and empathizing with others can greatly enhance your ability to maintain any relationship. As you

How comfortable are you expressing your emotions to others?

Think of specific people for each of the following categories: an acquaintance of the same sex, an acquaintance of the opposite sex, a friend of the same sex, a friend of the opposite sex, a close friend of the same sex, a close friend of the opposite sex, a parent or relative of the same sex, and a parent or relative of the opposite sex.

Using a scale from 1 (most comfortable) to 10 (least comfortable), for each person, indicate how comfortable you would be about sharing the following feelings:

_____ liking for the other person

_____ love for the other person

_____ anger with the other person

_____ disappointment with the other person

_____ liking for a third person

_____ love for a third person

_____ anger toward a third person

_____ disappointment with a third person

_____ anger toward yourself

_____ disappointment in yourself

_____ embarrassment

_____ your fears

_____ happiness

_____ enthusiasm

_____ pride

_____ uncertainty

Compare your scores for each person. With whom are most comfortable sharing your emotions? Compare the emotions you are most open about with the emotions you are most closed about. What makes you uncomfortable about sharing certain emotions?

recall, decentring and empathizing give you a better understanding of your partner. They allow you to select the most effective strategies to help you accomplish your communication goals—to adapt. To **adapt** means to adjust your behaviours in accord with the relationship or situation. When you modify your behaviour in anticipation of an event, you **adapt predictively**. For example, you might decide to buy a friend flowers before you break a date because you believe the flowers will soften the blow. When you modify your behaviour after an event, you **adapt reactively**. For example, you might buy your friend flowers to apologize for a fight. The purpose of both types of adaptation is to strengthen the relationship.

Table 9.2 contains nine common types of predictive and reactive communication adaptation behaviours. Use this table to examine your own behaviours. Which types do you use most frequently? Which types do you never use? Could these behaviours improve your relationships?

Although these adaptation behaviours are extremely beneficial to the development of a strong relationship, they also require a lot of effort. It is challenging to consciously consider each message we send. Normally, we use scripts and rituals to communicate mindlessly, without constantly monitoring or considering the impact of each message. As you learned in Chapter 1, we have a natural tendency to be egocentric, to focus on ourselves instead of others. Often, when we communicate, we create and send messages to others that make sense to us without truly considering whether those messages will make sense to others. If we are interacting with others who are quite similar to us, egocentric communication is usually functional. But it fails us if the other person is markedly different and cannot effectively decode

Table 9.2

Communication Adaptation Behaviours

Type	Examples
TOPICAL: Choosing a topic or issue to discuss because you know it will interest the other person.	Talking about a mutual friend, talking about a party you both went to, asking if he or she saw a particular play that was in town.
EXPLANATORY/ELABORATION: Providing additional information or detail because you recognize that the other person does not know it.	Explaining your mother's eating habits to a new friend, explaining to a neighbour who has squirrel problems how you keep them away from your bean plants.
WITHHOLDING EXPLANATION OR INFORMATION: Not providing explanation because your partner already knows the information; because it might hurt or anger your partner; because of fear of how the other person might misuse it; or to avoid violating a confidentiality.	Not elaborating on the parts of an auto-engine when you describe a car problem because you know the listener is knowledgeable about cars; not telling a friend you saw his or her lover with another person because he/she would be hurt; not telling someone about your interest in a mutual friend because you are afraid that person would blab about it to the mutual friend.
EXAMPLES/COMPARISONS/ANALOGIES: Choosing examples that you know your partner will find relevant.	Explaining roller blading by comparing it to ice skating, something your partner knows how to do.
PERSONAL REFERENCING: Referring to your partner's specific attitudes, interests, personality, traits, ethnic background, etc.	"I've got something to tell you I think you'll find funny." "Could you help me balance my chequebook; you're so good at math." "That's a behaviour I'd expect from you, given the way your parents raised you."
VERNACULAR/LANGUAGE: Choosing or avoiding certain words because of their potential effect on the receiver. Using words that have a unique meaning for you and your partner. Using words that you think are appropriate to the other person's level of understanding.	A wife asking her husband if he was catching flies during a movie, meaning he was asleep with his mouth wide open. A father telling his child that a criminal is someone who does bad things. Two computer jocks talking about "bytes," "ram," and "chips."
DISCLOSURE: Consciously deciding to share information about one's self that the other does not know about you.	Telling your lover about your sexual fantasies. Telling your instructor about family problems.
IMMEDIATE FOLLOW-UP QUESTIONING: Seeking additional information from the other person about information he or she shares during the interaction.	"So, what was it like growing up in small town Alberta?" "Tell me more about your vacation in Toronto." "Where are you going on your date?"
DELAYED FOLLOW-UP QUESTIONING: Seeking additional information from the other person about previous information he or she shared.	"How's your mother doing after her operation yesterday?" "How was your date Saturday night?"
ADAPTING TO IMMEDIATE REACTION/FEEDBACK: Modifying your words or behaviour because of your partner's reaction.	If your friend starts to cry when you talk about her mother's death, you might quickly change the topic.

our messages. You need to adapt if a person is from another culture, when your partner cannot understand your messages, and when you are trying to gain something from another person.

Develop and Apply Communication Sensitivity

Another skill that fosters good relationships, **communication sensitivity**, requires an awareness and appreciation of all the dynamics of an interpersonal interaction. A willingness and ability to adapt, combined with sensitivity and perceptiveness about yourself, the situation, and the other, is called **rhetorical sensitivity**.[12] A rhetorically sensitive person:

- Draws from a repertoire of flexible roles or selves in response to different situations without losing sight of his or her "core" self.

- Avoids stylized behaviour.

- Has an ability to handle the strain involved in adapting.

- Has an interaction consciousness about when to say things, when not to say things, and when to use placating comments.

- Appreciates the multiple ways ideas and feelings can be communicated.[13]

    In the following example can you identify the rhetorically sensitive speaker?

    Pat: I just found out that I don't have enought credits in social science. I can't believe it! It means I'll have to plan on another term before I can graduate.

    Sam: I know that's tough since you were so anxious to finish school. It'll be over before you know it, though.

    Pat: Yeah, you're right. I need to go to the bathroom, I'll talk with you later.

    Sam: Okay. See ya.

    Tonya: Hey, Sam, what's up?

    Sam: Hi, Tonya. How was the concert last night?

    Tonya: It was awesome. I'm still buzzing from it. The special effects were fantastic.

    Sam: I saw in the news that they had tons of lasers and stuff.

    Tonya: Oh, yeah! It was the best light show I've seen—it was really well coordinated with the music.

    Sam: It's really thrilling when everything works together like that.

In contrast to rhetorically sensitive individuals are the noble self and the rhetorical reflector.[14] **Noble selves** are inflexible and refuse to adapt. They believe that any departure from their true self or personal norms would be hypocritical. They say things like, "You don't want me to be someone I'm not, do you?" and "What you see is what you get," and "If it's what I think, then I should be able to say it." **Rhetorical reflectors**, on the other hand, mold themselves to whatever the situation dictates or the other person wants. These individuals have no real sense of themselves; they take on a completely new persona for each situation. Unlike rhetorically sensitive people, they do not have a strong core self. Try the Communication Experience on page 266 to see which type you are most like.

Rhetorically sensitive people are usually **conversationally sensitive** people. They are able to pick up meanings in what people say, remember what has been said, and compose multiple ways of saying the same thing.[15] They have a desire to listen, skill in interpreting the levels of liking and power in interactions, and an appreciation for subtleties.[16] You can acquire these skills through practice. To be

Rhetorical Sensitivity[17]

For each of the following items, decide whether you feel the item is (1) almost always true, (2) sometimes true, or (3) almost never true.

_____1. A person should tell it like it is.

_____2. You should tell someone if you think he or she is giving you bad advice.

_____3. Saying what you think is a sign of friendship.

_____4. It is better to speak your gut feelings than to beat around the bush.

_____5. When someone has an irritating habit, he or she should be told about it.

_____6. If people would open up to each other, the world would be a better place.

Count how many 1s you marked, how many 2s, and how many 3s. The 1s correspond to noble self communicators, the 2s correspond to rhetorically sensitive communicators, and 3s correspond to rhetorical reflectors. What do your responses indicate about you? How do they match with your own perception of yourself? How does your classification affect the way you communicate with others?

---

conversationally sensitive you must open your eyes and ears to all that goes on in your interactions. You must pay attention, try to minimize the impact of your perceptual biases, ask for confirmation of the subtle meanings you perceive, and try to process information in chunks instead of forming global impressions.

Nonverbal sensitivity is the ability to pick up and accurately interpret the variety of nonverbal cues that we display in interactions. To improve your skills, review the suggestions in Chapter 5: consider the context, look for clusters of cues, and check out the accuracy of your interpretations. As we have seen, the more intimate the relationship becomes, the greater the reliance on nonverbal messages for communication. Your close friends expect you to pick up and understand their nonverbal cues. If you are insensitive to those cues, you will have difficulty understanding their intended meanings and possibly in maintaining your relationships.

Be Tolerant and Show Restraint

The most satisfying relationships are those in which both partners refrain from continually disagreeing, criticizing, and making negative comments to each other. Both individuals learn to accept the other and do not feel compelled to continually point out flaws or failures. One study found that well-adjusted couples focus their complaints on specific behaviours, whereas maladjusted couples complain about one another's personal characteristics. Well-adjusted couples are also kinder, more positive, and have more humour in their interactions. The partners tended to agree with one another's complaints, whereas the partners in maladjusted relationships launched countercomplaints.[18] In addition, happy couples, when compared to unhappy couples, display more affection through positive nonverbal cues, display more supportive behaviours, and make more attempts to avoid conflict.[19]

Maintaining a relationship requires tolerance. You must learn to accept your partners for who they are and put up with some things you dislike. When relationships begin to deteriorate, couples often lose their tolerance. They begin focusing on and criticizing characteristics that they used to accept.

You must also be selective about disclosing your negative feelings about your partner. Research has found that marital satisfaction rises with the number of positive feelings the partners disclose, not with the number of negative ones.[20] Moreover, when we express negative feelings, we often put people on the defensive, as in the following dialogue:

Henry: Janice, look at all the crumbs in the new carpet. Did you vacuum today?

Janice: Of course I did. If you'd quit eating your meals in front of the TV, there wouldn't be all those crumbs on the floor. I don't see you vacuuming up after yourself, your highness.

As we learned in Chapter 6, and as we will see again in Chapter 10, statements like Janice's might clearly express negative feelings, but the accusatory "you" language will probably launch a full-fledged conflict. She could have said, "When you ask me that way, I feel as if you're treating me like a servant." Then Henry might have gained some "other-perspective," apologized, and thought twice about how he asked the next time.

Manage Conflict Cooperatively

Conflicts are inevitable in interpersonal relationships. As relationships develop, the individuals share more personal information and spend more time together, so the likelihood for conflict increases. The key to successful relational development and maintenance is *not* to avoid conflict altogether, but rather to manage it effectively. Because effective conflict management is a key to successful relationships, we have devoted an entire chapter to it. Since Chapter 10 discusses in detail the nature, causes, and methods of dealing with interpersonal conflict, we will simply mention at this time that using a cooperative management style can actually transform conflict into an experience that strengthens a relationship. It can clarify the definition of the relationship, increase the exchange of information, and create a cooperative atmosphere for problem solving.

Gain Compliance

The final skill for developing and maintaining relationships might seem somewhat contrary to the ones we have been discussing. Strictly speaking, to **gain compliance** is to use persuasive strategies to accomplish your personal goals—that is, to get your own way. We are not urging you to force your will upon others. We are, however, suggesting that it is sometimes ethical and moral to persuade others to go your way. In an ideal situation, the resulting interactions will fulfill both partners' goals.

You need compliance-gaining strategies if you encounter resistance to fulfilling your goal. For example, suppose you want to go out to a movie and you need to borrow money from one of your friends to pay for it. You may simply ask, "Can I borrow five dollars so I can go to a movie?" If your friend says, "Sure," the interaction is completed. If your friend says, "No, you haven't paid me back from last time," however, you will probably use one of the compliance-gaining strategies listed in Table 9.3. The strategy you choose will depend upon your skill level, the nature of

One technique for managing intimate relationships is to back off occasionally—periods of closeness must be balanced by periods of distance. We need time to ourselves in order to recharge and gain perspective. The following excerpt reflects the use of decentring, restraint, and effective conflict management to maintain intimate relationships.

The kinds of things we get upset about in intimacy tend to follow certain themes. Basically, we become hurt or resentful because we're getting "too much" or "too little" of something. Too many demands, too much criticism, too much domination. Or the converse, too little affectional, conversational, or sexual attention (which translates into "you don't feel I'm important" or "you don't love me"). Insufficient empathy is usually voiced as "you don't understand me," and too little responsibility translates into failure to take one's share of household and/or financial tasks. All these complaints require some attention, action, or retreat.

SHIFTING GEARS: It's not enough to identify the source of personal concern. You have to present your concerns in a way your partner can hear. If I say directly to my partner, "I'm afraid you're going to leave me," he has the opportunity to respond, "Darling, that's not true. What gave you that idea?" I get the reassurance I need. But if I toss it out in an argument, in the form of "you don't care about me," then my partner's emotional arousal keeps him from hearing me. And he is likely to back away—just when I need reassurance most.

If people were aware that intimate relationships are by nature characterized by ambivalence, they would understand the need to negotiate occasional retreats. They wouldn't feel so threatened by the times when one partner says, "I have to be by myself because I need to think about my life and where I'm going." Or "I need to be with my friends and spend time playing." If people did more backing off into constructive activities, including time to meditate or play, intimate relationships would be in much better shape today.

If couples could be direct about what they need, then the need for retreat would not be subject to the misrepresentation that now is rampant. The trouble is, we don't talk to each other that openly and honestly. What happens is one partner left behind doesn't know what the withdrawal means. But he or she draws on a personal history which provides room for all sorts of negative interpretations, the most common being "he doesn't care about me."

No matter how hard a partner tries to be all things to us, gratifying all of another's needs is a herculean task—beyond the human calling. Criticism, disappointment, and momentary rejection are intrinsic parts of intimate life; developing thicker skin can be healthy. And maintaining a life apart from the relationships is necessary. Energy invested in other people and activities provides a welcome balance.

From: Geraldine K. Piorkowski, *Psychology Today.* Reprinted with permission from *Psychology Today* magazine, copyright © 1995 (Sussex Publishers, Inc.).

the relationship, the amount of interaction time that is available, the likelihood of future interaction, opportunities for interaction, and concern for the relationship.

The shortcoming of the list in Table 9.3 is that it does not adequately reflect the ongoing, transactive nature of interpersonal persuasion.[21] Often, we plot strategies that develop over a number of interactions and modify them in accordance with others' responses. For example, before you ask to borrow money from your friend, you first might do a few favours for her during the day. Then if your friend says no, you might remind her that she owes you for all you've done for her. If she still says no, you might offer to help her over the weekend with her class project. The type of relationship you have established with the other person will also affect your strategy. If you often struggle for power, you will probably choose some of the negative strategies in Table 9.3. If your relationship is usually cooperative, you probably will attempt to find areas of agreement so that one partner's gain is not at the other's expense. Often we face little resistance to our requests from our partners, so we have no need for any compliance-gaining strategy.

Many of the communication skills that we have already discussed will play a role in your compliance-gaining attempts. In Chapter 4, we discussed the listening steps: stop, look, and listen. Those three steps can facilitate effective compliance gaining. You need to stop and focus your attention on what you want to gain and on your partner. Look at cues about your partner, and your partner's reactions to your compliance-gaining attempts. And finally, listen for information from your partner that can be incorporated in your strategies. Your abilities to listen and perceive cues from your partner, to use decentring to adapt to your partner's needs, and to use your communication sensitivity will enhance your ability to gain compliance.

Seeking to gain compliance from another person raises a number of ethical concerns. To what degree is it ethical to manipulate an individual in order to further your own self-interests? At what point does the ability to gain compliance mean that you are exploiting the other person? Is it ethical to lie or deceive another person in order to achieve your goals? To what degree are threats and punishment ethical ways of gaining compliance? Being effective in gaining compliance carries a responsibility for not taking advantage of other people's vulnerabilities and confidences. For example, if someone has shared very personal information with you, there is an expectation and trust that you will not use that information for personal gain, as in compliance gaining.

COMMUNICATION EXPERIENCE

Compliance Gaining

Think of something you have been unsuccessful at getting from a friend. Look through the list of compliance-gaining strategies and choose one you have not tried before that you think might work on your friend. Then try it. What happened?

If it didn't work, how did your friend react to the strategy? Why did the strategy fail? Is there another strategy that might have worked better?

If it did work, why did your friend respond positively? Would this strategy work in other situations with other people? Why or why not?

Did it seem ethical to you to plot out a strategy for getting what you wanted from your friend? Should you feel guilty because you have manipulated your friend? What did your friend have to sacrifice? What did your friend gain? Did your friend actually forfeit something against his or her wishes?

Table 9.3

Compliance Gaining Strategies

Strategy	Description	Example
1. Promise	You promise to reward your partner if he or she complies.	"I'll help you study for your next stat class if you let me borrow your psych notes tonight."
2. Threat	You threaten to punish your partner if he or she does not comply.	"If you don't let me borrow your car I'll tell your boyfriend about how you cheated on him."
3. Positive Expertise	You tell your partner that if he or she complies, he or she will be rewarded because of the "nature of things."	"If you just studied harder you'd get good grades and you could become a lawyer."
4. Negative Expertise	You tell your partner that if he or she doesn't comply, he or she will be punished because of the "nature of things."	"If you don't stop talking back to your boss, you'll never get ahead."
5. Liking	You act friendly and helpful to get your partner in a "good frame of mind."	"Wow, what a great outfit. Red is really your colour. Let me help you carry those groceries upstairs."
6. Pre-Giving	You give your partner some reward before making your request.	"You sit down, I'll do the dishes tonight. By the way, do you need your car tonight?"
7. Aversive Stimulation	You continuously punish your partner until he or she complies.	"I know this is the third time in a row I've said you can't borrow my car. When are you going to stop playing your music after midnight like I've asked?"
8. Debt	You remind your partner that he or she owes you because of something you've done for him or her in the past.	"You know I've taken out the garbage for the last three weeks. So you should clean out the refrigerator, instead of me."
9. Moral Appeal	You tell your partner that if he or she doesn't comply, he or she will be acting immorally.	"You need to tell my father you broke his power saw when you return it. Otherwise, it's the same as stealing—you'd be a thief."
10. Positive Self-feeling	You tell your partner that he or she will feel good about him- or herself by complying.	"I know you don't want to go and visit your grandmother, but you'll feel better if you do."
11. Negative Self-feeling	You tell your partner that he or she will feel bad about him- or herself if he or she doesn't comply.	"If you don't go and visit your poor old grandmother, you're going to feel guilty about it all week."
12. Positive Altercasting	You tell your partner that people with "good" qualities would comply.	"People who are loving, caring, and considerate are always willing to lend a friend some money."
13. Negative Altercasting	You tell your partner that only people with "bad" qualities would not comply.	"Only a person who is selfish and mean would refuse to lend a good friend some money."
14. Altruism	You ask the other person to do something out of the kindness of his or her heart; to do it for you not for him- or herself.	"You know I've never asked you to do anything for me before, but I'm asking this time."
15. Positive Esteem	You tell your partner that he or she will gain the regard of others, and increase his or her status by complying.	"All of us who work for you will think you're a great boss if you try to convince the owners to increase our salaries."
16. Negative Esteem	You tell your partner that he or she will lose the regard of other people, and decrease his or her status by not complying.	"I know that everyone under your supervision will be really disappointed in you if you don't even try to convince the owners that we deserve a raise."

Adapted from Marwell and Schmitt.[22]

De-Escalating and Ending Relationships

As Figure 9.1 shows, one half of the model for relational stages that we first saw in Chapter 7 is devoted to the process of de-escalating and terminating relationships. **Relational de-escalation** involves a reduction in the level of intimacy, commitment, self-disclosing, and general resources necessary to hold a relationship together. A relationship can descend through several stages before it reaches termination, or the end of interpersonal communication. As we mentioned before, no relationship ever really comes to a complete end, because each has a lasting impact. The more intimate a relationship becomes, the greater its impact. Individuals who have been married and divorced are certainly affected for a long time by that experience, even though the two partners might never see each other again.

The de-escalation and termination of a relationship is not inherently bad. Not all relationships are meant to endure.

Figure 9.1

Model of Relational Stages

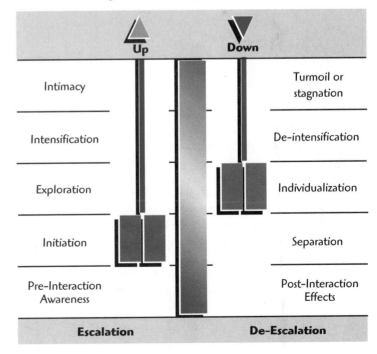

Escalation	De-Escalation
Intimacy	Turmoil or stagnation
Intensification	De-intensification
Exploration	Individualization
Initiation	Separation
Pre-Interaction Awareness	Post-Interaction Effects

Ending a relationship can be a healthy move if the relationship is harmful, or if it no longer provides confirmation of the self or satisfies interpersonal needs; it also can open the door to new relationships. Sometimes we choose not to end a relationship, but rather to de-escalate to a less intimate stage where there is a better balance between benefits and costs.

Breaking up an intimate relationship is hard because of the degree to which we become dependent upon the other person to confirm our sense of self. When a relationship ends, we may feel as if we need to redefine who we are. The most satisfying breakups are those that confirm both partners' worth rather than degrade it. "I just can't be what you want me to be"; "I'll always love you but . . . "; or "You're a very special person, but I need other things in life" are all examples of statements that do not destroy self-esteem.

The process of ending a relationship is considerably different when only one party wants out of the relationship (unilateral) than when both are agreeable to it (bilateral).[23] In **bilateral dissolutions**, both parties are predisposed to ending the relationship; they simply need to sort out details such as timing, dividing possessions, and defining conditions for the contact after the breakup. In a **unilateral dissolution**, the person who wants to end the relationship must use compliance-gaining strategies to get his or her partner to agree to the dissolution. Sometimes, however, people simply walk out of a relationship.

How Relationships End

A declining relationship usually follows one of several paths. Sometimes a relationship loses steam and runs down like a dying battery. Instead of a single event that causes the breakup, the relationship **fades away**—the two partners just drift further and further apart. They spend less time together, let more time go by between interactions, and stop disclosing much about themselves. You've probably had a number of friendships that ended this way—perhaps long-distance relationships. Long-distance relationships require a great deal of effort to maintain, so a move can easily decrease the level of intimacy. The artist Edward Hopper seems to have captured the essence of fading away in his oil painting at right. In this picture, the relationship seems lifeless and destined for eventual termination.

Some relationships end in sudden death.[24] As the name suggests, **sudden death** moves straight to separation. One partner might move away or die, or more frequently, a single precipitating event such as infidelity, breaking a confidence, a major conflict, or some other major role violation precipitates the breakup. Sudden death is like taking an express elevator from a top floor to ground level.

In between fading away and sudden death lies incrementalism. **Incrementalism** is the process by which conflicts and problems continue to accumulate in the relationship until they reach a critical mass that leads to the breakup; the relationship becomes intolerable or, from a social exchange perspective, too costly. "I just got to a point where it wasn't worth it anymore," and "It got to the point where all we did was fight all the time" are typical statements about incremental endings. For each of the three paths, individuals can choose from a variety of strategies to end the relationship.

Artist Edward Hopper often depicted fading relationships in his realistic paintings. (*Room in New York*, 1932; Sheldon Memorial Art Gallery, University of Nebraska–Lincoln, F. M. Hall Collection.)

UNDERSTANDING DIVERSITY

Men and women differ when it comes to dating and marital breakups. Women tend to be stronger monitors of the relationship, so they usually detect trouble before men do. Their sensitivity to the health of the relationship might be one factor that makes them more likely to initiate the termination of a relationship as well.[25] However, when some men want out of a relationship they engage in behaviours that women find totally unacceptable. This allows both partners to feel as if they were the ones who initiated the breakup and therefore to "save face."

Problems are sometimes associated with behaviours that appear early in a relationship. Marriages in which the men avoid interaction by stonewalling and responding defensively to complaints are more likely to end in divorce.[26]

In one study of divorce, men tended to see the later part of the process as more difficult, whereas the women said the period before the decision to divorce was more difficult. In addition, two-thirds of the women were likely to discuss marital problems with their children as compared to only one-fourth of the men; and men were twice as likely to say that no one helped them during the worst part of the process.[27]

Strategies for Ending Relationships

When the vitality in long marriages fades away over a period of years, the individuals move slowly through the de-escalation stages before finally divorcing. Brand new relationships are far more likely to end abruptly. As you saw in Figure 9.1, the farther up the relational highrise you take the elevator, the longer the ride down.

But no matter what stage a relationship is in, partners use both direct and indirect strategies when they wish to end it. **Indirect strategies** represent attempts to break up a relationship without explicitly stating the desire to do so. **Direct strategies** involve explicit statements. The strategy that a person chooses will depend upon the level of intimacy in the relationship, the level of desire to help the partner save face, the degree of urgency for terminating the relationship, and the person's interpersonal skills. The Cathy cartoon illustrates the difficulties we all face in coming up with a unique and nonthreatening strategy for ending a relationship.

INDIRECT STRATEGIES

One researcher identifies three strategies that people use to indirectly disengage: withdrawal, pseudo-de-escalation, and cost escalation. *Withdrawal* involves reducing the amount of contact and interaction without any explanation.[28] This strategy is the most dissatisfying for the other partner.[29] Withdrawal represents an attempt to avoid a confrontational scene and to save face.

In *pseudo-de-escalation* one partner claims that he or she wants to redefine the relationship at a lower level of intimacy, but in reality, he or she wants to end the relationship. Statements such as, "Let's just be friends" or "I think of you as more of a sister" might be sincere, or they might reflect an unspoken desire to disengage completely. When both parties want to end the relationship, they sometimes use mutual pseudo-de-escalation and enter into a false agreement to reduce the level of intimacy as they move to disengagement.

Cost escalation is an attempt to increase the costs associated with the relationship in order to encourage the other person to terminate it. A dissatisfied partner might ask for an inordinate amount of the other person's time, pick fights, criticize the other person, or violate relational rules. As the Understanding Diversity box on page 273 indicates, this is a strategy that men apparently use more often than women.

■ DIRECT STRATEGIES

The same researcher also identified four direct strategies that we use to terminate relationships: negative identity management, justification, de-escalation, and positive tone.[30] *Negative identity management* is a direct statement of the desire to terminate the relationship. It does not take into account the other's feelings, and it might even include criticisms. "I want out of our relationship"; "I just can't stand to be around you anymore"; and "I'm no longer happy in this relationship and I want to date other people" reflect negative identity management.

Justification is a clear statement of the desire to end the relationship accompanied by an honest explanation of the reasons. Justification statements may still hurt the other person's feelings: "I've found someone else that I want to spend more time with who makes me happy" and "I feel as if I've grown a great deal and you haven't." But a person who uses justification does not fault the other person, and he or she makes some attempt to protect both parties' sense of self. One researcher found that most people on the receiving end like this strategy best.[31]

De-escalation is an honest statement of a desire to redefine the relationship at a lower level of intimacy or to move toward ending the relationship. One partner might ask for a trial separation so that both people can explore other opportunities and gain a clearer understanding of their needs:[32] "Neither of us seems to be that happy with the relationship right now, so I think we should cool it for a while and see what happens."

Positive tone is the direct strategy that is most sensitive to the other person's sense of self. This strategy can seem almost contradictory because the initiator tries to affirm the other's personal qualities and worth at the same time that he or she calls a halt to the relationship. "I love you; I just can't live with you"; "I'm really sorry I've got to break off the relationship"; and "You really are a wonderful person, you're just not the one for me" are examples of positive tone statements.

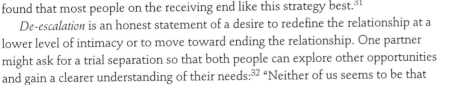

COMMUNICATION EXPERIENCE

How Your Relationships Have Ended

I dentify two relationships that you have ended and two relationships that the other person ended. For each relationship try to determine which of the indirect or direct strategies were used to end the relationship. What differences were there in how the relationships ended? What effects do you think the choice of strategy had upon you and your partner?

Conduct a survey of your friends by asking them these same questions. What conclusions can you draw about how people feel concerning different relationship termination strategies?

Components of the Human Communication Process

	Term	Explanation
How Relationships End	Fading Away	The relationship dissolves slowly as intimacy declines.
	Sudden Death	The relationship ends abruptly, usually in response to some precipitating event.
	Incrementalism	Relational conflicts and problems accumulate until they become intolerable, then the relationship ends.
Indirect Strategies	Withdrawal	Reducing the amount of contact without any explanation.
	Pseudo-de-escalation	Claiming a desire for less intimacy when you really want out.
	Cost Escalation	Increasing relational costs to encourage the other to end the relationship.
Direct Strategies	Negative Identity Management	Directly stating a desire to end the relationship without concern for the other person's feelings.
	Justification	Directly stating a desire to end the relationship with an explanation of the reasons.
	De-escalation	Directly stating a desire to lower the level of intimacy or move toward termination.
	Positive Tone	Directly stating a desire to end the relationship while affirming the other person's value.

Causes of De-Escalation and Termination

The reasons for ending an interpersonal relationship are as varied as relationships themselves. In general, we end relationships when they cost us more than they reward us. This does not mean that as soon as a relationship becomes difficult we dump it. Relationships are somewhat like savings accounts. If the relationship is profitable, you deposit your excess rewards into an emotional savings account. Then at times when the costs exceed the rewards, you draw from your savings account to make up the deficit. In other words, if you have had a strong, satisfying relationship with someone for a long period of time, you will be more inclined to stay in the relationship during rough times. There might be a point, however, at which your savings account will run out, and you will decide to close your account—end the relationship. Of course, if you can foresee that you will reap more benefits in the future, you might decide to keep the account open, even when it is overdrawn. In addition, if you have had even less satisfying relationships in the past, or if your alternatives seem more dismal than your current relationships, you might decide to stick it out.[33] Of course, under those relational circumstances, when attractive alternatives do appear, relationships often suffer a sudden death.

Table 9.4

Reasons Given for Breakups[34]

Faults
I realized that he/she had too many personality faults.
He/she behaved in ways that embarrassed me.
His/her behaviours were more to blame for the breakup than anything else.

Unwillingness to Compromise
I realized she/he was unwilling to make enough contributions to the relationship.
I felt that he/she no longer behaved towards me as romantically as she/he once did.
I felt that he/she took me for granted.
I felt that he/she wasn't willing to compromise for the good of the relationship.

Feeling Constrained
I felt that the relationship was beginning to constrain me, and I felt a lack of freedom.
Although I still cared for him/her, I wanted to start dating other people.
Although this relationship was a good one, I started to get bored with it.
He/she made too many contributions, and I started to feel suffocated.

One researcher found that most people attribute breakups to one of three main causes.[35] As Table 9.4 shows, "faults" are the number one cause. These are problems with personality traits or behaviours that one partner dislikes in the other. The number two cause, "unwillingness to compromise," represents a variety of failings on the part of one or both partners, including failure to put enough effort into the relationship, a decrease in effort, or failure to make concessions for the good of the relationship. The final cause, "feeling constrained," reflects one partner's desire to be free from the commitments and constraints of a relationship. But a variety of other elements can contribute to the breakup of both romantic and non-romantic relationships, including loss of interest in the other person, desire for independence, and conflicting attitudes about the definition of the relationship in areas such as sexual conduct, marriage, and infidelity.

A Model for Ending Relationships

Steve Duck developed a model to show stages in ending a relationship.[36] As Figure 9.2 shows, first one partner reaches some threshold of dissatisfaction that prompts him or her to consider ending the relationship. In this **intra-psychic phase**, you focus on evaluating your partner's behaviours, often fixing on the reasons in Table 9.4 to justify withdrawing. You don't intentionally communicate these thoughts to your partner, however, and you often decide not to dissolve the relationship. From time to time we all become frustrated with a relationship that we consider terminating, but never proceed further than this phase. However, we might "leak" our thoughts and feelings through our communication, displaying such emotions as hostility, anxiety, stress, or guilt. We might decide to confide to a third party about our dissatisfaction. During this phase we might consider various strategies for ending the relationship. Note the nonverbal "leakage" behaviours in this passage about a fictional love affair.

He dropped my hand, which he had been clasping, and signalled to the waiter for the bill.

We went home in silence. Outside my flat, which I did not invite him to enter, he offered me his cheek to kiss. The gesture was so completely dismissive that I knew it for what it was, the gesture that indicated the end of the affair.

At some point we might decide to move from our internal contemplations about the relationship to confronting our partner. This is the **dyadic phase** in the model. If your partner feels challenged and intimidated by your desire to end the relationship, you might have to justify your thoughts and feelings. Your partner might also criticize your behaviour and identify your failings. He or she might raise

Figure 9.2

A Model for Ending Relationships

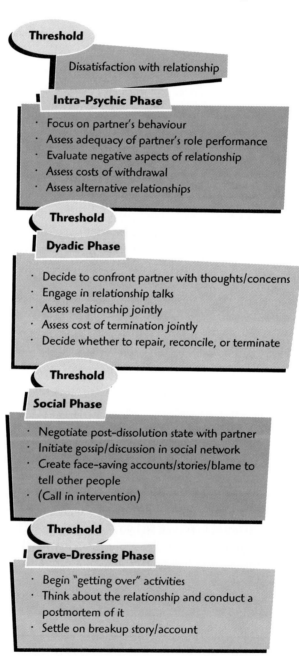

Threshold

Dissatisfaction with relationship

Intra-Psychic Phase

- Focus on partner's behaviour
- Assess adequacy of partner's role performance
- Evaluate negative aspects of relationship
- Assess costs of withdrawal
- Assess alternative relationships

Threshold

Dyadic Phase

- Decide to confront partner with thoughts/concerns
- Engage in relationship talks
- Assess relationship jointly
- Assess cost of termination jointly
- Decide whether to repair, reconcile, or terminate

Threshold

Social Phase

- Negotiate post-dissolution state with partner
- Initiate gossip/discussion in social network
- Create face-saving accounts/stories/blame to tell other people
- (Call in intervention)

Threshold

Grave-Dressing Phase

- Begin "getting over" activities
- Think about the relationship and conduct a postmortem of it
- Settle on breakup story/account

issues that cause you to re-evaluate the relationship, your partner, and the costs of dissolving the relationship. You might decide instead to work on improving and repairing the relationship.

If you and your partner agree to end the relationship, you enter the **social phase** and begin making the information public. Sometimes a person's social network will mobilize to preserve the relationship. Friends might act as mediators, encouraging reconciliation and suggesting ways to repair the relationship. Of course, friends can also reinforce a decision to separate. Rumours and stories about what happened and what is happening can fuel bad feelings and hasten the end of the relationship.

In the **grave-dressing phase**, one or both partners may attempt to place flowers on the grave of their relationship to cover up the hurt and pain associated with its death. They need a public story that they can share with others about what happened: "We still love each other; we just decided we needed more in our lives." Such a story often places blame on the other partner: "I knew he had his faults, but he thought he could change, and he just wasn't able to." During this phase, our friends encourage us to get back into social activities; they might even try to fix us up with dates. Most importantly, we go through an internal stage in which we come to accept the end of the relationship. We let go of feelings of guilt, failure, and blame.

Identifying and Acting upon Trouble Signs in Relationships

As the Understanding Diversity box on page 273 indicates, women usually sense trouble in a relationship earlier than do men, but what exactly do they sense? Because each stage in a relationship has unique communication qualities, specific verbal and nonverbal cues can tip us off when a relationship begins to de-escalate.[37] There is a decrease in touching and physical contact (including less sexual activity), physical proximity, eye contact, smiling, tonal variety in the voice, and ease of interaction. In addition, there is a decrease in the amount of time spent together, an increase in time between interactions, and more separation of possessions. The interactions become less personal, and so does the language.

Couples use fewer intimate terms; they use less present tense and more past tense; they make fewer references to their future in the relationship; they use more qualified language ("maybe," "whatever," "we'll see"); make fewer evaluative statements; and spend less time discussing any given topic. They fight more, and they disclose less. If one person becomes less open about discussing attitudes, feelings, thoughts, and other personal issues, he or she is probably signalling a desire to terminate, or at least redefine, the relationship. Can you pick up the signals of the couple's difficulty reflected in the painting on page 280?

When you pick up signals of relational problems, you have three choices: just wait and see what happens; make a decision to end the relationship; or try to repair the relationship. Repairing the relationship involves applying all the maintenance skills we talked about earlier. Some of the strategies for dealing with conflict that you will learn in Chapter 10 will also help you. Underlying the success of any repair

When one partner wants to end a relationship, he or she typically sends clear signals to that effect. This poignant painting by artist Eduard Manet depicts a relationship on a downward journey. (Erich Lessing/Art Resource)

effort, however, is the degree to which both partners want to keep the relationship going. The nature of the problem, the stage of the relationship, and the commitment and motivation of the partners all affect the success of repair efforts. There is no single quick solution to relational problems because so many factors influence each one. You need to focus on the specific concerns, needs, and issues that underlie the problem; then adapt specific strategies to resolve it. Professional counselling might be an important option. If you do choose to end the relationship, consider your goals. Do you want to continue the relationship at a less intimate level, or terminate it altogether? Do you care enough about the other person to want to preserve his or her self-esteem? Are you aware of the costs involved in ending the relationship? There is no one correct or best way to end a relationship. Ending relationships is also not something you can practice in order to improve. But you can practice the effective relational management skills such as decentring and empathy, adaptation, and compliance gaining. These skills will also help you in ending relationships.

The final issue to consider is how to deal with someone who wants to end his or her relationship with you. Again, there is no pat answer. If a friend stops calling or visiting, should you just assume the relationship is over and leave it alone, or should you call and ask what's up? People lose contact for a myriad of reasons. Sometimes it is beneficial to ask an individual directly if he or she is breaking off the relationship, although such direct requests place your self-concept on the line. How should you react if your friend confirms a desire to end the relationship? If possible, try to have a focused discussion on what has contributed to his or her decision. You might get information you need to repair the relationship. Or you might gain information that will help you in future relationships.

When intimate relationships do end, we rely on our social networks for support and self-confirmation. Advice about how to handle the loss of a close relationship is plentiful (see the article below), but basically each person must find a way to compensate for the loss of intimacy and companionship. The loss of an important relationship hurts, but it need not put us out of commission if we make the most of our friends and family.

Loss of a Friend Can Hurt More than a Romantic Split

You can't think of the person without a sickening lurch in your gut. You alternate between angrily wishing you'd never met the Judas and agonizing over what went wrong. It hurts when mutual friends bring up the person's name, when they tell you about the fun times you weren't invited to and wouldn't attend even if you were.

You have all the sloppy symptoms of a broken heart.

But you don't go to marriage counselling—you're not married.

You don't go to family counselling—you're not related.

You don't go to couples counselling—you're not lovers.

You don't even suggest to the person any counselling at all, lest you be thought insane.

You're "just friends," so there's no one to talk to about your shattered psyche, no words like "ex-lover" or "ex-husband" to legitimize your nemesis, no socially acceptable ritual to mourn the loss of the trusted confidant you once held dear.

Friendship—in other times and places lauded as passionately as romantic love—today takes a cultural back seat to every other important relationship.

Yet despite society's alleged nonchalance, the loss of a friend can cut more deeply than losing a lover.

"I felt totally betrayed and completely lost," says editor Justine Kaplan, 33, whose best friend, hurting from a Kaplan matchmaking attempt that went awry, told her that she no longer wanted to be friends. "I didn't understand. You're not supposed to just stop being friends with someone.

"I wanted to say, 'What the hell is this—you're breaking up with me?'"

She sighs, "With a lover, you can call them up later and say 'Let's be friends,' but when a friend rejects you, what's left to do?"

Any review of the popular media yields reams of articles on how to survive breakup of a lovematch, but almost none on losing a friend. That doesn't surprise University of South Carolina social psychologist Keith Davis, who has been researching friendship breakups for a decade.

"It's just a cultural bias," he says. "Researchers don't look at it, and people don't write about it."

He says his in-depth studies revealed two typical ways friendships end.

One is a "gradual growing apart, like when someone moves and doesn't stay in touch," he says. "The other is a betrayal, which in many ways feels quite similar to the experience with a lover."

The betrayals fall into three categories: stealing one's lover; not being there when needed, and the misuse of personal things, including property and secrets.

But whatever the betrayal, Davis says, working it through can transform the friendship into something better than it was.

"About half of my subjects said they were able to successfully repair the relationship," Davis says. "In the other half, what's learned is that the person can't be trusted, and they don't want to be around the person ever again."

Not surprisingly, Davis says anger and sadness are the most common emotions when friendships end.

"The nature of the emotion depends a lot on the specifics of the relationship," he says. "At the minimum you're angry beause you've been let down. And you become very sad because you thought you had a friend you could count on."

Still, most people in our culture don't really suffer over losing friends, says Gene Gordon, a Washington, D.C., psychoanalyst and clinical professor at George Washington University.

"Friendship is just not highly valued here," he says. "Breaking up means you're close to someone, but since most people aren't close, they don't feel the breakup. It's not like in places like Central America, where friendship is taken much more seriously. Here, friendships are taken vary casually."

In genuinely close friendship, Gordon says, it's natural to feel "extremely attached and very dependent." Therefore, breakups of those relationships are indeed traumatic.

"It's scary and lonely and awakens all the traumas of separation we've ever experienced in childhood," he says. "This doesn't mean one is immature. Very often, it speaks paradoxically to the maturity of the adult, that the friendship was that intimate to them."

When Laverne Left Shirley: How to Ease Breakup with a Buddy

Advice for the friend-lorn:

- Remember that it's natural to feel sad, angry, or guilty when you lose an important relationship.
- Give yourself permission and time to grieve.
- Give yourself credit for having cared enough about your friend to mourn the loss.
- Talk about your feelings. If talking to other friends doesn't help, seek professional counselling.
- Know that as painful as it may feel now, time will help.
- When the pain subsides, keep yourself open and willing to make new friends and cherish the ones you already have.
- Remember that it's rarely too late to forgive or ask for forgiveness.

From: Leslie Knowlton, *Los Angeles Times*. Copyright © 1995, Los Angeles Times. Reprinted by permission.

Summary

We use a variety of skills to escalate, maintain, and terminate interpersonal relationships. We disclose more intimate and risky information as the relationship continues to escalate. Strategies for maintaining relationships include avoidance, directness, and balance. The range of skills we need for relationship maintenance includes monitoring perceptions, listening actively, and responding confirmingly; being open and expressing emotions; empathizing and adapting; developing and applying communication sensitivity; being tolerant and showing restraint; managing conflict cooperatively; and gaining compliance.

UNDERSTANDING INTERPERSONAL RELATIONSHIPS

The other side of relationship escalation and maintenance is de-escalation and termination. On the way down, relationships can take three paths: fading away, sudden death, and incrementalism. Whether the disengagement is unilateral, with only one partner desiring it, or bilateral, with both wanting it, we can use direct or indirect strategies. Indirect strategies include withdrawal, pseudo-de-escalation, and cost escalation to end the relationship. Direct strategies are negative identity management, justification, de-escalation, and positive tone.

In general, relationships seem to end when the costs exceed the rewards over some period of time. The relationship no longer confirms an individual's sense of self enough to outweigh the demands the relationship places on the individual. The causes we give for ending a relationship fall into three categories: faults, unwillingness to compromise, and feeling constrained. We might communicate a desire to end the relationship intentionally or unintentionally through changes in our language and nonverbal communication.

A model for ending relationships has four phases: intra-psychic, dyadic, social, and grave-dressing. First, we internally assess the value of the relationship and consider termination; then we discuss it with our partner; we proceed by announcing the termination and interacting with friends and family; and finally, we come to grips with the consequences of separation.

Certain trouble signs signal changes in relationships. A decrease in physical contact, eye contact, smiling, the amount of time spent together, intimate language, and openness in discussing thoughts and feelings are signals that a relationship is de-escalating. The partners can try to repair the relationship by applying maintenance skills, but the results will depend upon their degree of mutual commitment. When we decide to end relationships, friends and family can provide comfort and support.

For Discussion and Review

■ FOCUS ON COMPREHENSION

1. Identify and explain three strategies for maintaining interpersonal relationships.

2. What seven interpersonal skills are associated with maintaining and escalating relationships?

3. What are direct and indirect strategies for ending a relationship?

4. What are the four phases identified in the model for ending relationships?

■ FOCUS ON CRITICAL THINKING

5. Which two skills are probably the most important for escalating a relationship and which two are least important? Why?

6. How do the strategies for maintaining a relationship relate to the indirect and direct strategies used for terminating a relationship?

7. How might the skills that are used for maintaining or escalating a relationship also be used for effectively terminating a relationship?

■ FOCUS ON ETHICS

8. How ethical is it for a person who is very skilled at compliance gaining to convince another person to escalate the relationship if that person has a strong initial resistance to escalation?

9. Under what circumstances might it be ethical for a person in an intimate relationship to use sudden death withdrawal as a strategy for ending a relationship? Under what circumstances would it be unethical?

Learning with Others

1. Working in groups of four or five students, use your own experiences to develop an answer to the following question: Do the reasons for breaking up a relationship change as the relationship becomes more intimate? To answer this question, start with casual relationships and identify reasons that people end those relationships. Next, talk about friendships, and discuss reasons for ending them. And finally, talk about intimate relationships and the reasons they break up. What are the similarities and differences among these different types of relationships and why they break up?

2. In groups of four or five, develop a survey of questions about what skills are critical for maintaining close relationships. Have each student conduct this survey with four or five of their friends. Then come back together as a group and total your survey results. How many of the communication skills that we identified in this chapter were named by the respondents? What new skills were identified? Report your results to the rest of the class.

3. In groups of four or five, videotape a five-minute conversation between two of your team members who know each other the best. They should try to carry on as natural a conversation as they can over anything they want. Watch the replay of the videotape, stopping it as necessary, as you evaluate which forms of adaptation from the list in Table 9.2 were present. Which types were easiest to identify? Why? Which were hardest? Why? How much of the time did the two team members actually adapt what they were saying to one another? What effect did adapting have upon the interaction?

1. At the end of each day for three or four days, stop and assess which of the seven interpersonal communication skills (refer to the Recap on page 271) you used the most in your interactions that day. Try to see if there is a consistent pattern in the skills you rely on. What skills do you seem to use the most? What skills do you use the least? How might using other skills affect your interactions and relationships?

2. Think about a close relationship you had that you ended. What strategy did you first use? How well did this strategy work? What was your partner's reaction to this strategy? How did you feel using this strategy? What other strategies were used, if any? What were the reactions to those? If you had it to do over again, what other strategy might you have chosen to use? How do you think your partner would have reacted to that strategy? Why? If you can't think of any relationship that you have ended, use one in which your partner has ended the relationship, and adapt the questions accordingly.

■ GLOSSARY

AVOIDANCE: A strategy for maintaining a relationship that involves ignoring discussions or opportunities for redefining the relationship.

DIRECTNESS: A strategy for maintaining a relationship that involves coming out and saying you want things to remain the same.

BALANCE: A strategy for maintaining a relationship that involves providing enough support to keep the relationship at a particular level.

ADAPTATION: Adjusting your behaviour in accordance with the relationship or situation.

PREDICTIVE ADAPTATION: Adjusting your behaviour in anticipation of another's reaction or of an event.

REACTIVE ADAPTATION: Adjusting your behaviour in response to another's behaviour or to an event.

COMMUNICATION SENSITIVITY: An awareness and appreciation of all the dynamics of interpersonal interactions.

RHETORICAL SENSITIVITY: A willingness and ability to adapt combined with a sensitivity and perceptiveness about your own self, the situation, and the other.

NOBLE SELF: An individual who is inflexible and refuses to adapt because he or she thinks that would be hypocritical.

RHETORICAL REFLECTOR: An individual who overadapts, taking on a self to fit each situation.

CONVERSATIONAL SENSITIVITY: The ability to pick up meanings in what is said, remember what was said, and compose multiple ways of saying the same thing.

NONVERBAL SENSITIVITY: The ability to pick up and accurately interpret nonverbal cues.

COMPLIANCE GAINING: The use of persuasive strategies to accomplish interpersonal goals.

RELATIONAL DE-ESCALATION: The downward movement of a relationship from one level to another through the reduction of intimacy, commitment, self-disclosing, and general resources.

BILATERAL DISSOLUTION: Ending a relationship when both parties are agreeable.

UNILATERAL DISSOLUTION: Ending a relationship when only one party is agreeable.

FADING AWAY: Ending a relationship by slowly drifting apart.

SUDDEN DEATH: Ending a relationship abruptly and without preparation.

INCREMENTALISM: Ending a relationship when conflicts and problems finally reach a critical mass.

INDIRECT RELATIONAL TERMINATION STRATEGIES: Attempts to break up a relationship without explicitly stating the desire to do so.

DIRECT RELATIONAL TERMINATION STRATEGIES: Explicit statements of a desire to break up a relationship.

INTRA-PSYCHIC PHASE: The first phase in a model of relationship termination: an individual engages in an internal evaluation of the partner.

DYADIC PHASE: The second phase in a model of relationship termination: the individual discusses termination with the partner.

SOCIAL PHASE: The third phase in a model of relationship termination: members of the social network around both parties are informed and become involved.

GRAVE-DRESSING PHASE: The final phase in a model relationship termination: the partners generate public explanations and move past the relationship.

Bridging Differences in Interpersonal Relationships

Even in the best of relationships, conflicts arise. The next two chapters focus on skills and frameworks for bridging relational chasms. Chapter 10 presents an overview of why conflicts occur and offers specific strategies for managing differences. Chapter 11 builds upon our ongoing examination of how gender, cultural, and ethnic differences can result in communication challenges. We explore the origins of these challenges and offer several concrete suggestions for meeting them.

Managing Conflict in Interpersonal Relationships

After studying this chapter, you should be able to:

1. Define conflict.

2. Compare and contrast three types of interpersonal conflict.

3. Identify commonly held myths about interpersonal conflict.

4. Describe differences between destructive and constructive approaches to managing conflict.

5. List and describe five stages of conflict.

6. Identify five types of power.

7. Describe three types of conflict management styles.

8. Identify and use conflict management skills to help manage emotions, information, goals, and problems when attempting to resolve interpersonal differences.

his house stinks," said Paul, wrinkling up his nose. "It smells like day-old garbage."

"Take it out yourself. It's your job," said Simone, turning her back on him to scrub furiously at an imaginary morsel of food on a frying pan that was already polished clean.

"Hey, hey," said Paul, holding up both hands in front of him, "I wasn't accusing you. I just said it smelled bad in here. Don't be so touchy."

"Oh, no? Well, you're always criticizing me. You think just because you have a big important job that you can come in here and say anything you like. And I come home from work feeling tired, too, you know, but you don't do anything to help, not even the things you agree to!" shouted Simone, turning around to confront her mate, planting her soapy hands on her hips.

"Well, you're always hocking me for no reason. I'm not putting up with this bad treatment from you anymore," snarled Paul. As he turned on his heel to stalk out of the kitchen, Simone burst into tears.

Does this conflict have a ring of familiarity? Do you know why Paul and Simone reached an impasse in their attempt to communicate? If you answered yes and then no, read on.

Eventually all relationships experience conflict. In the previous chapters we have focused on principles that explain how we develop and maintain relationships. Now we turn our attention to the issue of managing differences in our relationships with others. Paul and Simone's exchange is complicated, seething with conflicting goals and underlying resentments. How do we avoid the same kind of outcome in our own complicated exchanges?

The best route to success in resolving conflict effectively is acquiring knowledge about what conflict is, what makes it happen, and what we can do about it. We will begin by defining conflict, then examine some of the myths about it and focus on some of its constructive functions. We will also discuss the relationship among conflict, power, and conflict management styles. And finally, we will present conflict management skills that draw upon listening, responding, and problem solving.

What Is Conflict?

Simply stated, **interpersonal conflict** is a struggle that occurs when two people cannot agree upon a way to meet their needs. When the needs are incompatible, if there are too few resources to satisfy them, or if the individuals opt to compete rather than cooperate to achieve them, then conflict occurs. The intensity level of a conflict usually relates to the intensity of the unmet needs. One researcher developed the "struggle spectrum," shown in Figure 10.1, to describe conflicts ranging from mild differences to fights.[1] But at the bedrock of all conflict are differences—different goals, experiences, genders, cultures, and other factors.

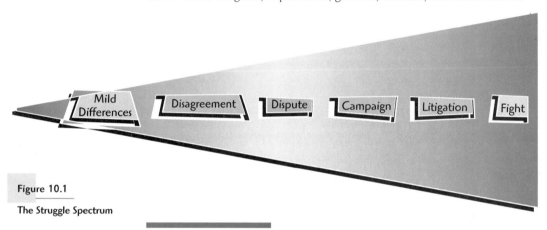

Figure 10.1

The Struggle Spectrum

Goals and Conflict

Psychologists agree that we are need-driven, goal-oriented individuals. Since most of what we do is based upon achieving a desirable goal, it is not surprising that most conflict is goal driven. You want something; your partner wants something else. If your partner interferes with your achievement of your goal, there may be a fight.

Suppose you are trying to find a parking spot in a busy shopping centre. Just as you find one, another shopper zips into "your" space. Your blood boils, and you get out of your car fighting mad. Or suppose you have had a difficult day at work. All you want to do is hunker down with a bowl of popcorn and watch MTV. But your spouse announces that a friend and his six-year-old son are coming over for dinner. "That's not what *I* feel like doing tonight. Why didn't you ask *me* before you invited them?" you shout. In both instances, your goals are colliding head on with someone else's, and you feel as if you have lost control of the situation.

Experiences and Conflict

Our inherent differences, coupled with our experiences, provide fuel for conflict. Consider the conflict that newlyweds Christy and Matt are having about how to celebrate the upcoming winter holidays. They have only two days to spend in their parents' town before returning to their new home in another city. Christy's family always exchanges presents and has a huge gathering on Christmas Eve and a family dinner on Christmas Day. Matt's family is Jewish. They celebrate Hanukkah quietly and do not feel comfortable either exchanging gifts for Christmas or trying to fit in at someone else's traditional celebration. Matt would like to celebrate Hanukkah on either Christmas Eve or Christmas Day at his parents' house, but Christy cannot understand why his family does not want to join her family's festivities. The conflict between Christy and Matt is not based upon different goals: they both want to see each set of parents and both want to celebrate the holidays. The conflict stems from their different backgrounds and experiences.

Interpersonal conflicts can range from mild disagreements to knock-down, drag-out fights. Many conflicts, however, stem from clashes in goals. (Superstock)

Types of Conflict

At some time or another, many close relationships go through a conflict phase. "We're always fighting," complains a newlywed. But if she were to analyze these fights, she would discover important differences among them. One research duo found that most conflicts fit into three different categories: (1) **pseudo conflict**—triggered by a lack of understanding; (2) **simple conflict**—stemming from different ideas, definitions, perceptions, or goals; and (3) **ego conflict**—based upon personal differences.

Pseudo Conflict

Will: Meet me at the fountain.

Sean: No, that's too far. Meet me by the administration building.

Will: The fountain is closer and more convenient.

Sean: No it's not.

Will: Yes it is. It's just off Market Street.

Sean: Oh, you mean the fountain by the administration building.

Will: Sure, that's exactly what I mean.

Sean: Oh, no problem. That's the place I had in mind.

Pseudo means false or fake. Pseudo conflict occurs when we simply miss the meaning in a message. But unless we clear up the misunderstanding by asking for more information, a real conflict might ensue. Note that in this example, Will offers helpful information ("It's just off Market Street") and Sean checks it with feedback ("Oh, you mean the fountain by the administration building").

Gender and Conflict

Throughout our discussion of interpersonal relationships we have noted that men and women learn different ways of relating to others. Research suggests that women are more likely to focus on relationship issues, whereas men typically focus on tasks.[2] Women often interact with others to achieve intimacy and closeness, but men interact to get something done or to accomplish something apart from the relationship. Men are often more aggressive and assertive than women when pursuing a goal or conquest.[3] The following list summarizes key differences that researchers have observed between some men's and women's responses to conflict.

Perceived Gender Differences in Responding to Conflict[4]

Females	Males
Concerned with equity and caring; connect with and feel responsible to others.	Concerned with equality of rights and fairness; adhere to abstract principles, rules.
Interact to achieve closeness and interdependence.	Interact for instrumental purposes; seek autonomy and distance.
Attend to interpersonal dynamics to assess relationship's health.	Are less aware of interpersonal dynamics.
Encourage mutual involvement.	Protect self-interest.
Attribute crises to problems in the relationship.	Attribute crises to problems external to the relationship.
Are concerned with the impact of the relationship on personal identity.	Are neither self- nor relationship-centred.
Respond to conflict by often focusing mainly on the relationship.	Respond to conflict by often focusing on rules and being evasive until a unilateral decision is reached.

Listening well and testing your understanding of a message with questions and feedback can help you keep these kinds of conflicts from escalating.

Simple Conflict

Simple conflict stems from differences in ideas, definitions, perceptions, or goals. You want to go to Lake Louise for your vacation; your spouse wants to go to Quebec City. Your spouse wants to fly; you would rather take the train. You understand each other, but you disagree.

A key to unravelling a simple conflict is to keep the conversation focused on the issues at hand so that the expression of differences does not deteriorate into a battle focusing on personalities.

The following exchange between Mark and Nick illustrates a conflict over a simple difference of opinion; notice how both partners stick to the issues and figure out a way to resolve their differences.

Although these findings provide a starting point for analyzing our conflicts with members of the opposite sex, we caution you against lapsing into "allness" statements such as, "Oh, you're just like all women. That's why you disagree with me." Or, "You're just like all men. You never want to focus on how I feel." Even thinking in these ways can prevent you from listening to what your partner is saying.

The most recent perspective on analyzing gender differences is called the *partnership perspective*. Rather than viewing gender differences as a gulf to be bridged, this perspective suggests that men and women are not locked into particular styles or approaches.[5] The partnership approach emphasizes the importance of keeping channels open and avoiding the tendency to stereotype communication styles by gender.

Culture and Conflict

An individual's culturally learned assumptions influence his or her conflict behaviour. In some cultures, most of the conflict is **expressive**; it focuses on the quality of relationships, and on managing interpersonal tension and hostility. In other cultures, conflict is more **instrumental**. It centres less on relationships and more on achieving a specific goal or objective.[6] One researcher noted that for people from low-context cultures, (those who derive more meaning from words than from the surrounding context), conflicts are most often instrumental.[7] Most North Americans come from low-context cultures. Many Asian cultures, on the other hand, are high-context cultures. They are also collectivist: they value group effort over individual achievement.[8] For people from these cultures, conflicts often centre on expressive, relational concerns. Keeping peace in the group or saving face is often a higher priority than achieving a goal.

Managing culture-based conflict requires a strong other-orientation. One research team suggests that North Americans of European descent receive little training in how to develop solutions to problems that are acceptable to an entire group.[9] They are often socialized to stick up for their own rights at any cost, and they approach conflict as a win-lose situation. In contrast, people from collectivist cultures approach conflict management situations from a win-win perspective; it is important that both sides save face and avoid ridicule. Such differences in approaches provide a double challenge. In addition to disagreeing over the issue at hand, people from different cultures may also have different strategies for reaching agreement.

Mark: I want to watch The Simpsons *tonight. It's their Christmas show.*

Nick: No way, man. I have to watch a documentary about textiles for my history class. It's an assignment.

Mark: But I've worked all weekend. I'm beat. The last thing I want to watch is some stuffy old documentary on the history of weaving.

Nick: Tell you what. Go ahead and watch The Simpsons. *I'll videotape the documentary and watch it later. Deal?*

Mark: Okay. Thanks. And I'll go grill some burgers so we can have supper together first.

This next exchange between Sue and Nadiya is a bumpier one. What starts as a simple conflict deteriorates into a series of personal attacks.

Nadiya: Sue, can I borrow your skirt? I have a date tonight. It would look great with my new jacket.

Sue: Sorry, Nadiya. I'm going to wear it tonight. I've got to give a presentation to the school board about our new volunteer program.

Nadiya: In case you don't remember, when you brought it home you said I could borrow it anytime. Besides, you haven't paid back the twenty bucks I loaned you to buy it.

Sue: Yes, but I bought the skirt especially for this occasion.

Nadiya: Well, don't ask to borrow anything from me ever again. You're just plain selfish.

Sue: Oh, yeah? Well you're the one who hogs all the space in the refrigerator. Talk about someone who's selfish. If that's not the pot calling the kettle black!

Nadiya: All right, now that we're being honest about who hogs what, you're the one who monopolizes the bathroom in the morning.

And so it escalates. The original disagreement about the skirt is forgotten and egos become attacked and bruised.

Ego Conflict

As you can see from the preceding example, a personal attack puts your partner on the defensive, and many people behave according to the adage, "The best defence is a good offence." When you launch a personal attack, you are "picking a fight." And as Sue and Nadiya's exchange illustrates, fights that begin as pseudo or simple conflicts can easily lapse into more vicious ego conflicts. Here's another example:

Michael: I don't think you should allow students to wear Halloween costumes to school. What can I do with a bunch of monsters and witches in P.E. class?

Julia: Well, all the parents are calling me up about it, and the kids are excited.

Michael: Is that how you make decisions? By responding to pressure from parents and kids?

Julia: You're just disagreeing with me because you wanted to be chair of this committee.

Michael: Not true! I just don't think you have the ability to chair it!

Note that as each person in the conflict becomes more defensive about his or her position, the issues become more tangled.

Remember Paul and Simone's argument at the beginning of this chapter? It started with what was probably an offhand remark and escalated into a major argument because both participants began attacking each other and bringing up other sensitive issues instead of focusing on the original comment.

If you find yourself involved in ego conflict, try to refrain from hurling personal attacks and emotional epithets back and forth.[10] Instead, take turns expressing your feelings without interrupting each other, then take time to cool off. It is difficult to use effective listening skills when your emotions are at a high pitch.

RECAP	Types of Conflict	
PSEUDO CONFLICT	Individuals misunderstand each other.	
SIMPLE CONFLICT	Individuals disagree over which action to pursue to achieve their goals.	
EGO CONFLICT	Individuals feel personally attacked.	

Myths About Conflict

Although not all conflict is destructive to our relationships, many cultures have taboos against displaying it in public. According to one researcher, many of us were raised with five **myths** that contribute to our negative feelings about conflict.[11] As you read the following sections, you may shake your head and say, "That's not where I came from." In some families, conflict is expressed openly and often. But even if your experience has been different, reading about these prevailing myths may help you understand your emotional responses to conflict or your partner's response when conflict occurs.

Myth 1: Conflict Can Always Be Avoided

"If you can't say anything nice, don't say anything at all." Many of us learned early in our lives that conflict is unnatural and that we should eliminate it from our conversations and relationships. Yet evidence suggests that conflict arises in virtually every relationship. Because each of us has a unique perspective on our world, it would be extraordinary for us *always* to see eye-to-eye with another person. One researcher found that contentment in marriage relates not to the amount of conflict, but to the way in which partners manage it.[12] Conflict is also a normal and productive part of interaction in group deliberations.[13] It is a myth that we should view conflict as inherently unproductive and something to be avoided. It happens, even in the best of relationships.

Myth 2: Conflict Always Occurs Because of Misunderstandings

"You just don't understand what my days are like. I need to go to sleep!" shouts Janice as she scoops up a pillow and blanket and stalks off to the living room. "Oh yeah? Well, you don't understand what will happen if I don't get this budget in!" responds Ron, who is hunched over the desk in their bedroom. It is clear that Ron and Janice are having a conflict. They have identified the cause of their problem as a lack of understanding between them, but in reality they *do* understand each other. Ron knows that Janice wants to sleep; Janice knows he wants to stay up and work. Their problem is that they disagree about whose goal is most important. Conflicts do sometimes flare up because of a lack of understanding or empathy for the other person, but there are times when individuals simply have different needs or goals. These differences, not lack of understanding, are the source of the conflict.

Myth 3: Conflict Is Always a Sign of a Poor Interpersonal Relationship

It is an oversimplification to assume that all conflict is rooted in underlying relational problems. Although it is true that constant bickering and sniping can be symptomatic of deeper problems, disagreements do not necessarily signal that the relationship is on the rocks. Overly polite, stilted conversation is more likely to signal a problem than are periodic disagreements. In fact, the free expression of honest disagreement is a hallmark of a healthy relationship.

Myth 4: Conflict Can Always Be Resolved

Consultants and corporate training experts often offer advice about how to eliminate conflict so that all will be well and harmony will prevail. Some people claim that with the application of a few skills and how-to techniques, conflicts can disappear, much like a stain from a shirt laundered with the right kind of detergent. This is simply not true. Not all differences can be resolved by listening harder or paraphrasing your partner's message. Some disagreements are so intense and the perceptions so fixed that individuals may have to agree to disagree and live with it.

Myth 5: Conflict Is Always Bad

It's a common fantasy to dream of eliminating all interpersonal conflict from our relationships. It would be bliss, we think, if we could live without disagreement, hassle, haggling, and tension. But conflict is a healthy component of our relationships. In fact, if a relationship is conflict-free, the individuals are probably not being honest with each other. Although it can be destructive, conflict can also help us identify issues that need further discussion and lead to negotiations that give us fresh insights into the relationship.

Constructive and Destructive Conflict

To construct something is to build or make something new. Characterized by greater cooperation in dealing with differences, **constructive** conflict helps build new insights and establishes new patterns in a relationship. As the For Better or For Worse comic demonstrates, the airing of differences can lead to a more satisfying relationship in the long run.

Conflict can suggest which elements of a relationship need to change or be improved. Here's an example:

Jenni: You know, I'm so tired of talking about what we're going to buy, what we're going to eat, where we're going next weekend. It's been weeks since we've had a real conversation.

Rex: What do you mean? We talk all the time.

Jenni: Yes, but that's just the point. We talk about everyday concerns, nothing else.

Rex: I don't know what you want, Jenni. But let's get a baby-sitter and go have dinner tomorrow night so we can talk. If I can figure out what's bothering you, maybe I can do something about it.

Note that Rex recognizes the need for further dialogue about Jenni's complaint. He transforms the issue of disagreement into a topic for discussion and relational adjustment. If Jenni had not expressed her dissatisfaction, the issue might have assumed larger proportions.

A well-managed disagreement that includes sharing personal needs or revising goals can lead couples or friends to first examine and then repledge their commitment to one another. It can revitalize the relationship, enabling both people to view its elements from different perspectives, even if the information shared seems negative at first.

Destructive conflict dismantles relationships without restoring them. If both individuals are dissatisfied with the outcome of the conflict, then it has been more destructive than constructive. The hallmark of destructive conflict is a lack of flexibility in responding to others.[14] Conflict can become destructive when people view their differences from a win-lose perspective, rather than looking for solutions that allow each individual to gain. If the combatants assume that one person will lose, the resulting competitive climate precludes cooperation and flexibility.

A rapidly spiralling conflict can be as destructive as a tornado churning through a trailer park. As with the conflict between Paul and Simone at the beginning of this chapter, it may start over a seemingly small issue, but it increases in intensity as other issues and differences are brought into the discussion. Such destructive escalations reduce flexibility, block off options for managing differences, and make a win-win solution more elusive. One way to minimize destructive conflict cycles is to understand the sequence of conflict-triggering causes so you can stop them at an early stage.

Understanding Conflict As a Process

Cathy was reading the Sunday paper, enjoying a second cup of coffee, and listening to her favourite classical music station. All seemed well. Suddenly, for no apparent reason, her roommate Barb brusquely stormed into the room and shouted, "I can't stand it anymore! We have to talk about who does what around here." Cathy was taken completely off guard. She had no idea her roommate was upset about the division of household chores. To her, this outburst seemed to come out of the blue; in reality, however, several events led up to it.

Most relational disagreements have a source, a beginning, a middle, an end, and an aftermath.[15] Let's find out how they function.

Source: Prior Conditions

The first phase in the conflict process is the one that sets the stage for disagreement; it begins when you become aware that there are differences between you and another person. The differences may stem from role expectations, perceptions, goals, or resources. In the previous example, Barb perceived that she and Cathy played different roles in caring for the household.

In interpersonal relationships, *many* potential sources of conflict may be smoldering below the surface. It may take some time before they flare up into overt conflict. Moreover, they may be compounded with other concerns, making them difficult to sort out.

Beginning: Frustration Awareness

At this stage, at least one of you becomes aware that the differences in the relationship are increasingly problematic. You may begin to engage in self-talk, noting that something is wrong and creating frustration. Perhaps you realize that you won't be able to achieve an important goal or that someone else has resources you need to achieve it. Or you may become aware of differences in perceptions. Barb knew that Cathy's family always used weekends for relaxation. In Barb's family, on the other hand, everyone pitched in on weekends to get household chores done for the week. She may have recognized that difference, even as her frustration level rose.

Becoming aware of differences in perception does not always lead to increased frustration. But when the differences interfere with something you want to accomplish, then your frustration level rises. In Barb's case, she wanted to get the house clean so she could turn her attention to studying for a test she had the next day. Cathy's apparent indifference to helping Barb achieve that goal was a conflict trigger.

Middle: Active Conflict

When you bring your frustration to the attention of others, a conflict becomes an active, *expressed struggle*.[16] If frustrations remain only as thoughts, the conflict is passive, not active. Active conflict does not necessarily mean that the differences are expressed with shouting or emotional intensity. An expression of disagreement may be either verbal or nonverbal. Calmly asking someone to change an attitude or behaviour to help you achieve your goal is a form of active conflict; so is kicking your brother under the table when he starts to reveal your secret to the rest of the family.

Cathy was not aware of the division of labour problem until Barb stormed into the room demanding a renegotiation of roles. Barb had been aware of her frustration for some time, yet had not acted on it. Many experts advocate that you do not wait until your frustration level escalates to peak intensity before you approach someone with your conflict. Bottled-up frustration tends to erupt like soda in a bottle that has just been shaken. Intense emotions can add to the difficulty of managing a conflict.

End: Resolution

When you begin to try to manage the conflict, it has progressed to the resolution stage. Of course, not all conflicts can be neatly resolved. Couples who divorce, business

T hink about a recent conflict that you have had or are having with someone and trace its development through the stages of conflict escalation. Perhaps it is a conflict that hasn't yet been resolved. Plot the evolution of the conflict to its current state. If no resolution exists, consider some possible solutions. Share your analysis of your conflict with one of your classmates.

1. Prior conditions: What is the source of the conflict?

_____

_____

_____

_____

2. Frustration awareness: When did you become aware of the conflict?

_____

_____

_____

_____

3. Active conflict: When and why did the conflict become an active conflict?

_____

_____

_____

_____

4. Resolution: Is there a resolution? If so, what is it? If not, what are some ways the conflict could be managed?

_____

_____

_____

_____

5. Follow-up: Is the conflict over? Do you still harbour some resentment? If so, what are strategies to help you manage the resentment?

_____

_____

_____

_____

partners who dissolve their corporation, or roommates who go their separate ways have all found solutions, even though they may not be amicable.

After Barb's outburst, she and Cathy were able to reach a workable compromise about the division of their household labour. Cathy agreed to clean the house every other week; Barb promised not to expect her to do it on weekends.

Aftermath: Follow-Up

As Yogi Berra once said, "It ain't over 'til it's over." After a conflict has been resolved, the follow-up stage involves dealing with hurt feelings or managing simmering grudges, and checking with the other person to confirm that the conflict has not retreated into the frustration awareness stage. As we noted in Chapter 7, interpersonal relationships operate as interactive processes rather than as linear, step-by-step functions. Conflict does progress in stages, but your resolutions can backslide unless you confirm your understanding of the issues with your partner.

The Friday after their discussion, Cathy proudly showed off a spotless apartment to Barb when she came home from class. Barb responded with a grin and a quick hug and privately resolved to get up early on Sunday morning so that she could go out to get Cathy pastries and the Sunday papers before she awoke. This kind of mutual thoughtfulness exemplifies a successful follow-up in a conflict.

RECAP	Understanding Conflict As a Process
PRIOR CONDITIONS STAGE	The stage is set for conflict because of differences in the individuals' actions or attitudes.
FRUSTRATION AWARENESS STAGE	One individual becomes aware that the differences are problematic and becomes frustrated and angry.
ACTIVE CONFLICT STAGE	The individuals communicate with each other about the differences; the conflict becomes an expressed struggle.
RESOLUTION STAGE	The individuals begin seeking ways to manage the conflict.
FOLLOW-UP STAGE	The individuals check with themselves and each other to monitor whether both are satisfied with the resolution.

Conflict and Power

As we saw in Chapter 7, in interpersonal communication, **power** refers to the resources an individual has to influence another person. Even if the person does not use it, sometimes just having power determines a person's role in the relationship. The person with more resources to control the conflict management process will have more influence in shaping the outcome of a disagreement. Knowing what the sources of power are and how those sources can be tapped in a conflict can help you both to predict how you and others will behave in conflicts and to resolve conflicts more effectively.

Power does not reside in individuals; it is a product of our interpersonal interactions. If both individuals possess relatively equal power and resources, their interactions are likely to be productive. Relationships with unequal power bases, however, are often lopsided and filled with conflict.

One pair of researchers developed a classic framework for defining bases of power that has been tested in several communication contexts, including classrooms and small group communication settings. The framework includes five power sources that we use to influence others.[17]

Legitimate Power

There's an old joke about a driver and a police officer who were arguing over a car wreck: "I had the right of way when he ran into me. How come you're blaming me? It wasn't my fault," said the driver.

"It certainly was," said the officer.

"Why?" asked the driver.

"Because his father is the mayor, his brother is the chief of police, and I'm engaged to his sister," was the reply.

Although they are not elected to their positions, parents do have a legitimate claim to power over their children until they can function on their own. (Alan and Linda Detrick/Photo Researchers, Inc.)

The driver who caused the accident wielded power of a sort, but **legitimate power** is power based upon an appointed, elected, or designated position. The Prime Minister of Canada, senators, provincial premiers, mayors, deans, and principals, have all had power bestowed upon them. In our interpersonal relationships, however, we do not usually elect one partner to be in charge of the relationship or to make the decisions. Of course, in parent-child and certain other dependent relationships, one person does assume a kind of natural legitimate power. And in some relationships among peers, the individuals explicitly define their roles and tasks. Sometimes the roles conflict, as in the example below:

Jenna: I'm in charge of the chequebook, so I am going to decide whether we spend sixty dollars a ticket to see the Stones next month.

Pierre: Oh no you're not. I'm in charge of entertainment, and I say we are not going to see them.

Often what we fight about is not what we fight about. While it may seem that this couple is disagreeing about whether or not to go to a concert, in reality the struggle is over who has the power to make the decision. Until they discuss that issue, they are unlikely to make much headway on resolving either this or future conflicts.

Referent Power

Referent power is based on interpersonal attraction. If people like us and value our company, friendship, and advice, then we have power and influence that we can use to manage conflicts.

Suppose, for example, that your best friend wants to have dinner at an expensive restaurant. You're a bit short on cash and would be content with pizza or a sandwich, but because you like your friend, you decide to go. Knowingly or not, your friend has used the power of interpersonal attraction to get his way. People rarely acknowledge the role of interpersonal attraction in managing conflicts, but this referent power may be enough to tip the balance in that person's favour.

Expert Power

If you are an expert, you have superior knowledge about, and experience with, some specialized field. This affords you greater influence in how decisions are made about matters relating to this field. **Expert power** is based upon the influence derived from a person's knowledge and experience. Suppose you are good at fixing cars and your friend is not. When the car in which you're riding stalls, your friend says, "I think it's the spark plugs." But you say it's the carburetor, so your friend gives in. You'd be surprised if your friend challenged your mechanical diagnosis. After all, you are the expert, so you expect your opinion to prevail. Of course, when both individuals assume expert status, clashes can result in heated controversy.

Reward Power

People who have the resources to give us gifts, money, status, power, or other things we might desire have **reward power**. They have the ability to manage a conflict with their resources. Your boss, your parents, your teacher, or others may have this power over you.

Suppose that you have been working long hours all week on an important project, but today is your four-year-old's birthday. You promised you would be home by 5:00 P.M. Your boss comes in at 4:30 P.M. and announces that a report has to be on her desk by 8:00 A.M. the next day. You are not pleased. Your goal conflicts with that of your boss, and your dialogue becomes heated. Your boss draws upon her reward power by promising, "If you stay late tonight and finish this report, I will give you a week off with pay to spend with your family." Even though your goal of spending the evening with your family has not changed, the offer causes you to relent and finish the report before the deadline. The conflict still exists, but her use of reward power has influenced your behaviour. Of course, those who exercise this kind of power must know what rewards will be meaningful to the person they are trying to influence, or the power will be useless.

Coercive Power

Just as offering rewards can influence the outcome of a conflict, so can the use of punishment. **Coercive power** involves the use of sanctions and punishments to influence outcomes. Often the same individuals who can reward you can also dish out punishment.

In interpersonal relationships, some people follow a similar strategy. If they have no legitimate power base and their referent, expert, and reward power bases are negligible, they may try coercion. At first they may inflict a mild punishment, such as not returning phone calls, to communicate irritation. Or they may try the silent treatment when they see the person. If they still do not achieve their goal, they may resort to verbal assaults.

Using Power

The conscious use of any type of power should be based on careful consideration of the short-term effect it will have upon your partner and the long-term effect it is likely to have upon your relationship. Any application that intimidates another or devastates his or her sense of self is not only unethical, but also destructive to the bond of trust between you.

We are not endorsing any of these power bases as either useful or not useful to draw upon when you are locked in interpersonal combat. But if you can analyze the balance of power that characterizes each of your relationships and anticipate the sources of influence during a conflict, then you may be able to select effective, other-oriented conflict management strategies.

COMMUNICATION EXPERIENCE

Power Checklist

Rate your own power and the power of your partner in relation to a conflict in which you are involved. Write the number 3 for high power, 2 for medium power, or 1 for low power in the appropriate blank.

SCORING: If your total power score and that of your partner are within 4 points of each other, you are in an equal-power situation. A difference greater than 4 points suggests an unequal balance of power.

Self		Other
_____	Legitimate Power (Position)	_____
_____	Referent Power (Reputation)	_____
_____	Coercive Power (Ability to Punish)	_____
_____	Reward Power (Resource Control)	_____
_____	Expert Power (Knowledge and Skill)	_____
_____	TOTALS	_____

Adapted from R. Hopper, *Between You and Me* (Glenview, IL: Scott Foresman, 1984).

RECAP Bases of Power

LEGITIMATE POWER	Influence is based upon being appointed, elected, or selected by someone to exercise control.
REFERENT POWER	Influence is based upon being well liked and respected.
EXPERT POWER	Influence is based upon knowledge and experience.
REWARD POWER	Influence is based upon ability to provide positive rewards and favours.
COERCIVE POWER	Influence is based upon ability to punish another person.

Sexual Harassment: It's About Power

What Is Sexual Harassment?

Any unwelcome sexual advances, requests for sexual favours, or other inappropriate verbal or physical behaviour of a sexual nature may be classified as sexual harassment. Examples include:

- repeated and unwanted requests for dates, sexual flirtations, or propositions of a sexual nature;

- unwanted sexual remarks or questions about a person's clothing, body, or sexual activity;

- unnecessary touching, patting, hugging, or brushing against a person's body;

- direct or implied threats that failure to submit to sexual advances will affect employment, work status, grades, letters of recommendation, or residential choice;

- physical assault;

- a pattern of conduct that causes humiliation or discomfort, such as use of inappropriate terms of greeting, sexually explicit or sexist comments, questions or jokes, or leering at a person's body.

What to Do if You Are Sexually Harassed

- Be direct and candid with the person.

- Use "I" messages (e.g., I don't like those kinds of jokes made about me).

- Avoid being overly dramatic; remain confident that the incident will be dealt with.

- If the incident happens at school or work, use the grievance procedure.

- Report the harasser to your supervisor, department chair, or dean.

- If the harasser is your supervisor or an administrative official, report the incident to his or her supervisor.

- Report the harassment immediately after it occurs. The longer you wait the less credible your story will be.

- When the harassment occurs, write down important facts.

- Report the incident as if you were a journalist: give the who, what, when, where, and how. Keep to the facts.

- Be prepared to give the interviewer names of witnesses.

- Put aside your anger and be thorough when telling the story.

Information adapted from Southwest Texas State University policy and procedure statement on sexual harassment and Vicki West, "Sexual Harassment: Identify, Stop, and Prevent" Seminar.

Conflict Management Styles

What's your approach to managing interpersonal conflict: fight or flight? Do you tackle conflict head-on or seek ways to remove yourself from it? Most of us do not have a single way of dealing with differences, but we do have a tendency to manage conflict following patterns that we have used before. The pattern we choose depends on several factors: our personality, the individuals with whom we are in conflict, the time and place of the confrontation, and other situational factors. For example, if your boss gives you an order, you respond differently than if your spouse gives you an order.

Several researchers have attempted to identify the patterns or styles of conflict. One model distinguishes only two dimensions: (1) how concerned you are for others and (2) how concerned you are for yourself.[18] Another more widely accepted approach organizes conflict styles into three types: (1) nonconfrontational (avoiding, withdrawing, being indirect); (2) controlling (attempting to use power strategies to control or manipulate outcomes); and (3) cooperative (seeking a solution that both individuals will find acceptable).[19] Before you read the following sections, try the Communication Experience on page 304 to see what style you typically use in managing conflict.

Nonconfrontational Style

One approach to handling conflict is to back off, either avoiding the conflict or giving in to the other person. Virginia Satir, author of *Peoplemaking*, a popular book about family communication, suggests that we learn conflict response patterns early in life.[20] Placating, distracting, computing, withdrawing, and giving in are responses that typify a **nonconfrontational style**.

A *placating* response is an attempt to please; generally placaters are uncomfortable with negative emotions and may adopt this approach because they fear rejection if they rock the boat. Typically, they seek approval and try to avoid threats to their self-worth. Placaters never seem to get angry, are so controlled that they seem unresponsive to the intensity of the situation, quickly agree with others to avoid conflict, and try to avoid confrontation at all costs. They appear to be other-oriented, but in fact they are simply seeking self-protection. Satir describes them as "syrupy, martyrish, and bootlicking." In the following exchange, note Hillary's placating response to Leslie's complaint:

Leslie: Hillary, I'm not in agreement with you on the QCN merger. I think the merger should be called off.

Hillary: Okay. Whatever you think is best. I just want you to feel good about your decision.

Another nonconfrontational style that Satir identifies is *distracting*. Distracters attempt to change the subject and avoid conflict or stress, rather than face issues directly. They hope that eventually the problem will just go away if it can be put off long enough.

A third nonconfrontational style is called *computing*; computers remove themselves from conflict by remaining aloof and cool. They avoid emotional involvement and refuse to be provoked or ruffled, even under intense pressure. This detachment allows them to avoid expressing genuine feelings about issues and ideas. Instead, they respond to emotional issues with impersonal words and phrases, such as "One would tend to become angry when one's car is dented, wouldn't one?" The computing style is characterized by low empathy and minimal involvement with the issues at hand.

Withdrawing from conflict, either physically or psychologically, is another nonconfrontational approach. "I don't want to talk about it," "It's not my problem," "Don't bother me with that now," or "I'm not interested in that" are typical responses from someone who uses this style.

Finally, some people consistently *give in* when faced with conflict. They are so uncomfortable that they surrender before the conflict escalates. Reggie hates westerns. Yet when Pam wants to rent *How the West Was Won*, Reggie says, "Okay, fine," just to avoid a confrontation.

Controlling Style

"You're wrong!" shouts Ed. "Here's how to get our project in on time. We can't waste time in the library. We just have to write up what we have."

"But Ed," suggests Derrick, "the assignment calls for us to have three library sources."

"No. We just don't have time. Just do it," argues Ed.

Ed wants to control, not collaborate.

You learned in Chapter 7 that each of us has some need to control and be controlled by others. But some people almost always want to dominate and make sure that their objectives are achieved. In managing conflict, **controlling** people have a win-lose philosophy. They want to win at the expense of the other person, to claim victory over their opponents. They are focused on themselves and usually ignore the needs of others. Controllers often resort to *blaming*, or seeking a scapegoat, rather than assuming responsibility for a conflict. "I didn't do it"; "Don't look at me"; and "It's not my fault" are typical controlling statements.

If this strategy does not work, controllers may resort to coercive power. They may try hostile name-calling, personal attacks, or threats and warnings. Threats refer to actions they can actually carry out.[21] Warnings are negative prophecies they cannot actually control. The boyfriend who says, "If you don't stop calling me names, I'm going to leave you," has issued a threat; he has the power to leave. If he were to say, "Don't call your parents names or they'll write you out of their will," that would be a warning. In reality, he has no control over his girlfriend's parents.

Obviously, threats are more powerful than warnings in changing behaviour, and then only if the other person would genuinely find the threatened actions punishing or disruptive. If a parent threatens a spanking, a child will take the threat seriously only if he or she knows the parent will carry it out. If the parent has administered only light raps on the wrist in the past, the child will probably not pay much attention to the threat.

Cooperative Style

Those who take a **cooperative** approach to conflict management view conflicts as a set of problems to be solved, rather than games in which one person wins and another loses. They use other-oriented strategies and foster a win-win climate by using the following techniques:[22]

Separate the people from the problem. They leave personal grievances out of the discussion, describing problems without making judgmental or evaluative statements about personalities.

Focus on shared interests. They ask questions such as: What do we both want? What do we both value? Where are we already agreeing? to emphasize common interests, values, and goals.

Generate many options to solve the problem. They use brainstorming and other techniques to generate alternative solutions. (You will learn more about problem-solving techniques later in this chapter).

Base decisions on objective criteria. They try to establish standards for an acceptable solution to a problem—these standards may involve cost, timing, and other factors. Suppose, for example, that you and your neighbour are discussing possible ways to stop a nearby dog from barking endlessly into the night. You decide upon these criteria: the solution must not harm the dog; it must be easy for the owner to implement; the owner must agree to it; it should not cost more than fifty dollars; and it must keep the dog from disturbing the sleep of others. Your neighbour says, "Maybe the dog can sleep in the owner's garage at night." This solution meets all but one of your criteria, so you call the owner, who agrees to put the dog in the garage by 10:00 P.M. Now everyone wins because the solution meets a sound, well-considered set of objective criteria.

People who take a cooperative approach to conflict management focus on shared interests and encourage others to generate options in order to solve problems. (Walter Hodges/Tony Stone Images)

Conflict Management Skills

As we saw in the previous section, the nonconfrontational and controlling styles of conflict management do not solve problems effectively, nor do they foster healthy long-term relationships. The skills we will review here are those we touched upon in our discussion of the cooperative style.[23]

Managing conflict, especially emotion-charged ego conflict, is not easy. Even with a fully developed set of skills, you should not expect to melt tensions and resolve disagreements instantaneously. The following skills can, however, help you generate options that promote understanding and provide a framework for cooperation.

Manage Your Emotions

For weeks you have been working on a brochure with a tight deadline. You turned it over to the production department with instructions two weeks ago. Today you call to check on its progress, and you discover that it is still sitting on the production coordinator's desk. You feel angry and frustrated. How should you respond? You may be tempted to march into her office and scream at her, or to shout at her supervisor.

Try to avoid taking action when you are in such a state. You may regret what you say, and you will probably escalate the conflict.

Often the first sign that we are in a conflict situation is a feeling of anger, frustration, fear, or even sadness, which sweeps over us like an ocean wave. If we feel powerless to control our own fate, then we will have difficulty taking a logical or rational approach to managing the conflict. Expressing our feelings in an emotional outburst may make us feel better for the moment, but it may close the door to logical, rational negotiation.

When we are emotionally charged, we experience physical changes as well. One researcher found that

> . . . our adrenaline flows faster and our strength increases by about 20 percent. The liver, pumping sugar into the bloodstream, demands more oxygen from the heart and lungs. The veins become enlarged and the cortical centres where thinking takes place do not perform nearly as well. . . . the blood supply to the problem-solving part of the brain is severely decreased because, under stress, a greater portion of blood is diverted to the body's extremities.[24]

Such changes fuel our fight-flight responses. If we choose to stay, verbal or physical violence may erupt; if we flee from the conflict, we cannot resolve it. Until we

Identifying Your Conflict Management Style

Different people learn different ways of managing conflict. This exercise gives you an opportunity to increase your awareness of what strategies you use and how they compare with strategies of others.

1. With your classmates, form groups of six. Make sure you know the other members of the group; do not join a group of strangers.

2. Working by yourself, respond to the twenty-four statements under How You Act in Conflicts, below.

3. Still working by yourself, read the descriptions of the conflict styles on the Scoring

portion of this exercise. Then make five slips of paper. Write the names of the other five members of your group on the slips of paper, one name to a slip.

4. On each slip of paper, identify that person's conflict strategy.

5. After all group members are finished, pass out your slips of paper to the people whose names are on them. Each member of your group should end up with five slips of paper describing his or her conflict strategy.

6. Score your questionnaire, using the table that follows the discussion of conflict strategies. Rank the five conflict strategies from the

one you use the most to the one you use the least.

7. After drawing names to see who goes first, ask one member to describe the results of his or her own self-assessment. Then ask him or her to read off the strategies on each of the five slips of paper. He or she should ask other group members what specific examples led to their conclusions, and group members should use the rules for constructive feedback. The person to the left of the first member should then repeat this procedure, and so on around the group.

8. Each group should discuss the strengths and weaknesses of each of the conflict strategies.

How You Act in Conflicts

The proverbs listed below can be thought of as descriptions of different strategies for resolving conflicts. Read each one carefully. Using the following scale, indicate how typical each proverb is of your actions in a conflict.

5 = very typical of the way I act in a conflict

4 = frequently typical of the way I act in a conflict

3 = sometimes typical of the way I act in a conflict

2 = seldom typical of the way I act in a conflict

1 = never typical of the way I act in a conflict

_____ 1. Smooth words make smooth ways.

_____ 2. If you cannot make a person think as you do, make him or her do as you think.

_____ 3. Soft words win hard hearts.

_____ 4. Come now and let us reason together.

_____ 5. When two quarrel, the person who keeps silent first is the most praiseworthy.

_____ 6. Might overcomes right.

_____ 7. He hath conquered well that hath made his enemies flee.

_____ 8. You can catch more flies with honey than vinegar.

_____ 9. A fair exchange brings no quarrel.

_____ 10. No person has the final answer, but every person has a piece to contribute.

_____ 11. Fields are won by those who believe in winning.

_____ 12. Tit for tat is fair play.

_____ 13. Only the person who is willing to give up his or her monopoly on truth can ever profit from the truths that others hold.

_____ 14. Kind words are worth much and cost little.

_____ 15. One gift for another makes good friends.

_____ 16. Bring your conflicts into the open and face them directly; only then will the best solution be discovered.

_____ 17. The best way of handling conflicts is to avoid them.

_____ 18. Put your foot down where you mean to stand.

_____ 19. Getting part of what you want is better than not getting anything at all.

_____ 20. Frankness, honesty, and trust will move mountains.

_____ 21. There is nothing so important that you have to fight for it.

_____ 22. There are two kinds of people in the world, winners and losers.

_____ 23. When someone hits you with a stone, hit him or her with a piece of cotton.

_____ 24. When both give in halfway, a fair settlement is achieved.

SCORING: Next to the proverb number, fill in the rating you gave yourself in the How You Act in Conflicts section. Then total each column.

Nonconfrontational Style

Avoids conflict or minimizes differences. Is uncomfortable directly facing conflict. Tries to make everyone happy or uses distracting nonconfrontational style.

1. _____
3. _____
5. _____
8. _____
14. _____
17. _____
21. _____
23. _____
Total _____

Controlling Style

Tries to blame, coerce, or threaten to manage differences and resolve conflicts.

2. _____
6. _____
7. _____
11. _____
12. _____
16. _____
18. _____
22. _____
Total _____

Cooperative Style

Seeks a win–win solution by separating people from the problem, focusing on common goals, generating multiple solutions, and basing decisions on objective criteria.

4. _____
9. _____
10. _____
13. _____
15. _____
19. _____
20. _____
24. _____
Total _____

The higher the total score for each conflict strategy, the more frequently you tend to use that strategy. The lower the total score for each conflict strategy, the less frequently you tend to use that strategy.

Adapted from: David W. Johnson and Frank P. Johnson, _Joining Together: Group Theory and Group Skills_ (Englewood Cliffs, NJ: Prentice-Hall, 1987), 270.

Empathy Can Span the Abyss

Intergenerational conflicts and misunderstandings can cause pain and emotional bruises. Instead of finding nurturing and love within the family circle, some people encounter exactly the opposite.

For example, one elderly reader writes: "I don't look forward to family gatherings because I come back with my self-esteem reduced to zero and feeling like a stereotypical old geezer. I'm rebuffed by my own children, giggled at, and made to feel my thoughts aren't important."

Another elderly reader describes in detail a truly unhappy situation. "I gave my money to my children, trusting them to take care of my needs when I grew older. But now that I have no money left, they have discarded me. How stupid I was not to take care of my security! I'm alone now, really alone, I need to understand what I did wrong. I guess I gave too much, cared too much."

Many letters from elderly people tell similar stories. I also hear from their sons and daughters, members of the so-called sandwich generation, whose reports have a different focus. A 54-year-old woman writes about the "hard burden" she bears in caring for her 88-year-old mother: "I'm angry that I am increasingly having to be a parent to someone whose self-centredness and narcissism made her unable to be a mother to me. The simple, awful fact is that I respect my mother and love her as my flesh and blood, but I don't like her and I wish she weren't in my life. My fear is that she's going to live on and on, growing more and more needful of my 'parenting,' and that I won't be free of her presence until I'm approaching 70 myself."

Another letter from a member of the sandwich generation reads: "My challenge involves my relationship with my mother-in-law of 29 years. She's 89. She has lost all semblance of a positive outlook. She speaks only of her aches and pains and the bleakness of her life. I cannot deal with this negative approach to living. Whatever I try to do for her, nothing is ever right."

Reflecting on these letters, I find the key word for what *both* sides need is empathy—which the dictionary defines as identification with and understanding of the situation, feelings, and motives of another person. Without this empathy, a great abyss can exist where there should be communication. Can we overemphasize that there's no substitute for honest communication between people? *Tell* others what you feel! Try to explain *why* you feel as you do. This can lead to real understanding.

One woman offers a promising, creative role model for others: "Sometimes I'm not delighted to hear what my mother needs and wants because it impinges on my time and energy. However, I prefer to know what she's thinking and feeling, even if it results in conflict. The resolution of such conflicts has strengthened our friendship and the community that is our family. Love, I believe, is being open and seeking a resolution that may require mutual sacrifice."

An extremely helpful, sound definition. Speaking of love, one reader writes: "Many years ago my mother gave me a book that set my life on a self-respecting, self-valuing course. It says it's quite okay to love yourself. If you don't, how can anyone else love you? If you think you're not worth loving, then, by cracky, you're not. If you think you're not worth much, you will always be a problem—if not a pain—to be around. Is that what you want for yourself? Not I."

A final intergenerational note from a grandmother: "My life was lonely after I lost my husband. I volunteered at the hospital, bowled twice a week, was active at my church and kept my home. But there was still a terrible void in my life. Then my 23-year-old granddaughter told me to keep Wednesday evenings open for her. We take turns cooking, or sometimes we go out. You have no idea what this has done for me. We share a meal, talk, and just enjoy our friendship. Our talk may be about her work or what I've done the past week—just nice conversation. We sometimes cry together. But we laugh together as well."

This grandmother and granddaughter have found a happy way to bridge the generation gap. Others could profit from their example.

From: Malcolm Boyd, *Modern Maturity.* Reprinted with permission from *Modern Maturity.* Copyright © 1992, American Association of Retired Persons.

can tone down (not eliminate) our emotions, we will find it difficult to apply other skills. Let's look at some specific strategies that you can draw upon when an intense emotional response to conflict clouds your judgment and decision-making skills.[25]

■ SELECT A MUTUALLY ACCEPTABLE TIME AND PLACE TO DISCUSS A CONFLICT

If you are upset, or even tired, you are at risk for an emotion-charged shouting match. If you ambush someone with an angry attack, don't expect him or her to be in a productive frame of mind. Instead, give yourself time to cool off before you try to resolve a conflict. In the case of the lapsed deadline, for example, you could call both the production coordinator and her boss and schedule an appointment to meet with them later in the day. By that time you could gain control of your feelings and also think the issue through. Of course, sometimes issues need to be discussed on the spot; you may not have the luxury to wait. But whenever it is practical, make sure the other person is ready to receive you and your message.

■ PLAN YOUR MESSAGE

If you are approaching someone to discuss a disagreement, take care to organize your message. Identify your goal and determine what outcome you would like; do not barge in and pour out your emotions.

You might also consider talking with a trusted friend or colleague first. A good friend with empathic listening skills can help you clarify the issues in the conflict. If you don't talk with a friend, consider writing down the key ideas you want to express to help you prepare for your face-to-face discussion. The purpose of the notes is not to deliver a speech when you meet your conflict partner. But taking time to plan your message with a friend or in writing can help you frame the issues of the disagreement.

■ MONITOR NONVERBAL MESSAGES

As you learned in Chapter 5, your actions play a key role in establishing the emotional climate in any relationship. Monitoring your nonverbal messages can help to de-escalate an emotion-charged situation. Speaking calmly, using direct eye contact, and maintaining a natural facial expression will signal that you wish to collaborate rather than control. Your nonverbal message should also support your verbal response. If you say you are listening to someone, but you continue to read the paper or work on a report, you are communicating a lack of interest in the speaker and the message.

■ AVOID PERSONAL ATTACKS, NAME-CALLING, AND EMOTIONAL OVERSTATEMENT

Using threats and derogatory names can turn a simple conflict into an ego conflict. When people feel attacked, they will respond by protecting themselves. Also try to avoid exaggerating your emotions. If you say you are irritated or annoyed rather than furious, you can still communicate your feelings, but you will take the sting out of your description.

■ USE SELF-TALK

When Tom was chairing the committee meeting, Monique accused him of falsifying the attendance numbers at the last fine arts festival. Instead of lashing back at Monique, he paused, took a slow, deep yet unnoticed breath, and thought, "I'm tired. If I snarl back, all we will do is escalate this issue out of proportion. I'll talk with Monique later after we have both cooled down." Perhaps you think that talking to yourself is an eccentricity. Nothing could be further from the truth. As you saw in Chapter 2, thoughts are directly linked to feelings,[26] and the messages we tell ourselves play a major role in how we feel and respond to others. Ask yourself whether an emotional tirade and an escalating conflict will produce the results you want. When Eleanor Roosevelt noted that "No one can make you feel inferior without your consent," she was acknowledging the power of self-talk in affecting our emotional response to what others say and do.

Manage Information

Because uncertainty, misinformation, and misunderstanding are often byproducts of conflict and disagreement, skills that promote mutual understanding are an important component of cooperative conflict management. Based on the describing, listening, and responding skills discussed in Chapter 4, the following specific suggestions can help you reduce uncertainty and enhance the quality of communication during conflict.

■ CLEARLY DESCRIBE THE CONFLICT-PRODUCING EVENTS

Instead of just blurting out your complaints in random order, think of delivering a brief, well-organized minispeech. When Marsha almost had a car accident, she came home and told her husband, "Last week you said you would get the brakes fixed on the car. On Monday, when you still hadn't taken the car in, you said you would do it on Wednesday. Now it's Friday and the brakes are in even worse shape. I had a close call this afternoon when the car almost wouldn't stop. We've got to get those brakes fixed before anyone drives that car again."

Public speaking teachers recommend that you describe events in chronological order. Use the same technique when describing a conflict. Offer your perspective on what created the conflict, sequencing the events like a well-organized story. Think of yourself as a journalist who is reporting on a news event. Your job is to describe the events dispassionately so that the other person shares your understanding of the problem.

■ "OWN" YOUR STATEMENTS BY USING DESCRIPTIVE "I" LANGUAGE

"I feel upset when you post the week's volunteer schedule without first consulting with me," reveals Katrina. Her statement describes her feelings as her own. If she had said, "You always prepare a schedule without telling anyone first. All of us who volunteer are mad about that," her statement would have had an accusatory sting. Beginning the statement with "you" sets the listener up for a defensive response. Also, notice that in the second statement, the speaker does not take responsibility for the problem; she suggests that it belongs to several unidentified people as well. If you narrow the issue down to a conflict between you and the other person, you put the conflict into a more manageable framework.

■ USE EFFECTIVE LISTENING SKILLS

Managing information is a two-way process. Whether you are describing a conflict situation to someone, or that individual is bringing a conflict to your attention, good listening skills will be invaluable.

Give your full attention to the speaker and make a conscious point of tuning out your internal messages. Sometimes the best thing to do after describing the conflict-producing events is simply to wait for a response. If you don't stop talking and give the other person a chance to respond, he or she will feel frustrated, the emotional pitch will go up a notch, and it will become more difficult to reach an understanding.

Finally, focus not only on the facts or details, but also analyze them so you can understand the major point the speaker is making. Try to use your understanding of the details to interpret the speaker's major ideas. Remember to stay other-oriented and "seek to understand rather than to be understood."[27]

■ USE EFFECTIVE RESPONSE SKILLS

Respond clearly and appropriately. Your response and that of your conflict partner will confirm that you have understood each other. Checking perceptions is vital when emotions run high.

If you are genuinely unsure about facts, issues, or major ideas addressed during a conflict, ask questions to help you sort through them instead of barging ahead with solutions. Then summarize your understanding of the information; do not parrot the speaker's words or paraphrase every statement, but check key points to ensure that you have understood the message. Note how Ted adeptly paraphrases to check his understanding:

Maggie: I don't like the conclusion you've written to the conference report. It doesn't mention anything about the ideas suggested at the symposium. I think you have also misinterpreted the CEO's key message.

Ted: So, if I understand you, Maggie, you're saying the report missed some key information and may also include an inaccurate summary of the CEO's speech.

Maggie: Yes, Ted. Those are the concerns I have.

Communities and Families Working to Prevent Youth Crime: A Snowball's Chance?

A small but articulate movement is starting to snowball in communities across Canada. The issue is public concern over youth crime. You don't need a pollster to know that one of the "hot buttons" for widespread public insecurity is youth crime. Public panic grows as headlines report sensational crimes.

Despite the harsh climate, there is growing support for youth crime remedies that focus not on punishment and reprisal but on the root causes of crime.

A lot of people believe we need to "get tough with young people," says Memorial University of Newfoundland professor Joan Pennel, a member of Canada's National Crime Prevention Council. "'Getting tough' means locking young people up, and when you lock them up, you disrupt their position in the community. This approach hasn't decreased criminal activity."

Another simple answer that some have seized on is to send offending youth to strict, military-style "Boot camps." "[But] the research finds that it really doesn't reduce re-offending, or reduce the prison population," according to Barb Hill of the John Howard Society in Kingston, Ontario.

What are the most appropriate ways to address youth crime? Anne Sherman, also of the National Crime Prevention Council, believes that justice system reform begins with community involvement. She also believes that "a restorative justice system is more appropriate than a punitive justice system, something that combines community involvement, victim involvement and restoration to the victim." Sherman believes that alternatives to court trials and incarceration must provide offending youth with meaningful ways to take responsibility and to make amends.

For example, the Ambassador Program in downtown Toronto has been described as a "retrieval program" for street youth who have dropped out of school and lived through drug abuse. Youth in the program spend their mornings in class working toward high school credits. Additional credits are earned in the afternoons by doing work placements in various job settings. In the "Speak Out" component of the program, the youth are trained to visit senior elementary schools in high-risk neighbourhoods and talk about life on the street and on drugs, based on their own experiences.

The Bent Arrow Traditional Healing Society's program for Aboriginal youth in Edmonton is aimed at urban youth who have had some involvement with the criminal justice system. The program draws heavily upon traditional Aboriginal culture and spirituality, while the students also do a five-week placement with employers who agree to hire them if they meet the requirements of the workplace. At the heart of the project, however, are the personal relationships with the students. "This place is more like an extended family," says Executive Director Shauna Seneca, "and that's by design. These kids need people in their lives who will care for them, come hell or high water. Many have never known that before."

In Prince Edward Island, "CRIME BEAT" was initiated to show youth that the rest of the community recognizes the good they are doing. "A lot of youth think the rest of the world is down on them," says coordinator Diane Barnes. One group of program youth produced a musical play about the impact of drunk driving among youth. Another group organized a successful "taxi-token" campaign during the Christmas season: tokens worth $5 (enough to get anyone in Charlottetown a ride home) were sold throughout the community for use as gifts.

Another "restorative" community solution to youth crime across Canada includes "family conferences," which are based on Aboriginal traditions. In a family conference, a young offender meets with a group of family and community members to discuss his or her offence, its impact on victims, and means to make amends.

Barb Hill, of the John Howard Society, sees hope that local crime prevention councils are springing up across Canada. "People are starting to say 'we want to do something different here'... [They] want to talk about what their community can do instead of sending their youth away."

Excerpts from *Transition*, Vanier Institute of the Family, Ottawa, March 1996, 4–10.

Manage Goals

As we have seen, conflict is goal-driven. Both individuals involved in an interpersonal conflict want something. And for some reason, be it competition, scarce resources, or lack of understanding, the goals appear to be in conflict. To manage conflict, it is important to seek an accurate understanding of these goals and to identify where they overlap.

IDENTIFY YOUR GOAL AND YOUR PARTNER'S GOAL

After you describe, listen, and respond, your next task should be to identify what you would like to have happen. What is your goal? Most goal statements can be phrased in terms of wants or desires. Consider the following examples:

Problem	Goal
Your boss approaches you and wants you to work overtime; you need to pick up your son from day care.	You want to leave work on time; your boss wants the work completed ASAP.
Your spouse wants to sleep with the window open; you like a warm room and sleep better with the window closed.	You want a good night's rest; your spouse wants a good night's rest.
Your six-year-old son wants to go to a swim party with no lifeguards.	You want your son to be safe; your son wants to have a good time.

Often in conflicts you will be faced with balancing the achievement of your goal against the goal of maintaining the relationship that you have with your partner. Eventually, you may decide that the latter goal is more important than the substantive conflict issue.

Next, it is useful to identify your partner's goal. In each of the problems in the preceding list, you would need to know what the other person wants in order to manage the conflict. Use effective describing, listening, and responding skills to determine what each of you wants and to verbalize your goals. Obviously, if you both keep your goals hidden, it will be difficult to manage the conflict.

10 MANAGING CONFLICT IN INTERPERSONAL RELATIONSHIPS

■ IDENTIFY WHERE YOUR GOAL
AND YOUR PARTNER'S GOAL OVERLAP

Roger Fisher and William Ury stress the importance of focusing on shared interests when seeking to manage differences.[28] Armed with an understanding of what
you want and what your partner wants, you can then determine whether the goals
overlap. In the conflict over whether the window should be open or closed, the goal
of both parties is the same: each wants a good night's sleep. Framing the problem as
"how can we achieve our mutual goal" rather than arguing over whether the
window should be up or down, moves the discussion to a more productive level.

 If you focus on shared interests (common goals) and develop objective, rather
than subjective, criteria for the solution, there is hope for finding a resolution that
will satisfy both parties.

Manage the Problem

You can apply all of the skills described so far to pursue a proven method for
problem solving, which is shown in Table 10.1. First, *define the problem*. Most problems boil down to something you want more or less of.

Next, *analyze the problem*. To analyze is to break something down into its components. With your partner, begin by describing the conflict-producing events in
chronological order (see page 314). Then decide whether it is a pseudo conflict, a
simple conflict, or an ego conflict (see page 291). Attempt to ferret out symptoms,
effects, and obstacles; decide whether the conflict stems from several subproblems
rather than from one major issue. As you proceed with your analysis, you and your
partner may decide that you need more information to help clarify the issues.

Cara and Vaughn have been going together for over a year. Lately they have been
fighting over small issues, so they decide to spend some time talking about what is
wrong and trying to understand one another. At the root of their conflicts, they
discover, is a basic problem: Cara wants to get married to Vaughn now. Vaughn
wants to stay with Cara, but he wants to wait until he feels ready for marriage. He
also wants to feel financially secure before he marries.

Table 10.1

Solving Problems: One Method of Organizing Problem-Solving Discussions

1. Define the Problem	What's the issue?
2. Analyze the Problem	What are the causes, symptoms, effects, and obstacles?
3. Determine the Goal	What do you want? What does your partner want? How do the goals overlap?
4. Generate Many Solutions	List many options rather than debating one or two strategies for achieving the goal.
5. Select the Best Solution	Eliminate options that are not mutually agreeable. If possible, take the best ideas from several generated to reach an amicable resolution.

After some discussion, they analyze the problem. They realize they come from different family backgrounds and have different expectations about marriage. Cara's folks were high school sweethearts and got married when they were eighteen. Vaughn's parents are older; they met after each of them had been divorced, and they married after a long, slow-paced relationship. Cara and Vaughn's different frames of reference help explain their feelings about the timing of marriage.

The next step in managing the problem is to *determine the goals* of you and your partner, following the suggestions on page 318. Also, generate objective criteria for a solution (see page 308). The more measurable, verifiable, and objective the criteria, the greater the likelihood that you and your partner will be able to agree when the criteria have been met. Cara and Vaughn decide that, ultimately, they have the same goal: to get married. The issue boils down to timing. So they decide to seek a course of action that will make them both feel secure.

Their next step is to *generate multiple solutions*. Simply understanding the issues and the causes, effects, symptoms, and history of a problem will not enable you to manage a conflict. It takes time and creativity to find mutually satisfactory solutions to most problems. It stands to reason that the more solutions you generate, the greater the probability that you can manage the conflict constructively. One way to generate options is through brainstorming. To use brainstorming, try the following suggestions:

1. Make sure the problem and the goals are clear to both of you.

2. Try to temporarily suspend judgment and evaluation; do not censor your thoughts.

3. Specify a certain time period for brainstorming.

4. Consider having each partner brainstorm ideas separately before a meeting, or write ideas down before verbalizing solutions.

5. Try to develop at least one unique or far-out idea. You can always tame wild ideas down later.

6. Piggyback off the ideas of your partner. Encourage your partner to use or modify your ideas.

7. Write down all of the ideas suggested.

8. Review each idea, noting ways to combine, eliminate, or extend them.

If the goal is to find the best way to manage the difficulty, it may take only one good idea to help move the conflict forward to a constructive resolution.

When they brainstorm, Cara and Vaughn generate the following options: save money for a year and then get married; take turns going to college; take turns working to support the family while the other gets a degree; get married now, get jobs and postpone college; get married now and take out college loans.

Finally, they decide to *select the best solution*. Sometimes it may take several attempts at defining, analyzing, goal-setting, and generating multiple ideas before a mutually agreeable solution emerges. It is always appropriate to recheck your understanding of the issues and goals. Cara and Vaughn decide to combine the best of several ideas. They agree to get engaged, but not to set a date. Instead, they set a financial goal of five thousand dollars in savings. When they hit that goal, they will set a wedding date. If they are both attending college, they will get part-time jobs so that they have income, and they will also apply for college loans.

If, after repeated attempts, you cannot arrive at a mutually acceptable solution, you may decide to keep trying. Or you may agree to take the issue to an impartial person who can help you identify conflict management strategies and solutions. At work, your immediate superior may be called in to help settle the matter. Or, occasionally, you may agree to disagree and drop it.

Even though we have presented these conflict management steps as prescriptive suggestions, it is important to remember that *conflict rarely follows a linear, step-by-step sequence of events*. These skills are designed to serve as a general framework for collaboratively managing differences. But if your partner does not want to collaborate, your job will be more challenging.

In reality, you don't simply manage your emotions and then move neatly on to developing greater understanding with another person. Sorting out your goals and your partner's goals is not something that you do once and then put behind you. It will take time and patience to balance your goal of maintaining a relationship with your immediate achievement goals. In fact, as you try to manage a conflict, you will more than likely bounce forward and backward from one step to another. This framework gives you an overarching perspective for understanding and actively managing disagreements, but the nature of interpersonal relationships means that you and your partner will respond—sometimes in unpredictable ways—to a variety of cues (psychological, sociological, physical) when communicating. Think of the skills you have learned as options to consider rather than as hard-and-fast rules to follow in every situation.

Practicing Conflict Management Skills

In this activity you will be paired with another person and invited to roleplay a conflict that you have had with another person. A third person will observe and provide feedback about the communication skills you use to manage the conflict.

Person A.

Think about a recent incident in which someone offended you. Make a few notes about the conflict. Then approach person B, who will play the person who has offended you. Describe the conflict, remembering to manage your emotions.

Person B.

You have offended person A. Your job is to listen, reflect, and help to manage the conflict. Start a dialogue to identify each other's goals and see how they overlap; then try to generate strategies to achieve the goals.

Person C.

Your job is to observe the roleplay. Use the following checklist to help you evaluate the participants. When the roleplay is over, tell the participants what they did well. Ask them how they could improve, and offer suggestions as well.

If time permits, switch roles and conduct another roleplay.

Conflict Management Roleplay Checklist

	Person A	Person B
Managing Emotions		
Makes direct eye contact.	_____	_____
Maintains open body posture.	_____	_____
Uncrosses arms and legs.	_____	_____
Has a slight forward lean.	_____	_____
Uses a calm voice.	_____	_____
Uses reinforcing head nods.	_____	_____
Has appropriate facial expression.	_____	_____
Managing Information		
Paraphrases content accurately.	_____	_____
Paraphrases feelings accurately.	_____	_____
Clearly describes the problem.	_____	_____
Uses appropriate lead-in ("So," or "You seem to be saying").	_____	_____
Managing Goals		
States the goals clearly.	_____	_____
Identifies how goals overlap.	_____	_____
Managing the Problem		
Identifies several options.	_____	_____

When Others Aren't Other-Oriented:
How to Be Assertive

Even if you master collaborative conflict management skills, others may make irrational, inappropriate demands that create conflict and tension. In these instances, you will need to assert yourself, especially if someone has aggressively violated your rights.

To **assert** yourself is to let your communication partner know that his or her behaviour or message is infringing on your rights. We each have rights. In interpersonal communication, you have the right to refuse a request someone makes of you, the right to express your feelings as long as you don't trample on the feelings of others, and the right to have your personal needs met if they don't infringe upon the rights of others.

Some people confuse the terms assertiveness and aggressiveness. **Aggressiveness** means pursuing your interests by denying the rights of others. Assertiveness is other-oriented; aggressiveness is exclusively self-oriented. Aggressive people are coercive. They blame, judge, and evaluate to get what they want. They use intimidating nonverbal cues such as steely stares, a bombastic voice, and flailing gestures. Assertive people can ask for what they want without judging or evaluating their partner.

In Chapter 4 we talked about using "I" messages to express your thoughts and feelings rather than "you" messages. "I" messages describe what you want by expressing your feelings and goals. "You" messages lead with an attack on the person. "You creep! You ate the last breakfast taco" is an aggressive "you" statement. "I asked you to save one taco for me; now I won't have anything to eat for breakfast" is an assertive statement that states your rights and describes the consequences of violating them.

RECAP   Assertiveness versus Aggressiveness

Assertiveness	Aggressiveness
Expresses your interests without denying the rights of others.	Expresses your interests and denies the rights of others.
Is other-oriented.	Is self-oriented.
Describes what you want.	Evaluates the other person.
Discloses your needs, using "I" messages.	Discloses your needs, using "you" messages.

Five Steps in Assertive Behaviour

Many people have a tendency to withdraw in the face of controversy, even when their rights are being violated or denied. But you can develop skill in asserting yourself by practicing five key suggestions.[29]

Describe how you view the situation. To assert your position, you first need to describe how you view the situation. You need to be assertive because the other person has not been other-oriented. For example, Doug was growing increasingly frustrated with Laurie's tardiness at the weekly staff meeting. He first approached Laurie by describing his observation: "I have noticed that you are usually fifteen minutes late to our weekly staff meetings." A key to communicating your assertive message is to monitor your nonverbal message, especially your voice. Avoid sarcasm or excessive vocal intensity. Calmly yet confidently describe the problem.

Disclose your feelings. After describing the situation from your perspective, let the other person know how you feel.[30] Disclosing your feelings will help to build empathy and avoid lengthy harangues about the other person's unjust treatment. "I feel as if you don't take our weekly meetings seriously," continues Doug as he asserts his desire for Laurie to be on time to the meeting. Note that Doug does not talk about how others are feeling ("Every member of our group is tired of you coming in late."); he describes how *he* feels.

Identify effects. Next, you can identify the *effects* of the other person's behaviour upon you or others. "When you are late it disrupts our meeting," says Doug.

Wait. Then you can simply wait for a response. Nonassertive people find this step hard. Again, be sure to monitor your nonverbal cues. Make sure your facial expression does not contradict your verbal message. Delivering an assertive message with a broad grin might create a double bind for your listener, who may not be sure what the primary message is—the verbal one or the nonverbal one.

Reflect content and feelings. After the other person responds appropriately, reflect your understanding of both the content and feelings of the message. "Oh, I'm sorry. I didn't realize I was creating a problem. I have another meeting that usually goes overtime. It's difficult for me to arrive at the start of our meeting on time," says Laurie. Doug could respond, "So the key problem is a time conflict with another meeting. That must make you feel frustrated to try to do two things at once."

If the other person is evasive, unresponsive, or aggressive, you'll need to cycle through the steps again: clearly describe what the other person is doing that is not acceptable; disclose how you feel; identify the effects; wait; then reflect and clarify as needed. A key goal of an assertive response is to seek an empathic connection between you and your partner. Paraphrasing feelings is a way of ensuring that both parties are connecting.

If you tend to withdraw from conflict, how do you become assertive? Visualizing can help. Think of a past situation in which you wished you had been more assertive and then mentally replay the situation, imagining what you might have said. Also practice verbalizing assertive statements. When you are appropriately assertive, consciously congratulate yourself for sticking up for your rights. To sharpen your assertiveness skills, try the following Communication Experience.

Practice: How to Assert Yourself

Working with a partner, describe a situation in which you could have been more assertive. Ask your partner to assume the role of the person toward whom you should have been more assertive. Now replay the situation, using the following skills:

1. Describe: Tell the other person that what he or she is doing bothers you. Describe rather than evaluate.

2. Disclose: Then tell the other person how you feel. For example, "I feel X, when you do Y . . . "

3. Identify Effects: Tell the other person the effects of his or her behaviour upon you or your group. Be as clear and descriptive as you can.

4. Wait: After you have described, disclosed, and identified the effects, wait for a response.

5. Reflect: Use reflective listening skills: question, paraphrase content, paraphrase feelings.

Observation of Assertiveness Skills

Ask your classmates to observe your roleplay and provide feedback, using the following checklist.

When you have finished asserting your point of view, reverse roles.

Clearly describes what the problem was.	_____
Effectively discloses how he or she felt.	_____
Clearly describes the effects of the behaviour.	_____
Pauses or waits after describing the effects.	_____
Uses effective questions to promote understanding.	_____
Accurately paraphrases content.	_____
Accurately paraphrases feelings.	_____
Has good eye contact.	_____
Leans forward while speaking.	_____
Has an open body posture.	_____
Has appropriate voice tone and quality.	_____

RECAP   How to Assert Yourself

Step	Example
1. Describe	"I see that you haven't completed the report yet."
2. Disclose	"I feel that the work I ask you to do is not a priority with you."
3. Identify Effects	"Without that report, our team will not achieve our goal."
4. Be Silent	Wait for a response.
5. Use Reflective Listening	
Question	"Do you understand how I feel?"
Paraphrase content	"So, you were not aware that the report was late."
Paraphrase feelings	"Perhaps you feel embarrassed."

Fighting Fairly

Consider the following suggestions to keep you focused on issues rather than personalities when you experience interpersonal conflict:

1. Be specific when you introduce a complaint.

2. Don't just complain; ask for a reasonable change that will make the situation better.

3. Give and receive feedback about the major points of disagreement to make sure you are understood by your partner.

4. Try tolerance. Be open to your own feelings, and equally open to your partner's feelings. Openness means that you accept change and can verbalize that attitude to your partner.

5. Consider compromise if appropriate. Many conflicts involve issues that are neither right nor wrong. Your partner may even have some good ideas.

6. Deal with one issue at a time.

7. Don't "mind rape." Don't assume to tell your partner what he or she knows or feels. Never assume you know what your partner thinks. Ask.

8. Attack the issue, not each other.

9. Don't call each other names or use sarcasm.

10. Don't "gunny sack." Just as farmers use a gunny sack to carry feed, many people carry past hurts into the conflict and then unleash them from the "gunny sack." Forget the past and stay with the issue at hand.

11. Don't burden your partner with too many issues.

12. Think about your thoughts and feelings before speaking.

Adapted from George R. Bach and Ronald M. Deutsch, *Pairing* (New York: Peter Wyden, 1970).

Summary

Interpersonal conflict is an expressed struggle that occurs when two people cannot agree upon a way to meet their needs or goals. At the root of all conflicts are our individual perspectives, needs, and experiences.

Conflict can result from misunderstanding someone (pseudo conflict), or it can stem from a simple difference of opinion or viewpoint (simple conflict). Ego conflict occurs when personalities clash; the conflict becomes personal and you may feel a need to defend your self-image.

Myths about the conflict management process tell us that conflict should always be avoided; that conflict always occurs because of misunderstandings; that conflict always occurs because of a poor interpersonal relationship; and that conflict can always be resolved. But conflict in interpersonal relationships is not always destructive. It can actually play a constructive role by identifying areas that need attention and transformation.

Although conflict seems to erupt suddenly, it often originates in events that occur long before the conflict manifests itself. It evolves from these prior conditions into frustration awareness, active conflict, solution, and follow-up stages. Understanding conflict as a process also involves recognizing how people seek and are given control over others. Power in interpersonal relationships can be legitimate, referent, expert, rewarding, or coercive. Decisions about using power should consider the effect upon the other person and the relationship.

Nonconfrontational approaches to conflict include placating, distracting, computing, and withdrawing. Controlling approaches employ blaming and threats. Cooperative approaches involve separating the person from the problem, focusing on shared interests, generating many options to seek a solution, and basing the decision on objective rather than subjective criteria. Skills for managing conflict focus on managing emotions, information, goals, and ultimately on managing the problem.

The goal of this chapter is not to eliminate conflict from your interpersonal relationships; that would be unrealistic and even undesirable. But knowing principles and skills for bridging differences can give you greater flexibility in maintaining satisfying relationships with others.

For Discussion and Review

■ FOCUS ON COMPREHENSION

1. What are pseudo, simple, and ego conflict?

2. What are five myths about conflict?

3. What are the five stages of the conflict management process?

4. Identify and describe the five types of power.

5. What are the four essentials skills of managing conflict?

■ FOCUS ON CRITICAL THINKING

6. Richard has an explosive temper. He consistently receives poor performance evaluations at work because he lashes out at those who disagree with him. What strategies might help him manage his emotional outbursts?

7. Melissa and Jake always seem to end up making personal attacks and calling each other names when they get into a disagreement. What type of conflict are they experiencing when they do this, and how can they avoid it?

8. Brian is a whiz at computers. When he, his sister, and his brother are shopping for a new computer for their parents, Brian's sister complains that he ignores her suggestions. What type of power is Brian exercising? What could he do to include his siblings in the decision process?

9. Analyze the opening dialogue in this chapter. What are Simone and Paul doing wrong in managing their differences? Are they doing anything right?

■ FOCUS ON ETHICS

10. Is it ethical to mask your true emotions in order to get along with others? Is honesty in a relationship always the best policy? Explain your response.

11. When a conflict arises between two people, are certain types of power more ethical to draw upon than others? Explain your answer, describing conditions that would justify the use of certain types of power.

12. Are there situations when you should *not* assert your point of view? Provide an example to support your answer.

For Your Journal

1. Analyze several recent conversations in which you were trying to convince someone to do something. Discuss the types of power you used in your efforts.

2. Consider a recent conflict you have had with someone. Determine whether it was a pseudo, simple, or ego conflict. Describe the strategies you used to manage the conflict. Now that you have read this chapter, discuss the other strategies you could have used to help manage the disagreement.

3. Identify a current or recent conflict you are having or have had with a friend or acquaintance. Use the problem-solving steps presented in this chapter to seek a solution to the problem that is creating the conflict. Define the problem: Identify the issues. Analyze the problem: What are the causes, symptoms, effects, and obstacles that keep you from achieving your goal? Determine your goal: What do you want? What does your partner want? Generate many possible solutions that would solve the problem. Finally, select the solution(s) that would permit each person to achieve his or her goal.

4. Briefly describe a conflict during which you did *not* do a good job of managing your emotions, that is, one in which you became angry and upset and lost your cool. Respond to the following questions: Why did you lose control of your emotions? If you could go back in time, what would you do differently to better manage your emotions before and during the conflict? Consider incorporating some of the suggestions discussed in this chapter.

Learning with Others

1. Win As Much As You Can[31]

   This activity is designed to explore the effects of trust and conflict on communication. You will be paired with a partner. There will be four partner teams working in a cluster.

4 Xs: Lose $1 each
3 Xs: Win $1 each 1 Y: Lose $3
2 Xs: Win $2 each 2 Ys: Lose $2 each
1 X: Win $3 3 Ys: Lose $1 each
4 Ys: Win $1

   Directions: Your instructor will provide detailed instructions for playing this game. For ten successive rounds you and your partner will choose either an X or a Y. Your instructor will tell all partner teams to reveal their choices at the same time. Each round's payoff will depend on the decision made by others in your cluster. For example, according to the scoring chart shown above, if all four partner teams mark X for round one of this game, each partner team loses $1. You are to confer with your partner on each round to make a joint decision. Before rounds 5, 8, and 10, your instructor will permit you to confer with the other pairs in your cluster. Keep track of your choices and winnings on the score sheet below. When you finish the game, compare your cluster's results with those of others. Discuss the factors that affected your balances. There are three key rules:

   1. Do not confer with the other members of your cluster unless you are given specific permission to do so. This applies to nonverbal and verbal communication.

   2. Each pair must agree on a single choice for each round.

   3. Make sure that the other members of your cluster do not know your pair's choice until you are instructed to reveal it.

Round	Time Allowed	Confer with	Choice	$ Won	$ Lost	$ Balance	
1	2 min.	partner	_____	_____	_____	_____	
2	1 min.	partner	_____	_____	_____	_____	
3	1 min.	partner	_____	_____	_____	_____	
4	1 min.	partner	_____	_____	_____	_____	
5	3 min.	cluster					Bonus Round:
	1 min.	partner	_____	_____	_____	_____	Pay x 3
6	1 min.	partner	_____	_____	_____	_____	
7	1 min.	partner	_____	_____	_____	_____	
8	3 min.	cluster					
	1 min.	partner	_____	_____	_____	_____	Pay x 5
9	1 min.	partner	_____	_____	_____	_____	
10	3 min.	cluster					
	1 min.	partner	_____	_____	_____	_____	Pay x 10

2. Agree-Disagree Statements about Conflict

Read each statement once and mark whether you agree (A) or disagree (D) with it. Take five or six minutes to do this.

_____ 1. Most people find an argument interesting and exciting.

_____ 2. In most conflicts someone must win and someone must lose. That's the way conflict is.

_____ 3. The best way to handle a conflict is simply to let everyone cool off.

_____ 4. Most people get upset at a person who disagrees with them.

_____ 5. If people spend enough time together, they will find something to disagree about and will eventually become upset with one another.

_____ 6. Conflicts can be solved if people just take the time to listen to one another.

_____ 7. If you disagree with someone, it is usually better to keep quiet than to express your personal difference of opinion.

_____ 8. To compromise is to take the easy way out of conflict.

_____ 9. Some people produce more conflict and tension than others. These people should be restricted from working with others.

After you have marked the above statements, break up into small groups and try to agree or disagree unanimously with each statement. Especially try to find reasons for differences of opinion. If your group cannot reach agreement or disagreement, you may change the wording in any statement to promote consensus. Assign one group member to observe your group interactions. After your group has attempted to reach consensus, the observer should report how effectively the group used the guidelines suggested in this chapter.

■ GLOSSARY

INTERPERSONAL CONFLICT: A struggle that occurs when two people cannot agree upon a way to meet their needs or goals.

EXPRESSIVE CONFLICT: Conflict that focuses on issues about the quality of the relationship and managing interpersonal tension and hostility.

INSTRUMENTAL CONFLICT: Conflict that centres on achieving a particular goal or task and less on relational issues.

PSEUDO CONFLICT: Conflict triggered by a lack of understanding and miscommunication.

SIMPLE CONFLICT: Conflict that stems from different ideas, definitions, perceptions, or goals.

EGO CONFLICT: Conflict that is based upon personal issues; conflicting partners attack one another's self-esteem.

CONFLICT MYTHS: Inappropriate assumptions about the nature of interpersonal conflict.

CONSTRUCTIVE CONFLICT: Conflict that helps build new insights and establishes new patterns in a relationship.

DESTRUCTIVE CONFLICT: Conflict that dismantles relationships without restoring the relationship.

POWER: The resources an individual has to influence another person.

LEGITIMATE POWER: Influence based upon being appointed, elected, or selected by someone to exercise control.

REFERENT POWER: Influence based upon being well liked and respected.

EXPERT POWER: Influence based upon knowledge and experience that an individual possesses.

REWARD POWER: Influence based upon a person's ability to provide positive rewards and favours.

COERCIVE POWER: Influence based upon someone's ability to punish another person.

SEXUAL HARASSMENT: Unwanted sexual advances, requests for sexual favours, or other inappropriate verbal or physical behaviour of a sexual nature.

NONCONFRONTATIONAL STYLE: A style of managing conflict that includes placating, distracting, computing, withdrawing, and giving in.

CONTROLLING STYLE: A style of managing conflict motivated by a desire to dominate. Behaviours include blaming, threatening, warning, and other forms of verbal abuse.

COOPERATIVE STYLE: A style of managing conflict that seeks win-win solutions to problems. Cooperative people separate the people from the problem, focus on shared interests, generate multiple solutions, and base decisions on objective criteria.

ASSERTIVENESS: Pursuing your best interests without denying your partner's rights.

AGGRESSIVENESS: Expressing your interests while denying the rights of others by blaming, judging, and evaluating the other person.

Interpersonal Communication and Cultural Diversity

After studying this chapter, you should be able to:

1. Define culture.

2. Identify four components of culture.

3. Discuss differences and similarities in verbal and nonverbal communication in different cultures.

4. Discuss barriers that inhibit effective intercultural communication.

5. Identify strategies for bridging cultural differences.

■ THE NATURE OF CULTURE

■ BARRIERS TO EFFECTIVE INTERCULTURAL COMMUNICATION

■ BRIDGING DIFFERENCES IN BACKGROUND AND CULTURE

verheard before class begins: "I've had it with all this cultural diversity stuff. It seems like every textbook in every class is obsessed with it. My history textbook talks about all these obscure people I've never heard of before. In English lit all we're reading is stuff by people from different cultures. I'm tired of all this politically correct nonsense. I mean, we're all Canadians. Why don't they just teach us what we need to know and cut all this diversity garbage?"

Perhaps you've encountered this kind of "diversity backlash" among some of your classmates, or perhaps you even share this attitude yourself. It may seem unsettling that all of our textbooks are changing, and that educators are so concerned with cultural diversity. But these changes are not motivated by an irrational desire to be politically correct. They are taking place because Canada is changing. As the statistics in the Diversity Almanac below suggest, it is becoming an increasingly culturally diverse country. And with this growing diversity, there is also a growing awareness that learning about cultural differences can affect every aspect of our lives in positive ways. You may not plan on travelling the world, but the world is travelling to you. Your boss, teacher, religious leader, best friend, or marriage partner may have grown up with different cultural traditions than your own. Our textbooks and courses are reflecting the change, not initiating it.

In collective cultures, cooperative activity is a way of life. Among Kenyan tribespeople, community goals take precedence over individual ambitions. (Peter Carmichael)

Diversity Almanac

- While Canada holds a widespread public perception of soaring immigration over the past years, there has actually been little deviation from Canada's 1994 rate of accepting 5.9 new immigrants per 1,000 people. In fact, this rate is lower than Canada's historical "peaks," including 1957 (16 per 1,000), 1966 (11 per 1,000), and 1974 (8 per 1,000).

- In 1991, 94 percent of Canada's total population were Canadian citizens. The majority obtained their citizenship by birth, while 12 percent were naturalized citizens.

- Canada's current rate of immigration is nonetheless still higher than in the other two leading immigration destinations, the United States (2.8 per 1,000), and Australia (3.5 per 1,000), and of the same order of magnitude as New Zealand (6.2 per 1,000).

- In 1991, Europeans made up the largest share of all immigrants living in Canada, accounting for 54 percent of all immigrants.

... But the picture is changing.

- The proportion of new immigrants to Canada who are European-born has declined steadily since 1961. Before 1961, 91 percent of new immigrants to Canada were born in Europe. This proportion fell dramatically to 25 percent for those new immigrants who arrived between 1981 and 1991.

Where are the recent immigrants to Canada coming from?

- In 1994, Asian-born persons, most from Hong Kong, China, the Philippines, and India, represented 64 percent of Canada's new immigrants.

Where are Canada's recent immigrants planning to settle?

- In 1994, 52 percent of Canada's new immigrants planned to settle in Ontario (predominantly Toronto), while 22 percent planned to settle in British Columbia (predominantly Vancouver), and 12.5 percent planned to settle in Quebec (predominantly Montreal).

From: *Report on the Demographic Situation in Canada 1995: Current Demographic Analysis,* Statistics Canada (1996), 68–69. ISSN 0715-9293; and from *The Daily,* December 8, 1992, Statistics Canada, Cat. No. 96-304E.

Throughout this book we have presented examples and research conclusions that emphasize how cultural differences affect our interpersonal relationships. In this chapter we will examine in more detail the impact culture has upon our lives and suggest some skills for bridging cultural differences in your interpersonal communications and relationships. With these skills, you will be equipped to understand and value the diversity inherent in our population. In order to live comfortably in the twenty-first century, we can learn ways to accommodate and understand cultural differences instead of ignoring them, suffering because of them, or wishing that they would disappear.

Canada is a multicultural country.
(National Capital Commission)

IV   BRIDGING DIFFERENCES IN INTERPERSONAL RELATIONSHIPS

Identify the intercultural encounters you have had during the past week. Use the space below to organize your experiences.

Friends or family members who are from a culture other than my own:

_____ _____

_____ _____

_____ _____

People I have met from a culture other than my own:

_____ _____

_____ _____

_____ _____

Ethnic foods I have eaten (not counting pizza):

_____ _____

_____ _____

_____ _____

Situations in which I have heard someone speaking a language other than my own:

1. _____

2. _____

3. _____

4. _____

The Nature of Culture

Exactly what is culture? **Culture** is a learned system of knowledge, behaviour, attitudes, beliefs, values, and norms that is shared by a group of people.[1] According to noted anthropologist Edward T. Hall, communication and culture are inseparable. How you interact with others is inextricably linked to how you learned to be a member of your group. Basically, we derive our cultural identity from three factors: elements, values, and contexts.

Cultural diversity includes more than differences in ethnic background or gender. To become other-oriented is to consider a range of differences that affect how we communicate and respond to others. Note the following differences that affect our inter-actions with others.

AGE   Different generations, because they share different cultural and historical events, often view life differently. If your grandparents experienced the Great Depression of the 1930s, they may have different attitudes about savings accounts than you or even your parents. Today's explicit song lyrics may shock older Americans who grew up with such racy lyrics as "makin' whoopee." The generation gap is real.

LANGUAGE   By far the majority of Canadians outside of Quebec claim English as their "native tongue," and most Quebecers claim French as their native tongue. However, a sizable minority of Canadians report a wide range of other languages as their native tongue, and this range reflects the diversity of cultures that are integrally formed by their language. The following is a breakdown of the twenty most popularly reported minority-languages spoken in Canada.

Top 20 Home Languages, Canada, 1991, Excluding English and French

1. Chinese
2. Italian
3. Portuguese
4. Spanish
5. German
6. Polish
7. Punjabi
8. Greek
9. Vietnamese
10. Arabic
11. Cree
12. Tagalog
13. Ukrainian
14. Persian
15. Korean
16. Hungarian
17. Tamil
18. Gujarati
19. Croatian
20. Armenian

RELIGION   Eating habits and attitudes toward abortion and use of alcohol are just a few of the factors in a person's religious beliefs and traditions that can affect relationships.

Here is a breakdown of the top denominations by percent of total population:

Roman Catholic	45.2%
Protestant	36.2%
United Church	11.5%
Anglican	8.1%
Presbyterian	2.4%
Lutheran	2.4%
Baptist	2.5%
Pentecostal	1.6%
Eastern Orthodox	1.4%
Jewish	1.2%
Islam	.9%
Hindu	.6%
Buddhist	.6%
Sikh	.5%

From: *The Daily*, June 1, 1993, Statistics Canada, Cat. No. 96-304E.

DISABILITY   Although you may not think of the disabled as part of the cultural diversity equation, there is evidence that we uncon-sciously alter our communication style when we converse with disabled people. For example, we make less eye contact with people who are in wheelchairs; we also afford them more

Cultural Elements

Categories of things and ideas that identify the most profound aspects of cultural influence are known as **cultural elements**. According to one research team, cultural elements include the following:

- Material culture: things and ideas
- Social institutions: schools, governments, religious organizations
- Individuals and the universe: system of beliefs
- Aesthetics: music, theatre, art, dance
- Language: verbal and nonverbal communication systems[2]

personal space when conversing. We often speak more loudly and more slowly to those who are blind. Many disabled people find these behaviours insulting.

SOCIAL CLASS The constitution declares that all people are created equal, but there is dramatic evidence that class differences exist and affect communication patterns. Social psychologist Michael Argyle reports that the cues we use to make class distinctions are: (1) way of life, (2) family, (3) job, (4) money, and (5) education. Class differences influence whom we talk with, whether we are likely to invite our neighbours over for coffee, and whom we choose as our friends and lovers. Most of us must make a conscious effort if we want to expand beyond our class boundaries.

GENDER In this book we emphasize how gender affects the way we listen, use words, and send and interpret nonverbal messages. Sex differences are biological differences between males and females: only men can impregnate, only women can menstruate, gestate, and lactate.

But gender differences focus on learned behaviour that is culturally associated with being a man or a woman. Gender role definitions are flexible: a man can adopt behaviour that is associated with a female role definition in a given culture and vice versa.

SEXUAL PREFERENCE During the past decade gays and lesbians have become more assertive in expressing their rights within society. Issues such as whether gays belong in the military, in the clergy, and in the teaching professions have stirred the passions of many. Being gay has become a source of pride for some, but it is still a social stigma for others. The incidence of suicide among gay teenagers is significantly higher than among non-gay teens. Although gay people are gaining legal rights and protections, they are still subject to discriminatory laws and social intolerance. The gay and lesbian community functions as a **co-culture** or a culture within the larger culture.

RACE According to the dictionary, race is based upon the genetically transmitted physical characteristics of a group of people classified together on the basis of a common history, nationality, or geographical location. Skin colour and other physical characteristics affect our responses and influence the way people of different races interact. Racial prejudice still has a devastating effect upon interpersonal communication patterns and relationships.

ETHNICITY Ethnicity refers to a social classification based upon a variety of factors such as nationality, religion, language, or ancestral heritage. Nationality and geographical location are especially important in defining an ethnic group. Those of Irish ancestry are usually referred to as an ethnic group rather than as a race. The same could be said of Britons, Norwegians, and Spaniards. Ethnicity, like race, fosters common bonds that affect communication patterns. On the positive side, ethnic groups bring vitality and variety to our society. On the negative side, members of these groups may experience persecution or rejection from members of other groups in our society.

Pomp and Circumstance. Which **elements of culture** are conveyed through Canada's changing of the guard ceremony on Parliament Hill? How do these cultural elements combine to shape the identity of Canadians?

CONSIDERING OTHERS

Think About the Other Person When You Get Impatient

DEAR ANN LANDERS: After reading the letters of complaint about thoughtless customers who slow down the checkout line, I needed to write.

When I was initially diagnosed with multiple sclerosis, the area most affected was my hands. They were extremely stiff and clumsy, but I could, with effort, manage to write.

Although my disability was not apparent to others, performing simple, everyday tasks was difficult and exhausting. I particularly remember the checkout line at the supermarket. Trying to manipulate the checkbook and write out a check took a great deal of effort.

I could sense the impatience of the customers behind me and felt anxious and embarrassed, even though I was holding up the line for only an additional minute or two. But it taught me a lesson. I realized how often I had been impatient and judgmental of others.

Compassion is often learned the hard way. I hope the next time an exasperated shopper is stuck in line behind someone who may not proceed at the normal rate of speed, he or she will give a thought to these questions: What do I really know about the person who is holding up the line? How important is that extra minute, anyway?—Still Learning in Ashland, OR.

DEAR ASHLAND: You have raised questions that we all need to keep in mind when patience runs thin. Thank you for reminding us.

Permission granted by Ann Landers and Creators Syndicate, published in 1994.

COMMUNICATION EXPERIENCE

Assessing Your Communication with Strangers

Your comfort level in communicating with strangers is related to your ability to communicate with people from other cultures. Respond to each statement by indicating the degree to which it is true of your communication with strangers: Always False (answer 1), Usually False (answer 2), Sometimes True and Sometimes False (answer 3), Usually True (answer 4), or Always True (answer 5).

_____ 1. I accept strangers as they are.

_____ 2. I express my feelings when I communicate with strangers.

_____ 3. I avoid negative stereotyping when I communicate with strangers.

_____ 4. I find similarities between myself and strangers when we communicate.

_____ 5. I accommodate my behaviour to strangers when we communicate.

To find your score, add the numbers you wrote next to each statement. Scores range from 5 to 25. The higher your score, the greater your potential for developing a strong relationship with someone from a different background.

From: William B. Gudykunst, _Bridging Differences: Effective Intergroup Communication_ (Newbury Park: Sage, 1991), 143.

As we grow, we learn to value these cultural elements. You were not born with a certain taste in music, clothes, and automobiles. Through **enculturation**, the process of communicating a group's culture from generation to generation, you learned what you liked by choosing from among the elements that were available within your culture. Your friends, colleagues, the media, and most importantly, your family, communicate information about these elements and advocate choices for you to make.

Cultures are not static; they change as new information and new influences penetrate their stores of knowledge. We no longer believe that bathing is unhealthy, or that we can safely use makeup made with lead. These changes resulted from scientific discoveries. But other changes take place through **acculturation**; we acquire other approaches, beliefs, and values by coming into contact with other cultures. Today, acupuncture, yoga, t'ai chi, and karate studios are commonplace in most cities across North America. Taco shells are available in every supermarket, and salsa sales are rising. In less obvious ways, "new" perspectives from other cultures have also influenced our thoughts, actions, and relationships. The article, "Cultural Differences in Marriage," describes the breadth of variation in one important cultural element, as well as changes occurring because of cross-cultural influences.

This girl's clothing and pets reflect the esthetics and lifestyle of her Inuit culture.

Cultural Values

Identifying what a given group of people values or appreciates can provide insight into the behaviour of an individual raised within that group. Although there are great differences among the world's **cultural values**, one researcher identified four variables for measuring values that are significant in almost every culture.[3] According to Geert Hofstede, each culture places varying degrees of value upon masculine and feminine perspectives, avoidance of uncertainty, distribution of power, and individualism. Hofstede's research conclusions for ten countries on these four dimensions are reflected in Table 11.1. High scores indicate greater value for the dimension; low scores suggest that less value is placed on the dimension.

Table 11.1

A Comparison of Cultural Values across Ten Countries

Country	Masculinity	Uncertainty Avoidance	Power Distance	Individualism
Costa Rica	21 L	86 H	35 L	15 L
France	43 M	86 H	68 H	71 H
Germany	66 H	65 M	35 L	67 H
Great Britain	66 H	35 L	35 L	89 H
Indonesia	46 M	48 L	78 H	14 L
Japan	95 H	92 H	54 M	46 M
Netherlands	14 L	53 M	38 L	80 H
USA	62 H	46 L	40 L	91 H
Russia	40 L	90 H	95 H	50 M
China	50 M	60 M	80 H	20 L

L= Low; M=Medium; H=High

From: Geert Hofstede, *Cultures and Organizations*. London: McGraw Hill, 1991.

Cultural Differences in Marriage

Within a culture, people know what is meant by the word "marriage," but for many years, researchers have been seeking a definition of the term that will cover the enormous variation in institutional arrangements found all over the world. The task has not been an easy one because the way in which one society defines the relationship can be quite different from that of another.

Such differences reflect the historical needs of each society—for example, inheritance of land and property, large families to work the land—as well as religious and other considerations. What does seem to be true is that the romantic aspects of marriage are by no means universal, and that, as societies change, so does the institution of marriage.

Purposes of Marriage

In Western society, if you have two spouses you are a bigamist and have committed a crime for which you may be sent to prison. Would this happen everywhere else in the world? Not in areas with polygamy. Polygyny is the most common form of this: in many societies, it is the norm for men to take more than one wife, and the number of wives a man has is often an indication of his status. This is far more common than polyandry—when a woman can marry more than one husband. Polyandry exists in an institutionalized form only in the Himalayan region, where a woman may go through a marriage ceremony with more than one man, and a further ceremony is required to recognize formally which is the father of each of her children. Group marriage, or the state of uncontrolled sexual promiscuity—a type of marriage much loved by historians who speculate on the evolution of social life—has never been recorded.

There is no simple explanation to account for the variable distribution of marriage practices. Having a number of wives may be to a man's economic and political advantage through the productivity of the women (and the children they bear) or the network of relationships that such marriages create. Throughout history, the creation and maintenance of dynasties have often depended on strategically arranged marriages. Almost everywhere, this institution is concerned with the transmission of rights and property, and marriage practices reflect this fact.

For example, marriage has to do with the identification of heirs, which for us usually means the legitimacy of our children. The Christian churches have always seen sexual intercourse and marriage as indissolubly linked, to the extent that it is wrong for the first to occur outside the second, and they have stated that the function of both is the production of children. Legitimate offspring are those conceived in wedlock, and the biological and social relationships together define the family.

In fact, much of the variation found in marriage practices can be traced to differing ideas and expectations about the relationship between social and biological fatherhood—known respectively as "pater" and "genitor." A great number of marital arrangements may exist once these two roles become separate and the legitimacy of offspring is defined by their relationship to the pater. For example, there is the widow inheritance practiced by the Hebrews in Old-Testament times, when a dead man's brother had the duty to have children by the widow, who were then regarded as the deceased's, not the genitor's. Or, perhaps more exotic, there is the so-called "ghost marriage" of the Chinese. If an unmarried man dies without issue, particularly without a son, a woman might go through a marriage ceremony with his "ghost" and the children she bears by a lover would be his.

These cases, and others like them, depend for their existence not only on the separation of the roles of pater and genitor, but also on certain social arrangements and religious ideas. Thus, in the Chinese case, not only is it important that a man should have sons in order to continue his line; a man without sons to worship him also has no existence as an ancestor.

The Limits of Choice

If the forms of marriage vary, so too do the practices associated with it—for example, how people choose a partner and where they live after marriage. We might think that those of us in industrialized countries are free to marry whom we like as long as we avoid committing incest, but in practice, this is not so. We have first to meet someone before we can marry them—and those we meet will be restricted by a whole range of factors including education, employment, and leisure interests.

Then there are the social pressures that intervene to make marriages between certain people that much more difficult. Commonly, this occurs when there is a great difference in the wealth, status, religion, ethnic background or age of the partners. Generally speaking, the higher the status, the more restricted the choice. This is clear in the case of the British Royal Family, but the Pharaohs of ancient Egypt were even more restricted—they were expected to marry their sisters.

Small-scale egalitarian societies, in which many of these factors do not apply, produce their own kinds of limitation. For example, young men may be highly dependent on the goodwill of their seniors in order to obtain the bridewealth that makes marriage possible. (A man's claim to his own children will not be socially recognized without this payment to his wife's family.) There are also societies in which marriages are arranged; the bride and groom have little or no say in the matter, and may not even meet each other face to face until after the ceremony has taken place.

In the latter case, it is clear that those involved are not marrying for love. In fact, for the majority of humanity, the reasons for marriage were and are much more down to earth and practical—often quite explicitly economic. In societies where the nature of the economy and the division of labor make the involvement of both men and women crucial to survival, there is little room for a romantic image of marriage.

Patterns of postmarital residence also vary greatly throughout the world. Ideally in our society, newly married couples go to live in their own home. Often, for financial reasons, this is not possible and in such cases it is usual for the couple to reside with the wife's parents. This pattern is adopted on the argument that it produces less tension for a mother and daughter to share the same kitchen than a woman and her daughter-in-law. In some societies, the bride lives with the groom's family, in others vice versa. Occasionally both types of residence are found in the same society, although one—that where the bride joins her husband—is regarded as being of higher status, the other form suggesting the relative poverty of the groom (perhaps an inability to pay bridewealth).

Marriage and Change

The form marriage takes in any given society is a reflection of the wider political, social, economic, and religious setting. Just as these alter over time, so does marriage. Although it is often claimed that the institutions of family and marriage are threatened, they usually are merely becoming transformed along with other aspects of society.

Marriages in the Western world are constantly changing. The relative ease with which divorce can be obtained has increased the amount of serial polygamy—in which men and women have a number of marriages, but one after the other—and the number of step-relationships. (It is not generally realized that only in the past decade has the number of broken marriages reached the 19th-century rate—although then the cause was death, not divorce.)

Age at first marriage and at first child has oscillated over the years, and despite widely encouraged contraception, the illegitimate birth rate remains high and has even increased in recent years. Tax laws in the United Kingdom make cohabitation an attractive and advantageous alternative to marriage for some couples. In Canada, the U.S., and the United Kingdom, evidence is beginning to accumulate to show that a significant minority of intelligent women with good careers are not marrying, but this is not precluding them from having children.

From: Peter Marsh, *Eye to Eye: How People Interact* (Topsfield, MA: Salem House Publishers, 1988), 21-22.

MASCULINE VERSUS FEMININE PERSPECTIVES

Some cultures emphasize traditional male values, whereas others place greater value on female perspectives. These values are not really about biological sex differences but overarching approaches to interacting with others. **Masculine cultures** value achievement, assertiveness, heroism, and material wealth. **Feminine cultures** value relationships, caring for the less fortunate, and overall quality of life.[4] Of course, rarely is a culture on the extreme end of the continuum; many are somewhere in between. For centuries most countries in Europe, Asia, and the Americas have had masculine cultures. Men and their conquests dominate history books; men have been more prominent in leadership and decision making than women. But today many of these cultures are moving slowly toward the middle—legal and social rules are encouraging more gender balance and greater equality between masculine and feminine roles.

TOLERANCE OF UNCERTAINTY VERSUS AVOIDANCE OF UNCERTAINTY

Cedric works for the phone company as a customer service representative. He grew up in Jamaica where there is sometimes a higher tolerance for bureaucratic uncertainty than there is Canada. Jake is from Toronto; he expects (sometimes demands) that his problems be resolved quickly. Cedric's higher tolerance for uncertainty and Jake's desire for straight, prompt answers to questions created an oil-and-water confrontation. Jake phoned Cedric to complain about the slow response to his request to have a new phone line installed for his fax machine. Cedric tried to be reassuring, but Jake got the distinct impression that Cedric was not sympathetic and thought that a week's wait for a new line was perfectly reasonable. Jake expected his new line within twenty-four hours. Both had difficulty tuning in to the cultural difference in their expectations about how quickly a bureaucracy should respond to an individual request.

Some cultures tolerate more ambiguity and uncertainty than others. Those in which people need certainty to feel secure are more likely to have and enforce rigid rules for behaviour and develop more elaborate codes of conduct. People from cultures with a greater tolerance for uncertainty have more relaxed, informal expectations for others. "Go with the flow" and "it will sort itself out" are phrases that describe their attitudes. One study showed that people from Portugal, Germany, Peru, Belgium, and Japan have high certainty needs, but people from Scandinavian countries tend to tolerate uncertainty.[5]

CONCENTRATED VERSUS DECENTRALIZED POWER

Some cultures value an equal or decentralized distribution of power, whereas others accept a concentration of hierarchical power in a centralized government and other organizations. In the latter, hierarchical bureaucracies are common, and people expect some individuals to have more power than others. Russia, France, and China are all high on the concentrated power scale. Those that often strive for greater equality and distribution of power and control include many (but not all) citizens from Australia, Denmark, New Zealand, and Israel. People from these latter countries tend to minimize differences in power between people.

Cealy: We've got this group project to do. Let's divvy up the work and then meet back here next week to see what each of us has done.

Ayako: Wait a minute, Cealy. It might seem to be more efficient to divide up the work into little separate pieces, but in the end we'll have a better report if we work on every section.

Cealy: Are you kidding? We'll be here all night! Josh, you take the history of the problem. Bert, you look at problem causes and effects. Ayako, why don't you do a literature search on the CD-ROM in the library and start looking up articles.

Ayako: All right. But I still think it would be better to go to the library together. I think we'd have better luck if we worked on each aspect of the problem as a team.

Cealy and Ayako clearly have different strategies for working together. Cealy approaches the project from an individualistic perspective; Ayako prefers a collective or group strategy to achieve the goal. Traditionally, North Americans champion individual accomplishments and achievements. People from Asian backgrounds often value collective or group achievement more highly. One researcher summed up the North American goal system this way:

> *Chief among the virtues claimed . . . is self-realization. Each person is viewed as having a unique set of talents and potentials. The translation of these potentials into actuality is concurred the highest purpose to which one can devote one's life.*[6]

In a collectivistic culture, conversely, people strive to attain goals for all members of the family, group, or community. In Kenyan tribes, for example:

> *. . . nobody is an isolated individual. Rather, his [or her] uniqueness is secondary fact. . . . In this new system group activities are dominant, responsibility is shared and accountability is collective . . . Because of the emphasis on collectivity, harmony and cooperation among the group tends to be emphasized more than individual function and responsibility.*[7]

Individualistic cultures tend to be more loosely knit socially; individuals feel responsible for taking care of themselves and their immediate families.[8] In collectivistic cultures, individuals expect more support from others, also more loyalty to and from the community. Because collectivistic cultures place more value on "we" than "I," teamwork approaches usually succeed better in their workplaces. As you will see in Chapter 14, North American businesses have tried to adopt some of Japan's successful team strategies for achieving high productivity.

RECAP	Dimensions of Cultural Values
Masculine versus Feminine	Does the culture place the highest value on assertiveness, heroism, and wealth or on relationships, caring for others, and overall quality of life?
Tolerance of Uncertainty versus Avoidance of Uncertainty	Does the culture value or appreciate ambiguity and uncertainty or does it hold more rigid and explicit behavioural expectations?
Concentrated versus Decentralized Power	Does the culture tolerate or accept hierarchical power structures or does it favour a more equal distribution of power?
Individual versus Group Achievement	Does the culture value individual achievement more than collective group accomplishments or vice versa?

What can be inferred about the use of *cultural context cues* to enhance message and meaning in Canadian aboriginal culture?

Cultural Contexts

As we discussed in Chapter 6, individuals from different cultures use **cultural contextual** cues in varying degrees to enhance messages and meaning. This led Edward T. Hall to categorize cultures as either high- or low-context.[9] In **high-context cultures** nonverbal cues are extremely important in interpreting messages. **Low-context cultures** rely more explicitly on language, and use fewer contextual cues to send and interpret information. Individuals from high-context cultures may perceive persons from low-context cultures as less attractive, knowledgeable, and trustworthy, because they violate unspoken rules of dress, conduct, and communication. Individuals from low-context cultures often are not skilled in interpreting unspoken, contextual messages.[10] Refer back to pages 339–342 to review other ways in which the use of cultural context affects communication.

Assessing Your Stereotypes

The purpose of this questionnaire is to help you understand how you stereotype members of other groups, as well as your own. Think of a group with which you identify closely (for example, your cultural or ethnic group). Then in the "My Group" column check off five adjectives that apply to that group. Then, think of another group that you do not identify with, and put check marks in the column marked "Other Group" next to five adjectives. After you enter your check marks, go back through the list and rate each adjective you checked in terms of how favourable the quality is: 1 = very unfavourable, 2 = moderately unfavourable, 3 = neither favourable nor unfavourable, 4 = moderately favourable, and 5 = very favourable. Enter these ratings first in the column to the left of the adjectives, and then next to your check marks.

Favourable-ness rating	Adjectives	My Group	Score	Other Group	Score
_____	Intelligent	_____	_____	_____	_____
_____	Materialistic	_____	_____	_____	_____
_____	Ambitious	_____	_____	_____	_____
_____	Industrious	_____	_____	_____	_____
_____	Deceitful	_____	_____	_____	_____
_____	Conservative	_____	_____	_____	_____
_____	Practical	_____	_____	_____	_____
_____	Shrewd	_____	_____	_____	_____
_____	Arrogant	_____	_____	_____	_____
_____	Aggressive	_____	_____	_____	_____

Favourable-ness rating	Adjectives	My Group	Score	Other Group	Score
_____	Sophisticated	_____	_____	_____	_____
_____	Conceited	_____	_____	_____	_____
_____	Neat	_____	_____	_____	_____
_____	Alert	_____	_____	_____	_____
_____	Impulsive	_____	_____	_____	_____
_____	Stubborn	_____	_____	_____	_____
_____	Conventional	_____	_____	_____	_____
_____	Progressive	_____	_____	_____	_____
_____	Sly	_____	_____	_____	_____
_____	Tradition-loving	_____	_____	_____	_____
_____	Pleasure-loving	_____	_____	_____	_____
	Totals:	_____	_____	_____	_____

Add up the numbers next to your check marks. Compute separate Favourableness scores for your group and the other group. Scores should range from 5 to 25. The higher the score, the more favourable your stereotype.

Adapted from: William B. Gudykunst, *Bridging Differences: Effective Intergroup Communication* (Newbury Park: Sage, 1991), 75. The list of adjectives is adapted from Kate and Brady (1933).

Barriers to Effective Intercultural Communication

The first step to bridging differences between cultures is to find out what hampers effective communication. What keeps us from connecting with people from other cultures? Sometimes it is different meanings created by different languages or by different interpretations of nonverbal messages. Sometimes it is our inability to stop focusing on ourselves and begin focusing on the other. We'll examine some of these barriers first, then discuss strategies and skills for overcoming them.

Ethnocentrism

Marilyn had always been intrigued by Russia. Her dream was to travel the country by train, spending time in small villages as well as exploring the cultural riches of Moscow, Kiev, and St. Petersburg. Her first day in Russia was a disappointment, however. When she arrived in Moscow, she joined a tour touting the cultural traditions of Russia. When the tour bus stopped at Sparrow Hills, affording them a breathtaking hilltop view of the Moscow skyline, she was perplexed and mildly shocked to see women dressed in elegant wedding gowns mounted on horseback and galloping through the parking lot. Men in suits were cheering them on as a crowd of tipsy revellers set off fireworks and danced wildly to a brass band. "What kind of people are these?" sniffed Marilyn.

"Oh," said the tour guide, "it is our custom to come here to celebrate immediately following the wedding ceremony."

"But in public with such raucousness?" queried Marilyn.

"It is our tradition," said the guide.

"What a backwards culture. They're nothing but a bunch of peasants!" pronounced Marilyn, who was used to more refined nuptial celebrations at a country club or an exclusive hotel.

For the rest of the tour Marilyn judged every Russian behaviour as inferior to those of westerners. That first experience coloured her perceptions, and her ethnocentric view served as a barrier to effective communication with the Russian people she met.

Ethnocentrism stems from a conviction that your own cultural traditions and assumptions are superior to those of others. In short, it is the opposite of an other-orientation that embraces and appreciates the elements that give another culture meaning. This kind of cultural snobbism is one of the fastest ways to create a barrier that inhibits rather than enhances communication.

Different Communication Codes

You are on your first trip to Calgary. You step off the bus and look around for Stampede Park, and you realize that you have gotten off at the wrong stop. You see a corner grocery store with "Stampede Park" painted on a red sign. So you walk in and ask the man behind the counter, "How do I get to the Calgary Stampede, please?"

The man smiles, shrugging his shoulders. But he points to a transit map pasted onto the wall behind the counter.

Today, even when you travel within Canada, you are likely to encounter people who do not speak your language. Obviously, this kind of intercultural difference poses a formidable communication challenge. And even when you do speak the same tongue as another, he or she may come from a place where the words and gestures have different meanings. Your ability to communicate will depend upon whether you can understand each other's verbal and nonverbal codes.

In the example above, although the man behind the counter did not understand your exact words, he noted the cut of your clothing, your backpack, and your anxiety, and he deduced that you were asking directions. And you could understand what his gesture toward the transit map meant. Unfortunately, not every communication between the users of two different languages is this successful.

Even when language is translated, there can be missed or mangled meaning. Note the following examples of mistranslated advertisements:

■ A General Motors auto ad with "Body by Fisher" became "Corpse by Fisher" in Flemish.

■ A Colgate-Palmolive toothpaste named "Cue" was advertised in France before anyone realized that *Cue* also happened to be the name of a widely circulated pornographic book about oral sex.

■ Pepsi-Cola's "Come Alive With Pepsi" campaign, when it was translated for the Taiwanese market, conveyed the unsettling news that, "Pepsi brings your ancestors back from the grave."

■ Parker Pen could not advertise its famous "Jotter" ballpoint pen in some languages because the translation sounded like "jockstrap" pen.

■ One American airline operating in Brazil advertised that it had plush "rendezvous lounges" on its jets, unaware that in Portuguese (the language of Brazil) "rendezvous" implies a special room for making love.[11]

Where English Is Spoken

Of the world's 4.8 billion people, nearly 750 million are familiar with English. English is the native tongue of barely a dozen countries, but it is widely spoken or studied in more than 90 others. A list follows of those countries in which English is (1) the native language, (2) the official or semiofficial language, or (3) studied widely.

The Native Language

English is the native language in 12 nations with 345 million people:

North America	*Canada (except Quebec), United States*
South America:	*Guyana*
Caribbean:	*Bahamas, Barbados, Grenada, Jamaica, Trinidad and Tobago*
Europe:	*Ireland, United Kingdom (England, Scotland, Wales, Northern Ireland)*
Pacific:	*Australia, New Zealand*

Official or Semiofficial Language

In 33 other countries and Puerto Rico, English is considered an official or semiofficial language. This means it is often used in the conduct of government business. Those nations are:

Africa:	*Botswana, Cameroon, Ethiopia, Gambia, Ghana, Kenya, Lesotho, Liberia, Malawi, Mauritius, Namibia, Nigeria, Sierra Leone, South Africa, Sudan, Swaziland, Tanzania, Uganda, Zambia, Zimbabwe*

Stereotyping and Prejudice

Europeans dress fashionably.

Asians are good at math.

Canadians are overly apologetic.

These statements are stereotypes. They are all inaccurate. To **stereotype** someone is to push him or her into an inflexible, all-encompassing category. In Chapter 3, you saw how our tendency to simplify sensory stimuli can lead us to adopt stereotypes as we interpret the behaviour of others. When we do so, we "print" the same judgment over and over again, failing to consider the uniqueness of individuals, groups, or events. This becomes a barrier to effective intercultural communication. Two anthropologists suggest that every person is, in some respects (1) like all other people, (2) like some other people, and (3) like no other people.[12] Our challenge when meeting others is to sort out how they are alike and how they are unique.

Can stereotypes play a useful role in interpersonal communication? The answer

Asia, Pacific:	Bangladesh, Burma, Fiji, India, Malaysia, Pakistan, Philippines, Singapore, Sri Lanka, Tonga, Western Samoa
Mideast, Mediterranean:	Israel, Malta

Where English Is Studied Widely

English is required in school or studied widely in at least 56 other nations:

North America:	Mexico
Central America, Caribbean:	Costa Rica, Cuba, Dominican Republic, Honduras
South America:	Brazil, Colombia, Venezuela
Europe:	Austria, Belgium, Denmark, Germany, Finland, France, Greece, Iceland, Italy, Luxembourg, Netherlands, Norway, Portugal, Romania, former Soviet Union, Sweden, Switzerland
Africa:	Algeria, Angola, Burkina Faso, Burundi, Central African Republic, Chad, Gabon, Guinea, Ivory Coast, Libya, Madagascar, Morocco, Niger, Senegal, Togo, Zaire
Mideast:	Egypt, Jordan, North Yemen, Saudi Arabia, Syria, Turkey
Asia:	Afghanistan, China, Hong Kong, Indonesia, Japan, Nepal, South Korea, Thailand

From Roger E. Axtell, *Do's and Taboos of Hosting International Visitors* (New York: John Wiley & Sons, 1989), 213–214.

is a resounding "no" if our labels are inaccurate or if they assume superiority on our part. But sometimes it may be appropriate to draw upon generalizations. If, for example, you are alone and lost in a large city at two o'clock in the morning and another car repeatedly taps your rear bumper, it would be prudent to try to drive away as quickly as possible rather than to hop out of your car to make a new acquaintance. You would be wise to prejudge that the other driver might have some malicious intent. In most situations, however, **prejudice**—prejudging someone before you know all of the facts—inhibits effective communication. If you decide that you like or dislike (usually dislike) someone simply because he or she is a member of a certain group or class of people, you will not give yourself a chance to communicate with the person in a meaningful way.

Certain prejudices are almost universal. Although there are more females than males in the world, in many societies females are prejudged to be less valuable than males. One study found that even when a male and a female hold the same type of job, the male's job is considered more prestigious than the female's.[13] Today, gender and racial discrimination in hiring and promotion is illegal in Canada. But our social attitudes have not kept pace with the law. Stereotyping and prejudice are still formidable barriers to effective interpersonal communication.

Assuming Similarity

Just as it is inaccurate to assume that all people who belong to another social group or class are worlds apart from you, it is usually erroneous to assume that others act and think as you do. Even if they appear to be like you, all people are not alike. While this statement is unprofound, it has profound implications. Like Sari, who *assumed* that others would value punctuality as she did, we often make the mistake of assuming that others value the same things we do, maintaining a self-focused perspective instead of an other-oriented one. As you saw in Chapter 3, focusing on superficial factors such as appearance, clothing, and even a person's occupation, can lead to false impressions. Instead, we must take the time to explore the person's background and cultural values before we can determine what we really have in common.

Bridging Differences in Background and Culture

Intercultural communication occurs when individuals or groups from different cultures communicate. The transactional process of listening and responding to people with different cultural backgrounds can be challenging. The greater the difference in culture between two people, the greater the potential for misunderstanding and mistrust.

Misunderstanding and miscommunication occur between people from different cultures because of different coding rules and cultural norms, which play a major role in shaping our patterns of interaction. The greater the difference between the cultures, the more likely it is that they will use different verbal and nonverbal codes. When you encounter a culture that has little in common with your own, you may experience **culture shock**, or a sense of confusion, anxiety, stress, and loss. If you are visiting or actually living in the new culture, your uncertainty and stress may take time to subside as you learn the values and codes that characterize the culture.

Travelling to foreign countries means encountering people who use verbal and nonverbal codes that are different from your own. The greater the differences, the more challenging the communication process becomes. (David Austen)

But if you are simply trying to communicate with someone from a background very different from your own—even on your home turf—you may find the suggestions in this section helpful in closing the communication gap.[14]

Seek Information about the Culture

Knowledge is power. Prejudice stems from ignorance. Learning about another person's values, beliefs, and behaviours can help you understand his or her messages and their meaning. Every person has a **world view** based upon cultural beliefs about the universe and key issues such as death, God, and the meaning of life.[15] According to Carley Dodd, "A culture's world view involves

All good people agree,
  And all good people say,
All nice people like Us,
  are We,
  And everyone else is They.

In a few short lines, Rudyard Kipling captured the essence of what sociologists and anthropologists call ethnocentric thinking. Members of all societies tend to believe that "All nice people like Us, are We . . ." They find comfort in the familiar and often denigrate or distrust others. Of course, with training and experience in other climes, they may learn to transcend their provincialism, placing themselves in others' shoes. Or, as Kipling put it,

  . . . if you cross over the sea,
  Instead of over the way,
  You may end by (think of it!)
    looking on We
  As only a sort of They.

In a real sense, a main lesson of the sociology of intergroup relations is to begin to "cross over the sea," to learn to understand why other people think and act as they do and to be able to empathize with their perspectives.

Adapted from: Faun B. Evans, Barbara Gleason, and Mark Wiley, *Cultural Tapestry: Readings for a Pluralistic Society* (HarperCollins, 1992).

finding out how the culture perceives the role of various forces in explaining why events occur as they do in a social setting."[16] These beliefs shape our thoughts, language, and behaviour. Only through intercultural communication can we hope to understand how each individual views the world. As you speak to a person from another culture, you should think of yourself as a detective, watching for implied, often unspoken messages that provide information about the values, norms, roles, and rules of that person's culture.

You can also prepare yourself by studying the culture. If you are going to another country, courses in the history, anthropology, art, or geography of that place can give you a head start on communicating with understanding. Learn not only from books and magazines, but also from individuals whenever possible. Even in a high-context culture, no one will fault you for asking directly for help if you show a sincere desire to learn. If you are trying to communicate with someone closer to home who is from a different background, you can study magazines, music, food, and other readily available sources of information about his or her culture. Or exchange visits to one another's homes or hangouts to observe and learn more about the person.

Given the inextricable link between language and culture, the more you learn about another language, the more you will understand the traditions and customs of the culture. Politicians have long known the political value of an adaptive approach toward international relations. Many Canadians can recall how former Prime Minister Trudeau displayed statesmanship by sampling the language and customs of whatever culture he was visiting. Speaking even a few words can signify your interest in learning about the language and culture of others.

Be Other-Oriented

When you encounter someone who comes from a very different background, remind yourself of Dorothy's famous line from *The Wizard of Oz*: you are not in Kansas anymore. You can no longer rely only on the assumptions of your own cultural heritage. People do not typically verbalize their cultural beliefs and values

Mind Your Manners —and Theirs

If it be appropriate to kiss the Pope's slipper, by all means do so.

—Lord Chesterfield, founder of modern etiquette, in 1750

The saying "When in Rome do what the Romans do" suggests that international travellers should adopt an other-oriented approach to the host country's manners and customs. After interviewing hundreds of international businesspersons, Roger Axtell offers the following tips on etiquette when visiting with people from other countries or travelling to international destinations.[17] Realize, of course, that these observations are not true of all individuals. As in Canada, in many of these countries there are dozens of different cultural groups with their own sets of values and customs.

Austrians
- Are punctual
- Use a firm handshake (both men and women)
- Consider keeping your hands in your lap when dining to be impolite
- Are uncomfortable with first names until a friendship is established

English, Scots, Welsh
- Tend to use understatement in business matters
- Value punctuality
- Are accustomed to cooler room temperatures than Americans
- Call a Scot a Scotsman, not a Scotchman or Scottish

French
- Rarely use first names, even among colleagues
- Frequently shake hands but their grip is less firm than most

- Eat their main meal of the day usually at midday
- Make decisions after much deliberation

Irish
- Are not overly conscious about time and punctuality
- Do not typically give business gifts
- Regard refusing a drink or failing to buy your round as bad manners

Italians
- Use strong and frequent hand and body gestures
- May grasp your elbow as they shake hands
- Do not consider punctuality a virtue, at least for social events
- Do not talk business at a social event

Russians
- Want to know what Americans really think

during early encounters. But fortunately, the skills we have discussed—listening with empathy, watching for nonverbal cues, responding to check your understanding—can help you.

Being other-oriented does not mean that you should try to communicate in ways for which you are not equipped. Trying to use slang or jargon from another culture to impress someone may result in embarrassing errors and do more harm than good. But if you try to respond to the other person's interests, needs, and rules, you can establish mutual trust and pave the way for effective communication.

Ask Questions

When you encounter a person from another background, asking questions is a simple technique for gathering information and also for confirming the accuracy of your expectations and assumptions. Some cultures, such as the Japanese, have rigid

- When greeting, shake hands and announce their name

- Among friends, some give "bear hugs" and kiss cheeks

Egyptians
- Like all Muslims, rest on Friday

- Regard friendship and trust as a prerequisite for business

- Social engagements usually held late in the day

Zambians
- Often shake hands with the left supporting the right

- When dining, may ask for food; it is impolite not to

- Consider it improper to refuse food

Australians
- Speak frankly and directly; they dislike pretensions

- Will not shy away from disagreement

- Appreciate punctuality

- Have good sense of humor, even in tense situations

Indians
- When greeting a woman, they put palms together and bow slightly

- They do not eat beef and regard the cow as a sacred animal

- Show great respect to elders

Japanese
- Exchange business cards before bowing or shaking hands

- Consider it impolite to have long or frequent eye-to-eye contact

- Rarely use first names

- Avoid the word "no" to preserve harmony

Thais (Thailand)
- Regard displays of either temper or affection in public as unacceptable

- Have a taboo against using your foot to point, or showing your sole

- Don't like pats on the head

Brazilians
- Like long handshakes

- Like to touch arms, elbows, and backs

- When conversing, view interruption as enthusiasm

- Attach a sexual meaning to the OK hand signal

Mexicans
- Are not rigidly punctual

- Take their main meal at about 1:00 or 4:00 P.M.

- Refrain from using first names until they are invited to do so

- Consider hands in pockets to be impolite

Adapted from: Roger E. Axtell, *Do's and Taboos of Hosting International Visitors* (New York: John Wiley & Sons, 1989).

expectations regarding gift giving. It is better to ask what these expectations are than to assume that your good old down-home manners will see you through.

When you ask questions, be prepared to share information about yourself, too. Otherwise, your partner may feel as if you are interrogating him or her as a way to gain power and dominance rather than from a sincere desire to learn about cultural rules and norms.

Communication helps to reduce the uncertainty that is present in any relationship.[18] When you meet people for the first time, you are highly uncertain about who they are and what they like and dislike. When you communicate with someone from another culture, the uncertainty level is particularly high. As you begin to interact, you exchange information that helps you develop greater understanding. If you continue to ask questions, eventually you will feel less uncertain about how the person is likely to behave.

What are typical rules and manners for most people native to Canada? Try to identify generally held rules of etiquette in the following situations.

Expectations regarding punctuality at meetings: _____

Greetings between good friends: _____

Greetings between business or professional colleagues: _____

Gift giving and receiving among friends: _____

Gift giving and receiving among business associates: _____

Typical times for daily meals: _____

Appropriate use of someone's first name: _____

Inappropriate use of someone's first name: _____

Share your answers with your classmates. Note similarities and differences in your responses. If you and your classmates have different expectations in these situations, what does this suggest about how reliable the suggestions are for other countries listed in the previous Understanding Diversity box?

Develop Mindfulness

"Our life is what our thoughts make it," said Marcus Aurelius in *Meditations*. To be **mindful** is to be consciously aware of cultural differences, to acknowledge that there is a connection between thoughts and deeds when you interact with a person from a background different from your own. William Gudykunst suggests that being mindful is one of the best ways to approach any new cultural encounter.[19] Remember that there are and will be cultural differences, and try to keep them in your consciousness. Also try to consider the other individual's frame of reference or world view and to use his or her cultural priorities and assumptions when you are communicating.[20] Adapt your behaviour to minimize cultural noise and distortion.

You can become more mindful through self-talk, something we discussed in Chapter 2. Self-talk consists of rational messages you tell yourself to help you manage your emotions or discomfort with a certain situation. Imagine that you are working on a group project with several of your classmates. One classmate, Suji, was born in Iran. When interacting with others, he consistently gets about a foot away from them, whereas you are more comfortable with three or four feet between you. When Suji encroaches on your space, you could "be mindful" of the difference by mentally noting, "Suji sure likes to get close to people when he talks to them. This must represent a practice in his culture." This self-talk message makes you consciously aware that there may be a difference in your interaction styles. If you still feel uncomfortable, instead of blurting out, "Hey, why so close?" you could express your own preferences with an "I" message: "Suji, I'd prefer a bit more space between us when we talk."

The article "Across the Divide" below discusses racial tension as experienced by our American neighbours, and provides a progressive remediation approach which may apply to many groups in conflict with each other. It describes how one group in New Orleans is attempting to develop greater cultural understanding by encouraging others to be mindful of racial similarities instead of emphasizing racial differences. The group was founded by Brenda Thompson, an African American freelance writer, and Rhoda Faust, a white bookstore owner.

The simplest way to gather information about someone with a background different from your own is to ask questions. By sharing information about yourself as well, you can quickly reduce feelings of uncertainty.
(M. Autman/
The Image Works)

Across the Divide

White people feel victimized—by affirmative action, quotas, and crime. Black people feel victimized—by racism, economic exclusion, and being viewed as criminals.

The battle lines between the races harden. People who feel like victims blame someone, an enemy. And everyone seems to gather like-minded people around them, a fortress against fear.

Then a group of black and white people get together and start to talk. They have no illusions about saving the world. They just can't bear to stand by anymore as race relations sour day by day.

Their modest goal is to exchange views and experiences, to talk across the racial divide, to seek understanding and, most of all, common ground . . . The group has grown to about 20 members who get together to share personal racial experiences and talk about ways to make a change. [Brenda] Thompson said she has made new friends.

"I want other people to see that people of different racial groups can talk and be friends and get past the colour differences and see that people are people," Thompson said.

Lucia Milling, a psychotherapist who lives in Covington, said she began attending the meetings to make friends.

"When I moved here from Nicaragua, I had lots of black friends," she said.

"But I moved to Covington, and they moved away too. I feel I've lost something in my life. Since I moved to this country in 1971, I have seen things get worse. Both blacks and whites are pulling away from each other, and I find it very discouraging."

Milling's husband, Bob, said he believes talking and sharing experiences can clear the way to better race relations.

"I'm not certain what can be done about it," he said. "But I believe the solutions are to be found in sitting around, getting to know each other, like people do when they socialize and communicate in a genuine way.

"It's like a David and Goliath kind of phenomenon. But I strongly believe it's worth it."

So do Don and Kim Marshall, a white couple who have been driving from their home in Covington to the meetings.

Mrs. Marshall, a graphic artist and former actor, suggested that the group consider creating a slavery museum in New Orleans someday to commemorate the slaves. At first, she wasn't sure how the concept would be accepted, but members listened and gave her the feedback she wanted.

"It's the kind of group where people can say what they want," she said. "I've learned a lot from everybody, and a few of us are hearing things we hadn't heard before."

Marshall said he joined the group to encourage racial interaction among children at a young age.

"I didn't go to school with blacks until I was in college," he said. "Today, you hear so much about college students not interacting, and everybody seems to be so shocked. No one is looking at the fact that these kids never really interacted."

The group is distributing bumper stickers that say "ERACISM," and members soon will begin wearing the [ERACISM] pins. Agreeing on a mission statement— a definition of what the group stands for and against—is the next step. So far, the process has not been easy.

"I think it's hard because it's important as hell that the exact language does reveal what each of us has in our hearts," [Rhoda] Faust said. "I think a lot of us are still groping to know what's in our hearts.

"But it's the only starting point I can think of. If we are able to go out into the world, our little group, and start saying this is our mission and this is what we have to work with, whether it's bumper stickers or pins, more people will get hope from how many others are out there," she said.

"If we get no further than distributing 5,000 bumper stickers, people will see them every day and think there's a force for good in the world."

—LISA FRAZIER, *THE TIMES-PICAYUNE*, OCTOBER 18, 1993.

Develop Flexibility

When you interact with someone from another background, your responding skills are crucial. You can only learn so much from books; you must be willing to learn as you communicate. Every individual is unique, so cultural generalizations that you learn from research may not always apply. It is not accurate to assume, for example, that _all_ French people are preoccupied with food and fashion. Many members of minority groups find it draining to correct these generalizations in their encounters with others. Pay close attention to the other person's nonverbal cues when you begin conversing; then adjust your communication style and language if necessary to put the person at ease. And avoid asking questions or making statements based on generalizations.

Tolerate Ambiguity

While exercising your flexibility, you may also need to remind yourself that communicating with someone from another culture produces uncertainty. It may take time and several exchanges to clarify a message. Be patient and try to expand your capacity to tolerate ambiguity if you are speaking to someone with a markedly different world view.

When Ken and Rita visited Miami for their winter vacation, they asked their hotel concierge to direct them to a church of their faith, and they wound up at one with a predominantly Haitian congregation. They were not prepared for the exuberant chanting and verbal interchanges with the minister during the sermon. They weren't sure whether they should join in or simply sit quietly and observe. Ken whispered to Rita, "I'm not sure what to do. Let's just watch and see what is expected of us." In the end, they chose to sit and clap along with the chanting rather than to become actively involved in the worship. Rita felt uncomfortable and conspicuous, though, and had to fight off the urge to bolt. But after the service, several members of the congregation came up to greet Ken and Rita, invited them to lunch, and expressed great happiness in their visit. "You know," said Rita later in the day, "I'm so grateful that we sat through our discomfort. We might never have met those terrific people. Now I understand why their worship is so noisy—they're just brimming over with joy."

Avoid Negative Judgments about Another Culture

Unfortunately, negative judgments about other cultures abound, and the kind of ethnocentrism that underlies these negative judgments poses a serious communication barrier. It is also an underlying cause of suspicion and mistrust and, in extreme cases, a spark that ignites violence. So instead of making judgments about another culture, try simply to acknowledge differences and to view them as an interesting challenge rather than as an obstacle to be eradicated.

COMMUNICATION EXPERIENCE

Can You Tolerate Ambiguity?

Respond to each statement with a number from 1 to 5: (1) Always False, (2) Usually False, (3) Sometimes False and Sometimes True, (4) Usually True, or (5) Always True.

_____ 1. I am comfortable in new situations.

_____ 2. I deal with unforeseen problems successfully.

_____ 3. I experience little discomfort in ambiguous situations.

_____ 4. I am relaxed in unfamiliar situations.

_____ 5. I am not frustrated when things do not go the way I expected.

To find your score, add the numbers you wrote next to each statement. Scores range from 5 to 25. The higher your score, the greater your tolerance for ambiguity.

From: William B. Gudykunst, *Bridging Differences: Effective Intergroup Communication* (Newbury Park: Sage, 1991), 121.

RECAP   How to Bridge Cultural Differences

Seek Information About the Culture	Learn about a culture's world view.
Be Other-Oriented	Put yourself in the other person's mindset.
Ask Questions	Reduce uncertainty by asking for clarification.
Develop Flexibility and Tolerate Ambiguity	Learn to "go with the flow"; take your time and expect some uncertainty.
Avoid Negative Judgments	Resist thinking that your culture has all the answers.

Summary

A culture is a system of knowledge that is shared by a larger group of people. It includes cultural elements, values, goals, and contexts. Cultural elements are categories of things and ideas that identify key aspects of cultural influence. Cultural values reflect how individuals regard masculine and feminine behaviours and individual and collective achievements. They also reflect whether individuals can tolerate ambiguity or need a high degree of certainty, and whether they believe in concentrated or decentralized power structures. The goals of a culture depend upon the way it values individual versus group achievement. In high-context cultures, the meaning of messages depends heavily upon nonverbal information; low-context cultures rely more heavily upon words than upon context for deriving meaning.

Intercultural communication occurs when individuals or groups from different cultures communicate. There are several barriers that inhibit effective intercultural communication. Ethnocentrism is the belief that our own cultural traditions and assumptions are superior to those of others. Differences in language and the way we interpret nonverbal messages also interfere with effective intercultural communication. We stereotype by placing a group or a person into an inflexible, all-encompassing category. A related barrier is prejudice—we often prejudge someone before we know all of the facts. Stereotyping and prejudice can keep us from viewing people as unique individuals and therefore hamper effective, honest communication. Finally, assuming that we are similar to others can also be a barrier to intercultural communication. All humans have some similarities, but our cultures have taught us to process the world differently.

Although it is reasonably easy to identify cultural differences, it is more challenging to bridge those differences. To enhance understanding between cultures, we suggest the following: seek information about the unfamiliar culture, be other-oriented, ask questions to clarify what you don't understand; be flexible and tolerant of ambiguity, and avoid negative judgments about other cultures.

For Discussion and Review

FOCUS ON COMPREHENSION

1. What is culture?

2. What are four contrasting cultural values?

3. What are the differences between high-context and low-context cultures?

4. What are differences between individualistic and collectivistic cultures?

5. What is ethnocentrism?

6. Christine, a Canadian, has just been accepted as a foreign exchange student in Germany. What are potential cultural barriers that she might face? How should she manage these potential barriers?

7. What's the problem in assuming that other people are like us? How does this create a barrier to effective intercultural communication?

8. If you were to design a lesson plan for elementary age students about how to deal with racial and ethnic stereotypes, what would you include?

9. What are appropriate ways to deal with someone who consistently utters racial slurs and evidences prejudice toward racial or ethnic groups?

■ FOCUS ON ETHICS

10. Marla is the director of the campus multicultural studies program. She wants to require all students to take at least four courses in a four-year degree program that focuses on multicultural issues. Is it appropriate to force students to take such a concentration of courses?

11. Should an individual always speak out upon hearing a racist, sexist, or otherwise offensive remark? What if the listener is not a member of the target group? Are there contextual factors to consider before speaking out?

12. Is it ethical or appropriate for someone from one culture to attempt to change the cultural values of someone from a different culture? For example, culture A practices polygamy: one husband can be married to several wives. Culture B practices monogamy: one husband can be married to only one wife. Should a person from culture B attempt to make someone from culture A change his or her ways?

For Your Journal

1. Describe your perceptions of your cultural values, based upon the discussion of cultural values beginning on page 339 in this chapter. On a scale of 1 to 10 rate yourself in terms of the value of masculine versus feminine perspective, individual versus group achievement, tolerance of uncertainty versus need for certainty, and centralized versus decentralized power. Provide an example of your reaction to an interpersonal communication encounter to illustrate each of these values.

2. Write a journal entry discussing how you have experienced one of the barriers to effective intercultural communication described in this chapter. Have you been ethnocentric in your thoughts or behaviour or a victim of ethnocentrism? Describe a situation in which communication was difficult because you and your communication partner spoke different languages. Have you been a victim of stereotyping or prejudice? Have you assumed someone was similar to yourself and later found that there were more differences than you suspected?

3. This chapter presented seven specific strategies or skills to help bridge differences in background and culture. Rank order these skills and strategies in terms
of what you need to improve in your interactions with people from different
backgrounds. Give a rank of 1 to the skill or strategy that you most need to
develop, a rank of 2 to the next area you feel you need to work on, and so on.
Rank yourself on all seven strategies.

Seek information about the culture   _____

Be other-oriented   _____

Ask questions of others   _____

Be mindful   _____

Be flexible   _____

Tolerate ambiguity   _____

Avoid negative judgments about
another culture   _____

Based upon the areas in which you need greatest improvement, write a journal entry about how you will develop skill in these areas. How will you put what
you have learned in this chapter into practice?

Learning with Others

1. Bring to class a fable, folktale, or children's story from a culture other than your
own. As a group, analyze the cultural values implied by the story or characters in
the story.

2. Working with a group of your classmates, develop an ideal culture based upon
the combined values and elements of people in your group. Develop a name for
your culture. Suggest foods, recreational activities, and other leisure pursuits.
Compare the culture your group develops with those that other groups in your
class develop. How would the communication skills and principles discussed in
this chapter help you bridge differences between those cultures?[21]

3. As a group, go on an intercultural scavenger hunt. Your instructor will give you a
time limit. Scavenge your campus or classroom area to identify influences of as
many different cultures as you can find. For example, you could go to the cafeteria and make note of ethnic foods that you find. Identify clothing, music, or
architecture that is influenced by certain cultures.

4. In small groups, identify examples from your own experiences for each barrier to
effective intercultural communication discussed in the text. Use one of the examples to develop a skit to perform for the rest of the class. See if the class can identify which intercultural barrier your group is depicting. Also suggest how the
skills and principles discussed in the chapter might have improved the communication in the situation you roleplay.

CULTURE: A learned system of knowledge, behaviour, attitudes, beliefs, values, and norms that is shared by a group of people.

CO-CULTURE: A culture that exists within a larger cultural context (e.g., the gay and lesbian culture).

CULTURAL ELEMENTS: Categories of things and ideas that identify the most profound aspects of cultural influence (e.g., schools, governments, music, theatre, language).

ENCULTURATION: The process of communicating a group's culture from generation to generation.

ACCULTURATION: The process through which an individual acquires new approaches, beliefs, and values by coming into contact with other cultures.

CULTURAL VALUES: What a given group of people values or appreciates.

MASCULINE CULTURAL VALUES: Achievement, assertiveness, heroism, and material wealth.

FEMININE CULTURAL VALUES: Relationships, caring for the less fortunate, and overall quality of life.

CULTURAL GOALS: A culture's objectives in terms of individual or collective achievement.

CULTURAL CONTEXT: Information not explicitly communicated through language, such as environmental or nonverbal cues.

HIGH-CONTEXT CULTURE: A culture that derives much information from nonverbal and environmental cues.

LOW-CONTEXT CULTURE: A culture that derives much information from the words of a message and less information from nonverbal and environmental cues.

ETHNOCENTRISM: The belief that your cultural traditions and assumptions are superior to others.

STEREOTYPE: To place a person or group of persons into an inflexible, all-encompassing category.

PREJUDICE: Prejudging someone before you know all of the facts or background of that person.

INTERCULTURAL COMMUNICATION: Communication between or among people who have different cultural traditions.

CULTURE SHOCK: The feeling of stress and anxiety a person experiences when encountering a culture different from his or her own.

WORLD VIEW: A perception shared by a culture or group of people about key beliefs and issues, such as death, God, and the meaning of life, which influences interaction with others.

MINDFULNESS: An awareness of cultural differences and the connection between thoughts and deeds when interacting with someone from a background different from your own.

Developing Relationships with Family, Friends, Lovers, and Colleagues

Most of our interpersonal relationships are not single interactions with strangers. Ongoing relationships with family, friends, lovers, and colleagues occupy most of our time and energy. In this final unit we present principles and skills for enhancing those relationships through more effective communication. Chapter 12 examines how we form our relationships with family members, and how family life can be enriched by recognizing the role that interpersonal skills can play in our domestic activities. Chapter 13 applies information from Chapters 7, 8, and 9 to our friendships and intimate relationships. The final chapter looks at the role interpersonal communication plays in the workplace, offering suggestions and strategies for effective communication in leadership and teamwork.

Relating to Family

A fter studying this chapter, you should be able to:

1. Define the term family and describe four types of families.

2. List and describe four approaches to studying family communication.

3. Identify the key principles of family systems theory.

4. Describe the cohesion and adaptability model of family functioning.

5. Identify and describe the communication characteristics of a healthy family.

■ THE NATURE OF FAMILIES

■ THE NATURE OF FAMILY COMMUNICATION

■ IMPROVING FAMILY COMMUNICATION

lisha: Hi Daddy.

Albert: Hi Sugarplum. Where is everyone?

Elisha: Well, Martha took Francine and Mikey to see their Nanna. She said to tell you that she loves you, and that she'll be home around four. Jackie's upstairs watching TV. When are we going to see Grandma Ruthie?

Albert: We're going to have dinner with her and her new boyfriend tonight at around six o'clock. I wonder what he'll be like.

Elisha: But, what if she marries him? Then I'll have three grandpas: Nanna's husband, Grandma Shirley's new husband, and Mr. Mystery Man. But none of them will be my real grandpa.

Albert: Maybe all of them will be, Lisha. In this family, love is what makes things real.

As this snatch of conversation illustrates, today's families are clearly undergoing a metamorphosis, and so are their communication patterns. In the 1950s a majority of Canadian families were like the Cleavers from the TV sitcom *Leave It to Beaver*; most of them consisted of a working father, a stay-at-home mother, and at least two of their biological children. Since that time, divorce has dramatically increased; in 1961, there were fewer than 200 divorces per 100,000 couples, while in 1990, there were more than 1,200. And many people have never been married. Although most of them will eventually marry, many are waiting until later in life to do so. Women's roles are changing, too. More are working outside the home, and couples now spend more time clarifying and negotiating domestic roles and responsibilities. In 1977, only 38 percent of mothers with children under the age of six were in the labour force, while in 1992, 63 percent were labour force participants. In these homes, 33 percent of the children under six years were cared for by nonrelatives.

"Blended families"—married or common-law couples with at least one step-child—are becoming increasingly common in Canada as divorce and remarriage rates go up. In 1990, about 7 percent of all families raising children were blended, and that number is expected to rise significantly in the years to come.

Parents today face different societal expectations about child rearing than did your grandparents when they were raising your parents. Families have changed from primarily agriculture-based enclaves to consuming entities. Most families do not grow and harvest their own food; they go to the mall and the market for their needs. In times past, family teamwork was vital for family survival. Today, family members function with greater autonomy. In addition, the increased mobility of families affects communication patterns with relatives. If family members find themselves living in cities distant from their families of origin, friendships develop with others who become a surrogate family.

Despite all of these changing cultural and societal conditions, however, communication still plays a pivotal role in family life. In fact, these changes should encourage us to understand how communication can reduce uncertainty as we struggle to define new roles and responsibilities for family members. In this chapter we will describe the nature of both families and family communication. We will provide an overview of different approaches to studying family communication and frameworks for studying how we talk, listen, and respond to each other in families. We will conclude with some research-based observations about improving family communication. But as we describe principles and perspectives, it is important to keep in mind that there is *no single best way to communicate in a family*. Each unique family comes with its own particular challenges for understanding and improving communication.

The Nature of Families

You might think that because families are basic to our existence, we do not need a formal definition of a family. Yet considerable controversy exists as to what constitutes a family unit.

The Family Defined

Traditional definitions of a family focus on the roles of husbands, wives, and children who all live together under one roof. Here is one written by a sociologist in 1949:

> *The family is a social group characterized by common residence, economic cooperation and reproduction. It includes adults of both sexes, at least two of whom maintain a socially approved sexual relationship, and one or more children, of one's own or adopted, of the sexually cohabiting adults.*[1]

More recently, Statistics Canada defined a family as:

> *a now-married couple (with or without never-married sons and/or daughters of either or both spouses), a couple living common-law (again with or without never-married sons and/or daughters of either or both spouses), or a lone parent of any marital status, with at least one never-married son or daughter living in the same dwelling.*[2]

Other definitions of a family de-emphasize the traditional role of mother, father, and children, placing more emphasis upon interpersonal relationships and personal commitment. Canada's Vanier Institute of the Family defines a family as:

> any combination of two or more persons who are bound together over time by ties of mutual consent, birth and/or adoption/placement and who, together, assume responsibilities for variant combinations of some of the following:
>
> ■ physical maintenance and care of group members;
> ■ addition of new members through procreation or adoption;
> ■ socialization of children;

- social control of members;
- production, consumption, and distribution of goods and services; and
- affective nurturance—love.[3]

Perhaps another modern sociologist's definition of a family best captures this relational emphasis. For him, the family is "an organized, naturally occurring relational inter-action system, usually occupying a common living space over an extended time period, and possessing a confluence of interpersonal images which evolve through the exchange of messages over time."[4]

For our purposes in this chapter, we synthesize these two perspectives to define the **family** as a unit made up of any number of persons who live in relationship with one another over time in a common living space, who are usually, but not always, united by marriage and kinship.

Family Types

Virginia Satir, a well-known expert in family therapy, has identified four types of families: natural, blended, single-parent, and extended.[5] The traditional family—a mother and father and their biological children—is often considered to be the **natural family**, or nuclear family. But changes in culture, values, economics, and other factors have rendered this family type no longer typical.

An increasingly common family type today is the **blended family**. This family type consists of two adults and their children. But because of divorce, separation, death, or adoption, the children may be the product of other biological parents or of just one of the adults who is raising them. As the guidelines for step-parents on page 368 suggest, it takes both skill and patience to assume the role of a step-parent.

The **single-parent family** is self-explanatory. This type of family has one parent and at least one child. Lone parents accounted for 20 percent of all families with children in 1991, up from 17 percent in 1981. The vast majority of lone parents in Canada are women, representing 92 percent of all lone parents of children under the

Today's families are often defined by interpersonal relationships and commitment rather than traditional roles. How would you describe the three families shown in these photographs? (Top left, Jon Riley/Tony Stone Images; top right, Motaksaki/Eastcott/Woodfin Camp & Associates; bottom, S. Gazin/The Image Works)

age of 13. Divorce, separation, desertion, and death of one parent are the traditional causes of single parenthood. More recently, single parenthood may also be a lifestyle of choice, as with the planned pregnancy of a single woman, or the adoption of a child by a single adult.[6]

Step-parenting 101

- Nurture and enrich the couple relationship.

- Reveal and understand emotions. This can be accomplished through dealing with and resolving the loss/pain from the previous relationship so that it does not interfere with the present one. Rid yourself of the bitterness that often exists after a divorce. Encourage the children to express and process their feelings in a productive manner.

- Have realistic expectations by getting to know all members of the stepfamily before a remarriage takes place.

- Understand that a new family is being created and that all members will be developing some new roles and changing others. Former spouses must learn to co-parent, which is often very difficult.

- Don't use children as pawns in a power struggle or as messengers between households.

- The non-custodial parent needs to develop a new role and continue to demonstrate love and concern.

- Step-parents need to develop a type of parenting role. Step-parents' roles will depend on custodial arrangements. The role of friend is a positive one and can be assumed if the children do not spend much time in the household of the step-parent.

- Democratic discipline works better than authoritarian or permissive discipline in a stepfamily.

- Don't neglect grandparents, who can play an instrumental role in stepfamily success.

- Seek support from family, friends, or local support groups.

—BARR: BRONSTON, *TIMES PICAYUNE*

(Adapted from the Stepfamily Association of America's "Stepping Ahead" manual.)

The **extended family** typically refers to the relatives—aunts, uncles, cousins, or grandparents—who are part of the family unit. Some extended families also include individuals who are not related by marriage or kinship but are treated like family or share a common identity with the family. These surrogate family members may even be called Mom, Dad, Aunt, or Uncle, honouring them as part of the family circle.

V DEVELOPING RELATIONSHIPS

In addition to Satir's categories, there is at least one other that can encompass any of her definitions. The family in which you were raised—no matter what type it is—is your **family of origin**. It is in your family of origin that you learned the rules and skills of interpersonal communication and developed your basic assumptions about relationships.

RECAP	Family Types
NATURAL FAMILY	The traditional family: mother, father, and their biological children.
BLENDED FAMILY	A family consisting of two adults and children operating as a family. Due to divorce, separation, or death, the children may be the product of other biological parents or of just one of the adults in the family.
SINGLE-PARENT FAMILY	One parent with children, either biological or adopted.
EXTENDED FAMILY	Family members related to the parents or children: grandparents, aunts, uncles, and other relatives.

The Nature of Family Communication

The study of family communication is the study of sending, receiving, and interpreting messages in the context of a family system. How do families negotiate differences and manage conflict? How do family communication patterns develop? Are there differences between the ways blended and natural families communicate? These are some of the questions that family communication scholars investigate. They also study how the behaviour of family members affects the meaning of words and actions, and how the messages we send and receive affect other family members.

Communication plays a major role in determining the quality of family life. As shown in Table 12.1, one research team found that over 86 percent of the families who reported family difficulty and stress said that communication was the key source of the problem.[7] Virginia Satir thinks good family communication is so important that she calls it "the largest single factor determining the kinds of relationships [we make] with others."[8] Another researcher found that the more positively premarital couples rated their communication with their partner, the more satisfied they were with their marriage relationships more than five and one-half years later.[9]

Approaches to Studying Family Communication

Over the years, researchers have developed four different approaches to the study of family communication. The **social-descriptive** approach attempts to understand how families function by investigating the rules, roles, patterns, traditions, and

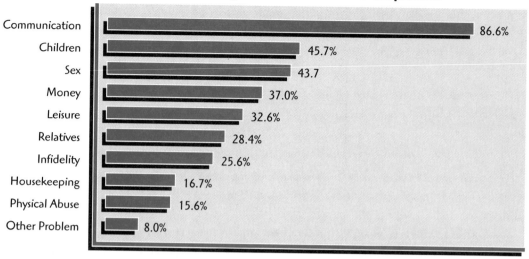

Percentage of all cases with a marital problem

Category	Percentage
Communication	86.6%
Children	45.7%
Sex	43.7
Money	37.0%
Leisure	32.6%
Relatives	28.4%
Infidelity	25.6%
Housekeeping	16.7%
Physical Abuse	15.6%
Other Problem	8.0%

Table 12-1

Sources of Family Difficulties

norms of family life. Many sociologists and anthropologists use this approach, employing survey techniques and other descriptive research methods. They compile statistical profiles of family behaviour to explain how the family unit has evolved and to predict how families will affect society in the future.

The **communication skills and enrichment** approach emphasizes prescriptive principles and skills that are designed to help even well-functioning families improve their communication skills. Professional psychologists, social workers, communication professors, and others in related fields often hold communication skill development workshops and marriage and family enrichment retreats to help people improve their listening, responding, conflict management, and problem-solving skills in the family context. Researchers have found that these experiential training sessions have enduring beneficial effects. As long as four years after they attend a workshop, couples report that what they learned there still helps them through communication difficulties.[10]

The **therapeutic** approach to family communication tries to help dysfunctional families identify and manage problematic communication issues. Family therapy can involve one or all family members, including members of the extended family. Generally, therapy is more successful if all family members are involved. In regularly scheduled sessions over an extended period of time, a trained counsellor or therapist listens to family members, and encourages roleplaying to help them untie the knots of dysfunctional communication.[11]

The **systems** approach is the most widely accepted among those who study family communication. This holistic approach considers the entire family as a unit, rather than focusing on specific remedies for individual family members. It analyzes how each family member functions in relationship to every other member, and how the family environment affects communication patterns. The underlying assumption is that whatever happens to one family member affects the entire family system, so attempting to isolate specific behaviours or single issues will not provide a complete understanding of how the family operates. We will examine this approach in more detail in the next section.

Understanding the Family Communication System

As we saw in Chapter 3, just as we use punctuation in writing to signal the ends of sentences, pauses, and other nuances that give language meaning, so do most of us punctuate, or divide up, sequences of behaviour in an effort to determine what the behaviours mean.[12] But this tendency leads us to attribute our behaviour to single causes. You may have heard someone say, "It all started when I moved away from home" or "When I took that second job, our lives became unbearable." These statements imply that a single, specific turn of events unleashed a whole sequence of feelings, problems, or other events.

Often conflicts erupt because family members punctuate events from different perspectives. Consider this exchange:

Eric: Why are you so late again tonight?

Melissa: I had a big accounting report to finish up for tomorrow.

Eric: Well, Shawna has been waiting for you to help her with her math—she wouldn't do it with me. And you left all the breakfast dishes in the sink this morning.

Melissa: I know, I know. I just got home and already you're jumping on me again. You're pushing me away. Give me a little slack, and maybe I'll make more of an effort to get home earlier.

Eric: Maybe if you came home earlier, I wouldn't have to jump on you. These days, it seems as if you've lost interest in your family.

Although they are both unhappy about the same problem, Eric and Melissa each attribute it to a different cause. And each is using a controlling strategy—attempting, as we learned in Chapter 10, to consolidate a power base for him- or herself by blaming the other. Studies suggest that married couples who are most dissatisfied with their relationships are more likely to blame their spouses for problems than to assume responsibility themselves.[13]

In fact, the problem this couple is experiencing is probably far more complex than either one of them has acknowledged. Dysfunctional events in families generally have multiple and interwoven causes because family systems themselves are complex. As one family therapy team puts it, "family systems, like all social systems, are organizationally complex, open, adaptive, and information-processing systems."[14] Let us examine these characteristics in greater detail.

■ FAMILY SYSTEMS ARE MORE THAN THE SUM OF THE INDIVIDUAL MEMBERS

To understand family dynamics, you must consider more than the individual family members. A key tenet of systems thinking is that the whole is greater than the sum of the parts. The family assumes a collective identity that incorporates the individual goals, needs, and personalities of the members. In order to truly understand family relationships, you must observe family members interacting together.

■ FAMILY SYSTEMS ARE INTERDEPENDENT

An interdependent system is one in which the parts are related to, and affected by, the other parts of the system. Family members are affected by the behaviour and attitudes of other family members. If a parent suffers from alcoholism, the children and spouse will be affected. Virginia Satir uses the analogy of a mobile that hangs over a child's crib to illustrate this interdependence. Touch one part of the mobile and the rest of the pieces move. So it is with family members.

■ FAMILY SYSTEMS ARE COMPLEX

Thayne: If you hadn't taken that job, Mom, you'd be able to pick me up after school. Now I have to ride the bus for an hour.

Julie: Yeah, Mom, me too. I have to walk home from school. Last week when it rained, my school papers got all wet and I couldn't do my homework.

Mom: But both of you have end-of-the-year field trips to Ottawa. The only way we can afford to get you there is for me to take this extra job. I'm doing it for you.

Thayne: Well, all I can say is, I don't like riding the bus.

Julie: And I don't like walking in the rain.

Mom: Well, I don't like working all the time, either. I'm doing it so you can do what your friends do.

As this situation shows, the complexity of family life may lead to misunderstandings about the meaning of family members' messages and actions. Because many factors influence the family system, and because family members punctuate behaviours and events in different ways, it is a challenge to determine what an

V   DEVELOPING RELATIONSHIPS

isolated statement or behaviour means; few have single causes or effects. In this instance, the mother and children may need to stop holding on to their individual complaints and brainstorm ways to make all of their lives more comfortable.

■ FAMILY SYSTEMS ARE OPEN

As an open system, your family is affected by the economy, your neighbourhood, your occupation, your religion, your friends, and other external influences. If, for example, a large factory in your town closes, which employs one of your parents, it would undoubtedly have an impact upon your family's standard of living.

■ FAMILY SYSTEMS ARE ADAPTIVE

Families adapt to change; some do this better than others. The ability to roll with the punches or stay the course depends primarily on how well a family communicates. Whether the changes are positive (such as marriage, graduation, or a promotion) or negative (such as divorce, death of a family member, or a criminal conviction), family members process the change through their interaction with each other.

■ FAMILY SYSTEMS PROCESS INFORMATION

Daryl: Mom, I need to be at ball practice at seven o'clock tonight.

Marge: Okay, but I have to be at the parent volunteer coffee at seven. Bill, can you get Daryl to ball practice at seven o'clock?

*Bill: I'm supposed to chair the brotherhood finance committee meeting at seven. I **have** to be there a few minutes early to prepare the agenda. Daryl, if I can drop you off at half past six, I can make my meeting. Will that be okay?*

Daryl: Sure, Dad, that will be fine.

Missy: Mom, Dad, I forgot to tell you that tonight is open house at our school, and I'm singing in the choir. I can't wait for you to hear us! We've been practicing all week. It starts at seven o'clock.

This family has just learned that its unsystematic method for keeping track of who is doing what isn't working very well. To avoid situations like this one, some families leave notes for one another on the refrigerator; others use answering machines, computers, or cellular phones. Regardless of the method of communication, families need to exchange information. Whether they are dealing with mundane issues, such as who will pick up the laundry, or with monumental issues, such as whether to have another child, family members must gather and use information to function effectively within the family system.

In addition to processing personal information among themselves, families must also gather and process information from outside sources. As the Electronic Connections box on page 374 suggests, many of today's parents are reaching beyond traditional sources for advice about parenting.

The Family Communication System

Characteristic	Phenomenon
Family systems are more than a collection of individual members:	The whole is greater than the sum of the parts.
Family systems are interdependent:	What happens to one affects all family members.
Family systems are complex:	Family members punctuate events in different ways; most events have multiple causes.
Family systems are open:	What happens outside the family affects all family members.
Family systems are adaptive:	Family members use communication to adapt to change.
Family systems process information:	Family members develop methods for communicating with other family members as well as outside networks.

ELECTRONIC CONNECTIONS

Parents Turn to Online Communities for Advice on Everything from Child Rearing to Home Repair and Pets

For many parents, online services are the best place to turn for advice and information on parenting—everything from health and school issues to how to handle the stresses that occur in families where both parents work outside the home.

For these people, online services serve as an extended virtual neighbourhood, a community with some of the comforts people enjoyed when they lived in extended families or in neighbourhoods where everyone had children. Then, to get a good piece of advice (or just to blow off steam), you needed only to stop at your next-door neighbour's house for a cup of coffee. Today, when you're looking for a place to chew the fat (or commiserate with other parents), often the best place to turn to is your computer—your pipeline to parents all over the world.

The range of parental information online is impressive. When a friend of mine believed his wife was about to give birth to a premature baby, he wanted to talk to other parents who had been in the same situation, but he didn't know anyone who had been through it. He not only wanted advice on what to expect, he also was in search of a community of other parents who could offer support and a certain amount of hand-holding.

Another friend went looking for similar advice and succor after his niece was diagnosed with childhood diabetes.

Recently, when I had trouble with the way the principal was chosen for the public school that my kindergarten-age son and fourth-grade daughter attended, I found myself wishing I had the advice of other parents on ways to deal with what appeared to be an uncaring public school bureaucracy.

Though our problems were different, we all ended up turning to commercial online services, where we sought networks of parents and concerned professionals interested in sharing advice and comfort. In addition to informal advice (the kind you'd share over coffee), we also sought—and found—reference information on the issues that embroiled us, as well as travel tips, advice on family-friendly restaurants and hotels, and even tips on helping a child develop better study skills.

From: Preston Gralla, "Parent Communities Online," published in *Family PC*, January/February 1995, p. 194.

A Model for Family Interaction

More than a century ago, the Russian author Leo Tolstoy observed, "All happy families are alike. Each unhappy family is unhappy in its own way." More recently, a pair of family therapists observed, "Unhappy people came from families where there were a lot of other unhappy people."[15] As they attempted to identify causes for the problems in dysfunctional families, the therapists discovered that usually the major source of a family problem "was not buried in the deep complexes and super-egos and egos of the individuals, but was evident in plain daylight to the therapists. It lay in the family system: in the way the family was organized; in the way its members communicated; in the way they worked out their daily interactions."[16]

A few years later, another pair of researchers developed a model called the **circumplex model of family interaction** to explain the dynamics of effective functioning and dysfunction within family systems.[17] The model's three basic dimensions, as indicated in Figure 12.1, are adaptability, cohesion, and communication. **Adaptability**, shown on the model ranging from chaotic to rigid, refers to the family's ability to modify and respond to changes in its own power structure and roles. For some families, tradition, stability, and historical perspective are important to their sense of comfort and well-being. Other families that are less tradition-bound are better able to adapt to new circumstances.

Cohesion refers to the emotional bonding and feelings of togetherness that families experience. Family cohesion ranges from excessively tight, or enmeshed, to

Figure 12-1

A Circumplex Model of Family Systems Adapted from: David Olson and Hamilton I. McCubbin, *Families: What Makes Them Work* (Newbury Park: Sage Publications, Inc. 1983).

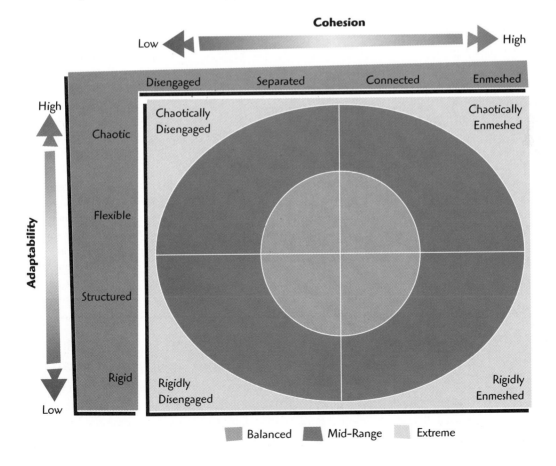

disengaged. Because family systems are dynamic, families usually move up and down the range from disengaged to enmeshed. The originator of the circumplex model selected the three poems below to characterize families who are disengaged (in one of the black sections on the left side of the model), enmeshed (in one of the black sections on the right side of the model), and balanced (in the white section at the centre of the model), respectively.

Disengaged:

I do my thing, and you do your thing
I am not in this world to live up to your expectations
And you are not in this world to live up to mine
You are you and I am I
And if by chance we meet, it's beautiful
If not, it can't be helped.

—FRITZ PERLS

Enmeshed

We do our thing together
I am here to meet all your needs and expectations
And you are here to meet mine
We had to meet, and it was beautiful
I can't imagine it turning out any other way.

—JERRY GILLIES

Balanced:

Sing and dance together and be joyous,
    but let each one of you be alone
Even as the strings of a lute are alone
    though they quiver with the same music
And stand together yet not too near together;
For the pillars of the temple stand apart,
And the oak tree and the cypress grow
not in each other's shadow
But let there be spaces in your togetherness
And let the winds of the heavens dance between you.

—KAHLIL GIBRAN, *THE PROPHET*

The third key element in the model—and the most critical one—is communication. It is not labelled in the model because *everything* in the model is influenced by communication. It is through **communication** that families are able to adapt to change and maintain either enmeshed or disengaged relationships. Communication is what determines whether families are cohesive or adaptable. Communication keeps the family operating as a system.

V   DEVELOPING RELATIONSHIPS

The circumplex model helps us understand relationships among family cohesiveness, adaptability, and communication at different stages of family development. In general, families with balanced levels of cohesion and adaptability function better across the entire family life cycle than do those at the extremes of these dimensions. A balanced family has a moderate amount of cohesion and adaptability—represented by the centre circle on the model. Balanced families are often better able to adapt to changing circumstances and to manage stressful periods, such as the children's adolescence. Not surprisingly, these balanced families usually have better communication skills.

As we have already emphasized, however, research suggests that *there is no single best way to be a family*. At some stages of family life, the balanced ideal of the circumplex model may not apply. Older couples, for example, seem to operate more effectively when there is more rigid structure and a lower level of cohesiveness. Families with younger children seem to function well with high levels of both cohesion and adaptability. Only one thing is constant as we go through family life: Effective communication skills play an important role in helping families change their levels of cohesiveness or adaptability. These skills include active listening, problem solving, empathy, and supportiveness. Dysfunctional families—those that are unable to adapt or alter their levels of cohesion—invariably display poor communication skills. Family members blame others for problems, criticize one another, and listen poorly.

Communication and Family Roles

One of the most important questions to ask your intended mate is this: Who will take out the garbage?[18] Embedded in the answer is a sense of your understanding of your future role in the family. Whether you can reach agreement about this seemingly minor issue will predict how well you can discuss role expectations and negotiate changes later on. As we saw in the dialogue at the beginning of Chapter 10, agreement about who is supposed to do what in a family enhances family satisfaction; disagreement about role expectations can be a major source of conflict and dissatisfaction.

How do we form our role expectations? According to two sociologists, we formulate an idealized version of our parents, but we also draw upon TV, movies, books, our religious traditions, and our friends for images of how to behave in a family.[19] Understanding the origin and development of the roles we expect to play and those we actually perform can provide insight into our sense of family satisfaction. If our own roles and those of our partners are consistent with both our own **role expectations** and our partner's, then we are likely to feel satisfied and fulfilled. If, on the other hand, we expect to behave one way and other family members expect us to behave differently, then dissatisfaction on both sides is the likely result.

For example, if you and your partner have equal roles as wage earners, you may also expect to share equal responsibility for keeping your home tidy and clean. But if your partner's role expectations and behaviour are different from what you expect, then you must try to manage the conflict. *One of the best predictors of marital and family satisfaction is the degree to which our roles match the role expectations of others.*

One of the first research teams to investigate the effect of role relationships on family communication identified two basic types of marriages.[20] **Institutional marriages** define husband-wife responsibilities along traditional lines. Husbands

Family Readjustment Scale

Because families are interdependent, if there is a major event in your life, your family must cope with the changes it fosters. Follow the directions below. After you calculate your score, discuss how the events you included affected your family. Try to recall how you communicated about these events. Where would you place your family on the adaptability continuum? On the cohesion continuum?

1. Under Number of Occurrences, indicate how many times in the past year each of the events has occurred.

2. Multiply the number under Scale Value by the number of occurrences of each event and place the answer under Your Score.

3. Add the figures under Your Score to find your total for the past year.

Your Score	Scale Value	Number of Occurrences	Life Event
_____	100	_____	Death of spouse
_____	73	_____	Divorce
_____	65	_____	Marital separation
_____	63	_____	Death of close family member
_____	53	_____	Personal injury or illness
_____	50	_____	Marriage
_____	47	_____	Fired at work
_____	45	_____	Marital reconciliation
_____	45	_____	Retirement
_____	44	_____	Change in health of family member
_____	40	_____	Pregnancy
_____	39	_____	Sex difficulties
_____	39	_____	Gain of new family member
_____	39	_____	Business readjustment
_____	38	_____	Change in financial state
_____	37	_____	Death of close friend
_____	36	_____	Change to different line of work
_____	35	_____	Change in number of arguments with spouse
_____	31	_____	Mortgage over $10,000
_____	30	_____	Foreclosure of mortgage or loan
_____	29	_____	Change in responsibilities at work
_____	29	_____	Son or daughter leaving home

work and fix things; wives manage the home and are more emotive and expressive. **Companionship marriages** have more flexible roles that consider the partners' individual preferences. In North America, companionship marriages seem to be on the rise, whereas institutional marriages are decreasing.[21]

Another researcher identifies three primary role types for couples—independents, traditionals, and separates—based upon eight different variables:[22] conflict

Your Score	Scale Value	Number of Occurrences	Life Event
_____	29	_____	Trouble with in-laws
_____	28	_____	Outstanding personal achievement
_____	26	_____	Wife begins or stops work
_____	26	_____	Begin or end school
_____	25	_____	Change in living conditions
_____	24	_____	Revision of personal habits
_____	23	_____	Trouble with boss
_____	20	_____	Change in work hours or conditions
_____	20	_____	Change in residence
_____	20	_____	Change in schools
_____	19	_____	Change in recreation
_____	19	_____	Change in church activities
_____	18	_____	Change in social activities
_____	17	_____	Mortgage or loan less than $10,000
_____	16	_____	Change in sleeping habits
_____	15	_____	Change in number of family get-togethers
_____	15	_____	Change in eating habits
_____	13	_____	Vacation
_____	12	_____	Christmas
_____	11	_____	Minor violations of the law
_____			This is your total life change score for the past year.

Researchers Holmes and Rahe suggest that if you score at least 150, you have about a 50-50 chance of developing an illness or stress-induced health change. A score above 300 points increases the likelihood of a health change to almost 90 percent.

From: Holmes and Rahe, "The Social Readjustment Rating Scale," *Journal of Psychosomatic Research*, 216.

avoidance, assertiveness, sharing, traditionalism, management of uncertainty and change, use of time, use of space, and autonomy. **Independent** couples, the most autonomous of the three types, are able to take change and uncertainty in stride. Both partners tend to define roles for themselves that contain traditionally male and traditionally female elements. Independents are also comfortable managing conflict and negotiating differences in family relationships.

Indicate which of the behaviours listed below are the *primary* responsibility of the wife (W), the husband (H), or both (H/W). Discuss your reasons for responding as you do.

_____ taking out the garbage

_____ writing thank you notes

_____ initiating sexual activity

_____ balancing the chequebook

_____ changing diapers

_____ bringing home a paycheque

_____ disciplining the children

_____ starting up the barbecue

_____ doing the laundry

_____ planning for retirement

_____ cooking

_____ cleaning the bathrooms

_____ changing the oil in the car

_____ driving children to school

_____ mending clothes

_____ maintaining gutters

_____ buying Mother's Day and birthday presents for parents

Traditional couples resist change and dislike uncertainty. They share things both physically and emotionally with their partners. They are highly interdependent and try to avoid conflict rather than manage it. These couples prefer stable, traditional sex roles.

Separate couples maintain more distance than traditionals, both physically and psychologically, although they also follow fairly regular routines and tend to avoid conflict. They also disclose less to one another. Like traditionals, they are more comfortable with traditional sex roles.

Many relationships, of course, combine the traits of these three types of couples. This researcher found that around 60 percent of the couples she studied could be classified as independent, traditional, or separate. The other 40 percent were some combination of these three types.[23] Which type of relationship is the most satisfying? Traditionals tend to have more satisfying and stable relationships than independents, but separates are even less stable. The key factor for success in all of these types of relationships seems to be agreement about role expectations. Couples who agree on how their relationship is defined tend to agree on other issues as well.

Independents who have flexible roles need to renegotiate responsibilities more often, so communication skills are especially crucial in this type of relationship. But renegotiation of roles and expectations is a normal part of all couples' relationships, especially when they undergo major changes such as the birth of a child, a new job for either partner, or a child's leaving home. In the next section, we will provide pointers for effective renegotiating as well as suggestions for communicating effectively in other family situations.

Independents	Accept change and uncertainty.
	Have high role flexibility.
	Are more comfortable managing conflict than other role types.
	Assume less conventional gender roles.
Traditionals	Resist change.
	Do not like uncertainty.
	Share physically and emotionally with their partner.
	Have an interdependent relationship.
Separates	Maintain more physical and psychological distance between partners.
	Follow regular routines.
	Are more likely to avoid conflict.

Improving Family Communication

Wouldn't it be fantastic if you could share special secrets guaranteed to enrich your family life? But, alas, there are no sure-fire prescriptions for transforming your family system into one that a TV sitcom family would envy. Instead, we can pass on some skills and principles that researchers have either observed in healthy families or applied successfully to improve dysfunctional ones. Before you read on, take the test in the Communication Experience on page 382 to see which skills you need to improve.

Those who have compared dysfunctional marriages with healthy ones have noted some important differences. One researcher found that couples who are more satisfied with their marriages follow certain patterns.[24]

Sharing meals together is one way that healthy families avoid lapsing into mundane exchanges. The dinner table provides an ideal forum for conversation about each family member's daily life, relationships, and feelings.

Complete the following Family Communication Diagnostic Test to assess your communication skills.

Family Communication Diagnostic Test

	Usually	Sometimes	Seldom
1. Is it difficult for you to converse with other family members?	___	___	___
2. Do you feel other family members lack respect for you?	___	___	___
3. During family discussions, is it difficult for you to admit that you are wrong when you recognize that you are wrong about something?	___	___	___
4. Is it difficult to accept constructive criticism from other family members?	___	___	___
5. Do you pretend that you are listening to other family members when you are not really listening?	___	___	___
6. Do you find yourself being inattentive while in conversation with other family members?	___	___	___
7. Do you misunderstand other family members?	___	___	___
8. Are you dissatisfied with the way you settle your disagreements with members of your family?	___	___	___
9. Do you fail to express disagreement with other family members because you are afraid they will get angry?	___	___	___
10. When a problem arises between you and another family member, do you become emotionally upset?	___	___	___
11. Does it upset you a great deal when another family member disagrees with you?	___	___	___
12. Is it difficult to confide in other family members?	___	___	___
13. Do you feel other family members wish you were a different type of person?	___	___	___
14. Do other family members fail to understand your feelings?	___	___	___

If you checked Usually more than three times, your family communication skills clearly need sharpening.

From: S. A. Beebe, *Family Communication* (Independence, MO: Herald Publishing House, 1983), 98.

1. They more frequently talk over pleasant things that happened during the day.

2. Both partners more frequently feel they are understood by their spouse.

3. They discuss shared interests.

4. They are less likely to break off communication by pouting.

5. They more often talk with each other about personal problems.

6. They make more frequent use of words that have a private meaning for them.

7. They talk most important things over together.

8. They are more sensitive to each other's feelings and make adjustments to take these into account when they speak.

9. They feel freer to discuss intimate issues without restraint or embarrassment.

10. They are better able to tell what type of day their spouse had without asking.

11. They intentionally communicate nonverbally to a greater degree.

The consistent theme in the above list is that satisfying couple relationships involve more supportive interaction than do less satisfying relationships.

Results from another study that sought to identify why marriages succeed are summarized in Table 12.2.[25] Note that the first seven reasons are the same for both husbands and wives.

Other researchers took a broader look at entire family systems. One travelled extensively in search of the attributes of a "good family."[26] She too found that members of "good" families follow consistent patterns:

1. They have a chief, heroine, or founder—someone around whom others cluster.

2. They have a switchboard operator—someone who keeps track of who is doing what.

3. They maintain strong bonds within the family, but have other group associations as well.

4. They are hospitable.

5. They deal directly with stress and tragedy.

6. They cherish family rituals and traditions.

7. They express affection in a way that is meaningful to other family members.

8. They have a sense of place.

9. They find some way to connect with future generations.

10. They honour their elders.

Members of "good" families connect with future generations and honour their elders.
Courtesy of Tourism Nova Scotia.

Virginia Satir also found that in healthy families, "the members' sense of self-worth is high; communication is direct, clear, specific, and honest; rules are flexible, humane,

Table 12.2

Reasons for Marital Success Reported by Husbands and Wives

Husbands	Wives
My spouse is my best friend.	My spouse is my best friend.
I like my spouse as a person.	I like my spouse as a person.
Marriage is a long-term commitment.	Marriage is a long-term commitment.
Marriage is sacred.	Marriage is sacred.
We agree on aims and goals.	We agree on aims and goals.
My spouse has grown more interesting.	My spouse has grown more interesting.
I want the relationship to succeed.	I want the relationship to succeed.
An enduring marriage is important to social stability.	We laugh together.
We laugh together.	We agree on a philosophy of life.
I am proud of my spouse's achievements.	We agree on how and how often to show affection.
We agree on a philosophy of life.	An enduring marriage is important to social stability.
We agree about our sex life.	We have a stimulating exchange of ideas.
We agree on how and how often to show affection.	We discuss things calmly.
I confide in my spouse.	We agree about our sex life.
We share outside hobbies and interests.	I am proud of my spouse's achievements.

Lauer & Lauer (1985). Reprinted with permission from *Psychology Today* magazine. Copyright © 1985 (Sussex Publishers, Inc.).

and subject to change; and the family's links to society are open and hopeful."[27] In such families, she notes, people listen actively; they look *at* one another, not *through* one another or at the floor; they treat children as people; they touch one another affectionately regardless of age; and they openly discuss disappointments, fears, hurts, angers, and criticism, as well as joys and achievements.[28]

A study by Pearson entitled *Lasting Love: What Keeps Couples Together* also sought to identify what explains marital satisfaction and stability.[29] Pearson interviewed several couples who had been together from forty to seventy years. She reports the following eight factors as hallmarks of happily married couples: (1) lowered expectations (realistic understanding of what being married means); (2) unconditional acceptance of one another; (3) seeing others in a positive way (what Pearson calls positive distortion); (4) viewing themselves as a united team (becoming one); (5) remaining separate, unique individuals (remaining two); (6) mutually satisfying sexual relations; (7) the skills to manage conflict; and (8) persistence.

These studies are descriptive rather than prescriptive. They report what satisfied married couples *do*, rather than recommend specific actions or suggestions. Perhaps you have noticed, however, that several communication-related behaviours keep cropping up in these reports. Let's explore their usefulness as skills.

V   DEVELOPING RELATIONSHIPS

Take Time to Talk about Relationships and Feelings

Healthy families talk.[30] The sheer quantity of communication depends upon family members' needs, expectations, careers, and activities. But the talking extends beyond idle chatter to focus on issues that help the family adapt to change and maintain a sense of cohesiveness.

Often, because of the crush of everyday responsibilities and tasks, family members may lapse into talking only about the task-oriented, mundane aspects of making life work: yard mowing, grocery shopping, errand running, and other uninspiring topics. Healthy families communicate about much more: their relationships; how they are feeling; how others are feeling. They make time to converse, no matter how busy they are. They have an other-orientation in these conversations, instead of focusing on themselves. In addition, they enjoy one another and don't take themselves too seriously.[31]

Of course, honestly sharing feelings about relationships won't necessarily result in the issues being managed successfully. Sometimes a professional therapist may be needed to help a family sort out serious relationship problems. The article "When Gay Parents Come Out" on page 386 describes how therapy helped one couple cope with the aftermath of a husband and father's disclosure that he was gay.

Healthy families have topics of conversation about things other than functional tasks; their communication reflects other-oriented messages about family members and family relationships. This suggests that being empathic and other-oriented is as important in families as it is in other interpersonal situations.

Listen Actively and Clarify the Meaning of Messages

Since talking about relationships is important in healthy families, it is not surprising that effective listening is also important. In the often stressful context of family life, good listening skills are essential.

Good listening requires an other-orientation. In Chapters 4, 5, and 6, we presented fundamental skills for listening and responding to messages. Family members will communicate with greater accuracy if they learn to stop, look, and listen. Stop mental and outside distractions: don't try to carry on a conversation over a TV blaring, a video game bleeping, or a stereo's distracting rhythmic pulse. Look: constantly monitor the rich meaning in nonverbal messages; remember that the face and voice are prime sources for revealing emotional meaning; body posture and gestures provide clues about the intensity of an emotion. Listen: focus on both details and major ideas. Asking appropriate follow-up questions and reflecting content and feelings are other vital skills for clarifying the meaning of messages. And remember the importance of checking your perceptions of the meaning of nonverbal messages.

Good listeners try to understand the feelings behind another person's words—to read between the lines. One pair of researchers suggests that you should try to interpret messages according to the sender's code system, not your own. Because you are in intimate daily contact with other family members, you have every reason and opportunity to learn their code systems. Then you can avoid becoming involved in diversionary arguments about the proper meaning of a word, phrase, or gesture.[32] Of course, after you attempt to understand your partner's meaning, you then need

When Gay Parents Come Out

Three years ago, Julie was convinced that Larry, her husband of 20 years was seriously ill. For four months he couldn't eat or sleep. He was losing weight. He was pale and clammy.

When he announced that he was going to the doctor, she knew he would come home with news that he was dying.

Instead, Larry told Julie and soon afterward their two sons and daughter that he is gay. Reactions ran the gamut, from relief, then rage, then compassion on the part of Julie to confusion but acceptance on the part of their youngest son, then 9.

Initially, their daughter, then 15, wanted nothing to do with her dad and stormed out of the room. Months of therapy have changed some of her feelings.

Their middle son, 16, continues struggling to accept Larry's sexual orientation. He attended three therapy sessions and then quit. Julie says he probably feels threatened by the things his peers say and may be questioning his own sexuality.

In fact, it is because of their middle child's struggles that Larry and Julie asked that their full names not be used for this story. If they knew it would not upset him, they said, they would be completely open. They've declined invitations to tell their story on national talk shows.

Now divorced, Julie and Larry remain close friends, often spending holidays together or socializing over dinner.

Larry, who lives with a male partner, tries to spend as much time as possible with his kids, taking them to the movies, attending their athletic events, and spending time at his former home with them.

Their youngest son occasionally spends the night at Larry's house, and has accompanied him and his companion on business trips.

Larry and Julie won't go so far as to say they are living happily ever after, but they will say that things are working out better than they could have imagined.

"Not many stories are this good," said Larry, who with Julie credits therapy as well as a series of support groups with helping them come to terms with their new lives. The support groups, which meet at different times monthly, are for gay spouses, straight spouses, and their children, who are grouped according to age.

Gay and lesbian activism is prompting more homosexuals to come out of the closet. When they do, their straight spouses and children are often shocked and traumatized. The straight partner often feels rejected sexually and deceived, as if their marriage has been a lie. Typically, they believe that they are alone in feeling such pain.

When Julie looks back on the day that Larry told her the news, she said she felt a sense of relief knowing that he wasn't ill: Soon after, though, the anger set in.

"There's a sense of betrayal, a sense of mistrust. I was very angry at Larry. I was like a volcano. I remember at one point saying, 'We were living a lie,' and he said, "We didn't live a lie. We loved each other and we still do.'

"We've had the benefit of some really good therapy. He's allowed me to yell at him and let out all my venom and that's what has gotten me through. As for the kids, I thought they should be privy to the same information. This has always been a warm and loving relationship, and not to tell them why we were getting divorced wouldn't make any sense."

From: Barri Bronston, *Times-Picayune*, Sept.19, 1994.

---

to relate the message to your own system of meaning. Another research team identified a listening technique called **documentation**, in which you describe the experiences that led you to attach a certain meaning to another person's statement.[33] For example, if you say, "I can see that you're not looking at me, so I take it that you're not interested in what I'm telling you," the other person will become aware of the behaviour that led to your interpretation, and will also be able to verify whether your interpretation is correct.

What Do You Talk About?

One evening, between the time you get home from work or school and bedtime, make a log categorizing what you and the members of your household talk about. You don't need to record the actual subject matter, just the types of messages you used. Consider the following categories:

1. Topic messages: information about basic events, ideas, or tasks that need to be performed.

2. Individual feeling messages: any messages in which you or your family members verbalize a specific feeling (e.g., I'm pleased or I'm exhausted). Be sure to record what feelings were verbalized.

3. Partner messages: Statements that focus on the nature of the relationship, such as "we have a lot of fun together" or "we always seem to fight a lot."

Write an essay or journal entry, if you keep a journal for class, in which you discuss what you learned from your analysis.

Imagine this scene: you are greeted at the door by your partner who can hardly wait to tell you about the trials and tribulations of his or her day. Nothing went well, or so it seems from your partner's perspective. The litany of problems is impressive: oversleeping; getting a traffic ticket on the way to work; missing an important meeting; working through lunch; getting a reprimand from the boss; and forgetting to get groceries on the way home from work. You may be tempted to respond, "Don't worry, I'll take care of everything." Genuinely wanting to help, you might say, "I'll buy you a new alarm clock and we can order out for pizza tonight. Just let me take over." Although your partner might appreciate your efforts to "fix it," what he or she needs *first* is to be assured that someone cares. Focus on the person before focusing on the problem. "You must feel awful" or "How frustrating!" would express your understanding of his or her feelings. Before rushing in to solve the problem, be other-oriented. Let your family member know you empathize.

STOP:	Concentrate on your family members' messages rather than on personal evaluations of them.
	Minimize outside distractions.
	Seek a quiet place to talk.
LOOK:	Monitor your family member's face and voice for clues about the emotion he or she is expressing.
	Look at his or her posture and gestures to gauge the intensity of the emotion.
	Use eye contact to signal that the communication channel is open.
LISTEN:	Listen for both details and major ideas.
	Mentally summarize key ideas.
	Don't interrupt. Just listen.
ASK QUESTIONS:	Ask appropriate questions to seek more information.
	Ask questions to clarify what you don't understand.
REFLECT CONTENT:	Paraphrase the essential meaning of your family member's message.
	Use your own words with a lead-in such as, "What I hear you saying is . . ." or "You seem to be saying . . ."
	Don't overuse the skill of paraphrasing.
REFLECT FEELINGS:	Selectively summarize how you think your family member is feeling.
	Don't over-reflect feelings; reflect when you are genuinely uncertain about what someone feels or means.
CHECK PERCEPTIONS:	Ask the meaning of a specific nonverbal expression or behaviour.
DOCUMENT:	Tell your family member what specific behaviour caused you to reach a specific conclusion.

Support and Encourage One Another

A smoothly functioning family can be a supportive, encouraging sanctuary from everyday stresses. Through communication, we can let others know that we support and value them. Satir suggests that many, if not most, sources of dysfunction in families are related to feelings of low self-worth.[34] Healthy families take time to nurture one another, express positive feelings, and take a genuine interest in each person's unique contributions to the family. It is important to learn the guidelines we discussed in Chapters 2 and 10 concerning the types of messages—verbal and nonverbal—that help establish positive, supportive relationships and an open climate for conversation.[35] It is also important to remember, however, to be selective in providing feedback and disclosing your feelings and attitudes about other family

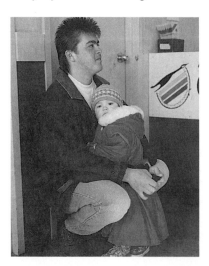

Wise parents use support and encouragement rather than coercion as a primary strategy for shaping their children's behaviour. The challenge is to find a middle ground that tempers support with appropriate control. (Fred Cattroll)

members.[36] As we saw in Chapter 8, although trust is important in developing support, total honesty and candidness, however well intended, will not necessarily strengthen your relationships. After a point, too much disclosure can lower satisfaction.[37]

Parents have a special obligation to disclose responsibly to their children. Too much negative and controlling feedback can cause permanent damage.[38] Researchers have found that supportive messages—those that offer praise, approval, help, and affection—can lead to higher self-esteem in children, more conformity to the wishes of the parent, higher moral standards, and less aggressive and antisocial behaviour.[39]

Parents frequently deliver control messages to get children to do what the parents want. Often these messages involve coercion or threats. One research team found a curvilinear relationship between a parent's use of control messages and the child's willingness to obey. Control messages are effective in shaping a child's behaviour up to a point; an overemphasis on control often results in rebellion.[40] The challenge is for parents to strike a balance between genuine support and appropriate control. Kahlil Gibran's timeless advice to parents below suggests that children need a balance of control and support as they seek their independence from parents.

COMMUNICATION EXPERIENCE

We have suggested that it is not a good idea to tell a family member everything you may think or feel about him or her. Self-disclosing too much can result in hurt feelings and dissatisfaction with the relationship. Write your true feelings about a family member in your notes or a journal, if your teacher is asking you to keep a journal. Then decide which information would be useful to disclose and which would be unproductive to disclose.

On Parenting

Your children are not your children.
They are the sons and daughters of Life's longing for itself.
They come through you but not from you,
And though they are with you, yet they belong not to you.
You may give them your love but not your thoughts,
For they have their own thoughts.
You may house their bodies but not their souls,
For their souls dwell in the house of tomorrow,
    which you cannot visit, not even in your dreams.
You may strive to be like them, but seek not to make them like you,
For life goes not backward nor tarries with yesterday.
You are the bows from which your children as living arrows are sent forth.

The archer sees the mark upon the path of the infinite,
      and He bends you with His might that
      His arrows might go swift and far.
Let your bending in the archer's hand be for gladness;
For even as He loves the arrow that flies,
      so He loves also the bow that is stable.

—KAHLIL GIBRAN, *THE PROPHET*

Use Productive Strategies for Managing Conflict, Stress, and Change

All too often parents resort to violence when their children balk at their orders. The "Family Violence Almanac" below includes statistics and research conclusions about the increase in child abuse and violence in today's families. Actor Tom Cruise has self-disclosed how his father physically abused him as a child. "As a kid," says Tom, "I had a lot of hidden anger about that. I'd get hit, and I didn't understand it." When his father was dying of cancer, Cruise said, he was finally able to address the issue directly with his dad. "He allowed me to go to the hospital to talk to him under the condition of not asking him any questions. I loved my father very much."

Learning to manage conflict with siblings is also a challenge in many families. It is with our siblings that we first learn how to manage the complexities of relationships and especially how to manage conflict. One study reported that more than half of all adolescent conflicts are between siblings.[41] The most typical method of managing sibling conflict is withdrawal. However, there is evidence that some siblings resort to violence when they run out of things to say. One survey found that 62 percent of senior high students said they had hit a brother or sister within the past year.[42] Sibling conflicts, as well as other family conflicts, often have a special intensity. Maybe that is because we drop our guard in the privacy and security of a family; we know our family members will love us no matter what, so we may express our feelings with an intensity that would be inappropriate in other social settings. Another reason conflict flares up is that we often communicate with family members when we are tired and stressed, so emotions are less controlled.

Family Violence Almanac

When words are not enough to communicate anger and frustration, physical violence often takes their place in today's families. Consider the following statistics and research conclusions about family violence in Canada:

- According to Statistics Canada's 1993 National Survey on Violence Against Women, three in ten women who are currently or previously married, or living in a common-law relationship, have experienced at least one incident of physical or sexual violence at the hands of their current or former partner.
- The highest rates of wife assault are found among young couples (18–24 years) and among marital or common-law partnerships of fewer than two years.
- Men who had witnessed their fathers' violence toward their mothers inflicted more severe and repeated violence on their own wives than men whose fathers were not violent.

V DEVELOPING RELATIONSHIPS

- In the more serious violent incidents against female partners, the abuser was likely to have been drinking.
- Women are at greater risk of severe violence just after they leave their husbands or partners.
- A study in Toronto of adolescent runaways found that nearly 75 percent of them had been physically beaten as children.
- A study of male prostitutes found that 72 percent of them had been physically or emotionally abused by family members.
- While there are no national statistics for child abuse in Canada, 11 percent of children in the United States are estimated to have been physically abused by a parent.

From: Health Canada, National Clearinghouse on Family Violence, *Wife Abuse* (Cat. # H72-22/4-1995E) & *Child Abuse & Neglect* (Cat # H72-22-1-1990E).

As we saw in Chapter 10, all close relationships undergo periods of conflict and stress, so families should be prepared to handle them. Satisfied couples report just as many conflicts as dissatisfied couples. The difference is that satisfied couples have learned skills and strategies for managing interpersonal differences. One research team found that couples who lack constructive argumentation skills are those who resort to verbal aggression (attacking their partner's self-worth to inflict psychological pain)[43] and even physical violence.[44]

Another researcher who studied couples relationships for over twenty years suggests that we be on the alert for four key warning signs in our communication behaviour.[45] These signs indicate that we need to work on the kinds of conflict management skills we discussed in Chapter 10.

WARNING SIGNS

1. Criticism: Attacking someone's personality or character rather than specific behaviour, usually with blame and personal comments.

2. Contempt: Intending to insult and psychologically abuse your partner; contempt may be verbal or nonverbal.

3. Defensiveness: Denying responsibility, making excuses, whining, repeating yourself, saying "yes, but."

4. Stonewalling: Withdrawing, not responding; becoming minimally engaged in the relationship.

Most couples experience some of these behaviours during their relationship, but the single best predictor of divorce is stonewalling. If all four warning signs are consistently present, there is a 94 percent chance the couple will eventually divorce.

Based on his extensive observations, the same researcher offers the following suggestions for managing couples conflicts. Many of them apply to parent-child and sibling conflicts as well:[46]

1. Pick your battles carefully.

2. Schedule discussions.

3. Structure your conflicts: build the agenda, persuade and argue, resolve.

4. Acknowledge your partner's viewpoint before expressing your own.

5. Moderate your emotions.

6. Trust your partner and communicate nondefensively.

7. Soothe your partner; learn how to comfort and provide positive reinforcement.

8. Take stock in your partnership.

9. Find the glory in your story as a couple and enhance romance.

10. Know when to get help or when to give up.

Couples who have a more volatile relationship, in which emotions override rational approaches to managing differences, can try the following:

1. Tell your partner what you can or won't do: set limits and develop rules.

2. Offer sincere and positive appreciation.

3. Express interest in your partner; avoid phony flattery.

4. Choose to be polite, regardless of your partner's actions.

5. Be direct and honest.

6. Be careful about teasing.

And couples who have developed a pattern of avoiding conflict can try these suggestions:

1. Get in touch with your feelings.

2. Reaffirm your basic beliefs about your relationship.

3. Learn to level with your partner when necessary.

4. Create strategies that function like "suggestion boxes" to express ideas and suggestions.

5. Turn to other friends and professionals for support.

Developing strategies to negotiate conflict over family roles is especially important, since evidence suggests that the match between roles and expectations largely determines family satisfaction. One framework for renegotiating family roles calls for family members to consider four action steps: (1) take responsibility; (2) describe the expected behaviours; (3) engage in mutual renegotiation; and (4) establish a time frame for renegotiation.[47] First, rather than leaving a change in role behaviour to chance, assume responsibility for talking about your expectations. Take special care to describe what you expect, rather than evaluating, blaming, or criticizing behaviour you don't like. Then continue the dialogue with family members by discussing their needs and responses to your expectations. And finally, establish a mutually agreeable time and place to resume negotiations. The place should be free from distraction and interruption; the time should be one when all individuals are rested and relaxed.

Most couples who use effective communication skills will be able to see positive results, even with respect to long-standing issues. Notice how Brad and Samantha use their skills to renegotiate who handles some of the household chores.

Samantha: Brad, is this a good time to talk?

Brad: Sure, what's up?

Samantha: Do you remember how we agreed that you would help out a bit more around the house since I've started back to school?

Brad: Well, yes.

Samantha: I've noticed that several of the things you said you would do just aren't getting done. Lately, it seems like I've had to go back to doing the shopping, cooking, and laundry. Those were things you said you could handle.

Brad: Yes, I agree I said I'd do them. But with my boss out and the new project at the plant, I've had to spend more time in the early mornings and evenings at work. When I get home I have just enough energy to nuke a TV dinner and crash.

Samantha: I know you're stretched to the limit, too. How about this? You do the shopping and cooking like you agreed. Let's take turns doing the laundry. When the hamper is full, you take a load to the washer; I'll do the next one. Does that sound reasonable?

Brad: Yes, I'm exhausted. But I know you are, too. I'll try to keep up with the meals and help more with the laundry.

Samantha: Good. Thanks Brad. I think this will work. Let's see how it goes for a week, and then we may need to talk about it some more.

No list of do's and don'ts will miraculously manage all differences in a family relationship. The suggestions offered here provide only a starting point. As we have emphasized, you will need to adapt these skills and suggestions to the context of your unique family system. But research consistently shows that listening skills and empathy are strong predictors of family satisfaction.

RECAP   **How to Improve Family Relationships**

Take time to talk about relationships and feelings.

- Be other-oriented in your focus.
- Don't take yourself too seriously.

Listen and clarify the meaning of messages.

- Learn and interpret messages according to the sender's code system.

- Document your interpretation of messages.

Support and encourage one another.

- Use confirming messages.
- Be selective in disclosing your feelings.

Use productive strategies for managing conflict, stress, and change.

- Watch for communication warning signs.
- Learn to renegotiate role conflicts.

Summary

A family is a unit made up of any number of persons who live in relationship with one another over time in a common living space and are usually, but not always, united by marriage and kinship. The nature of family life has undergone significant changes during this century, so we can describe four types of families: A natural family consists of a mother and father and their biological children. Blended families also consist of two adults and their children, but the children may be products of other marriages or unions. Single-parent families are being created by a wider variety of circumstances than ever before. Extended families include relatives such as aunts, uncles, cousins, and grandparents.

A variety of studies suggest the importance of communication in contributing to the overall quality of family life. A social-descriptive approach to families investigates the rules, roles, patterns, traditions, and norms of family life. Skill and enrichment approaches to family communication emphasize teaching family communication skills, such as listening, self-disclosure, and conflict management. Therapeutic models of family intervention are based upon helping dysfunctional families identify and manage family relationship problems. The systems perspective views families as open, complex, adaptive information-processing systems, in which family members are interdependent and the family equals more than the sum of the individual members.

One model for describing family systems assesses family cohesion and adaptability and the role of communication in affecting family members' roles and relationships. Cohesion refers to the emotional bonding and the feeling of closeness that families experience. Family adaptability refers to the flexibility of family members in responding to changes in family roles, rules, and relationships. Although there is no single ideal balance between cohesion and adaptability for all families, those that are moderate on both dimensions are usually better able to manage stress and communicate effectively.

The ability to understand and negotiate family members' roles is key to family satisfaction. Research suggests that couples relationships can be classified into three types: independent couples, who prefer personal autonomy; traditional couples, who like routines and tend to resist change; and separate couples, who maintain more physical and psychological distance and follow fairly regular routines. When there is a significant difference between a person's expected role in the family and his or her role performance, dissatisfaction is the likely result.

The chapter concludes by reviewing principles and skills that can enhance family communication: take time to talk with other family members about relationship issues; listen to others and adopt an other-orientation; support and encourage one another; use productive strategies for managing conflict and stress. Learn to renegotiate family roles and expectations by taking responsibility for the change, describing the expected behaviours, engaging in mutual renegotiation, and establishing a time and place for renegotiating roles.

For Discussion and Review

■ FOCUS ON COMPREHENSION

1. What is a family?

2. Identify four approaches to studying family communication.

3. What are elements of a family communication system?

4. Identify interpersonal communication skills that can enhance the quality of family life.

■ FOCUS ON CRITICAL THINKING

5. How is a sports team like a family communication system? Use the principles of systems thinking to make your comparison.

6. Steve and Yvette both have full-time jobs and are raising two children. A lot of the household chores simply aren't getting done, and this bothers Steve. How should Steve initiate and manage a discussion about how these chores should be handled?

7. Do you think the institution of the family is deteriorating, or is it just changing? Support your answer.

■ FOCUS ON ETHICS

8. Twelve-year-old Nathan consistently does not get along with his other brothers and sisters. He also is not doing well in school. His parents want to take him to a counsellor, but Nathan does not want to go. Should Nathan's parents insist that he attend counselling?

9. Valentina is six-year-old Will's stepmother. Will does not want Valentina to attend his first grade open house next week. He wants his "real mother" to attend, even though she now lives 300 miles away. Should Valentina attend the open house anyway to show that she wants to be involved in Will's activities?

10. Is it ethical to withhold honest thoughts and feelings from other family members? Should family members always "tell it like it is"? Should parents encourage their children to "tell everything" they know and feel?

1. Select two TV situation comedies or dramas that revolve around a family. The program could be a current show or one that is still broadcast in reruns, such as *Leave It to Beaver*, *All In the Family*, or *The Brady Bunch*. Describe the communication patterns in the TV programs that you observe. Draw upon the principles and skills presented in this chapter as you describe the family communication patterns. You may even want to discuss which of your TV families seem to do a more effective job of communicating with one another.

2. Describe what someone would learn about your family if they were to view only the nonverbal elements of the way your family interacts. For example, imagine someone viewing a videotape of your family's daily activities with the "sound turned off." Consider not only such factors as facial expression, eye contact, touch, and use of personal space, but also the way your home is arranged and the overall appearance of your family's dwelling.

3. The text identifies several conclusions about families that are thought to be healthy or effective on pages 381–384. Select one of the studies mentioned in the text and evaluate your own family's communication effectiveness, based upon the research conclusions presented in the chapter.

Learning with Others

1. After you have indicated whether you agree or disagree with the following statements, break into small groups and try to agree or disagree *unanimously* with each statement. Try to find reasons for differences of opinion. If your group cannot reach agreement or disagreement, you may change the wording in any statement to promote unanimity.

■ AGREE-DISAGREE STATEMENTS ABOUT FAMILIES

_____ 1. Most family members know how to communicate effectively; they just don't take the time to practice what they know.

_____ 2. Family conflict is a symptom rather than a cause of deteriorating family relationships.

_____ 3. Family conflict is harmful to family harmony, and all conflict should be avoided at all costs.

_____ 4. Most family conflict occurs because we don't understand the other family member; we fail to communicate effectively.

_____ 5. Families function best if there is one central leader of the family.

_____ 6. Ineffective communication is the single most important cause of family conflict, divorce, and family tension.

_____ 7. Nonverbal communication (facial expression, eye contact, tone of voice, posture, etc.) is more important than verbal communication; what you do is more important than what you say.

_____ 8. It is sometimes necessary to ignore the feelings of others in order to reach a family decision.

_____ 9. The best way to love your marriage partner is to care more for your partner than you care for yourself.

_____ 10. Generally speaking, the quality of family life is deteriorating today.

_____ 11. There is one best approach or set of rules and principles that will ensure an effectively functioning family.

2. In groups of five or six, brainstorm a list of destructive conflict-management behaviours that will have effects opposite from those suggested in this text. Role-play a situation in class that illustrates your list of destructive behaviours. Then have class members try to describe them. Consider the following situations for roleplays:

a. One member of a couple is watching a football game on TV.

b. A couple is deciding whether to have a baby.

c. One member of a couple is drinking and flirting at a party.

d. A teenager is spending too much money for clothes.

e. A mother or father is spending too much time at work.

f. A family member is smoking, drinking, or eating too much.

Ask another team of students to roleplay these same situations, using constructive methods for managing conflict. Ask the class to identify the effective conflict-management principles used in the roleplays.

FAMILY: A unit made up of any number of persons who live in relationship with one another over time in a common living space who are usually, but not always, united by marriage and kinship.

NATURAL FAMILY: A mother, father, and their biological children.

BLENDED FAMILY: Two adults and their children. Because of divorce, separation, death, or adoption, the children may be the product of other parents, or of just one of the adults who is raising them.

SINGLE-PARENT FAMILY: One parent raising one or more children.

EXTENDED FAMILY: Relatives such as aunts, uncles, cousins, or grandparents who are part of the family unit.

FAMILY OF ORIGIN: The family in which you were raised.

SOCIAL-DESCRIPTIVE APPROACH: An approach to studying family communication by investigating the rules, roles, patterns, traditions, and norms of family life.

COMMUNICATION SKILLS AND ENRICHMENT APPROACH: An approach to studying family communication that focuses on the prescriptive principles and skills designed to help even well-functioning families improve their communication skills.

THERAPEUTIC APPROACH: An approach to studying family communication that tries to help dysfunctional families identify and manage problematic communication issues.

SYSTEMS APPROACH: A holistic approach to studying family communication that views a family as an interdependent system of related individuals.

CIRCUMPLEX MODEL OF FAMILY INTERACTION: A model that shows the relationships between family adaptability, cohesion, and communication.

FAMILY ADAPTABILITY: Refers to a family member's ability to modify and respond to changes in the family's power structure and roles.

FAMILY COHESION: Refers to the emotional bonding and feelings of togetherness that families experience.

FAMILY COMMUNICATION: The way in which family members mutually influence each other.

ROLE EXPECTATION: The consistent way we expect someone to behave.

INSTITUTIONAL MARRIAGE: A marriage in which partners assume traditional husband and wife roles.

COMPANIONSHIP MARRIAGE: A marriage in which partners have flexible roles.

INDEPENDENT COUPLES: A marriage relationship in which the couples accept change and uncertainty, have high role flexibility, and may assume less conventional gender roles.

TRADITIONAL COUPLES: A marriage relationship in which the husband and wife operate with a well-defined interdependent relationship.

SEPARATE COUPLES: A marriage relationship in which the husband and wife maintain more physical and psychological distance between themselves and their partner.

DOCUMENTATION: A listening technique in which you state what behaviour led to your understanding or interpretation of your partner's behaviour.

Relating to Friends

*J*onah: *Alex, you look awful! What's up?*

Alex: *You wouldn't believe the day I had. First, I get the kids all bundled up and ready for school. We go outside, and my car door wasn't closed completely all night, so I guess the inside light was on, and it drained the battery. So I go back in the house with the kids, call a tow truck, wait at the garage for a recharge, and wind up three hours late for work.*

Jonah: *Sounds gruesome. How did the kids get to school?*

Alex: *Suzanne had to call a friend to pick them up. She missed her bus to work. But that's not all. I get to work and start trying to catch up, and fifteen minutes later the fire alarm goes off. So we all traipse down five flights of stairs, and what do you think it is? A short in the electrical system. Back upstairs, I get this coffee stain on my new pants, I get caught in traffic on the way home, and now—now—I find out that this miserable convenience store is out of milk! How can they be out of milk, for crying out loud? I mean, what are convenience stores for, anyway?*

Jonah: *Al, here's a quarter. Go call Suzanne and tell her you'll be home in an hour. You come home with me. We'll talk, we'll listen to my new CDs, we'll have something warm to drink. I've got milk—you can take it home for the kids. If you go there now, you'll just act like a bear.*

Alex: *Okay, yeah. You're right, Jonah. I'm so glad I ran into you. I'll be right back.*

Friends like Jonah make life bearable. For most of us, our friendships are one of our most valuable sources of support. In a survey of more than 100,000 men and women, single women rated friends and social life as the most important source of happiness in their lives. Single men rated friends second only to their job duties.[1] The importance of friendship is as old as the human race; more than two thousand years ago Aristotle defined the nature of friendship in his classic work, the *Nicomachean Ethics*. The motives for friendship, he wrote, are usefulness, pleasure, and a commitment to common goodness; these motives still drive us to develop friendships today. Look at the exchange between Jonah and Alex, for example. Jonah is serving a useful purpose for Alex by listening to his story, offering pleasure and relaxation at his home, and preparing him to be a better husband and father when he returns to his own home.

In this chapter we will examine the nature and characteristics of friendship as well as how people win and lose friends. We will also explore the relationship between liking and loving, and how these feelings affect our interpersonal communication.

The Nature of Friendship

A friend is someone we like and who likes us. We trust our friends. We share good and bad times with them. We want to be with them and we make time for that purpose. Or, as one armchair philosopher observed, a real friend is one who will continue to talk to you over the back fence even though he knows he's missing his favourite television program.

We expect this kind of self-sacrifice from our friends. Here are some other ideals that we hold out for friendship:

A friend will see you through after others see you are through.

A friend is one who'll tell you what you should be told even if it momentarily offends you.

A friend thinks of you when all others are thinking of themselves.

A friend is one who sticks by you even when he or she gets to know you well.

A friend is one who, when you've made a fool of yourself, doesn't feel that you've done a permanent job.

Although not every friendship we form lives up to these ideals, by nature, a friend is someone whom we choose to be with, not someone we associate with because we have to. Friendship is a relationship that exists over time between people who share a common history.[2] It is a relationship of choice, as we defined the term in Chapter 7. Or, as one researcher suggests, "Chance makes our parents, but choice makes our friends." Friendship develops naturally into an interdependent

Figure 13-1

A Common Pattern of Friendship and Acquaintance

Adapted from: Peter Marsh, *Eye to Eye: How People Interact* (Topsfield, MA: Salem House, 1988).

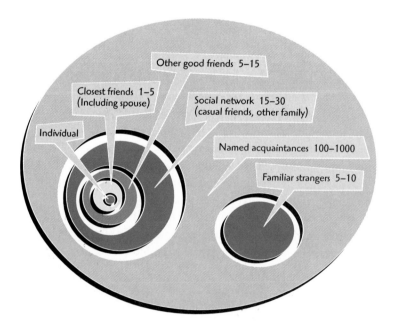

V   DEVELOPING RELATIONSHIPS

relationship that is different from other interpersonal relationships. In friendship, we have no external constraints that keep us together, such as a job, school, or family, even though we often make friends with people in these relationships. Usually we form friendships with our equals, whereas we often form other types of relationships with people of different ages or social backgrounds.[3]

Reasons for Friendship

As we discussed in Chapter 1, friends are not just incidental to our lives. We develop friendships because we need to. According to Will Schutz, we have three primary social needs that make us initiate and sustain friendships with others: the need for inclusion, the need for control, and the need for affection.[4] The **need for inclusion** suggests that each of us has a need to be included in the activities of others. We all need human contact and fellowship. We need to be invited to join others, and perhaps we need to invite others to join us. Of course, the level and intensity of this need differ from person to person, but even loners desire some social contact.

The second need, the **need for control**, suggests that we also need some degree of dominion over the relationships we establish with others. We must exercise control in order to predict how others will respond. We may also have a need to be controlled because we desire some level of stability and comfort in our interactions with others. And, finally, we each have a **need for affection**. We need to give and receive love, support, warmth, and intimacy, although the amounts vary enormously from person to person. The greater your inclusion, control, and affection needs are, the more likely it is that you will actively seek others as friends.

Because of these needs, social isolation can negatively affect our physical and mental health. Research suggests that the most stressful event in life is losing a friend or companion.[5] Besides helping us enjoy a healthy life, friends help us cope with stress, take care of physical needs, and even help in the development of our personality. Friends also help shape our attitudes and beliefs. Especially during periods of change and crisis in our lives, such as adolescence and retirement, friends help us cope with uncertainty and have a profound influence on our behaviour.[6] How many friends do we need? Typically, as shown in Figure 13.1, people have up to five close friends, fifteen other friends, twenty or more members in a social network (which could include family members), and many more people who are simply acquaintances.[7] In all of our social interactions, we are happiest when we are in the company of our friends. Perhaps Cicero said it best: A friend multiplies our joys and divides our sorrows. The classic story of Damon and Pythias on page 406 suggests that true friends will be there when we need them.

Friends also perform other functions, such as bolstering our self-esteem. Most of us need people who provide encouragement and tell us that we are decent and likable. It is confirming to have a friend become indignant for us when we have

Although we all have a need to feel included and accepted throughout our lives, this requirement typically intensifies during adolescence. (R. Sidney/ The Image Bank)

experienced an injustice. Friends can help keep a stream of positive acceptance flowing to counteract the numerous nicks and bruises that our self-worth suffers in the course of daily living.

Friends also provide material help when we need it. When you are away on vacation, you might ask a friend to feed your cat and water your plants. If you run out of gas, you might call a friend to bring you some or pick you up.

One of the most important functions that friends perform, however, is to help us manage the mundane. Most friendships are not based upon unusual activities. On the contrary, most of us seek out friends just to talk, have a meal, or be entertained together. In a survey of more than 40,000 respondents, *Psychology Today* reported that the following were most often mentioned as activities to do with friends:[8]

1. Have an intimate talk

2. Have a friend ask you to do something for him or her

3. Go out to dinner in a restaurant

4. Ask your friend to do something for you

5. Have a meal together at home or at your friend's home

6. Go to a movie, play, or concert

7. Go drinking together

8. Shop together

9. Participate in sports

10. Watch a sporting event

How Satisfying Are Your Friendships?

Do your friendships make you feel less lonely? The following items are taken from the most frequently used research measure of loneliness, the University of Los Angeles Loneliness Scale. For each question in the list, indicate how often you feel as though the statement applies to you.

	Never	Rarely	Sometimes	Often
I feel in tune with the people around me.	4	3	2	1
No one really knows me well.	1	2	3	4
I can find companionship when I want to.	4	3	2	1
People are around me but not with me.	1	2	3	4

Total your score for all four items. The average total for 250 Los Angeles respondents was 4.2; higher scores reflect greater loneliness and may indicate that your friendships are not as satisfying as they could be.

From: Peter Marsh, *Eye to Eye: How People Interact* (Topsfield, MA: Salem House, 1988).

Doing Something About Loneliness: Reaching Out to Others

The first step in overcoming loneliness is to resist the passive attitude that you can easily lapse into if you are always alone. Loneliness is a temporary condition if you are willing to take constructive actions. In order to form satisfying friendships, it is necessary to be other-oriented, to reach out and cultivate the interest of other people instead of waiting for them to come to you.

What to Do

- Accept invitations when they are offered.
- Call on someone or invite someone to visit.
- Be responsive in conversation. Let people know that you are interested in what they say by smiling and nodding.
- Ask questions to keep the conversation flowing. Others will find it rewarding to talk to you.
- Ask questions that help people to present themselves in their best light.
- Be open to the interests of other people.
- Draw attention to interests you have in common.

What Not to Do

- Do not stay away from people to hide your loneliness.
- Do not make negative remarks about yourself.
- Do not harbour critical thoughts about the people you meet.
- Do not think that you have to be exceptionally clever or attractive to be liked.

Adapted from: Peter Marsh, *Eye to Eye: How People Interact* (Topsfield, MA: Salem House, 1988).

Gender Differences in Friendships

Women form friendships differently than do men.[9] Consider these two friendly conversations between strangers who are watching their children at a playground.

Conversation 1:

Darleen: How old is your baby? She's so precious with that big smile and her little "Hewwo."

Roselyn: Fourteen months. She's just starting to say a few words. It's such an exciting time, but I'm exhausted today. I can't wait for her nap.

Darleen: I know what you mean. Mine is sixteen months, and he's pulling everything out of the cupboards. I get so frustrated trying to watch him every second, sometimes I want to scream.

Roselyn: Does your husband ever take over on weekends?

Darleen: Oh, I'm not married. Sometimes my boyfriend watches him, but he's not really into it, you know. He doesn't live with us or anything.

Conversation 2:

Derek: Nice weather for a baseball game. Looks like your daughter's a good hitter.

Byron: Yes, she played in Little League this summer. Sixteen games and twelve home runs. Was your son in the league?

Derek: No. My wife and I couldn't get home in time to take him to the games—they started so early.

Byron: I know, I know. What line of work are you in?

As you can see, women tend to self-disclose more than do men; they do it early, and with a greater depth and breadth as they develop intimate relationships. Men appear to be less expressive and more instrumental in their conversations with others; they talk less about emotions and more about work and achieving goals. Women also seem to be more vigilant in monitoring the progress of a relationship than are men. They are more aware of problems and think more about the possibility of ending the relationship. If they do end the relationship, they can provide more detailed descriptions about the exchange than can men.[10]

Damon and Pythias: An Ancient Example of Friendship

Damon and Pythias had been the best of friends since childhood. Each trusted the other like a brother, and each knew in his heart there was nothing he would not do for his friend. Eventually the time came for them to prove the depth of their devotion. It happened this way.

Dionysius, the ruler of Syracuse, grew annoyed when he heard about the kind of speeches Pythias was giving. The young scholar was telling the public that no man should have unlimited power over another, and that absolute tyrants were unjust kings. In a fit of rage, Dionysius summoned Pythias and his friend.

"Who do you think you are, spreading unrest among the people?" he demanded.

"I spread only the truth," Pythias answered. "There can be nothing wrong with that."

"And does your truth hold that kings have too much power and that their laws are not good for their subjects?"

"If a king has seized power without permission of the people, then that is what I say."

"This kind of talk is treason," Dionysius shouted. "You are conspiring to overthrow me. Retract what you've said, or face the consequences. "

"I will retract nothing," Pythias answered.

"Then you will die. Do you have any last requests?"

"Yes. Let me go home just long enough to say good-bye to my wife and children and to put my household in order."

"I see you not only think I'm unjust, you think I'm stupid as well," Dionysius laughed scornfully. "If I let you leave Syracuse, I have no doubt I will never see you again."

"I will give you a pledge," Pythias said.

"What kind of pledge could you possibly give to make me think you will ever return?" Dionysius demanded.

At that instant Damon, who had stood quietly beside his friend, stepped forward.

"I will be his pledge," he said. "Keep me here in Syracuse, as your prisoner, until Pythias returns. Our friendship is well known to you. You can be sure Pythias will return so long as you hold me."

Dionysius studied the two friends silently. "Very well," he said at last. "But if you are willing to take the place of your friend, you must be willing to accept his sentence if he breaks his promise. If Pythias does not return to Syracuse, you will die in his place."

"He will keep his word," Damon replied. "I have no doubt of that."

Pythias was allowed to go free for a time, and Damon was thrown into prison. After several days, when Pythias failed to reappear, Dionysius's curiosity got the better of him, and he went to the prison to see if Damon was yet sorry he had made such a bargain.

"Your time is almost up," the ruler of Syracuse sneered. "It will be useless to beg for mercy. You were a fool to rely on your friend's promise. Did you really think he would sacrifice his life for you or anyone else?"

"He has merely been delayed," Damon answered steadily. "The winds have kept him from sailing, or perhaps he has met with some accident on the road. But if it is humanly possible, he will be here on time. I am as confident of his virtue as I am of my own existence."

Dionysius was startled at the prisoner's confidence. "We shall soon see," he said, and left Damon in his cell.

The fatal day arrived. Damon was brought from prison and led before the executioner. Dionysius greeted him with a smug smile.

"It seems your friend has not turned up," he laughed. "What do you think of him now?"

"He is my friend," Damon answered. "I trust him."

Even as he spoke, the doors flew open, and Pythias staggered into the room. He was pale and bruised and half speechless from exhaustion. He rushed to the arms of his friend.

"You are safe, praise the gods," he gasped. "It seemed as though the fates were conspiring against us. My ship was wrecked in a storm, and then bandits attacked me on the road. But I refused to give up hope, and at last I've made it back in time. I am ready to receive my sentence of death."

Dionysius heard his words with astonishment. His eyes and his heart were opened. It was impossible for him to resist the power of such constancy.

"The sentence is revoked," he declared. "I never believed that such faith and loyalty could exist in friendship. You have shown me how wrong I was, and it is only right that you be rewarded with your freedom. But I ask that in return you do me one great service."

"What service do you mean?" the friends asked.

"Teach me how to be part of so worthy a friendship."

From: William J. Bennett, *The Book of Virtues* (New York: Simon & Schuster, 1994).

Rules for Friendship

Friendships, like other types of relationships, operate within the bounds of certain rules. A rule, as you may recall, is a prescription that tells us what behaviour is obligated, preferred, or prohibited in certain contexts. We label someone as socially inexperienced if he or she does not know the rules for interacting with others. According to some researchers, your ability to understand and follow friendship rules is key to establishing and maintaining the friendship.[11] But friendship rules are not tacked on a wall for all to see; they are based upon learned social and cultural expectations. They are also remarkably similar across cultures. Here are the rules that one research team identified for establishing relationships:[12]

1. Respect the other's privacy.

2. Do not discuss what is said in confidence with anyone else.

3. Look the other person in the eye during conversation.

4. Do not criticize the other person publicly.

5. Do not force sexual activity upon the other person.

6. Seek to repay debts, favours, or compliments no matter how small.

7. Stand up for the other person in his or her absence.

8. Share news of success with the other person.

9. Address the other person by his or her first name.

To maintain friendships, we have additional expectations. We expect our more intimate friends to do the following:[13]

V   DEVELOPING RELATIONSHIPS

1. Volunteer to help in time of need.

2. Trust and confide in us.

3. Stand up for us in our absence.

4. Show emotional support.

5. Strive to make us happy when we are in each other's company.

6. Not to be jealous or critical of our other relationships.

7. Ask for personal advice.

8. Not to nag.

9. Joke or tease with us in a friendly way.

10. Disclose personal feelings or problems.

As a relationship becomes more intimate, we expect our friends to be more aware of, and active in, meeting our personal needs.

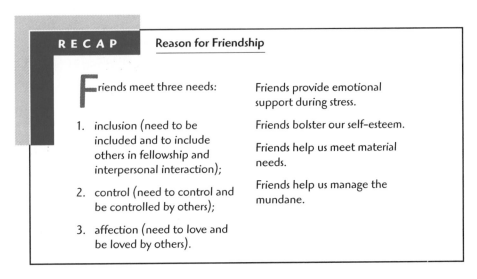

RECAP   **Reason for Friendship**

Friends meet three needs:

1. inclusion (need to be included and to include others in fellowship and interpersonal interaction);

2. control (need to control and be controlled by others);

3. affection (need to love and be loved by others).

Friends provide emotional support during stress.

Friends bolster our self-esteem.

Friends help us meet material needs.

Friends help us manage the mundane.

Three Types of Friendships

George Washington observed, "True friendship is a plant of slow growth, and must undergo and withstand the shocks of adversity before it is entitled to the appellation." Although some of our friendships do blossom suddenly, most proceed according to the stages we described in Chapter 7. And as we saw in Chapters 8 and 9, not all friendships become **intimate**. The intensity of our affection for our friends and the intimacy of our conversations determines whether we view someone as an acquaintance, a casual friend, or a close friend.

▪ ACQUAINTANCES

As we saw in Figure 13.1, most of us have many acquaintances—people whom we know but do not consider friends. For example, we do not send them birthday cards or write them postcards when we travel. Depending upon your occupation and daily activities, you may have dozens of acquaintances. Some people report having more than one thousand acquaintances.[14] The factors we described on page 409 usually determine whether these acquaintances will become friends.

Communication with acquaintances tends to be functional and superficial. You may talk with them about work, school, or what you have done or will do over a holiday or weekend. As you do in the early stages of a friendship, when you speak to acquaintances, you limit your self-disclosure to facts keeping your feelings and attitudes to yourself.

■ CASUAL FRIENDS

The key difference between acquaintances and casual friends is the level of intimacy in your conversations. You are more likely to reveal personal information to a casual friend than to an acquaintance. Perhaps among your many acquaintances at school there is a small group of people who meet together to study. This study group may eventually begin to do such things as have a meal together or go to a movie or a concert. You move from being acquaintances to being casual friends. Casual friends are more likely to volunteer to help one another in time of need. They also are more likely to plan get-togethers than to depend upon chance meetings in the street or at the movies. As Figure 13.1 shows, casual friends are part of a social network that may also include relatives.

■ CLOSE FRIENDS

As the name implies, close friends are near and dear to you. They may literally live close to you, or they may move miles away from you. At one time, however, you were probably interacting with your close friend frequently. More often than not, your closest friends are people of your gender.

Your conversations with close friends are highly **intimate**. You confide in those that you trust. You also try to see them often. Close friends are those that help the most when we are stressed or troubled. You enjoy their company when all is well; when you have problems, your close friends want to help ease your burdens and pain.

Achieving intimacy is not the goal of all of your friendships, however. Attempts to force it or to manipulate others in the hopes that they will cling to you and no one else usually backfire. People don't like to be smothered. True friendships are more likely to blossom when disclosure evolves naturally in small increments, when trust is high, and when both individuals have the freedom to leave the relationship.

Friendships at Different Stages in Life

As we saw in Chapters 7, 8, and 9, establishing intimacy with another person takes time, so most of us have a limited number of intimate relationships. We also have different needs for intimacy at various stages of our lives. One pair of researchers examined the differences among friendships at four stages in life: childhood, adolescence, adulthood, and old age.[15]

V DEVELOPING RELATIONSHIPS

Who's your "best" friend? Write his or her name below and then use the questions to help you analyze your relationship.

My best friend is _____.

How we met: _____

_____

_____

_____

_____

_____

Why we became friends: _____

_____

_____

_____

_____

_____

How my friend meets my needs: _____

_____

_____

_____

_____

_____

_____

How I meet my friend's needs: _____

_____

_____

_____

_____

_____

_____

CHILDHOOD FRIENDSHIPS

At about the age of two, when we start to talk, we begin parallel play with others. As toddlers we perceive our playmates as others who can help meet our needs. Our first friendships are usually superficial and self-centred. Childhood friendships can be categorized into five sometimes overlapping stages.[16] From ages three to seven, we have *momentary playmates*—we interact with those in our presence. From ages four to nine, we have *one-way assistance*. We still view friendships from a "take" perspective, as instruments to help meet our needs, rather than from a "give" or "give-and-take" perspective.

The third stage, ages six to twelve, is the *fair-weather friend* stage. There is more give and take in friendships, but the reciprocity occurs when things are going well; the relationship is likely to end if problems and conflicts develop. The fourth stage, ages nine to fifteen, is called *mutual intimacy*. With the closeness that develops, relationships become more possessive. The last stage (twelve through adulthood) allows for more *independence* in friendships, as well as deepening interdependence with friends that permits greater levels of intimacy and sharing.

ADOLESCENT FRIENDSHIPS

During adolescence, beginning with the onset of puberty around age twelve, we move away from relationships with parents and other adults and toward greater intimacy with our peers. During adolescence, peer relationships are the most important social influence on our behaviour. We develop cliques of friends and form friendship networks. Boys are more likely to join gangs—which might be socially acceptable groups such as a sports or debate team, or less socially desirable groups bent on violence and destruction of property. Girls are more likely to develop intimate relationships with one or two good friends. Friendship relationships usually peak in late adolescence and early adulthood, before we select a mate.[17]

During adolescence boys seem to have more friends, whereas girls appear to develop closer, more intensive and intimate relationships. The patterns of making and keeping friends we learn as children continue to affect the formation of friendships during adolescence.

Here is how one researcher described the nature of teenage friendships:

> There is order in the chaos, and chaos in the order, of teenage friendships. We want to hang out with the gang, but we want to be close to somebody too. We want to be close to somebody, but we don't want to shut anybody out, either. We want to trust fully, but discover that people let you down—while at the same time we are ready to drop the friendship if our needs aren't being met.[18]

ADULT FRIENDSHIPS

Adult friendships are among our most valued relationships. Henry Van Dyke summarized the virtues of developing a trusting, intimate relationship with a friend when he wrote the following:

> But, after all, the very best thing in good talk, and the thing that helps most, is friendship. How it dissolves the barriers that divide us, and loosens all constraint, and diffuses itself like some fine old cordial through all the veins of life—this feeling that we understand and trust each other, and wish each other heartily well. Everything into which it really comes is good.[19]

One researcher identifies four explanations as to why friendships dissolve during adulthood:[20] First, they may cool because of physical separation. One person may move to a new community, or even if the person hasn't moved, he or she may no

V   DEVELOPING RELATIONSHIPS

longer travel in the same social circles. Second, new friends may replace old. Changing jobs, joining a new club or religious organization, or having new neighbours move in next door, may diminish the amount of time you can spend with former friends. A third and obvious reason for ending a friendship is that you may simply dislike something your friend did. Perhaps he or she did not help you in a time of need, betrayed a confidence, or violated another friendship rule. And, finally, if and when we begin the process of selecting a mate for life, our friendship relationships may change.

Friendships can sometimes have an adverse effect upon a couple if one partner feels that the other's friends are competing for time and intimacy. If one partner's desire to go out alone with friends becomes more important than marriage and family, then conflict flares up.

Elderly people may make new friends, but they usually rely most on their spouses and oldest friends to fulfill their need for companionship. (Sandra Rice)

■ THE ELDERLY AND FRIENDSHIPS

Although the elderly make new friends, they value old ones most. During retirement, when individuals have more time for socializing, friendships become increasingly important; but older adults form fewer new friendships. Instead, they tend to maintain a small, highly valued network of friends.

■ SIMILARITIES AND DIFFERENCES AMONG STAGES

Despite these differences, there are also common behaviours across age groups. One research team found that self-disclosure, one of the most important components of friendship, did not seem to change in either depth or amount from young adulthood through age ninety-one.[21] They did report, however, that as friends get older, there is more negative self-disclosure; we are more willing to tell our friends less positive things about ourselves rather than limiting our disclosures to information that makes us "look good."

COMMUNICATION EXPERIENCE

Make lists of the friends you had in childhood and during adolescence, and of those you have now in the columns below. Are any friends in all three columns? If so, why? If not, what changed?

My Childhood Friends	My Adolescent Friends	My Friends Today
_____	_____	_____
_____	_____	_____
_____	_____	_____
_____	_____	_____
_____	_____	_____
_____	_____	_____

Making Friends

In Chapters 7, 8, and 9 we presented some suggestions for initiating and maintaining relationships, including friendships. Some of the ideas presented in the following sections are variations on those suggestions. As you read them, however, keep Dale Carnegie's simple advice in mind: "You can make more friends in two months by becoming interested in other people than you can in two years by trying to get other people interested in you."[22]

Recognize, Select, and Make the Most of Friendship Opportunities

A "friendship opportunity" is a situation in which you are likely to meet other people who may become your friends. People who develop friendships with others are good at judging where and when to meet others and with which individuals they will be compatible. We can't tell you precisely where you will meet someone who is likely to become your friend. But knowing your own interests, likes, and dislikes is a first step in choosing places to look.[23] As implied by Robert Frost in his poem "The Pasture," friendship opportunities need not always be major, preplanned events; they could involve simply inviting others to share in everyday activities.

The Pasture

I'm going out to clean the pasture spring;
I'll only stop to rake the leaves away
(And wait to watch the water clear, I may):
I sha'n't be gone long.—You come too.
I'm going out to fetch the little calf
That's standing by the mother. It's so young,
It totters when she licks it with her tongue.
I sha'n't be gone long.—You come too.

—ROBERT FROST

From: *The Poetry of Robert Frost*, edited by Connery Lathem. Copyright © 1994 by Robert Frost. Copyright © 1916 ©1969 by Henry Holt and Co., Inc. Reprinted by permission of Henry Holt and Co., Inc.

Encourage Others to Be Your Friend

To develop a friendship with another person, you must show him or her something that will encourage interaction. You need skills to assess his or her interests and background, and then to communicate your interest in them.

Your encouragement may be explicit or implicit. You may explicitly ask for a date or initiate a conversation. To do this, you need effective conversation skills.

How do you start a conversation? Here are several approaches:

- Volunteer your name or information about yourself followed by a question about the other person ("Hello, I'm from Regina. Where are you from?").

- Make a comment about the other person or ask him or her a question ("That's a beautiful tie. Where did you buy it"?).

- Talk about where you are, the weather, something that you are both observing ("Do you think it will ever stop raining"?). There are no sure-fire, prerehearsed lines for initiating conversation. Effective conversation emerges from the situation and the people involved.

Once the conversation begins, you can try out these suggestions:

- Ask questions that are open-ended and keep the conversation rolling.

- Adapt to your listener; be other-oriented.

- Remember what you talk about. Focus on what both you and your conversation partner are discussing.

- Take turns initiating and responding so that you are sharing responsibility for the conversation.

- Don't only talk about yourself.

- Don't say or do something that will cause the other person to value him- or herself less. Being rude, interrupting, and not considering the feelings of others inhibits conversation.

- Reveal information about yourself so that the other person can get to know you. If you tell nothing about yourself, your partner may perceive you as aloof. Of course, if you reveal too much too quickly, you can also violate your listener's expectations and make him or her uncomfortable.

Classic conversation stoppers

These suggestions are consistent with the standard "script" that we follow in our culture for initial conversations, as we noted in Chapter 8. Remember that if you deviate from this script, you may make your partner feel uneasy. The *Far Side* cartoon provides some examples of disconcerting deviations.

You can also communicate your desire to make friends and to be a friend to someone through your nonverbal behaviour.[24] As we discussed in Chapter 5, the following nonverbal cues communicate a friendly attitude:

Proximity:	Move closer and lean forward if you are seated.
Orientation:	Sit directly in front of or closely beside the person.
Gaze:	Look the person in the eyes, especially when he or she looks at you.
Facial expression:	Smile.
Gestures:	Nod your head; use lively movements.
Posture:	Keep an open posture, with your arms stretched toward the other person, rather than placing your arms on your hips or folding them.
Touch:	Touch the person in a friendly, nonsexual way.
Tone of voice:	Higher pitch, rising inflection, clear pure tone.

Understand How Friendships Develop and Grow

This course in interpersonal communication may be your first formal education in how interpersonal relationships develop. You learn about relationships through your experience as well as occasional tips from parents, friends, and teachers along the way.

The information we presented in Chapters 7, 8, and 9 explained how relationships develop, are maintained, and sometimes deteriorate. Knowing these textbook principles is no substitute for human experience, but understanding such things as the typical pace of relationship development, why we are attracted to others, the function and purpose of self-disclosure, and some of the reasons relationships deteriorate can help make you a wiser friend.

What do friends talk about? A study by two researchers reports five major areas of conversation:[25]

1. Social talk about events, jokes, and just enjoyment of one another's company;

2. Gossip about others;

3. Common interests;

4. Sharing information and solving problems;

5. Support and encouragement in times of stress.

What do you and your friends discuss? If you are focusing on one of these areas to the exclusion of others, you may want to assess where you are in the friendship. As we discussed in Chapter 8, the depth and breadth of your self-disclosure characterizes your level of intimacy with others. John Powell suggests that conversations with others take place on one of five levels, as shown in Figure 13.2.[26] Powell refers to the opening moves in the scripted conversations just described and discussed in Chapter 8 as "cliché" conversation. Their main purpose is to make contact. The subtext or implied meaning of such talk is, "I'm interested in you. Let's communicate."

Much of our conversation either remains at a very basic level or proceeds to the second level of conventional conversation that involves the exchange of other non-threatening information, such as your name, or where you went to high school. At level three the conversation becomes more personal. Here you begin to reveal your ideas and judgments. These revelations take more courage because others may disapprove of your judgments. Powell calls the fourth level "gut level" communication. This conversation is usually reserved for good friends; at this level you share emotions and feelings. Level five, or "peak communication," is rare. Only with your most intimate friends or lovers do you self-disclose your most personal thoughts. This level requires considerable trust and carries a high risk of rejection. In Powell's words, "But if I tell you who I am, and you do not like who I am, that is all that I have."[27]

The goal of interpersonal conversation is not to raise every friendship to level five. Nor do we usually set conscious goals based on these levels. You don't come home from the first night out with a new friend and say, "Well, I got to level two today and I hope to get to level four by tomorrow." As we discussed in Chapter 8, developing deep, meaningful conversation with friends takes time and occurs in small increments. A meaningful friendship unfolds as you explore, through conversation, your personal thoughts and feelings, and as you listen and respond to others' thoughts and feelings.

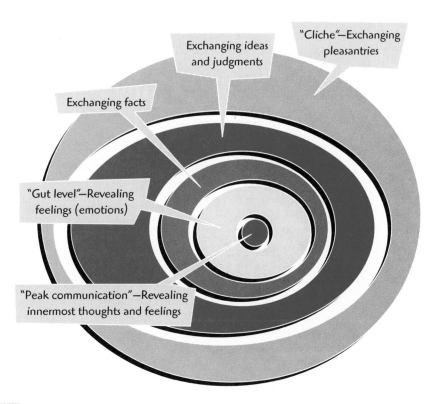

Figure 13-2

Powell's Five Levels of Communication

A Time to Talk

When a friend calls to me from the road
And slows his horse to a meaning walk,
I don't stand still and look around
On all the hills I haven't hoed,
And shout from where I am, What is it?
No, not as there is a time to talk.
I thrust my hoe in the mellow ground,
Blade-end up and five feet tall,
And plod: I go up to the stone wall
For a friendly visit.

—ROBERT FROST

From: *The Poetry of Robert Frost,* edited by Connery Lathem. Copyright © 1994 by Robert Frost. Copyright © 1916 ©1969 by Henry Holt and Co., Inc. Reprinted by permission of Henry Holt and Co., Inc.

COMMUNICATION EXPERIENCE

Who Are Your Friends?

Who are the friends you would turn to for support or to celebrate a major event? Answer the questions to do a "friendship inventory."[28]

1. You have an extra ticket to a concert or major sports event. List the three people you would call, in order of preference.

1._____

2._____

3. _____

2. You have just learned of the unexpected death of a family member. Who would you call first? Second? Third?

1._____

2._____

3._____

3. You are going on a cruise and have learned that you can bring a friend along for free. List in order of preference the first three people you would invite to be your guest.

1._____

2._____

3._____

4. As you are driving through a small town, you get a traffic ticket and you don't have your car registration or driver's licence with you. You are taken to jail. List in order the first three people you would call.

1. _____

2. _____

3. _____

Use Skills That Help Maintain and Repair Relationships

Friends become friends not just because they understand how relationships work, but also because they are able to put into practice behaviours that enhance and enrich the friendship. The skills of listening and reflecting we discussed in Chapter 4 are especially important. Listen so that you can provide encouragement and support, especially in time of trouble. Also use the confirming responses you learned in Chapter 6 and the relationship maintenance strategies described in Chapter 9. Most importantly, be other-oriented and practice decentring and empathy in your exchanges.

Even in the best of relationships, there are differences that result in conflict. Long-time friends develop strategies for overcoming these differences. You can try out some of the conflict management skills we discussed in Chapter 10 to work through disagreements.

RECAP   **How to Make Friends**

- Recognize, select, and make the most of friendship opportunities. — Look for friends at events and activities that are compatible with your own interests.

- Encourage others to be your friend. — Develop effective conversation skills.

- Understand how friendships develop and grow. — Know principles of relationships and rules for establishing and maintaining relationships.

- Use skills that help maintain and repair relationships. — Stop, look, listen, respond, and empathize with others. Provide confirming responses. Be open, adaptive, and sensitive to your partner.

Losing Friends

We have discussed how friendships are won, but it is equally useful to know how friendships are lost. Clues about how not to make friends and influence people can be found in the pioneering work of two British researchers, Michael Argyle and Monika Henderson. They studied people who described themselves as lonely and friendless. Their research suggests that these people had developed communication patterns that discouraged close personal relationships.

If you meet someone who seems aloof or untalkative, it might be that the person is actually in a lot of pain because he or she is saddled with a portfolio of self-defeating behaviours that stem from a poor self-image. Those who are lonely have the following tendencies as compared to less lonely people:

1. Engage in less self-disclosure and are less likely to respond when others self-disclose to them.

2. Take less interest in others during conversation. They tend to ask fewer questions and generally are less talkative.

3. Are less assertive and more passive in standing up for their rights.

4. Blame their interpersonal failures on their lack of social skill. They also feel they will not be likely to develop skills no matter how hard they may try.

5. Are viewed by others as having low self-esteem and as difficult to meet and get to know. They are also perceived as uninterested in other people.

6. Lack the nonverbal skills to show positive emotions, especially through the facial expressions and voice.[29]

But maybe it is worth the effort to push beyond your initial perceptions; to make an attempt to draw the person out, and put him or her at ease by starting a conversation. You may discover a very interesting complex individual who is simply too shy to be conventionally sociable.

Just as there are behavioural rules for making and maintaining friends, there are behaviours which, if you pursue them, will almost certainly cost you a friendship. Listed in order of offensiveness, they are as follows:[30]

1. Acting jealous or being critical of your relationship;

2. Discussing with others what your friend said in confidence:

3. Not volunteering help in time of need;

4. Not trusting or confiding in your friend;

5. Criticizing your friend in public;

6. Not showing positive regard for your friend;

7. Not standing up for your friend in his or her absence;

8. Not being tolerant of your friend's other friends;

9. Not showing emotional support;

10. Nagging your friend.

In Chapters 7, 8, and 9 we saw how relationships intensify and sometimes become less intense in predictable stages. Relationship dissolution is not an event but a process. Love relationships usually end more abruptly and with more emotional intensity than friendships. When one researcher asked individuals to identify why their friendships with a friend of the same sex ended, first on the list was physical separation.[31] When we move away from our friends, it apparently takes a toll on the intensity of the relationship. Second, subjects reported that new friends replace old friends as circumstances change. Third, people often just grow to dislike a characteristic of the friend's behaviour or personality. And finally, interference from dating or a couples relationship often contributes to the decay of a friendship. It should come as no surprise that casual friendships are more likely to end than are those with close or intimate friends. Close friendships are better able to withstand change, uncertainty, and separation.

Friendship and Love

When most of us think of love, we think of the head-over-heels, romantic, "love at first sight" variety. Some of our love relationships do involve this kind of passionate sexual attraction. But we also love people with whom we share no sexual chemistry. We love our parents, our children; we have loving friends of the same or the opposite sex with whom we do not share our bed. Love is not a one-dimensional feeling. But there are differences between our relationships with friends and those with lovers.[32] One pair of researchers suggests that love differs from friendship "in the identity of interest that the partners share. Love exists to the extent that the outcomes enjoyed or suffered by each are enjoyed or suffered by both."[33]

Another key difference between friends and lovers lies in how they talk about their relationship. Friends are less likely to talk about what attracted them to each other than are lovers. Friends are also less likely to celebrate anniversaries and mark the passage of time in formal ways, such as a card or a special dinner. Love involves an increase in a sense of "we-ness," of passionate solidarity and identification with the other.

One researcher attempted to identify differences between love and friendship by developing two scales—one to measure love and the other to measure liking.[34] He found that people made distinctions between love and liking based upon these scales. Love relationships are more passionate and intimate than friendships, but interestingly, people like their lovers only slightly more than they like their friends. And women make greater

Do you assume the couple in this photo are lovers or friends? Upon what clues did you base your judgment? (Esbin-Anderson/ The Image Works)

Loving, Liking, and Feeling

Love is not a special kind of liking. Just as it is possible to like someone without loving him or her, so it is possible, though unusual, to love someone without liking him or her very much. To measure your regard for a friend, dating partner, lover, or spouse in terms of loving and liking, insert his or her name in each of the following statements; then give each statement a rating from 1 to 9, depending on how strongly you agree or disagree with it (for example: disagree completely = 1; agree completely = 9; agree to some extent = 5). For scoring instructions, see below.

1. I feel responsible for ———'s well-being.
2. If I could never be with ——— I would feel miserable.
3. I have great confidence in ———'s good judgment.
4. I feel I can confide in ——— about virtually anything.
5. If I were lonely, my first thought would be to seek ——— out.
6. I think ——— is one of those people who quickly wins respect.
7. I think that ——— is unusually well-adjusted.
8. ——— is the sort of person who I would like to be.
9. I would do almost anything for ———.
10. In my opinion ——— is an exceptionally mature person.
11. It would be hard for me to get along without ———.
12. ——— is one of the most likable people I know.
13. I would forgive ——— for practically anything.
14. Most people would react favourably to ——— after a brief acquaintance.
15. I would highly recommend ——— for a responsible job.
16. One of my primary concerns is ———'s welfare.
17. It seems to me that it is very easy for ——— to gain admiration.
18. I would greatly enjoy being confided in by ———.

Scoring. The total score for statements 3, 6, 7, 8, 10, 12, 14, 15, and 17 is the measure of liking, the total for the others is the measure of loving. The higher the "liking" score the greater likelihood that this person is more a friend than a lover.

From: Peter Marsh, *Eye to Eye: How People Interact* (Topsfield, MA: Salem House, 1988).

distinctions between loving and liking than do men. Try the Communication Experience above to see how much you like or love one of your friends or partners.

Two other researchers analyzed survey results of several hundred college students and identified three primary factors that determine the kind of love relationship we share with another person: intimacy, commitment, and passion.[35] Intimacy includes such attributes as trust, caring, honesty, supportiveness, understanding, and openness. As we have seen, it is a factor in all kinds of love. The second factor, commitment, includes loyalty, devotion, putting the other first, and needing one another. Commitment, too, characterizes all kinds of love relationships. Passion, however, is linked to romantic relationships. It includes excitement, sexual passion, and butterflies in the stomach.

The closest relationship you develop with another human being will probably be a romantic one. When one research team asked a group of students, "With whom do you share your closest relationship?" 47 percent said it was with a romantic partner.[36] Thirty-six percent said they were closest to their friends, 14 percent said they were closest to a family member, and 3 percent reported "other."

Types of Love

Love, of course, means different things to different people. Many studies use the following six categories to classify types of love: eros, ludis, storge, mania, pragma, and agape.[37] To find out which type you favour in your relationships, do the Communication Experience on page 425.

■ EROS

He: Your eyes. I could get lost in your eyes. And your laugh. I feel so alive when I'm with you. I want to make love to you.

She: Yes. When I'm with you I feel this great desire sweep over me. You take my breath away. I want you more than anything.

Eros is sexual love based upon the pursuit of beauty and pleasure. The physical need for sex brings many couples together. Erotic lovers crave sexual intimacy and passionately seek sexual activity to satisfy their need. Sexual attraction brings special needs and emotions to a relationship, sometimes obscuring other concerns. Shakespeare described this phenomenon when he wrote, "But love is blind, and lovers cannot see the folly that themselves commit."

Love Before and After Marriage

After marriage, the passion in a relationship usually cools slightly. One survey recorded the following changes in frequency in certain behaviours during the first year of marriage.[38]

During your first year of marriage . . .

Your Partner

■ approved or complimented you	30% less often
■ did or said something to make you laugh	34% less often
■ said "I love you"	44% less often
■ initiated sex	39% less often
■ did something nice for you	28% less often

You and Your Partner

■ had sex	38% less often
■ were physically affectionate without sex	39% less often
■ shared emotions, feelings, problems	34% less often
■ talked about the day's events	6% less often

◼ LUDIS

He: Phoebe, I'd like to take you bowling Saturday night if you've never been. It's such a gas at those lanes across town where they still do the setups by hand.

She: Terrific idea. I'll put on my mom's poodle skirt for you. Then later we can go by the lake and park.

For some, love is a game, something to pursue to pass the time. **Ludis** lovers are not seeking long-term relationships; rather, they seek immediate gratification and to win their partner's affection. Their goal is to be in love and to enjoy their partner rather than to achieve a sexual victory.

Early dating relationships are often of the ludis type. Going on a date to a junior high dance is a casual pleasure, not a prelude to a lifelong commitment. Ludis love lasts as long as the couple has fun and finds the relationship mutually satisfying.

◼ STORGE

She: Allen, I have to talk with you about Clara. She's acting as if she wants to get rid of me.

He: I know she's been really tense lately about taking her licensing exam. She hasn't been all that nice to me, either.

She: Really? You know, I so appreciate being able to call you up like this to talk about it. What did she do to you?

He: Well, she's just been quiet, kind of withdrawn, like she's thinking about something else. When I talk to her, she kind of scowls.

She: That's just what she does to me. Maybe it's not personal. You know, maybe we should just leave her alone until the exam's over. I was going to call her up to have dinner, but maybe we should just go ourselves instead. I want to catch up on news from home, anyway.

Storgic love is the sort we find in most friendships and in relationships with siblings and other family members. Sexual consummation is not a factor in this sort of love, although sexual attraction may be present. A storgic relationship usually develops over a long period of time, and it is solid and more resistant to change than erotic love. Trust, caring, and compassion are high. Selfishness is low.

Discovering Your Own Love Profile

Using the six types of love discussed in the section you just read, one research team asked people questions designed to show the relative prominence of each type in an individual's "love profile." An abbreviated version of the questionnaire is given here.

Rate each of the following statements on a scale from 1 to 5 (1 = strongly disagree, 2 = disagree, 3 = neutral, 4 = agree, 5 = strongly agree) to determine your own love profile. Scoring instructions are given after the list of statements.

1. You cannot love unless you have first had a caring relationship for a while.

2. The best kind of love grows out of a long friendship.

3. Kissing, cuddling, and sex should not be rushed into; they will happen naturally when intimacy has grown.

4. Love is really deep friendship, not a mysterious, mystical emotion.

5. I believe that "love at first sight" is possible.

6. We kissed each other soon after we met because we both wanted to.

7. Usually the first thing that attracts my attention to a person is a pleasing appearance.

8. Strong physical attraction is one of the best things about being in love.

9. When things are not going right with us, my stomach gets upset.

10. Once when I thought a love affair was over, I saw him or her again and the old feelings came surging back.

11. If my partner ignores me for a while, I sometimes do really stupid things to try to get his or her attention.

12. When my partner does not pay attention to me, I feel sick all over.

13. I try to use my own strength to help my partner through difficult times, even when he or she is behaving foolishly.

14. I am usually willing to sacrifice my own wishes in favour of my partner's.

15. If my partner had a baby by someone else, I would want to raise it and care for it as if it were my own.

16. I would rather break up with my partner than stand in his or her way.

17. For practical reasons, I would consider what he or she is going to become before I commit myself.

18. You should plan your life before choosing a partner.

19. A main consideration in choosing a partner is how he or she reflects on my family.

20. I would not date anyone that I would not want to fall in love with.

21. At least once I had to plan carefully to keep two of my lovers from finding out about each other.

22. I can get over love affairs pretty easily and quickly.

23. My partner would get upset if he or she knew some of the things I have done with other people.

24. What he or she does not know about me will not hurt my partner.

Scoring. Divide your total for statements 1 through 4 by 4. This is your score for the friendship factor (storge). Recent surveys indicate that the average score for women is 2.9. For men it is 2.5.

Similarly, divide your total for statements 5 through 8 by 4. This is your score for the passionate factor (eros). The average score for men is 2.9, for women 2.7.

To get your score for the possessive factor (mania), divide your total for statements 9 through 12 by 7. The average for women is 2, for men 2.2.

To get your score for the selflessness factor (agape), divide your total for statements 13 through 16 by 4. The average for women is 2.5, for men 2.3.

To get your score for the practical factor (pragma), divide your total for statements 17 through 20 by 4. The average for women is 2.1, for men 1.8.

To get your score for the game-playing factor (ludis), divide your total for statements 21 through 24 by 4. The average for men is 1.9, for women 1.7.

From: Peter Marsh, *Eye to Eye: How People Interact* (Topsfield, MA: Salem House, 1988).

He: You know I can't live without you, Darla. Why do you treat me so mean?

She: Baby, it's in my bones. You know I love you, but I need a little freedom, too. I'm just going out with my pal. I'll be back to give you all my love in a few hours.

He: I can't let you go. I just don't trust you when you say you love me. Who is this friend, anyway?

A **manic** lover is one who is obsessed over the relationship with the other person. The relationship swings wildly between extreme highs and lows. Each of the lovers may have an insatiable need for attention, often fueled by a low self-concept.

UNDERSTANDING DIVERSITY

Jealousy in Many Languages

What makes people jealous? One research team studied the behaviours of people from seven countries to identify activities that arouse this disturbing emotion. They found significant differences across cultures.[39]

Behaviour	Country in Which the Behaviour Has the Strongest Effect in Making Someone Jealous	Country in Which the Behaviour Has the Weakest Effect in Making Someone Jealous
Flirting	Yugoslavia	Hungary
Kissing	Hungary	Yugoslavia
Dancing	Former Soviet Union/Russia	Netherlands
Hugging	Hungary	United States
Sexual Relationship	Former Soviet Union/Russia	Mexico
Sexual Fantasy	Netherlands	Yugoslavia

■ PRAGMA

He: Look, you have two kids, a lousy job, and no husband. I make more money than I know what to do with, I love kids, and I love bungee jumping just as much as you do. Why don't we get married?

She: But I don't love you, Harold. Doesn't that matter?

He: You'll start to love me if you get to know me. Believe me, I'm a great guy.

Pragma is the root word for practical. This kind of relationship works because the partners' personal requirements, personalities, backgrounds, likes, and dislikes are compatible. In some cultures, parents prearrange marriages because of pragmatic concerns, and if the children are lucky, passion develops later on, as the relationship takes its course.

AGAPE

He: I hate you, Mommy! You're always saying I can't do this, I can't do that. It's not fair! I hate you!

She: Well, I can understand why you feel that way about me now. But I still love you. Would you like to come read a story with me instead of throwing those marbles in the toilet? We can cuddle up and maybe you'll feel better.

He: No! I hate you!

She: Well, you let me know when you want me to read to you.

Agape love is based upon a spiritual ideal of love. It involves giving of yourself and expecting nothing in return. The famous passage in 1 Corinthians, Chapter 13 describes this love:

> *Love is patient, love is kind. It does not envy, it does not boast, it is not proud. It is not rude, it is not self-seeking. It is not easily angered, it keeps no record of wrongs. Love does not delight in evil but rejoices with the truth. It always protects, always trusts, always hopes, always perseveres. Love never fails.*[40]

This kind of "pure" love may characterize the relationship between a parent and a child, or the relationship between a spiritual leader and his or her followers.

How Love Develops and Grows

Most relationships do encompass more than one kind of love. And relationships evolve. One based upon storgic love may evolve into an erotic relationship, for example. Several studies have found that men and women have different styles of loving. Men gravitate toward ludic and erotic relationships, whereas women are more likely to be manic, storgic, or pragmatic. Clyde and Susan Hendrick found that most people consider eros, agape, and storge love the most important kind for them.[41] Manic and pragmatic were next in importance, and ludis love was the least important. The Hendricks also report that:

> *men fell in love more easily than women (eros), who were more cautious about entering relationships (pragma). Once involved in a love relationship, men were less likely than women to break it off, and it was easier for women to remain friends after the breakup (storge).*[42]

Passion and love are such highly individual phenomena that we will not presume to teach you a set of skills to cultivate them. We do, however, urge you to keep in mind the skills and principles that we have emphasized throughout the book for initiating and maintaining healthy interpersonal relationships. Become other-oriented by stopping, looking, and listening to your partner. Consider his or her feelings, and try to decentre and empathize. Understand how we develop relationships through conversation. Also be mindful of the typical patterns that most meaningful relationships follow. In general, the ability to develop loving relationships with others requires sensitivity to their unique needs and personalities.

RECAP	Types of Love
EROS	Sexual, erotic love based upon the pursuit of beauty and pleasure.
LUDIS	Playful, game-playing love based upon immediate gratification and enjoyment.
STORGE	Solid love of friendship based upon trust and caring.
MANIA	Obsessive love driven by the mutual needs of both partners.
PRAGMA	Practical love based upon mutual benefits for both partners.
AGAPE	Selfless love based upon giving of oneself for others.

Summary

Friends are an important source of help and comfort in times of stress. They also make life more enjoyable even when all is well and we simply seek the joy of companionship. Friends are people we like and with whom we have a relationship over time, based upon our own choices. Through both verbal, and especially, nonverbal communication, we express interest in our friends.

We develop friendships because we need to develop close relationships with others. It is a basic need. Friendships offer emotional support and even affect our physical health. Friends also enhance our self-esteem.

Friendships, like all interpersonal relationships, operate within certain rules and culturally learned expectations. Some of the most important friendship rules include the following: respecting the other's privacy; keeping confidences; maintaining eye contact when speaking; not criticizing a friend in front of other people; not forcing unwanted sexual activity; repaying debts and favours; standing up for the other person even when they are not present; sharing good news; and addressing the person by his or her first name.

Friendships evolve over time and develop in stages. Not all of your friends are good friends. Some you would probably classify as acquaintances, others as casual friends, and a smaller group as close friends. Intimacy is one of the key factors that determines whether someone is merely an acquaintance or a close friend.

Friendships differ in importance at various stages in your life. Childhood friendships develop in intimacy and intensity through a series of stages. At around the age of twelve, family relationships often become less important, and adolescent friendships become more intense. Adult friendships often focus first on the selection of a life mate, which may supplant other relationships. Other reasons for the dissolution of adult friendships include physical separation; new friends replacing old; and developing a dislike for a friend's behaviour. Adult friendships can have a negative affect upon a couple if one partner believes friendships with others are taking the place of an intimate relationship at home. As you age you continue to develop friendships, but there is evidence that the elderly value old friends best. Older adults appear to form fewer new friendships and to have a smaller network of friends, yet the friends that the elderly have are very important to them.

There is no list of do's and don'ts that will help you win friends and influence others. Yet there are four principles that may help you understand how to gain and maintain friendships. First, recognize, select, and make the most of your opportunities to make friends. Second, develop skills for encouraging others to be your friend. Conversational skills are important for both establishing and maintaining friendships. Third, try to understand how friendships evolve and grow. And, finally, knowing skills for repairing relationships can help to keep a relationship strong. Knowing and avoiding communication patterns that lead to the loss of friendship can also help you maintain your friendships.

There are important differences between friendship and love relationships. All loving relationships, including those with close friends, involve intimacy and commitment. But only romantic relationships involve passion. Our closest relationships are often romantic ones, but some people feel closer to their friends. Many studies define six categories of love: eros, or erotic love, ludis, or playful love, storge, the love of a friend, mania, obsessive love, pragma, practical love, and agape, selfless love. Most relationships encompass more than one of these categories.

For Discussion and Review

■ FOCUS ON COMPREHENSION

1. Why do we develop friendships?

2. What are three types of friendships, and how are they different from one another?

3. What are the attributes of friendships at different stages in life (e.g., during childhood, adolescence, adulthood, and old age)?

4. What are the six types of love, and how would you characterize them?

■ FOCUS ON CRITICAL THINKING

5. Bob has difficulty making friends. He is interested in outdoor activities and is a good student, but he struggles to find others who share his interests. What suggestions would you give Bob for capitalizing on "friendship opportunities"?

6. Allyce is a single mother with two children. In addition to working part-time as a lawyer, she volunteers at the AIDS Centre in her community to help victims. Last year she anonymously donated one thousand dollars for AIDS research. Madeleine is a caterer. Each year her friend Louise asks her to set up a table at a benefit party for the Junior League and serve each patron a free helping of Madeleine's Famous Mock Turtle Soup. Madeleine always obliges. How would you characterize Allyce's behaviour? How about Madeleine's? What are the differences and similarities between the kinds of love they offer?

7. What type of love is illustrated in the story about Damon and Pythias presented on page 406?

■ FOCUS ON ETHICS

8. Is it ethical to consciously use strategies to cultivate a friendship? Shouldn't friendships develop naturally rather than by design? Explain your answer.

9. You are at a party and you overhear a group making negative comments about one of your best friends. They are not talking to you, but you hear them. Should you intervene and stick up for your friend or just ignore them?

10. Your best friend asks you to listen to her speech before she gives it to her speech class because you are a communication major and excel in public speaking. You

V   DEVELOPING RELATIONSHIPS

hear her speech, and it is awful. She, however, thinks she has an excellent speech. Any criticism of her performance would hurt her feelings. How honest should you be in helping your friend improve her speech?

11. You learn that your best friend is cheating on his or her mate. You are also good friends with your best friend's mate. Should you mind your own business (MYOB) or tell your friend's mate what you know?

For Your Journal

1. Write your own definition of friendship. Select three of your good friends and discuss how their behaviour illustrates your definition. What forms of support that your friends provide do you value most?

2. Rank order the list of friendship rules on page 408, based upon your own preferences. Add any other behaviours that are important to you and your friendships.

3. Think of two people you love. Looking at the six types of love discussed on pages 423-427, identify the kind of love that best describes the relationship you have with each person. Provide examples to support your choices.

4. Consider someone whom you have loved or currently love. Identify the interpersonal skills that were most important in initiating and escalating the love relationship. You can review other chapters in this text as you formulate your answer.

Learning with Others

1. *Agree-Disagree Statements about Relationships:* Read each of the statements below and indicate whether you agree or disagree. After you have made your individual response, work with a group of your classmates and try to reach complete agreement on each item. If agreement isn't possible, you may change the wording so that you all either agree with the item or disagree with it. Use this activity as a chance to compare your attitudes and assumptions about relationships with those of others in your class.

_____ 1. Loving is based mostly on giving.

_____ 2. The best way to love in a marriage is to care more for your partner than you care for yourself.

_____ 3. People who become too involved in their love relationships and give too much of themselves will probably feel empty.

_____ 4. I want a girl/boy just like the girl/boy who married dear old Dad/Mom.

_____ 5. Marriages work best if both partners are totally honest with one another.

_____ 6. Familiarity breeds contempt.

_____ 7. No one relationship is really irreplaceable. An emotionally healthy person who loses a loved one will find a replacement.

_____ 8. "Give until it hurts" is the best philosophy upon which to build a marriage.

_____ 9. Mature love can overcome all obstacles in any relationship.

_____ 10. Some people don't need people and will never develop intimacy with another person.

2. The Rules of Friendship

In this chapter we talked about friendship rules. Make a list of the rules that operate in your friendships and share them with others in class. Note rules that you and several of your classmates have in common.

3. Acts of Love

Working in small groups, develop a skit that includes dialogue to illustrate one of the six kinds of love discussed in this chapter: eros, ludis, storge, mania, pragma, and agape. Perform your skit for the class without telling your classmates which type of love your group is illustrating; see if your classmates can correctly identify the type.

4. Metaphors of Love[44]

Think of several people whom you love; not only romantic partners, but also family and friends. Then think of a metaphor that describes each of these love relationships. For example, a roller coaster, a chess game, a jet plane, a car stuck in traffic, a sunset, a sunrise. Share your metaphors with others. Identify which of the six kinds of love you feel in each relationship.

NEED FOR INCLUSION: The need to be included and to include others in group activities.

NEED FOR CONTROL: The interpersonal need for some degree of dominion in our relationships as well as the need to be controlled.

NEED FOR AFFECTION: The need to give and receive love, support, warmth, and intimacy.

INTIMACY: The degree of closeness we feel with another person.

EROS LOVE: Sexual, erotic love based upon the pursuit of physical beauty and pleasure.

LUDIS LOVE: Playful, game-playing love based upon the enjoyment of others.

STORGE LOVE: Solid love of friendship based upon trust and caring.

MANIA LOVE: Obsessive love driven by mutual needs.

PRAGMA LOVE: Practical love based upon mutual benefits.

AGAPE LOVE: Selfless love based upon giving of yourself for others.

Relating to Colleagues

After studying this chapter, you should be able to:

1. List and describe principles of upward, downward, horizontal, and outward communication.

2. Compare and contrast five different leadership styles.

3. Identify skills that enhance leadership and followership ability.

4. Discuss four strategies for preparing for an effective job interview.

5. Describe three strategies for interviewing others for a job.

6. Understand how to give and receive feedback during a performance review.

7. List and describe eight characteristics of an effective team.

8. Identify skills, tools, and steps for solving problems in teams.

9. Describe the role and effects of technology upon interpersonal relationships in the workplace.

lthough you may purchase a Lotto 649 ticket each week with dogged optimism, chances are that you will continue to have to earn your living. In fact, although a forty-hour work week is allegedly the norm, many people work considerably more than eight hours a day, five days a week. If you are typical, you will spend more than one-third of your adult life working with other people. Even with today's greater use of fax machines, computers, and teleconferencing, most of your working hours will involve face-to-face interpersonal contact with others. Review the graphs on page 437, which list the twelve most frequent jobs held by Canadian men and women. For most of these jobs, it would be difficult to imagine success and happiness without mastering the basics of sound interpersonal communication skills. The quality of the relationships you establish with your co-workers and customers is directly related to your ability to communicate effectively with them.

In this chapter we will examine research conclusions about relationships in the workplace. We will see how communication flows up, down, horizontally, and out. We will examine principles and skills for leading and following. We will also review basic communication skills for job interviews and giving and receiving performance interviews. And we will present team communication skills to help you work effectively with others in groups. Finally, in today's world, much of the communicating we do with others on the job is via fax, phone, or computer messages. We will conclude the chapter by providing some tips for making the most of your interactions with others when your messages are mediated by technology.

With lobster fishing being a clear exception, the success of most jobs is dependent on successful interpersonal communication skills. Courtesy Tourism Nova Scotia.

The Importance of Relationships with Colleagues

Although some of our work-related problems result from such things as a broken copy machine or an uncooperative computer, most of the problems that keep us up nights involve issues or decisions about others. One researcher estimated that 98 percent of the problems that we worry about at work are "people problems."[1] Whether this statistic is accurate or not, it is clear that "people skills" are important.

Surveys of employers have sought to answer the question: what are the most important skills people need to be successful on the job? The results of these research efforts are dramatically consistent. The number one skill you need to perform your job well, according to the experts and practitioners, is an ability to communicate effectively with others.[2] You get your job through a face-to-face interview. You keep your job based upon your ability to do

Table 14.1

Factors Most Important in Helping Graduating College Students Obtain Employment[3]

Rank/Order	Factors/Skills Evaluated
1	Oral (speaking) communication
2	Listening ability
3	Enthusiasm
4	Written communication skills
5	Technical competence
6	Appearance
7	Poise
8	Work experience
9	Résumé
10	Specific degree held
11	Grade point average
12	Part-time summer employment
13	Accreditation of program
14	Leadership in campus/community activities
15	Participation in campus/community activities
16	Recommendations
17	School attended

the work, which usually involves a large measure of interpersonal interaction. One study specifically asked employers to identify the most important factors in helping graduating college students obtain employment. The number one skill: speaking.[4] The number two skill: listening. The entire list of important factors is presented in Table 14.1. These survey results suggest that interpersonal communication skills are more highly valued, more cherished, in fact, than your grade point average, the specific degree you hold, or the school you attended.

The higher you go in an organization, the more your job involves communicating with others. One researcher who observed chief executive officers for five weeks found that managers spend most of their time communicating with others. Here are the specific activities and corresponding percentages of time they devote to each:[5]

Attending scheduled meetings	59%
Handling mail and memos	22%
Attending unscheduled meetings	10%
Talking on the phone	6%
Visiting others	3%

In all, managers spend almost 80% of their day communicating orally with others.

Review Table 14.2, which lists the twelve most frequent jobs held by Canadian men and women. For most of these jobs, it would be difficult to imagine success and happiness without mastering the basics of sound interpersonal communication skills.

V   DEVELOPING RELATIONSHIPS

Twelve Most Frequent Jobs for Canadian Women, 1991

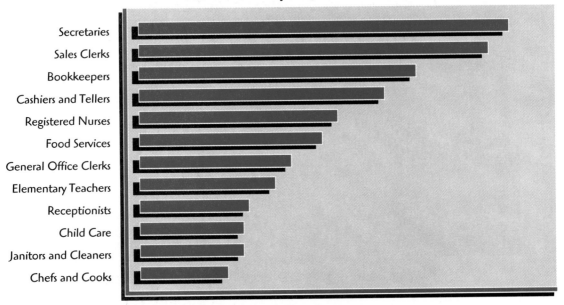

- Secretaries
- Sales Clerks
- Bookkeepers
- Cashiers and Tellers
- Registered Nurses
- Food Services
- General Office Clerks
- Elementary Teachers
- Receptionists
- Child Care
- Janitors and Cleaners
- Chefs and Cooks

Twelve Most Frequent Jobs for Canadian Men, 1991

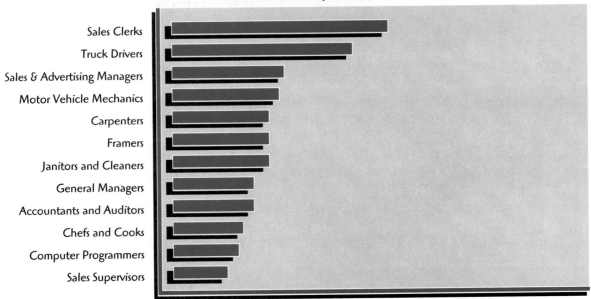

- Sales Clerks
- Truck Drivers
- Sales & Advertising Managers
- Motor Vehicle Mechanics
- Carpenters
- Framers
- Janitors and Cleaners
- General Managers
- Accountants and Auditors
- Chefs and Cooks
- Computer Programmers
- Sales Supervisors

From: *The Daily*, March 2, 1993, Ottawa: Statistics Canada, Cat. # 96-304E.

Charles Redding, a pioneer in teaching and research about communication in organizations, recommends the following bare minimum competencies for anyone who manages others:[6]

1. Be an effective speaker and listener.

2. Possess the ability to be an empathic listener and effective reader.

3. Have an understanding of how corporate decisions are made.

4. Identify the communication roles of both superiors and subordinates.

5. Have an understanding of the communication policies and programs of an organization.

6. Develop a knowledge of how to communicate in an organization using various media and methods (such as computers, public speaking, and memos).

Working with Others in Organizations

In most organizations, working is communicating; communicating is working. Understanding the role and function of your communication with others can help you get your job done well and efficiently. Researchers who study how communication flows in the workplace perceive four directions: upward, downward, horizontal, and outward. We'll consider the function of each.

Upward Communication: Talking with Your Boss

"Please place your suggestions in the suggestion box," announces the boss. The suggestion box is the symbol for upward communication. **Upward communication** involves the flow of communication from subordinates up to superiors. The only person in an organization who does not communicate upward is the boss, president, or chief executive officer (CEO). And even those individuals usually answer to a governing board or to stockholders. Although today's organizational emphasis on quality encourages communication from lower levels to higher levels, effective upward communication is still far from the norm. Many employees fear that their candid comments will not be well received. Others may wonder, "Why bother?" If managers offer no incentive for sharing information up the line, it is unlikely that their subordinates will make the effort. If a supervisor stays holed up in an office away from his or her employees, opportunities for sharing ideas will be limited. Remember the proximity hypothesis described in Chapter 8? We are more likely to talk with those people who are physically close to us.

If there is little upward communication, the organization may be in a precarious situation. Those lower down in the organization are often the ones who make contact with the customer, make the product, or work most closely with the development and delivery of the product or service; they hear feedback about the product's virtues and problems. If supervisors remain unaware of these problems, productivity or quality may suffer. In addition, if employees have no opportunities to share problems and complaints with their boss, their frustration level may be dangerously high. Upward communication helps managers to deal quickly with problems and to hear suggestions for improving processes and procedures.

A popular Broadway show called "How to Succeed in Business Without Really Trying" suggests that you can get ahead by manipulating your boss. Although we do not encourage you to try this approach, we do suggest that developing a positive relationship with your supervisor can help you succeed. One pair of researchers suggest that subordinates can "manage up" by being sensitive to the needs of supervisors.[7] If you know what your boss's most important goals are, along with his or her strengths, weaknesses, and preferred working style, you will be in a good position to establish a more meaningful relationship that will benefit both of you.

If you are a manager yourself, encourage your subordinates to share both good news and bad. Be visible and cultivate their trust by developing a system that elicits feedback and comments. Use a suggestion box (real or electronic), informal discussions, or more formal meetings and presentations. Making time for these exchanges will pay off in the long run.

Downward Communication: Talking with Your Subordinates

When the dean of your college tells your department chair that a course has to be canceled because of low enrollment, the department chair tells your instructor, and your instructor tells you, you have experienced downward communication. **Downward communication** is the flow of information from those higher up in an organization to those of lower rank. It can happen via memo, newsletters, posters, video, or, of course, face-to-face. Most downward communication consists of instruction about how to do a job, rationales for doing things, statements about organizational policies and procedures, feedback about job performance, and information that helps develop the mission or vision of the organization.[8]

What is the best way to communicate with employees—in writing or face-to-face? It depends upon the situation. Often the best method is oral, with a written follow-up. Table 14.3 suggests both effective and ineffective ways to communicate various categories of information to employees. In all of these situations, the best managers take care to develop and send ethical, other-oriented messages. Then they follow up to ensure that the receiver understood the message, and that it achieved its intended effect. Managers need to be especially other-oriented when they are sharing sensitive information or broaching personal topics. The article "Dealing with an Employee's Hygiene Problem" on page 441 provides tips about how to discuss a delicate personal problem without wounding the person's ego.

At the opposite end of the spectrum, the worst managers indulge in an egocentric abuse of the legitimate power that accompanies their rank within an organization. Sexual harassment, which often takes place through downward communication channels, appears to be a growing problem in the workplace. In a 1991 survey of 1,500 Canadians, 37 percent of the women indicated that they had personally experienced what they considered to be sexual harassment in the workplace. More than one-third of the women surveyed indicated that they thought if they reported sexual harassment, people at their work would consider it an over-reaction and an unnecessary complaint.[9]

There are two types of harassment. The first type is **quid pro quo**, which translates from Latin as, "you do something for me and I'll do something for you." A supervisor who says or implies, "Have sex with me or your job is in jeopardy" or "If you want the promotion you should have sex with me," is obviously using his or her power as a boss to trade sex for something the employee wants.

Table 14.3

Most Effective versus Least Effective Methods for Communicating with Employees in Ten Different Situations

Situation	Most Effective	Least Effective
1. Communicating information requiring immediate employee action	Oral followed by written	Written only
2. Communicating information requiring future employee action	Written only	Oral only
3. Communicating information of a general nature	Written only	Oral only
4. Communicating a company directive or order	Oral followed by written	Oral only
5. Communicating information on an important company policy change	Oral followed by written	Oral only
6. Communicating with your immediate supervisor about work progress	Oral followed by written	Oral only
7. Promoting a safety campaign	Oral followed by written	Oral only
8. Commending an employee for noteworthy work	Oral followed by written	Written only
9. Reprimanding an employee for work deficiency	Oral only	Written only
10. Settling a dispute among employees about a work problem	Oral only	Written only

From: D. A. Level, Jr., "Communication Effectiveness: Method and Situation," *The Journal of Business Communication*, 10 (Fall 1972), 19–25.

The second type of harassment involves creating a **hostile environment**, in which an employee feels his or her rights are being violated because of working conditions or offensive behaviour on the part of other workers. Telling lewd or obscene stories or jokes about members of the opposite sex, using degrading terms to describe women or men, or displaying risqué photographs of nude or seminude people can contribute to a hostile working environment. A supervisor who either creates, or fails to change, work situations that are threatening to a subordinate, is a party to sexual harassment. Jokes are not innocent and pictures are not "all in fun" if they make an employee feel degraded. Supervisors must adopt an other-oriented approach with respect to this issue; it is the receiver, not the sender, of the message who determines whether the behaviour is hostile. Court cases have been won by defendants who were able to prove that a supervisor tolerated a hostile work environment, even if the supervisor did not directly participate in the offensive behaviour. Wise supervisors do not wait for a problem to occur. They take a proactive approach, offering all workers seminars on how to avoid engaging in sexually offensive behaviour and explicitly discussing what workers should do if they become the victims of sexual harassment.

Dealing with an Employee's Hygiene Problem

Having to tell an employee that her breath or his body odor is offensive may be one of the most awkward situations in a manager's career. Yet sometimes it's essential to take action, not only for the comfort of co-workers but for the employee's future as well. Start with the assumption that the offender is not aware of the problem. First try a subtle suggestion: Offer breath mints and remark on how much they help you after an aromatic lunch, or mention how crucial a morning shower is to getting you going every day. If there's no noticeable improvement within a few days, however, be more direct. Frame the problem as an obstacle to the person's progress. If he accepts the advice, drop the matter. If he offers a reasonable excuse, be understanding but press for immediate action. If he gets angry or defensive, make it clear that this concerns the company and other employees. Underscore that careful grooming is part of everyone's job description.

ICEBREAKER There are times when personal matters can hinder our careers. Maybe it shouldn't be that way, but it is. And because that's the case, I've got to tell you that you have a problem: bad breath [or body odour].

GETS ANGRY OR DEFENSIVE What? Are you suggesting I smell? No one has ever said anything like that to me. This is just a way to humiliate me, isn't it?

ACCEPTS THE CRITICISM Oh, I'm so embarrassed. I never realized . . . I'm sorry. I'll take care of it right away.

OFFERS EXCUSE I've been having extensive dental work done. Or: I've been taking a prescription and was told this might be a side effect.

MAKE COMMON CAUSE Look, this is embarrassing for us both. I'm not trying to put you down—this is a problem that was brought to my attention, and it's correctable. We've all got to work together comfortably, even if it means making a few adjustments.

REASSURE THE EMPLOYEE Don't be embarrassed—we all have our shortcomings, and this is easier than most to correct. There's no need to apologize.

SUGGEST PROFESSIONAL HELP I thought it must be something like that. Maybe you could give your dentist [or doctor] a call and ask for advice on how to counteract this. Or switch medications, if it doesn't interfere with the treatment.

WRAP-UP I'm glad we've been able to deal with this. Let's put the whole matter behind us now and move on.

From: Stephen M. Pollan and Mark Levine, *Working Woman*, Sept. 1994, 69.

What Is Sexual Harassment?

Read each of the following situations and write an A in the blank if you agree that the situation depicts some form of sexual harassment, or D if you disagree. Share your answers with your classmates and discuss those situations over which you disagree. For those situations that everyone marked with an A, discuss whether the harassment is quid pro quo or whether it relates to a hostile environment.

_____ 1. Marcia is wearing a low-cut blouse and a miniskirt; a male co-worker whistles at her as she is walking down the hall. The male co-worker is guilty of sexual harassment.

_____ 2. Susan is the branch manager of an insurance firm. She asks one of her employees, Steve, to stay after work and discuss some work-related ideas with her. When Steve arrives, the lights are dimmed, the door is locked, Susan offers Steve a glass of wine, and she asks Steve to sit next to her on the couch. Susan is guilty of sexual harassment.

_____ 3. Jed, Lee, and Craig usually meet for lunch in the company cafeteria. They like to tell each other sexually explicit jokes that often portray women as sex objects. Cheryl overhears the jokes and complains to her supervisor. Jed, Lee, and Craig are guilty of sexual harassment.

_____ 4. Manny is a college professor who has a *Playboy* calendar displayed in his office. He requires all of his students to visit him in his office for a private tutorial session in each of his classes. Manny is guilty of sexual harassment.

_____ 5. Cathy, Manny's department chair, has received several complaints from female students about the calendar that Manny displays on his wall. She has not asked Manny to remove the calendar. Cathy is guilty of sexual harassment.

_____ 6. At the weekly staff meeting several of the male workers secretly rate their female co-workers on a scale from 1 to 10 in terms of their physical attractiveness and then compare notes after the meeting. The supervisor knows this occurs but does not say anything about it. The supervisor is guilty of creating a hostile work environment.

_____ 7. Barbara has left Brian several notes asking him for a date. Brian keeps refusing Barbara's requests. Now Barbara sends him E-mail messages about three times each week asking Brian for a date. Brian asks Barbara to stop sending him messages, but she persists. Barbara is guilty of sexual harassment.

Horizontal Communication: Talking with Your Colleagues

You poke your head into your co-worker's office and say, "Did you hear about the possible merger between Byteware and Datamass?" Or while you are tossing a crust at the Pizza Palace, one of your fellow workers asks how much pepperoni to put on a Super Duper Supreme. Both situations illustrate horizontal communication. **Horizontal communication** refers to communication among co-workers at the same level within an organization. In larger organizations you may talk with other workers in different departments or divisions who perform similar jobs at a similar level; that, too, is horizontal communication. Most often you communicate with your colleagues to coordinate job tasks, share plans and information, solve problems, make sure you understand job procedures, manage conflict, or to get a bit of emotional support on the job.[10]

"I Heard It Through the Grapevine," a popular song from the 1960s, describes the way gossip travels among friends. Messages travel through the workplace the same way. Grapevine messages tend to circulate within groups and departments rather than across departmental lines. One research team found that information travels quickly through the organizational grapevine, and that it is also accurate from 75 to 90 percent of the time.[11] But errors do creep into these messages; details get lost and embellishments are added, much as when children play "Whisper Around the World."

Although grapevine errors can cause problems for an organization, most continue to encourage co-worker communication because it enhances teamwork and allows the work group to develop a certain degree of independence. Some organizations even try to formalize it by forming *quality circles*, or groups of employees who meet together on a regular basis. These groups usually talk about such issues as how to improve the quality of services or products, reduce mistakes, lower costs, improve safety, or develop better ways of working together. This active participation in the work process encourages workers to do a better job. Moreover, the training they receive to participate in these groups—in group problem solving, decision-making skills, listening, relating, speaking, and managing conflict—applies to other areas of their work as well.

Outward Communication: Talking with Your Customers

"Attention, K-Mart shoppers: submarine sandwiches are now a blue light special, on sale for one dollar each for the next fifteen minutes." This is one kind of communication with customers. But in addition to just pitching to their customers, today's organizations are also asking customers what they think about the quality of the goods and services the organization produces. Increasingly, successful organizations are those that are other-oriented; they focus on the needs of those they serve through **outward communication**. They are spending time and money to find out what the *customer* perceives as quality, rather than relying solely upon the judgments of their corporate executives. And they are training their staffs to develop more empathy, better listening skills, and more awareness of nonverbal messages from customers.

Outward Communication

When a high-tech icon communicates to the financial world, his emotional expression is key.

One of the best gauges of the relative health of Kanata-based Newbridge Networks Corp. is the mood of its mercurial founder and chairman, Terry Matthews.

When his company's finances or share prices are weak, Matthews presents a sullen, uncommunicative face to the world. But when business is looking up and financial analysts are finally becoming convinced Newbridge is on the right track, Matthews becomes an expansive, mischievous bundle of energy.

For months now, Matthews has treated colleagues and competitors alike to the sunnier side of his complex personality. He can be found on more public podiums and no longer loses patience when asked less-than-intelligent questions. His inner confidence, always high, is reaching flood tide.

James Bagnall, *Ottawa Citizen*, Tues., June 4, 1996, p. A1.

RECAP **Communication Flow Within an Organization**

Flow	Definition
Upward Communication	Communication from subordinates to superiors
Downward Communication	Communication from superiors to subordinates
Horizontal Communication	Communication among co-workers of similar rank
Outward Communication	Communication to those outside the organization

Working with Leaders and Followers

Leadership is behaviour that influences, guides, controls, or inspires others to take action. Former U.S. Secretary of State Henry Kissinger said the task of the

V   DEVELOPING RELATIONSHIPS

leader is "to get people from where they are to where they have not been." And the Emperor Napoleon claimed that "There are no bad soldiers, only bad officers." In the workplace, leaders have a high degree of responsibility; they make more money, have larger offices, and enjoy more special privileges than their subordinates. Researchers have found that they behave differently in groups as well. They talk more, have more influence, and take on more responsibility than lower-status employees.[12] When we say that some people are "born leaders," we mean that their background and personality make it easy for them to assume these behaviours. Other people feel uncomfortable in leadership roles and genuinely prefer to be followers. But in certain situations, even "born followers" may be called upon to lead. No matter which role you usually play, the discoveries of researchers who have studied leadership approaches and communication styles can provide you with options if you are asked to become a leader in your workplace.[13]

Approaches to Leadership

Studies show that some leaders are **task-oriented**; they initiate work, provide information, summarize the progress of the workers, develop plans, and help to coordinate all aspects of achieving a goal. Other leaders are more **relationship-oriented**; they encourage others, compliment or praise good work, and tell jokes to help release tension and manage conflict. The most effective leaders are adept at directing both the task and the relationship functions of a group.

Both task-oriented and relationship-oriented leaders may use different methods to influence others. **Authoritarian leaders** assume primary responsibility for making decisions and giving orders; they seek to control others. Although this leadership style is efficient, especially during a crisis, most workers prefer **democratic leaders**, who consult with workers rather than issue edicts and orders. **Laissez-faire leaders** are even more laid back. They assume the group has more information and skill than they do as leaders, so they provide very little, if any, direction. **Situational leaders** respond to the conditions under which they must work.[14]

As the Understanding Diversity box on page 446 points out, situational leadership may be the most effective approach for both men and women in the workplace. No single style works well in every situation. If a leader is well liked and enjoys the support of the work group, he or she has a wide range of options in leadership style. If the group is attempting to tackle a highly structured task (there is one best way to solve the problem), such as putting the parts together to build a lawn mower, a task-oriented approach that is fairly authoritarian might work best. However, if the group is trying to decide among three well-qualified candidates to fill a job vacancy, the leader might take a more democratic, relationship-oriented approach. In general, the more structured the task, the more useful is a task-oriented approach. This approach is also useful for unstructured tasks if the leader does not get along well with the group. Table 14.4 provides some examples of suitable approaches for different tasks.

He Said, She Said: Gender Styles Differ at Work

So you think you're bilingual, do you? You say you speak English and French, or Chinese or German.

Impressive, but not good enough—not in today's workplace anyway. To be truly successful in the '90s, you also must be fluent in Femalespeak and Malespeak.

Conversation is rife with ritual, according to Deborah Tannen, author of *You Just Don't Understand* and *Talking From 9 to 5*. And men and women's conversational rituals often clash, leading to misinterpretation and, in the worst cases, hindering women's progress up the male-dominated corporate ladder.

On page after page in her latest tome, Tannen reiterates her theme: Both conversational styles—men tend to be direct, blunt; women indirect and vague—are valid. Either style can work well with others who share that style. But neither works well in every situation.

Tannen repeatedly pleads for both sexes to understand each other's style and to develop flexibility within those styles.

Men and women have very definite expectations of how members of their own sex should behave, Tannen writes.

Studies show that "individuals of both sexes who departed from the norms for their own sex were viewed negatively by subordinates of the same sex," she says.

In one study, "a male manager whose style approximated those of the women was seen as 'fairly meek' and 'weak' by men who worked for him, though he was highly praised by women subordinates," Tannen writes.

Conversely, or perversely, women managers whose style was more like those of the men in that study were criticized by female subordinates who saw them as cold and haughty.

What's a person to do?

Adapt to your audience, Tannen and others say.

For Moira Jamieson, a business consultant, the adapting has taken the form of becoming more comfy with Femalespeak, since Malespeak is her natural style.

"One of the comments I've received throughout my life is that I'm blunt, I'm direct, I'm domineering like a man," says Jamieson, 39. "For this reason, I've had great relationships with men."

But not so great with women.

"Most women find me too pushy, assertive, forceful," she says. "On several occasions, I've been called a bitch for just being blunt."

So Jamieson is modifying her style.

"It takes a great deal of conscious effort," she says. "I think about things for a couple days before I know I'll have to say them."

RECAP — Leadership Approaches

Approach	Assumption
Task-Oriented	Focuses on initiating work, providing information, and setting the task to be accomplished.
Relationship-Oriented	Focuses on encouraging others and maintaining a supportive, friendly climate.
Authoritarian	Gives orders, seeks to control others.
Democratic	Consults workers and considers other viewpoints.
Laissez-faire	Provides minimal direction.
Situational	Adapts approach to suit the situation.

'Til Speech Do We Part

According to Deborah Tannen, these are the conversational rituals of women and men:*

Women

- Speaking indirectly, couching criticism and commands in praise or vagueness to avoid causing offence or hurt feelings.

- Maintaining an appearance of equality.

- Playing down their authority to avoid appearing egotistical or "bossy."

- Saying "I'm sorry" not as an apology but as a way of restoring balance to a conversation.

- Feeling discomfort with boasting; downplaying their accomplishments.

- Asking questions to elicit more information

Men

- Speaking directly, whether giving criticism or orders.

- Using banter, teasing, and playful put-downs.

- Striving to maintain a one-up position in any interaction.

- Perceiving "I'm sorry" as putting oneself down or accepting blame.

- Boasting or "blowing their own horn" to highlight their accomplishments.

- Seeking information elsewhere rather than asking questions, for fear of appearing to lack knowledge.

According to Tannen and other researchers, here are some ways to bridge the gap between these different rituals:

Tips for Women

- Be cautious in offering unsolicited advice. Often, when men are given advice, they take it as criticism.

- Don't soften your opinions with qualifiers such as "I think" or "Maybe we should" or "Wouldn't it be a good idea if." Using such qualifiers weakens your message.

- Be wary of going into long explanations. Get to the point quickly—if more explanation is needed, provide it.

Tips for Men

- Don't minimize the importance of women's feelings with statements such as, "Why are you so upset about that?" Women express their feelings more quickly and easily and need to have those feelings taken seriously.

- Don't remain silent and assume a woman will know you're absorbing what she's saying. Ask questions to show that you're interested and listening.

*Note: Remember that these generalizations do not represent *all* men or *all* women.

Excerpted and adapted from: Loraine O'Connell, *Austin American-Statesman*, January 24, 1995.

Enhancing Leadership Skill

Around 700 B.C., Homer warned his Athenian audience to be selective in their attempts to assume control: "You will certainly not be able to take the lead in all things yourself, for to one man a god has given deeds of war, and to another the dance, to another the lyre and song, and in another widesounding Zeus puts a good mind." The first qualification for leadership, as he was trying to tell them, is skill and knowledge about the task at hand. In addition, however, you need the skills necessary to motivate, inspire, and instruct others in their work. Because not all of us are born with these skills, Stephen Covey wrote a book called *Seven Habits of Highly Effective People* to help those of us who want to sharpen our leadership skills. To be successful as a leader, Covey suggests the following:[15]

Table 14.4

Selecting a Leadership Style

Note how different tasks call for different approaches to leading others.

Task	Leadership Style	Rationale
Develop a new food product with a creative team.	Laissez-faire, with a combined task and relationship orientation.	Allows for creative thinking in a nonjudgmental, supportive atmosphere.
Organize a fundraising program to support the new library.	Democratic	All individuals need to feel they can make a contribution.
Escort a group of elementary students on a field trip.	Authoritarian	Strong, directive leadership is important to ensure the safety of the children.
Try out a new recipe at a gourmet club member's home.	Relationship-oriented	The focus is on enjoying each other's company rather than achieving a task-oriented goal.
Supervise a housing construction project.	Task-oriented, with some attention to worker relationships as well.	The key goal is to accomplish the task, but group members' feelings and relationships should not be ignored.

"That was a fine report, Barbara. But since the sexes speak different languages, I probably didn't understand a word of it."

V   DEVELOPING RELATIONSHIPS

1. *Be proactive*: Don't wait until a situation becomes a problem to solve before starting to solve it. Don't simply react to problems, but anticipate them. Don't blame others. Accept responsibility for making decisions yourself.

2. *Begin with the end in mind*: Effective people have a vision of where they are going and what they want to accomplish.

3. *Put first things first:* In Covey's words, "Make sure the main thing is the main thing." Manage your time so that you can manage your life.

4. *Think win/win:* Don't assume someone must lose and someone must win. Approach situations attempting to maximize the benefits for all.

"These pine cones represent scores of potential Scoutrees!"

5. *Seek first to understand, then to be understood.* Listen effectively. Listening skills are essential in being other-oriented.

6. *Synergize:* Synergy means that working together results in more creativity than working alone.

7. *Sharpen the saw*: Take time out to enhance your skills rather than continuing to work with "unsharpened" tools.

As we have already noted, the most effective leaders combine a task orientation with a relationship orientation to perform the following functions:[16]

Task Functions

1. *Initiate* new ideas or approaches to achieving the task.

2. *Provide information*, such as facts, examples, statistics.

3. *Seek information* by asking for facts and other data that can help get the work done.

4. *Seek opinions* and ask for clarification of opinions expressed by others.

5. *Offer opinions* about issues and ideas under consideration.

6. *Elaborate* and amplify the ideas of others.

7. *Evaluate* the advantages and disadvantages of issues, ideas, or proposed solutions.

8. *Energize* and motivate the group to take action and be productive.

Relationship Functions

9. *Encourage* others and offer praise and acceptance of others' ideas.

10. *Harmonize* and mediate disagreements and conflict.

11. *Compromise* and seek ways of finding common ground among group members.

12. *Be a gatekeeper* by encouraging less talkative members to participate and limiting lengthy orations from big talkers.

Despite gains in overall participation in the Canadian work force, women continue to face special social and communication challenges in corporate leadership roles. Less than one percent of Canada's top corporations are led by a woman. Among more than 500 companies surveyed in 1993, only seven held the position of chair, CEO, or president. Furthermore, only 1.6 percent of corporate vice-presidents in Canada are women, suggesting women are not in line to assume the highest positions on the corporate ladder in the near future.[17] The article "It's Lonely Near the Top" on page 451 discusses one woman's experience of isolation in assuming an important leadership role. To counteract their isolation, many professional women join support groups to discuss work-related challenges and strategies.

Enhancing Followership Skill

If you find yourself playing the role of follower in a group, remind yourself that you can still make an enormous contribution. Consider the following:

1. Seek opportunities to provide input and suggestions to leaders. Look for ways to communicate your interest in the goals of the group.

2. Listen well. This skill appears on any list for leaders or followers. Listening effectively and being able to comprehend and evaluate information is an essential followership skill.

3. Provide appropriate feedback. If you are not sure you understand directions from your superior, ask for further clarification.

4. Support your suggestions with evidence rather than with off-the-cuff opinions. Be able to document your suggestions with data, rather than relying only upon emotion-based hunches. Although you should not ignore intuitive thoughts, most supervisors will respond more positively to those ideas you can support with evidence.

5. Don't abandon your ethical principles. If you are being asked to do something that violates your sense of right and wrong, you may need to suggest tactfully that the orders you have been given by your boss are not consistent with your ethical principles. "I was only following orders," or "I was just doing what I was told," usually don't hold up in court as an excuse for violating the law.

COMMUNICATION EXPERIENCE

Working in a group with other classmates, facilitate a discussion on the following topic: How can we improve communication between students and faculty at our college or university? Have different members of the group take turns leading the discussion, deliberately using different leadership styles. One person could use an authoritarian style; another could use a democratic style or a laissez-faire style. Appoint someone in your group to make notes about the group interaction, recording both leader behaviours and group members' responses to their leader. After several members have led the group, discuss which style worked best and why.

It's Lonely Near the Top

Ellen McCoy knows well what it's like to face isolation on the job because of gender. Back in the mid-'80s, she worked in Mobil's trading units in London and New York, high-stress environments where vulgarity often bubbled up with the intensity of a newly tapped gusher. McCoy didn't mind, she says, until "it became clear that the men were playing a kind of game to see how gross they could get before I would object." When she finally took the bait, the men responded by retreating to the corner to talk—and laugh. "It was clear and visible exclusion," says McCoy, who reacted by quietly charting a course to another post at Mobil.

McCoy, 44, says that such blatant exclusion is a thing of the past. Still, as one of a handful of senior women executives at the company, she feels a lingering sense of isolation. She's the only woman on the 12-member executive committee of Mobil's supply-and-trading division, and only seven women hold ranks equal to or higher than hers company wide. So when subtle gender bias comes up, she finds herself struggling with split-second decisions about whether to object. "I'm torn between not wanting to seem like a nag and giving good stewardship on women's issues," she says. "I don't want to be seen as a sensitive person, or to be seen as a one-issue person."

McCoy says she loves working at Mobil's Fairfax, Va., headquarters, where she is the manager of financial and information services for her division. But when she walks into a meeting to find 10 or 12 male peers assembled, she braces herself. "They'll be chatting, patting each other's back. Whatever sport is in season is being discussed," she says. "It's like a language among them—a style that is very male and therefore somewhat exclusionary." McCoy, not a sports fan, usually keeps quiet, "unless some fellow skiers are there," she says. Then, as soon as possible, she steers the talk to business.

McCoy is not alone in this predicament. A 1992 Center for Creative Leadership study found that both female and male executives see a sense of intense scrutiny and isolation as a major barrier to women's advancement. Catalyst, the research organization, estimates that women still account for less than 5 percent of managers at the VP level or above in the largest U.S. companies.

To counter the impression that she's all business, McCoy makes a point of informally socializing with male colleagues individually, making brief visits to their offices or inviting them to lunch. "It's fun," she says. "I really like these people—it's not all calculated." But relationship building can't eliminate the strain she feels in group settings. Longer encounters, like a recent five-day management retreat, can be plain exhausting. "While other people are relaxing and having fun," she says, "I have to make an effort."

Even when talk turns to business, McCoy often feels the stress of being the only woman present, especially when personnel issues are discussed. Occasionally she finds herself shifting uncomfortably in her seat when her colleagues presume that a woman with young children would not be interested in an assignment involving travel, for example. "I say we should ask the woman and let her decide whether she's interested." says McCoy. "I feel like I'm the only one there listening for women's issues." When she feels compelled to "call someone on something," she tries to use humor. "It's clear to me that any exclusions are not personal—my peers have really good intentions, and they feel bad when they do something wrong." Still, she is often left to wonder whether she handled a situation in the best way. "If I leave a meeting thinking, 'Was I eloquent or was I shrill?,' I have no one to bounce things off of."

In her 18-year career at Mobil, she has held many positions at the core of the company's business operations, including scheduling global oil exports, buying crude-oil futures on the commodities market and managing worldwide crude-oil operations and pricing policy. Her current job, though, is a support function that involves accounting and back office services. She is aware that many men also serve temporary stints in such positions to broaden their experience. "So I wonder: Do I have this job for developmental reasons? Or because I got high enough and someone decided it's time to put me in a staff position?"

Working to Get and Keep a Job

All of our discussions about leading and following in the workplace may be hypothetical for you if you have not yet landed your first "real job." But whether you are a recent high school graduate or you have been employed for several years and have come back to school to finish your degree and get a new job, you can apply the skills and principles that we have discussed throughout this book to perform well during job interviews. First, we'll discuss communication issues that relate to being interviewed for a job; then we'll present information to help you if you have the opportunity to interview others.

When You Are Interviewed for a Job

Just as interpersonal relationships develop in stages, so does a job interview proceed through stages before, during, and after the interview. Job interviews, like all of your other interpersonal communications, will be successful if you are other-oriented. The following steps can help you maintain this orientation.

ASSESS YOUR SKILLS AND ABILITIES

Chapter 2 of this book invited you to consider your sense of self as you interact with others. Before you go into an interview, you should consider who you are and identify your skills and talents. Many people select a career because they think they might like to be a lawyer, doctor, or teacher. But rather than thinking about what you want to *be*, we suggest considering what you like to *do*. Ask yourself these questions:

1. What do I like to do in my free time?

2. What are my best skills and talents?

3. What special education and training do I have?

4. What experiences or previous jobs have I had?

In addition to these questions, write down responses to complete this statement: "I can . . . " For example, you might respond: "I can cook, write, relate well to others." List as many answers as possible. Here's another statement to complete: "I have . . . " "I have travelled, worked on a farm, sold magazine subscriptions." Responding to the "I can" and "I have" statements will help you develop an awareness of your skills and experiences to keep on tap when you are asked about them during the interview.

IDENTIFY THE NEEDS OF YOUR EMPLOYER

Armed with an analysis of your skills and abilities, you should now find out how they can fit into the organization. Practice "organizational empathy." Identify what type of work others need to have performed by looking up information in the library about the products and services the organization offers. In addition, rely upon your interpersonal network to find out as much as you can about what the organization does.

■ LISTEN, RESPOND, AND ASK APPROPRIATE QUESTIONS

An **interview** is a structured, planned discussion, usually between two people. During this discussion, you can apply all the skills related to listening, responding, and asking appropriate questions that you learned in Chapter 4. But in addition, you must try to project your enthusiasm and competence. Give special attention to your personal appearance, using an other-oriented perspective. Not all job interviews require that you dress up—if you are interviewing for a position as a maintenance worker, for example, you may not need to wear a suit. But it is always best to dress conservatively so that your clothing does not create "noise" that distracts the interviewer's attention.

One of the best ways to prepare for an interview is to anticipate the interviewer's questions. Also be sure to get a good night's sleep and eat well so that you can stay alert. Long interviews can be physically demanding. Table 14.5 lists typical questions asked during an interview. We don't recommend that you develop canned, rehearsed answers, but it may be helpful to think about possible responses to these questions.

Also be prepared to answer questions about special activities in your background such as military service, vocational training, sports teams, and the like.

Consider the interview an opportunity to ask questions as well as to answer them. Asking questions about an organization is a way to display enthusiasm for the job as well as a means of assessing whether you really want to join the organization. You will want to know the following:

- Will there be any job training for this position?

- What are the opportunities for advancement?

- What is the atmosphere like in the workplace? (You will observe this as well during the interview.)

- What hours do people work?

- Is there flexibility in scheduling the work day?

- When do you anticipate making a decision about this position?

Usually the interviewer will discuss salary and benefits with you during the interview. If this is a preliminary interview, and you may be called back for another, you may want to defer questions about salary and benefits until you know that the organization is seriously considering you for the position.

During the interview, maintain eye contact and speak assertively. The goal in an interview is to project a positive attitude to the interviewer. As motivational speaker Zig Ziglar once noted, "Your attitude, not your aptitude, will determine your altitude."

Table 14.5

Typical Questions and Follow-up Questions for Job Interviews

I. Education

1. Why did you select your major area of study?

2. Why did you select your college/university?

3. If you were starting college again, what would you do differently? Why?

4. What subjects were most interesting? Useful? Why?

5. What subjects were least interesting? Useful? Why?

6. Other than the courses you studied, what is the most important thing you learned from your college experience?

7. How did you finance your college education?

II. Experience

8. What do you see as your strengths as an employee?

9. You say that a strength you have is _____. Give me some indication, perhaps an example, that illustrates this strength.

10. What special skills would you bring to this position?

11. Describe your last few work experiences. Why did you leave each one?

12. What were the best aspects of your last job?

13. What were the worst aspects of your last job?

14. What were some of your achievements in your last job?

15. What were some of your disappointments in your last job?

16. Do you see yourself as a leader/manager of people? Give me an example.

17. What kinds of work situations would you like to avoid? Why?

18. What frustrations have you encountered in your work experience? How have you handled these frustrations?

19. Do you think the progress you made in your last job is representative of your ability? Why or why not?

20. What do you look for in a boss?

21. What areas did your last boss suggest you improve? What did you do to improve?

22. Most employees and bosses have some disagreements. What are some things that you and your boss have disagreed about?

III. Position and Company

23. Why did you select this company?

24. Why did you decide to apply for this particular position?

25. How do you see yourself being qualified for this position?

26. Why should I hire you?

27. Sometimes a work assignment requires frequent travel. How do you react to the prospect of frequent travel?

28. Are you willing to relocate?

IV. Self-Evaluation

29. Tell me a little bit about yourself. Describe yourself.

30. What do you see as your personal strengths? Talent? How do you know that you possess these? Give examples of each.

31. What do you see as your weak points? Areas for improvement? Things you have difficulty doing? What have you done to deal with these?

32. In what areas of work are you most confident?

33. Describe a specific work problem you had. Tell what you did to solve this problem.

34. What traits or skills are most important to being successful? Why? Evaluate yourself in relation to these traits and skills.

35. What do you consider to be your greatest work achievement? Why?

36. What does it mean to you to be a self-starter? Do you see yourself as a self-starter? Explain.

V. Goals

37. Where do you see yourself being in your profession in five years? In ten years? How did you establish these goals? What will you need do to achieve these goals?

38. What are your salary expectations for this position? Starting salary? Salary in five years?

Adapted from: Michael S. Hanna and Gerald L. Wilson. *Communicating in Business and Professional Settings.* New York: McGraw Hill, 1991, 263–265. Used with permission of McGraw-Hill, Inc.

After the interview it is wise to write a brief letter to thank the interviewer and to provide any additional information that he or she requested. You may also want to send a thank you note to others in the organization, such as a secretary or administrative assistant, for helping you arrange the interview. If the interviewer asked for references, make sure you contact your references quickly and ask them to send letters of recommendation to the organization. Expedite this process by providing addressed, stamped envelopes and a copy of your résumé so that they can personalize their letters with specific information.

Is it appropriate to call the person who interviewed you to ask when a decision will be made about hiring someone? Some employers abide by the philosophy: don't call us, we'll call you. But many others would interpret your call as a sign of your interest in the position and a testament to your ability to follow through. You may want to take the direct approach and simply ask your employer toward the end of the interview, "Would it be all right if I called you in a few days to see if you have made a decision or if you need additional information?" If the date on which the interviewer told you a decision would be made passes by, it is probably okay to call and find out whether they've offered the job to someone else and to express your continued interest in the position if it hasn't been filled.

Speaking assertively, maintaining eye contact, and projecting a positive attitude through your posture and facial expression will help you make a good impression during a job interview.

RECAP   **Jop Interview Communication Skills**

Assess your skills and abilities.	Ask yourself "What can I do?" "What have I done?"
Identify the needs of the employer.	Focus on what the employer values and wants.
Listen, respond, ask questions.	Anticipate typical questions; project a positive attitude during the interview.
Follow up after the interview.	Write thank you notes; help your references send meaningful recommendation letters.

When You Interview Others for a Job

Today your primary focus may be on getting a job, but eventually you may find yourself having to interview others for employment. To do this well, you will need to structure the interview, ask appropriate questions, and use effective interpersonal communication skills. It is just as important for you to be other-oriented as it is for the applicant.

An interview is not a random conversation. Effective interviewers prepare for the interview, considering ways to conduct the session that will put the interviewee at ease, enable both people to obtain the information they need, and allow the interview to conclude on a confirming note.

To prepare for an interview, remember that your first objective is to hire the best person for the job. Review the credentials of the person you are interviewing and consider the specific questions you have for him or her. Select a quiet, private, attractive room to ensure that the prospective employee will have a favourable impression of the organization.

Just as a speech or an essay has a beginning, middle, and end, so does an interview. At the beginning of the interview, establish rapport and develop a positive climate for communication. Don't immediately start firing substantive questions. Engage in small talk; put the interviewee at ease. Provide some background information about the organization and the job, but don't talk too long. If you talk for ten minutes straight at the start of a thirty-minute interview, you will establish a you listen–I talk format. Interviews should be interactive. Some experts recommend that you talk less than 30 percent of the time when interviewing others. Your goal is to establish a relationship so that you can get your questions answered and learn as much as you can about the style and skill of the interviewee.

When you see that the applicant is ready, ask questions and obtain the information you need to make a decision about him or her. You may want to take notes, but don't take so many that you lose eye contact with the applicant. Use the questions listed earlier in Table 14.5 to plan your queries, but also be flexible enough to pursue other paths of inquiry that the candidate's background suggests.

During the closing part of an interview, give the applicant a chance to ask questions about the organization or about your personal observations as an employee of the organization. Asking, "Is there anything else you'd like to tell me about yourself" is a good signal that you are heading for the close of the interview. Summarize what will happen next. Tell the candidate what next steps he or she should take and the approximate time frame for making a decision. Try to end the interview on a positive note, but don't make the candidate feel like the job is "in the bag" if that is not the case.

■ ASK APPROPRIATE QUESTIONS

The essence of a good interviewing technique involves asking appropriate questions. Questions are like mental can openers; they help you reveal the skills and abilities of the interviewee.[18] There are three basic types of questions to ask during an interview: open questions, closed questions, and probing questions. An **open question** is one that prompts a wide range of possible responses. "Tell me about your key strengths" or "What do you think you would find most challenging about working for Bell Northern Research?" are examples of open questions. You have no specific answer in mind; you want the interviewee to share ideas, information, or opinions.

A **closed question** is one for which there is a limited range of possible answers. "Where were you born?" "How long have you lived in Edmonton?" and "How long did you work at your last job?" are examples of closed questions. If interview time is limited and you want to know specific information, closed questions are effective.

A **probing question** encourages the candidate to provide more information and elaborate on brief answers. It takes a good listener to ask effective probing questions. "Could you tell me a bit more about why you went to school in Halifax?" and "Could you elaborate on your job responsibilities?" are examples of probing questions.

Experienced interviewers often use the *funnel structure* for organizing an interview, starting with open questions followed by increasingly closed ones. They ask probing questions as needed to find out the answers to specific questions. Here's an example of the funnel sequence:

Open question: "What are your key strengths for this job?"

Open question: "What do you know about selling and marketing?"

Open question: "In what areas might you need more education to do this job?"

Closed question: "Did you take any business courses in college?"

Closed question: "What experience have you had in direct sales?"

Closed question: "How much did you make in commissions?"

Some interviewers use an inverted funnel sequence; they ask closed questions first and then end with open ones, using a mix of probing questions to seek more detail when needed. Which sequence works best? It depends upon your objective and how much you already know about the applicant. Asking open questions first is a way to gauge the candidate's communication skills. But if you need specific information before you can ask more general questions, you may need to lead with closed questions.

As an interviewer, you need to be aware that some questions are illegal. For example, the Canadian Human Rights Code (which legislates hiring practices by federal government departments, agencies, crown corporations, Canada Post, chartered banks, national airlines; interprovincial communication, telephone, and communication companies, and any other federally regulated industries) prohibits discrimination in hiring on the basis of:

- race
- national or ethnic origin
- colour
- religion
- sex, including pregnancy or childbirth
- marital status, family status
- pardoned conviction
- physical or mental disability, including dependence on alcohol or drugs
- sexual orientation

■ USE EFFECTIVE INTERPERSONAL COMMUNICATION SKILLS

The most effective interviewers are those who listen actively and respond appropriately to the candidate. Effective listeners are able to glean both details and key characteristics of the candidate; mentally summarizing the candidate's responses can enhance your comprehension. Your ability to establish rapport will depend upon your ability to be other-oriented. Because most interviews are an hour or less, your skill in assessing nonverbal cues is also important. Does the interviewee maintain eye contact and use appropriate facial expressions? Does he or she have distracting mannerisms? Interviews are high-stress situations, but watch for an unusual number of vocal nonfluencies ("and . . . er . . . uh") and other distracting nonverbal cues. Effective interviewers are observant, responsive, and sensitive to the words and unspoken messages of others.

RECAP   **How to Interview Others for a Job**

Structure the interview.	Have a beginning, middle, and end.
Ask appropriate questions.	Ask open, closed, and probing questions.
Use interpersonal skills.	Listen, respond, and relate to the interviewee.

Types of Interview Questions

	Why Use It	Example
Open Question	To prompt a wide range of responses.	"Would you tell me about your strengths?"
	To assess values, opinions, and attitudes.	"What are your interests and hobbies?"
Closed Question	To get straight yes or no answers.	"Do you live in Regina?"
	To force a response.	"How long have you lived in Regina?"
Probing Question	To follow up.	"Tell me more about what you did last summer."
	To get someone to elaborate and talk more.	"Elaborate on why you chose communication as your major."

Performance Review Interviews

After you have worked in a job for some time, you will probably receive a performance review. A **performance review** represents an opportunity for upward and downward communication. During this interview, your supervisor provides feedback about your skills and abilities. This enables you to see how others perceive your effectiveness and to assess whether you are likely to get a promotion or a pink slip. In this interview you can also express your observations about the organization and your desires for the future. Usually a supervisor begins by preparing a written report summarizing your strengths and weaknesses, then meets with you to review it.

Despite the opportunities for growth provided by performance reviews, these opportunities are often lost to poor communication, misunderstandings, and damaged relations between employees and their supervisors. As a result of the growing recognition of these counterproductive results, some organizations are seeking alternatives to the traditional performance reviews. For example, the Public Service Commission of Canada has abandoned the requirement of mandatory performance reviews, and offers Commission employees the option of ongoing, mutual feedback as necessary. For most Canadian employees, however, the formal performance review is still the order of the day, and the following advice may be heeded:

When receiving feedback from a supervisor, the best approach is to listen and gather as much objective information about his or her perceptions as possible. Most performance reviews involve evaluating or rating employees. As we learned in Chapter 6, in an evaluation situation it is easy to become defensive; try to manage your emotions and use the information to your benefit instead.

Key questions to ask when you are receiving feedback include:

1. What do you see as my strengths and accomplishments?

2. What are areas in which I can improve my work?

3. Are my goals consistent with the goals of the organization or department?

4. What new skills do I need to enhance my job performance?

5. What training opportunities exist for me to enhance my job performance?

6. What can I do to enhance my value to the organization or department?

You can also suggest new ways for your supervisor to use your talents or structure your responsibilities.

What is the best way to respond if you disagree with your supervisor's evaluation? Consider the suggestions for managing conflict offered in Chapter 10. Manage your emotions, manage the communication, manage the goals, and then manage the problem. Stay calm and seek specific information or examples that will help you understand why someone has perceived your work differently than you do. Launching into a defence of your skills will only escalate the tension and inhibit effective communication. Instead, use your skills to ask questions and reflect what your supervisor is saying before you develop a response.

Usually you will have an opportunity to provide a written response to the evaluation. Before writing your response, take an honest, objective look at what your supervisor has said. Where you disagree, provide specific evidence or examples to support your position. Otherwise, just saying you don't like the review will do nothing to advance your position.

■ PROVIDING FEEDBACK TO EMPLOYEES

If you are a boss, remember that the purpose of the performance appraisal interview is to share strengths and areas for improvement. Your communication goal is

to provide helpful information. Too much negative feedback may create so much internal "noise" for the employee that he or she will not hear the message. Don't overlook the power of positive feedback in improving performance. As Mark Twain said, "I can live for two months on a good compliment." One research team offers ten suggestions for giving effective feedback to employees:[19]

1. *Make feedback specific rather than general.* "You are 10 percent behind on your sales quota" is a better response than "You just don't seem to be performing well."

2. *Deliver the feedback face-to-face before you present it in writing.* Give the person a chance to respond in a friendly setting.

3. *Present the feedback in a straightforward manner (for North Americans).* Most North Americans want to know what the issues are. Individuals from more high-context cultures (for example, those from China or Japan) may prefer more indirect feedback.

4. *Time the feedback carefully.* Feedback is usually more effective when it is immediate. Sometimes, however, it may be advisable to provide feedback when it will do the most good: just before the employee is ready to write the annual report this year, provide suggestions for improvement based upon the strengths and weaknesses of last year's report.

5. *Focus on behaviour rather than on the worth of a person, especially if the feedback is negative.*

6. *Make the session interactive.* Establish a dialogue with the employee rather than just pronouncing your ideas and opinions.

7. *Be sure your verbal and nonverbal messages are consistent.* Don't say positive things while providing negative nonverbal cues such as no eye contact and fidgeting.

8. *Apply the 80/20 rule.* Spend 80 percent of the time on the 20 percent of the issues that will have the most impact. Focus on what is important. Don't spend excessive time on trivial, less important issues.

9. *Give each issue the proper emphasis.* Don't make less important issues seem earth-shattering. On the other hand, don't trivialize important issues by trying to brush them off as not important.

10. *Make the feedback noncoercive.* Don't threaten. Describe areas of concern, but resist delivering ultimatums. The goal should be to develop an understanding of how to improve rather than to induce fear.

The most effective feedback helps rather than hinders the employee's effectiveness. The article "Co-Workers' Comments Can Help" below notes that comments from peers, as well as a boss, can help improve job proficiency.

Co-Workers' Comments Can Help

No matter how much self-esteem we have, what others say about us matters, if we're normal human beings. The trick is to separate the good from the bad, take in the good, then objectively evaluate anything negative we hear about ourselves.

V DEVELOPING RELATIONSHIPS

"I worked very hard to make myself into a good salesperson," said a friend. "I'm enthusiastic about the products I sell, I'm knowledgeable, I push, but in a soft-spoken way. I know when to back off, and I know how to make people feel good about buying the products and buying them from me.

"Then my sales manager let me know that he's had complaints from the front office that I haven't been making the complete cost picture clear to a lot of my customers. I'd been going away thinking I'd answered all their questions, but when they got their first bills, the front office took a lot of flak, and sometimes customers canceled their orders," she said.

"Now the sales manager tells me I have to go to a selling seminar on my own time and develop a way to make sure customers know exactly what they'll be paying, and when."

Even though her sales manager's timely warning may seem like bad news, it has given this woman a chance to change her ways BEFORE her entire career is jeopardized.

What we hear from co-workers can prove useful, as well. If people who are reliable and kindly disposed toward us say we're not much fun to be around lately, or that they've noticed that we're not smiling anymore, we need to take what they say seriously, and ask questions.

We may need to change our attitudes about our jobs, or make some changes in the way we approach our work.

And if people tell us we're looking tired all the time, we might think of ways to put more rest and relaxation into our schedules, or even seek medical advice.

If a supervisor comments that we always act as if we're the exception to every rule, or that she can't understand what we're trying to prove by the way we approach our work, it may be time to consider how our conduct appears to others.

Do people tell you that:

- You don't play by the rules?

- You're not working with the rest of the team?

- The quality of your work has deteriorated?

- Your work habits are causing problems for others?

- You often act as if you're harassed, tense, or in a bad mood?

- Your personal affairs are getting in the way of your work?

- Your behaviour with clients is unprofessional?

- You display a chip-on-the-shoulder attitude?

- Your work/appearance/office manners are causing problems for your colleagues?

Comments like these are often timely warnings, not put-downs. If they come from supervisors or co-workers you respect and know to be truthful, they're telling you about things that can affect your job and your life.

Your own feelings can be a valuable guide as well. Do you often:

Feel put-upon, or that everyone's against you?

Feel you have to go out of channels to get things done?

Feel unappreciated, isolated, or out of touch?

If you feel continually dissatisfied and defensive about the way you do your job, it may be time to reconsider how you think and operate when you're at work. It may be time to accept the offers of help that are often implicit in the comments of co-workers and supervisors as well.

—NIKI SCOTT, *TIMES–PICAYUNE*, OCTOBER 16, 1994.

Working in Teams

This book focuses on developing one-on-one relationships with others. But as the article on page 466 indicates, more and more businesses are turning to teamwork as a strategy for strengthening workplace effectiveness. When you work with groups or teams, you can use the same types of listening, responding, and conflict management skills to develop effective relationships. Some researchers suggest that you will spend from 30 to 60 percent of your working day in meetings, groups, or teams, or in preparing to work in groups.[20]

Characteristics of Effective Teams

A **team** is a group of individuals organized to work together to achieve a common goal.

Anthropologist Margaret Mead said: "Never doubt that a small group of thoughtful, concerned citizens can change the world. Indeed, it's the only thing that ever has." One pair of researchers spent several years studying effective teams, such as the Dallas Cowboys, McDonald's, and NASA, and concluded that there are eight primary characteristics that they all share:[21]

■ A CLEAR, ELEVATING GOAL

The single most important attribute of an effective team is having a common, well-defined goal that all members of the team value. The goal should raise team members' sights because they consider it important and worthwhile. Winning the Stanley Cup, sending an astronaut into space, or selling more hamburgers than anyone else are all examples of clear, elevating goals.

Good teamwork is no accident. Both in the workplace and on the basketball court, effective teams share clear goals and structures, high standards, a collaborative spirit, and a strong sense of commitment. (NBA Photos)

DEVELOPING RELATIONSHIPS

When Receiving a Performance Review

- Seek clarification of your strengths and weaknesses.

- Ask how you can improve.

- Assess whether your goals are consistent with those of the organization.

- Identify whether you need more training or skills.

- Ask how you can increase your value to the organization.

When Giving a Performance Review

- Be specific.

- Meet face-to-face.

- Be straightforward and honest.

- Offer feedback at the right time.

- Focus on behaviour rather than on the worth of a person.

- Interact rather than lecture.

- Match your verbal and nonverbal messages.

- Spend 80 percent of the time on the 20 percent that will have the most positive effect.

- Give issues appropriate emphasis.

- Don't coerce or threaten.

COMMUNICATION EXPERIENCE

Practicing Performance Interview Skills

Roleplay a performance interview with one of your classmates. One of you should play the role of the employer or supervisor, the other the role of the employee. Select an employment situation that is meaningful to both of you. For example, if both you and your partner have worked at a fast-food restaurant or retail store, held an office job, or worked on a farm, develop a similar work situation with which both of you can identify. Use the following checklist to evaluate the roleplay. Check all of the behaviours that are illustrated in the roleplay. If time permits, switch roles so that each of you plays the roles of both supervisor and employee.

Did the supervisor:

Offer specific rather than general feedback? _____

Present areas for improvement in a clear, straightforward way? _____

Offer feedback at the right times? _____

Focus on behaviour rather than the employee's self-worth? _____

Give the employee time to respond? _____

Keep nonverbal behaviour consistent with verbal behaviour? _____

Focus on important rather than trivial information? _____

Use appropriate verbal and nonverbal emphasis for each issue? _____

Avoid threats and coercion? _____

Did the employee:

Ask what the supervisor perceived as his/her strengths and accomplishments? _____

Ask how his/her work could be improved? _____

Ask whether his/her work goals are perceived to be consistent with those of the organization? _____

Ask if he/she needs new skills to enhance job performance? _____

Use consistent verbal and nonverbal behaviour during the interview? _____

Respond calmly if negative feedback about job performance was offered? _____

A RESULTS-DRIVEN STRUCTURE

If you have ever seen a house built, you know that underneath the exterior bricks and siding is the framework of the home. To be effective, a team also needs a structure, a support system, that holds things in place. A clear division of labour, rules for operating efficiently, and adequate information are critical elements of a team structure. The tasks that the team undertakes should be structured to achieve the team's clear, elevating goal.

COMPETENT TEAM MEMBERS

A competent team member is one that has adequate knowledge, is skilled in achieving the task, and is also willing and eager to get the job done. Teams need adequate training to help them get the job done. They also need training in how to work together as a team. The training should give team members information to do the job, skill to perform the tasks, and inspiration to do their best.

UNIFIED COMMITMENT

Effective teams develop a common bond and a feeling of mutual support and esprit de corps. A unified team means that all team members are willing to work to achieve the clear, elevating goal of the group. The motto "All for one and one for all" characterizes that unity.

A COLLABORATIVE CLIMATE

In Chapter 6 we compared supportive versus defensive approaches to developing effective relationships with others. In a collaborative climate, team members describe rather than evaluate, seek to solve problems rather than control, respond with spontaneity rather than plot strategies, are empathic rather than neutral, seek equality rather than superiority, and state their conclusions provisionally rather than with certainty.

STANDARDS OF EXCELLENCE

A team is more likely to produce quality results if it sets high standards for itself. Last year's Grey Cup champs would probably not have emerged victorious if they had said, "Let's just try to win our division." More than likely, the ultimate prize was in their sights during the entire season. Effective teams set goals that make them stretch in order to achieve their highest potential.

EXTERNAL SUPPORT AND RECOGNITION

Because most workers want to feel appreciated, effective team members are those who recognize and reward success. They celebrate when they win and provide encouragement to one another when they lose. Effective teams also recognize outstanding individual achievement, but they avoid focusing exclusively on any one member. The goal is to help all team members feel supported and appreciated.

V DEVELOPING RELATIONSHIPS

■ PRINCIPLED LEADERSHIP

Teams need effective leaders who are flexible and can adapt to the unique needs and talents of the team. Decision making is usually shared among group members, but during periods of high uncertainty, or during a crisis, the team may need bold, decisive leadership.

RECAP — **Characteristics of Effective Teams**

Characteristics	Example
A clear, elevating goal.	Select a goal that excites the team.
Results-driven structure.	Be organized, with clear role assignments.
Competent team members.	Train team members to be skilled, knowledgeable, and motivated.
Unified commitment.	Develop team cohesiveness.
Collaborative climate.	Encourage team members to support one another.
High standards of excellence.	Settle only for the best results.
External support and recognition.	Celebrate when the team is successful.
Principled leadership.	Develop responsive, well-informed leaders.

Skills for Developing Effective Teams

Just knowing the characteristics of an effective team is not enough to ensure effectiveness. Team members need skills for managing relationships, and a set of problem-solving skills and tools to develop a well-functioning team. The relationship skills they need are those that we emphasize throughout this book for developing other-oriented relationships. The tools for achieving the task include a variety of subtasks that are unique to the organization and the specific job the team wishes to accomplish. The skills a baseball team needs may be quite different from those that a Fortune 500 technology corporation team needs. But both must follow a structured plan for making decisions and solving problems.

■ TEAM RELATIONSHIP SKILLS

Team relationship skills are people skills—those that help maintain team climate and enhance communication: listening and responding; verbal and nonverbal interpretive skills; conflict management skills; skills that foster interaction. Team members should give special consideration to the use of personal space, seating arrangements, and territoriality. They should also develop facilitation skills that help team members manage interaction and provide needed structure for discussions to keep team members on track. Some teams take turns designating one team member as the facilitator for each meeting—to call the meeting to order and help the team stick to the agenda. Other teams may appoint a permanent leader to serve as a verbal gatekeeper. The article "The Lone Ranger as Team Player" on page 466 provides additional tips for working with your teammates.

Tools that team members need to work together include a structured problem-solving approach, strategies for analyzing problems and generating solutions, and methods for comparing pros and cons to evaluate decisions. Each of these tools gives the team the structure it needs to accomplish the team task. For any problem-solving approach, the team's first task is to identify and define the problem, making sure that everyone understands its sources.[22]

The Lone Ranger as Team Player

Like the cowpoke on the lonesome prairie, the image of the corporate superstar, single-handedly riding a project to completion, fuels a favorite myth: Rugged individualism gets the job done.

With North America's steady decline in trade competitiveness, however, many businesses are encouraging their lone rangers to gather round the camp-fire—adapting the Japanese concept of teamwork while preserving the strengths of North American ingenuity. Instead of a herd mentality, the new team setup more closely resembles a jazz ensemble, with group members providing backup while exchanging solos of improvisational creativity.

In its New Product Lab, the Graduate School of Business has championed the new approach, as teams of a dozen or so students work together to solve a problem posed by a corporate client. Although coaches—usually an experienced business executive—are assigned to each team, their purpose is to advise, not lead. Within teams, there is no consistent hierarchy: If leadership roles are assigned, they are on a rotating basis.

There are no rigid protocols for running an NPL group, but a few rules of thumb have emerged to help stimulate the productive tension between team-work and personal initiative.

1. Trust your teammates. Working collaboratively means you have to take a leap of faith, giving others responsibility and trusting them to come through.

2. Strive to make decisions by consensus, not by voting. Over time, team members defeated in earlier votes are likely to reciprocate, even unconsciously, by knocking down others' suggestions. Consensus takes more time, but is far less divisive.

3. Learn to let go of ideas, however cherished. The team will inevitably have to kill ideas as it moves through the creative process. If your own concept is abandoned, don't take it personally. A corollary: Be willing to explore ideas that aren't your own.

4. Encourage unconventional thinking and individual "genius." In most groups, someone emerges whose inspired muse acts as a spark plug, igniting the entire group. While giving attention to such individuals, keep an open mind: A bright idea often sounds "weird" the first time it's uttered.

5. Accept conflict. Contention is to be expected—and even encouraged, since it often helps the team move toward a superior solution. Techniques that foster sharp, productive differences in thinking include asking for evidence when team members state their points of view, encouraging members to take the other side of an issue, and keeping at least one really tough question on each meeting's agenda.

6. Divide and conquer. Two heads are often better than 12. To study specific problems or proposals, create subgroups that meet outside of regularly scheduled full-team meetings.

7. Speak in one voice. Once a consensus has been reached, the team needs to present its ideas in a coherent, unified fashion. In the New Product Labs, a team "editor" is chosen who compiles, sharpens, and condenses information for the client to digest.

—TIM ANDREW OBERMILLER, *UNIVERSITY OF CHICAGO MAGAZINE*

■ ANALYZING THE ISSUES

Next, the team needs to analyze the issues involved in the problem. One tool for teams is the **journalist's six questions** technique.[23] Team members can ask themselves the six questions that every journalism student is taught to answer in the first paragraph of a news story: who, what, when, where, why, and how. Once their analysis is complete, team members can brainstorm to generate possible solutions. **Brainstorming** is a process that involves generating many ideas through free association before you evaluate them. To brainstorm, a team can do the following: (1) identify a specific problem; (2) tell the group to put aside judgments and evaluations; (3) tell the group to identify as many solutions as possible (team members can also write ideas first—hold a period of silent brainstorming—before sharing them with the team); (4) set a time limit for the brainstorming; (5) encourage wild and zany ideas; (6) ask the team to build on the ideas of others; (7) record all ideas; (8) acknowledge all ideas; and (9) evaluate the ideas after sharing all of them.[24]

Another way to generate possibilities is to use the **6M technique**.[25] For any problem or obstacle that they face, the team assesses which of the following issues will help manage it:

■ Manpower (people)—Do you need more or fewer people?

■ Machinery—Do you need equipment?

■ Methods—Do you need to learn techniques to solve the problem?

■ Materials—Do you need things?

■ Money—Do you need dollars?

■ Minutes—Do you need time?

Effective team problem-solving requires careful planning. Meetings should follow a well-planned agenda and have clear-cut goals that team members can examine and agree upon in advance.

Once the team has generated a list of possible solutions using one or both of these techniques, it needs to **analyze the pros and cons** of each one. Perhaps when you want to buy a car or make some other big decision, you write down the pros—the reasons you like the car—on one side of a sheet of paper, and record the cons—the things you do not like—on the other side. By comparing the pros with the cons, you can then make a more rational decision.

Teams can use the same simple technique when considering one or more solutions or options to manage a problem. Pro-and-con analysis helps a team base decisions on rational rather than emotional criteria.

Finally, the team should select a solution, then test and implement it, ensuring that each team member understands his or her role in the plan. Throughout the implementation process, team members should meet and maintain close interpersonal contact to monitor the results and revise the plan if necessary.

■ CONDUCTING MEETINGS

Of course, to use these problem-solving techniques effectively, team members also need to know how to run effective meetings. The first step toward keeping a meeting on track is to develop and use an agenda. Determine what the overarching goal of the meeting is. Do you want to share information, discuss issues, or take action? Next, identify items that you need to discuss in order to achieve the goal. Third, organize your agenda items to achieve the goal. Decide whether you should put high-priority items first, or place less contentious issues first on the agenda, and then address the more challenging issues after the team has reached agreement on others. Don't wait until the meeting to distribute the agenda; send it to other team members in advance so that all can be prepared when the meeting starts.[26]

Team Steps, Tools, and Skills

Problem-Solving Steps	Team Tasks	Team Relationship Skills
1. Define the problem.	Use journalist's six questions. Use 6M analysis. Brainstorm. Establish team goals. Clarify roles and responsibilities.	Listen and respond. Speak clearly. Interpret nonverbal messages. Manage conflict.
2. Analyze the problem.	Gather data. Select criteria. Use the journalist's six questions. Use 6M analysis.	Listen and respond. Speak clearly. Interpret nonverbal messages. Manage conflict.
3. Generate solutions.	Brainstorm.	Listen and respond. Speak clearly. Interpret nonverbal messages. Manage conflict.
4. Select the best solution.	Analyze pros and cons of brain-stormed solutions. Use criteria to help make a decision.	Listen and respond. Speak clearly. Interpret nonverbal messages. Manage conflict.
5. Test and implement the solution.	Decide who does what. Develop a work plan. Test the solution on part of the problem to see if it works. Reinforce good work. Celebrate when the team accomplishes its goal.	Listen and respond. Speak clearly. Interpret nonverbal messages. Manage conflict.

Technology and Workplace Communication

The workplace of today is quite different from that of your parents or grandparents. Anthropologists suggest that working with tools is one of the hallmarks of any civilized society, but today's technological advances can help us transcend time and space themselves. As we noted in Chapter 1, and as you have seen in Electronic Connections features throughout the text, these days fax machines, computers, modems, beepers, and cellular telephones permit technological connections that mediate our interpersonal relationships. Marriages between computers, video, fibre optics, and electronic messaging now make it possible to interact with others when we are not in their presence. As these new technologies develop, they will have a potent effect upon the interactions we have with others, not just in the workplace, but also in our homes, schools, places of worship, and other arenas.

The Role of Technology in the Workplace

Imagine that it's time for work. But instead of hopping in your car for a forty-minute commute—the national average time for getting to work—you stroll into your media room, flip on your computer, and comb your hair so that when you talk to your boss via TV you will make a good impression. You push a button and collect your E-mail from your computer, then settle down to write your reports and talk to clients. Our homes are still our castles, but increasingly, our homes are also our workplaces, thanks to the power and ingenuity of today's technology. Even if face-to-face interaction is still required for complicated, unstructured tasks, we will undoubtedly prepare for interpersonal contacts by gathering information from a computer data base, sending and receiving faxes, or communicating with others via E-mail. The pace at which we use technology to help us do our work will quicken. As students and teachers, many of us are already using technology to increase our efficiency and to enhance learning and teaching.

ELECTRONIC CONNECTIONS

As the first article shows, electronic technology is creating new options for managing workplace communication off site. Some employees are taking the next logical step and becoming part-time telecommuters. The second excerpt below provides tips for proposing such an arrangement to your boss.

Stay Connected After Hours

One of the most frustrating experiences for a working parent is the tug of war you feel at the end of a long day. On one side, there's a stack of important documents to review and a stuffed electronic-mail message box pulling to keep you in the office. On the other side, there's dinner and kids to tuck in pulling you home. Thanks to your family PC, you can deal with those documents and answer those E-mail messages without missing a precious moment with your kids. Equipped with a host of onboard communications tools, your PC can serve as your office away from the office, allowing you to get home for dinner and tackle your day's-end chores after the kids are asleep.

With a fax modem and the E-mail (via online services) and faxing capabilities that came bundled with your computer (or that you've added on to it), you can send and receive electronic messages and files, send faxes, and tap into other computers, including the one at work. If your PC is not equipped with a fax modem, you can easily add an external modem.

E-mail management tops the list of tasks that are well suited for being done from a family computer. In fact, you can often do it better and faster after hours. Many managers habitually handle the bulk of their E-mail first thing in the morning and last thing before closing down for the day, so shifting that task to a home-based computer is a minor change in routine with big benefits on the family front.

The best strategy for setting yourself up to handle E-mail at home depends to some extent on whom you need to communicate with—whether it's with your colleagues on an internal network or with far-flung contacts outside your company—and what E-mail resources you intend to use.

Thanks to your family PC, you don't have to feel guilty about work left undone or about missing your kids' bedtime. With the right connections, you can make your time at the family PC as productive as the time you spend at the office. In fact, you're likely to discover that in the still of the night, away from interruptions, your efficiency improves dramatically.

Peter Scisco, *Family PC*.

Yet there is evidence that some workers are reluctant to embrace the new technology. According to a recent Gallup poll, 49 percent of the 600 white-collar workers surveyed said they were cyberphobic—afraid of computers—or resistant to new technology. Only 12 percent thought of themselves as "early adopters" who eagerly buy new hardware and software. Women (39 percent) tend to fear technology more than men (27 percent). What are some of the reasons for the anxiety? Over 56 percent said they were worried about losing their privacy, 38 percent feared information overload, and another 38 percent were worried about diminished face-to-face contact with colleagues. Thirty-five percent were afraid of having to constantly learn new skills, and 19 percent were worried about being passed over for a promotion because they lacked computer skills.[27] Despite these concerns, the same poll found that two-thirds of those surveyed are using computers, and almost 70 percent thought the information superhighway will help their company in the future.[28]

Computers and modems have had perhaps more far-reaching effects upon workplace communication than any other technology.[29] Today, workers from the top level on down in an organization use a computer to write, track data, compute, and

---

If you think a full day of uninterrupted work time at home sounds even better, you may want to approach your boss about telecommuting.

Getting the Idea Across to a Boss

The biggest hurdle you're likely to face as a telecommuter is persuading your boss to let you try it.

"Even managers who are supportive of the concept in their heads have butterflies in their stomachs," quips Gil Gordon, a telecommuting consultant with Gil Gordon Associates in Monmouth Junction, New Jersey.

Gordon and Nick Sullivan, the telecommuting senior editor of *Home Office Computing* magazine offer these tips to telecommuting wannabes when negotiating with the boss:

- Look at telecommuting from your boss's perspective. How

will a telecommuting schedule help your company and your supervisor? Perhaps telecommuting will help you do better-quality work, shift your hours to provide improved service for your company's customers, or help you stay in a job you might otherwise have to leave.

- Sell your boss on quantity and quality. You'll get more and better work accomplished from home.

- Define your goals. Write a formal proposal that includes detailed information on your telecommuting schedule, how you will accomplish the work, and anticipated expenses.

- Devise a foolproof way to stay in touch with the office. Send daily E-mail and fax messages to keep the office updated on your work progress. Encourage your colleagues to call you at

home, and be available to them when they do.

- Begin telecommuting with a modest request, such as working from home one day a week for a month. That's a trial period of just four days with minuscule risk. Or, suggest an initial telecommuting period in order to complete a special project or report.

- Once the trial is successful, gradually expand the time you telecommute.

- The boss may counter all of your good arguments with: "If you telecommute, everyone will want to. And we can't have that." The fact is, not everyone will want to telecommute, not everyone's job is suited to it, and not everyone has the self-discipline and independence to work from home.

Cathryn Conroy, *CompuServe* magazine, February 1995.

---

perform other daily functions. A **modem** lets you connect your computer to other computers via a telephone line, so you can send written messages as well as pictures and even videos. A **scanner** lets you insert photographs or text into a computer, which you can then incorporate into documents and reports or send to others over the phone lines. A scanner looks like a photocopier, but instead of putting photos or words on a sheet of paper, it transfers them into digital signals to be "read" by your computer. It is also possible to store movies and videos in a computer, which you can then send by modem around the world to others. A **facsimile machine**, popularly called a fax, makes it possible to transmit written documents via telephone lines anywhere in the world.

Interactive TV broadcasting systems now permit you to talk to others "face-to-face" over great distances. Using **electronic messaging**, or E-mail, you can type a message on your computer to be read by anyone who is connected to your network. Internet, a popular and vast computer network, is one of the most widely used E-mail networks in the world. Many organizations also have developed internal computer networks that permit employees to communicate with each other. If you have a computer and modem at home, you can interact with anyone who has a similar system.

The Effects of Technology on Workplace Communication

The net result of these technological advances is that your workplace is no longer confined to your own office, store, or plant, nor to people who work for your organization. Once you log onto the information superhighway, you can exchange information such as research findings, statistics, historical facts, and new ideas with others in your profession around the world. As the Electronic Connections box below suggests, your home computer can help you to plow thorough routine correspondence more efficiently, and may occasionally even permit you to avoid commuting. This, in turn, can give you more time to spend with family and friends.

Will these new technologies, and others yet to be developed, replace the need for face-to-face interpersonal relationships? Early evidence suggests that the answer is no. Communication technology is not new. Gutenberg's movable type, Morse's telegraph, and Bell's telephone all affected the speed with which we interacted with others, but they have not replaced direct interaction.

A growing collection of research studies show that we still use electronic media selectively for workplace communication:[30]

1. The more positive the message, the more immediate the media we use to communicate it. We like to tell someone good news in person. We are more likely to select some other medium to communicate bad news.

2. We prefer mediated communication (E-mail) when we need to communicate data and content-rich messages, and we like face-to-face meetings for relationship messages.

3. Mediated messages work best in the workplace if the task is highly structured or involves sequential steps. Less structured tasks seem to be managed better face-to-face.

4. Groups who use video conferences and E-mail messages are more likely to have polarized opinions than those who meet face-to-face.

5. Groups and individuals will be more productive if they have someone to help them when they experience either hardware or software problems.

6. The use of sophisticated technology does not necessarily result in improved quality. It may let us make mistakes faster.

7. In the future, people will still solve complex issues and problems face-to-face rather than through mediated messages.

The Chronicle of Higher Education

"All this E-mail . . I miss schmoozing."

Summary

For most people, work involves a great deal of communication with others. In this chapter we have identified principles and skills that can help you establish more effective interpersonal relationships on the job, which in turn can make your communication in the workplace more effective.

In most organizations, communication flows up, down, horizontally, and out to customers. Through upward communication you can share ideas and strategies for improving the work process; you can also enhance your relationship with your boss. Downward communication involves making contact with those who work for you. You should decide whether you will send messages in writing, in person, or through mediated channels. Horizontal communication concerns the communication you have with your colleagues on your level throughout the organization; most of the time, however, horizontal communication will occur with those who work in your immediate vicinity. The grapevine is an informal channel of horizontal communication that carries information quickly and often, though not always accurately. Most organizations are encouraging better communication with customers and clients. Contacting those outside the organization who receive the organization's goods and services is an important way of ensuring that what the organization offers is of high quality.

Leadership skills are important for success in most jobs. Some leaders are highly task oriented, some are more relationship oriented, and the best leaders are skilled at both orientations. Authoritarian leaders favour downward communication; democratic leaders encourage upward communication and a participative, consensual style of decision making. Laissez-faire leaders lead only when asked for direction or information. Situational leaders recognize that there is no single best way to lead all the time. They adapt their leadership style according to their relationship with the group members and the structure of the task.

To enhance your leadership style, you will need to cultivate such people management skills as listening, responding, organizing, and inspiring others. Leaders also need to know how to organize work, accomplish the task, and relate well to others. An effective follower, a role most people play in organizations, makes relevant contributions, listens, follows directions, supports suggestions with evidence, and doesn't abandon ethical principles.

To land a job in any organization, you must make a good impression when you interview for a position. When you are interviewed for a job, you should do the following: assess your skills and abilities, identify the needs of your employer, listen and respond appropriately during the interview, and follow up after the interview. When you interview others, you should give thought to how you will structure the interview; interviews have a beginning, middle, and end. Use an effective mix of open, closed, and probing questions, and listen and respond with an other orientation.

A performance review is the standard way most managers or supervisors tell their employees how well they are performing key job skills. When you receive feedback during a performance review, listen, ask questions, and paraphrase when appropriate to make sure you understand what the reviewer is saying. When you offer feedback to others, consider such factors as timing and the tone of the interview.

In today's workplace you will undoubtedly find yourself working with others in teams. Effective teams have a clear, elevating goal, a results-driven structure, competent team members, a unified commitment, a collaborative climate, standards of excellence, external support and recognition, and principled leadership. To be an effective team member, you also need skills for managing relationships and tools for problem solving and accomplishing the work.

Technology has a growing presence in the workplace. Although mediated interaction will not replace face-to-face interpersonal contact, it clearly plays an important role in sending and receiving messages. Instead of talking to someone in person, you can send a fax, E-mail message, or a video; or you can contact him or her on your portable phone. Although we use these technologies for much of our work, we still prefer face-to-face interaction when dealing with relationship issues and untangling complex problems.

For Discussion and Review

▆ FOCUS ON COMPREHENSION

1. What are some suggestions for improving upward, downward, horizontal, and outward communication?

2. Identify and describe authoritarian, democratic, and laissez-fare leadership styles.

3. What topics are legally off-limits during an employment interview?

4. What are the four elements of the job interview process?

5. What are the eight characteristics of effective teams?

■ FOCUS ON CRITICAL THINKING

6. Alberta is the supervisor of a ten-person workstation in a large manufacturing plant. She must provide performance appraisal interviews for each employee. One of her workers, Pierre, is having difficulty getting his work done because he often makes personal calls on company time. How should Alberta structure her performance appraisal interview with Pierre?

7. Paula is having difficulty getting her work team to be productive. She has excellent employees, but they seem unmotivated and cannot seem to work cooperatively. Referring to the characteristics of effective teams that we discussed in this chapter, suggest a plan that Paula could implement to get better results.

8. Jerry is president of West Coast Computing. He has a sense that his managers are not tapping the wealth of ideas and suggestions that lower-level employees might have for improving productivity. What specific strategies could Jerry implement to improve upward communication?

■ FOCUS ON ETHICS

9. Delynn is being interviewed for a job that she really wants. Her interviewer asks her what her religious beliefs are and whether she is married. How should Delynn handle these inappropriate questions?

10. Imagine that your boss has provided an unflattering and, from your perspective, untrue assessment of your work skills. What is the best way to respect the authority of your supervisor yet set the record straight about your job performance?

11. Clayton has E-mail at work but not at home. His brother has E-mail at his home. Is it ethical for Clayton to use the computer at work on company time to send and receive E-mail messages from his brother three or four times a week?

For Your Journal

1. Whether you are currently employed or are a student at a college or university, monitor each of your interactions at your institution for a four-hour period on a busy day. Categorize each one as upward, downward, horizontal, or outward, and record how your behaviour changes when you shift categories.

2. Select a job that you now hold or have held in the past. Imagine that you are the person who will interview the person to take your place. Develop interview questions that would assess whether someone should be hired for your position.

3. Identify a team that you have belonged to sometime during your life that was exceptionally successful. It could be a team you are a member of now, including a sports team. Identify why that team was successful. Compare your reasons with the attributes of an effective team described on page 462 of your text.

4. Make a list of the workplace technology that you can now use with some skill (e.g., telephone, personal computer, fax machine, etc.). Make a second list of workplace technology with which you are familiar but do not know how to operate. Which list is longer? How has your use of technology affected your relationships with colleagues and friends?

Learning with Others

1. Pair up with one of your classmates and plan an employment interview. Develop a real or hypothetical situation that is realistic for both of you. The interviewer should plan the questions he or she will ask. Rehearse your interview, then perform it for the class and ask for feedback.

2. Divide into teams of two or three people. Each team will interview a business person or supervisor in a nonprofit organization such as a hospital or school about the issues covered in this chapter. Ask such questions as:

   ■ What do you do to enhance upward communication among the people you supervise?

   ■ What is your approach to leading others? What works and what doesn't work with your subordinates?

   ■ How do you foster teamwork among your employees? How does the organization foster it among supervisors?

   ■ How has the use of technology (e.g., fax machines, E-mail, etc.) affected the way workers communicate in your organization?

   After the interview, present to your class a brief report about what you learned. Or, write a short report or journal entry (if your instructor has asked you to keep a journal) summarizing your findings.

3. Divide into teams and use the brainstorming method suggested in this chapter to develop solutions for *one* of the following questions:

   ■ What can be done to curtail the use of illegal drugs in Canada?

   ■ What strategies can we use to reduce crime in our community?

   ■ How can we improve the curriculum in our school?

   ■ How could busy parents juggle work, home life, and school responsibilities more effectively?

- What are some strategies for reducing family violence?

- What can be done to reduce sexual harassment on the job?

- What strategies could improve the antagonistic relationships among Members of Parliament?

- What teaching methods would foster teamwork between teachers and students?

- How can we improve the communication climate among individuals with different ethnic and racial backgrounds?

Consider using the silent brainstorming technique before asking group members to verbalize their solutions. Have someone record each idea on a chalkboard or flip chart. Ask the group to rate each idea on a ten-point scale. Identify the top two most popular ideas and analyze the pros and cons of each one.

GLOSSARY

UPWARD COMMUNICATION: Communication in an organization that flows from subordinates to superiors.

DOWNWARD COMMUNICATION: Communication in an organization that flows from superiors to subordinates.

QUID PRO QUO: A Latin phrase that can be used to describe a type of sexual harassment. The phrase means "you do something for me and I'll do something for you."

HOSTILE ENVIRONMENT: A type of sexual harassment that threatens an employee's rights through offensive working conditions or behaviour on the part of other workers.

HORIZONTAL COMMUNICATION: Communication among colleagues or co-workers at the same level within an organization.

OUTWARD COMMUNICATION: Communication that flows to those outside an organization (e.g., customers).

LEADERSHIP: Behaviour that influences, guides, controls, or inspires others to take action.

TASK-ORIENTED LEADERSHIP: A leadership approach that focuses on initiating work, providing information, and getting the job accomplished.

RELATIONSHIP-ORIENTED LEADERSHIP: A leadership approach that encourages others and maintains a supportive, friendly work climate.

AUTHORITARIAN LEADERSHIP STYLE: A leadership style that involves directing, giving orders, and seeking to control others.

DEMOCRATIC LEADERSHIP STYLE: A leadership style that involves consulting workers and considering many points of view.

LAISSEZ-FAIRE LEADERSHIP STYLE: A leadership style that involves minimal direction on the leader's part.

SITUATIONAL LEADERSHIP STYLE: An approach to leadership that lets the situation and the needs of followers dictate the leadership style.

INTERVIEW: A structured, planned discussion, usually between two people.

OPEN QUESTION: Type of interview question for which there is a wide range of possible answers.

CLOSED QUESTION: Type of interview question for which there is a more limited range of possible answers.

PROBING QUESTION: A question that an interviewer uses to seek more detailed information.

PERFORMANCE REVIEW: An interview between an employee and supervisor designed to provide feedback about the employee's skills and abilities.

TEAM: A group of individuals organized to work together to achieve a common goal.

JOURNALIST'S SIX QUESTIONS: A technique for analyzing and defining issues by answering the questions, who? what? where? when? why? and how?

BRAINSTORMING: A process of generating many ideas through free association separate from the process of evaluating the ideas.

6M TECHNIQUE: A method for structuring the analysis of a problem or issues by assessing manpower, machinery, methods, materials, money, and minutes.

ANALYZE PROS AND CONS: Simple technique for considering the advantages and disadvantages of a solution or proposal.

MODEM: Computing hardware that allows users to send and receive information via the phone line.

SCANNER: A machine that permits you to insert photographs or text into a computer, which you can then incorporate into documents and reports or send to others over phone lines.

FACSIMILE MACHINE: Often called a fax, this machine transmits written documents over telephone lines.

INTERACTIVE TV: A television broadcasting system that allows users to communicate face-to-face over great distances.

ELECTRONIC MESSAGING (E-MAIL): A system that allows users to generate and transmit messages via computer.

Notes

Chapter 1

1. E. T. Klemmer and F. W. Snyder, "Measurement of Time Spent Communicating," *Journal of Communication* 20 (June 1972): 142.

2. F. E. X. Dance and C. Larson, *Speech Communication: Concepts and Behavior* (New York: Holt, Rinehart and Winston, 1972).

3. Ibid.

4. J. T. Masterson, S. A. Beebe, and N. H. Watson, *Invitation to Effective Speech Communication* (Glenview, IL: Scott, Foresman, 1989).

5. S. W. Duck, *Understanding Relationships* (New York: The Guilford Press, 1991), 9.

6. Mikhail Bakhtin, *Speech Genres and Other Late Essays* (Austin: University of Texas Press, 1986).

7. H. Lasswell, "The Structure and Function of Communication in Society," in *The Communication of Ideas*, ed. L. Bryson (New York: Institute for Religious and Social Studies, 1948), 37.

8. See: V. E. Cronen, W. B. Pearce, and L. M. Harris, "The Coordinated Management of Meaning: A Theory of Communication," in *Human Communication Theory: Comparative Essays*, ed. F. E. X. Dance (New York: Harper & Row, 1982), 61–89.

9. See: D. Barnlund, *Interpersonal Communication: Survey and Studies* (Boston: Houghton Mifflin Company, 1968).

10. Ibid.

11. O. Wiio, *Wiio's Laws—and Some Others* (Espoo, Finland: Welin-Goos, 1978).

12. Masterson, Beebe, and Watson, *Invitation to Effective Speech Communication*, 6.

13. R.B. Adler and N. Towne, *Looking Out Looking In*, 8th ed. (Toronto: Harcourt Brace, 1996), 356.

14. S. Wahlroos, *Family Communication* (New York: Signet Books, 1976), *xi*.

15. V. Satir, *Peoplemaking* (Palo Alto, CA: Science and Behavior Books, 1972).

16. R. Hill, *Family Development in Three Generations* (Cambridge, MA: Schenkman, 1970).

17. K. E. Davis and M. Todd, "Assessing Friendship: Prototypes, Paradigm Cases, and Relationship Description," in *Understanding Personal Relationships*, eds. S. W. Duck and D. Perlman (London: Sage, 1985).

18. B. Wellman, "From Social Support to Social Network," in *Social Support: Theory, Research and Applications*, eds. I. G. Sarason and B. R. Sarason (Dordrecht, Netherlands: Nijhoff, 1985).

19. R. Hopper, M. L. Knapp, and L. Scott, "Couples' Personal Idioms: Exploring Intimate Talk," *Journal of Communication* 31 (1981): 23–33.

20. J. L. Freedman, *Happy People* (New York: Harcourt Brace Jovanovich, 1978).

21. M. Argyle and M. Hendershot, *The Anatomy of Relationships* (London: Penguin Books, 1985), 14.

22. W. M. Kephard, "Some Correlates of Romantic Love." *Journal of Marriage and the Family* 29 (1967): 470–74.

23. M. Argyle, *The Psychology of Happiness* (London: Routledge, 1987).

24. J. J. Lynch, *The Broken Heart: The Medical Consequences of Loneliness* (New York: Basic Books, 1977).

25. D. P. Phillips, "Deathday and Birthday: An Unexpected Connection," in *Statistics: A Guide to the Unknown*, ed. J. M. Tanur (San Francisco: Holden Day, 1972).

26. F. Korbin and G. Hendershot, "Do Family Ties Reduce Mortality: Evidence from the United States 1966–68," *Journal of Marriage and the Family* 39 (1977): 737–45.

27. Ibid.

28. M. Argyle, *The Psychology of Interpersonal Behaviour* (London: Penguin, 1983).

29. Korbin and Hendershot, "Do Family Ties Reduce Mortality."

30. G. Miller and M. J. Sunnafrank, "All Is for One but One Is Not for All: A Conceptual Perspective of Interpersonal Communication," in *Human Communication Theory: Comparative Essays*, ed. F. E. X. Dance (New York: Harper & Row, 1982), 220–42. Also see: G. R. Miller and M. Steinberg, *Between People: A New Analysis of Interpersonal Communication* (Chicago: Science Research Associates, 1975).

31. T. Watzlawick, J. Beaving Bavelas, and D. Jackson, *The Pragmatics of Human Communication* (New York: W. W. Norton, 1967).

32. F. E. Millar and L. E. Rogers, "Relational Dimensions of Interpersonal Dynamics," In *Interpersonal Processes: New Directions in Communication Research*, ed. M. E. Roloff and G. R. Miller (Newbury Park, CA: Sage, 1987), 117–39.

33. S. B. Shimanoff, *Communication Rules: Theory and Research* (Beverly Hills: Sage, 1980).

34. M. Argyle, *Interpersonal Communication*, 44.

35. M. Argyle, M. Hendershot, and A. Furnham, "The Rules of Social Relationships," *British Journal of Social Psychology* 24 (1985): 125-39.

36. Argyle, *The Psychology of Interpersonal Behaviour*.

37. M. Argyle is widely acknowledged as the first scholar to suggest a systematic approach to apply learning theory to the development of social skills, including interpersonal communication skills. See: M. Argyle, *The Psychology of Interpersonal Behaviour*.

38. M. V. Redmond, "The Functions of Empathy (Decentering) in Human Relations," *Human Relations* 42 (1993): 593–606. Also see: M. V. Redmond, "A Multidimensional Theory and Measure of Social Decentering," *Journal of Research in Personality* (1995).

Chapter 2

1. K. Horney, *Neurosis and Human Growth* (New York: W. W. Norton & Co., 1950), 17.

2. For an excellent discussion of the role of gender and communication see: J. C. Pearson, L. H. Turner, and W. Todd-Mancillas, *Gender and Communication,* 3d ed. (Dubuque, IA: Wm. C. Brown, Publishers, 1995). Also see: D. K. Ivy and P. Backlund, *Exploring Genderspeak* (New York: McGraw-Hill, 1994).

3. Ibid.

4. D. G. Ancona, "Groups In Organizations: Extending Laboratory Models" in *Annual Review of Personality and Social Psychology: Group and Intergroup Processes,* ed. C. Hendrick (Beverly Hills: Sage, 1987): 207–31. Also see: D. G. Ancona and D. F. Caldwell, "Beyond Task and Maintenance: Defining External Functions in Groups," *Group and Organizational Studies* 13 (1988): 468–94.

5. S. L. Bem, "The Measurement of Psychological Androgyny," *Journal of Consulting and Clinical Psychology* 42 (1974): 155–62.

6. This adaptation of S. L. Bem's work is from: R. M. Berko, L. B. Rosenfeld, and L. A. Samovar, *Connecting: A Culture-Sensitive Approach to Interpersonal Communication Competency* (Fort Worth: Harcourt, Brace College Publishers, 1994).

7. E. Berne, *Games People Play* (New York: Grove Press, 1964).

8. M. V. Redmond, "The Functions of Empathy (Decentering) in Human Relations," *Human Relations* 42 (1993): 593–606. Also see: M. V. Redmond, "A Multidimensional Theory and Measure of Social Decentering," *Journal of Research in Personality* (1995).

9. B. Siegel, *Love, Medicine and Miracles* (New York: Harper & Row, 1986).

10. "Pooh Does a Good Deed," *Pooh Sleepytime Stories* (New York: Golden Press, 1979), 44.

11. Summarized by D. E. Hamachek, *Encounters with the Self* (New York: Holt, Rinehart and Winston, 1982), 3–5, and edited by R. B. Adler and N.Towne, *Looking Out/Looking In* (Fort Worth: Harcourt, Brace Jovanovich College Publishers, 1993). Also see: C. R. Berger, "Self-Conception and Social Information Processing", in *Personality and Interpersonal Communication,* eds. J. C. McCroskey and J. A. Daly (1986): 275–303.

12. "Owl Finds a Home," *Pooh Sleepytime Stories* (New York: Golden Press, 1979), 28.

13. Hamachek, *Encounters with the Self,* and Berger, "Self-Conception and Social Information Processing."

14. R. Norton, *Communicator Style: Theory, Applications and Measures* (Beverly Hills: Sage Publications, 1983), 58.

15. J. L. Bledsoe, "Your Four Communicating Styles," *Training* (March 1976): 18–21. Also based upon materials presented by Wilson Learning Corporation (Eden Prairie, MN: 1976).

16. R. Edwards, "Sensitivity to Feedback and the Development of Self," *Communication Quarterly* 38 (Spring 1990): 101–11.

17. F. E. X. Dance and C. Larson, *The Functions of Human Communication* (New York: Holt, Rinehart and Winston, 1976), 141.

Chapter 3

1. C. R. Berger, "Self-Conception and Social Information Processing," in *Personality and Interpersonal Communication,* eds. McCroskey, J. C. & J. A. Daly (Newbury Park, CA.: Sage, 1987), 275–304.

2. P. R. Hinton, *The Psychology of Interpersonal Perception* (New York: Routledge, 1993).

3. P. Watzlawick, J. Beavin, & D. Jackson, *Pragmatics of Human Communication* (New York: Norton, 1967).

4. A. L. Sillars, "Attribution and Communication: Are People Naive Scientists or Just Naive?" in *Social Cognition and Communication,* eds. M. E. Roloff, & C. R. Berger, (Beverly Hills: Sage, 1982), 73–106.

5. R. D. Laing, H. Phillipson, & A. R. Lee, *Interpersonal Perception* (New York: Springer, 1966).

6. C. R. Berger & J. J. Bradac, *Language and Social Knowledge* (Baltimore: Edward Arnold, 1982).

7. S. Asch, "Forming Impressions of Personality," *Journal of Abnormal and Social Psychology,* 41 (1946): 258–90.

8. D. M. Wegner & R. R. Vallacher, *Implicit Psychology: An Introduction to Social Cognition* (New York: Oxford University Press, 1977).

9. J. S. Bruner & R. Tagiuri, "The Perception of People" in *Handbook of Social Psychology,* ed. G. Lindzey, (Cambridge, MA: Addison-Wesley, 1954).

10. F. Heider, *The Psychology of Interpersonal Relations* (New York: Wiley, 1958).

11. E. E. Jones & K. E. Davis, "From Acts to Dispositions: The Attribution Process in Person Perception," in *Advances in Experimental Social Psychology* Vol. 2, ed. L. Berkowitz (New York: Academic Press, 1965).

12. G. A. Kelly, *The Psychology of Personal Constructs* (New York: Norton, 1955).

13. R. Nisbett & L. Ross, *Human Inference: Strategies and Shortcomings of Social Judgment* (Englewood Cliffs, NJ: Prentice-Hall, 1980).

14. Ibid.

15. Ibid.

16. E. E. Jones & R. Nisbett, "The Actor and the Observer: Divergent Perceptions of the Causes of Behavior," in *Attribution: Perceiving the Causes of Behavior,* E. E. Jones et al. (Morristown, NJ: General Learning Press, 1972), 79–94. D.E. Kanouse & L.R. Hanson, Jr., "Negativity in Evaluations," in E.E. Jones et al., 47–62.

17. Hinton, *The Psychology of Interpersonal Perception.*

18. Asch, "Forming Impressions of Personality."

19. M. V. Redmond, "The Functions of Empathy (Decentering) in Human Relations," *Human Relations* 42, no. 4 (1993): 593–606.

Chapter 4

1. L. Barker et al., "An Investigation of Proportional Time Spent in Various Communication Activities of College Student," *Journal of Applied Communication Research* 8 (1981): 101–09.

2. A. Tan, *The Joy Luck Club* (New York: Ivy Books, 1989), 197.

3. W. Winter, A. J. Ferreira, and N. Bowers, "Decision-Making in Married and Unrelated Couples," *Family Process* 12 (1973): 83–94.

4. O. E. Rankis, "The Effects of Message Structure, Sexual Gender, and Verbal Organizing Ability upon Learning Message Information," Ph.D. dissertation, Ohio University, 1981; C. H. Weaver, *Human Listening: Process and Behavior* (New York: The Bobbs-Merrill Company, 1972); R. D. Halley, "Distractibility of Males and Females in Competing Aural Message Situations: A Research Note," *Human Communication Research* 2 (1975): 79–82; Our discussion of gender-based differences and listening is also based upon a discussion by: S. A. Beebe and J. T. Masterson, *Family Talk: Interpersonal Communication in the Family* (New York: Random House, 1986).

5. J. Thurber, "The Secret Life of Walter Mitty," in S. Barnet et al., *Literature for Composition*, 3d ed. (Glenview, IL: Scott, Foresman and Company, 1992), 43.

6. R. Montgomery, *Listening Made Easy* (New York: Amacon, 1981).

7. R. G. Owens, "Handling Strong Emotions," in O. Hargie (ed.) *A Handbook of Communication Skills* (London: Croom Helm/New York University Press, 1986).

8. R. G. Nichols, "Factors in Listening Comprehension," *Speech Monographs* 15 (1948): 154–63; G. M. Goldhaber and C. H. Weaver, "Listener Comprehension of Compressed Speech When the Difficulty, Rate of Presentation, and Sex of the Listener are Varied," *Speech Monographs* 35 (1968): 20–25.

9. J. Harrigan, "Listeners, Body Movements and Speaking Turns," *Communication Research* 12 (1985): 233–50.

10. S. Strong et al., "Nonverbal Behavior and Perceived Counselor Characteristics," *Journal of Counseling Psychology* 18 (1971): 554–61.

11. See: R. G. Nichols and L. A. Stevens, "Listening to People," *Harvard Business Review* 35 (September-October 1957): 85–92.

12. O. Hargie, C. Sanders, and D. Dickson, *Social Skills in Interpersonal Communication* (London: Routledge, 1991).

13. J. B. Weaver III and M. B. Kirtley, "Listening Styles and Empathy," *The Southern Communication Journal* 60 (1995): 131–40.

14. C. W. Ellison and I. J. Fireston, "Development of Interpersonal Trust as a Function of Self-Esteem, Target Status and Target Style," *Journal of Personality and Social Psychology* 29 (1974): 655–63.

15. O. Hargie, C. Sanders, and D. Dickson; R. Boulton, *People Skills* (New York: 1981).

16. Boulton. We also acknowledge others who have presented excellent applications of listening and responding skills in interpersonal and group contexts: Dennis A. Romig and Laurie J. Romig, *Structured Teamwork ® Guide* (Austin, TX: Performance Resources, 1990); Sam Deep and Lyle Sussman, *Smart Moves* (Reading, MA: Addison-Wesley, 1990); Peter R. Scholtes, *The Team Handbook* (Madison, WI: Joiner Associates, 1988).

17. S. Gilbert, "Self-Disclosure, Intimacy, and Communication in Families, *Family Coordinator* 25 (1976).

Chapter 5

1. A. Mehrabian, *Nonverbal Communication* (Chicago: Aldine-Atherton, 1972), 108.

2. M. Zuckerman, D. DePaulo, and R. Rosenthal, "Verbal and Nonverbal Communication of Deception," *Advances in Experimental Social Psychology* 14 (1981): 1–59.

3. P. Ekman and W. V. Friesen, "The Repertoire of Nonverbal Behavior: Categories, Origins, Usage and Coding," *Semiotica* 1 (1969): 49–98.

4. E. Hess, *The Tell-Tale Eye* (New York: Van Nostrand Reinhold Company, 1975).

5. R. L. Birdwhistell, *Kinesics and Context* (Philadelphia: University of Pennsylvania Press, 1970).

6. N. Zunnin and M. Zunnin, *Contact: The First Four Minutes* (New York: Signet, 1976).

7. J. H. Bert and K. Piner, "Social Relationships and the Lack of Social Relations," in *Personal Relationships and Social Support*, ed. S. W. Duck with R. C. Silver (London: Sage, 1989).

8. P. Ekman, "Communication Through Nonverbal Behavior: A Source of Information About an Interpersonal Relationship," in *Affect, Cognition and Personality*, eds. S. S. Tomkins and C. E. Izard (New York: Springer, 1965).

9. P. Ekman and W. V. Friesen, "Constants Across Cultures in the Face and Emotion," *Journal of Personality and Social Psychology* 17 (1971): 124–29; Argyle, *Bodily Communication*, 157; I. Eibl-Eibesfeldt, "Similarities and Differences Between Cultures in Expressive Movements," in *Nonverbal Communication*, ed. R. A. Hinde (Cambridge: Royal Society & Cambridge University Press, 1972); P. Collett, "History and Study of Expressive Action," in *Historical Social Psychology*, eds. K. Gergen and M. Gergen (Hillsdale, NJ: Erlbaum, 1984); E. T. Hall, *The Silent Language* (Garden City, NY: Doubleday, 1959); R. Shuter, "Gaze Behavior in Interracial and Intraracial Interaction," *International and Intercultural Communication Annual* 5 (1979): 48–55; R. Shuter, "Proxemics and Tactility in Latin America," *Journal of Communication* 26 (1976): 46–52; E. T. Hall, *The Hidden Dimension* (New York: Doubleday, 1966). For an excellent discussion of world view and the implications for intercultural communication see: Carley H. Dodd, *Dynamics of Intercultural Communication* (Dubuque, IA: Brown & Benchmark, 1995).

10. M. Argyle, *Bodily Communication* (New York: Methuen & Company, 1988).

11. W. G. Woodal and J. K. Burgoon, "The Effects of Nonverbal Synchrony on Message Comprehension and Persuasiveness," *Journal of Nonverbal Behavior* 5 (1981): 207–23.

12. Argyle, *Bodily Communication*.

13. N. Blurton-Jones and G. M. Leach, "Behavior of Children and Their Mothers at Separation and Parting," in *Ethological Studies of Child Behavior*, ed. N. Blurton-Jones (Cambridge: Cambridge University Press 1972).

14. G. W. Beattie, *Talk: An Analysis of Speech and Non-Verbal Behavior in Conversation* (Milton Keynes: Open University Press, 1983).

15. This example originally appeared in Collett, "History and Study of Expressive Action."

16. R. Birdwhistell, *Kinesics and Context* (Philadelphia: University of Philadelphia Press, 1970).

17. A. E. Scheflen, "Quasi-Courtship Behavior in Psychotherapy," *Psychiatry* 28 (1965): 245–57.

18. M. Moore, *Journal of Ethology and Sociology* Summer 1994; also see: D. Knox and K. Wilson, "Dating Behaviors of University Students," *Family Relations* 30 (1981): 255–58.

19. M. Reece and R. Whitman, "Expressive Movements, Warmth, and Verbal Reinforcement," *Journal of Abnormal and Social Psychology* 64 (1962): 234–36.

20. A. Mehrabian, *Silent Messages* (Belmont, CA: Wadsworth Publishing Company, 1972), 108.

21. P. Ekman and W. V. Friesen, "The Repertoire of Nonverbal Behavior: Categories, Origins, Usage and Coding," *Semiotica* 1 (1969): 49–98.

22. A. T. Dittman, "The Body Movement–Speech Rhythm Relationship as a Cue to Speech Encoding," in *Studies in Dyadic Communication*, eds. A. W. Siegman and B. Pope (New York: Pergamon, 1972).

23. A. A. Cohen and R. P. Harrison, "Intentionality in the Use of Hand Illustrators in Face-to-Face Communication Situations," *Journal of Personality and Social Psychology* 28, (1973): 276–79.

24. C. Darwin, *Expression of Emotions in Man and Animals* (London: Appleton; reprinted University of Chicago Press, 1965).

25. A. Mehrabian and M. Williams, "Nonverbal Concomitants of Perceived and Intended Persuasiveness," *Journal of Personality and Social Psychology* 13 (1969): 37–58.

26. M. Argyle, F. Alkema, and R. Gilmour, "The Communication of Friendly and Hostile Attitudes by Verbal and Nonverbal Signals," *European Journal of Social Psychology* 1 (1972): 385–402.

27. A. Kendon, "Some Functions of Gaze-Direction in Social Interaction," *Acta Psychologica* 26 (1967): 22–63.

28. S. W. Duck, *Understanding Relationships* (New York: The Guilford Press, 1991), 54.

29. Knapp, *Nonverbal Communication in Human Interaction* (New York: Holt, Rinehart and Winston, 1978), 313.

30. P. Ekman, W. V. Friesen, and S. S. Tomkins, "Facial Affect Scoring Technique: A First Validity Study," *Semiotica* 3 (1971): 37–58; P. Ekman and W. V. Friesen, *Unmasking the Face* (Englewood Cliffs, NJ: Prentice-Hall, 1975).

31. A. Mehrabian, "Significance of Posture and Position in the Communication of Attitude and Status Relationships," *Psychological Bulletin* 71 (1969): 363.

32. Ekman and Friesen, *Unmasking the Face*; Ekman, Friesen and Tomkins, "Facial Affect Scoring Technique: A First Validity Study."

33. Ibid.

34. R. Buck, R. E. Miller and C. F. William, "Sex, Personality, and Physiological Variables in the Communication of Affect Via Facial Expression," *Journal of Personality and Social Psychology* 30 (1974): 587–96.

35. M. Zuckerman et al., "Face and Tone of Voice in the Communication of Deception," *Journal of Personality and Social Psychology* 43 (1982): 347–57.

36. G. J. McHugo, "Emotional Reactions to a Political Leader's Expressive Displays," *Journal of Personality and Social Psychology* 49 (1985): 513–29.

37. J. R. Davitz, *The Communication of Emotional Meaning* (New York: McGraw-Hill, 1964).

38. Ibid.

39. K. K. Sereno and G. J. Hawkins, "The Effect of Variations in Speakers' Nonfluency upon Audience Ratings of Attitude Toward the Speech Topic and Speakers' Credibility," *Speech Monographs* 34 (1967): 58–74; G. R. Miller and M. A. Hewgill, "The Effect of Variations in Nonfluency on Audience Ratings of Source Credibility," *Quarterly Journal of Speech* 50 (1964): 36–44; Mehrabian and Williams, "Nonverbal Concomitants of Perceived and Intended Persuasiveness."

40. T. Bruneau, "Communicative Silences: Forms and Functions," *Journal of Communication*, 23 (1973): 17–46.

41. S. J. Baker, "The Theory of Silence," *Journal of General Psychology* 53 (1955): 145–67.

42. E. T. Hall, *The Hidden Dimension* (Garden City, NY: Doubleday & Company, 1966).

43. R. Sommer, "Studies in Personal Space," *Sociometry* 22 (1959): 247–60.

44. Ibid.

45. See: B. Stenzor, "The Spatial Factor in Face-to-Face Discussion Groups," *Journal of Abnormal and Social Psychology* 45 (1950): 552–55.

46. A. Montague, *Touching: The Human Significance of the Skin* (New York: Harper & Row, 1978).

47. Ibid.

48. Nancy M. Henley, *Body Politics: Power, Sex, and Nonverbal Communication* (Englewood Cliffs, NJ: Prentice-Hall, 1977).

49. J. Kelly, "Dress as Non-Verbal Communication," Paper presented to the annual conference of the American Association for Public Opinion Research, May 1969.

50. J. Lefkowitz, R. Blake, and J. Mouton, "Status Factors in Pedestrian Violation of Traffic Signals," *Journal of Abnormal and Social Psychology* 51 (1955): 704–06.

51. For an excellent review of gender and nonverbal cues see: J. Pearson, L. Turner, and W. Todd-Mancillas, *Gender & Communication* (Dubuque, IA: William C. Brown, 1991); D. Ivy and P. Backlund, *Exploring Gender Speak: Personal Effectiveness in Gender Communication* (New York: McGraw-Hill, 1994).

52. Mehrabian, *Nonverbal Communication*.

53. Argyle, *Bodily Communication*.

54. Mehrabian, *Nonverbal Communication*.

55. Argyle, *Bodily Communication*.

56. See: Birdwhistell, *Kinesics in Context*.

Chapter 6

1. C. K. Goden and I. A. Richards, *The Meaning of Meaning* (London: Kegan, Paul Trench, Trubner, 1923).

2. E. T. Hall, *Beyond Culture* (Garden City, NY: Doubleday, 1976).

3. L. A. Samovar and R. E. Porter, *Communication Between Cultures* (Belmont, CA: Wadsworth, 1991), 234.

4. A. Tan, "The Language of Discretion," in *About Language*, 3d ed., ed. W. H. Roberts and G. Turgeon (Boston: Houghton Mifflin, 1992), 142.

5. See: G. H. Mead, *Mind, Self and Society* (Chicago: University of Chicago Press, 1934); H. Blumer, *Symbolic Interactionism: Perspective and Method* (Englewood Cliffs, NJ: Prentice Hall, 1969).

6. *The American Heritage Dictionary of the English Language* (Boston: Houghton Mifflin Company, 1969), 1162.

7. A. Korzybski, *Science and Sanity* (Lancaster, PA: Science Press, 1941).

8. G. Gusdorff, *Speaking* (Evanston, IL: Northwestern University Press, 1965), 9.

9. A. Ellis, *A New Guide to Rational Living* (North Hollywood, CA: Wilshire Books, 1977).

10. C. Peterson, M. E. P. Seligman, and G. E. Vaillant, "Pessimistic Explanatory Style is a Risk Factor for Physical Illness: A 35-Year Longitudinal Study," *Journal of*

Personality and Social Psychology 55 (1988): 23–27.

11. F. K. Heussenstaunn, "Bumper Stickers and Cops," *Transaction* 35 (1971): 32–33.

12. B. L. Whorf, "Science and Linguistics," in *Language, Thought and Reality,* ed. J. B. Carroll (Cambridge, MA: M.I.T. Press, 1956), 207.

13. R. L. Howe, *The Miracle of Dialogue* (New York: The Seqbury Press, 1963), 23–24.

14. H. S. O'Donnell, "Sexism in Language," *Elementary English* 50 (1973): 1067–72, as cited by J. Pearson, L. Turner, and W. Todd–Mancillas *Gender & Communication* (Dubuque, IA: William C. Brown, 1991), 96.

15. See: D. K. Ivy and P. Backlund, *Exploring Genderspeak* (New York: McGraw Hill, 1994).

16. J. R. Gibb, "Defensive Communication," *Journal of Communication* 11 (1961): 141–48. Also see: R. Bolton, *People Skills* (New York: Simon and Schuster, 1979), 14–26.

17. E. Sieburg and C. Larson, "Dimensions of Interpersonal Response," paper delivered at the annual conference of the International Communication Association, Phoenix, April 1971.

Chapter 7

1. F. E. Millar and L. E. Rogers, "A Relational Approach to Interpersonal Communication," in *Explorations in Interpersonal Communication,* ed. G. R. Miller (Newbury Park, CA: Sage, 1976), 87–103.

2. Ibid.

3. Ibid.

4. C. R. Berger, "Social Power and Interpersonal Communication, in *Handbook of Interpersonal Communication,* eds. M. L. Knapp and G. R. Miller (Newbury Park, CA: Sage, 1985), 439–99.

5. A. M. Nicotera, "Summary of Studies on the Theory of Friendship and Consideration of Implications," in *Interpersonal Communication in Friend and Mate Relationships,* A. M. Nicotera & Associates (Albany, NY: State University of New York Press, 1993), 125–35.

6. I. Altman and D. A. Taylor, *Social Penetration: The Development of Interpersonal Relationships* (New York: Holt, Rinehart, & Winston, 1973).

7. Adapted from Altman and Taylor, *Social Penetration.*

8. M. L. Knapp, D. G. Ellis, and B. A. Williams, "Perceptions of Communication Behavior Associated with Relationship Terms," *Communication Monographs* 47 (1980): 262–78.

9. J. A. DeVito, *The Interpersonal Communication Book,* 5th ed. (New York: Harper & Row, 1989); M. L. Knapp, *Interpersonal Communication and Human Relationships* (Boston: Allyn & Bacon, 1984); B. Ruben, *Communication and Human Behavior,* 3d ed. (Englewood Cliffs, NJ: Prentice Hall, 1992); J. T. Wood, "Communication and Relational Culture: Bases for the Study of Human Relationships," *Communication Quarterly* 10 (1982): 75–83.

10. L. A. Baxter and C. Bullis, "Turning Points in Developing Romantic Relationships," *Communication Research* 12, 469–93.

11. Ibid.

12. C. R. Berger and J. J. Bradac, *Language and Social Knowledge: Uncertainty in Interpersonal Relations* (Baltimore: Edward Arnold, 1982).

13. W. Douglas, "Question Asking in Same and Opposite Sex Initial Interactions: The Effects of Anticipated Future Interaction," *Human Communication Research* 14, 230–45.

14. S. W. Duck, "A Topography of Relationship Disengagement and Dissolution," in *Personal Relationships, 4: Dissolving Relationships,* ed. S. W. Duck (New York: Academic Press, 1982).

15. Ibid.

16. D. DeStephen, "Integrating Relational Termination into a General Model of Communication Competence," paper presented at the annual meeting of the Speech Communication Association, 1985.

17. T. L. Morton, J. F. Alexander, and I. Altman, "Communication and Relationship Definition," in *Explorations in Interpersonal Communication,* ed. G. R. Miller (Newbury Park, CA: Sage, 1976), 105–25.

18. R. D. Laing, H. Phillipson, and A. R. Lee, *Interpersonal Perception: A Theory and a Method of Research* (New York: Springer, 1966).

19. Laing, Phillipson, & Lee.

20. Altman and Taylor, *Social Penetration*; Morton, Alexander, and Altman, "Communication and Relationship Definition."

Chapter 8

1. B. Pym, *Excellent Women* (first published in 1952; New York: E.P. Dutton, 1988), 50.

2. C. R. Berger and J. J. Bradac, *Language and Social Knowledge: Uncertainty in Interpersonal Relations* (Baltimore: Edward Arnold, 1982)

3. W. Stoebe, "Self Esteem and Interpersonal Attraction, in *Theory and Practice in Interpersonal Attraction,* ed. S. Duck (London: Academic Press, 1977).

4. S. W. Duck, *Personal Relationships and Personal Constructs: A Study of Friendship Formation* (New York: John Wiley & Sons, 1973).

5. M. Sunnafrank, "A Communication-Based Perspective on Attitude Similarity and Interpersonal Attraction in Early Acquaintance," *Communication Monographs* 51 (1984): 372–80.

6. M. Sunnafrank, "Interpersonal Attraction and Attitude Similarity: A Communication-Based Assessment," in *Communication Yearbook* 14, ed. J. A. Anderson (Newbury Park, CA: Sage, 1991), 451–83.

7. Ibid.

8. M. Sunnafrank, "Predicted Outcome Value During Initial Interactions: A Reformulation of Uncertainty Reduction Theory," *Human Communication Research* 13 (1986): 3–33.

9. Ibid.

10. M. V. Redmond and D. A. Vrchota, "The Effects of Varying Lengths of Initial Interaction on Attraction and Uncertainty Reduction," paper presented at the annual meeting of the Speech Communication Association.

11. R. A. Bell and J. A. Daly, "The Affinity Seeking Function of Communication," *Communication Monographs* 51 (1984): 91–115.

12. S. Anderson, "The Egg," in *Literature for Composition,* eds. S. Barnet, et al. (Glenview, IL: Scott, Foresman, 1988).

13. C. R. Berger and R. J. Calabrese, "Some Explorations in Initial Interaction and Beyond: Toward a Developmental Theory of Interpersonal Communication," *Human Communication Research* 1

(1975): 99–112; Berger and Bradac, *Language and Social Knowledge*.

14. Berger and Bradac, *Language and Social Knowledge*.

15. M. Sunnafrank, "Predicted Outcome Value During Initial Interactions" and "Interpersonal Attraction and Attitude Similarity."

16. Berger and Bradac, *Language and Social Knowledge*.

17. F. S. Fitzgerald, *The Great Gatsby* (New York: Charles Scribners' Sons, 1925), 1.

18. L. B. Rosenfeld, J. M. Civikly, and J. R. Herron, "Anatomical and Psychological Sex Differences," in *Self-Disclosure: Origins, Patterns, and Implications of Openness in Interpersonal Relationships*, G. J. Chelune (San Francisco: Jossey-Bass, 1979), 80–109.

19. I. Altman and D. A. Taylor, *Social Penetration: The Development of Interpersonal Relationships* (New York: Holt, Rinehart, & Winston, 1973).

20. J. Luft, *Group Processes: An Introduction to Group Dynamics* (Palo Alto, CA: Mayfield, 1970).

21. Adapted from K. Kellerman et al., "The Conversation MOP: Scenes in the Stream of Discourse," *Discourse Processes* 12 (1989): 27–61.

Chapter 9

1. K. Dindia, "A Multiphasic View of Relationship Maintenance Strategies," in *Communication and Relational Maintenance*, eds. D.J. Canary, and L. Stafford (San Diego: Academic Press, 1994): 91–112.

2. S. Duck, "Steady as (s)he goes: Relational maintenance as a shared meaning system," in *Communication and Relational Maintenance*, eds. D. J. Canary, D. J. and L. Stafford (San Diego: Academic Press, 1994): 45–60.

3. D. J. Canary and L. Stafford, "Preservation of Relational Char-acteristics: Maintenance Strategies, Equity, and Locus of Control," in *Evolving Interpersonal Relationships*, ed. P. J. Kalbfleisch (Hillsdale, NJ: Erlbaum, 1993): 237–59.

4. Ibid.

5. J. Ayers, "Strategies to Maintain Relationships: Their Identification and Perceived Usage," *Communication Quarterly* 31 (1983): 62–67.

6. Canary and Stafford, "Preservation of Relational Characteristics."

7. D. J. Canary and L. Stafford, "Maintaining Relationships Through Strategic and Routine Interaction," in *Communication and Relational Maintenance*, eds. D. J. Canary, and L. Stafford, (San Diego: Academic Press, 1994): 3–22.

8. Ibid.

9. Ayers, "Strategies to Maintain Relationships."

10. B. R. Burleson, and W. H. Denton, "A New Look at Similarity and Attraction in Marriage: Similarities in Social-Cognitive and Communication Skills as Predictors of Attraction and Satisfaction," *Communication Monographs* 59 (1992): 268–87.

11. A. L. Vangelisti, "Communication Problems in Committed Relationships: An Attributional Analysis," in *Attributions, Accounts, and Close Relationships*, eds. J. H. Harvey, T. L. Orbuch, and A. L. Weber, (New York: Springer-Verlag, 1992), 144–64.

12. R. P. Hart and D. M. Burks, "Rhetorical Sensitivity and Social Interaction," *Speech Monographs* 39 (1972): 75–91; R. P. Hart, D. M. Burks, and W. F. Eadie, "Attitudes Toward Communication and the Assessment of Rhetorical Sensitivity," *Communication Monographs* 47 (1980): 1–22.

13. Ibid.

14. Ibid.

15. J. A. Daly, A. L. Vangelisti, and S. M. Daughton, "The Nature and Correlates of Conversational Sensitivity," *Human Communication Research* 14, no. 2, 167–202.

16. Ibid.

17. Adapted from Hart, Burks, and Eadie, 6–7.

18. J. K. Alberts, "An Analysis of Couples' Conversational Complaints," *Communication Monographs* 55 (1988): 184–97.

19. M. A. Fitzpatrick and D. M. Badzinski, "All in the Family: Interpersonal Communication in Kin Relationships," in *Handbook of Interpersonal Communication*, eds. M. L. Knapp & G. R. Miller (Beverly Hills: Sage Publications, 1985), 687–736.

20. G. Levinger, and D. J. Senn, "Disclosure of Feelings in Marriage," *Merrill-Palmer Quarterly* 12 (1967): 237–49. A. Bochner, "On the Efficacy of Openness in Close Relationships," in *Communication Yearbook 5*, ed. M. Burgoon (New Brunswick, NJ: Transaction Books, 1982), 109–24.

21. G. R. Miller and F. Boster, "Persuasion in Personal Relationship, in *A Handbook of Personal Relationships*, ed. S. Duck (New York: Wiley, 1988): 275–88; M. G. Garko, "Perspectives and Conceptualizations of Compliance and Compliance Gaining," *Communication Quarterly* 38, no. 2 (1990): 138–57.

22. G. Marwell and D. R. Schmitt, "Dimensions of Compliance-Gaining Behavior: An Empirical Analysis," *Sociometry* 30 (1967): 350–64.

23. G. R. Miller and M. R. Parks, "Communication in Dissolving Relationships," in *Personal Relationships 4: Dissolving Personal Relationships*, ed. S. W. Duck (Academic Press: London, 1982), 127–54.

24. S. W. Duck, "A Topography of Relationship Disengagement and Dissolution," in *Personal Relationships 4: Dissolving Personal Relationships*, ed. S. W. Duck (Academic Press: London, 1982).

25. S. W. Duck, *Understanding Relationships* (New York: Guilford, 1991).

26. J. M. Gottman and S. Carrere, "Why Can't Men and Women Get Along? Developmental Roots and Marital Inequities," in *Communication and Relational Maintenance*, eds. D. J. Canary, D. J. & L. Stafford (San Diego: Academic Press, 1994): 203–29.

27. G. O. Hagestad and M. A. Smyer, "Dissolving Long-Term Relationships: Patterns of Divorcing in Middle Age," in *Personal Relationships, 4: Dissolving Personal Relationships*, ed. S. W. Duck (Academic Press: London, 1982).

28. L. A. Baxter, "Accomplishing Relationship Disengagement," in *Understanding Personal Relationships: An Interdisciplinary Approach*, eds. S. Duck and D. Perlman (Beverly Hills: Sage, 1984): 243–65.

29. D. DeStephen, "Integrating Relational Termination into a General Model of Communication Competence," paper presented at the annual meeting of the Speech Communication Association.

30. Baxter, "Accomplishing Relationship Disengagement."

31. DeStephen, "Integrating Relational Termination into a General Model of Communication Competence."

32. M. J. Cody, "A Typology of Disengagement Strategies and an Examination of the Role Intimacy, Reactions to Inequity and Relational

Problems Play in Strategy Selection," *Communication Monographs* 49, no. 3, 148–70.

33. Miller and Parks, "Communication in Dissolving Relationships."

34. Adapted from Cody, "A Typology of Disengagement Strategies."

35. Cody, "A Typology of Disengagement Strategies."

36. Duck, "A Typography of Relationship Disengagement and Dissolution."

37. Miller and Parks, "Communication in Dissolving Relationships."

Chapter 10

1. J. W. Keltner, *Mediation: Toward a Civilized System of Dispute Resolution* (Annandale, VA: Speech Communication Association, 1987).

2. For a discussion of male and female gender roles see: B. Bate, *Communication and the Sexes* (Englewood Cliffs, NJ: Prentice Hall, 1988); J. Pearson, L. Turner, and W. Todd-Mancillas, *Gender & Communication* (Dubuque, IA: Wm. C. Brown, 1991); D. Ivy and P. Backlund, *Gender Speak* (New York: McGraw-Hill, 1994).

3. C. M. Hoppe, "Interpersonal Aggression as a Function of Subject's Sex, Subject's Sex Role Identification, Opponent's Sex, and Degree of Provocation," *Journal of Personality* 47 (1979): 317–29.

4. R. M. Berko, L. B. Rosenfeld, and L. A. Samovar, *Connecting: A Culture-Sensitive Approach to Interpersonal Communication Competency* (Fort Worth, TX: Harcourt, Brace College Publishers, 1994).

5. J. Hocker and W. Wilmont, *Interpersonal Conflict* (Dubuque, IA: Brown and Benchmark, 1994).

6. M. Olsen, *The Process of Social Organization* (New York: Holt, Rinehart, & Winston, 1978).

7. S. Ting-Toomey, "A Face Negotiation Theory," in *Theories in Intercultural Communication*, eds. Y. Kim and W. Gudykunst (Newbury Park, CA: Sage Publications, 1988).

8. Ibid.

9. G. R. Miller and M. Steinberg, *Between People: A New Analysis of Interpersonal Communication* (Chicago:

Science Research Associates, 1975), 264.

10. Hocker and Wilmont, *Interpersonal Conflict*, 15–16.

11. R. J. Doolittle, *Orientations of Communication and Conflict* (Chicago: Science Research Associates, 1976), 7–9.

12. E. H. Mudd, H. E. Mitchell, and J. W. Bullard, "Areas of Marital Conflict in Successfully Functioning and Unsuccessfully Functioning Families," *Journal of Health and Human Behavior* 3 (1962): 88–93; N. R. Vines, "Adult Unfolding and Marital Conflict," *Journal of Marital and Family Therapy* 5 (1979): 5–14.

13. B. A. Fisher, "Decision Emergence: Phases in Group Decision-Making," *Speech Monographs* 37 (1970): 60.

14. M. Deutsch, *The Resolution of Conflict* (New Haven: Yale University Press, 1973).

15. A. C. Filley, *Interpersonal Conflict Resolution* (Glenview, IL: Scott, Foresman, 1975); R. H. Turner, "Conflict and Harmony," *Family Interaction* (New York: John Wiley and Sons, 1970); K. Galvin and B. J. Brommel, *Family Communication: Cohesion and Change* (New York: HarperCollins, 1991).

16. Hocker and Wilmot, *Interpersonal Conflict*, 10.

17. J. R. P. French and B. H. Raven, "The Bases of Social Power," in *Group Dynamics*, ed. J. D. Cartwright and A. Zander (Evanston, IL: Row, Peterson, 1962), 607–22.

18. R. Kilmann and K. Thomas, "Interpersonal Conflict-Handling Behavior as Reflections of Jungian Personality Dimensions," *Psychological Reports* 37 (1975): 971–80.

19. L. L. Putnam and C. E. Wilson, "Communicative Strategies in Organizational Conflicts: Reliability and Validity of a Measurement Scale," in *Communication Yearbook* 6, ed. M. Burgoon (Beverly Hills, CA: Sage Publications, International Communication Association, 1982).

20. V. Satir, *Peoplemaking* (Palo Alto: Science and Behavior Books, 1972).

21. J. T. Tedeschi, "Threats and Promises," in *The Structure of Conflict*, ed. P. Swingle (New York: Academic Press, 1970).

22. R. Fisher and W. Ury, *Getting to Yes: Negotiating Agreement Without Giving In* (Boston: Houghton Mifflin, 1988).

23. Our discussion of conflict management skills is based upon several excellent discussions of conflict management prescriptions. We acknowledge: Fisher and Ury, *Getting To Yes*; R. Boulton, *People Skills* (New York: Simon & Schuster, 1979); D. A. Romig and L. J. Romig, *Structured Teamwork ® Guide* (Austin, TX: Performance Resources, 1990); O. Hargie, C. Saunders, and D. Dickson, *Social Skills in Interpersonal Communication* (London: Routledge, 1994); S. Deep and L. Sussman, *Smart Moves* (Reading, MA: Addison-Wesley, 1990); and J. L. Hocker and W. W. Wilmont, *Interpersonal Conflict* (Madison, WI: Brown & Benchmark, 1994); M. D. Davis, E. L. Eshelman, and M. McKay, *The Relaxation and Stress Reduction Workbook* (Oakland, CA: New Harbinger Publications, 1982). W. A. Donohue and R. Kolt, *Managing Interpersonal Conflict* (Newbury Park: CA: Sage Publications, 1992).

24. Boulton, *People Skills*, 217.

25. Fisher and Ury, *Getting to Yes*; Boulton, *People Skills*, Romig and Romig, *Structured Teamwork® Guide*; T. Gordon, *Leader Effectiveness Training (L.E.T.): The No-Lose Way to Release the Productive Potential of People* (New York: Wyden Books, 1977).

26. A. Ellis, *A New Guide to Rational Living* (North Hollywood, CA: Wilshire Books, 1977).

27. S. R. Covey, *The Seven Habits of Highly Effective People* (New York: Simon & Schuster, 1989), 235.

28. Fisher and Ury, *Getting to Yes*.

29. Our prescriptions for assertiveness are based upon a discussion by R. Boulton, *People Skills*. Also see: J. S. St. Lawrence, "Situational Context: Effects on Perceptions of Assertive and Unassertive Behavior," *Behavior Therapy* 16, 1985: 51–62.

30. D. Cloven and M. E. Roloff, "The Chilling Effect of Aggressive Potential on the Expression of Complaints in Intimate Relationships," *Communication Monographs* 60, 1993: 199–219.

31. J. W. Pfeiffer and J. E. Jones, eds. *A Handbook of Structured Expereiences for Human Relations Training* (La Jolla, CA: University Associates, 1974), Vol. 2, 62–76.

Chapter 11

1. A. G. Smith, ed., *Communication and Culture* (New York: Holt, Rinehart & Winston, 1966).

2. P. Cateora and J. Hess, *International Marketing* (Homewood, IL: Irwin, 1979), 89; as discussed by L. A. Samovar and R. E. Porter. *Communication Between Cultures* (Belmont, CA: Wadsworth, 1991), 52.

3. G. Hofstede, *Culture's Consequences: International Differences in Work-Related Values* (Beverly Hills, CA: Sage, 1980).

4. G. Hofstede, "Cultural Dimensions in Management and Planning," *Asia Pacific Journal of Management* (January 1984): 81–98.

5. Ibid.

6. Hofstede, *Culture's Consequences*.

7. W. B. Gudykunst, *Bridging Differences: Effective Intergroup Communication* (Newbury Park, CA: Sage, 1991), 45.

8. Ibid.

9. E. T. Hall, *Beyond Culture* (Garden City, NY: Doubleday, 1976).

10. Samovar and Porter, *Communication Between Cultures*, 234.

11. R. E. Axtell, *Do's and Taboos of Hosting International Visitors* (New York: John Wiley & Sons, 1989), 118.

12. C. Kluckhohn and Murry, 1953, as quoted by J. S. Caputo, H. C. Hazel, and C. McMahon, *Interpersonal Communication* (Boston: Allyn and Bacon, 1994), 304.

13. S. Kamekar, M. B. Kolsawalla, and T. Mazareth, "Occupational Prestige as a Function of Occupant's Gender," *Journal of Applied Social Psychology* 19 (1988): 681–88.

14. M. V. Redmond and J. M. Bunyi, "The Relationship of Intercultural Communication Competence with Stress and the Handling of Stress as Reported by International Students," *International Journal of Intercultural Relations* 17 (1993): 235–54; R. Brislen, *Cross-Cultural Encounters: Face-to-Face Interaction* (New York: Pergamon Press, 1981).

15. For an excellent discussion of world view and the implications for intercultural communication see: C. H. Dodd, *Dynamics of Intercultural Communication* (Dubuque, IA: Brown and Benchmark, 1995).

16. Ibid, 75.

17. Axtell, *Do's and Taboos*, 168.

18. C. R. Berger and R. J. Calabrese, "Some Explorations in Initial Interactions and Beyond," *Human Communication Research* 1 (1975): 99–125.

19. W. B. Gudykunst and Y. Kim, *Communicating with Strangers* (New York: Random House, 1984); W. B. Gudykunst, *Bridging Differences: Effective Intergroup Communication* (Newbury Park, CA: Sage, 1991).

20. L. B. Szalay and G. H. Fisher, "Communication Overseas," in *Toward Internationalism: Readings in Cross-Cultural Communication*, ed. E. C. Smith and L. F. Luce (Rowley, MA: Newbury House Publishers, 1979).

21. Adapted from Samovar and Porter, *Communication Between Cultures*.

Chapter 12

1. G. P. Murdock, *Social Structure* (New York: Free Press, 1965), 1.

2. Statistics Canada (1992), *Families, Number, Type and Structure*. Cat. No. 93-312. Ottawa: 133.

3. The Vanier Institute of the Family (1994), *Profiling Canada's Families*. Ottawa: 10.

4. A. P. Bochner, "Conceptual Frontiers in the Study of Communication in Families: An Introduction to the Literature," *Human Communication Research* 2, 4 (Summer 1976): 382.

5. V. Satir, *Peoplemaking* (Palo Alto, CA: Science & Behavior Books, 1972).

6. Status of Women Canada, *Women in Canada: A Statistical Profile*, Sept. 1994. Ottawa: 6.

7. D. F. Beck and M. A. Jones, *Progress on Family Problems, A Nationwide Study of Clients' and Counselors' Views on Family Agency Services* (New York: Family Service Association of America, 1973).

8. Satir, *Peoplemaking*.

9. H. J. Markman, "Prediction of Marital Distress: A 5-Year Follow-Up," *Journal of Consulting and Clinical Psychology* 49 (1981): 760.

10. L. A. Costa, "The Effects of a Marriage Encounter Program on Marital Communication, Dyadic Adjustment and the Quality of Interpersonal Relationship" (Doctoral dissertation, University of Colorado, Boulder, 1981).

11. D. Kantor and W. Lehr, *Inside the Family* (San Francisco, CA: Jossey-Bass Publishers, 1975), 10.

12. P. Watzlawick, J. Beavin, and D. Jackson, *Pragmatics of Human Communication: A Study of Interactional Patterns, Pathologies, and Paradoxes* (New York: Norton, 1967).

13. G. Bernal and S. Golann, "Couple Interaction: A Study of the Punctuation Process," *International Journal of Family Therapy* 2 (1980): 47.

14. A. Napier and C. Whitaker, *The Family Crucible* (New York: Bantam, 1978).

15. Ibid.

16. Ibid.

17. D. H. Olson et al., *Families: What Makes Them Work* (Beverly Hills: Sage Publications, 1983), 17.

18. We thank John Masterson for suggesting this diagnostic question based upon his research: "Speech Communication in Traditional and Contemporary Marriages" (Doctoral dissertation, University of Denver, 1977).

19. E. W. Burgess and P. Wallin, "Engagement and Marriage" in *Studies in Marriage and the Family*, ed. R. R. Bell (New York: Thomas T. Crowell, 1968).

20. E. W. Burgess, H. J. Locke, and M. M. Thomas, *The Family: From Institution to Companionship* (New York: American Books, 1963).

21. M. A. Fitzpatrick, *Between Husbands and Wives: Communication in Marriage* (Beverly Hills: Sage Publications, 1988).

22. Ibid.

23. Ibid.

24. L. Navaran, "Communication and Adjustment in Marriage," *Family Process* (1967): 173–74.

25. J. Lauer and R. Lauer, "Marriages Made to Last," *Psychology Today* 7 (1985): 22–26.

26. J. Howard, *Families* (New York: Simon & Schuster, 1978), 286–91.

27. V. Satir, *The New Peoplemaking* (Mountain View, CA: Science & Behavior Books, 1988), 4.

28. Satir, *Peoplemaking*, 1972, 13–14.

29. J. C. Pearson, *Lasting Love: What Keeps Couples Together* (Dubuque, IA: Wm. C. Brown, 1992).

30. J. Stachowiak, "Functional and Dysfunctional Families," in *Helping Families to Change*, eds. V. Satir, J. Stachowiak, and H. A. Taschman (New York: Jason Aronson, 1975).

31. A. Bockner and E. Eisenberg, "Family Process: Systems in Perspectives," in *Handbook of Communication Science*, eds. C. Berger and S. Chaffee (Beverly Hills: Sage Publications, 1987).

32. R. A. Hunt and E. J. Rydman, *Creative Marriage* (Boston: Holbrook Press, 1976), 43.

33. S. Miller, E. W. Nunnally, and D. B. Wachman, *Talking Together* (Minneapolis, MI: Interpersonal Communication Programs, 1979).

34. Satir, *The New Peoplemaking*.

35. E. Sieburg, "Interpersonal Confirmation: A Paradigm for Conceptualization and Measurement," paper presented at the International Communication Association, Montreal, Quebec, 1973, ERIC Document No. ED 098 634, 1975.

36. S. Gilbert, "Self-Disclosure, Intimacy and Communication in Families," *Family Coordinator* 25 (1976), 221–29.

37. Ibid.

38. B. C. Rollins and D. Thomas, "Parental Support, Power and Control Techniques in the Socialization of Children," in *Social Support: Theory, Research and Application*, eds. W. R. Burr, et al. (New York: The Free Press, 1979).

39. P. Noller and M.A. Fitzpatrick, *Communication in Family Relationships* (Englewood Cliffs: Prentice Hall, 1993), 202.

40. R. Montemayor and E. Hanson, "A Naturalistic View of Conflict Between Adolescents and Their Parents and Siblings," *Journal of Early Adolescence* 5 (1985): 23–30.

41. R. J. Gelles, "Violence in the Family: A Review of Research in the Seventies," *Journal of Marriage and the Family* 42 (1980): 873–85.

42. S. K. Steinmetz, "The Use of Force for Resolving Family Conflict: The Training Ground for Abuse," *Family Coordinator* 26 (1977), 19–26.

43. These statistics were compiled from: Noller and Fitzpatrick, *Communication in Family Relationships*, 202; Rollins and Thomas, "Parental Support, Power and Control Techniques in the Socialization of Children"; Montemayor and Hanson, "A Naturalistic View of Conflict Between Adolescents and Their Parents and Siblings," 23–30; Gelles, "Violence in the Family: A Review of Research in the Seventies," 873–85; Straus, Gelles, and Steinmetz, *Behind Closed Doors* (New York: Doubleday, 1980); Steinmetz, "The Use of Force for Resolving Family Conflict, 19–26; Burnett and Daniels, "The Impact of Family-of-Origin and Stress on Interpersonal Conflict Resolution Skills in Young Men," *American Mental Health Counselors Association Journal* (1985): 162–71; K. Galvin and B. Brommel, *Family Communication: Cohesion and Change* (New York: HarperCollins, 1991).

44. See: D. A. Infante, S. A. Myers, and R. A. Buerkel, "Argument and Verbal Aggression in Constructive and Destructive Family and Organizational Disagreements," *Western Journal of Communication* 58 (Spring 1994): 73–84; D. A. Infante, *Arguing Constructively* (Prospect Heights, IL: Waveland, 1988); D. A. Infante, "Teaching Students to Understand and Control Verbal Aggresion," *Communication Education* 44 (1995): 51–63.

45. D. Infante, T. A. Chandler, and J. E. Rudd, "Test of an Argumentative Skill Deficiency Model of Interspousal Violence," *Communication Monographs* 56 (1989).

46. For a summary and application of John Gottman's work, see: J. Gottman with N. Silver, *Why Marriages Succeed or Fail* (New York: Simon & Schuster, 1994).

47. S. A. Beebe and J. T. Masterson, *Family Talk: Interpersonal Communication in the Family* (New York: Random House, 1986), 309–10.

Chapter 13

1. J. L. Freedman, *Happy People* (Orlando, FL: Harcourt Brace Jovanovich, 1978).

2. For an excellent review of the nature of friendship see: M. Argyle, *The Psychology of Interpersonal Behaviour* (London: Penguin, 1983).

3. M. Argyle, *The Social Psychology of Everyday Life* (London: Routledge, 1991).

4. M. Argyle and M. Henderson, *The Anatomy of Relationships* (London: Penguin, 1985).

5. S. W. Duck, *Understanding Relationships* (New York: The Guilford Press, 1991).

6. Argyle, *The Social Psychology of Everyday Life*, 49.

7. W. Schutz, *The Interpersonal Underworld* (Palo Alto, CA: Science & Behavior Books, 1958).

8. M. B. Parlee, "Conversational Politics," *Psychology Today* 12 (1979): 48.

9. For a review of gender differences in friendship development, see: Duck, *Understanding Relationships* and D. Ivy and P. Backlund, *Genderspeak* (New York: McGraw-Hill, 1994).

10. Duck, *Understanding Relationships*, 171.

11. M. Argyle and M. Henderson, *The Anatomy of Relationships*.

12. M. Argyle, M. Henderson, and A. Furnham, "The Rules of Social Relationships," *British Journal of Social Psychology* 24 (1985): 125–39.

13. Argyle and Henderson, *The Anatomy of Relationships*.

14. Argyle, *The Social Psychology of Everyday Life*.

15. W. J. Dickens and D. Perlman, "Friendship Over the Life-Cycle," in *Personal Relationships 2: Developing Personal Relationships*, eds. S. W. Duck and R. Gilmour (London: Academic Press, 1981).

16. R. L. Selman, "Toward a Structural Analysis of Developing Interpersonal Relations Concepts: Research with Normal and Disturbed Preadolescent Boys" in *Minnesota Symposia on Child Psychology* 10, ed. A. D. Pick (Minneapolis, MN: The University of Minnesota Press, 1976).

17. Dickens and Perlman, "Friendship Over the Life-Cycle."

18. Z. Rubin, *Children's Friendship* (Cambridge, MA: Harvard University Press, 1980), 74.

19. Henry Van Dyke from E. Doan *The Speaker's Sourcebook* (Grand Rapids, MI: 1960), 107.

20. S. M. Rose, "How Friendships End: Patterns Among Young Adults," *Journal of Social and Personal Relationships* 1 (1984): 267–77.

21. H. J. Markman, F. Floyd, and F. Dickson, "Towards a Model for the Prediction of Primary Prevention of Marital and Family Distress and Dissolution," in *Personal Relationships 4: Dissolving Personal Relationships*, eds. S. W. Duck and R. Gilmour (London: Academic Press, 1982).

22. D. Carnegie, *How to Win Friends and Influence People* (New York: Simon & Schuster, 1937).

23. Duck, *Understanding Relationships*.

24. Ibid.

25. Argyle and Henderson, *The Anatomy of Relationships*.

26. J. Powell, *Why Am I Afraid to Tell You Who I Am?* (Chicago: Argus Communications, 1969).

27. Ibid.

28. This activity is adapted from J. Stewart and G. D'Angelo, *Together: Communicating Interpersonally* (New York: Random House, 1988), 328.

29. Ibid.

30. Ibid.

31. Duck, *Understanding Relationships*.

32. We have drawn upon the research summary for our discussion of love and interpersonal communication from: S. S. Hendrick and C. Hendrick, *Liking, Loving & Relating*. (Pacific Grove, CA: Brooks/Cole, 1992).

33. J. D. Cunningham and J. K. Antill, "Love in Developing Romantic Relationships," in *Personal Relationships 2: Developing Personal Relationships*, eds. S. W. Duck and R. Gilmour (London: Academic Press, 1981).

34. Based upon research by D. M. Buss, "Conflict between the Sexes: Strategic Interference and the Evocation of Anger and Upset," *Journal of Personality and Social Psychology* 56 (1989): 735–47.

35. Z. Rubin, *Liking and Loving, An Invitation to Social Psychology* (New York: Holt, Rinehart & Winston, 1973).

36. Referenced by A. Aron and E. N. Aron, "Love," in *Perspectives on Close Relationships*, eds. A. Weber and J. Harvey, (Boston: Allyn and Bacon, 1994).

37. For an excellent summary of this research see: C. Hendrick, *Closer Relationships* (Beverly Hills: Sage Publications, 1989).

38. J. A. Lee, "A Typology of Styles of Loving," *Personality and Social Psychology Bulletin* 3 (1977): 173–82.

39. Based upon research by B. Buunk and R. B. Hupka, "Cross-Cultural Differences in the Elicitation of Sexual Jealousy," *Journal of Sex Research* 23 (1987): 12-22.

40. *Holy Bible*, New International Version (London: Hodder and Stoughton, International Bible Society, 1973), 1153–54.

41. Hendrick and Hendrick, *Liking, Loving & Relating*.

42. Ibid.

43. Based upon survey results presented in P. Marsh, *Eye to Eye: How People Interact* (Topsfield, MA: Salem House Publishers, 1988), 22.

44. This activity is adapted from J. Stewart and G. D'Angelo, *Together: Communicating Interpersonally* (New York: Random House, 1988), 340.

Chapter 14

1. J. M. Juran, *Juran on Planning for Quality* (New York: The Free Press, 1988).

2. D. B. Curtis, J. L. Winsor, and R. D. Stephens, "National Preferences in Business and Communication," *Communication Education* 38 (January 1989): 6–14.

3. Ibid.

4. Ibid.

5. H. Mintzberg, "The Manager's Job: Folklore and Fact" *Harvard Business Review* 53, no. 4 (July-August 1975): 26–41.

6. W. C. Redding, *The Corporate Manager's Guide to Better Communication* (Glenview, IL: Scott, Foresman, 1984).

7. J. Gabarro and J. Kotter, "Managing Your Boss," *Harvard Business Review* 58 (1980): 92–100.

8. D. Katz and R. Kahn, *The Social Psychology of Organizations* (New York: John Wiley, 1966).

9. Angus Reid poll, October 1991, as described in *Women in Canada: A Statistical Profile*, Ottawa: Status of Women Canada, 18.

10. R. W. Pace and D. F. Faules, *Organizational Communication* (Englewood Cliffs, NJ: Prentice Hall, 1994).

11. W. L. Davis and J. R. O'Connor, "Serial Transmission of Information: A Study of the Grapevine," *Journal of Applied Communication Research* 5 (1977): 61–72.

12. T. J. Peters and R. H. Waterman, *In Search of Excellence* (New York: Harper & Row, 1982).

13. Research summarized by S. A. Beebe and J. T. Masterson, *Communicating in Small Groups: Principles and Practices* (New York: HarperCollins, 1994), 76.

14. See: A. P. Hare, *Handbook of Small Group Research*, 2d ed. (New York: The Free Press, 1976). Also see: Beebe and Masterson, *Communicating in Small Groups: Principles and Practices* (New York: HarperCollins, 1994); F. Fiedler, *A Theory of Leadership Effectiveness* (New York: McGraw-Hill, 1967).

15. S. R. Covey, *The 7 Habits of Highly Effective People* (New York: Simon & Schuster, 1989).

16. K. D. Benne and P. Sheats, "Functional Roles of Group Members," *Journal of Social Issues* 4 (Spring 1948), 41-49.

17. "The Boy's Club," *Financial Post Magazine*, Sept. 1993, pp. 16–24. Cited in *Women in Canada: A Statistical Profile*. Ottawa: Status of Women Canada, Sept. 1994.

18. R. Hopper, *Guide to Effective Interpersonal Communication* (Glenview, IL: Scott, Foresman, 1984).

19. Curtis, Floyd, and Winsor, *Business and Professional Communication* (New York: HarperCollins, 1992).

20. R. K. Mosvick and R. B. Nelson, *We've Got to Start Meeting Like This!* (Glenview, IL: Scott, Foresman, 1987).

21. C. E. Larson and F. M. J. LaFasto, *TeamWork: What Must Go Right/What Can Go Wrong* (Beverly Hills: Sage Publications, 1989).

22. Most contemporary approaches to structuring group problem solving are based upon the model identified by J. Dewey, *How We Think* (Boston: D. C. Heath, 1910). Our discussion of applications of problem solving and group communication principles and techniques is based upon: Beebe and Masterson, *Communicating in Small Groups*. For an excellent discussion of teamwork skills and principles, see: P. R. Scholtes, et al. *The Team Handbook: How to Use Teams to Improve Quality* (Madison, WI: Joiner Associates, 1988).

23. J. E. Eitington, *The Winning Trainer* (Houston: Gulf Publishing Company, 1989), 157.

24. A. F. Osborn, *Applied Imagination* (New York: Charles Scribner's Sons, 1962). Applications of silent brainstorming based upon nominal group technique as suggested by A. L. Delbecq, A. H. Van de Ven, and D. H. Gustafson, *Group Techniques for Program Planning: A Guide to Nominal Group and Delphi Processes* (Glenview, IL: Scott, Foresman, 1975). Also see: A. B. VanGundy, *Techniques of Structured Problem Solving* (New York: Van Nostrand Reinhold, 1981); J. K. Brilhart and L. M. Jochem, "Effects of Different Patterns on Outcomes of Problem-Solving Discussion," *Journal of Applied Psychology* 48 (1964):174–79; W. E. Jurma, "Effects of Leader Structuring Style and Task Orientation Characteristics of Group Members,"

Communication Monographs 49 (1979): 282–95; S. Jarboe, "A Comparison of Input-Output, Process-Output, and Input-Process-Output Models of Small Group Problem-Solving Effectiveness," *Communication Monographs* 55 (June 1988): 121–42.

25. Eitington, *The Winning Trainer*, 158.

26. See: Mosvick and Nelson, *We've Got to Start Meeting Like This!*; M. Doyle and D. Straus, *How to Make Meetings Work* (New York: Playboy Press, 1976); D. B. Curtis, J. J. Floyd, and J. L. Winsor, *Business and Professional Communication* (New York: HarperCollins, 1992); T. A. Kayser, *Mining Group Gold* (El Sequndo, CA: Serif Publishing, 1990).

27. These statistics are based upon a Gallup Poll sponsored by MCI. Our summary of these statistics appeared in R. Resnick, "Technofear Need Not Keep Businesses From Thriving," *Austin-American Statesman* (January 9, 1995): C3.

28. Ibid.

29. A. Gumpert and R. Cathcart, eds. *INTERMEDIA: Interpersonal Communication in a Media World* (Oxford: Oxford University Press, 1986).

30. S. R. Hiltz, K. Johnson, and M. Turoff, "Experiments in Group Decision Making: Communication Process and Outcome in Face-to-Face Versus Computerized Conferences," *Human Communication Research* 13, no. 2 (1986): 225; M. S. Poole and G. Desanctis, "Microlevel Structuration in Computer-Supported Group Decision Making," Human Communication Research 19 (1992): 5–49. Also see Beebe and Masterson, *Communicating in Small Groups*, 296–97.

Index

and perception, 79–80
Generalized-other perspective, 47
Generation gap, 336
Gestures, 134, 136–138
  gender and interpretation of, 152
Ghost marriage, 340
Gibb, Jack, 186
Gibran, Kahlil, 376, 389–390
Gillies, Jerry, 376
Giving in conflict management style, 307
Gleason, Barbara, 351
Goals
  and conflict, 290, 317–318
  of teams, 462
Golden Rule, 40
Gordon, Gene, 282
Gordon, Gil, 471
Gralla, Preston, 374
Grapevines, 443
Grave dressing phase of relationship, 278–279
The Great Gatsby (Fitzgerald), 236, 239
Griffith, Georgia, 189
Group achievement, 343
Group associations, 41
Group marriage, 340
Gudykunst, William B., 48, 101, 102, 338, 345, 354
Gusdorff, Georges, 173
Gut level communication, 417
Gut reactions, 135

H

Hall, Edward T., 146, 148, 169
Hall, Rich, 166, 168
Halo effect, 70
Ham, Wayne, 40
Ham radio operators, 179
Hanna, Michael S., 454
Happiness, facial expression for, 143
Having Our Say (Delaney & Delaney), 57
Health, 18
Hearing, defined, 96
Heider, Fritz, 77
Henderson, Monika, 419–420
Hendrick, Clyde, 427
Hendrick, Susan, 427
HIDDEN quadrant, Johari Window, 243–244
High-context cultures, 169, 344, 351
Hill, Anita, 439
Hill, Barb, 316–317
Hinduism, 40
Hofstede, Geert, 339
Homer, 447
Homosexuality. *See* Sexual orientation
Honesty, 16
  perception and, 85
  self-esteem and, 58
Hopper, Edward, 248, 273
Horizontal communication with colleagues, 442–443
Horney, Karen, 33
Hostile environment harassment, 440
How to Use Sign Language Interpreters Effectively, 115
Human communication, 4
  as action, 6–7
  as interaction, 8

as transaction, 9
Human Rights, 173
Huxley, Aldous, 33

I

"I," development of, 47
Ignoring details, 79
Illustrators, 138
"I" messages, 315, 322–323
Immediacy cues, 153
Impersonal response, 192
Impervious responses, 191
Implicit personality theory, 76
Implicit rules, 21
Impressions
  implicit personality theory, 76
  perception and, 75–76
Improving interpersonal communications, 23–25
Inclusion, 230
  friendship and need for, 403
Incoherent response, 192
Incongruous response, 192
Incrementalism, 273
Independence in friendships, 412
Independent marriage, 379
Indexing comments, 180
Indian etiquette, 353
Indirect perception checking, 84–85
Individual achievement, 343
Individualization stage, 217
Inescapability of interpersonal communication, 11
Information
  about culture, 350
  overload, 109
  source, 6
Initial interactions, 249
Initiating norms for relationships, 248–249
Initiation stage of interpersonal relationship, 215
Institutional marriages, 377–378
Instrumental conflict, 293
Intended effect of message, 16
Intensification stage of interpersonal relationship, 215–216
Intentional messages, 7
Interactive TV systems, 472
Intercultural communication, 350
Intergenerational conflict, 312
Interpersonal communication
  defined, 4–5
  goals for, 14–16
  principles of, 11–13
Interpersonal perception, 68–69
Interpersonal power, 207–209
Interpersonal relationships, 19. *See also*
  Attraction; Ending relationships;
  Escalating relationships;
  Maintaining relationships; specific
  types of relationships
  balance in, 260
  comfort and intimacy, balance between, 221
  conflict management, 267
  continual renegotiation of, 219–220
  defined, 203
  initiating norms for, 248–250

mutuality of, 219
observing and acting on cues, 247
past experience and, 221
perception of relationship and, 220–221
principles of, 218–222
  as processes, 218–219
  qualities of communication in, 211–213
  relational de-escalation of, 216–218
  relational escalation, 214–216
  roles in, 220
  self-disclosure and, 236–245
  stages of, 213–218
  suggestions for initiating, 245–250
  as systems, 219
  trouble signs in, 279–282
Interpersonal trust, 205–206
Interrupting response, 191
Interviews. *See also* Job interviews
  performance review interviews, 458–459
Intimacy, 206–207
  comfort and intimacy, balance between, 221
  friendships and, 409, 410
  self-disclosure and, 237
  stage of personal relationship, 216
  touch and, 148–149
Intimate space, 146
Intrapersonal communication, 55–56
Intra-psychic stage, 277
Irish etiquette, 352
Irrelevant information, credit to, 82
Irrelevant response, 192
Irreversibility of interpersonal communication, 12
Islam, 40
Italian etiquette, 352

J

James, William, 35, 38, 39
Japanese etiquette, 353
Jargon, 179, 181
  computer jargon, 181
Jealousy and culture, 426
Job interviews
  appropriate questions in, 456–466
  follow up after, 455
  interviewee skills, 452–455
  interviewer skills, 455
  structuring interview, 456
Job performance interviews, 458–462
Johari Window, 243–245
John Howard Society, 316–317
Johnson, David W., 310–311
Johnson, Frank P., 310–311
Johnston, Lynn, 297
Journalist's size questions technique, 467
The Joy Luck Club (Tan), 97
Judaism, 40
Judgments, confirmation of, 190
Jumping to conclusions, 183
Justification, 275
Just-in-time approach to feedback, 122

K

Kahlo, Frida, 38
Kennedy, John F., 351

to conflict, 315
   descriptive vs. evaluative feedback, 122
   with empathy, 116–120
   listening and, 99
   supportive responses, 190
   timing responses, 121–122
   unnecessary details, avoidance of, 122
   with usable information, 122
Responsiveness, 52
Restricted codes, 179, 181
Reward power, 303
Rhetorical reflectors, 265
Rhetorical sensitivity, 265–266
Roberts, Paul, 171–172
Rockwell, Norman, 67, 136
Rogers, Carl, 101
Roles
   expectations about, 377
   for interpersonal relationships, 220
   self–concepts and, 41–42
Romantic relationships, 17
Roosevelt, Eleanor, 314
Rules for interpersonal relationships, 21
Russian etiquette, 352–353

■ S

Sadness, facial expression for, 143
Samovar, Larry, 169
Sandwich generation, 312
Sargeant, John Singer, 131
Satir, Virginia, 17, 45–47, 306–307, 367, 369, 383–384, 388–389
Scanners, 472
Schiele, Egon, 38
Schmitt, 270
Schuman-Heink, Madame, 58
Schutz, Will, 403
Science and Sanity (Korzybski), 172
Scisco, Peter, 470
Scot etiquette, 352
Scott, Niki, 461–462
Screamers, 179
Selecting sounds, 96
Selective exposure, 51
Selective perception, 69–70
Self-concept, 33–35
   affecting interpersonal communication, 46–55
   appearance and, 149, 151
   communication style and, 51–52
   development of, 39
   differences in, 35
   group associations and, 41
   individual interactions and, 39–41
   labels and, 42–43
   looking back and, 58–59
   material self, 36
   message interpretation and, 50–51
   roles and, 41–42
   self-esteem compared, 38
   social self, 38
   spiritual self, 38
   support for, 59
Self-confidence, 145
Self-disclosure
   costs and rewards analysis of, 240–241
   in friendship, 406
   intimacy and, 237–238

Johari Window, 243–245
   patterns of, 238–239
   principles of, 237–241
   reciprocity of, 240
   relationship development and, 228
   risks, assessment of, 240
   social penetration model, 242–243
   starting relationships and, 249
Self-esteem, 45–46
   affecting interpersonal communication, 46–55
   communication style and, 51–55
   "Declaration of Self-Esteem," 45–46
   in ending relationship, 280
   improvement of, 55–62
   looking back and, 58
   message interpretation and, 50–51
   self-concept compared, 46
   support for, 59
Self-fulfilling prophecies, 49
Self-labels, 42–43
Self-pity, 58
Self-reflexiveness, 42–43
Self-talk, 55, 173
   in conflict, 314
   mindfulness through, 354–355
Self-worth, 45
Sensations, 69
Sensitivity
   communication sensitivity, 264–266
   nonverbal sensitivity, 266
   self-disclosure and, 240
Separate marriage, 380
Separation stage, 218
Serial polygamy, 341
Seven Habits of Highly Effective People (Covey), 447–449
Sex. *See also* Gender
   attitudes about, 43–44
Sexist language, 183–184
Sex roles, 42–43
Sexual harassment, 439–440
   evaluation of, 442
   and power, 305
Sexual orientation, 337
   diversity and, 337
   in family, 386
   of parents, 386
Shakespeare, 35, 165
   Hamlet's soliloquy, 165
Shannon, Claude E., 7
Shared tasks, 260
Shaw, George Bernard, 49
Sherman, Robert, 198
Shimanoff, Susan, 21
Short-term initial attraction, 227–228
Sibling conflict, 390
Siegel, Bernard, 49
Silence, 145
Similarity
   assumption of, 350
   and attraction, 229–230
Simple conflict, 292–293
Simplification and perception, 81
Simultaneous interaction, 4–5
Single-parent family, 367
Sipher, Ray, 86–87
Situational context, 13
Situational leaders, 445

6M technique, 466
Slogans for communication, 193
Sniglets, 168
Social class, 337
Social-descriptive approach to family communication, 369–370
Social institutions, 336
Social networks, 260
Social penetration model, 242–243
Social rules, 21
Social self, 38
Social space, 146
Sociological information, 19
Space, personal. *See* Personal space
Specific-other perspective, 47
Spiritual self, 38
Stabilized relationships, 256
Stages of interpersonal relationships, 21–22, 213–218
Stagnation stage, 217
Static evaluation, 182
Step-relationships, 341, 342, 378
Stereotypes, 70
   male/female labels, 43
   prejudice and, 348–349
   self-assessment exercise, 345
Stimuli
   attribution of action to, 78
   perception and, 69–70
Stonewalling in family, 391
Storgic love, 424
Struggle spectrum, 290
Submissive relationships, 20
Sudden death of relationship, 273
Sullivan, Gordon, 471
Sullivan, Harry Stack, 39
Sullivan, Nick, 471
Sunnafrank, Michael, 19
Supportive responses, 188
Surprise, facial expression for, 143
Surrogate family members, 368
Swearing, 106–107
Symbolic interaction theory, 170
Symbols, 12
   words are, 166
Symmetrical relationships, 20
   power and, 208
Sympathy cards, 101
Synchronized communicators, 212
Systems
   families as, 370
   interpersonal relationships as, 219

■ T

Tactile channels, 7
Tailhook scandal, 439
Talking From 9 to 5 (Tannen), 446
Talks-Responsive, 53
Tan, Amy, 97
Tangential response, 192
Tannen, Deborah, 104, 446–447
Taoism, 40
Task-oriented leaders, 445
Taylor, Dalmas, 211–212, 242–243
Teams
   analyzing issues by, 467–468
   characteristics of, 462, 464–465
   leadership of, 465
   meetings of, 468